DRINK

DRINK

A CULTURAL HISTORY
OF ALCOHOL

IAIN GATELY

G O T H A M   B O O K S

GOTHAM BOOKS
Published by Penguin Group (USA) Inc.
375 Hudson Street, New York, New York 10014, U.S.A.
Penguin Group (Canada), 90 Eglinton Avenue East, Suite 700, Toronto, Ontario M4P 2Y3, Canada (a division of Pearson Penguin Canada Inc.); Penguin Books Ltd, 80 Strand, London WC2R 0RL, England; Penguin Ireland, 25 St Stephen's Green, Dublin 2, Ireland (a division of Penguin Books Ltd); Penguin Group (Australia), 250 Camberwell Road, Camberwell, Victoria 3124, Australia (a division of Pearson Australia Group Pty Ltd); Penguin Books India Pvt Ltd, 11 Community Centre, Panchsheel Park, New Delhi–110 017, India; Penguin Group (NZ), 67 Apollo Drive, Rosedale, North Shore 0632, New Zealand (a division of Pearson New Zealand Ltd); Penguin Books (South Africa) (Pty) Ltd, 24 Sturdee Avenue, Rosebank, Johannesburg 2196, South Africa

Penguin Books Ltd, Registered Offices: 80 Strand, London WC2R 0RL, England

Published by Gotham Books, a member of Penguin Group (USA) Inc.

First printing, July 2008
10 9 8 7 6 5 4 3 2 1

Photo credits: British Museum: pp. 4, 22, 55. British Library: pp. 158, 173, 303, 324. Bodleian Library: p. 99. Wikimedia: p. 108. Rijksmuseum: p. 135. Ardent Spirits Exhibition: pp. 234, 310. Saint Louis Art Museum: p. 265. The Virtual Absinthe Museum: p. 336. Women's Organization for National Prohibition Repeal: p. 394. Fulchester Industries/Dennis Publishing: p. 470.

LIBRARY OF CONGRESS CATALOGING-IN-PUBLICATION DATA
Gately, Iain, 1965–
Drink : a cultural history of alchol / Iain Gately. – 1st ed.
    p. cm.
    ISBN 978-1-592-40303-5 (hardcover)   1. Brewing–History.   2. Alcoholic beverages–History.   3. Alcoholic beverages–Social aspects.   4. Drinking customs.   5. Drinking of alcoholic beverages–History.   6. Drinking of alcoholic beverages–Social aspects.   I. Title.
    TP573.A1.G38 2008
    641.2'1–dc22   2007046210

Printed in the United States of America
Set in Caslon Book BE with Bodoni and Campanile
Designed by Sabrina Bowers

While the author has made every effort to provide accurate telephone numbers and Internet addresses at the time of publication, neither the publisher nor the author assumes any responsibility for errors, or for changes that occur after publication. Further, the publisher does not have any control over and does not assume any responsibility for author or third-party Web sites or their content.

CONTENTS

ACKNOWLEDGMENTS

My most sincere thanks to Anne Hedley, who made California seem my home, and to Jeff Grossman for his aid and inspiration. The Alcohol Research Group in Berkeley were models of friendliness and efficiency; Andrea Mitchell, in particular, guided me toward works favoring the creed of Homer. The staff of the British Library maintain their reputation for excellence. Finally, my particular thanks to Jim Rutman at Stirling Lord Literistic and Simon Trewin in London for their advice and assistance at every stage.

INTRODUCTION

The first time I ever saw my grandmother drink alcohol was when she accepted a small glass of champagne on her hundredth birthday. She pronounced it to be pleasant but not so good as to want more. My uncle teased his mother over waiting so long to take a drink and she replied with a concise sermon on its dangers to the young: It made them vain and indolent—and what was the value in that? She had been steadfast in her indifference to drink, and in her outright opposition to drunkenness since her childhood. Born in 1906, in Kilmarnock, in Scotland, the home of Johnnie Walker whisky, she emigrated to America in the 1920s. Her new country was dry at the time: National Prohibition had commenced a few years before, and it was illegal to sell alcohol as a recreational beverage. In the event, she found herself one of the few willingly sober people in the immigrant community. Upon arrival in Brooklyn she shared an apartment whose other occupants, as was the custom, had annexed the bathtub for making home brew. Late one evening the doorbell rang, one of her flatmates opened the door, and Gran caught sight of a uniform. She rushed to the bathroom, locked herself inside, and drained away the hooch—to the fury of her companions, and the policeman, who had dropped by for a drink.

"They made such a fuss," she said.

They have my sympathies.

My own experience of alcohol has been very different from that of my grandmother. I am certain that I had drunk more of it before my twenty-first birthday than she had throughout her entire century. To her it was a useless substance, which changed people's characters for the worse, whereas to me it has been a source of pleasure, which has made celebrations brighter, friendships deeper, and which has served on occasions as a temporary relief from sorrow. Such contrasting views may be found among people of both our generations, indeed, throughout history.

DRINK

1 THE GRAIN AND THE GRAPE

Alcohol is a fundamental part of Western culture. It is the most controversial part of our diet, simultaneously nourishing and intoxicating the human frame. Its equivocal influence over civilization can be equated to the polar characters of Dr. Jekyll and Mr. Hyde. At times its philanthropic side has appeared to be in the ascendant, at others the psychopath has been at large. Throughout history, the place of alcohol in our meals, medicines, and leisure activities has been a matter of fierce debate. Whereas some cultures have distinguished it as a sacred fluid, whose consumption should be limited to ceremonial occasions, others have treated it as a kind of food and ignored, or accommodated, any incidental effects that it might have upon the psyche, and a few have even tried to exclude it from society altogether. Such differing views have often been concurrent, thus increasing the mystery surrounding alcohol. In both ancient Greece, and the present millennium, it has been credited with the powers of inspiration and destruction.

The substance at the center of this controversy, the chemical soul of all alcoholic drinks, is *ethanol,* which in its pure state is a colorless and highly volatile liquid. It is classified as a depressant, in the sense that it inhibits the functions of the central nervous system. It is also biphasic, meaning that its effects on the drinker vary in accordance with the quantity consumed. In small doses, ethanol generates a sense of euphoria and diminishes inhibitions. Larger quantities cause slowed brain activity, impaired motor function, slurred speech, and drowsiness; and in very high doses it is fatal. Moreover, when the body metabolizes ethanol, it is broken down into acetaldehyde, a far more toxic substance, which generates headaches, nausea and lethargy, and a heightened sensitivity to loud noises and sudden movements, which can persist for days after drinking.

Alcohol occurs naturally as a by-product of fermentation–the action of sugar-eating yeasts on fruits. It is a highly nourishing substance–one ounce of pure ethanol contains 224 calories–75 percent more than refined sugar. It is also sweet in flavor when diluted, making it attractive to most living creatures. Insects, birds, and even elephants have been observed to seek it out in the wild and to exhibit signs of drunkenness after consuming it. It is certain that humanity, and indeed our predecessor species, were exposed to alcohol and its side effects in the process of feeding themselves.

So how did we fall in love with this equivocal fluid? When did we begin to prepare it for ourselves? For most of the 160,000 years of our existence as a species, we lived in small bands of hunter-gatherers. The only mementos these distant ancestors have left are their own bones, a few tools chipped out of stone, and evidence that they had fire and perhaps a belief in an afterlife, for they buried their dead with care. It is impossible to know what part alcohol played in their lives, but to judge by the habits of existing tribes of hunter-gatherers, it is likely that they had a taste for it and that they assembled to enjoy nature's bounty in places where fruits were ripening. In Mexico, for example, tribes in marginal regions who did not grow their own food nonetheless would travel great distances in order to be present when certain cacti came into fruit so that they could make alcohol. Those tribes who lacked the technology of pottery used hollowed-out logs as fermentation vessels. One tribe that lacked both pottery and access to tree trunks had discovered a method of weaving watertight baskets to contain the cherished fluids.

Definite evidence of the preparation of alcoholic drinks first appears around 8000 BC after humanity took up agriculture and established sedentary communities. The earliest proof that they were converting some of their produce into brews derives from the chemical analysis of the residues found inside pottery jars discovered in a grave in Jiahu, in northern China, and dating to 7000–6600 BC. These clay vessels, coincidentally the most ancient of their kind, contained a fermented drink made with rice, honey, grapes, and hawthorn berries. Further evidence of prehistoric brews comes from Transcaucasia, part of present-day Georgia, where grape pips have been discovered around Neolithic settlements with shapes that differ slightly from those of wild grapes, suggesting that they had been cultivated. Moreover, pottery fragments from the same area, decorated with what appear to be human figures raising their arms in celebration, and dating circa 6000 BC, confirm that its inhabitants had the technology, and the desire, to store liquids, and thought fit to adorn their containers with joyful images.

Proof that people were cultivating plants to manufacture alcohol first appears in the so-called Fertile Crescent, a geographical area curving between the Mediterranean and the Persian Gulf. The analysis of a yellow residue found on the inside of a jar at a Neolithic settlement in Haji Firuz Tepe (Iran), dating to 5400–5000 BC, revealed that the jar had once held wine. The residence in which it was discovered had six such jars, and other houses in the same hillside village also had similar vessels, in comparable quantities. The amount of wine each household might have produced suggests that it was a small but significant part of their diet. In such communities, winemaking was the best technology they had for storing highly perishable grapes, although whether the resulting fluid was intended for intoxication as well as nourishment is unknown. It is likely that the inhabitants of the Fertile Crescent were also making mead from honey and beer from their surplus grain in the same era. The first proof that beer was being brewed in the region derives from the residues of an alcoholic barley brew found in a pottery vessel at Godin Tepe, in the Zagros Mountains of Iran, and dating to 3100–2900 BC. As is the case with the wine of Haji Firuz Tepe, whether this ur-beer was made to stimulate or simply as a kind of food remains a mystery.

However, by the middle of the third millennium BC, evidence begins to appear which shows that alcohol was very much more than mere sustenance to the inhabitants of the Fertile Crescent. As its little agricultural settlements developed into villages, then towns, so their material culture became increasingly sophisticated. In Sumeria, at the confluence of the rivers Tigris and Euphrates, in present-day Iraq, the decorative arts flowered and writing appeared. Both of these mediums were used to record the social roles played by alcoholic drinks.

In Uruk, the principal city of Sumeria and probably the largest in the world at the time, brewing was practiced on an epic scale. The Sumerians documented both the quantity and the type of beer, or *kash,* that they brewed. They distinguished eight styles made from barley, eight from wheat, and three more from mixed types of grains. They appointed a goddess, Ninkasi, to rule over the art of brewing and associated both the production and distribution of beer with women. The fragments of their laws that have survived, incised on clay tablets, tell us that they had regulated drinking places; their material culture shows us that they staged formal drinking sessions and associated alcohol with ceremony and rank. A banquet scene engraved on a lapis lazuli seal, recovered from a royal tomb in Ur, adjacent to Uruk, and dating circa 2500 BC, depicts two tiers of aristocratic tipplers, indulging in the preferred recreation of their caste. The centerpiece of the top tier shows a pair of seated figures in regal postures, sucking beer through straws perhaps a yard long from a vessel the size of, and faintly reminiscent in its shape to, a modern beer keg. In the lower level, equally patrician individuals raise conical cups to their mouths, and are waited on by a functionary carrying a spouted jug. The same tomb contained examples of drinking straws made of gold and silver, and a solid gold drinking set consisting of a fluted bowl, a jug, and a cup. Its occupant, Queen Puabi, also priestess of the moon god Nanna, was buried with her court as well as her drinking apparatus—eighty other bodies, dressed up to serve her in the afterlife, filled a death pit adjacent to her final resting place.

The artifacts, laws, and records of the Sumerians show that alcohol was abundant in their society, that access to it was regulated, and that it was a favorite of its elite and offered to its gods. The epic Sume-

Sumerian seal

rian poem *Gilgamesh* (c. 2000 BC), perhaps the oldest literary work in existence, which recounts the exploits of the eponymous king, a semi-legendary ruler of Uruk, further shows that the Sumerians were no strangers to drunkenness. After setting out its hero's semidivine ancestry, the poem proceeds to the recruitment of the wild man Enkidu, whom Gilgamesh wishes to have as a companion-in-arms on an expedition to slay the resident demon of a distant cedar forest. The wild man is persuaded to join civilization by the charms of Shanhat the harlot, who proceeds to educate him in the ways of men:

> Enkidu knew nothing about eating bread for food,
> And of drinking beer he had not been taught.
> The harlot spoke to Enkidu, saying:
> "Eat the food, Enkidu, it is the way one lives.
> Drink the beer, as is the custom of the land."
> Enkidu ate the food until he was sated,
> He drank the beer—seven jugs! and became expansive and sang with joy!

Clearly alcohol was not just fodder in Sumeria—it was also, in the right quantities, a source of happiness.

Gilgamesh provides further insights into Sumerian attitudes toward alcohol. Its characters drink water when about their daily or heroic tasks but resort to alcohol whenever they are celebrating. Intoxication, it implies, was also de rigueur at their new year festivities, which, according to other sources, were very drunken indeed. Their highlight was a ceremonial and public act of coitus between the king of Uruk and the high priestess of the temple of Ishtar, goddess of procreation. The union was symbolic as well as real, and the mythical coupling that it reenacted was believed to have resulted in Ninkasi, the beer goddess. A hymn to her, the so-called Prayer to Ninkasi (c. 1800 BC), which has survived from the period, gives a detailed picture of how *kash* was made in Sumeria. It was a complex process—the grain was converted into *bappir* bread before being fermented, and both grapes and honey were added to the brew. The resulting gruel was drunk unfiltered, hence the need for straws at banquets.

Similar styles of brew were common in ancient Egypt, whose writings and artifacts likewise provide a detailed record of what its inhabitants drank and hint at some of their reasons for doing so. The story of Egyptian drinking begins in the city of Hierakonpolis, whose ruins contain the remains of the world's oldest brewery, dating to circa 3400 BC. It was capable of producing up to three hundred gallons per day of a Sumerian-style brew. Heirakonpolis was also the site of a thriving pottery industry whose principal products were beer jugs and cups, the shards of which litter the ruins of the city. The sheer abundance of such relics and the relative scale of the brewing operations imply that beer was a vital part of the diet of the people who lived there.

While the common people of Heirakonpolis drank beer, its rulers were distinguished by a taste for wine, which was an imported luxury and an emblem of power. The tomb of King Scorpion, who ruled the city in the same age that its brewery was constructed, held seven hundred or so wine jars, made from various types of clay and embellished with different designs, most of which can be traced to what is now Israel and Palestine. The presence of so many jars, so far from their places of origin, confirms that the art of winemaking had spread throughout the Fertile Crescent and that the wine trade was a stimulus to civilization in the Middle East.

By the time that Egypt entered its dynastic era (c. 3100 BC), beer, known as *hqt*, had been established as the beverage for workers, whereas wine, or *irp*, was the drink of the elite. Beer, in keeping with its plebeian associations, was treated principally as a kind of food. Egyptian tomb paintings and clay models depicting its manufacture feature bare-breasted peasant women up to their elbows in their brews; papyrus scrolls bearing financial accounts state that the laborers who built the pyramids of the Giza Plateau were provided with a daily ration of one and a third gallons. A modern re-creation of Egyptian beer, brewed in accordance with written and pictorial evidence, weighed in at 5 percent ABV–the strength of the average contemporary pint, implying that, by the standards of the present day, the pyramids were built by an army of drunks. However, while the Egyptians have left us plenty of practical information about their brewing, they were almost silent on the matter of intoxication. The very few descriptions as to the effect of ten or more pints of beer every day are positive, if enigmatic: "The mouth of a perfectly contented man is filled with beer."

We can, however, be certain that the average Egyptian became intoxicated on certain ceremonial occasions. These included the annual bash celebrating the Drunkenness of Hathor, goddess of fertility, motherhood, and the Milky Way. The Egyptians considered the swath of stars under her special protection to be a river across the sky, and hence Hathor was associated with the yearly inundation of the Nile. She also possessed some of the attributes of Sekhmet, a destroyer goddess of the old kingdom of Upper Egypt, and the drunkenness festival celebrated both the beginning of the annual flood and the mythical occasion on which Sekhmet was diverted from the extermination of humanity by her fellow gods, who provided her with beer disguised to look like blood. After drinking seven thousand jars, she lapsed into a drooling slumber, and while she slept, the gods who had opposed her consolidated their hold on creation. In celebration of their ingenuity, a special red-colored beer was drunk at the festival, in sufficient quantities to induce similar stupors.

The annual rise of the Nile was also associated with Osiris, god of the dead, of life, of vegetable regeneration, and of wine. In the dynastic era, Egypt had become a producer as well as an importer of *irp*. It remained an elite beverage, hence its protection by the most important deity in the Egyptian pantheon. After a fashion, Osiris and wine were made for one another. According to legend, he had died and been reborn, and the vine was a natural example of renewal—every winter it withered back to its roots, every spring it put forth new shoots. The end and resurrection of Osiris were celebrated over the Oag festival, immediately preceding that of the Drunkenness of Hathor. For the duration of its festivities Osiris was known as "the lord of *irp* through the inundation," and the hieroglyphics that constitute the event's name show three wine jars on a table, with a fourth being offered by a human hand. In the latter stages of the dynastic era, the worship of Osiris, and consumption of wine, became even more closely intertwined. His devotees, after prayers and rituals, would eat bread and drink wine in the belief that these were the transubstantiated flesh and blood of their divinity.

Wine, as befits its status as a luxury with divine associations, was manufactured with much more sophisticated methods, and with a great deal more care, than any other agricultural product. The Egyptians dedicated many slaves, and much land, toward perfecting its quality. Their fascination with wine marks the appearance of a new bond between mankind and a type of alcoholic beverage. Not only was it food, and liquid inspiration, it also was capable of stimulating the taste buds in a manner that no other edible substances could. Whereas a loaf of bread was more or less the same all over Egypt, the *irp* from neighboring vineyards might taste radically different, and the Egyptians set about classifying these variations.

A large number of amphorae of their ancient vintages have survived in the graves of pharaohs and other potentates, where they were placed to refresh the dead in the afterlife, and as offerings to Osiris. Most were marked with a description of their contents–where, when, and by whom they had been made. An early example from the burial chamber of King Zoser, the first Egyptian ruler to be entombed in a pyramid, announced that its wine came from the "vineyard of the red house of the king's house in the town of Senpu in the western nomes." As the dynastic era progressed, labeling became more sophisticated, and included reflections on the merit of the wine as well as its provenance. Good *irp* was described as *nfr*, very good as *nfr nfr*, and very very good as *nfr nfr nfr*. Moreover, instead of spoiling over time like other ingredients of the pharaonic diet, the flavors of *nfr*, or better *irp*, were believed to improve with age, and some of the wines discovered alongside the mummified remains of their owners have labels declaring them to be several decades old at the time of their interment. Given that the average life expectancy at the time was only forty, such senior vintages most likely were buried after their creators.

The analysis of the residues in various graveside amphorae has enabled us to augment the information provided by the ancient labels and to determine what color of wine each one contained. Recent tests carried out on amphorae from the tomb of King Tutankhamen (d. 1322 BC) confirm that he drank both reds and whites, from different estates within his dominions. The boy king was buried with twenty-six wine jars, containing vintages up to thirty-six years old, produced by fifteen different winemakers. One such, labeled "Year 5. Wine of the House-of-Tutankhamen Ruler-of-the-Southern-On, l.p.h.[in] the Western River. By the chief vintner Khaa," proved to have contained a red, whereas "Year 5. Sweet wine of the Estate of Aton of the Western River. Chief vintner Nakht" was white. The different colors were stacked at opposite cardinal points of the tomb, suggesting a further level of discrimination, whose meaning has been lost. The grave goods also included King Tut's favorite wine-cup–an alabaster chalice.

❖   ❖   ❖

The systematic preparation of alcoholic drinks was surprisingly quick to spread from the Middle East to northern Europe. In the same century that King Scorpion was accumulating jars of Levantine wine for his afterlife, the inhabitants of a distant island surrounded by a cold sea were making merry on truly psychoactive brews. The cultivation of cereals had reached Germany by 5000 BC and Britain a few centuries later. Crops originating in the Fertile Crescent had appeared in the Orkney Islands in the far north of Scotland by about 3800 BC, where they were used to make beer. It is not known if the Scottish discovered fermentation independently, or whether the process traveled alongside the Middle Eastern cereals they employed in their brews.

The settlement of Skara Brae in the Orkneys, whose stone dwellings have been preserved by virtue of having been buried beneath a sand dune for many thousands of years, provides much in the way of circumstantial evidence about the drinking habits of its Neolithic population. Pottery jars with a capacity of up to thirty gallons have been found in several dwellings, and the analysis of a greenish slime in the bottom of one such vessel confirms that it held an alcoholic beverage made from barley and oats, which had been flavored with meadowsweet and spiced up with deadly nightshade, henbane, and hemlock. These last additives are hallucinogenic, and lethal in the right quantities. Henbane induces blurred vision, dilated pupils, rapid heartbeat, dizziness, nausea, euphoria, and hallucinations in very small doses; hemlock is best know as a neurotoxin that paralyzes before it kills; and deadly nightshade, three juicy berries of which can be fatal, speeds the pulse and gives its consumer the sensations of flight. Clearly, the inhabitants of Skara Brae were drinking for effect rather than to satisfy their hunger or their thirsts.

Other Neolithic sites throughout the British Isles also provide evidence of both alcohol and drunkenness. At Durrington Walls, for instance, a settlement adjacent to Stonehenge, many hearths have been uncovered that are distinguished by the quantity of animal bones and smashed pottery vessels they contain—clearly visitors to the sacred complex feasted long and drank deep. Indeed, it is likely that a culture of intoxication existed in Britain and much of Europe prior to the introduction of cereal crops and beer. Paleobotanical remains, and the entoptic phenomena depicted in cave paintings dating to more than thirty thousand years ago, show that its inhabitants consumed cannabis and opium poppies for pleasure. It is easy to understand how alcohol was welcomed as a new method of generating an altered state of consciousness.

The conceit that the purpose of alcoholic beverages was to make people drunk rather than merely to nourish them was also apparent on the other side of the Atlantic Ocean during the late Neolithic era, notably among the Mayans of Central America. The Mayans were a sophisticated civilization who, by 1000 BC, had established large cities with monumental architecture and who had developed the arts to a very high degree of excellence. They were a mead-drinking culture, who flavored their mead with the bark of the balche tree. In addition to collecting wild honey, they kept hives of a native species of stingless bees in and around their huts to provide a secure source of raw materials for their brews. They also made a fermented drink from corn, whose intoxicating properties are confirmed in their creation myth, the *Popol Vuh*. Mayan drinking appears to have been a ceremonial as well as hedonistic activity. It was an act of communicating with the spirit world, and compulsory on certain ritual occasions. They do, however, seem to have viewed drunkenness in a comical as well as serious light, and produced beautiful glazed cups, some of which depict humorous scenes of drinkers, and also grotesque pottery figurines of inebriates.

Similar evidence as to the preparation of alcoholic drinks in ancient times has been found in India and other Asian countries, and in Nubia in Africa. Indeed, by about 1000 BC, all over the world, wherever humanity had settled in villages or towns, alcohol was consumed. The parallel evolution of drinking in such disparate cultures as Pharaonic Egypt and Neolithic Scotland implies that our predecessors in all these places made a special place for alcohol in their cultures, whether as food, as an intoxicant, as a medicine, or as a status symbol. Despite, however, the wealth of archaeological evidence, we have no direct proof as to their feelings about this equivocal fluid. Did they attribute a spiritual significance to every drop they swallowed, as if it were a magic potion? Were any of them critical of drinking and drunkenness, or was intoxication considered to be a commonplace and wholly natural condition?

2　BACCHANAL

But when Orion and Sirius are come into mid-heaven,
and rosy-fingered Dawn sees Arcturus, then cut off all
the grape-clusters . . . and bring them home. Show
them to the sun ten days and ten nights: then cover
them over for five, and on the sixth day draw off into
vessels the gifts of joyful Dionysus.
　　　　　　　　　—Hesiod, *Works and Days* (ll. 609–617)

The first civilization to leave a coherent account of its thoughts on alcohol, and to enumerate its benefits and detriments, was that of classical Greece—a loose association of city-states united by language, religious beliefs, and culture, located on the edges and islands of the Aegean Sea. These states appeared around the twelfth century BC and, by 700 BC, had so prospered that they had established a network of colonies throughout the Mediterranean—in Sicily, France, Spain, and North Africa. Alcohol, specifically wine, played a pivotal role in Greek culture. Our word *wine* derives from their *oin,* whose consumption was considered to be both one of the defining characteristics of *Hellenic* civilization and a point of difference between its members and the population of the rest of the world, whom they termed *barbaroi,* or barbarians. Wine was omnipresent in Hellenic society. It was used as an offering to their deities; as a currency to buy rare and precious things from distant countries; and it was drunk formally, ritually, as a medicine, and to assuage thirst. In some Greek states such as Athens its consumption could be a civic duty. At the great public feasts officials known as *oinoptai* oversaw its distribution and ensured that all present got their fair share, and such equality of portions was the seed from which grew the concept of *demokratia,* or "people power."

The central place of wine in Greek civilization was established during its heroic age and is apparent in its earliest literary works. The *Iliad* and the *Odyssey,* the two great epic poems of Homer, which tell of the siege of Troy by a Greek army and the voyage home of one of its leaders, Odysseus, are suffused with references to wine and its powers, and set out the etiquette surrounding its consumption. They evoke a warrior ethos, which venerated mortal combat, meat feasts, and the liberal consumption of wine. Wine was the drink of fighting men, the indispensable lubricant of their culture of death and honor, of sacking cities, of carrying off armor, cattle, and women. All their rituals were punctuated with libations of wine—the gods did not pay attention otherwise. Drink also had the power to sanctify the words of men. Wine made warriors speak the truth, and an oath sealed with wine had greater weight than one celebrated with a cup of water.

When Greece passed from its heroic to its classical age, its inhabitants were struck by an outburst of creativity unprecedented in the history of humanity. Science, philosophy, the decorative and figurative arts, and the concept of democracy were invented, examined, or practiced with more imagination and success than ever recorded before. The principal source of this torrent of inspiration was the city-state of Athens, acknowledged among its peers in the fifth century BC to be the leader in matters cultural. This century, so rich in stimulating events (Athens was at war on average once every decade), and this town, where it would have been possible to have known Socrates, Praxiteles, Plato, Sophocles, Aristophanes, Hippocrates, and Anaxagoras, together have left a treasure trove of opinions about alcohol, specifically wine. From this cultural age of gold a coherent portrait emerges. Poets, playwrights, politicians, and philosophers set down their feelings about wine, which generally were enthusiastic. Their compliments were almost universal, their warnings few, if dire. Wine was a force for good, a substance that enabled people to relax while simultaneously elevating their minds, inspiring drinkers to "laughter and wisdom and prudence and learning." According to the epic poet Panyasis:

> Wine is like fire, an aid and sweet relief,
> Wards off all ills and comforts every grief,
> Wine can of every feast the joys enhance,
> It kindles soft desire, it leads the dance.

Not only were the Greeks passionate about wine, they were also discriminating drinkers. Like the Egyptians, with whom they traded and from whom they may have learned some of the skills of winemaking, they believed certain vineyards had been blessed with magical soil and that their vintages cast a spell on people lucky enough to drink them. Instead, however, of labeling them *nfr nfr* and leaving it at that, Greek poets rhapsodized over their favorites:

> There is a wine which *Saprian* they call,
> Soon as the seals from whose rich amphorae fall,
> Violets and roses mix their lovely scent,
> And Hyacinths, in one rich fragrance blent;
> You might believe Jove's nectar sparkled there,
> With such ambrosial odor reeks the air.

While some vineyards produced wine with sensational flavors, others were believed to generate peculiar side effects, not all of them desirable. The wine of Heraea in Arcadia, for example, was reputed to "drive men out of their senses and make women inclined to pregnancy." Moreover, certain vintages were reckoned to possess specific medicinal qualities. There were special wines for loosening the bowels or calming their wind, for sweetening the breath, and for healing wounds and cancers. Indeed Hippocrates (d. 370 BC), the father of Western medicine, advocated the use of wine to treat every illness he had identified, bar one—should a patient be suffering from "an overpowering heaviness of the brain," then "there must be total abstinence from wine."

Notwithstanding the care taken in their manufacture, the taste and appearance of Greek wines would shock modern palates. Archaeological evidence suggests that most were resinated—i.e., were treated with and flavored by the gum of the terebinth tree. The purpose of this additive was to retard the oxidation process and prevent the wine from becoming vinegar. Other common additives included seawater, spices, and honey. Furthermore, wine was not filtered when it was made and had to be strained before being served, lest the drinker choke on stalks, pits, and other such detritus.

As a general rule, the Greeks did not drink their beloved nectar straight but mixed it with water. This habit, according to the physician Philomides, could be traced back to a happy accident—once upon a time in the heroic age, while a group of Greeks were drinking by the seashore, a violent thunderstorm broke out that drove them undercover and topped up their wine bowl with water. When they returned after the storm had passed, they tasted the mixture and found it to be far more pleasant, and far less inflammatory, than neat wine. Inspiration for the beverage was credited to Zeus, the Thunderer, king of the gods, who ruled the world from Mount Olympus; and who was toasted thereafter at formal gatherings "as the originator of rain-storms, [and] the author of the painless mixture derived from the mingling of wine and rain."

The Greeks considered the consumption of unmixed wine to be not only uncivilized but also perilous. The risk it posed to manners was documented by the philosopher Plato: "The Scythians and Thracians, both men and women, drink unmixed wine, which they pour on their garments, and this they think a happy and glorious institution." The danger it represented to unwary drinkers was proven by the example of the Spartan general Cleomenes, who had been sent to sack the city of Argos but had destroyed instead the shrine of the god of the same name, then led his forces home, claiming to have been distracted by an omen. Cleomenes went mad and died shortly afterward, and his "own countrymen declared that his madness proceeded not from any supernatural cause whatsoever, but only from the habit of drinking wine unmixed with water, which he learnt of the Scythians."

There were also risks associated with drinking mixed wine, and although the Greeks generally considered it to be liquid joy, they acknowledged it was capable of producing painful and sometimes dangerous side effects. The tendency of drinking to cause a hangover was noted, and Greek literature contains advice on how to avoid, and how to cure, the headaches and nausea that followed a binge. The key to avoidance was quality—good wine was less likely, according to the poet Philyllius, to make the drinker "feel seedy." As for cures, boiled cabbage eaten the following day was considered to be the best way to clear a fuzzy head, although some drinkers felt the cure was more painful than the ailment, and the combination of rank-smelling cabbage, a sore brain, and a sense of queasiness to be an unnecessary compound of evils—"stern misfortune's unexpected blow," in the words of the poet Amphis.

The usual way to recuperate after a bout of heavy drinking was to sleep it off. Indeed, sleeping late was considered to be a hallmark of the drunkard, as was a certain inattentiveness to serious matters. Habitual drunks were characterized by the description *apeles,* which means careless, and/or carefree. Being *apeles* was no disgrace. Many great men were honored with the title. It was, however, occasionally the subject of mild criticism. The historian Herodotus, for instance, pointed it out as a vice of foreigners and gave the example of Amasis, ruler of Egypt, who became *apeles* to the extent that he lost his kingdom.

The Greek word for drinker, *philopotes,* which also meant "lover of drinking sessions," bore no stigma. As drinking was an inherently pleasurable activity it was understandable that people would want to indulge in it as much as possible. Those who succumbed too often did so not out of dependency but rather from an inability to resist an entirely natural impulse. They were considered weak, not wrong. In contrast, inappropriate sobriety was thought highly suspect. Some skills, such as oratory, could only be exercised when drunk. Sober people were coldhearted—they meditated before they spoke and were careful about what they said, and therefore, according to *logic,* the new science of reason, did not really care about their subject. When the orator Demosthenes wanted to criticize the youth of Athens for their drinking habits he had to coin a new term—*akratokothones*—to distinguish their dangerous kind of drinking. "But even so it was the remark and not its target that became notorious, laying the orator open to the more serious charge of being a water drinker."

Water drinkers were believed not only to lack passion but also to exude a noxious odor. Hegesander the Delphian noted that when the two infamous water drinkers Anchimolus and Moschus went to the public baths everyone else got out. The different powers of the respective beverages were summed up in an epigram:

> If with water you fill up your glasses,
> You'll never write anything wise
> But wine is the horse of Parnassus,
> That carries a bard to the skies.

This is not to suggest that the Greeks, whenever possible, avoided drinking water—they wrote lovingly of certain springs and streams whose contents were distinguished by their delicious flavors or medicinal qualities. Indeed, scientific inquiry, then in its infancy, was prepared to defend the beverage to a limited degree: "But that water is undeniably nutritious is plain from the fact that some animals are nourished by it alone, as for instance, grasshoppers."

However, the same special quality in wine that raised its drinkers above water lovers was recognized as being a potentially dangerous force. The more extreme degrees of intoxication were conceived of as a kind of possession, during which an anarchic spirit took command of the drinker's reason, made them blurt out all sorts of truths, and forced them to reveal their secrets, even to absolute strangers.[1] According to a maxim of the period, "Wine lays bare the heart of man," and in the days when looking glasses were made from sheets of burnished metal:

> As brass is a mirror to the face,
> So is wine for the mind.

Indiscretion was not the only side effect of too much wine to be recognized by the Greeks. Excessive indulgence could make "an old man dance against his will" and was the "sire of blows and violence." Those who dedicated their lives to their amphorae, who went beyond *apeles,* were compared to rudderless ships, liable to drift with the wind and to wreck themselves on shoals. Finally, the Greeks also recognized that drinking could kill, albeit only suddenly. Their literature is littered with examples of men and mythical beasts who lost their lives to wine. In almost all such cases death was instantaneous—a pint or

---

[1] Aspiring Grecian politicians were warned off drunkenness: Pittacus, writing to Periander of Priene, cautioned him to steer clear of drink "so that it may not be discovered what sort of a person you really are, and that you are not what you pretend to be."

two too many and the drinker expired on the spot. Sudden death by drinking might strike anyone, anywhere, and there is evidence, in the form of a tombstone inscription, that public-spirited individuals sought to warn the living of the lethal potential of alcohol:

THIS IS THE MONUMENT OF THAT GREAT DRINKER,

ARCADION; AND HIS TWO LOVING SONS,

DORCON AND CHARMYLUS, HAVE PLACED IT HERE,

AT THIS THE ENTRANCE OF HIS NATIVE CITY:

AND KNOW, TRAVELER, THE MAN DID DIE

FROM DRINKING NEAT WINE IN TOO LARGE A CUP.

The Greeks attributed the perilous aspects of drinking to the work of a god—Bacchus, also known as Dionysus, who was the embodiment of their views about alcohol. Bacchus was a composite immortal, who had started life as a simple fertility idol and was built up over time into the sophisticated divinity of the classical period. He resembled Osiris in some aspects, and the Greeks acknowledged that they had borrowed from the Egyptians when crafting their god. The finished item was claimed to be the love child of the union between Zeus, the Thunderer, and Semele, a princess of Thebes. He was said to have been twice born, as Zeus had been forced to kill his pregnant lover to satisfy a technical point of Greek theology and had carried Bacchus in a special pouch in his thigh for the remainder of his term. After passing his infancy with the sea nymphs, the young demi-immortal spent his youth at Mount Nysa, which was reckoned to be in Africa or Arabia. Nysa, wherever it was, possessed a somewhat lax educational system. Instead of learning, like other little Greek boys, how to fight and debate, Dionysus passed his time in "dances and with troops of girls... and in every kind of luxury and amusement." His education over, he returned to Greece with the aim of initiating its people into the pleasures of the grape. He wore his hair and beard very long and sported a wreath of vine leaves and ivy. A fawn skin was draped over his shoulders, and he traveled in a chariot drawn by a pair of leopards. His languid behavior and slender body, in contrast to the dynamism and heroic proportions of the other bastard sons of Zeus, verged on the effeminate. His power, however, was truly divine, and exercised in a capricious manner, as is illustrated by the story of how he introduced wine to Greece.

◈ ◈ ◈

According to legend, upon his return to Hellenic soil, Bacchus had paused at a village where a goatherd named Ikarios offered him a drink of milk. In return, he presented Ikarios with some vines, together with directions as to how to cultivate them and how to turn their fruit into wine. The goatherd followed the god's instructions, created the first-ever Greek vintage, and invited his neighbors to share the new drink. They were amazed by its bouquet, stunned by its effects, and soon were dancing and singing its praises. However, one by one they lost control of their legs. Those still upright accused Ikarios of poisoning them, beat him to death, and threw his mutilated body into a well. His daughter, Erigone, went mad with grief and hanged herself. She was turned into a star, in the constellation of Virgo. Maira, her faithful dog who guarded her body, was likewise set in the heavens as Canis Minor, the lesser dog. Maira was a vindictive little creature and has yet to forgive humanity for the death of her mistress. She rules over the hottest days of summer, whose scorching sun and dusty winds drive men mad.[2]

The tale is typical of those involving Bacchus. Like wine, he brought happiness but sometimes also chaos and misery. Notwithstanding this duality, he had many devotees. He was a god who stood for the untamed side of human nature, for liberation from the conventions of communal living. The long-haired love child of Zeus was a favorite among women, who would leave off their normal occupation of weaving, retire to the countryside, and surrender themselves to their divinity. These devotees were known as *maenads*, "women who were driven mad," or *Bacchae*—the celebrants of Bacchus—and were distinguished by their cries of "OI!" The state of excitement they achieved was called *ecstasis*—hence our word *ecstasy*. They were famously outrageous. After enough wine they became inflamed with lust and bloodlust. The former they appeased by raping shepherds, the latter by tearing their flocks to pieces and eating them raw. They adorned trees with *phalloi*, they danced in a wild

---

[2] The only defense against the baneful influence of the dog star was to drink: Alcaeus, the Mitylenaean poet, says:

> Steep your heart in rosy wine, for see, the dog star is in view;
> Lest by heat and thirst oppressed you should the season's fury rue.

and abandoned manner, they threw away their clothing, and neither apologized nor repented when they deigned to return home,
exhausted, naked, and covered with blood, to their brothers, their
husbands, and their sons. The antics of these fair devotees were a
popular theme in the visual art of the period. Scantily clad maenads
appear painted on pottery, sculpted in bas relief and in the round in
marble, and cast in bronze, and are claimed to be the first representations of mortal female beauty ever to have been created by the
hands of man.

In addition to such impromptu forms of worship, Bacchus enjoyed
a number of formal rites. As befits the god of temporary amnesia, he
was patron of the Greek theater, and every year in Athens, and every
two or three years in other parts of Greece, festivals were staged in his
honor. His patronage of the dramatic arts was traced in legend to his
encounter with Ikarios, who had killed a goat that tried to eat his vines
and, when their grapes were ripe, had used its skin as a receptacle for
the new wine. Ikarios and his friends had danced around the goatskin
during the early stages of their drinking bout, thus inventing "the rit
ual dance of the *tragos,* the goat," which was the germ of the annual
festival of Athenian *tragodia,* or tragedy. Comedy, the other principal
theatrical genre in the ancient world, was likewise derived from the
spontaneous devotions of the followers of the god of wine. Their
drunken processions were termed *komos,* hence *komodia,* which celebrated the playful side of human nature, and which parodied the behavior of inebriates onstage.

Some of the tragedies and comedies written for the festival of Bacchus have survived and are still performed. They include one dedicated entirely to their patron—the *Bacchae,* by Euripides (484–406 BC),
which portrays its subject as lord of the ecstatic dance, as an advocate
of back-to-nature, and as an assassin. The *Bacchae* tells the story of the
arrival of Bacchus in Thebes and his attempts to introduce its population to his rites. The women of the city-state are fascinated, but its
ruler perceives the exotic and effete stranger to be a threat to his authority. The king challenges the god and loses—he is torn apart offstage by his mother and other drunken maenads, who have mistaken
him in their cups for a young lion, and congratulate themselves for
killing such difficult game as they share out his flesh. The message of
the play is that there exist some aspects of human nature that the state
cannot and should not try to control.

Notwithstanding the lessons in the *Bacchae,* and a generally enthusiastic attitude toward alcohol, the Greeks had strict rules as to who might consume the fluid. It was not customary for women to drink. Excepting the rare occasions on which they slipped out to worship Bacchus, they were expected to steer clear of wine. They were excused from formal participation in civic wine and meat feasts; for the wine was believed to make them *paroinos* (violent when drunk). Outside of the seasons for Bacchanalia, women who wanted wine were forced to make clandestine arrangements for its procurement. Many were ready to take the risk: According to the comic playwrights of the period, Greek women were secretive and dedicated drinkers.

Since access at home to drink was often controlled by a slave, with orders to keep it from the women, most slaked their thirsts in the *kapelion,* or taverns. According to archaeological evidence kapelion were widespread, and each neighborhood in the average town had a local wine bar. Their importance within the community is corroborated by the numerous *katadesmoi,* or hex tablets, which were pottery shards inscribed with curses against named persons and activated by the blessing of a magician, and which litter the ruins of Greek cities. These artifacts, each one bearing a line or two of vitriol, have as their usual targets tavern keepers, their wives, bar slaves, and married women.

Whereas custom held women and alcohol apart, philosophy alone kept it from the mouths of infants. A minimum drinking age was proposed by Plato in his *Laws,* which were intended to frame the legislation for an ideal society. According to Plato, no one under the age of eighteen should be allowed to touch wine, for the young were typified by "excitable" dispositions and it was an error to inflame this with wine, to "pour fire upon fire." Plato recommended further restrictions until middle age but limitless access thereafter: "When a man has reached the age of forty, he may join in the convivial gatherings and invoke Bacchus, above all other gods, . . . that thereby we men may renew our youth, and that, through forgetfulness of care, the temper of our souls may lose its hardness and become softer and more ductile."

Plato subsequently changed his mind about the minimum drinking age he'd proposed in the *Laws.* In his *Republic,* a revised blueprint for the ideal state, he argued, in the dialectic form he perfected, that youth must learn to drink. The reason given for the volte-face was that since wine was a necessary part of culture, it was best that young men gained early experience of its effects and disciplined themselves to manage them, as the following dialogue illustrates:

> ATHENIAN STRANGER: Are not those who train in gymnasia, at
>   first ... reduced to a state of weakness?
> CLEINIAS: Yes, all that is well known.
> ATHENIAN STRANGER: Also that they go of their own accord for the
>   sake of the subsequent benefit?
> CLEINIAS: Very good.
> ATHENIAN STRANGER: And we may conceive this to be true in the
>   same way of other practices?
> CLEINIAS: Certainly.
> ATHENIAN STRANGER: And the same view may be taken of the
>   pastime of drinking wine, if we are right in supposing that the
>   same good effect follows?
> CLEINIAS: To be sure.

In the opinion of Plato, the proper forum for training youth to tipple wisely, the gymnasium, so to speak, of wine, was the *symposium,* a formal, if convivial, drinking party. In order to emphasize the positive influence such gatherings could assert on society, he provided an ideal example of one in an eponymous prose work. His opinion was shared by most Greeks, who considered symposia to be the perfect expression of Hellenic culture. They were staged in accordance with strict rules that determined the order of proceedings, the number of guests, and that set a limit on the quantity of wine to be consumed. They were held in the *androns,* or men's rooms, of private houses. These were furnished with a squared circle of couches on which guests reclined in pairs. The number of couches was seven, eleven, or fifteen, meaning fourteen, twenty-two, or thirty people present. All the guests were male, for the Greeks considered the habit, current in other nations, of encouraging men to eat with their female relations by blood or marriage to be barbaric.

A symposium commenced with a banquet, which was consumed without wine. Dinner was followed by drinking. The drinking was subject to a precise etiquette. First, a *symposiarch* was elected from among the guests, whose duty was to choose how they would be entertained

while they drank. Next the guests, under the guidance of the symposiarch, decided how many *kraters* (a vessel the size of a garden urn) of
wine they would consume together, and in what proportion the wine
inside them would be mixed with water. The usual number of kraters
seems to have been three, the usual proportion three-to-one water to
wine, which would have resulted in a drink with a similar alcoholic
strength to modern beer. The wine was then served in drinking bowls
and drinking cups, decorated with Bacchic or other scenes. Some emphasized the bestial potential of wine with images of drunken centaurs
attempting to tread grapes or rape peasants; while others represented
its elevating qualities with beautiful girls in diaphanous robes, tossing
their heads and kicking their heels, lost in the ecstasy of the dance.

A variety of pastimes were enjoyed at symposia. The most common, a relic of the warrior feast, was the recital or composition of
poetry, which was accompanied by music. Guests took turns to
sing—a little like modern karaoke. The music was provided by
pornikes, or flute girls, who sometimes doubled up as prostitutes
(hence pornography—the graphic depiction of flute girls). Other

Detail of ancient Greek wine cup

popular entertainments included *aenigma*–playing at riddles–and a drinking game called *kottabus,* in which the player would throw the last drops of wine in his cup toward a metal bowl, while shouting out the name of his beloved. If all the wine hit the bowl with a clear, ringing tone, then all was well, but if it missed, Aphrodite, goddess of love, had blackballed him.

While in the ideal example of a symposium provided by Plato, the guests trundle off home in varying degrees of inebriation after a night of philosophizing, some of these gatherings ended in riot and disorder: It seems to have been part of their tradition that once the eating, sensible drinking, and entertainment had finished, the participants would quit the *andron* for the streets and perform a drunken *komos* through town. On the occasions when they were too drunk to leave the andron, they threw its furniture out the windows. Groups of well-bred young men formed drinking clubs, with names such as the Ithyphalloi (erections) and the Autolekythoi (wankers), which staged regular symposia, at which passions ran so high that one such caused a war:

> Some young fellows, made drunk at too many games of Kottabos, went to Megara and stole a whore named Simaetha; thereupon the Megarians, in agonies of excitement, as though stuffed with garlic, stole in revenge two whores of Aspasia; and with that began the war which broke out over all Greece, caused by three strumpets.

War was a constant in classical Greece and kept its best minds in motion: The playwright Euripides composed his *Bacchae* while in exile in Macedonia, a country to the northeast of its Greek neighbors, which was acknowledged to be imperfectly Hellenic–a friend of some Greek nations, but no more. Macedonia was a sort of buffer zone, where Greek was spoken, Greek gods were worshipped, and Greek culture thrived, but all these were tainted with barbarism–Macedonians had atrocious accents, their worship, centered on sacrifice, occasionally human, was savage enough to raise Greek eyebrows, and to cap it all, their neighbors on the other side were the gloriously brutish Thracians. Despite its cultural limitations, Macedonia under King Philip II rose to be a regional power in the fourth century BC and the leader of a forced alliance of the principal Greek states. Once he had achieved dominance, Philip took pains to represent himself as a philhellene, a champion of Greek civilization. Orators, historians, philosophers, and artists were invited to his palace, many of whom returned his hospitality with sneers. According to one such, the Macedonians "gamble, drink, and squander money. . . . More savage than the half-bestial centaurs, they are not restrained from buggery by the fact that they have beards." Indeed, the only matter in which Philip won unqualified approval was in his worship of Bacchus. The historian Theopompus described him as "a man of violent temper and fond of courting dangers, partly from nature, and partly too from drinking; for he was a very hard drinker, and very often he would attack the enemy while he was drunk."

Hard-drinking fathers breed hard-drinking sons. Alexander (356–323 BC), known to history as the Great, conqueror of most of the world known to antiquity, took after Philip in his fondness for wine. Indeed, his drinking habits, and their contribution to his early death, were the subject of scrutiny and controversy for centuries after the event. Alexander's tutor was the philosopher Aristotle, who is recognized as the founding father of the scientific method, and who produced a treatise on the nature of alcohol and its place in society. Unfortunately only a few fragments of this work survive to tell us what Aristotle thought of drink. These show that he came tantalizingly close to discovering distillation, although he succeeded only in turning wine into flavored water, rather than spirits: "If the wine be moderately boiled, then when it is drunk, it is less apt to intoxicate; for as some of its power has been boiled away, it has become weaker." They also show that he experimented with the effects of alcohol on animals and believed that "the man who commits a crime when drunk should be punished twice over, once for the crime, and once for being drunk," although this maxim had little influence on the behavior of his pupil.

Alexander assumed the throne of Macedonia after King Philip was murdered in 336 BC. Having secured his kingdom and control of Greece, Alexander invaded Persia in 334 BC. The Persians were the archenemies of the Greeks and had attempted their subjugation on two occasions in the fourth century BC. They were acknowledged to be a special sort of barbarian, whose civilization was older and culture more refined than that of the Greeks. They, too, were committed wine drinkers; indeed Darius I, their greatest king, had the inscription "I was able to drink a good deal of wine and to bear it well" engraved on his tomb. Wine was ubiquitous in Persian society, and according to the Greek historian Herodotus, in addition to slaking their thirsts and inspiring them to poetry, it was used as a decision-making tool: "If an important decision is to be made, they discuss the question when they are drunk, and the following day the master of the house where the discussion was held submits their resolution for reconsideration when they are sober. If they still approve it, it is adopted; if not, it is abandoned. Conversely, any decision they make when they are sober is reconsidered afterward when they are drunk."

The Persian empire consisted of a patchwork of subject states stretching from Anatolia to Afghanistan, incorporating the greater part of the Fertile Crescent, where the vine had first been cultivated. By 333 BC, Alexander had overcome its armies and occupied its capital, Persepolis, which he burned to the ground, quite possibly by accident, when his Bacchic victory celebrations got out of hand. He then proceeded to the conquest of Babylon and Egypt. Already the master of a greater territory than any previous Western ruler, he resumed his march to the east, reaching as far as the Punjab in India in 325 BC. In the process of his conquests, he introduced Greek culture, including a taste for wine, to a vast swath of territory. His armies were accompanied by philosophers, geographers, and historians, who compared their own observations to those of past travelers, and to legends, including that of Bacchus. Alexander himself "wanted the tales of the god's wanderings to be true" and, en route through the mountains of the Punjab, became convinced that he was indeed following in the footsteps of Bacchus. Some local tribesmen, captured in a skirmish and questioned through interpreters, called themselves Nysaeans and the mountain beside them Nysa. Could this be Mount Nysa, the legendary sanctuary of the god of wine in his youth? The presence of wild vines and ivy seemed confirmation, so Alexander made formal sacrifice and "many of the not unprominent officers around him garlanded themselves with ivy and . . . were promptly possessed by the god and raised the call of Dionysus, running in his frantic rout."

The Macedonians claimed to find the worship of Bacchus to be widespread in India, although it is likely that they confused the Hindu god Shiva with the son of Zeus. Shiva is often portrayed adorned with a tiger skin, in the style of Bacchus and his dappled cloak, and his followers, like bacchantes, were fond of dancing and drumming. Moreover, the Indian doctrine of reincarnation had a parallel in the birth and rebirth of the god of wine. In general, however, the Macedonians found the inhabitants of India temperate by their own standards. According to a doctor attached to their army, the Indians suffered from few diseases "on account of the simplicity of their diet and their abstinence from wine." They were, however, considered to be fond of binge drinking, and when the Indian swami Calanus, who had followed the army for two years, lecturing whoever would listen, burned himself to death, Alexander staged a games in his memory. Since the Indians were unfamiliar with Olympic disciplines, it was decided that the contest should be "as to who should drink the greatest quantity of unmixed wine." The consequences, as any Athenian would have predicted, were disastrous: "Of those who entered for the prize and drank the wine, thirty-five died at once by reason of the cold; and a little afterward six more died in their tents. . . . He who drank the greatest quantity and won the prize, drank four choes of unmixed wine . . . and he lived four days after it; and he was called the Champion."

The contest took place close to the outer limit of Alexander's conquests. Compelled to turn back by his Macedonian veterans, some of whom had been ten years from home, he led a disastrous march west through the Gedrosian Desert, where many of them were lost. The tragedy was attributed to Bacchus, who was believed to have a score to settle with Alexander. In his early Greek campaigns, Alexander had razed Thebes, which was under the official protection of the god of wine, but had failed to make the proper sacrifices in amends. When the source of his woes was pointed out to him, together with the corroborating evidence that he had killed his best friend when drunk—a sure sign of Bacchic displeasure—Alexander sought to appease the offended god with a triumphal procession of the remains of his army through Babylon. Perhaps the gesture of conciliation failed. He died of unknown causes in June 323 BC, at the age of thirty-two. While theories abounded as to what it was that killed him, including drinking a pair of eight-pint horns of neat wine in quick succession, the most likely cause was poison. Within twenty-five years his empire had been divided into four—Macedon, Thrace, Mesopotamia, and Egypt. Egypt fell to Ptolemy, one of his generals, whose descendants formed a dynasty that ruled it for fourteen generations and nearly three centuries. The last of the Ptolemaic line to rule Egypt was the seventeen-year-old Cleopatra VII, whose allure and bounteous possessions attracted the attention of a new Mediterranean power: Rome.

3 IN VINO VERITAS

Rome was the next great drinking civilization to emerge in the classical world. Founded in legend by the twins Romulus and Remus on the banks of the river Tiber, the city-state subdued first its neighbors–the Latins, the Samnites, and the Etruscans–so that by 275 BC it controlled most of the Italian peninsula. Over the next 150 years, following victories over the Carthaginians and the Macedonians, Rome established itself as the preeminent nation in the Mediterranean. The new superpower gained ascendancy through a genius for organization and republicanism. On the way up, it won the respect of its foes for its asceticism and single-mindedness; once it was on top, it distinguished itself, at home, through decadence.

Like the Greeks, the Romans have left us a comprehensive picture of their drinking habits. These changed drastically over time, for in its formative years, by Hellenic standards, Rome was almost dry. Romulus, its mythical first ruler, is said to have used only milk when making offerings to his gods. The situation was little better in 290 BC, when the dictator Papirius could only tender a single small cup of wine to the god Jupiter in order to win his favor in a battle against the Samnites. The scarcity of wine in early Rome is corroborated by the relative insignificance of Liber, their native deity of the grape, who was an altogether more modest immortal than Bacchus. His duties seem to have been limited to protecting vines and their fruit. The power to inspire divine madness in a drinker was far beyond his reach, and when the cult of Bacchus reached Roman territory in the second century BC it was received with suspicion, and its adherents were persecuted. It did not seem possible, to such a sober culture, that people should congregate in large bands merely for the purpose of becoming drunk together. The Romans decided that it was all a sinister plot to destabilize their rule, and in 186 BC their Senate issued a decree commanding the destruction of Bacchic shrines and the prohibition of Bacchic rites throughout Italy. With proscription came persecution: Spurius Postumius Albinus and Quintus Marcius Philipus were diverted from the "care of armies, and wars, and provinces, to the punishing of an intestine conspiracy." Nearly seven thousand devotees of Bacchus lost their lives in the ensuing purge. The slaughter was justified on the grounds that its victims were irredeemable villains, who left "no sort of crime, no kind of immorality" unattempted, and among whom "there were more obscenities practiced between men than between men and women."

Not only did the Romans of the time have a cultural blind spot for inebriation as a form of worship, they were also utterly opposed to any creed that encouraged drinking among women. Their traditional views on this matter were strong. According to one of their own historians, "at Rome women were not allowed to drink wine.... The wife of Egnatius Maetennus was clubbed to death by her husband for drinking from a large jar, and he ... was acquitted of murder by Romulus." The same source quoted, with approval, the example of a matron "who was starved to death by her family for having broken open the box containing the keys to the wine store." In addition to prohibiting women from drinking, the early Romans also restricted the access of slaves and young men under thirty to alcohol.

However, within a few decades of the anti-Bacchic purge, Roman attitudes toward drink had shifted. The change was driven by pragmatic, rather than cultural, reasons. Wine formed part of the rations of Roman legionaries, and a secure and increasing supply was necessary to support the efforts of ever larger and more active armies. Once it had been decided that they would get into viticulture, the Romans went about the business with their customary thoroughness. Their genius was standardization. Weapons, legions, sewers, and roads were assembled according to formula. This practical bent was now applied to the cultivation of the grape. Their first steps were to establish a uniform procedure for winemaking, and to achieve this they were forced to borrow from their enemies.

In 160 BC, in the midst of the throes of the final Punic War, the

Roman senate ordered the translation of a Carthaginian treatise on viticulture, resulting in *De Agri Cultura,* by Marcus Porcius Cato, which is the earliest surviving prose work in Latin. *De Agri Cultura* covered every aspect of vineyard management, right down to the rations of slaves, and their clothing allowances. It was circulated among landowners, and Rome very quickly became a significant producer of wine. By the standards of the time, the new model vineyards were large (Cato recommended sixty acres) commercial ventures, which required a substantial investment in slaves, plant, and buildings. They focused on producing bulk wines. *De Agri Cultura* speaks of only six different kinds of wine, against the fifty or so recognized by the Greeks. In addition to encouraging domestic production, Rome also set about stifling competition. In 154 BC the cultivation of vines beyond the Alps was banned. This protectionist measure stimulated domestic output further, and within a decade Roman-made wine was being exported in substantial volume to newly conquered territories.

A plentiful supply altered Roman attitudes toward drinking. They no longer need to count each cup when making offerings to their gods, and their largesse increased accordingly. They disposed of most of the surplus they produced by adopting the drinking culture of the Greeks, which both compensated for the poverty of their own and provided them with a wide range of reasons and rituals for consuming wine. By the middle of the first century BC, the transformation of Rome from a sober society, suspicious of both alcohol and drunkenness, to a major producer, populated with practiced and discriminating drinkers, was complete. The extent of change is apparent in the behavior of Mark Antony, a contender for the rule of Rome during the period of one of its civil wars (44–31 BC). Antony established his power base in the eastern part of Rome's possessions, conducted a long and fruitful love affair with Queen Cleopatra of Egypt, and went into his final battle disguised as Bacchus, right down to the fawn skin and tambourine. Such conduct would have been simply inconceivable to his disciplined and ascetic ancestors, who had been one of the most proper plebeian families of ancient Rome.

The ultimate victor of this conflict was Octavian, acknowledged as Augustus Caesar, the first Roman emperor, whose absolute rule commenced in 27 BC. Thereafter, a fashion for rare and costly foreign vintages appeared among the senior orders of citizens, and "the study of wines become a passion, and the most scrupulous care was be-

stowed upon every process connected with their production and pres-
ervation." Roman writers, moreover, dedicated an increasing quantity
of their output toward praising wine. Some even went so far as to
denigrate water drinking, which would have been treasonous in the
republican age, when Rome's magnificent aqueducts were a matter of
national pride. These new advocates of the grape borrowed heavily
from Hellenic culture and, in doing so, incorporated Bacchus within
their own. Poets began to call upon him in Latin as well as Greek to
fill them with the creative spirit: "Whither, O Bacchus, dost thou
hurry me, o'erflowing with thy power? Into what groves or grottoes
am I swiftly driven in fresh inspiration?"

Not only did the Romans adopt Bacchus, they also embellished
him with new myths and provided him with a sidekick–Silenus–a
bloated middle-aged inebriate who carried around a bulging wine
skin, and who served the drinks at mythical revels. However, while
the powers of the god of wine were extended in fiction, belief in their
truth diminished. The Roman Bacchus was less of a mystery than the
Greek variety. He was another statue on a crowded shelf, invoked as a
figure of speech rather than venerated as an object of faith. Wine became a secular substance, and the Romans no longer thought it necessary to blame drunkenness on possession by a god. In the absence of
such magical associations, the effects of drinking were scrutinized
with more critical eyes.

The poet Horace, in his *Epistles,* ridiculed the notion that since
wine inspired writers writers should be drunk. Noting that "from the
moment Liber enlisted brain-sick poets among his satyrs and fauns,
the sweet muses, as a rule, have had a scent of wine about them in the
morning," and that would-be poets "have never ceased to vie in wine
drinking by night and to reek of it by day," he pointed out that this was
to mistake the symptoms for the cause and was as futile as dressing up
like Cato without possessing Cato's virtues. Horace was, however, a
fervent advocate of alcohol per se, so long as it was consumed in accordance with his motto, "Let Moderation Reign!" In the right quantities, in his opinion, wine could be a miracle worker: "It unlocks secrets,
bids hopes be fulfilled, thrusts the coward onto the battlefield, takes
the load from anxious hearts. The flowing bowl–whom has it not
made eloquent? Whom has it not made free even amid pinching poverty?"

In addition to ridiculing drunken poets and praising temperate drinking, Horace also satirized the prevailing fashions for fine wines and for consuming too much of them. He singled out for especial ridicule the trend toward ever more elaborate drinking rituals in the style of the Grecian symposium and poured scorn upon the vogue for ceremony. He was, however, swimming against the tide. The Romans of the imperial era had fallen in love with ostentation–magnificence was in as much as Hellenism–and they developed a domestic version of the symposium at which they might display their wealth and taste.

The Roman dinner party, or *convivium,* differed from its model in many aspects. Wine was served before, with, and after food, whereas in Greece the drinking had begun only after eating had ended. Most significantly, women were admitted to the dinner table, where they drank with the same gusto as their male counterparts. Rome, once noted for the sobriety of its women, became known for its drunkardesses. Their excesses attracted the attention of its satirists. The poet Martial pictured one such Latin maenad trying to hide the alcohol on her breath by not speaking; to no avail for her uncontrolled belching released its odor.

A measure of the difference between entertaining in imperial Rome and classical Athens is provided by the *Satyricon* of Petronius Arbiter, written during the reign of the emperor Nero. The story of two young men of good families who philander their way around the empire accompanied by a handsome catamite, and pursued by a nymphomaniac, the high priestess of Priapus, god of erections, and a gay but vengeful sea captain, the *Satyricon* features a convivium at the house of a rich ex-slave named Trimalchio, which is the polar opposite of the ideal symposium depicted by Plato. Whereas the Greek example focuses on the inventive wine-inspired after-dinner speeches of its participants, the Roman version is distinguished by coarse and venal conversation and the uglier forms of drunkenness.

The tone for this latter feast is set when the heroes of the *Satyricon* meet their host at the baths, where he is playing ball. Exercise over, Trimalchio urinates in a silver chamber pot carried around by a dedicated eunuch, wipes his fingers in the eunuch's hair, and leads his guests home in a little dogcart pulled by a matching pair of slaves. The former have their toenails cut on arrival and are offered a glass of sweet wine as an aperitif. The dinner that follows is comprised of a series of culinary prodigies accompanied by spectacular vintages. Trimalchio opens a glass jar of Opimian Falernian ("Guaranteed one hundred years old!"), while his guests talk about money and death. He leaves the table midmeal to ease his bowels and advises his guests to follow his example ("There's not a man been born yet with solid insides"). His wife, meanwhile, an equal paragon of bad taste, drinks herself into a frenzy in his absence. Upon his return to the table, she accuses him of preferring the bodies of young boys to her own, then attacks him with her fingernails. Peace is only restored when Trimalchio commands for his will to be brought in and read out. It frees some of the slaves present, who burst into tears of gratitude. The dinner ends in drunken chaos: Trimalchio commands his band to play a funeral march; the neighbors mistake it for a fire alarm and break down the door with axes, enabling the better-mannered guests to escape.

Trimalchio, the epitome of the new Roman model of inebriate, made his money in the wine trade, which had gone from strength to strength under the early emperors. Its vintners, like their Greek and Egyptian predecessors, had begun to focus on quality as well as volume. Around AD 60, a Roman Spaniard, Columella, wrote a new treatise on winemaking, which superseded Cato's *De Agri Cultura*. While much of his advice regarding the situation of vineyards and the management of slaves was little different, Columella recognized at least twenty types of wine grape, including the Bumast ("full breasted"), and the "wooly" Aminean, against Cato's mere half dozen. Moreover, their juices could be combined to make more than a hundred kinds of wine, a figure confirmed by the historian Pliny.

Columella was also an early prophet of genetics and advised his readers to consider each vine as an individual and to breed only from the best of them, for just as "those who contend in the sacred games protect with watchful care the progeny of their swiftest race horses, and upon the multiplying of offspring of noble stock they base their hope of future victories, we, too, for a reason like theirs in selecting the progeny of victorious Olympic mares, should base our hope of a bountiful vintage upon the selection of progeny of the most fruitful."

His treatise was political as well as practical. Columella saw viticulture as the potential salvation of Rome, now up to its neck in decadence. Its emperors had gone from bad to worse: Whereas Augustus, the first Caesar, had been abstemious and had forced himself to vomit if occasion demanded he drink more than a pint of wine, his successors had gloried in excess. Caligula, the third emperor (d. AD 41), "assumed the entire garb of Bacchus and made royal progresses and sat in judgment thus arrayed"; Nero (d. AD 68), the next Caesar but one, had married himself, as a woman, to one of his knights, consecrated the marriage, also as a woman, and, when Rome had been devastated by a fire, had embarked on a drinking binge while he serenaded the flames with his harp. Rome's citizens, meanwhile, as the *Satyricon* implied, were hell-bent on following the examples set on high.

In the opinion of Columella, the empire could only save itself from decadence by making wine instead of drinking it. He pictured the vigorous good health enjoyed by vintners and contrasted it with the weakness of his fellow Romans who wasted their hours in the circuses and theaters rather than in the grainfields and vineyards. "We spend our nights in licentiousness and drunkenness, our days in gaming or sleeping, and account ourselves blessed by fortune in that 'we behold neither the rising of the sun nor its setting,'" he regretted, and concluded that in consequence "the bodies of our young men are so flabby and enervated that death seems likely to make no change in them."

The decadent style of drinking lamented by Rome's poets, satirists, and gentlemen farmers was nowhere more in evidence than in Pompeii, center of the Roman wine trade. The vine had first been cultivated in the region by Greek colonists, and by the age of the Caesars the town had become one of the principal sources of Italian wine. Although some of its vintages were respected by connoisseurs, its main business was in bulk wine for export. According to Pliny, "Wines from Pompeii are at their best within ten years and gain nothing from greater maturity. They are also observed to be injurious because of the hangover they cause, which persists until noon on the following day." Hangovers notwithstanding, Pompeiians were furious drinkers, who seem to have measured the appeal of wine by the quantity they drank. In order to realize their ideal, they cooked themselves in the municipal baths to sweat out previous binges, then, "without putting on a stitch of clothing, still naked and gasping, [would] seize hold of a huge jar . . . and, as if to demonstrate their strength, pour down the entire contents . . . vomit it up again immediately, and then drink another jar. This they repeat two or three times over, as if they were born to waste wine and as if wine could be disposed of only through the agency of the human body."

Pompeii and the neighboring town of Herculaneum were destroyed by the eruption of Mount Vesuvius on August 24, AD 79. Pliny

was killed by poison fumes, and the degenerate Pompeiians were buried alive under a layer of mud, lava, and ashes. The resulting time
capsule has preserved the scenes of their excess. The grander villas of
the town have frescoes depicting the production of wine, or the adventures of Bacchus, including one important series from the so-called
House of the Mysteries, which shows, in sequence, a young woman
being stripped, whipped, and initiated into the arcania of a Bacchic
sect. Also preserved are the town's 118 *tabernae,* or taverns, where the
poorer citizens drank. A typical example consisted of a single, open
room, with a counter to one side, behind which amphorae were stored
on their sides on racks, rather like the barrels of beer in an English
country pub. Wine was dispensed from these into pottery *cucumas,* or
carafes, and was available in a range of qualities—as evinced by the bill
of fare chalked onto the blackboard of one such establishment:

> For one [coin] you can drink wine
> For two you can drink the best
> For four you can drink Falernian.

The Romans continued the Greek habit of mixing their wine with
water, and despite the abundance in Pompeii of the former, *tabernae*
keepers were not above overdiluting their vintages with the contents of
the town aqueducts, as a piece of graffiti from another tavern indicates:
"Curses on you, Landlord, you sell water and drink unmixed wine
yourself." Some *tabernae,* known as *popinae,* also doubled as brothels
and were graced with splendidly candid frescoes of fornicating couples
on the walls of their back rooms.

While most of the public drinking in Pompeii took place in its *tabernae,* wine was also served, sometimes for free, in its amphitheater. The
Roman culture of spectacle entertainments, in particular the spectacle
of death, has few parallels in history. Tribal society everywhere was
brutal, public executions were a common feature of most ancient civilizations, but the organization, the scale, and the frequency of bestiaria
(shows in which wild animals were killed), gladiatorial contests, chariot races, and other such extravaganzas placed Rome in a category of
its own. These spectacles were staged to purchase the affection of the
masses. The republic was dead, but its façade was preserved and

Romans fought for election to various public offices through largesse. Whoever put on the best show gained the greatest number of supporters. The most extreme entertainments were staged in the capital and were accounted by the epigrammatist Martial to be the greatest wonder of the world, which drew an audience from throughout the empire. Farmers from the provinces, Egyptians, Jews, Scythians, Greeks, and Gauls all flocked to Rome's amphitheaters to satisfy their curiosity and bloodlust. Since most of the spectacles were competitive, in that their sponsors vied with each other for attention, novelty was the watchword. According to Martial, "Whatever Fame sings of ... the arena makes real." Participants in the shows were dressed as historic or mythical figures, ancient battles on land and sea[3] were reenacted, people who had killed, or been killed by, lions in legend were impersonated in appropriate costumes, by criminals or slaves, who were compelled to slay or to die. The old myths were not only staged by the book, but also in sensational variations and ridiculous combinations. Martial records one combat between Daedalus, the legendary Greek who built himself a pair of wings to fly away from captivity, and a wild boar. The boar won: "Daedalus, now thou art being so mangled by a Lucanian boar, how would'st thou wish thou hads't now thy wings!"

Writers such as Martial and Columella were the sternest critics of Roman degeneracy. While they delighted in drawing attention to domestic vices, the reputation of the empire's legions suffered little among its enemies abroad. Roman armies seldom lost battles, and if they did, they were always avenged. The legions maintained the austere principles of the republic, and the depravity that characterized the capital and towns like Pompeii was absent from their camps. The wine rations that they carried served functional rather than hedonistic purposes: Wherever they campaigned they added wine to their drinking water, and its bactericidal properties protected many against the waterborne illnesses that were one of the greatest hazards of warfare in the ancient world. By the end of the first century AD, Roman rule had been extended over much of western Europe, and France, Belgium, parts of Germany, and the British Isles all paid tribute to or professed allegiance with the eternal city.

---

[3] Some of the venues could flood their arenas.

This western expansion had commenced with the step-by-step subjugation of the French Gauls. The process had been assisted by wine in several ways. In the first instance, its superior alcoholic strength had saved Rome at a crucial moment. The Gauls, like most other kinds of western barbarian, were a beer-loving culture with a binge-drinking mentality, and when they had invaded Italy in 105 BC, they had paused in the Alban district to drink it dry of wine. Although practiced inebriates, they were unready for the extra kick that wine possessed, and like the degenerates of imperial Rome, they went into speedy physical decline: "They gained so rapidly in corpulence and flabbiness and became so womanish in physical strength that whenever they undertook to exercise their bodies and to drill in arms their respiration was broken by continual panting, their limbs were drenched by much sweat, and they desisted from their toils before they were bidden to do so by their commanders." Thus compromised, they were slaughtered by the legions.

In addition to reducing the fighting ability of Gallic armies, wine also acted as a civilizing influence in times of peace. The Greek colony of Marseilles on the Mediterranean coast of Gaul had cultivated the grape since its inception, and when the Romans took it over they traded its vintages and their own imports with their former enemies. From the Gallic point of view the stronger the beverage the better, and their drinking habits became stratified through the availability of wine. According to the historian Poseidonius, "The liquor drunk in the houses of the rich is wine brought from Italy and the country round Marseilles, and is unmixed; though sometimes a little water is added. But among the needier inhabitants a beer is drunk made from wheat, with honey added; the masses drink it plain." This stratification, which associated wine with power and beer with servitude, was a godsend to Roman wine merchants, who took "wine to them by ship up the navigable rivers, or by chariot traveling overland" and received "incredible prices" for their wares. The going rate was one slave for one amphora of Pompeiian wine. A slave was worth three hundred times as much in Rome.

Notwithstanding their value as trading partners, the Gauls were difficult neighbors who persisted in launching raids into Roman territory. In order to put an end to such incursions, Julius Caesar took the war to Gaul in 58 BC. He found a few of his adversaries had learned the lesson of the Alban massacre and had banned wine. The Nervii, a

"savage people of great bravery" who lived in what is now the Champagne district of France, "suffered no wine and other things tending to
luxury to be imported; because they thought that by their use the
mind is enervated and the courage impaired." Clearly, the Nervii considered beer and wine to be fluids without anything in common, for
they still drank beer. The additional alcoholic strength of wine seems
to have persuaded them that it was not only dangerous but alien.
They were exterminated by Caesar's legions, as were every other tribe
who put up any resistance, and thereafter Gaul Romanized rapidly.
Emblematic of this progress was the dispersal of the vine. Bordeaux,
once a distant client of Pompeii, became a producer in its own right.

The northern limit of the Pax Romana in France was the river
Rhine, beyond which lurked numerous Germanic tribes. They, like the
ancient Gauls, were beer and binge drinkers. Both characteristics were
recorded by the historian Tacitus, who noted that their usual beverage
was "a liquor prepared from barley or wheat," and that their thirst for it
was not quenched with moderation: "It is no disgrace to pass days and
nights, without intermission, in drinking." Moreover, once they were
drunk, they started fighting, and "the frequent quarrels that arise
amongst them, when inebriated, seldom terminate in abusive language,
but more frequently in blood." The Germans practiced ritual as well as
recreational tippling. Like the Persians in the days of Alexander, they
considered intoxication to be an essential prelude to decision making.
After downing a sufficient quantity of their barley brews, they would
"deliberate on the reconcilement of enemies, on family alliances, on the
appointment of chiefs, and finally on peace and war; conceiving that at
no time is the soul more opened to sincerity, or warmed to heroism." In
the opinion of Tacitus, the Teutonic passion for intoxication was a
weakness that could be exploited: "If you will but humor their excess in
drinking, and supply them with as much as they covet, it will be no less
easy to vanquish them by vices than by arms." Interestingly, the tactic
of inebriating opponents before slaughtering them seems to have been
a standard Roman military stratagem and was employed with great
success over the centuries against various barbarian hordes.

The vast forests of Germania, teeming with beer-drinking savages,
held little interest to the Romans. Civilization had to end somewhere,
and they chose to draw a line to the north along the river Rhine. To
the west, however, lay an Atlantic archipelago, within easy reach of
Gaul, and which, although its sky was "obscured by continual rain and

cloud," was wonderfully fertile, looked promising enough to invade and subdue. The classical world knew very little about Britain or its peoples before Caesar had visited it with his legions in 55 BC. Tacitus admitted this ignorance in his *Agricola,* which contained a potted history of the place: "Who the first inhabitants of Britain were is open to question: We must remember we are dealing with barbarians." Archaeological evidence suggests that the equivocal barbarians were Celtic, and that their drinking habits were little different from those of the Neolithic inhabitants of the Orkney Islands, who had brewed up psychoactive ales by the gallon.

The Romanization of Britain commenced in AD 43 when the emperor Claudius picked up where Caesar had left off and sent four legions over to conquer it. By AD 96, most of England and Wales were part of the empire. Scotland, like Germany, was left to its brutish inhabitants. The subject territory was civilized according to the standard Roman formula. Taxes were imposed that obliged Britons to grow cash crops to sell to the legions in their garrisons; and cooperative local rulers were given Roman names, were encouraged to build country villas in the Italian style, and to plant vineyards. In the event, "competition for honor proved as effective as compulsion," and Britons vied in Romanizing themselves. They imported both wine and Bacchus as symbols of sophistication. His image appeared in villas up and down the land—in mosaic in Somerset, in a fresco in Dover, and in marble in Spoonley Wood, Gloucestershire, where he was carved naked, leaning against a vine-entwined tree trunk, dangling an empty cup over the head of a kittenish panther. The British were eager for Roman literature as well as its visual culture. Martial claimed that "Britain is said to hum my verses," with the intention of implying he was read wherever civilization existed, and proving at the same time the existence in England of a thirst for Latin eloquence.

However, many Britons resented Roman occupation, and while they paid lip service to the customs of their new rulers, their rebellious hearts inspired them to pervert their submission. In Northamptonshire, for instance, the natives superimposed classical shrines on the barrow graves of their ancestors but buried new bodies underneath in the traditional fashion. Moreover, beyond the Roman camps and towns, where Britons still plied their barbarism with impunity, they drank ale not wine, and their ale was so good that it became the staple of the Roman legions stationed in the country. The Augustan legion, which garrisoned a fortress at Vindolanda on the wall that divided England from Scotland, drank far more English ale than the wine supplied to them in their rations. They employed a certain Arrectus, the first named brewer in British history, to prepare them their liquid bread. Such examples of counter-Romanization, however, were rare throughout the empire. Rome had a dominant and lasting influence on the drinking habits of most of Europe. The culture once famed for its love of milk introduced wine to the parts of the continent where it had been absent, together with a bibulous ethos derived from the Greek model. Rome spread the name of Bacchus from the Libyan deserts to Ultima Thule.

4 WINE, BLOOD, SALVATION

**I am the vine, ye are the branches: he that abideth
in me, and I in him, the same bringeth forth much
fruit.**

—John 15:5

At about the same time that the *Satyricon* was composed, and the
wild Britons were developing a taste for wine, a rebellion commenced in one of Rome's more civilized provinces—Judea. The
future emperor Titus, fresh from a stint as military tribune in Britain,
was sent with four legions to subdue the revolt and, in AD 70, sacked
Jerusalem, killed or enslaved much of its population, and burned down
its temple. His victory was commemorated with the construction of a
triumphal arch in Rome, which still stands, and which depicts various
sacred objects taken from the Jews as booty. Religion had been the
cause of the differences between Rome and its Jewish subjects. The
latter were monotheistic and iconoclastic, and had refused to erect a
sculpture of the emperor Caligula in their temple, as required by imperial edict. Their obstinacy in such matters was thought to be a
shame, for in most other aspects, they behaved like a civilized race.
They were a wine-drinking culture, indeed, had been enamored of the
grape for millennia prior to the foundation of Rome. Archaeological
evidence suggests that their Semitic predecessors had carried out an
extensive wine trade with Egypt and probably were responsible for
the vintages found in the tomb of King Scorpion in Hierakonpolis.

The ancient connections of the Jews to viticulture were reflected
in their sacred texts: Wine makes its debut in the Tanakh alongside

Noah. After the flood, the original patriarch disembarked from his ark, planted a vineyard, and "he drank of the wine, and was drunken, and was uncovered in his tent." Thereafter, references to wine flow thick and fast. The promised land—the homeland selected by God for his chosen race—is identified by the presence of vines bearing giant bunches of grapes; the prophets of the Tanakh discuss its consumption, and its patriarchs and kings gave conspicuous examples of how and how not to drink. The Tanakh even provides practical advice in the Book of Isaiah (5:1–5) as to the best way to lay out a vineyard, in the guise of a metaphor that illuminates the love of God for his chosen people. This sacred text is generally very positively disposed toward drinking, albeit with the odd warning: "A laboring man that is given to drunkenness shall not be rich," cautions Ecclesiasticus 19:1, for instance. Such sentiments aside, alcohol, in the form of wine, is usually represented as the gift of god—a source of wealth and happiness, a substance with the power to "soothe the heavy-hearted." Furthermore, the cultivation of the grape is portrayed as a dignified occupation—appropriate work for a prophet or a patriarch.

Wine played an important part in the personal rituals of the Jews. The weekly Sabbath commenced with a prayer delivered over a cup of wine; circumcisions, weddings, and funerals were celebrated with prescribed measures, the consumption of which was obligatory for every man present. In addition to such moderate imbibing, on the annual festival of Purim the faithful were instructed by their rabbis to drink so much wine that they could "no longer distinguish between the phrases 'Cursed be Haman' and 'Blessed be Mordechai,'" respectively their most deadly enemy and most devoted friend at a critical point in their history.

Wine, and the Jewish Tanakh, likewise played vital roles in the lives of the adherents of a new religion, Christianity, which had arisen in the first century AD in Roman Judea. Christians were thought at first to be a breakaway sect of Jews, whose clandestine rituals were a cloak for witchcraft, and which also concealed a conspiracy to overthrow Rome and her empire. The emperor Nero blamed them for the fire that ruined much of his capital in AD 64, and crucified or burned as many of them as he could find. Any stragglers were sewn into the skins of wild beasts and fed to the lions at the circus. Notwithstanding such an inauspicious debut in the history books, the new religion made converts at so rapid a rate that despite imperial hostility, within a century of the death of its founder, Christians could be found in almost every corner of the empire.

The rapid dissemination of Christianity was in part a consequence of the duty Christ had laid upon his followers to propagate his message. This was something of a theological innovation. Judaism, which Christianity acknowledged as its source, and as sharing the same single God, did not seek converts. Moreover, it laid obstacles in the path of those wishing to become Jews, including circumcision for men and strict dietary taboos. Christianity had no such barriers to entry. The matter had been debated and settled by the apostles: Anyone could become a Christian, and every convert was expected to spread the good news.

The early rituals of the new faith were also far simpler than those of Judaism. The single most important rite of the Christians was the ceremony of the Eucharist, at which they gathered to share bread and wine, in accordance with the instructions of their founder. This ceremony placed the consumption of wine at the heart of the new religion and made it a duty to drink. Christianity added a new dimension to the relationship between humanity and alcohol. Not only could it relieve thirst, inspire joy, and ruin livers, but it might also, in the form of wine, represent the transubstantiated blood of the son of God. This potential was made apparent by Christ to his disciples at the last supper he spent with them, to celebrate the Jewish feast of Passover. After filling his cup with wine, he shared it with them and explained the significance of this act: "And he took the cup, and when he had given thanks, he gave it to them and they all drank of it. And he said unto them, This is my blood of the new testament which is shed for many." (Mark 14:23–25)

The Eucharist was not the only link between Christianity and wine. Jesus had used the care of a vineyard as the theme for one of his most famous parables, and the grapevine as a metaphor for the relationship between himself and his converts. Moreover, the first miracle he had performed had been the transformation of six jars of water into wine at a wedding feast in Cana. Indeed, so pervasive was wine in the teachings of the new religion that the apostle Paul had felt it necessary to make clear that its role was principally symbolic and that the Eucharist should not be taken as an invitation to gluttony or drunkenness, "For he that eateth or drinketh unworthily, eateth and drinketh damnation to himself [for] not discerning the Lord's body."

By AD 139, Christians were common enough for the emperor Marcus Aurelius to commission Pliny the Younger, nephew of the historian killed at Pompeii, to investigate the sect. Were they terrorists? Did they kill people and eat their bodies and drink their blood? Pliny ordered the torture of two Christian deaconesses and found them to be simple, respectable, and poor, as were the cousins of Jesus, who owned and worked a small farm. This inquisition prompted a response. Christians were growing in confidence as well as numbers. Justin Martyr (AD 100–165), an uncircumcised Syrian convert, addressed a letter to Marcus Aurelius in which he advised him that his traditions, gods, and institutions were all absolutely worthless and that he, his friends, and family were condemned to go to hell after death, where they would suffer forever in the company of their most distinguished ancestors, and their slaves. The letter, styled as an *apologia,* ended with a warning to the most powerful man in the world: Christianity was now everywhere. "We are but of yesterday, and we have filled every place among you—cities, islands, fortresses, towns, marketplaces, the very camp, tribes, companies, palace, senate, forum— we have left nothing to you but the temples of your gods."

The proliferation of which Tertullian boasted had been accompanied by an increase in the sophistication of the Christian canon. The fathers of the church had been forced to devise official doctrines, including appropriate provisions toward alcohol, in order to guide their plethora of converts. The New Testament was silent on the secular use of wine, beyond St. Paul's advice to St. Timothy to "drink no longer water, but use a little wine for thy stomach's sake." Should all Christians therefore use wine to settle their stomachs? The matter was addressed by St. Clement of Alexandria (AD 150–215), who produced a comprehensive Christian etiquette on drinking in his *Pedagogia.* Clement was Greek by origin and Alexandria, where he taught in the early 200s, was an important center of learning, with schools of classical, Judaic, and Christian philosophy. His work shows the particular influence of Plato, and illustrates how much the author of the *Symposium* contributed to Christian thinking about alcohol.

The *Pedagogia* commenced with a brief history of what the Christian canon permitted the faithful to drink. In the beginning, Clement argued, the natural, temperate, and healthy beverage for the thirsty was water, because water was supplied by the Lord to the Hebrews on their journey to the promised land. However, once they had reached their destination, indicated by the presence of the giant grapes, it became a sacred duty to drink wine, a duty confirmed by Jesus, who compared wine to his own blood, and "to drink the blood of Jesus is to become partaker of the Lord's immortality." Having established a Christian obligation to drink, Clement proceeded to examine how this obligation should be met. He was of the opinion that the duty to consume (with the exception of sacramental wine) varied with age. Young Christians should be kept away from recreational drinking altogether, for it caused their "members of lust" to come to maturity sooner than they ought. "The breasts and organs of generation," he explained, "inflamed with wine, expand and swell in a shameful way, already exhibiting beforehand the image of fornication." Such tumescence was inevitably accompanied by "shameless pulsations." Ergo youth plus alcohol equaled un-Christian behavior. Proceeding from adolescents to adults, Clement recommended that the latter steer clear of wine during meals and while at work, but that they might take a cup to ward off the cold evening air. The elderly, however, and Clement was of advanced years at the time of writing, were advised that wine was the "milk of old age" and that they should drink every day for the sake of their health, in order to "warm by the harmless medicine of the vine the chill of age, which the decay of time has produced."

Lest Christians were tempted to disregard his guidelines, Clement provided a portrait of the damage drink could wreak. Heavy topers who ignored the rules were distinguished by their red demonic eyes, like those of corpses, which signified that they were dead to both the Word and the Lord. They made an ugly, if instructive, spectacle: "You may see some of them, half-drunk, staggering, . . . vomiting drink on one another in the name of good fellowship." Their red eyes rolling and seeing double, these monsters found it impossible to stay upright or speak anything but "maudlin nonsense." "It is well, my friends," Clement concluded, "to make our acquaintance with this picture at the greatest possible distance from it, and to frame ourselves to what is better, dreading lest we also become a spectacle and laughingstock to others."

Clement also addressed the matter of women drinking, on which he also followed Plato. While female Christians must, of course, drink sacramental wine, they should otherwise be kept away from the fluid: "An intoxicated woman is great wrath." Sexual discrimination in terms of access to wine was a retrograde step. Women had played a prominent part in the early church, enjoying an equality they were denied by other faiths. This freedom, however, was eroded as the Christian church grew in power and sophistication, and shaped its doctrines to Hellenic models, which accorded a diminished status to the fairer sex. Clement did, however, differ from his Greek authorities on the matter of fine wines. He warned good Christians not to fret if they could not get their hands on "the fragrant Thasian wine, and the pleasant-breathing Lesbian, and a sweet Cretan wine, . . . and Mendusian, an Egyptian wine, and the insular Naxian, the 'highly perfumed and flavored,'" or other such rare and costly vintages, with which he betrayed an evident familiarity. Luxurious tastes were as sinful as overindulgence. The old men Clement envisaged as doing most of the drinking in Christendom were advised to accept whatever was put in front of them and to consume it in a dignified manner: "We are to drink without contortions of the face, not greedily grasping the cup, nor before drinking making the eyes roll with unseemly motion; nor besprinkle the chin, nor splash the garments while gulping down all the liquor at once. . . . Eagerness in drinking is a practice injurious to the partaker. Do not haste to mischief, my friend. Your drink is not being taken from you. It is given you, and waits you."

The third century AD, in which Clement had composed his *Pedagogia,* was a period of mixed fortunes for the Christians. While they continued to multiply in number, they were subject to sporadic persecution under the emperors Maximin, Decius, and Diocletian. The last great purge of Christians occurred in the final two years of the reign of Diocletian, who instructed his officials "to tear down the churches to the foundations and to destroy the sacred scriptures by fire." Before, however, they could complete their task, Diocletian abdicated, and his resignation marked a turning point in the history of Christianity.

Diocletian's final act as emperor had been to divide his empire into three portions comprising western Europe, Italy and North Africa, and the Roman East. The division was implemented because imperial Rome had become too unwieldy to be managed by a single ruler. Whereas its hinterlands had once been home to submissive barbarians who kept to their hovels and paid their taxes, centuries of Roman occupation had been a significant economic stimulant, and the barbarians had taken to growing cash crops, drinking wine, wearing togas, and building cities. Former backwaters such as Gaul demanded the full-time attention of the imperial administration–it was no longer sufficient to send a letter or a legion every now and then. Moreover, the non-Romanized barbarians beyond the outer limits of the empire were becoming more numerous, and more aggressive. In the East, the Sasanids of Persia were seeking to reclaim the empire Asia had lost to Alexander the Great; in the center and to the west, various tribes were making raids across the Danube and the Rhine. No single ruler could counter all these threats at the same time.

No sooner had Diocletian partitioned his dominions and retired to a splendid villa in Salona than the rulers of the new divisions attacked one another, each with the aim of governing the entire empire alone. The victor was Constantine, the first Roman Christian ruler. A vision on the eve of an engagement at Milvian Bridge, in which a cross had appeared in the heavens, persuaded him to adopt it for the standards of his legions. He won the battle and converted to Christianity out of gratitude. Thereafter, the fortunes of his adoptive religion flourished. It received the imperial seal of approval in 313, when Constantine issued the Edict of Milan, which proclaimed that it would be legal throughout his dominions.

However, at the time of the edict, the Christian population was no more than a fifth of the total of the western part of the empire and a third of that of the East. The pagan majority resented the preference that had been given to what they saw as an intolerant and upstart creed. They bombarded Constantine and his successors with petitions: Pagan senators demanded that they be allowed to worship their ancestors in a traditional manner, souvenir sellers from the temple of Diana at Ephesus complained that Christianity was driving them out of business. They found a last champion in a brilliant, if short-lived, emperor, Julian, who confiscated the wealth of the Christian church and revoked the privileges of its clergy. But Julian ruled for only two years, and no subsequent emperor supported the pagan cause. In AD 392 the coemperors Theodosius and Valentinian II prohibited any form of pagan worship, even sacrifice to the *lares* (the household gods), who used to receive daily offerings of incense, flowers, and a few drops of wine. The temples of antiquity were converted to churches or left to fall to ruin. Their demise, and the neglect of the idols they contained, was celebrated by the Christian historian St. Jerome: "They who were once the gods of the nations...dwell with the owls and bats under their lonely roofs."

Not every deity in the Roman pantheon was left to the company of owls and bats. Bacchus survived the purge, at first in abstract form. His journey to respectability commenced in the catacombs—the labyrinth graveyards underneath Rome where Christians, in the days that they were clandestine, assembled to worship and laid their dead to rest. The themes of renewal and salvation, central to their faith, could not be expressed with overtly Christian symbols, so they resorted to metaphor, and the vine—Bacchic emblem of rebirth—adorned many of the stone sarcophagi in which they were entombed. Moreover, the paintings that decorate later tombs in these refuges, when the faith of their occupants could be expressed, also contain Bacchic references. The last supper, a popular theme, usually showed Jesus and his disciples arranged and posed as if they were participating in a symposium. This borrowed imagery continued to be incorporated into the symbolism of the church as it developed its own visual identity.

The integration of the pagan god of wine into Christianity extended beyond the figurative. Some of the poetry written in his praise was found to contain sufficient Christian sentiments to inspire St. Gregory of Nazianzus (AD 325–389) to use entire passages from the *Bacchae* of Euripides in his *Passion of Christ*. Moreover, the name Dionysus[4] never fell out of fashion, indeed, was common, and graced a number of saints, commencing with St. Dionysus, first bishop of Paris, who had been martyred in AD 274.

The influence of Christianity, in its formative centuries, over the drinking habits of the inhabitants of the Roman Empire was evolutionary, rather than revolutionary. The new religion assumed the generally positive views toward wine held by Judaism, to which it added a duty to drink, yet differentiated this sacred obligation from secular tippling, which it discouraged, except in moderation. This adopted philosophy had a calming effect on drinking in general. Moreover, as the Christian church grew in power, it organized its hierarchy along imperial lines and adopted classical imagery to express its precepts, so

---

[4] Its modern English equivalent is Dennis.

that by the time that it had become the official religion of the empire, it had been transformed from the faith of a breakaway sect of Jews to a thoroughly Romanized institution, whose bishops owned vineyards and slaves and splendid cellars, and whose adherents were buried in tombs adorned with vine leaves carved in stone.

5   BARBARIANS

The public halls were bright, with lofty gables,
Bathhouses many, great the cheerful noise . . .
Till mighty fate brought change upon it all.
Slaughter was widespread, pestilence was rife,
. . . And so these halls
Are empty, and this red curved roof now sheds
Its tiles, decay has brought it to the ground,
Smashed it to piles of rubble, where long since
A host of heroes, glorious, gold-adorned,
Gleaming in splendor, proud and flushed with wine,
Shone in their armor, gazed on gems and trea-
sure. . . .
　—"The Ruin," *The Exeter Book of Anglo-Saxon Verse*

In AD 369, the Christian poet Decimius Ausonius composed his mag-
num opus–*Mosella*, or the *Moselle*–an ode dedicated to the river of the
same name. The ode describes at length the beautiful villas and vineyards that line the river's banks and pays tribute to the civilizing forces
that had combined to produce so charming a scene. Ausonius, a native
of Bordeaux, was an exemplary neo-Roman. He wrote impeccable
Latin, held estates and vineyards, exchanged homoerotic poetry with
Bishop Paulinus of Nola, was tutor to the emperor Gratian, and was
elected consul, the highest office in the imperial administration, in AD
379. The town of Trier, on the banks of the Moselle, where he conceived his most famous ode, was likewise an archetypal example of the
cultural impact the combination of Rome and Christianity had had on

the once-barbarous lands of western Europe. It possessed palaces, baths, chapels, and a basilica, and had served as an imperial residence during the reigns of Constantinus II, Valerian I, and Theodosius.

This civilized idyll was not destined to last. Within ten years of the death of the poet, the tranquil scenes he had described had become a war zone. On New Year's Eve AD 406, the Vandals, a Germanic tribe, rolled across the frozen Rhine and devastated Roman Gaul. Trier was sacked; the villas Ausonius had praised were reduced to smoking ruins and the vineyards that surrounded them, populated, in the poet's fancy, with satyrs and nymphs, were burned to their roots. According to an observer of the period, "All Gaul was filled with the smoke of a single funeral pyre." Its population was slaughtered or enslaved, and the grandson of Ausonius was reduced to working in chains on the ancestral estates. By AD 450, the entire Roman Empire in the west had been shattered into fragments by the cumulative impact of wave after wave of barbarian invasions.

The trouble had begun in AD 376, when two bands of Goths had appeared at the edge of Roman territory on the banks of the river Danube. They wanted sanctuary from the Huns, an even more barbaric species of barbarian, who had invaded their own country. In return for a place to settle within the Roman Empire, they pledged to support it with their arms. The offer was accepted, and perhaps two hundred thousand people crossed the Danube. They were disarmed, fed with refuse and dog meat, robbed of their children, and shunted around like cattle. Unsurprisingly, they revolted. They commenced by plundering the Balkans, and although they did not have the science to lay siege to cities, they destroyed the agriculture of the area and decimated its population. It required several Roman armies and ten years of campaigning to control them. Shortly afterward the Huns themselves invaded Roman territory via the Caucasus. In 401, the Goths revolted once more and marched into Italy. Thereafter, the barbarian incursions came thick and fast. The Ostrogoths attacked in the east, the Vandals in the west, and the Visigoths through the center. In 410 Rome itself was sacked.

Worse was to come. The barbarians started fighting one another, and a hundred conflicts, some trivial, others major engagements, occupied the next generation, until they were distracted from their squabbles by the reappearance in force, in AD 446, of the Huns. The Huns were Eurasian nomads who were expert horsemen, superb archers, and intelligent tacticians, as capable of laying siege to cities in the best Roman style as of massacring their populations. They were objects of especial terror to Christians, who suspected them of being the harbingers of the Apocalypse. Their leader, Attila, was identified as "the Scourge of God," sent to chastise unbelievers and to test the faithful.

The short-term influence of the Huns on the production and consumption of alcohol in Europe was significant. They destroyed vineyards, butchered their workers, and drank the cellars dry. They possessed a number of their own rituals for drinking, centered around the consumption of *kumis*–fermented mare's milk. Kumis is a rare example of alcohol obtained from animal, as opposed to vegetable, sources. It was weak–around 2 percent ABV–and was neglected by the Huns in favor of wine when the latter was available. Despite, however, being the conquerors of substantial tracts of cultivated land, the Huns remained true to their nomadic roots. They neither liked nor understood metropolitan life, so did not linger in the cities that they sacked, some of which survived their visit with little more damage, albeit depopulated of their inhabitants, than scorch marks and bloodstains. Attila died in AD 453, his empire collapsed within ten years, and the Huns vanished–as if they had indeed been evil spirits.

The barbarian invasions split the western Roman Empire into a collection of warring states. The trade links that had supplied, for instance, Britain with Falernian wine were broken. The use of currency collapsed. The homogeneity that Rome had imposed across the continent dissolved, and the nations of modern Europe together with their different languages and customs were born amid ashes and slaughter. The invaders established new systems of manners and government, which placed a different worth on drink from the classical and Christian ideals that had prevailed throughout Europe. The Germanic tribes who had become the new rulers of the western empire possessed heroic ideologies, which promoted vigor and activity above organization and piety. Their heroes were monsters–of superhuman strength and appetite–binge drinkers as well as serial killers. Their impact on drinking habits was most pronounced in the peripheral parts of the empire, particularly in Britain. Whereas in Italy and Gaul vestiges of Roman taste and Roman administration lingered on under the new rulers, they all but vanished in Rome's most western province.

Rome had lost control over Britain around AD 412, when the emperor Honororius issued an edict advising its inhabitants that they must fend for themselves. They made a last desperate appeal to the metropolis in AD 446—the province was being torn apart: "The barbarians drive us into the sea, and the sea drives us back to the barbarians. Between these, two deadly alternatives confront us—drowning, or slaughter." But the appeal went unanswered, and thereafter Britain slipped back over the horizon into the Dark Ages. The principal tribes to profit from the collapse of Roman authority in Britain were the native Picts and Celts, and the immigrant Angles and Saxons who arrived from what are now Denmark and Germany. The Anglo-Saxon invasion was piecemeal and began around the middle of the fifth century when Vortigen, a Kentish warlord, invited Horst and Hengist, the leaders of bands of Saxon mercenaries, to take land in the Thames Estuary and protect him against the Picts who were running riot through the island. Negotiations were carried out at a banquet, and a later record of the event notes the introduction of a new drinking custom to England. The mercenaries were the hosts, and after they had feasted Vortigen, a "young lady came out of her chamber bearing a golden cup full of wine, with which she approached the king and, making a low courtesy, said to him, 'Lauerd King, wassail!'" Vortigen was struck by her beauty and asked his interpreter how he should answer. "She called you Lord King," said the interpreter, and "offered to drink your health. Your answer to her must be 'Drinc heil!'" Vortigen accordingly answered "Drinc heil" and bade her drink, after which he took the cup from her hand, kissed her, and drank himself. The girl was Hengist's daughter and so captivated Vortigen that he asked for her hand in marriage, and gave over Kent as the bride price.

The Saxons and the other warrior bands that followed Horst and Hengist into Britain were keener to plunder than teach its inhabitants the proper way to wassail. The country was broken up into fiefdoms, and society reverted to tribal values. In the absence of the uniform law and order that the Romans had imposed, trade collapsed, the ports were empty, the roads and sewers fell into disrepair, and without a critical mass of artisans, merchants, their servants, and their slaves to populate them, the towns were abandoned. The new arrivals brought their own social unit, the clan, and own style of settlement, the village. The population of these communities numbered in their hundreds, in contrast to the tens of thousands who had lived in the Roman cities.

A corresponding shift in drinking habits occurred. Whereas the

Romanized Briton's ideal tipple might have be a krater of fifteen-year-old Falernian wine mixed with water, consumed at a leisurely pace and accompanied by a discussion of the latest literature out of Rome, Anglo-Saxons drank for the glory of intoxication—for a joyride to the stars—and did not care overmuch what vehicle they used for transportation. They distinguished four generic kinds of alcoholic drink: *medu* (mead), *ealu* (ale), *win* (wine), and *beor,* whose identity is a matter of debate. Mead had the most cachet. Rather as the Hellenic hero Prometheus had stolen fire from the sun god, so the chief Anglo-Saxon deity had undertaken a quest for the good of mankind whose object was the Mead of Wisdom. In poetry, heroes yearned for and returned to mead halls, where they might make mead boasts and take mead oaths that held a particular sanctity. Ale, however, was the common drink. It was a quintessentially Germanic beverage, common to all the Teutonic tribes who now ruled over continental Europe. But whereas many of these, in particular in Gaul and Spain, had taken to wine and were beginning to blend Roman drinking habits with their own, in Britain ale ruled supreme. Wine and its associated rituals were all but forgotten. To judge by archaeological records, in the form of amphorae shards, the supply dried up in the century following the fall of Rome.

Grave goods show that the Anglo-Saxons employed a variety of drinking vessels—cups, mugs, glasses, and cattle horns. These last were decorated with bands of silver or gold and had the quality that they could not be put down unless they were empty, and so were passed from hand to hand or drained in a single draft. Smaller vessels have also been recovered from the graves of warriors and princes—Anglo-Saxon shot-cups—whose diminutive size implies they were used to hold a more potent brew than mead, ale, or wine. This might have been the mysterious *beor,* which was stronger and sweeter than ale and rarer than mead and, while not wine, ranked at least in strength with wine, and whose consumption led to a state known in Old English as *beordruncen,* i.e., very drunk. Two culprits have been identified as *beor*: a type of super-strength cider, which, in theory, can be fermented to almost 18 percent ABV; and a concentrated liquor freeze-distilled out of ale, mead, or cider, which can be as strong as 50 percent ABV, and which requires little more effort to make than leaving a barrel of whichever brew out of doors over winter.

Whatever the potion and the measure, alcohol was generally consumed in a mead hall. Every village contained one or more of these edifices that were the houses of the elite, who used them to perpetuate their wealth, fame, and power through the liberal distribution of food, drink, and gifts. Halls were the epicenters of Anglo-Saxon culture. Gladiators, the theater, chariot races, and other similar spectacle entertainments had vanished with the Romans. Leisure time—and there was plenty of it, at least half of every year—was spent in hunting, in playing games, in practicing how to fight, and in drinking. The mead hall was a communal gathering place—both kitchen and cultural center—where people were fed, where they declared their allegiances, and where they celebrated their collective identity. Halls varied greatly in size—the smallest were perhaps ten by fifteen feet, the largest a hundred or more yards in length. All were symbolic of the relative power of their owner. A sense of the status they conferred, and the desire to build them, is preserved in *Beowulf,* the first epic poem to be written in Old English. The poem begins with the raising of a hall by King Hrothgar, who, after success as a raider, and in winning treasure and followers, wished to celebrate his triumphs:

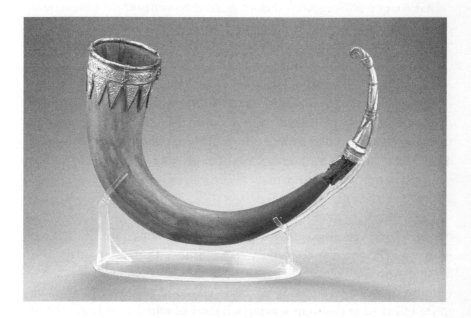

Anglo-Saxon drinking horn

So his mind turned
to hall building: He handed down orders
for men to work on a great mead hall
meant to be the wonder of the world forever;
it would be his throne room and there he would dispense
his God-given goods to young and old.

Although halls were built for formal purposes, they were nonetheless lively places whose ceremonies revolved around drinking. Hall-
goers were serenaded by bards, who were inspired to sing by their
particular god, Kvasir, whose name is a derivation of "strong ale." Kvasir, according to legend, was slain by two malicious dwarfs who mixed
his blood with alcohol to make "the mead of inspiration." Anyone who
drank of this magic potion could thereafter compose poetry and speak
wise words. The warriors in the hall who listened to the odes of heroism responded by making mead- or ale-pledges, oaths of a sacred nature, which usually nominated acts of rapine or slaughter as their aim
and which they were expected to fulfill on pain of shame. According to
a saying of the period: "In war is proved what was pledged over ale."
Women also had a clearly defined role in hall etiquette. They acted as
cupbearers and were referred to by the bards as "peace weavers," in the
sense that by passing a drink from warrior to warrior, they maintained
the friendship between them. The cup, or horn, was handed to the
drinker in strict order of precedence—first to the hall lord, often with
the injunction to be joyful at drinking, then to the *duguo*—the elder
retainers—next the *geoguo*—young retainers—and finally to guests.

Morale in the mead hall, among the warriors and the women who
served and who drank with them, was the barometer of happiness for
the clan. In *Beowulf,* disorder in the hall is presented as a kind of sacrilege. A monster by the name of Grendel appears in the poem. He kills
and eats Hrothgar's retainers, who, despite repeated oaths, are unable
to defend themselves:

Time and again when the goblets passed
and seasoned fighters got flushed with beer
they would pledge themselves to protect Heorot
and wait for Grendel with their whetted swords
But when dawn broke and day crept in
over each empty, blood spattered bench,

the floor of the mead hall where they had feasted
would be sick with slaughter.

The scribe of *Beowulf* was a Christian and decorated the pagan tale
of monsters, blood feuds, and stolen treasure with Catholic sentiments. Christianity was the brightest light in the Dark Ages. Its
egalitarian creed, and the fervor of its missionaries, won over the
beer-drinking barbarians who now ruled in place of Rome, and forged
links between their disparate and antagonistic kingdoms. However,
its clergy were forced to adapt their doctrines to accommodate the
tastes and habits of their new flocks, and European Christianity acquired its own peculiar flavor. It was considered impossible to make
barbarians live by the recommendations of Clement of Alexandria
and give up heavy drinking, which was so central to etiquette in the
case of princes, and the principal form of leisure for everyone else, so
this aspect of their culture had to be tolerated at the risk of losing
souls.

While the ecclesiastical writers of the age were diligent in their
condemnation of drunkenness, almost all of them condoned drinking.
Most belonged to various monastic orders, which multiplied at an explosive rate in the middle of the first millennium. Western Christian
monasticism was established by St. Benedict of Nursia (c. AD 480–543),
a wellborn Italian, who studied in Rome then fled to seek enlightenment as a laborer in the countryside. The lessons he drew from isolation and hard work inspired him to compose a rule for those disposed
to imitate him. Despite promoting the virtues of poverty, chastity, and
obedience, his rule was wonderfully popular, and Benedictine monasteries sprang up all over western Europe. Critical historians have asserted that their rapid increase was no surprise: The politics of the age
were complex, the governments oppressive, famines were frequent,
and so the opportunity to withdraw from the perils of civilian life and
to spend one's days in tranquility, engaged in prayer and physical or
mental labor according to one's temperament, was well-nigh irresistible.

Benedict, despite his emphasis on self-denial, did not expect abstinence from his followers: "Although we read that wine is not at all
proper for monks, yet because monks in our times cannot be persuaded
of this, let us agree to this, at least, that we do not drink to satiety, but

sparingly; because 'wine maketh even wise men fall off.'" His rule allowed each monk a ration of one *hemina*[5] of wine per day; though an abbot might issue more "if the circumstances of the place, or the work, or the summer's heat, should require" it. This generous ration could be withdrawn as a punishment: Anyone "tardy in coming to the work of God or to the table" was condemned to eat alone, "his portion of wine being taken from him, until he hath made satisfaction and hath amended."

The conversion of the British Isles to Christianity by the Benedictines and their fellow religious orders commenced in Ireland, which never had been conquered by the Romans and so had retained its indigenous values untainted. Its pagan inhabitants lived in tribes, and their drinks were ale or mead. They seem to have been master brewers: A Dark Ages poem describing the life and deeds of Cano, an Irish prince of the era, lists more than a dozen different sorts of ale and names the regions in which they were consumed:

> Ale is drunk around Loch Cuain
> It is drunk out of deep horns
> In Magh Inis by the Ultonians
> Where laughter rises to loud exultation....
> The Saxon ale of bitterness
> Is drunk with pleasure about Inber in Rig,
> About the land of the Cruithni, about Gergin
> Red ales, like wine, are freely drunk

The Irish were evangelized by St. Patrick in the fifth century, around the same time that the Kentish warlord Vortigen was being taught to wassail. The saint defeated the magic of hostile Druids with miracles, converted kings, and founded monasteries the length and breadth of Ireland. While his views on alcohol have not been preserved, those of his contemporary divines show a marked bias in favor of it—indeed, a desire to associate drinking with faith. Several of them worked miracles using ale as a prop, in particular St. Brigit (c. AD 450–520), who, like Christ at the wedding feast of Cana, turned water into alcohol on several occasions, once managing to change the dirty

---

[5] According to a sixteenth-century English translation of the rule, a *hemina* equated to one pint.

bathwater of a leper colony into good red ale. St. Brigit could, moreover, multiply ale. Faced with a shortage of grain, and the proximity of Easter, she prayed over her brew, which produced enough ale to last through Holy Week and for some days thereafter.

Alcohol also appears in the rules produced by Irishmen, in the style of St. Benedict, for use in their native monasteries. St. Gildas (AD 504–570) was responsible for the earliest example of these, in which he acknowledged that monks must be allowed to drink, and that even if they did so to excess then this was no great sin: "If anyone because of drunkenness is unable to sing the psalms, being stupefied and without speech," they were to be "deprived of dinner," which was a modest penalty in an age when fasting was thought to be a laudatory activity. This policy of toleration was extended to the lay population. St. Gildas is on record as stating that his mission included drunkards. As he pointed out in a letter to a fellow cleric, "Our Lord Jesus Christ did not avoid the feasts of publicans, so that he might save all sinners and harlots."

Irish Christians were responsible for the reconversion of much of Europe, and their native tolerance of drinking contributed to their successes abroad. Their missionaries left for France and Germany armed with inspirational tales of not one but three Irish saints who had had the power to convert water into ale, for Mochuda and Cronanus had developed the same miraculous skill as Brigit. Their examples were followed on the continent by saints Arnuld and Goericus, to the amazement of their audiences, and numerous pagan souls were saved for Christ by the spontaneous creation of alcohol. Irish missionaries were prepared to work miracles against, as well as with, their favorite beverage. St. Columban (521–579) won many converts by casting Satan out of an ale cask that a band of heathen Austrians were about to offer to their native deity: "They had placed in their midst a large [cask] ... filled with ale. When the man of God approached and asked what they intended to do with it, they said that they intended to make an offering to their god, Wotan.... Hearing of this abominable deed, at a distance he breathed upon the vessel, and through a miracle the vessel was shattered into pieces ... and the [force of the blast expelled] the ale.... It was clear that the devil had been hidden in this vessel, and he would have captured the souls of the participants through the heathen offering. The barbarians, seeing this, were stunned, and said that the great man had the breath of God, since he was thus safely able to shatter the vessel into pieces." Interestingly, the supernatural ability to explode casks predates

St. Columban in Irish myth. Athairne the Fierce, a legendary hero, was said to have developed an urgent thirst for ale while still in his mother's womb and, after taking control of her faculties, prompted her to ask a brewer to draw some from his barrel. She was refused, whereupon the unborn hero caused the barrel to explode and enjoyed secondhand the spilled brew his mother licked off her fingers.

The pious endeavors of Irish and other missionaries led to the creation of a Christian empire of souls, whose European dominions closely matched those of imperial Rome, and which shared the same capital. Christian channels of communication were the conduits through which news of Britain, the abandoned province, reached Rome, more than a century and a half after silence had fallen. It seems that Rome had forgotten as much about its former possession as the inhabitants of Britain had of their past ruler. The persistence of Ultima Thule was revealed by the appearance of some of its youth in the papal slave market, where they were spotted by Pope Gregory I. Struck by their beauty, he inquired as to their place of origin and, when told they were Angles, from England, resolved to convert such appealing pagans. In AD 597 he sent a Benedictine monk, St. Augustine of Canterbury, on this important mission. It was successful, after numerous martyrdoms, and within a century most of England had become Christian. Bishoprics and monasteries were founded and endowed with land, bishops and abbots grew in temporal as well as spiritual power, and their refectory tables were laden with as much food and alcohol as any pre-Christian mead hall. Not only did the plenty of the halls infiltrate the monasteries, but also their drinking culture. The Anglo-Saxon abbot Alcuin, writing circa AD 800 to a Mercian bishop, admonished him for overindulging, as if he were a hall lord: "It is surely better that Christ's bishop is more praised for his performance in church than for the pomp of his banquets. . . . The continual pursuit of drunkenness . . . [is] insanity: In the words of the prophet, 'Shame on you, you mighty wine drinkers and bold men in mixing your drinks.' Whoever takes pleasure in such things will, as Solomon says, 'never be wise.'"

Monasteries were islands of literacy in an analphabetic country. Their monks made exquisite copies of the gospels and the other sacred texts of the Christian canon. They wrote, by and large, in Latin and preserved some of the most famous of the imperial authors for the sake of their instructive writing styles. Exposure to Ovid and Virgil made them familiar with the Roman pantheon, and they incorporated classical metaphors and imagery within their own works. Bacchus was resurrected as a synonym for wine; they referred to vineyards as Nysa after the mountain where he had spent his adolescence. The clerics also revived the dormant classical hierarchy of drinks with wine at the top. Their prejudice is evident in the *Colloquy of Aelfric,* written by an English bishop in the late 900s and intended to serve as a phrase book for Anglo-Saxon novices learning Latin. It takes the form of a Q & A between teacher and pupil and illustrates the drinking habits of the monastery:

> ABBOT: "What does the novice drink?"
> NOVICE: "Ale if I have it, water if I have no ale."
> ABBOT: "Does he not drink wine?"
> NOVICE: "I am not so wealthy that I may buy myself wine; and wine
>   is not the drink of children or fools but of the old and wise."

Note that the novice, probably a teenager, welcomed ale when he could get it, suggesting that Clement's advice on adolescent drinking carried as little weight in England as his strictures against bingeing. The irrepressible thirst of the Anglo-Saxons was confirmed elsewhere in Aelfric's work. His sermon *De Populo Israhel* was written as a model to show his fellow clerics how to explain to the bibulous English why an omnipotent deity had supplied Moses with water in the wilderness instead of something alcoholic. God, according to Aelfric, had he been so minded, could just as easily have caused a flow of wine "or, what is more, of ale" to spring forth from the rock, but that he chose not to do so was simply proof of the inscrutability of his ways.

In addition to reviving Bacchus, and formulating appropriate policies toward drinking for Anglo-Saxon Christians, the religious orders were instrumental in collecting and preserving English medical lore in documents known as *leechdoms.* These used alcoholic beverages in almost every cure; indeed, the only condition for which they were not recommended as medicine was pregnancy. According to one such tract, "pregnant women should not drink to excess nor drink *beor* at all."

Just as civilization was enjoying a second spring in England, a fresh batch of barbarians appeared from the north. The Vikings arrived by sea, and since most of the fighting in the country over the past two centuries had been land-based, the English were entirely unprepared for them. The most unready were the monasteries, many of which were situated on little islands just off the coast, so as to be at a safe distance from the conflicts that rolled up and down the land and the temptations it contained in times of peace. Lindisfarne, an islet off the coast of Northumbria, which had been selected by St. Aiden in AD 635 as the ideal site for a religious colony and had flourished to the extent that it had a church the size of a cathedral, more than a hundred monks, an alumni roll that included several saints, a brewery, and a treasure of gold and silver, was the first to be attacked. The Vikings hit Lindisfarne in AD 793, and in the words of Simeon of Durham, they "laid everything waste with grievous plundering, trampled the holy places with polluted feet, dug up the altars, and seized all the treasures of the holy Church. They killed some of the brothers; some they took away with them in fetters; many they drove out, naked and loaded with insults; and some they drowned in the sea."

The Vikings were a rude reminder to the Christian Anglo-Saxons of just how civilized they had become since their conversion. Ethnically, Vikings were very similar to the warrior bands who had settled Britain after the end of Roman rule—they had matching tribal gods, an identical veneration for mead halls, and an equal obsession with battle and excess. They launched their *snaken*—snake boats, long ships—not only against the coasts of Britain but also those of Germany, France, Portugal, and Spain. Wherever they visited they left the same reputation as a race of psychopaths who respected neither property nor person. Their swords, spears, battle-axes, and war hammers were responsible for the creation of a host of new martyrs. They put down roots in some of the places they attacked. In England they took Northumbria and Mercia, and fought legendary wars against King Alfred of Wessex; in France, the Norsemen founded the kingdom of Normandy; and they were probably the first humans ever to reach and settle Iceland. In between raiding and colonization, the Vikings traded their plunder for luxuries via river through the Baltic states and Russia to the Black Sea, where they established contact with Constantinople, the last outpost of the old Roman Empire. Their trade goods in the main consisted of furs, slaves, amber, and walrus ivory, which they exchanged for gold, silver, and wine.

Alcohol was central to Viking culture. Their gods drank heavily; their paradise consisted of a battlefield, where dead heroes might fight all day every day for eternity, and a celestial hall, Valhalla, where the deceased repaired each dusk to enjoy a perpetual menu of roast pork and mead served by awesome blonde Valkyries. The Vikings had the same categories of alcoholic drink as the Anglo-Saxons—mead, ale, wine, and *beor*. Like the Anglo-Saxons, they venerated mead but drank mostly ale. Modern attempts to reproduce a Viking brew have resulted in a strong (9 percent ABV), dark, and malty beverage, sweet in taste— which would have seemed even sweeter in an age when sugar was rare. In polite Viking society ale was strained before being served—ale strainers have been found amid the grave goods of well-bred ladies, who performed the role of cupbearers in the Viking halls.

The Norse sagas, which contain their creation myths, their gene- alogies, and record the deeds of their greatest warriors, provide a sense of the pervasiveness of drink in Viking society. A striking number of their heroes and kings died from alcohol-related accidents—King Fjolne, for instance, fell into a vat of mead below his hall and was drowned; the prince Swegde and his train of warriors were lured by a dwarf into the pit of hell after a drinking binge; kings Alf and Yngve, brothers, mur- dered each other in Yngve's mead hall when drunk, and so on. Rather as the Romans had made a tactic of intoxicating barbarians before at- tacking them, Vikings often settled their feuds by killing each other in mead halls, or burning them to the ground when their occupants were drunk. An example of both metasolutions appears in the Yngling saga, in the story of King Ingjald, who marked the beginning of his reign with an heirship feast: "It was the custom at that time that he who gave an heirship feast . . . should sit upon the footstool in front of the high seat, until the full bowl, which was called the Brage-beaker, was brought in. Then he should stand up, take the Brage-beaker, make solemn vows to be afterward fulfilled, and thereupon empty the beaker. Then he should ascend the high seat which his father had occupied; and thus he came to the full heritage after his father. Now it was done so on this occasion. When the full Brage-beaker came in, King Ingjald stood up . . . and made a solemn vow to enlarge his dominions by one half, toward all the four corners of the world, or die." King Ingjald realized his pledge by intoxicating his guests, burning down his own hall with them all inside, then confiscating their kingdoms.

In their prime, between about AD 850 and 1100, the Vikings had a significant influence over the fortunes of Europe and beyond. Their voyages of trade and exploration took them farther north and west than any prior Europeans. They were the first to reach the coast of North America, and *Vinland* ("land of wine") was the first European name for that portion of the continent. The Vikings got to America by using their colonies in Iceland and Greenland as stepping-stones over the Atlantic Ocean. They established a summer trading camp in New-foundland, then coasted south until they came to a land of plenty. These voyages, pioneered by Leif Eriksson, are described in the Graenlendinga saga, which records the discovery of grapes in the new land by Tyrkir, a German Viking, who was familiar with wine from his native country. Eriksson accordingly named the place after its most promising feature, and loaded up his *snaken* with a cargo of grapes to take home to Greenland, where the vine did not grow and wine, if it ever reached there, was a fabulously rare import. He also took back timber, which Greenland likewise lacked. There were subsequent voyages in quest of grapes and lumber, but hostile Native Americans drove them away and they gave up on the American continent.

Meanwhile, in the parts of Europe that they had settled, they, too, succumbed to Christianity. They adjusted their drinking habits to accommodate the new religion, which, in its turn, incorporated some Viking customs, especially those pertaining to the year-end feast of Yule, which King Hakon of Norway shifted so as to coincide with Christmas. Whereas the Christian celebration had focused on quiet prayer, the Viking festival emphasized gift giving and self-indulgence. King Hakon decreed that for the new, combined festival "everyone was to have ale for the celebration, or else pay fines, and had to keep the holidays while the ale lasted."

6 ISLAM

How I wish today that
My share of life's provisions
Was a wine on which to squander
My earnings and inheritance.
   —Abu "Ali al-Hasan Ibn Hani" al-Hakami (c. AD 757–814)

In the course of their river voyages through Europe toward the Black
Sea, the Vikings established contact with the followers of a new religion whose conquests during the same period that the Vikings had
terrorized the West made the Norsemen's own achievements seem
trivial. One such encounter was recorded for posterity by Ibn Fadlan, a
native of Baghdad, and a disciple of Islam. Ibn Fadlan was a pious and
literate man who traveled in the entourage of a Muslim ambassador,
and his account of his meeting with a band of Vikings in AD 922, by the
banks of the river Volga, is a mixture of admiration and horror. They
were "perfect physical specimens, tall as date palms, blond and ruddy."
They were also "the filthiest of all Allah's creatures," who did not wash
after eating, excreting, or sexual intercourse, all of which acts they performed before the astonished Muslim's eyes. Their drinking habits
were equally repugnant: "They are addicted to alcohol, which they
drink night and day. Sometimes one of them dies with the cup still in
his hand." While this was scarcely news to the peoples whom the
Vikings raided, Ibn Fadlan expected it to disturb his readers in Baghdad, whose faith had placed an absolute ban on the consumption of
alcohol.

   Islam, the revelation of Allah, the one true God, via his prophet

Muhammad, was born in the harsh climate of Arabia, in the middle of the first millennium AD. Muhammad (c. AD 570–632), a native of the town of Mecca, received a visit in his fortieth year from the archangel Gabriel, who informed him that he was the last of a line of Judeo-Christian prophets whose pedigree stretched from Noah to Jesus, and instructed him to spread the word of Allah and to convert, extermi-nate, or tax unbelievers. Initially, he was poorly received in Mecca, which contained the most sacred object in Arabia–the Kaaba, a black cubic rock adorned with the images of 360 different gods, most of them petty immortals, possessed of no very great powers and wor-shipped, individually, by very few people. They did, however, draw the Arab nation together once a year for their veneration, so that polythe-ism was an important business in the city, and the monotheism preached by Muhammad unwelcome. After retreat to the town of Me-dina, where he continued to communicate with Allah and raised an army, Muhammad subdued Mecca, converted his fellow tribesmen, and by the time of his death, the principal places in Arabia, and its foremost clans, recognized the rule of Islam.

The basic precepts of new religion were simple–to acknowledge the supremacy of Allah, to pray five times a day, to fast during a specified period each year, to give alms, and, if possible, to make a pilgrimage to Mecca. Further instructions as to how Muslims were expected to behave were contained in the *Koran,* revered as the word of God, as spoken to his prophet. This sacred text was set down some years after the death of Muhammad, in the first in-stance inscribed on palm leaves and the shoulder blades of dead sheep. It contains 114 suras, or chapters, each composed of an un-even number of verses. It is not chronological, in that it does not record the utterances of Allah in the sequence that they were made. The Koran provides the faithful not only with general guidance on how to live, but also gives particular directions regarding dress, personal hygiene, and diet. Among these is a total ban on the con-sumption of alcoholic drinks.

Subsequent commentators have unraveled the correct order in which advice was given by Allah to mankind, and it can be de-duced that his attitude toward alcohol changed from approbation into censure over time. Islam was born in a region of drinkers: The Greek historian Herodotus had claimed that the Arabs worshipped only two gods—"Bacchus and Urania." Strabo, writing four centuries later, noted that they drank wine when they could, and palm liquor in those parts of their territory unsuited to the cultivation of the grape. Arabian poetry had a minor genre dedicated to the celebration of wine, and perhaps as a concession to this heritage, alcohol is first mentioned in the Koran as a good thing, alongside water, milk, and honey. However, by its next appearance its status had become equivocal: It was labeled as sinful but also pronounced as having some useful qualities, albeit unspecified: "They ask concerning wine and gambling. Say, 'In them is great sin and some profit, for men; but the sin is greater than the profit.'" The news that drinking was a sin was not enough to deter the faithful, some of whom refused even to sober up for prayers. The prophet consulted his god again and was advised that no Muslim could attend prayers if drunk. Given the frequency of prayer sessions, this could be read as a de facto ban. However, it seems the Arabs persisted in their old ways and continued to drink heavily at their frequent feasts. An affair of blood at one such led to a third consultation and complete and unequivocal prohibition. At the event in question, Hazrat Saad Ibn Abi Waqquas was busy reciting poetry that eulogized the excellence of his own tribe while belittling the merits of the Ansars of Medina, when an enraged and drunken Ansari youth threw a lamb bone at him, wounding his head. From such trifling incidents flow momentous consequences. Muhammad conferred with God once more and was told, "Strong drink, games of chance, idols, and divining arrows are an abomination of Satan; avoid them, that you might prosper," for "Satan's plan is to excite enmity and hatred between you, with intoxicants and gambling, and hinder you from the remembrance of Allah and from prayer: Will ye not then abstain?"

And that was that.

Interestingly, this third and final directive was tested by some of the faithful: Was it permissible to drink only a little bit? No, Muhammad is reported to have answered: Any is too much. And besides, wine would be available in heaven. The Islamic paradise is described in some detail in the Koran and appears to have been designed to appeal to the ascetic inhabitants of a barren land. Good Muslims were encouraged to expect an afterlife of sensual excess, spent in a fertile

Arcadia: "As for the righteous...theirs shall be gardens and vine-yards, and high-bosomed virgins for companions, a truly overflowing cup." Anyone thirsty after a mortal life of abstinence could chose between "rivers of wine, delicious to drinkers," and a packaged variety ("pure wine, securely sealed, whose very dregs are musk"), upon arrival in paradise. This was deferred gratification on a grand scale, far beyond the Christian version, which left the delights of heaven unspecified, beyond one's being in the presence of God. Even the most visionary of Christian saints had lacked the confidence to depict their paradise as wet.

With such clear limitations to work with, Islam set about conquering the drinking world. Under the command of the caliphs, the lineal descendants of Muhammad or his generals, Muslim victories were numerous, rapid, and convincing. Within a hundred years of the death of the Prophet they controlled Egypt, North Africa, most of the Persian Empire, Sicily, Corsica, Spain, and Portugal, and had made incursions into France as far as Bordeaux. In accordance with their creed, their new subjects were offered the alternatives of the sword, the Koran, or of paying tribute. Those who converted immediately gained all the privileges and duties of being a Muslim. In some areas, notably North Africa and Persia, a majority of the population switched to Islam; in others, those who preferred taxation to circumcision remained in the majority, and laws were formulated to circumscribe their conduct.

The first version of the laws for non-Muslims resident in Islamic lands were set out in the *Umar Pact* made between the second caliph, Umar Ibn Khetib, and the Christians of Syria, in AD 637. The pact created the notion of a *dhimmi*–a Jew or Christian who lived under Muslim rule, paid a poll tax, and who was bound to observe its regulations. Surprisingly, in the light of the Muslim abhorrence of alcohol, dhimmis themselves were allowed to continue to drink, and to produce and sell wine to each other for sacred and secular purposes. In the Spanish town of Córdoba, for instance, there was a state-operated market for wine in the Christian quarter during the rule of al-Hakam I (AD 796–823). As a consequence, the impact of a dry religion on mankind's love affair with alcohol was not so colossal as might have been expected. Taverns continued to operate, albeit they were forbidden to serve Muslims. Although the pact of Umar was tightened up in subsequent versions ("They shall not drink wine in public, nor display their crosses or their swine"), alcohol remained available throughout the Islamic world.

With so much temptation at hand it is unsurprising that many Muslims succumbed to Satan's wiles and took up or, in the case of converts, resumed drinking. Although pious sobriety was venerated, and examples of heroic restraint were held up to the faithful, including that of a cousin of Muhammad who, after being captured by Christians, was "celebrated for refusing, after an abstinence of three days, the wine and pork, the only nourishment that was allowed by the malice of the infidels," and despite the prescription under Islamic law of eighty lashes for anyone caught drinking, alcohol, especially wine, was widely consumed, and even celebrated.

Muslim poets made a significant contribution to the philosophy of drinking. Collectively, their work gave a new face to alcohol. The composite portrait was drawn, in the main, in Persia, whose ancient relationship with wine had continued beyond its conversion to Islam. It pictured the act of drinking as one of defiance and as a pleasure made all the sweeter for being sinful. The master hand responsible for the best parts of the portrait, who registered every cup of wine that he drank as a vote in favor of Satan and against piety, was Abu Nuwas (c. 756–813), a decadent genius whose name means "curly locks" in Arabic. His mother was a Persian seamstress, his father an Arab soldier who had served in the campaigns of the caliph Umar. He studied the Koran at Basra, in Iraq, and spent the rest of his life, by his own admission, drinking, fornicating, and writing poetry.

His audience was huge. The Islamic world was united by a single language, Arabic, a lyrical idiom wonderfully suited to the expression of creative thinking. Arabic possessed pre-Islamic traditions of verse, including the minor genre of *khamriyya,* wine poetry, which Abu Nuwas adopted and perfected:

> Drink the wine, though forbidden,
> For God forgives even grave sins.
> A white wine, forging bubbles when mixed—like pearls set in gold,

>   Such as was on the ark in Noah's time–
>   Best of his cargo while the Earth was still awash.

The poet found his inspiration in the taverns of his native Basra, which were run by Jewish merchants, and in Egypt when in exile, where Christian religious orders supplied the drinks. He was especially fond of the young male acolytes who served the wine in Christian establishments. Indeed, he wrote of attending mass just so that he could fantasize over an altar boy as he drank communion wine, and succeeded in insulting both Christianity and Islam in the same poem:

>   I wish that I were the Eucharist which he is given or the chalice from
>   Which he drinks the wine! No, I wish I were the very bubbles of wine!
>   So that I might gain the benefit of being closer to him.

The poems of Abu Nuwas, and the writers who followed his example, are not only useful markers of attitudes toward alcohol under Islam in its heartland at its zenith, but also tell us the what, how, and where of Arab drinking. The what, for poets, was wine, of which they recognized four colors–red, white, amber, and golden. Some of it was naturally effervescent–Abu Nuwas wrote of a red variety that "shoots out sparks like rubies" and compared its bubble trails to falling stars. Wine was drunk mixed with water, often starting in the morning ("Quick to your morning drink and delight yourself, my man!"), and drinking binges lasted days, sometimes weeks. The beverage itself in Arabic was a she–the daughter of the vine. A good vintage could provoke not just the thirst, but also the lust of the poet:

>   I have become insane for [this] delicate virgin
>   Who is excessively violent in the glass and headstrong.

Virgin wines were thought to improve with age. When praising one such spinster, still "preserved for the day she is pierced," Abu Nuwas dwelt on the traditional Arab association of age with wisdom:

>   She is so antique that were she to acquire
>   An eloquent mouth and tongue

She would sit like an elder among the people, upright,
And regale them with tales of ancient nations.

Finally, discrimination in the classical style was apparent in Islamic wine writing: Specific vintages were eulogized in the vivid language of a classical oenophile:

A wine both frisky and quiet
As if lines of Himyarite or Persian appear on its surface,
Which, with time, become almost intelligible....

A pre-Islamic convention of *khamriyya* was the expression by the poet of a longing to die drinking, and this was the death rumored to have overtaken Abu Nuwas. Although he spent time in prison and in exile, Abu Nuwas was not just tolerated but accepted as a good Muslim during his life. He passed most of his years around the court of the caliphs in the new city of Baghdad (founded AD 762) and produced a number of panegyrics in praise of his rulers. These, combined with his habit of satirizing anyone who crossed him in perfect, memorable verse, probably saved him from execution. Moreover, his poetry is not devoid of repentance, and Islam is a forgiving religion to its adherents. According to legend, Abu Nuwas's epitaph, which was embroidered on his shroud, was "My excuse, Lord, will be to admit that I have no excuse."

❖ ❖ ❖

In addition to contributing to the philosophy of drinking, the Islamic world introduced a practical innovation to the pastime that was to have a far greater impact than the concept that wine on earth was a sin. While Christian Europe trundled through the Dark Ages, Muslim scientists picked up where the Greeks had left off and made substantial contributions to medicine, physics, mathematics, astronomy, and chemistry. The process of distillation was among their many discoveries. While Aristotle had worked it out in principle and succeeded in turning wine into water, it was Muslims who perfected its practice and who managed to extract alcohol from wine. The pioneer was Jabir Ibn Hayyan (721–815), known as Geber[6] in the West, who is

[6] Geber's habit of writing in symbolic code, incomprehensible to the casual reader, is the source of our word *gibberish*.

acknowledged to be the father of the science of chemistry. He established the principle of classifying substances by their properties and invented equipment and techniques for isolating them. His technical innovations included the alembic still, whose principles still govern the production of alcoholic spirits. Geber tried his still on various fluids, including wine, which he found released a flammable vapor that he described as "of little use but of great importance to science." It is possible that the condensed vapor was put to good use by Abu Nuwas, who listed, among his other forms of liquid inspiration, a wine that "has the color of rainwater but is as hot inside the ribs as a burning firebrand." Further research on the vapor was carried out by Al Razi (865–925), a Persian polymath who specialized in medicine. He described the process of distilling in his book *Al Asrar* ("The Secret"), and the isolation of a substance he called "al-koh'l of wine," which translates literally as "mascara of wine"–koh'l was the powdered antimony Arab women used to blacken their eyelids. It was also slang for substances isolated by distillation, and it is in this sense–as the chemical soul of strong drinks–that it passed into use outside the Arabic-speaking world.

Muslim advances in science also contributed to mankind's understanding of the effects of alcohol on the human frame. Al Zahrawi, Islam's greatest surgeon (936–1013), despite working in a society where alcohol was prohibited, nonetheless had sufficient patients who were heavy users to identify its detrimental effects: It could be a cause of convulsions, apoplexy, dementia, partial and total paralysis, difficulties in articulation, gout, and "disturbances of the liver." Notwithstanding such glum news, some scientific Muslims attempted to soften, or to qualify, the Koranic ban on drinking. Avicenna (980–1039), a Persian philosopher whose commentaries on Plato and Aristotle were the sources for the reintroduction of their thinking to western Europe, confessed to using wine as an aid to study: "When sleep overcame me or I became conscious of weakening, I would turn aside to drink a cup of wine, so that my strength would return to me." He promoted Platonic views on alcohol and believed them to be as valid for Muslims as for Athenians: "To give wine to youths is like adding fire to a fire already prepared with matchwood. Young adults should take it in moderation. But elderly persons may take as much as they can tolerate." The concept that old and responsible Muslims might enjoy unlimited access to wine was extended by Averroës (d. 1198), who attempted to reconcile Aristotle with Islam. Averroës claimed that the Koranic ban did not apply to him: "Wine is forbidden because it excites wickedness and quarrels; but I am preserved from those excesses by wisdom. I take it only to sharpen my wits." By extension, any intelligent and reasonable Muslim should feel free to drink.

Such sentiments were shared by Omar Khayyam (d. 1122), the great Persian mathematician, astronomer, and poet. Renowned in his lifetime for his scientific work, Khayyam's poetry, which he wrote in the *Rubaiyat,* or quatrain, form, is responsible for his posthumous fame. Much of it is in praise of wine and the pleasures of intoxication. His ethos, however, was very different from that of Abu Nuwas. He was not interested in portraying himself as a sinner or degenerate; indeed, he was entirely dismissive of faith. Drinking was the only truth:

> Tonight I will make a tun of wine,
> Set myself up with two bowls of it;
> First I will divorce absolutely reason and religion,
> Then take to wife the daughter of the vine.

Khayyam also ruled out the repentance Abu Nuwas had flirted with. Forget paradise and hell, heaven is here and now:

> They say there is Paradise with the houris and the River,
> Wine fountains, milk, sweets, and honey:
> Fill the wine-cup, put it in my hand—
> Cash is better than a thousand promises.

Finally, medical, rational, and poetical protests against the Koranic ban on alcohol were joined by theological objections. Islam had been riven by sectarianism since the death of its prophet, who had left no son and heir to guide his converts. Disputes as to who should succeed to the command of the faithful quickly resulted in the division of the Muslim world into Shias and Sunnis, the former of whom believed that spiritual authority devolved from the blood of the Prophet, in the shape of his daughter Fatima and her descendants, and that therefore only the fourth caliph, Ali, grandson of the Prophet, had been authentic, whereas the Sunnis held that the first three caliphs had been legitimate rulers. The once-united Arab lands fractured into smaller kingdoms, often at war with one another. In the midst of this turbulence, the Carmathian sect appeared. They were an offshoot of the Shiites and flourished between the ninth and eleventh centuries. They believed that spiritual leadership of the Islamic world should have gone to Ismail, the eldest son of the sixth iman, who had been passed over in the succession as a punishment for drinking wine. Since, in Carmathian eyes, Ismail could do no wrong, wine drinking could not be a sin, so they positively encouraged it. The Carmathians caused considerable disorder within Muslim domains, besieging Baghdad, sacking Mecca, and stealing the Kaaba. However, for reasons unknown, by AD 1050 they had melted away. The sacred stone was restored to the holy city, and wine to the list of sins.

At the same time as the ban on drinking was causing strife in the heartlands of Islam, it was denting its reputation abroad. In AD 988 Prince Vladimir of Kiev, whose kingdom formed the nucleus of modern Russia, decided that his subjects should be united under a single religion. He sent to the Jews, the Christians, and the Muslims, requesting details of their faiths. The Muslims told him that they believed in one God, were circumcised, ate no pork, drank no wine, and would enjoy the carnal embraces of over seventy women each in paradise. According to the *Russian Primary Chronicle,* "Vladimir listened to them, for he was fond of women and indulgence, regarding which he heard with pleasure. But circumcision and abstinence from pork and wine were disagreeable to him. 'Drinking,' said he 'is the joy of the [Russians]. We cannot exist without that pleasure.'"

Vladimir chose Christianity, and Islam lost a potentially useful ally. The Dark Ages in Europe were over, and Europeans started to push Islam out of their continent. Battles raged across central and eastern Spain, and El Cid Campeador, astride his horse Babieca, put Muslims and their Christian allies to the sword from Barcelona to Valencia. In 1085, the Normans took Sicily, and with it the great still at the Medical School of Syracuse. Hitherto, the Christian world had been free of spirits. Thereafter, the secrets of their preparation spread gradually through Europe. Geber was translated into Latin by Robert of Chester in 1144. Al Razi was translated into the same language for Charles of Anjou in 1279. Although it took another century for spirits to escape the laboratories of alchemists and to reach to the public at large, the genie was out of the bottle.

7   BREWS FOR BREAKFAST

hristian Europe emerged from the Dark Ages as a heavy-drinking culture. Alcohol had the reputation of a saint. No medical prescription was complete without it, nor, indeed, was any meal. Mothers brewed ale for their children; alchemists used spirits in their search for the secrets of how to turn other substances into gold; priests held wine aloft in chalices and declared it to be the blood of Christ; and drunkenness, especially during the barbarian festivals that had been adopted by Mother Church, was regarded as a natural, indeed blameless, condition.

The difference between Christian and Islamic attitudes toward alcohol was a matter of mutual criticism when the two faiths collided in the course of the Crusades. Their official launch took place in AD 1095, at the Council of Clermont in France, when Pope Urban II called on all good Christians to venture forth against the *Saracens,* as those Muslims in present possession of the terrain where Christ had lived and died were known. Anyone who answered the call was offered a complete remission of all his sins and encouraged to distinguish himself by decorating his garments or shield with a cross. Hundreds of thousands responded, many of whom set off at once for the Holy Land, under the leadership of a hermit named Peter the Simple, and guided by a duck, a goose, and a goat. After massacring the Jews in various German cities, they themselves were slaughtered in Hungary and the survivors were finished off in Nicea. The First Crusade proper set off the following year and in 1099 achieved its objective with the capture of Jerusalem. There followed a further half dozen or so ventures over the following two hundred years, during which the Saracens gradually clawed back the Middle East from the infidel, culminating in 1291 with the fall of Acre and the withdrawal of the remaining Christians to Cyprus.

This prolonged contact enabled both sides to observe and remark on the drinking habits of the other. The crusaders were perceived by the merchants of the Levant who provisioned them to have prodigious, indeed unnatural, appetites for alcohol. Thirstiest of all were the knights who accompanied the English king, Richard the Lionheart, on the Third Crusade, whose suppliers "could scarce believe even what they saw to be true, that one people, and that small in number, consumed threefold the bread and a hundredfold the wine more than that whereon many nations of [Muslims] had been sustained." On the other side of the coin, Muslim abstinence was considered to be proof of their fundamental immorality. John Mandeville, for instance, an English knight who traveled to the Holy Land in the thirteenth century, argued that the Koranic prohibition would inevitably lead to the collapse of Islam and confusion to its sober pagans, for "as holy writ saith, ET IN VIRTICEM IPSIUS INIQUITAS EJUS DESCENDET, that is for to say, 'his wickedness shall turn and fall on his own head.'"

The cultural differences between crusader and foe were also explored in medieval literature. Alcohol had its own bibulous Romantic hero in the person of Huoun, Duke of Bordeaux, who marched against the Saracens equipped with a magic goblet he had been given by a dwarf named Oberon.[7] The goblet filled with excellent Bordeaux wine whenever a true Christian raised it to his lips but remained empty in the hands of Muslims. It accompanied Sir Huoun on many quests and may be seen as a device to introduce a substance the crusaders considered indispensable to a region where it was rare and bad. Many of them died of thirst in the deserts of the Holy Land, and those who survived brought the memory of it home with them.

Once they had returned to Europe and had hung up their spurs, the knights who had ventured forth in the service of the cross never again needed to pass as much as a morning without access to some form of alcoholic beverage. As has been noted, they had a plethora of

---

[7] A popular English translation (1540, Lord Berners) of the adventures of Sir Huoun gave Shakespeare the inspiration for his *Midsummer Night's Dream*.

cultural reasons to justify drinking, and they further possessed limitless opportunities to indulge them. Everyone in Europe, young and old, rich and poor, drank every day, and usually several times each day. What they consumed was determined by their status. The population of much of the continent was divided by the feudal system into three castes, or *estates*—the clergy, the nobility, and the commoners, each of which had different levels of access to various types of drinks.

Of the three estates, the clergy drank the least. Most belonged to some or other monastic order, whose rules limited the quantity of liquid sustenance in their diet. They were all, however, required by their occupation to drink wine every day in memory of their Savior, and in order to ensure security of supply, they cultivated the grape wherever the climate permitted. These two parameters, rationing and compulsion, caused the *religious,* as members of the clergy were known, to concentrate on the quality of the wine they made to be sipped at the altar, or swallowed in prescribed measures over meals in their refectories. In an age of ignorance and superstition they alone applied science, such as it was, to the manufacture of wine. The Cistercians, a new order of monks formed in AD 1112 by St. Bernard of Citeaux, led the field. His followers carried out their initial experiments with quality in the Burgundy region of France. Over the course of the twelfth century, they bought up, or were rewarded for their prayers (in the form of gifts from pious Catholics) with, many of the best vineyards in the region, which they turned into a vast laboratory. They studied in detail the vintages that each of these produced, and rediscovered the ancient Egyptian concept that a particular patch of earth might impart the same unique character to the wine that it grew, year in year out. Thereafter they paid especial attention to the *terroir*—the soil in which each vine was rooted.

Their discoveries benefited secular vintners, who made the best out of the remaining patches of land in the region, so that by 1285 when Fra Salimbene, an Italian cleric, visited Burgundy, he was astonished to discover that it had become a monoculture: "The people of the region do not sow or reap or gather into barns, but they send their wine to Paris ... [via river]. ... They sell it at a good price and from this they get all their food and clothing." He also waxed lyrical over the quality of the wines they produced: "They give off a delicate aroma, they are very comforting and very delicious; they give all who drink them peacefulness and cheerfulness."

The Cistercian rule possessed a breeder clause: As soon as any monastery had more than sixty monks, twelve of them had to leave to found a new one. There were four hundred Cistercian monasteries when St. Bernard died in AD 1153, and two thousand a century later. The breeder clause spread the Cistercians and their mania for wine-making far and wide. From France they moved on to Germany, where they founded the monastery of Eberbach on the banks of the Rhine. Within a hundred years Eberbach had itself spawned more than two hundred children and had become "the largest vine-growing establishment in the world." The Cistercians even had a go in England. Their abbey in Beaulieu, near Southampton, was planted out with vines, although the fluid these produced seems to have been atypically bad. When King John tried it in 1204 he instructed his steward to "send ships forthwith to fetch some good French wine forthwith for the abbot."

In those parts of Europe where it was hard to grow vines, or where the native drink was ale, the religious orders applied themselves to brewing. As had been the case with wine, they focused on quality, and the results were equally good. A number of twenty-first-century breweries and brews owe their origin to medieval monasteries, including Weihenstephan, founded in AD 1040, and Leffe (AD 1240). Religious enthusiasm toward brewing resulted in part from the understanding that ale, having the same ingredients as bread, could be drunk without sin when on a diet of bread and water, and that therefore the fasts that littered their calendar need not be too unpleasant. They were, however, limited to an allowance of eight pints per day. Nunneries had breweries, too, and it was a nun, the Blessed Hildegard von Bingen (d. 1179), abbess, brewster, botanist, and mystic, who first noted that hops had preservative qualities when added to ale. They also imparted a bitter flavor, which many found agreeable, and the practice of hopping ale spread from religious breweries to secular ones.

The steady drinking of the clergy was light in comparison to the constant guzzling of the nobility, who, together with their households, got through quantities of alcohol that would have stunned even the degenerate wine lovers of Pompeii. Those at the pinnacle of feudal society proclaimed their status through excess. They dressed magnificently and forbade the practice of doing so in the same style to the clergy and the commoners. They built ostentatious palaces, where they feasted their fighting men and other retainers and, if they could afford them, exotica such as jesters and midgets; and they drank like lords. Such extravagance was not merely hedonism but a duty. It was part and parcel of being upper class. The responsibility is apparent in an English allegorical poem of the period entitled "Winner and Waster," which represents acts of conspicuous distribution and consumption as being the perfect expressions of the aristocratic ethos.

In England, where wine was imported, expensive, and therefore noble, the demand of its gentry sparked a viticultural revolution in the Bordeaux region of France. This had become English soil following the marriage of Henry Plantagenet to Eleanor of Aquitaine in 1152, and both events proved to be love matches. In the case of Bordeaux wines, the desire of the English aristocracy to buy was equaled by the willingness of the Bordelaise to plant, harvest, ferment, and sell. The relationship was encouraged by the king of both places, who abolished some of the taxes on the wine trade, and by the first quarter of the thirteenth century, Bordeaux was exporting about twenty thousand tons of wine per year to England. Its target market was comprised of the English feudal lords, whose monarch, as principal aristocrat, led by example. In 1307, for instance, King Edward II ordered a thousand tons of claret for his wedding celebrations—the equivalent of 1,152,000 bottles. To place the number in its proper perspective, the population of London, where the celebrations took place, was less than eighty thousand at the time.

The volume of consumption, even by modern standards, was remarkable: Fourteenth-century levels of wine exports from Bordeaux to England were neither matched nor exceeded until the 1920s. However, the beverage at the heart of the trade was no Falernian. The classical concept that wine, if properly stored, could improve with age had been forgotten during the Dark Ages. Wine was fermented and transported in wooden barrels, instead of being sealed inside amphorae, and as a consequence Bordeaux's vintages were usually vinegar before they reached their second birthday. The oenophiles of the Middle Ages prized new wine over old, and this preference was reflected in the mechanics of the Bordeaux wine trade. Because of the instability of its product, the wine fleet delivered two shipments each year. The first, in late autumn, carried new wine, the second, in winter, brought *reek* wine, an inferior product fermented from the lees of the first pressing. When the new wine arrived in England there was panic selling of anything left over from last year's vintage, and panic buying of the new. All this for a thin, pink, fizzy fluid, with the generic name of *claret*, which might turn acidic at any moment.

Few commoners, the third category of human beings in feudal England, ever tasted claret. Their staple was ale, which, to them, was rather food than drink. Men, women, and children had ale for breakfast, with their afternoon meal, and before they went to bed at night. To judge by the accounts of the great houses and religious institutions to which they were bound by feudal ties, they drank a great deal of it—a gallon per head per day was the standard ration.[8] They consumed such prodigious quantities not only for the calories, but also because ale was the only safe or commonly available drink. Water was out of the question: It had an evil and wholly justified reputation, in the crowded and unsanitary conditions that prevailed, of being a carrier of diseases; milk was used to make butter or cheese and its whey fed to that year's calves; and cider, mead, and wine were either too rare or too expensive for the average commoner to use to feed themselves or to slake their thirsts.

Ale was so vital to the very existence of the third estate that its price and quality were regulated by law. In 1267, King Henry III issued a pioneering piece of consumer protection legislation—the Assize of Bread and Ale—which set the maximum retail price of town-brewed ale at one penny for two gallons; the same penny bought three gallons from a country brewer. Prices were to be reviewed each year and could be adjusted in accordance with fluctuations in the cost of grain. The assize also provided for the appointment of ale tasters, who were responsible for quality control. The ale tasters recognized two grades of ale—"good," or "clear," ale, and plain ale. The better sort could be sold at a premium, the plain variety had to pass certain minimum standards. Anyone producing inadequate ale could be punished with fines, time in the stocks, or a ducking in the nearest pond or river.

---

[8] About the same as that of the Egyptian laborers who build the pyramids at Giza.

The immense demand for ale was satisfied by many thousands of brewers, or rather brewsters, for the majority of them were female. Brewing was one of the few trades open to medieval women. It was generally practiced as a cottage industry—whenever a brewster brewed, there was usually a small surplus for sale, so a family might drink ale of their own manufacture one week, sell the excess to their neighbors, then buy their neighbor's ale the following week. The typical brewster sold less than a hundred gallons of ale each year. She brewed using buckets, jugs, and troughs—whatever she had on hand. A rare few ran substantial breweries, owned plant, employed servants, and enjoyed otherwise male privileges such as the ability to sign contracts on their own behalf.

Most home-brewed ale was sold locally and quickly. It had a shelf life of a week at best, and it spoiled if it was agitated in travel. This perishability accounts, in part, for the number of brewsters; indeed it has been estimated that "almost every other household [in England] brewed for profit in the countryside, and about one household in every fifteen brewed for commercial purposes in towns." The ale trade between commoners was divided into on- and off-premises sales. Peasants either brought their own containers to a brewster's door for her to fill; or a room, or area, in her household would be set aside and drinking vessels supplied for people to consume the ale they purchased in situ. Places offering on-sales were designated *alehouses* and were regulated by law. They were required to declare their presence, and that they had ale for sale, by hanging a bush from a pole outside their front doors. This was a signal and invitation to the local ale taster to come and verify the quality of the ale and set the price at which it might be sold. Ale had to be offered in fixed measures—the assize of 1277 declared, "No brewster henceforth

Hermit and ale house

shall sell except by true measures, viz., the gallon, the pottle,[9] and the quart."

Despite their impressive average intake of ale, English commoners were not considered to be perpetual drunkards by their rulers or their priests. This title was reserved for a subcategory of the feudal system—students. These privileged creatures were a by-product of the fundamental transformation of higher learning that had occurred in the late twelfth and early thirteenth centuries. Hitherto, education had been the province of monasteries, and had focused on the solution of such knotty metaphysical problems as how the Holy Ghost had impregnated the Virgin Mary. However, as the bureaucracies of both church and state evolved, a need arose for numerate, literate clerks to administer them, and universities sprang up across Europe—in Paris, Salerno, Oxford, Padua, and Toledo. In some of these places, their scholars formed a significant part of the population: At the end of the twelfth century, ten percent of the inhabitants of Paris were students.

Students enjoyed all the same privileges as the clergy. They could not be prosecuted in the secular courts, which effectively placed them above the law in the towns where they studied, and they were notorious for abusing their rights and running riot. When matters got out of hand, the nobility and clergy stepped in on their side. In Paris, for instance, after a series of riots over the price of wine in taverns had led to the death of both townspeople and scholars, the students were pledged the special protection of the pope, the king of France, and the Holy Roman Emperor. As a consequence of such favoritism, they were hated by the townspeople. They also infuriated pious clerics by the levity with which they treated Mother Church. Parisian students were notorious for their blasphemous frivolity. A preacher of that age observed that they respected neither the rituals of their faith nor the places in which it was practiced. He was particularly irked by the *herring game,* which students played during high mass every Sunday: A group of them would enter the church in single file, each trailing a raw herring on a string from the hem of his gown. The aim of the game was to tread on the herring of the person in front, while preventing anyone from stepping on your own. Fresh herrings were required for each new round.

---

[9] One-half gallon.

The students, both by their own admission, and to the disgust of their critics, were fanatical drinkers. They employed their learning to compose Latin songs and poems in praise of their favorite pastime, some of which have survived in a German manuscript written circa 1230, known as the *Carmina Burana*. The *Carmina Burana* is tantamount to a medieval student manifesto. Its contents reflect its authors' preoccupations—wine, love, nature and adventure, and a contempt for institutional authority. The students referred to themselves within the manuscript as the *goliards* (probably a corruption of the Latin word for "glutton"). The most famous of their number, known as "the Archpoet," summed up their philosophy in his masterpiece "The Confessions of Golias":

> In the public house to die
> Is my resolution
> Let wine to my lips be nigh
> At life's dissolution
> That will make the angels cry
> With glad elocution:
> Grant this drinker, God on high,
> Grace and absolution

The goliards were satirists in addition to being poets. They produced several parodies of divine service, called Missae de Potatoribus—Masses for Drinkers. These were Christian in their form but bacchanalian in spirit, as is apparent in their version of the Paternoster:

PRIEST: Our Father, who art in glasses, hallowed be thy wine. May the cups of Bacchus come, may thy storm be done in wine as it is in the tavern, give us this day our bread for the devouring, and forgive us our great cups, as we forgive not drinking, and lead us not into the absence of wine, but deliver us from our clothing.
CONGREGATION: Amen.

❖ ❖ ❖

Feudal patterns of drinking, and the principle of servitude, were disturbed by a human catastrophe in the middle of the fourteenth century. Between 1347 and 1385, at least one in three of every noble, cleric, student, and commoner in Europe was killed by a plague pandemic. While historians are undecided whether the pestilence in question was bubonic plague, pneumonic plague, or a combination of the pair—the *Black Death* spread quickly, struck suddenly, and was fatal to nine-tenths of the people it infected. There was no known cure—not even prayer and a blameless life could stay the disease. All sorts of preventatives and remedies were tried—people bathed themselves in vinegar and holy water, adorned themselves with herbs, amulets, and crosses, altered their habits, took refuge in the country, all to no avail. Alcohol was many people's first and last resort. As the epidemic spread westward, ale was used as a prophylactic and was believed to have won some small if notable battles against it. When the Black Death appeared in Oudenburg in Belgium, Arnold, the local abbot, forced Christians to drink his brews instead of water. Survival rates were high among his congregation, and after death he was canonized. He is now the patron saint of brewers.

The Black Death took fifty years to die away, blossoming into minor epidemics in the interim and killing a third of the remainder of the population of Europe in the process. It was not the only problem facing the continent: The climate was changing—the Little Ice Age (c. 1350–1850) had begun; the church was being torn apart in a power struggle between pope and antipope; the Hundred Years' War between England and France was in full swing, as were conflicts in Italy, Germany, the Low Countries, and on various Mediterranean islands.

So much upheaval shattered the foundations of feudalism. Instead of being plentiful and submissive, labor was scarce and flighty. In England, the serfs found they could pick and choose between employers and walk away from the obligations that had tied their ancestors to the service of a lord, or an abbey. Their wages leapt: even the meanest worker earned four and a half pence per day, which was enough to buy himself three loaves, a big joint of meat, and several gallons of ale. Labor, moreover, migrated to towns, and the consequent concentration of thirst made brewing feasible on a commercial scale. Brewsters were displaced by large breweries, usually run by men, and the common alehouses became their customers.

Hand in hand with the new concept of a free market for labor came the notion of leisure. Public drinking houses flourished as a consequence. A fresh ethos evolved around them: They were run by the people, for the people. They were places where men and women from different occupations and backgrounds might meet to drink and to enjoy each other's company, and where they might talk with candor about their rulers. Indeed, the common people enjoyed a freedom of speech and action in their drinking places that was denied to them elsewhere, and these institutions became the nucleus of a popular culture.

In England, the public places where people could buy alcohol came in three forms: (a) alehouses, (b) taverns, which sold wine as well as ale, and (c) inns, which, strictly speaking, were hostels for pilgrims. Whether alehouse, tavern, or inn, postplague urban pubs were built to a new architectural plan. Instead of a single drinking space, equipped with benches, reminiscent of the Anglo-Saxon hall, they became warrens, with galleries of rooms, and drinkers were distributed through these according to their wealth and status. Poor drunkards were kept downstairs or in the cellars, merchants and other respectable folk occupied the middle tiers, and whores plied their trade in the rafters. The clientele of drinking houses were mostly illiterate and so their signs were simple, visual, memorable. They used animals (e.g., the *Bear*) celestial bodies (the *Sun*), or heraldic devices from coats of arms including exotic or fantasy creatures such as lions, unicorns, dragons, and griffins to announce their presence.

The popularity of public drinking houses can be deduced not merely from their increasing numbers but also from the flood of criticism they attracted from the church, which considered them to be competition. English Christians were going to pubs instead of mass, and passed the most important festivals in the calendar in their cups instead of on their knees. Such godlessness knew no bounds. According, for example, to Master Rypon, prior of Finchdale, not even Lent was sacred: "When by law or custom of the Church men should fast, very few people abstain from excessive drinking: On the contrary, they go to the taverns, and some imbibe and get more drunk than they do out of Lent, thinking and saying–'Fishes *must* swim!'" Those who did attend divine service went to the pub afterward, where they could be found "drinking and singing, with many idle words,...and evil expressions...making the holy day a sinful day." Pubs also diverted people from the drinking parties that the church itself organized, which were an important source of its revenue. In country parishes throughout England, groups of parishioners, such as the young bachelors, arranged annual *church-ales,* usually to coincide with

Christian holidays, whose profits went toward church maintenance funds and to pay for new vestments for their priests.

In order to justify their antipathy toward pubs, the clergy reexamined holy scripture and found drunkenness to be a form of gluttony, one of the seven deadly sins. Once they had quantified the damage it caused to the immortal soul, they composed cautionary sermons, with vivid imagery, to scare their congregations away from their rivals. People who ventured into a "Develes temple" could expect to miss out on paradise. Temptation lurked in every pottle. The brimming mug of ale in this world would be replaced with a goblet of fiery brimstone in hell. As well as eternal torment after death, drinkers could expect to be disfigured in this life by their sin. According to their critics in the pulpit, they acquired an unhealthy complexion "paler than that of the infirm, so that amongst the living their flesh is as the flesh of the dead." These zombies were also cursed with corpse breath and a woeful sense of balance: "Oft as they go homeward towards their beds they drench themselves in ditches by the way." Once home, the drunkard/glutton could be expected to set himself on fire, see double or even treble, fall asleep among the hounds, and on occasions, murder his wife and children.

Moreover, gluttony introduced its victims to its fellow deadly sins *sloth, lechery,* and *pride.* Drinkers spent all day in bed, were careless of how they appeared, and grew fat through inactivity. Those who could rouse themselves to any degree were all lust and boast, but mostly the latter, for pride was construed to be the "devill's wine," the house red, of all his chapels. Drink made men brag—Satan entered them via their cups and whispered inside their heads: "Thou arte lord of great power. Thou arte stronger than another. Thou art comlier, fairer, wiser in working, more subtle in understanding, more abundant in riches than others be.... Why art thou so familiar with poor men?... (Lo, sirs! Lo, sirs! This is the drink the which the devil maketh many on drunken!)"

Great sins led to small. Swearing abounded in taverns, and false oaths were offensive to both the secular and sacred courts: Under common law, oaths were binding declarations; according to the second commandment, it was a sin to take the name of God in vain. The sacrilegious ejaculations that characterized the speech of drunkards were lambasted from the pulpit. A representative effort, from Brother Whitford of Sion, tells the story of a blasphemous squire named Mayster Baryngton, who retired to a tavern after a blank Sunday morning's hunting and, once he had quenched his thirst with ale, set to cursing his luck: "By God's blood, this day is unhappy!" No sooner had he spoken than his nose began to bleed. The sight of his own blood provoked the squire into a frenzy of further swearing, and at each fresh curse, he began to bleed somewhere else—from his ears, at his wrists, from under his fingernails, "in marvelous great quantity." Undeterred, Mayster Baryngton kept up his blasphemy, whereupon his tongue turned "black as pitch" and "he expired and was dead."

The negative sentiments of sermons were echoed in poetry. William Langland, whose *Piers Plowman* paints not merry but miserable England with a put-upon peasantry, takes pains to show the damage drunkenness could wreak among the illiterate masses—how they might ruin themselves even in the absence of feudal overlords. He sets one of his scenes of degradation in an alehouse, peopled with both real and allegorical characters. Its principal figure is Glutton, representing the deadly sin of the same name, who is intercepted on his way to church by Betty the brewster. Betty tempts Glutton into her den, where he finds a complete crosssection of postfeudal commoners already drinking: a shoe seller, a gamekeeper and his wife, Tim the tinker and his apprentices:

> Hick the horse dealer and Hugh the needle seller
> Clarice of Cock Lane and the clerk of the church
> Davy the ditcher and a dozen other;
> Sir Piers the priest and Pernel of Flanders
> A fiddler, a rat catcher, the street sweeper of Chepe,
> A roper, a riding man, and Rose the dish seller,
> Godfrey of Garlickithe and Griffith the Welshman . . .

The atmosphere is all bustle and cheer. Everyone welcomes Glutton, and ale is called for. Those with insufficient funds pawn their clothes or the tools of their trade in order to contribute to the round. And on this sinister note matters deteriorate. Glutton drinks deep and betrays his bestial nature:

> They sat so till evensong singing now and then,
> Til Glutton had gulped down a gallon and a gill.
> His guts 'gan to rumble like two greedy sows;

He pissed a potful in a paternoster-while[10]
And blew with the bugle at his backbone's end,
That all hearing that horn held their noses after
And wished it were stopped up with a wisp of furze.

Not to be outdone by the pulpit, Langland also succeeded in associating a fourth member of the seven deadly sins with drinking houses in his poem. Betty the brewster is married to *Avarice*, who ruins the poor by extending them credit to buy ale.

Despite such vociferous and disapproving opponents, alehouses were loved by the people. A preacher records, with disgust, that the men who drank deep at them were accounted "good fellowes" by their peers. Another, with equal repugnance, observed that the individuals who frequented them sang songs, played games, told each other jokes, fell in love, and consummated love on the premises, and were, in general, sinfully happy.

A sympathetic view of the English pub appears in the poetry of Geoffrey Chaucer (d. 1400), whose *Canterbury Tales* commence in the Tabard Inn at Southwark, where a group of pilgrims have gathered on their way to the tomb of St. Thomas à Beckett. The Tabard is a welcoming place, blessed with a genial landlord, who declares in the prologue of the poem that he hopes "never to drink anything but wine or ale." He advises his pilgrims to tell each other stories to pass the time along the way to Canterbury, and they oblige. *The Canterbury Tales* was something of an innovation in English literature. Instead of peopling his work with allegorical or mythical figures, or stereotypes, Chaucer sought to present individuals, and used their drinking habits as an aid to characterization—readers could form a better mental image of his heroes and heroines if they knew what they drank and what they thought of alcohol. The enigmatic Summoner, for instance, who loved "strong wine, red as blood," would "speak and cry as he were mad" in Latin, after imbibing enough of his beloved potion. The Miller, in contrast, is drunk throughout his tale, which itself is an example of the vulgar lechery that preachers railed against from their pulpits as being among the side effects of drinking. The Wife of Bath bares her soul when she speaks of the sweet wine she adores and the effect it has on her:

---

[10] The time it takes to say an Our Father.

> For after wine, of Venus must I think:
> For just as surely as cold produces hail,
> A liquorish mouth must have a liquorish tail.
> In women wine's no bar of impotence,
> This know all lechers by experience.

While some of Chaucer's characters comment on the dangers of drinking—the Parson, for instance, calls drunkenness "the horrible sepulcher of man's reasoning" and recommends abstinence—*The Canterbury Tales* as a whole presents alcohol in a sympathetic light. This positive approach reflects Chaucer's own feelings about the substance—his father was a wine merchant, and we know he drank regularly, for in 1374 King Edward III granted the poet a pitcher (eight pints) of wine per day for life, which was later supplemented with another royal grant of a ton of wine per year. It also reflects the spirit of the age. Preachers may have fulminated against pubs and drunkenness, but they did not dare attack drinking per se, which, as the pilgrims of *The Canterbury Tales* illustrate, was an essential part of life in late medieval England.

8   A NEW WORLD OF DRINKING

At the same time that clerical hostility to drunkenness was growing in England, the medical reputation of the fluid that caused it was going from strength to strength in continental Europe. Alcohol was the medieval panacea, recommended by such luminaries as Arnald of Villanova (d. 1315) as a cure for almost any ailment. A physician and alchemist by profession, Arnald set down the good news about drink in his *Liber de Vinis*. The *Book of Wine* was an enthusiastic champion of its subject and recommended plenty of it, both as a prophylactic and a medicine, because "it truly is most friendly to human nature." If taken in the right measure wine was suited to "every age, every time, and every region." In addition to blessing everyone with perfect health, from peasant infants to princes in their dotage, wine could help women to conceive and give birth, and best of all it was intoxicating. Arnald believed that periodic drunkenness was not just fun but also good for people, though not more often than twice a month. In the words of a man respected in his time for his learning: "There is undoubtedly something to be said for inebriation, inasmuch as the results which usually follow do certainly purge the body of noxious humors."

Arnald experimented with the Islamic science of distillation in the course of his alchemical work, and his pupil Raymund Lull, Franciscan monk, alchemist, and missionary, was the first European to write about spirits. He reckoned them to be a "Marvelous medicament," better even than wine, because, in his opinion, they were an entirely different fluid. Distillation did not so much separate as transform, and the substance it produced was "an emanation of the divinity, an element newly revealed to man, but hid from antiquity, because the human race was then too young to need this beverage [which is] destined to revive the energies of modern decrepitude." The element in question was the fabled *quintessence*–the fifth essence–the substance from which all heavenly bodies were believed to have been made, a sample of which Lull thought he had captured in his retort. His enthusiasm was shared by other early European distillers. Thaddeus of Florence (1223–1303) wrote a landmark tract on the matter whose title, "De Virtute *aquae vitae*, quae etiam dicitur *aqua ardens*" ("On the virtues of the water of life, which is also called firewater"), gave the new and elevating beverage the names by which it became known throughout Europe.

The first part of the continent in which distillation flourished was Germany, then comprised of dozens of petty kingdoms. In the fifteenth century, apothecaries in a number of these states started to sell spirits to the public by the shot, as a health tonic. They retailed them as *brandy,* which derives from the German *Gebrant wein*, or "burned wine," an allusion to the distillation process. As demand for their product grew, and the mythical element became an everyday beverage, it acquired a reputation for being dangerous if consumed in excess. A Nuremburg doctor, writing in 1493, advised would-be brandy drinkers that they had to treat the new fluid with caution: "In view of the fact that everyone at present has got into the habit of drinking aqua vitae it is necessary to remember the quantity that one can permit oneself to drink, and learn to drink according to one's capacities; if one wishes to behave like a gentleman." Clearly, this diplomatic warning was not enough, for in 1496 restrictions were placed on the retail and consumption of spirits in Nuremberg. They could not be sold on Sundays or feast days, and spirits bought on weekdays might be drunk only at home. Similar limitations were introduced in Munich a few years later.

Despite such warnings and restrictions, the popularity of spirits continued to grow. Their case was championed in print by Hieronymous Braunschweig, an Alsatian army doctor and author of the illustrated *Big Book of Distillation* (1512). The *Big Book* was aimed at the home distiller and lavished praises on "the mistress of all medicines." It claimed curative powers for aqua vitae to rival those attributed by Arnald of Villanova to wine: "It eases diseases coming of cold. It comforts the heart. It heals all old and new sores on the head. It causes a good color in a person...it eases the pain in the teeth and causes sweet breath...it heals the short-winded. It causes good digestion and appetite...and takes away belching. It eases the yellow jaundice, the dropsy, the gout, the pain in the breasts when they be swollen, and heals all diseases in the bladder.... It heals the bites of a mad dog." Last, but not least: "It gives also courage in a young person and causes him to have a good memory."

Most fifteenth-century German spirits were distilled from wine, of which the region now produced a considerable surplus. The Cistercian monasteries along the Rhine, and a number of aristocratic vintners, had discovered the Riesling grape was the perfect match for the terrain and climate and had planted it in abundance. The original Cistercian settlement in the region at Eberbach by now had over three hundred hectares of vineyards and was the largest single producer of wine in late medieval Europe. In celebration of this status, its monks constructed a giant wine barrel, or tun, in 1500, which had a capacity of about seventy thousand liters. The tun was described as the eighth wonder of the world by the poet Vincentius Obsopaeus, who salivated in his verses over the ocean of fine wine that it contained.

German, or Rhenish wine as it was known at the time, was sold all over Europe. It was typically light in color and weak in strength, and commanded a slight premium in price to the wines of Bordeaux in England. It was, however, far from being the most expensive wine in circulation, which distinction was reserved for vintages from the southern and eastern Mediterranean. The late medieval period witnessed a tremendous expansion in commerce, which was pioneered by the rising Italian city-states of Venice and Genoa. The Venetian trading empire extended from Christian Constantinople and various Saracen nations in the east, to Southampton and Antwerp in the west. It specialized in high-value goods—silks and spices from the Orient and powerful wines from the Levant, whose grapes had been allowed to dry a little in the sun after their harvest, thus concentrating their sugars and increasing their alcoholic potential. The principal Venetian brand was known in England as *Malmsey,* after the Byzantine town of Monemvasia in the Peloponnese. The Genoese focused on Chian wines, from the eponymous Greek Island, which they had captured from the Saracens in 1261. They also sourced wine from Catalonia, Valencia, and Málaga in Spain as these were successively reconquered for Christianity.

The Italian city-states explored as well as traded. Not only did they turn north into the Atlantic when they left the Mediterranean, toward Portugal, France, and the British Isles, they also ventured south into what, for fourteenth-century Europeans, were unknown waters. By 1339, the Genoese had reached the Canary Islands, which were populated by a people called the Guanches, of uncertain origin and stone age technology, who resisted initial attempts to settle but who were subdued by imported Normans from 1402 onward. The surviving Guanches were sold into slavery and their lands were planted with vines. The Madeira Archipelago was first visited in the same year that the Canaries were put on the map. It was "rediscovered" in 1419 by a Portuguese expedition sent by Prince Henry the Navigator and settled in 1425. Unlike the Canaries, Madeira was uninhabited and agriculture rather than slave taking was the priority of its immigrants. Within a decade it was exporting sugar and producing wine. The Azores were next to appear on nautical charts. They had first been spotted in 1427, visited in the 1430s, and had been settled by the 1450s. They were planted with vines from Crete, and soon produced a strong sweet wine similar to that which had made the Mediterranean island famous in classical times.

These early Atlantic ventures were of little initial importance in comparison to trade in the Mediterranean. However, in 1453, Constantinople, the ancient capital of the eastern Roman Empire and the last bulwark of Christianity in the region, fell to Islam. The loss of Constantinople had serious repercussions for commerce, as it had been the terminus for European trade with Asia and China. As a consequence, European eyes turned toward the Atlantic. Might it be possible to reach Asia by sea, by traveling south around Africa and thence east across the Indian Ocean? If so, the new island colonies would be important staging posts. The possibility fascinated Henry of Portugal. Between the discovery of the Azores and his death in 1460, he had sent fleets as far down the west coast of Africa as Sierre Leone. The Portuguese push south was continued by his successors, and in January 1488 Captain Bartolomeo Dias rounded Cape Horn and sailed into the Indian Ocean. These voyages brought the Europeans into direct contact with a number of African cultures for the first time. At each step south down the coast, the Portuguese had established trading stations. The Africans had ivory, gold, slaves, and palm oil to offer, and by a process of trial and error the Portuguese discovered which goods of their own were appealing to their counterparts. In the case of the Wolofs, who occupied what is now Senegal, the best articles of trade were wine, weapons, and horses. The Wolofs were a sophisticated culture, nominally Muslim, who maintained links with other members of their faith through a trans-Saharan land trade route, but who had chosen to disregard the Koranic ban on drinking. They had a number of native beverages, including palm wine and millet beer, and these two drinks were found to be common throughout sub-Saharan Africa. Indeed, at every point of the continent where the Portuguese landed, they found alcohol to be present and to have been integrated into the customs and rituals of the peoples with whom they made contact.

In addition to seeking a route to Asia by sailing around Africa, Europeans also contemplated the possibility of reaching it by traveling west. Although no one thought the world was flat, they disagreed as to just how big and round it was. In 1492, the Spanish king and queen, Ferdinand and Isabella, financed a fleet of three ships under a Genoese sea captain, Christopher Columbus, which sailed from Seville to the Canary Islands, and thence across the Atlantic to the Americas. Within fifty years of this voyage, the Spanish had established an American empire that stretched from Florida to southern Chile. The empire was created by conquest of two great civilizations, the Aztecs and the Incas, and the piecemeal annexation of the territories of various smaller cultures. During the same decades the Portuguese succeeded in their ambition of reaching Asia via Africa, established a colony in Brazil, and sponsored, under Ferdinand Magellan, the first expedition in history to sail around the world. Both Spain and her neighboring power provisioned their fleets with bounteous stocks of wine, sourced from Andalusía, or their respective Atlantic Island colonies. Wine was a significant part of the cost of fitting out an expedition. Magellan spent more on sherry than on armaments; indeed his wine rations cost nearly twice as much as his flagship, the *San Antonio*. In consequence, the Spanish and the Portuguese paid careful attention to the presence or absence of alcoholic drinks in the places where they traded or conquered, to their potential for vineyards, and to the drinking habits of the natives.

The Spanish found not one but a multitude of drinking cultures in their American possessions. These were concentrated in Middle or *Meso*america, between Mexico and Panama, and were as diverse among themselves as they were different from Spanish custom. Mesoamerican civilizations were perhaps the most ingenious in history in identifying potential sources of alcohol. They fermented cacti and their fruits, maize and its stalks, the sap of a good two-dozen species of agave, honey, sasparilla, the seed pods of the mesquite tree, hog plums, and the fruit and bark of various other trees. The ubiquity of alcohol was remarked upon by the conquistadores, who observed that in their new dominions "up to now no tribe has been found which is content to drink only water."

Among the novel types of fermentables observed by the Spaniards in Mesoamerica, four in particular stood out: the fruits, or *tunas,* of cacti; maize; tree bark; and *pulque.* The manufacture of alcoholic beverages from cacti proved widespread among hunter-gatherer tribes. Typically, the tribe in question would move to an area where cacti were in fruit and spend all their time brewing and drinking until the season was over. The Chichimeca of central Mexico, for instance, would work in short cycles, preparing then consuming "tuna wine": "every third day, the women make the wine and the men drink so much that they lose their senses." According to Spanish accounts, the Chichimeca were highly volatile when intoxicated, so that the women would hide their menfolk's bows and arrows lest they kill each other. Moreover, in order not to be surprised by their enemies when under the influence, the Chichimeca "never all [got] drunk at the same time" and appointed drink monitors, whose duty was to stay sober and keep a good lookout.

A more important source of fermentable material was maize, the principal cereal crop of the Americas, which hitherto had been unknown to Europeans. This was used to produce *tesguino*–maize beer. Tesguino was made by masticating corn kernels and boiling these for a prolonged period to produce a syrup, which was rediluted, then fermented for three to five days. The Spanish called it *vino de maíz*–maize wine–and noted the enthusiasm with which it was consumed by their new subjects: "They have solemn festivals of drunkenness for which the whole pueblo congregates." Tesguino was the drink of choice in central and western Mexico.

To the south, in the Yucatán Peninsula, the principal alcoholic drink of the once-great Mayas was *balche*–mead fermented with the bark of the balche tree. The resulting concoction has been described as "milky white, sour to the smell, and at first very disagreeable to the taste." Despite its unpleasant flavor, the Maya consumed balche in volume at their frequent "fiestas, dances, and weddings," where they would "dance after drinking repeatedly from small jars and in a short time become intoxicated and act as if they were crazy and childish."

Whereas many of the native types of alcoholic drink fell out of use after the Spanish conquest, one in particular remained common and grew in popularity. This was *pulque,* the fermented sap of the *maguey,* the Spanish generic name for a the agave plant. Like the poetical mead of the Anglo-Saxons, pulque had a special cachet, especially among the Aztecs, whom the Spanish had displaced as lords of Mexico. According to Aztec theology, pulque was blessed with a mother goddess, and a band of immortal guardians–the *Centzontotochtli*–the Four Hundred Moon Rabbit Gods of Pulque. Their number, and their place of residence, were both symbolic of fertility, and their principal sphere of influence, beyond the supervision of the manufacture of pulque, was breeding. The connection between the moon, the rabbits, fertility, and pulque was enhanced by the milky color of the fluid, which was liberally employed at planting and harvest festivals.

The manufacturing process of pulque was complex and required the death of the plant. Magueys mature when they are five to seven years old, whereupon the center, which resembles a giant artichoke, begins to swell prior to sending out a *quiote*–a single flower stalk. The quiote bud is cut out and a cavity scraped clean in the center of the plant, which fills with sap, called *aguamiel*–honeywater. The aguamiel is extracted two or three times a day–a large plant can yield seven liters per day, until it dies, and it may survive in this wounded state for up to six months, bleeding out a total of perhaps a thousand liters. This was an aesthetically pleasing process for the Aztecs–reminiscent of their usual method of human sacrifice–cutting out the victim's heart and draining the cavity of blood.

Once collected, the aguamiel was placed in clay pots and sealed for a period of four days, during which time it fermented. Pulque brewers were a superstitious lot. They would abstain from sex for the fermentation period, as they believed that intercourse made the brew sour. They also refrained from tasting the pulque, or drinking any other pulque during the brewing period, for the same reason. Anyone breaking abstinence was likely to be cursed with a twisted mouth or possessed by an angry rabbit god. Once pulque was ready, it had to be consumed quickly, as it had a shelf life of little more than twenty-four hours. Fresh pulque has a sweet odor said to be reminiscent of bananas. Off-pulque, however possesses a smell so noxious that, in the words of a Spanish observer, "there are no dead dogs, nor a bomb, that can clear a path so well." In order to circumvent such perishability, the aguamiel was sometimes boiled down into a syrup, which later could be rediluted and fermented.

The Aztecs appear to have had the strictest drinking laws in history outside Islam. Only men or women over the age of fifty-two could have a draft of pulque whenever and wherever they wished. Most Aztecs died before they were old enough to drink. Illicit drinkers had their hair cut off, their houses demolished, and/or were summarily executed. The Codex Mendoza (1541), a postconquest compilation of native beliefs, features a picture of three young people being stoned to death for drunkenness with a caption explaining that this was no less than they deserved. The old took advantage of their privileges, especially on the festive occasions when they were expected to drink deep. Bernadino de Sahagun, who compiled an account of Aztec civilization before it vanished, gives a touching picture of legal, albeit geriatric, drinkers in their cups: "Once they were all intoxicated they began to sing; some sang and cried, others sang to give pleasure. Each one would sing whatever he liked and in the key he fancied best, and none of them harmonized; some sang out loud, others softly, merely humming to themselves." The elderly were also issued cigarettes to smoke while they drank, for the combination of alcohol and tobacco was a popular one throughout Central America.

There were, however, numerous exceptions to such Draconian drinking laws. The nobility of either sex, warriors, pregnant women, pulque brewers and maguey cultivators, and various classes of priests and temple choirs were permitted to drink with differing degrees of freedom. The nobility drank pulque with their meals, as a privilege of their caste, and sometimes mixed it with their chocolate. Warriors and brewers helped themselves from stone troughs at various temples, which were filled to the brim in honor of a number of the denizens of the Aztec pantheon. Moreover, there was one festival at which the entire population, including babes in arms, were required to drink. This was the *Pillahuana* (Drunkenness of Children) festival, held every fourth new year, at which all the children born in the intervening period had their ears pierced and were taken to watch the human sacrifices by their godparents, who acted as chaperones throughout the event and who encouraged, or forced, their charges to drink liberal

An Aztec matron enjoys the milk of old age.

quantities of pulque. The results, according to a Spanish source, were ugly: "Once drunk, they would quarrel among themselves, they cuffed one another and fell on the floor on top of each other, or else they would go embracing each other."

In addition to the aforementioned exceptions, some people were cursed by the stars to drink. Rabbit served as an astrological marker—it was one of the signs of the Aztec zodiac, and anyone born on the day of *Umetochtli–2-Rabbit*–was destined to become a drunk, who "would not look for anything else in life save alcohol . . . and only drink it . . . in order to get intoxicated . . . even before breakfast." Two-Rabbits were easy to spot, as they were notoriously unkempt: "They totter along, falling down and getting full of dust, and red in the face. . . . They do not care, although they may be covered in bruises and wounds from falls, provided they can get drunk, nothing else matters." Interestingly, the Aztec legal process was unusually sympathetic toward them. Their drunkenness was a valid alibi for any crime. "He has become his rabbit" would be the judgment, and punishment would be left to fate. The defense of possession by one's rabbit was proof against every charge, though at the price of stigma—people born on luckier days had nothing but "loathing and hatred" for 2-Rabbits.

The Spanish did their best to exterminate Aztec and other New World religious practices and to replace them with Christianity. All the traditional drinking occasions were prohibited, as were the intricate laws governing who might drink and when. This cultural apocalypse resulted in an increase in tippling among their new subjects, to whom it became a secular, as opposed to ritual, pastime. Given the unpleasant living conditions that they were forced to endure after the conquest, it is likely that most of them resorted to alcohol for the purpose identified by Sophocles in classical Greece: to "banish woe." And while the traditional range of Mesoamerican additives to alcoholic drinks, including tobacco, peyote, *yage*, toad juice, and magic mushrooms, vanished from their brews, the drinks themselves lived on. In Mexico, the Spanish turned pulque into gold. They introduced licensing laws for its production and sale, and taxes on its consumption. A century or so after the conquest, levies on pulque were second only to the silver mines as a source of imperial revenues. They also introduced the technology of distillation, which the Mexicans were quick to adopt. They applied their ingenuity to building stills from the simplest of materials—clay and hollowed-out logs—which they used to extract elixirs from their traditional potations, creating new beverages in the process. Pulque, for example, was transformed into mescal.

A similar course of events occurred in Spain's dominions in South America, which they had subjugated with the same mixture of cunning and brutality as they had employed against the Aztecs. The Incas, their victims in the south, were rulers of an empire encompassing much of modern Peru, Chile, and Ecuador, and parts of Argentina. Their common beverage was maize beer. Its consumption was a vital part of their religious and social rituals. A few drops were offered to the sun god before drinking; and intoxication was encouraged at major ceremonies and feasts, especially those relating to the initiation of children. These last were celebrated by all parents on the second birthday of their first child, when it was given a name, received valuable presents from its relatives, its first haircut, and its last taste of breast milk, and was introduced to alcohol. According to a Spanish source, "As soon as the presentation of gifts was over, the ceremony of drinking began, for without it no entertainment was considered good. They sang and they danced until night, and this festivity continued for three or four days, or more."

Although the indigenous peoples of South America continued to drink their traditional maize brews postconquest, these were supplemented, as had been the case in Mexico, with distilled spirits, and also with new drinks introduced by the Spanish. The principal novelty was wine. The Spaniards planted the vine in every suitable part of the Americas that they controlled. It flourished best at first in Peru. Although the Spanish government latterly attempted to restrict the trade in South American wine, so as to protect the market for its own exports, by the 1570s Peru was sending its vintages to Chile (which was also a producer), Colombia, Venezuela, Mexico, and to the Philippines, to which a transpacific trade route had been opened in 1565.

While the Spanish were building an empire in Central and South America, the Portuguese had concentrated on trading with the Far East. In 1494, after mediation from Pope Alexander VI, the two maritime powers had divided the globe between them along a north-south meridian, with the Spanish allotted all "new" lands west of longitude 39' 53" and the Portuguese the other half of the world. Brazil fell into the Portuguese hemisphere, which they settled and to which they introduced sugarcane and distillation, but their principal efforts were focused on Asia. They established bases in Goa, in India, in 1510, and in Malacca, in Malaysia, the following year, with the intention of cornering the spice trade. In 1536, the Chinese permitted them to use Macau on their coast as a harbor and to purchase the silks and other luxury goods that fetched such colossal prices in Europe. From Macau the Portuguese voyaged to Japan, where they were granted permission to send one ship each year.

Japan had featured large in the European imagination since the publication of Marco Polo's largely fictional account of the gold-rich island of Zipangu. The gold was a myth, but the actual wealth, power, and sophistication of Japan, and moreover of China, came as a shock to Europeans and increased their fascination with these ancient and complex civilizations. European goods were shoddy in comparison to what China and Japan had to offer, and both places were conscious of their superiority. In consequence, their political organization, their religions, and the personal habits of their populations were scrutinized, with the aim of discovering how commerce could be advanced. As usual, careful attention was paid to their drinking customs.

The universal alcoholic beverage throughout China was rice wine. It had been described by Marco Polo as "a liquor which they brew of rice with a quantity of excellent spice in such fashion that it makes better drink than any other wine." Moreover, it was "clear and pleasing to the eye. And being very hot stuff, it makes one drunk sooner than any other wine." The Portuguese found the same substance common in Japan, where it was known as *sake* and was in such demand "that they say that more than one-third of the rice grown in Japan is used in making it." The rituals with which this popular fluid was drunk were set down in some detail by João Rodrigues, a Portuguese Jesuit who spent several decades in the country, commencing in 1577. His observations reveal some parallels, and some radical differences, with European drinking practices.

Japanese society was far more formal than that of Europe–the slightest contact between individuals was punctuated by convoluted rituals. As a consequence, their drinking etiquette was correspondingly more complex, especially in the higher echelons of society. Drinking parties and dinner parties were the usual entertainments of the upper classes, each of which was choreographed to the most intricate degree. Their "first and chief courtesy and token of interior love and friendship" was a *sakazuki*–a sake drinking session–at which two or three people drank in turns from the same cup "as a sign of uniting their hearts into one or their . . . souls into one." Such noble aims were accompanied by tortuous rituals. Stripped to its bones, a sakazuki held for a single distinguished guest, after greetings, a staged entry, an exchange of bows, compliments, and presents, required the host to send a cup of sake to his guest, who was required to return it untasted to the host, who returned it in turn, and so on several times, before the host reluctantly consented to take the first sip.[11] Despite the time such rituals consumed, their participants nonetheless managed to get roaring drunk. To Japanese minds, intoxication was the logical aim of drinking in company, and it was a condition that carried no stigma. Rodrigues contrasted this ethos with Jesuit views of alcohol, which perhaps did not represent those of all his native continent: "In Europe it is a great disgrace to get drunk. But it is esteemed in Japan. When you ask, 'How is the lord?' they answer, 'He is drunk.'"

Indeed, at drinking parties and tippling sessions after banquets, it was ill-mannered to stay sober, "and so they are obliged to drink even when it is injurious to their health." Those who really could not drink had to pretend to be drunk. It was also good form to feign a hangover. This was achieved by sending thank-you letters deliberately late, writ-

---

[11] The first Englishman to observe this procedure thought it so much humbug: "Before the master of the house begins to drink, he will proffer the cup to every one of his guests, making show to have them to begin though it be far from his intention."

ten in shaky characters, apologizing for the delay and excusing themselves on the grounds "that from the time they returned home up to the time of writing they had been intoxicated and incapable on account of the amount they had drunk. This is to show how great was the welcome and affection that the host had shown them. It was for his sake that they forced themselves to drink so as to afford him pleasure."

Despite the differences in ritual, the Japanese shared some opinions with Europeans as to the effect of drinking on the drinker. Like the classical Greeks, they believed alcohol made a person speak his mind. However, and unlike sixteenth-century Europeans, they considered drunkenness de rigueur for business transactions. According to Rodrigues, "They seem to do this on purpose in order to avoid deceit, for the [sake] does not allow any dissembling because it makes them blurt out everything hidden in their hearts and speak their minds without any duplicity."

Finally, a ceremonial drink was an important part of Japanese death rituals. Before committing *seppuku*, i.e., disemboweling themselves, Japanese suicides would take a farewell draft of sake and provide a cup for the second responsible for beheading them when the pain became too great. The practice was imitated by Christian martyrs (for after an initial welcome the Portuguese were discouraged and persecuted) to gain respect for their faith. A pair of friars martyred in Nagasaki in 1617 "brought wine reserved for mass and poured it into cups and, lifting them up high (for this is the courteous custom of Japan), each gave a cup to his executioner to drink."

In addition to recording the differences and similarities between Japanese and European attitudes toward alcohol, Rodrigues also drew attention to the passion in the Far East for a nonalcoholic beverage, which had no counterpart of similar significance in his own culture. He traveled extensively in China as well as Japan and, everywhere he went, found people drinking *cha*, or tea. The idea that a dry, i.e., alcohol-free, drink might confer similar benefits to, say, wine upon its consumers was almost unimaginable in Europe. True, there were such prodigies as healing springs; true, too, that infants drank milk and thrived on it. But the suggestion that boiling leaves in water was a worthwhile use of firewood seemed ridiculous. In consequence, the "various properties, natural powers, and benefits of Cha" and the extravagant praise lavished on it by two hard-drinking civilizations,

both of which, incidentally, scorned drinking hot water solo, were examined by Rodrigues in depth and one by one. His conclusions were
positive. Tea, as the Asiatics insisted, did indeed have useful properties. It was an aid to celibacy, to the digestion, and to sleepy people. It
had a calming influence–"As a cordial it eases the heart and relieves
melancholy"–and attractive organoleptic qualities: "The scent of excellent cha is most pleasing, and when a lot of it is drunk . . . it leaves in
the throat a very mellow taste." Best of all, it was an outstanding urine
trigger and thus "very good against the pain caused by the [kidney]
stone and strangury."

Rodrigues noted the particular importance of this unusual beverage to the old. The Japanese had a custom of renouncing their worldly
goods to their children upon reaching a certain age and station and
retiring to the countryside, where they lived in fantastically expensive
mock-hermitages, in which they entertained each other, with great
ritual, to tea. The ceremony was minimalist and required the patience
of age to appreciate its art. There were neither tea boasts nor tea
bards; indeed, the contemplation of a single flower or twig was considered the height of entertainment. Might high tea perform a similar
role in Europe? Rodrigues held back from making predictions: While
tea was appropriate to a Zen mind-set, even its most fervent Japanese
advocates still believed alcohol to be the appropriate beverage for the
hot-blooded people who had not yet given up on the world.

9 WATKIN'S ALE

Though I go bare,
Take ye no care,
I am nothing a-cold;
I stuff my skin,
So full within,
Of jolly good ale & old.
                    —Traditional English Drinking Song

In 1578, the cozy duopoly of Portugal and Spain over international trade beyond Europe was violated by an Englishman with a red beard and an unpleasant temper. Francis Drake, following the route pioneered more than fifty years before by Magellan and not attempted since, sailed into the Pacific, where he raided every Spanish settlement between Valparaiso and Acapulco. He burned down their houses, freed their slaves, sank their ships, and carried off their treasure. His greatest prize was the *Caca Fuego,* a Manila galleon laden with spices, silk, and bullion; his incidental captures yielded substantial quantities of Spanish- and South American–grown wine, including 1,770 skins of the Chilean vintage of 1577. Drake coasted up America as far as present-day San Francisco, where he claimed the land for his queen, received the submission of the native chiefs, and named the region Nova Albion. He, and the complement of his ship, the *Golden Hind,* were probably the first men ever to drink wine in northern California. After repairing his vessel, Drake reached off over the Pacific to Asia, where he gate-crashed the spice trade, before heading home for England and a knighthood.

The appearance of an English ship in those parts of the world that the pope had confirmed as belonging to Catholic Spain and Portugal was as unexpected as it was unwelcome. In retrospect, it was inevitable. During the same decades that they had been exploiting their respective spheres of influence, a schism among European Christians had thrown the home continent into disarray. Within a period of about thirty years between 1520 and 1550, northern Germany, Switzerland, Scandinavia, England, and parts of the Low Countries had rejected the authority in matters spiritual of the pope, and the customs of his church, in favor of new, radical versions of Christianity. As this upheaval–the *Reformation*–progressed, pitting Protestant reformers against Rome, a battle royal took place for the moral high ground. The consumption of alcohol entered the debate, at first in metaphor, as each side accused the other of behaving like drunks. The Catholics, claimed the Protestants, were inebriated with power, whereas Protestants, to Catholic minds, had the corrupted thought processes of terminal alcoholics. Such accusations caused both sects to scrutinize the place of drink in their version of a Christian society.

Martin Luther, if not the architect then at least the catalyst of the Reformation, had strong views about the matter. In his opinion, it was certainly wrong that Catholic monks should touch alcohol, for it turned them into inebriated onanists. He spoke from experience–he had started in religion as a black-robed monk. Everyone else, however, could drink with an easy conscience, just as their Savior had. Moreover, there were reasons to celebrate: "We ought to give thanks to God for providing us with food and drink and then besides, liberating us from the papacy....If you are tired and downhearted, take a drink."

Luther, in deed as well as word, was by and large proalcohol. He was provided with a barrel of Einbecker beer by the Duke of Brunswick to keep his spirits up during his first tussle with the Catholic Church, and his attitude to drink in general is summed up in one of his better-known sayings:

> Who loves not wine, women, and song
> Remains a fool his whole life long.

He did however, consider drunkenness to be un-Christian and it was sufficiently prevalent in the reformed German states, probably as a consequence of the spread of distilled spirits, to move him to speak against it. He depicted it as an epidemic, which had erupted among the commoners, and latterly had contaminated society at every level, so that "now those who are the greatest and best are beginning to fall, indeed, even the princes. Now the ten-year-old milksops ... are beginning, and ruining themselves in their flower.... We preach, but who stops it? Those who should stop it do it themselves.... Therefore Germany is a land of hogs.... If you were going to paint it, you would have to paint a pig."

Other Protestant reformers, notably Ludwig Haetzer (d. 1529), took a harder line toward alcohol than Luther. The aim, after all, was not merely to correct the abuses of the church but also to make society pure. Like the fire-and-brimstone preachers of the medieval English pulpit, Haetzer believed that drinking inevitably led to sin, and in 1525 he published a treatise, *On Evangelical Drinking,* which proposed total abstinence, not only from drunkenness but also from alcohol among Evangelical Christians. His views were echoed by Sebastien Franck in another treatise, *Concerning the Horrible Vice of Drunkenness,* which was printed in 1528, and which, after describing the disgusting effects the Horrible Vice had on humans, concluded that drinkers were "heathens and not Christian, who do not show forth the fruits of faith." His solution was to ban drink in Christian societies. These were, however, minority views; indeed, Haetzer was executed by other reformers for his radicalism. Protestants in the main considered drinking to be a secular rather than a sacred matter. They watered down the doctrine of transubstantiation, according to which the bread and wine of the Eucharist became the actual flesh and blood of Christ, to *consubstantiation,* whereby they remained food and drink, albeit infused with the spirit of divinity. This change effectively reduced the religious importance of wine. The best it could be, to Luther and his followers, was a vehicle for the Godhead.

The Catholics, in contrast, while happy to condemn their opponents as alcoholic heretics, said little against drink per se. Wine, in the hands of a Catholic priest, could still be the blood of Christ, and so many monasteries were in the wine or brewing trades that to lose the wealth these generated would be financial suicide. Moreover, there were numerous saints associated with the production, distribution, and consumption of alcohol. Could it be that these companions of God labored in vain? In consequence, whereas the Protestants had questioned drinking and would continue to do so as part of a general reassessment of what constituted a Christian way of life, Catholicism more or less ignored the issue. There was a scholarly debate in various Italian states about the nature of wine, whose participants, while unanimous in the opinion that wine was a healthy beverage, in particular the red variety, since of all foodstuffs it most resembled blood and therefore would convert easiest to this vital fluid, uttered a few mild criticisms against it. The critics, however, were very much in the minority. The reputation of alcohol, wine especially, was on the rise in Catholic countries during the Reformation. This, in part, was a consequence of the Renaissance, the intellectual and artistic movement that had begun in the Italian city-states the previous century and which had since spread through Europe.

The Renaissance revived Roman and Greek ideals and themes in the visual arts, and also represented Christian scenes in classical styles. Bacchus, whose emblems had for so long been employed as Christian symbols of resurrection, was himself resurrected and once again became a proper subject for artists. The rehabilitation of the god of wine was completed by the hand of Michelangelo, who was commissioned by Cardinal Raffaele Riario to produce a statue of the pagan demon for his palace. The resulting image, life-size in marble, is a masterful combination of myth and realism. Bacchus is cut from the rock in an unsteady pose. Although well muscled, he lacks the signature hard body of his creator's other works, rather is faintly androgynous, reflecting the effeminacy sometimes attributed to him in myth. The face, moreover, is unsettling: According to the English poet Percy Shelley, the statue "looks drunken, brutal, and narrow minded and has an expression of dissoluteness the most revolting." In the event it was rejected by the cardinal and sold instead to a banker. Its creator was partial to wine, especially that of his native Tuscany, every mouthful of which, he claimed, "Kisses, bites, licks, thrusts, and sings."

Michelangelo's Bacchus

Among other classical ideals, the Renaissance also revived the Platonic principle of moderation in drinking. This standard was proclaimed in works such as *The Book of the Courtier* (1528) by Balthazar Castiglione, a kind of Renaissance etiquette manual for the man about court. According to Castiglione, drunkenness was the enemy of continence and temperance, the two watchwords that should govern the behavior of the aspiring courtier. Interestingly, the princes or cardinals whose courts Castiglione's readers hoped to frequent still aimed at the medieval ideals of flamboyance and excess. The cardinals, in particular, were as continent as Viking raiders, and their bastard sons, whom they disguised as their nephews,[12] often excelled their fathers in dissipation. As for princes, while some expected their menials to be sober and alert, they considered themselves above such conduct, for they, after all, were no mere courtiers.

The old-fashioned virtues of conspicuous consumption and distribution were displayed to perfection at the court of King Henry VIII of England who, according to a French spy, was "constantly intoxicated." The staff and guests at his favorite palace in Hampton Court got through 4.8 million pints of ale and beer each year, and more than a hundred tons of wines from all over Europe, and this was but a fraction of the alcohol consumed at his other palaces and frequent, splendid pageants. Henry further distinguished himself from the Renaissance ideal by renouncing the Catholic Church, which he had once championed, and adopting Lutheran values, in order that he might divorce his first wife for a prettier, more fertile woman. He rejected the authority of Rome, authorized his second, of six, marriages, and, in 1534, established himself (with the consent of a dutiful Parliament) as the supreme head of the new Church of England. Once the religion of his kingdom was in safe hands, he moved against the servants of his Papist rival. Its monasteries in England were inspected and found to be populated with drunken sinners. Their assets were seized and distributed among his favorites, and their monks and nuns were pensioned off or told to find work.

As the dissolution of the monasteries progressed, it acquired a destructive nature. The images of saints and martyrs that had crowded English churches were smashed, pilgrims' shrines were demolished, theological libraries were burned, and colorful Catholic festivals were

---

[12] Hence our word *nepotism*.

banned. The church-ales, hitherto an important part of rural life, were prohibited in 1547, on the principle that they, too, were a species of idolatry. Marriage was demoted from a sacrament to a civil matter, so that the wassailing that had accompanied *bride-ale* (bridal) celebrations lost its sanctity. The consequent reduction of drinking occasions and places—for church halls had been the social centers of some rural communities—was compensated for by an increase in the number and importance of pubs. Confiscated church property was converted into secular drinking space. In London, for instance, the Chapel of St. Martin-le-Grand was refurbished as a wine tavern, the site of the Carmelite priory of Whitefriars was given over to alehouses, and land belonging to the Dominican order—the Blackfriars—became home to a pub named after the pre-Reformation owners, which still exists and still serves ale.

Between the death of King Henry VIII in 1547 and the ascension to the throne of Queen Elizabeth I in 1558, England was in turmoil. It had had a Protestant child monarch and a vituperative Catholic queen in the interim, whose respective advisors persecuted the opponents of their factions of Christianity with equal fanaticism. During this period, English pubs acquired the reputation of being places where the idle and discontented, whether Catholic or Anglican, depending upon which sect was out of power, might gather to foment discord. The reputation lingered for the first two decades of Elizabeth's reign, during which she consolidated power, and *their* numbers continued to grow. The official distrust of public houses derived from their egalitarianism, born in the age of Chaucer, which had since become part of English culture—anyone might meet at one and say what they felt about any subject with absolute freedom. The increase in the number of pubs, and the impossibility of controlling the hearts and tongues of the people who went to them, infuriated the ruling class. England suffered an economic depression in the middle of the sixteenth century, and this was blamed on drinking places, as was unemployment, vagrancy, and the appearance of syphilis. The damage they caused to the economy was explained to Parliament by William Cecil, secretary of state: "The multiplying of taverns is evident cause of the disorder of the vulgar people who by haunting thereto waste their small substance which they weekly get by their hard labor and commit all evils that accompany drunkenness." Their role in the dissemination of syphilis was the speculation of William Clowes, surgeon of St. Bartholomew's Hospital, who claimed to have treated over a thousand syphilitics and who believed that infection was transmitted not just by sex but also via "unwary... drinking" in "lewd alehouses," whose moral atmosphere alone might contaminate the innocent.

Neither Cecil or Clowes had any effect on the trade of public houses, whose numbers continued to grow. According to the first official census, carried out in 1577, England (less three counties) contained 14,202 alehouses, 1,631 inns, and 329 taverns. This equated to a pub per every 187 persons,[13] and excluded both the plethora of informal outlets such as tippling houses and the multitude of hucksters who sold ale by the mouthful or the pottle in the streets.

Many of the new drinking places stocked a different kind of beverage from ale–*beer*. Beer, in Elizabethan times, was ale brewed to a slightly more complicated process, and with the infusion of hops, as had been recommended by Abbess Hildegard von Bingen in the Middle Ages. Although these may seem small differences, they had important consequences. Hops had a threefold effect on ale–they imparted bitterness to its flavor, they increased the foaminess of its head, and most importantly, they possessed powerful antimicrobial properties. Whereas ale generally had a shelf life of a week or two, beer lasted for months. Beer was first recorded in England in 1361, when a trader from Amsterdam named James Dodynessone paid a toll on some firkins he had landed at Great Yarmouth. For the first century or so after its appearance in the country it was considered a drink for foreigners. However, its longevity recommended it as a provision for troops on campaign and ships on long voyages, and soldiers, sailors, and Londoners developed a taste for the alien brew. By 1493, the "berebrewers" of London were sufficiently numerous to found their own mystery, or guild, and by the time of the Reformation it was as common in metropolitan pubs as ale.

Despite the slight differences between the two, beer was viewed with a great deal of suspicion, especially by traditionalists, who labeled it a noxious foreign concoction. Andrew Boorde,[14] author of the

---

[13] The figure in 2004 was one per every 529.

[14] Boorde was quite a character–an Oxford scholar, a former monk, a spy who traveled all over Europe, the man who introduced rhubarb to England, whose written work included a guidebook for travelers to the continent and a treatise on beards. Interestingly, as well as condemning beer as downright dangerous to his fellow countrymen, he also advised them to steer clear of Adam's ale, for "water is not wholesome sole by itself for an Englishman."

immensely popular *Dyetary of Health* (1542), a diet-cum-home-doctor book, advised his readers to stick to good old ale, since "ale for an English man is a natural drink." Conversely, they should avoid beer at all costs, for "it is a natural drink for a Dutch man," and Dutchmen had radically different metabolisms from people born in the island kingdom. Boorde lamented the spread of beer, which "of late days is much used in England to the detriment of many Englisshe people; specially it killeth them the which be troubled with the colic and the stone and the strangulation." He warned any of his countrymen still tempted to try it that beer "doth make a man fat, and doth inflate the bely, as it doth appear by the Dutch-men's faces and belyes."

Beer gained ground against ale, despite such strident health warnings. It was, after all, in its common form, a better-made and more interesting brew. Ale brewers fought back by pushing up the alcoholic strength of their product, and beer brewers responded in kind. Elizabethan "maltbugs" could choose between such heady concoctions as "Huffecap, Mad Dog, Father Whoresonne, Angel's Food, Dragons Milk, . . . &c.," and made a spectacle of themselves when they tracked down a quality barrel, whether of beer or ale: "It is incredible to see how [they] lug at this liquor, even as pigs should lie in a row, lugging at their dame's teats, till they lie still againe, and be not able to wag."

While beer may have had the advantage in terms of shelf life, ale enjoyed a better image. In contrast to metropolitan beer, it was perceived of as a breath of country air, as the mainstay of stout and patriotic yeomen and their rosy-cheeked spouses and offspring. Moreover, like the pulque of the Aztecs, ale had symbolic or sentimental associations with fertility. The popular Elizabethan ballad "Watkin's Ale," for instance, tells the story of a girl who doesn't want to die a maid and so persuades a lusty youth to proof her against this eventuality. They court for a short while, and then:

> He took this maiden then aside,
> And led her where she was not spyed
> And told her many a pretty tale
> And gave her well of Watkins Ale

Not only was ale blessed by traditional ties to procreation, it also had the endorsement of England's greatest dramatist, William Shakespeare. His partiality toward it may be deduced from the respective drinking habits of his characters. His heroes quaff, or praise, ale, and criticize beer, which is the beverage of choice of his villains and weaklings. The playwright's preference may be interpreted as protonationalism. By the time that Shakespeare had started writing, Elizabethan England had developed a clear identity, and with it an archetypal Englishman. In addition to favoring ale over beer, this new paragon had definite tastes in other categories of drink, which are also apparent in Shakespeare's plays.

The fashionable drink, the darling of gallants, sea captains, and playwrights alike, was a sweet, strong golden wine called *sherris, sherris-sack,* or just plain *sack. Sherris* was an Anglicization of Jérez, the name of the town in Andalusía in Spain where this nectar was produced. *Sack* derived from the Spanish *sacar*–to take out, or export. Its popularity resulted in part from a promotional drive by its producers, the dukes of Medina Sidonia, who had encouraged trade in their wines with England by removing export duties and through offering special privileges to its merchants. The drive had coincided with war between France and England, which had put claret off-limits, and by 1570 the English, together with their fellow Protestants in the Netherlands, were taking out forty thousand butts of sack, or two-thirds of the annual vintage, every year. Their fondness for the fluid was not diminished by the outbreak of hostilities between England and Spain in 1585; indeed, sack seems to have become more attractive, on the understanding that any on sale in England had been captured from the Spaniards. This association was strengthened when Sir Francis Drake led a preemptive raid against the Spanish fleet as it lay in harbor in Cádiz. The sack, in the sense of investiture and despoliation of the town, yielded two thousand nine hundred butts of the eponymous wine as part of the booty. Englishmen queued up to drink "authentic Cádiz" when Drake brought it home. What could be more patriotic than to tipple on a beverage bought with English cannon and English blood?

Sack had its champion in the Shakespearean character of Sir John Falstaff, who has sack in front of him, or calls for more, almost whenever he is onstage. Perhaps his best known speech is in praise of this elixir, and its sentiments may be taken to reflect Elizabethan feelings about alcohol in general:

"A good sherris-sack hath a twofold operation in it. It ascends me into the brain, dries me there all the foolish and dull and cruddy vapors which environ it; makes it apprehensive, quick, forgetive, full of nimble, fiery, and delectable shapes; which, delivered o'er to the voice, the tongue, which is the birth, becomes excellent wit. The second property of your excellent sherris is the warming of the blood; which, before cold and settled, left the liver white and pale, which is the badge of pusillanimity and cowardice, but the sherris warms it and makes it course from the inwards to the parts extreme. It illumineth the face, which as a beacon gives warning to all the rest of this little kingdom, man, to arm," for "valour comes of sherris," and therefore: "If I had a thousand sons, the first human principle I would teach them should be, to forswear thin potations, and to addict themselves to sack."

Falstaff was Shakespeare's most popular comic creation–the embodiment of Elizabethan drinking, with all its perceived vices and virtues. He was so well-liked that he reappeared as star of his own show–*The Merry Wives of Windsor.* This play, graced with one of Shakespeare's few original plots, showcases drunkenness, and its pitfalls, and its champion. A rumor written down a century afterward claimed that it was composed in obedience to the wishes of Queen Elizabeth, implying that England high and low loved Sir John Falstaff. It is interesting that a character so defined by tippling could be so popular. Sir John has echoes of Silenus, the fat old drunken demigod who sometimes traveled with Bacchus, suggesting that both the Romans and the Elizabethans had a similar ideal drinker in their heads–a figure both comic and endearing.

Sir John had a variety of drinking companions, female as well as male, and the former presented lively exhibitions of feminine drunkenness, the stage symptoms of which included blushes and malapropisms. Doll Tearsheet, for instance, a prostitute invited by Falstaff to drinks in an upstairs room at the Boar's Head Tavern, his home from home (in *King Henry IV, Part II*), arrives for her assignation with an impressive color in her cheeks, the result of drinking "too much canaries...a marvelous searching wine."

Women of all conditions appear to have enjoyed a reasonable freedom to consume alcohol in Elizabethan times. While outright inebriation (except in stage whores played by boys) was frowned upon, it was considered normal for them to drink. The queen herself breakfasted on ale, took wine at her banquets, and permitted spirits to be kept in her palaces. In rural areas, brewsters still made ale by the trough, and in wealthy households, women experimented with distillation. Just as the farmer's wife brewed, so her equivalent in the gentry manufactured "strong waters." Lady Margaret Hoby, for instance, wife of Sir Thomas Posthumous Hoby, recorded in her diary (1559–1605) how she "went about my stilling; stilled aqua vitas." The fair amateurs occasionally needed guidance as to when to use the fluids they produced. In his *Delightes for Ladies* (1602) Sir Hugh Platt advised his readers that they should not try to clean their teeth with aqua vitae, lest these fall out and they be forced "to borrow a rank" in order to be able to eat their roast beef.

Whether their tipple was beer, ale, sherris-sack, or rosewater, the inhabitants of Elizabethan England drank deep and with gusto. Their passion for alcohol is reflected in the philosophical passages of Shakespeare about its effects on individuals and their performance when under its influence. *Macbeth* contains the perfect summary of its physiological consequences—nose picking, lechery, and urine; *The Merchant of Venice* depicts how it deludes drinkers; and *Twelfth Night* showcases its comic aspects. Like Aristophanes in classical Athens, Shakespeare influenced opinions toward alcohol and its effects for centuries to come, and the insights, or prejudices, toward the fluid apparent in his plays were those taken to Virginia, in North America, when the English decided to settle there.

10 PILGRIMS

The decision to establish English colonies in the Americas was prompted by the wealth that Spain was extracting from her New World domains. Might not England also find gold, pearls, and silver mines in the vast territory that the Spanish had yet to occupy? The Elizabethan prophet of colonization was Sir Walter Raleigh, who had a vision of a brave and prosperous new England on the far Atlantic coast, owned by the gentry and worked by industrious yeomen. Raleigh was not the first Englishman to have dreamed of, or to have promoted, colonies in the Americas. In 1497, a group of Bristol merchants had hired the Genoese captain John Cabot to investigate their prospects. He had reported that the fishing was good off a part of the North American coast that was christened Newfoundland, and his employers established summer camps along its shores. Cabot, however, vanished on his second voyage west, and for the next eighty years, the idea of colonization was put on ice. It was resuscitated in 1583, when Sir Humphrey Gilbert raised funds in London for an ambitious settlement in the New World, which was intended to revive feudalism on a scale that not even the Spaniards had attempted. Gilbert took a fleet to Newfoundland, which he claimed for England, but made no efforts to establish a permanent settlement and was lost at sea on his return voyage.

Indeed, England's New World ventures had been a series of failures—depressing precedents, which argued against their repetition, until Sir Walter Raleigh brought some glamour to the show. Not only was he beautifully dressed and experienced in planting (he had been involved in the colonization of Ireland by the sword), but he was also blessed with a talent for organization. In 1584, he obtained letters patent from Queen Elizabeth for the foundation of an American colony and, the same year, sent a reconnaissance expedition under captains Amidas and Barlow. His scouts were back in England within a few months, having explored a patch of what is now North Carolina, which they declared to be akin to the biblical promised land, and distinguished in a similar fashion by an abundance of vines: Their first landing place had been "so full of grapes that the very surge of the Sea sometimes over-flowed them." They had made contact with the native tribes, who were friendly; and Barlow had taken note of their drinking habits: "Their drinke is commonly water, but while the grape lasteth, they drinke wine, and for want of casks to keep it, all the year after they drink water, but it is sodden with ginger in it, and black sinamon, and sometimes sassaphras, and divers other wholesome and medicinable herbes and trees." Barlow's "wine" was grape juice, for unlike the inhabitants of central and southern America, the natives of the northern part of the continent did not drink alcohol.

According to the records of the Spanish who colonized Florida and explored the Gulf of Mexico, and of the French who settled in Florida and Canada, sobriety was universal among the cultures inhabiting the eastern and southern seaboards of North America. While the Spanish were careful, as usual, to write down the diets of the people they came across on the Terra Firma, alcohol only appears on their own provision lists, or in expressions of grief over its absence. For instance, the destruction of communion wine by belligerent Indians near Mobile was ranked an equal loss to that of gunpowder, bullets, and valiant comrades by Rodrigo Rangel, a participant in Hernando de Soto's crazed 1539 drive from Cape Canaveral to the Mississippi River.

Although they found no evidence of indigenous tippling, both the Spaniards and the French had commented on the potential of the land for making wine. Every tree seemed draped with vines; indeed, the original name for the Island of Orleans opposite Quebec was Bacchus Island. It is a matter of dispute as to whether it was the French or Spanish who were the first to make an American vintage. The evidence rests on the word of Sir John Hawkins, an English slave trader who dropped anchor by the French settlement in Florida in 1565. Sir John was disgusted by the inability of its starving inhabitants to support themselves by growing food, and noted that their token gesture toward self-sufficiency had been the manufacture and consumption of twenty butts of wine. However, René Laudonnière, the governor of the colony, makes no mention of the wine in his account of the settlement, indeed takes pains to make clear that the first drink he'd had since arriving was the one given to him by Hawkins, which "greatly refreshed me, forasmusch as, for seven months' space, I never tasted a drop of wine." The Spanish, however, were producing Floridian wine by 1570 from the native muscadine grape.

Cheered by the excellent reports that Amidas and Barlow had brought back, Raleigh followed up in 1585 with a full-scale expedition, whose mission was the plantation of an entire English village in the New World. This venture consisted of five ships, which together carried 108 settlers and most of the paraphernalia thought necessary to survive and thrive in America. It was commanded by Sir Richard Grenville, a violent Devonian, who had spent his youth fighting Turks. Sir Richard possessed idiosyncratic drinking habits, in keeping with his bellicose reputation. According to a contemporary, "He was of so hard a complection" that "he would carouse three or four glasses of wine, and in a braverie take the glasses betweene his teeth and crash them in pieces and swallow them downe, so that often times the blood ran out of his mouth."

Grenville was also a stickler for form. Dinner aboard the *Tiger,* his flagship, was served off gold plate and accompanied by martial music from the ship's band. There was plenty to drink, for in addition to beer rations for the settlers and sailors, the entire spectrum of Elizabethan alcohol was on board—ale, sack, other kinds of wine, cider, and *strong waters,* i.e., spirits. After crossing the Atlantic, the expedition paused in Hispaniola,[15] where it purchased livestock from the Spaniards, then continued to *Virginia,* as the territory it intended to settle had been named. Before, however, it could land the colonists and their supplies it was struck by a storm that drove the *Tiger* ashore, drowned the livestock, and ruined all the seed. Most of the alcohol supply was destroyed. Despite such grievous losses the colonists knuckled to and built a fort, a church, storehouses, and stables, and christened their settlement Roanoke. Mission accomplished, Grenville returned to England, capturing a rich prize en route.

---

[15] Now divided between Haiti and the Dominican Republic.

The colonists meanwhile set to planting, traded with the Indians, and even managed to brew ale from corn: "We made of the same in the country some mault, whereof was brued as good ale as was to be desired." Despite this show of industry, they were discontented—with one another and with Virginia. Their number included gentlemen, who, by definition, did not work. It also contained a tailor, a mathematician, and a former MP. Its practical men, however, were few. Accusations of bad attitudes and indolence flew back and forth; meanwhile, supplies ran short, and relations with the Indians deteriorated into conflict. When, by chance, Sir Francis Drake slid by a year later, fresh from sacking Spanish settlements in Hispaniola and Florida, his appearance was accounted providential. He offered the colony provisions, ships, and even people. With these fresh supplies, and their soon-to-be-ripe crops, the colonists felt optimistic over their prospects. Sadly, the same night a storm dispersed Drake's fleet and sank the boats he'd earmarked for Virginia. At this the settlers lost heart and went home with him.

Very shortly after Roanoke had been abandoned, a resupply fleet arrived under Grenville. He searched for the missing colonists, concluded they had been massacred by hands unknown, and left a token presence of fifteen soldiers, commanded by Master Coffin. Neither Coffin nor any other member of his team was buried in his namesake. When a new fleet of settlers arrived in 1587, complete with women, children, and farmyard animals, the only trace of Grenville's caretaking force was "the bones of one of those fifteen which the savages had slain long ago." The emigrants of '87 went the same way as master Coffin and his men and vanished without trace.

Serial failure, once again, gave American colonies a bad name in England and it was twenty years before another was attempted. After the death of Queen Elizabeth in 1603, Sir Walter Raleigh, their principal advocate, fell from grace and was imprisoned in the tower of London, where he wrote *The Historie of the World* and experimented with distillation with the Earl of Northumberland, a fellow prisoner. They christened their most palatable concoction *"spiritus dulcis,"* which they stilled from sack, "sugarcandie," and "spirits of roses."

However, by 1606, New World colonies were back on the English political agenda. Memories of failure were fading, and most of the written accounts of prior attempts, especially the *Brief and True Report of the New Found Land of Virginia* (1588) of Thomas Harriot, painted so attractive a picture of the potential of the Americas that it was decided to have another go. The superabundance of grapes was an important draw to the new generation of would-be colonizers. If wine could be produced in Virginia, it would lessen English reliance on imports from, and its trade deficit with, potentially hostile Catholic countries. A group of London merchants headed by some token peers set up a new Virginia Company, which was granted a royal charter by Elizabeth's successor, King James I, in 1606. The charter anticipated that settlers would direct their energy toward finding pearls and gold mines, and in planting vineyards and olive trees. An expedition was organized, and in 1607 it set out for the Chesapeake Bay. A hundred and four colonists (out of 144) survived the voyage, and they elected to start their empire on a small, waterlogged island, to the north of Roanoke, which they named Jamestown.

Their first impressions of their new home were marred by the rapid departure of the transport ships, which took with them much of the beer that had been intended to refresh them until they could manufacture their own. As the sails vanished over the horizon, those remaining on American soil questioned the wisdom of their decision to emigrate to a place with "neither taverne, [nor] beere-house." Ironically some of the colonists had been lured to the New World by the promise of a sober lifestyle and a healthy diet. Virginia, according to the promotional material of the eponymous Royal Company, was the perfect place to escape the temptations of London, with opportunity neither for drunkenness nor gluttony. The marketing proved true, as the colonists died in droves from famine or waterborne diseases. The absence of alcohol, and the consequent necessity of drinking water solo, was held to blame for their deaths in a later postmortem, which concluded: "To plant a Colony by water drinkers was an inexcusable error in those, who laid the first foundacion . . . which until it be laide downe againe, there is small hope of health."

In order to stem the tide of mortality, the governor and the council of Virginia advertised in 1609 for two brewers. It seems, however, that they failed to attract any applicants, for the absence of alcohol continued to be a matter for lamentation among the Virginians. It was also taken as a sign of potential weakness. The Spanish sent a spy to measure English progress on what they regarded as their soil. His report, to a Spaniard, made encouraging reading: "There are about three hundred men there more or less; and the majority sick and badly treated, because they have nothing but bread of maize, with fish, nor do they drink anything but water—all of which is contrary to the nature of the English—on which account they all wish to return [home], and would have done so if they had been at liberty."

The salvation of Jamestown was the discovery that it could produce something with a ready market in London—tobacco. England was in the grip of a smoking craze. Its poets and playwrights wrote eulogies in praise of tobacco with the enthusiasm they had hitherto reserved for sack and ale. Smoking was called drinking tobacco or dry-drinking by the English, who had no prior experience of smoking anything and so lacked the vocabulary to describe the act. In their enthusiasm they allotted it virtues—of suppressing appetite, of causing mild intoxication—and considered smokers to be elegant. In 1613, Virginia exported its first crop of the weed to England, in 1620 it shipped twenty thousand pounds of tobacco, and in 1627 it sent five hundred thousand pounds and had begun to prosper.

Experiments with winemaking as per charter were abandoned— the little wine the colony had produced was unpalatable. According to a governor of the Virginia Company, "We must confess our wine to have been more of an embarrassment than a credit to us," and the vines were grubbed up to make room for more tobacco. With the exception of a little maize beer, Jamestown relied on imported alcohol. Outbound ships in the tobacco trade filled their holds with wine from Madeira and the Canary Isles, and English beer. They were not at all particular as to the quality of their merchandise, for the thirsty colonists would exchange tobacco for whatever they brought. Indeed, the beer supplied by one provisioner named Dupper was so bad that it was reckoned to have "been the death of two hundred."

The improving fortunes of Virginia were closely monitored in England by its merchants and its dissidents. The proof that English people could live, and even prosper, in the New World inspired many with dreams of profits, or of freedom. King James I had chosen to enforce a very narrow view of Protestantism, centered on the duty of obedience owed by English Protestants to himself. Those who wished to worship otherwise were arrested or fled the country. A group of the latter, who had taken refuge in the Dutch town of Leyden, decided to attempt a colony in North America where they might practice their faith as they wished. They debated the matter at length before committing themselves. Their principal concerns about the proposed venture were that "the change of air, diet, and drinking of water would infect their bodies with sore sicknesses and grievous diseases." They had read of the damage water drinking had wreaked in Virginia and, once they had resolved to go, included a vast store of *booze* (a neologism for alcoholic drinks) in their provisions.

This group of men, women, and children came to an arrangement with a group of London merchants that gave their proposed voyage legitimacy, and chartered a claret ship from the Bordeaux wine trade named the *Mayflower* for their passage. The hundred and two pilgrims, under the leadership of John Carver, plus perhaps three dozen sailors, had an easy transatlantic voyage until they approached the American coast, when foul weather forced them north of Virginia to Cape Cod, which they sighted on November 19, 1620. On the twenty-first of the same month, the first of their number stepped ashore. Their initial impressions were of fear and wonder—the landscape was wild and forbidding. Like the Virginians of 1587, they mourned the absence of "inns to entertain or refresh their weather-beaten bodies."

Their sense of isolation was heightened when they started to explore their new home. Their first reconnaissance party, under Captain Standish, very quickly lost itself in the forest. One of its members recorded the panic when they realized they had no idea where they were and that "our victuals was only biscuit and Holland cheese, and a little bottle of aquavitae." Fortunately, they blundered upon "springs of fresh water, of which we were heartily glad," and set an important precedent: "[We] drunk our first New England water with as much delight as ever we drunk drink in all our lives." One of the party went so far as to claim the water had been "as pleasant ... as wine or beer." Hitherto, American water had been viewed with a distrust bordering on paranoia.

Winter was approaching and the pilgrims decided to settle where they were, because "we could not now take time for further research or consideration, our victuals being much spent, especially our Beere." The shortage of beer was a point of friction between them and the crew of the *Mayflower*, which remained at anchor while they went ashore daily to clear ground and build houses in the sleet and snow. The winter was fierce, epidemics broke out among the pilgrims and mariners, but the latter, wishing to guard their stock of beer for the journey home, refused to allow it to be given to the sick. William Bradford, chosen by the colonists to be their leader after the death of John Carver, recorded their intransigence: "As this calamity fell . . . the passengers that were to be left here to plant . . . were hasted ashore and made to drink water that the seamen might have the more beer, and one [Bradford himself] in his sickness desiring but a small can of beer, it was answered that if he was their own father he should have none."

When spring arrived only fifty-three pilgrims remained alive. They disembarked for the last time from the *Mayflower* in March 1621, and she returned to England. As the weather improved, the colonists went exploring again and found, or rather were found by, an English-speaking Indian, Samoset, who had picked up the language from passing fishermen and slave traders. After appropriate introductions, Samoset asked for some beer, which was evidently the thing he had missed most since his last contact with Englishmen. The colonists had none with them but "gave him strong water . . . which he liked well." Once refreshed, he told the pilgrims that "the place where we now live is called Patuxet, and that about four years ago all the inhabitants died of an extraordinary plague, and there is neither man, woman, nor child remaining, as indeed we have found none, so as there is none to hinder our possession, or to lay claim unto it."

Samoset introduced the pilgrims to the neighboring tribes, parlays were arranged, and peace and harmony were agreed among them. At the most important of these meetings, with Massasoit, "the great king," amity was sealed, in the English fashion, with a toast: "After salutations, our governor kissing his hand, the king kissed him, and so they sat down. The governor called for some strong water, and drunk to him, and he drunk a great draught that made him sweat all the while after; he called for a little fresh meat, which the king did eat willingly, and did give his followers. Then they treated of peace."

The peace they made lasted twenty-four years, which in its time was something of a New World record, for both Europeans and Americans. During that period the colonists flourished. They were quickly self-sufficient in food, had furs and cod to trade, and their success laid to rest the ghosts of failure that had haunted England's American endeavors. Among other matters, they were living proof that the English could drink water and enjoy good health. This latter achievement was a matter of pride, as is evident from a letter sent by Bradford to

London in 1624, countering various slanders that had been published against *New England:*

6TH OBJ.: The water is not wholesome.

ANS.: If they mean, not so wholesome as the good beer and wine in London (which they so dearly love) we will not dispute with them; but else for water it is as good as any in the world (for aught we know) and it is wholesome enough to us that can be content therewith.

Bradford's claims were corroborated by amazed newcomers, one of whom commented in a letter home that that New England water drinkers were "as healthful, fresh, and lusty as they that drink beer."

Fresh groups of pilgrims arrived in 1621, 1623, and 1629, and settled in and around the Plymouth Colony. By the time the last batch arrived, the original New Englanders were not only self-sufficient in food but produced a surplus of it, some of which was used to make alcoholic drinks. Although the colonists had discovered some merits in water, as soon as they could brew they did, using whatever fermentable material they could spare, as a ditty from the time reflects:

> If barley be wanting to make into malt,
> We must be content and think it no fault,
> For we can make liquor to sweeten our lips,
> Of pumpkins, and parsnips, and walnut tree chips.

Imported liquor was available in addition to home brews. The pilgrims traded their surplus food with the cod fishing fleets to the north and the tobacco planters in Virginia to the south. The fisheries were one of the largest industries on either side of the Atlantic at the time, and possibly the most efficient. English fishing boats traveled to Newfoundland each spring, where they caught, cured, and loaded cod, which they sold for wine in Spain, Portugal, or their Atlantic island colonies. The wine was then either exchanged in England for trading goods for the settlers in Newfoundland, New England, and Virginia, or carried straight back to the American coast.

In consequence, there was plenty of booze sloshing around the colonies, as evidenced by a curious little settlement established close to Plymouth named Mount Wollaston. Its inhabitants consisted of a

Captain Wollaston, Thomas Morton, and a number of indentured servants whom Wollaston hired out as laborers in Virginia for the tobacco harvest. In 1628, while the captain and his servants were absent, Morton turned the settlement into a Bacchic republic, much to the horror of his Puritan neighbors. According to Bradford, "Morton became Lord of Misrule and maintained, as it were, a School of Atheism. And after they had … got much by trading with the Indians, they spent it … in quaffing and drinking, both wine and strong waters in great excess…. They also set up a Maypole, drinking and dancing about it many days together, inviting Indian women for their consorts, dancing and frisking together like so many fairies or furies … [and] revived and celebrated … the beastly practices of the mad Bacchanalians."

The Maypole was an eighty-foot pine tree, topped off with a "pair of buckshorns." A poem, composed by Morton, was nailed to its base, which renamed the little settlement *Ma-re Mount,* or Merrymount, and proclaimed that henceforth May Day was to be a holiday in the settlement. Morton also wrote a song, complete with the Bacchic ejaculation Io! for holidaymakers to sing as they danced around his pole:

> Give to the Nymph that's free from scorn
> No Irish stuff nor Scotch over-worn.
> Lasses, in Beaver coats, come away.
> Ye shall be welcome to us night and day.
> Then drink and be merry, merry, merry boys
> Let all your delight be in Hymen's joys;
> Io! To Hymen, now the day is come,
> About the merry Maypole take a room.

In order to finance their merriment, Morton and his accomplices broke a colonial taboo by selling arms to the Native Americans for their furs. They received better value, and were on the edge of cornering the fur trade, when the other settlers in the area banded together and sent a force against them to bring them to their senses. The confrontation turned out comically. Morton had holed up in a fortified house on Merrymount and threatened to fight to the death. There followed a brief standoff, during which period he and his band became so drunk that they were incapable of fighting and gave up. The only blood shed in the entire event came from Morton, who wounded himself in the nose with his saber. He was sent back to England,[16] the Maypole was cut down, and the hill was rechristened Mount Dagon, after the god of the Philistines.

Morton was something of a maverick among emigrants. The majority left England in order to practice a particular style of Christianity, rather than to indulge in pagan revels. News of success in the New World traveled through underground conduits to their brethren at home and in exile in Holland, encouraging them to follow. In 1629 the Massachusetts Bay Company was chartered in London for the settlement of the eponymous area to the north of the Plymouth Colony, and English people flowed across the Atlantic to settle there in their hundreds, then their thousands. The first significant batch, under John Winthrop, arrived in Salem in June 1630 aboard the *Arbella* and ten other ships. The *Arbella,* in deference to contemporary prejudice, carried "42 tonnes of beere" (about ten thousand gallons) the same amount of wine, and only three thousand gallons of water. Her passengers—fearing, no doubt, a shortage of alcohol in Massachusetts—supplemented their rations with private caches. Winthrop recorded that a maidservant on board, because she was "stomach sick," had "drank so much strong water, that she was senseless, and had near killed herself," and commented, "We observed it a common fault in our young people that they gave themselves to drink hot waters very immoderately."

By the time that Winthrop's charges had settled down, New England was past the tipping point. A formula had been developed for self-perpetuation—someone might expect to emigrate and, within a few years, own land and make a profit from their work. With profit came progress, in the English sense, and the émigrés improved their new homeland with breweries and taverns. While brewing was under way by 1629, when John Smith claimed New England had two "brewhouses" that made "good ale, both strong and small" from Indian corn or barley, the first evidence of it occurring on a commercial scale dates to 1633, when a "furnace for brewinge" was shipped over from England. Thereafter, references to breweries come thick and fast, and

---

[16] Morton was a hard man to keep down. He returned to America, was deported again, spent time in Exeter jail, and composed the *New English Canaan* (1637), a vituperative account of the New World colonists.

much of their trade was wholesale. The absence of public drinking places, which had so disheartened the first pilgrims, had also been remedied. Inns, known as *ordinaries,* were constructed in most of the settlements in New England, and after 1634, every community was required by law to build one for "the receiving, refreshment, and entertainment of travelers and strangers, and to serve publick occasions." Ordinaries were usually sited in the center of each settlement, alongside the meetinghouse and the stocks. They sold local brews, and imported wines and spirits, in standard measures. Their prices were fixed by law: "It is ordered that no person that keeps an ordinarie shall take above 6d a meal of a person, and not above 1d for an ale quart of beer."

As breweries and ordinaries multiplied in number, so did drunkenness. The condition, pace Morton, seems to have been rare among settlers in the early years, and drunks were punished with fines, time in the stocks, or by naming and shaming. In 1633, for instance, Winthrop recorded in his journal that "Robert Cole, having been oft punished for drunkness, was now ordered to wear a red D about his neck for a year." Public humiliation, however, as a "Presentment by ye Grand Jury" in Plymouth in 1637 attests, was not always a sufficient deterrent: "1. Wm. Renolds is presented for being drunck at Mr. Hopkins his house, that he lay under the table, vomiting in a beastly manner."

In the same year that Wm. Renolds was hauled up for drunkenness, the regulations governing ordinaries were tightened up. Only licensed ordinaries might sell alcohol for consumption on their premises, and these could offer only wine, spirits, and beer in fixed measures for fixed prices. Furthermore, they could not brew their own beer but had to buy from a "common brewer," i.e., one with a special permit. Among the number of common brewers was Captain Robert Sedgwick, perhaps the first man to grow rich out of brewing in America. In 1637 he "set up a brew house at his great charge, & very commodious for this part of the countrey."

The drinks list in New England was supplemented by cider, whose manufacture grew to be a cottage industry, analogous to ale brewing in medieval England. Indeed, the drink came to be identified with the place—fermented apple juice[17] was more American than apple pie. The

---

[17] All colonial era cider was "hard," i.e., alcoholic, as the pilgrims lacked the technology to prevent it from fermenting.

first orchard in Massachusetts was planted in 1623 by William Blaxton—an eccentric clergyman, who for a number of years was the only English resident of Boston—on his farm on Beacon Hill. Cider orchards were also planted in Virginia and in *New Amsterdam,* an American settlement founded by the Dutch, in imitation of their English Protestant cousins.

The pilgrims had planned their colony while in Holland and had sent there for their families and friends once they had established a modus vivendi in New England, so that the Dutch had as good a picture of their progress as the English. Once it was clear to them that Europeans might prosper in the Americas, they formed a West India Company (1621), which established colonies at Fort Orange and Fort Nassau on the Delaware River. In 1625 work started on a fort on Manhattan Island, and the next year, Peter Minuit, the director general of Dutch interests in the region, bought the island itself from its native American owners.

The name Manhattan is reputed to be of bibulous origin: According to a Moravian missionary, writing some time after the event, when Henry Hudson was exploring the region in 1609, he met some Indians on an island in the river that bears his name and, as was the custom of the age, offered them a drink. The Indians, by their own account, did not like its smell and refused. One of their warriors, however, not wishing to appear ill-mannered in front of strangers, took the drink, bid his friends farewell (for they were convinced it was a poison), and swallowed it down in one. He collapsed on the spot but rose again to his feet shortly afterward and declared the beverage to be wonderful. His fellows imitated him; they, too, drank and became intoxicated, and thereafter the place was called *Manahachtanienk*—"the island where we drank liquor." The story has some corroboration from Hudson, who admitted to giving the Indians wine "in order to make a trial of their hearts."

Once they had possession of Manhattan, the Dutch completed their fort, whose southern limit was marked by Wall Street, and laid out farms. They were as fond of their booze as the English, and in 1632 their West India Company built a brewery on a lane that became known as "Brouwers Straet." They also planted vineyards, gathered wild hops from the woods, and Peter Stuyvesant, who became governor in 1647, cultivated cider apple trees imported from Holland on his farm in what is now the Bowery district of Manhattan. As had been the case with other European settlers in North America, the Dutch noted that the Indians with whom they traded for land and furs had no prior acquaintance with alcoholic drinks. In his *Description of the New Netherlands* (c. 1642) Adriaen van der Donck observed that while the local tribes drank fresh grape juice, "They never make wine or beer. Brandy or strong drink is unknown to them, except those who frequent our settlements, and have learned that beer and wine taste better than water. In the Indian languages, which are rich and expressive, they have no word to express drunkenness." Van der Donck believed that such innocent sobriety had benefits: the "rheumatic gout" and "red and pimpled noses" were unknown among Native Americans; nor did "they have any diseases or infirmities which are caused by drunkenness."

However, the innocence did not last. Once the indigenous peoples got their first taste of alcohol, they seemed to be eager to make up for lost time. Whereas initially, Europeans had made a point of offering drinks as a gesture of friendship to any natives they came across in the Americas, once they founded settlements and had had the opportunity to observe the effects of alcohol on peoples who had hitherto existed without it, they were no longer so free with their liquor. Their Indian neighbors seemed incapable of drinking for any other reason than to get as drunk as possible as quickly as possible. Once inebriated, they were violent and dangerous, albeit principally to themselves.

Europeans in the New World, especially French missionaries, were curious as to what it was that prompted this all-or-nothing approach to alcohol among Native Americans. It was a novelty, true–in 1633, a Montagnais brave told a Jesuit that when the people of his grandmother's time first had seen the French "covered with their cuirasses, eating biscuits, and drinking wine" they believed they were "dressed in iron, ate bones, and drank blood." But the tribe had adjusted to biscuits and armor far better than the heady red fluid the French used to slake their thirsts. It seems that instead of considering alcoholic beverages to be a kind of food, as did most Europeans, the Indian nations focused instead on the soul–the alcohol–and not the body in which it was hidden. When the Compte de Frontenac inquired of an Ottawa Indian "what he thought the brandy he was so fond of was made of, he said, of tongues and hearts, for, added he, after I have drunk of it I fear nothing and I talk like an angel." Similar sentiments were noted in the

1640s by a Jesuit among the Iroquois, who told him that they did not like the taste of alcoholic drinks, but drank them nonetheless "simply to become intoxicated—imagining, in their drunkenness, that they become persons of importance, taking pleasure in seeing themselves dreaded by those who do not taste this poison."

The problem was exacerbated by the relative abundance of spirits, versus other drinks, in the Americas. Their concentrated form made them easier to carry across the Atlantic than wine or beer, so that unlike most Europeans, who started drinking beer or watered wine while children, the first contact a Native American had with alcohol was likely to be with strong waters, a mouthful or two of which was enough to produce an altered state of consciousness. Thereafter, they would look to drink for stimulation rather than mere refreshment, and since their cultures did not possess rituals and safeguards as to when and how much to drink, many very quickly ruined themselves on the white man's wicked water.

11 RESTORATION

The thirsty earth soaks up the rain,
And drinks and gapes for drink again;
The plants suck in the earth, and are
With constant drinking fresh and fair;
The sea itself (which one would think
Should have but little need of drink)
Drinks twice ten thousand rivers up,
So fill'd that they o'erflow the cup.
The busy Sun (and one would guess
By 's drunken fiery face no less)
Drinks up the sea, and when he's done,
The Moon and Stars drink up the Sun:
They drink and dance by their own light,
They drink and revel all the night:
Nothing in Nature's sober found,
But an eternal health goes round.
Fill up the bowl, then, fill it high,
Fill all the glasses there—for why
Should every creature drink but I?
Why, man of morals, tell me why?
　　　　—"Drinking," Abraham Cowley

A significant proportion of the strong waters arriving in the Americas were there courtesy of the Dutch, who, by the middle of the seventeenth century, were the largest maritime trading nation in the world. Their rise to eminence had, in historical terms, been exceptionally rapid: Prior to 1566, their nation was a patchwork of duchies and bishoprics under the control of Spain. However, over the following decades, seventeen of these entities, mostly Protestant, combined together to form the *United Provinces,* and with the assistance of England they established a republic and drove the Spaniards from their lands. Overseas, meanwhile, they appropriated a number of Portuguese colonies and founded, as in America, new stations of their own. By 1648, when the Peace of Westphalia, a pan-European settlement of various conflicts, was agreed and their nation recognized, they had trading posts in Manhattan, the Caribbean, Africa, India, Sri Lanka, and various Indonesian Islands. They carried Virginian tobacco to Europe, African slaves to the Americas, French wine and brandy everywhere, and they had a near monopoly on Asian spices.

Their modus operandi, backed up by force if necessary, was similar wherever they traded. The breadth of their commercial network allowed them to match supply and demand however distant, and they encouraged suppliers to grow specific products and process them in a particular manner. They provided technical assistance to ensure the suppliers got it right, paid cash for their produce, and offered easy terms for those goods the suppliers themselves most valued and which they carried to them. The Dutch method was honed in the Bordeaux region of France, where they had long been buyers of its wines. In order to stimulate supply, they sent in engineers to reclaim land and build dykes (a Dutch specialty) and provided vines and loans and barrels and a guaranteed market to any vintners willing to work with them. In return, they wanted cheap sweet white wine, and plenty of it.

Their system created losers as well as winners. Traditional growers in Bordeaux exported via its port, which still levied medieval duties on ships bringing wine down the river Gironde. These were, in Dutch eyes, unnecessary costs. They therefore dropped their customary suppliers and transferred their attentions inland toward the Dordogne, and north, to the hinterland behind La Rochelle. Here they offered their standard incentives to growers and shipped their purchases around the tariff walls. The Dutch wanted their wine to be stable as well as inexpensive. To this end they introduced the technology of fumigating wine barrels with sulphur matches, and the practice of fortifying the wine itself with ardent spirits. These two measures extended its lifespan, and the taste of sulphur wore off as it aged.

In some economic-captive areas of France, the Dutch elected to export brandy instead of wine fortified with the same. The region they focused on was the Charente, in particular the district around the village of Cognac, which was perfectly situated for the manufacture of spirits. Its principal advantages were, in order of importance, the proximity of a duty-free port, the abundance of firewood (necessary to heat stills), and plenty of substandard wine. In the event, thanks to chalk in the soil, the wine of the region proved to be peculiarly well suited to distillation, and the finished item–*cognac*–acquired a reputation as a superior beverage. It had fans in England by 1594, Native American victims two decades later, and was used subsequently to prize open new markets elsewhere. In 1652, the Dutch purchased a substantial block of land in the Cape of Good Hope in South Africa for a few barrels of Cognac and some good Virginian tobacco. Cape Town became a vital staging post for their Asian trading fleet, and to save transport costs, they imported breeding livestock and planted their new colony with all the standard provision crops, including vines, perhaps the first to be cultivated in sub-Saharan Africa.

Go-betweens to most of the world, the Dutch kept the pick of the cornucopia of goods that they traded for themselves. The decades during which they flourished and won their independence were characterized by suffering in much of the rest of Europe. Wars religious, civil, and despotic rolled back and forth across the continent, so that by the time that Peter Stuyvesant was planting his cider apple orchard in Manhattan, his native land was "an island of wealth surrounded by a sea of want." The Dutch were conspicuous consumers on home soil, in both public and private life. They staged elaborate functions for their various civic bodies and militia, including feasts that lasted several days, at which mountains of delicacies were served out on gold and silver plate. These events took place in purpose-built halls whose walls were covered with tapestries and oil paintings, where their participants enacted rituals centered around the sharing of food and drink. Such rituals, all of which had been invented within the lifespan of the republic, and most of which involved communal intoxication, helped it to establish an identity. Heavy drinking was part of being Dutch. Despite the relative youth of these ceremonies, they were surprisingly sophisticated and amazed foreigners with their complexity. After attending one such formal binge, a French visitor commented, "All these gentlemen of the Netherlands have so many rules and ceremonies for getting drunk, that I am repelled as much by them as by the sheer excess." The sheer excess was striking. An English observer at a Dutch *schutter* party in 1634 reported, "I do not believe scarce a sober man was to be found among them, nor was it safe for a sober man to trust himself among them, they did shout so and sing, roar, skip, and leap."

Drunkenness was ubiquitous in the young republic. Its towns were packed with taverns, and the Dutch demonstrated their disdain for the medieval notion that these might lead them into sin by giving them provocative names, such as the *Beelzebub* in Dortrecht, and the *Duivel aan de Ketting* (Devil on a Chain) in Amsterdam. Drink and be damned was their ethos. The Dutch imbibed for nourishment as well as intoxication, and the alcoholic part of their diet reflected the wealth of choice they enjoyed in comparison to commoners elsewhere. Workingmen breakfasted not merely on beer but on such luxurious beverages as *Wip*, which was comprised of warm ale, nutmeg, sugar, egg whites, and brandy. They topped themselves up throughout the working day with various brews, with wine, and a shot or two of spirits. They drank with every meal, they sealed bargains over a drink— there was no occasion in which alcohol was inappropriate. Indeed, the Calvinist pastor Peter Wittewrongel, as part of a general philippic against sin, complained in 1655 that "men drink at the slightest excuse . . . at the sound of a bell, or the turning of a mill."

The Dutch celebrated their good fortune in their visual art. They commissioned tavern scenes from painters, showing ordinary people socializing, drinking, and smoking. This was an innovation. Hitherto, no one had wasted paint on peasants, unless as incidental figures in the background, present as an aid to perspective, or to direct the eye with their praise and diminished stature toward a saint or a noble. Moreover, these revolutionary canvases, depicting ordinary people in everyday clothes and unselfconscious postures, were affectionate without being sentimental in their treatment of their subjects. The spirit of the new genre is apparent, reduced to a single figure, in Gabriel Metsu's canvas of a Dutch drinker (c. 1660). This depicts an old soldier seated on a bench with one arm slung over a beer barrel, as if it were a lover or his best friend. He holds a long clay pipe in the fingers of his left hand, like an artist with a paintbrush. In his right hand is a shining pewter tankard. His expression is alert and mischievous. The beer barrel has a faded stencil of a red stag on its face. Technically, the painting is on a par with Italian Renaissance standards; philosophically, it is an aeon apart.

Gabriel Metsu's The Old Drinker

The luxury and plenty enjoyed by the Dutch in the middle third of the seventeenth century stands in stark contrast to the poverty and strife that the English endured over the same period. Two civil wars were fought between 1642 and 1649, which culminated in the execution of King Charles I and the declaration of a commonwealth by the remnants of Parliament. From 1653 to 1658, the country was a protectorate under the puritan Oliver Cromwell, during which period the theaters were closed, press censorship was imposed, and an *excise,* i.e., consumption, tax on beer and ale was introduced.

These austere times came to an end with the restoration of King Charles II in 1660. Known as the "Merrie Monarch," Charles had spent much of the preceding decade in exile at the French court, where his natural hedonism had flowered. Upon his return to England he reopened the theaters, encouraged the arts and sciences, and set an example as a libertine that his court strove to emulate. A spirit of decadence flourished, which included a passion for fine wines, and plenty of them. Daniel Defoe, passing comment on the initial years of the Restoration half a century later, noted that "our drunkenness as a national vice takes its epoch at the Restoration. . . . Very merry, and very mad, and very drunken the people were, and grew more and more so every day."

The Restoration ethos was embodied in the courtier and poet John Wilmot, first Earl of Rochester. His portrait shows a young man with a slim face, Mae West lips, and long fluffy chestnut hair, but does not do credit to his actual debauchery. His lyrical, often pornographic verse, much of which was topical, delighted English society. His life was short and alcoholic—"in a course of drunken gaiety and gross sensuality, with intervals of study perhaps yet more criminal, with an avowed contempt of all decency and order, a total disregard to every moral, and a resolute denial of every religious obligation . . . [Rochester] lived worthless and useless, and blazed out his youth and his health in lavish voluptuousness." Before, however, he died from syphilis aged thirty-three, Rochester made some graceful contributions to the drinking canon. He considered wine to be "Poetick Juice" and acknowledged its influence, together with sex, over his work:

> Cupid and Bacchus my saints are;
> May drink and love still reign:
> With wine I wash away my cares,
> And then to cunt again.

Wit, wine, and love were the Holy Trinity of Restoration lyrical poets. Their output was encouraged by gifts from the court and patronage by its nobles.[18] Similar themes prevailed in Restoration theater, whose principal genre was comedy. New plays were topical, with convoluted plots, rakish aristocratic characters, and plenty of tippling. Their contemporary settings provide a guide to prevailing drinking habits and highlight the fashion for wine, especially French wine. While sack was considered appropriate for poets, the court and nobil-

---

[18] The post of poet laureate was formalized, with an annual stipend of a butt of sack.

ity had moved on to *Haut-Brion* and *champagne*. The former was a red wine from Bordeaux, whose producers had discovered the concept of quality and the power of marketing. Haut-Brion was the antithesis of the pink rotgut the English had bought in spectacular quantities in the Middle Ages. Its appearance in England, and its memorable flavor, were recorded by Samuel Pepys, in his diary entry for April 10, 1663: "Drank . . . a sort of French wine, called Ho Bryan, that had a good and most particular taste that I ever met with." Haut-Brion was a deep ruby in color and, if properly kept, had a lifespan of several years. It was shipped to England in casks, where it was sold at exorbitant prices in taverns or carted off to stately homes and bottled.

The modern wine bottle was an English invention, its creator Sir Kenelm Digby, scholar, traveler, sometime pirate, and pioneer archaeologist. Digby discovered a method of making cheap, strong bottles out of glass, hitherto a costly and fragile material whose manufacture was the province of artisans. His bottles were square, and translucent green or brown, rather than globular and clear, but they were wonderfully durable. When sealed with corks, another innovation, they provided a system for storing wine and allowing it to mature in an oxygen-free environment. For the first time since the fall of Rome, Europe had the technology to age wine.

In the same years that English lords were laying down ranks of square bottles full of Bordeaux in their cellars, they were also buying casks of wine from the Champagne district of France. This fluid, which at the time was a still, sweet drink, gold-tinted red, as if someone had opened an artery and dripped a little blood into a glass of white wine, had been all the rage at the French court when King Charles II had lived there in exile. His fellow monarch, Louis XIV, had been crowned in Rheims cathedral at the heart of the Champagne region and had drunk its wines ever since. Immediately post-Restoration this "frantically fashionable" French elixir was touted in England by the émigré Marquis de Saint-Évremond, where it, too, became all the rage. However, the champagne the English came to know and love was very different from the wine the French court drank every day. It arrived in England each autumn and was consigned to cellars to sleep over winter. When spring came and temperatures rose, its yeasts woke up and it underwent a secondary fermentation, which made it fizzy and dry. It is described as "brisk champagne" in its debut in the English language in 1664, and whereas

Saint-Évremond considered bubbles in champagne to be sacrilege, in England they were de rigueur. Fizz made its stage debut in the comedy *Love and a Bottle* by George Farquhar, where its effervescence is commented on when poured out: "See how it puns and quibbles in the glass."

However, by the time that champagne was sparkling in London theaters, a portion of English society had turned against the fashion for things French. They were, after all, made by Catholic hands, and Parliament and the English people were staunchly anti anything that smacked of popery. When King Charles tried to push a bill through Parliament granting freedom of worship to Catholics, it was rejected, and in 1679, imports of French wine were banned altogether. This served to make them more expensive rather than unavailable, and their consumption or rejection became polarized on party political lines.

The politicization of drinking tastes is apparent in later Restoration comedies, which used them as an aid to characterization. Tory writers created little England ale-loving Whig Puritans, who hated foreign drinks. Their archetype was Dashit, a typically hypocritical Whiggish wine merchant in Aphra Behn's play *The Revenge* (1673). Their prejudices were expressed in the same work by Trickwell, who, disguised as a Puritan preacher, upbraids Dashit for selling French wine: "You have made us drunk with *the juice of the whore of Babylon:* For whereas good Ale, Perry, Cider, and Metheglin, were the Ancient British and Trojan drinks, you have brought in popery, mere popery— French and Spanish wines, to the subversion, staggering, and overthrowing of many a good Protestant Christian."

Outside of plays and the high society that they represented, ale or beer was still the drink of most English people, whether Whig or Tory, and unlike French wines, which were taxed or exempted in tune with the mood in Parliament, both brews were subject to continuous levies. The excise introduced to England to fund its civil conflicts generated too much money to be repealed: A petition from the Brewers Company in 1660 pleading for "freedom from the illegal and intolerable burden of excise, burdensome to the poor to whom ale and beer, next to bread, are the chief stay" had been rejected, and thereafter tax on liquid bread was a fact of life in England.

The Restoration was a period of innovation in drinks. Novel beverages appeared in London, some of which were recorded by Samuel Pepys in his diary. These included such exotica as orange juice. Pepys had his first taste of this curiosity at the house of his cousin, Thomas Strudwick, in 1669, and he clearly was suspicious of its potablity: "Here, which I never did before, I drank a glass, of a pint I believe, at one draught, of the juice of oranges of whose peel they make confits . . . and it is a very fine drink; but it being new, I was doubtful whether it might not do me hurt." While orange juice was rare, another novelty, *coffee,* very quickly became commonplace. Coffee was the first nonalcoholic beverage to be drunk regularly in England. People began to substitute a cup or two of this hot infusion for their morning pint of ale. It seemed to have all the invigorating properties of alcohol without inducing delinquency in the drinker.

Coffee originated in Ethiopia and for centuries had been a popular beverage in Islamic lands, which had held a monopoly on its production. The Dutch, however, had managed to obtain some coffee bushes in 1616, which they shipped to Amsterdam and thence to Sri Lanka, where they established a plantation of their own. From Sri Lanka they carried the plant to Java, where it flourished, and by the middle of the seventeenth century, they were growing enough to begin its export to Europe. The first coffee shop in England was opened in Oxford in 1651. London had one a year later, Venice followed in 1683, and Paris in 1686. The prophet of coffee in Paris was an Italian, Francesco Procopio dei Cotelli, whose Procope, which is still open, was the prototype of all French *cafés.*

The first coffee shop in England, that of Pasqua Rosee in Oxford, marked its debut with flyers, which explained the nature of the drink it sold and how it should be consumed. Coffee was "a simple innocent thing, compounded into a Drink, by being dried in an Oven, and ground to Powder, and boiled up with spring water, and about half a pint of it to be drunk . . . and to be take as hot as possibly can be endured." The flyer also listed some of the medical benefits to be reaped from drinking coffee: It protected against headaches and was "excellent to prevent and cure the *Dropsy, Gout,* and *Scurvy.*" Moreover, it was "a most excellent Remedy against the Spleen, *Hypocondriack Winds,* or the like." Finally, the flyers contained a warning as to psychoactive properties. While coffee would "prevent *Drowsiness,* and make one fit for business" it could also "hinder sleep for 3 or 4 hours."

London had its first coffee shop a year after Oxford, and more than a hundred a decade later. Despite such rapid proliferation they were controversial institutions, as was the beverage they sold. The principal objection to their product was its failure to intoxicate. According to the first English critic of coffee, it was a loathsome fluid, "thick as puddle water . . . ugly in color and taste," which had the nasty side effect of "qualifying wine," i.e., countering its effects. Moreover, in the opinion of the same critic, coffee made its users garrulous, treacherous, and impotent. Whereas, in the ages before Christians had drunk the stuff, "a Prince of *Spain* [was] forc'd to make an Edict, that the Men should not repeat the act of Coition above nine times a night, for before the Edict, belike Men did exceed that proportion; That in this Age, Men drink so many Spirits and Essences, so much Strong-water, so many several sorts of Wine, such abundance of Tobacco, and (now at last) pernicious Coffee, that they are grown as impotent as Age, as dry and as unfruitful, as the Deserts of *Africk*."

Despite the grave threat posed by coffee to the sex lives of English men and women, new coffeehouses kept appearing. From 1663 onward, the sale of coffee was regulated for the first time, alongside that of other new beverages, viz., tea, chocolate, and sherbet, and coffeehouses were licensed in a similar manner to alehouses. By modern standards the Java that they served was filthy stuff. Its active ingredient had spent months at sea before reaching England, and on arrival it was charred rather than roasted, ground into coarse lumps, and brewed up with river water in the proportions of one ounce per quart. Indeed, it is unlikely that the burgeoning popularity of coffee shops derived entirely from infusions, for they also sold a full range of alcoholic drinks. Their attraction rather seems to have been their egalitarian code. Just as pubs in the Middle Ages had served as sanctuaries from feudalism for the commoners, so coffee shops performed a similar role for England's mercantile and professional classes. They were places where people of any background might meet on equal terms to do business, or to discuss matters of common concern, without having to adhere to the stultifying rituals relating to precedent then current in England. Their informal code was spelled out in a pamphlet of the age, dedicated to the "Excellent virtues of that sober and wholesome drink called Coffee":

> First, Gentry, Tradesmen, all are welcome hither,
> And may without Affront sit down Together:
> Pre-eminence of Place, none here should Mind,
> But take the next fit seat that he can find:

Nor need any, if Finer Persons come,
Rise up for to assigne to them his Room.

Coffeehouses tended to specialize in different sorts of clientele. While some drew clergymen, others attracted scientists, artists, or lawyers. Each was like a little court, where trade, literature, metaphysics, philosophy, or politics ruled, and gossip flourished. They became known as "penny universities," as coffee cost a penny a cup[19] and newspapers and debate came free of charge. Groups of businessmen with similar interests gathered at specific coffeehouses to transact their affairs. Indeed, some such in the City of London quickly became the foci of both the domestic capital markets and international trade. From 1697 onward, most of the business of the London Stocks Exchange was carried out in a pair of coffeehouses–Jonathan's and Garraway's. London's shipowners, meanwhile, met at Lloyd's Coffee House, whose proprietor published a daily paper listing news of interest to the shipping world, held auctions of prize goods, and which evolved to become the headquarters of a global insurance market.

The net effect of the "salutiferous berry" on British drinking habits was considerable. For the first time in history, there was a safe, cheap, and respectable alternative to alcohol. It had its greatest impact in the morning: Instead of quaffing ale before going to work, people drank coffee by the dish, preferring to gibber rather than to stumble. The sobriety coffee fostered was welcomed, "for whereas formerly apprentices and clerks with others used to take their morning's draught in ale, beer, or wine, which by the dizziness they cause in the brain make many unfit for business, they use now to play the goodfellows [with] this wakeful and civil drink."

---

[19] The same as a pint of small beer.

12   RUM

Sugar and slave trading were among the principal topics of conversation at Edward Lloyd's Coffee House in London. Europeans had been found to have an insatiable appetite for the former substance, whose manufacture relied upon cheap labor supplied by the latter traffic. Sugar for the English market was produced in various Caribbean islands, which the English had begun to colonize at about the same time as New England. At first these had served as raiding stations from which to harry the shipping of other European nations, but once it was discovered that their soils were suited to sugarcane, they were cultivated with an intensity hitherto reserved for vineyards.

The manufacture of refined sugar for the home market created a by-product—molasses. Initially this was considered to be worthless and was fed to hogs, or dumped on the land as fertilizer. However, it was soon found that with the addition of water, molasses fermented readily. While the resulting brew had a few aficionados, further experimentation revealed that it was an ideal raw material for distillation, and *rum* was born. The first mention of the potation is contained in a description of Barbados, dating to 1651: "The chief fuddling they make in the island is *Rumbullion*, alias *Kill-Devil*, and this is made of sugar canes distilled, a hot, hellish, and terrible liquor."

The island of Barbados, the source of this diabolic fluid, had been an uninhabited, densely wooded Eden when an English ship had chanced upon it 1607. A base was established at Holetown in the 1620s, and it was settled in earnest in the 1640s, first to grow tobacco, then, to the exclusion of all else, sugarcane. By the time that rum had made its debut in the lexicon, Barbados had been deforested and plantations of the new wonder crop covered much of its surface. Its alcoholic by-product was used to perk up the indentured servants from Britain who comprised its initial workforce: "For when their spirits are exhausted, by their hard labor, and sweating in the Sun, ten hours every day, they find their stomacks debilitated and much weakened in their vigor every way, a dram or two of this Spirit, is a great comfort and refreshing to them."

However, free rum notwithstanding, competition for English indentured workers from Virginian tobacco growers caused a labor shortage, which was relieved by the importation of African slaves. Whereas in 1640 there had been more English slaves in Africa than vice versa, by 1660 the position was reversed, as English ships purchased tens then hundreds of thousands of Africans and carried them to the New World to work on plantations. Those who were landed in Barbados were provided a rum ration at work: "This drink is of great use to cure and 'fresh the poor negroes, whom we ought to have a special care of, by the labor of whose hands, our profit is brought in."

The governing class of Barbados also took to 'freshing themselves with rum. When Christopher Codrington arrived in the island in 1703 to commence his appointment as its governor, he complained that the local dignitaries thought "the best way to make . . . strangers welcome is to murther them with drinking." He also noted that their constitutions had been hardened by constant boozing to the extent that "the tenth part of that strong liquor which will scarce warme the blood of our West Indians who have bodies like Egyptian mummys, must certainly dispatch a newcomer to the other world." When the Barbadians began to export their embalming fluid alongside their cargoes of sugar, it quickly acquired a reputation as a superior drink on the other side of the Atlantic. In 1708, the historian John Oldmixon recorded the appearance of rum in England, where it had "lately supplied the Place of Brandy in Punch" and was "much better than the Malt spirits and sad Liquors sold by our distillers." Indeed, Oldmixon rated rum on a par with French Cognac in terms of quality, and more highly as a medicinal drink. It was "certainly more wholesome, at least, in the sugar islands; where it has been observed, that such as drink of . . . [brandy] freely, do not live long, whereas the Rum-Drinkers hold it to a good old age."

One particular group of rum drinkers did not, however, make it to a good old age. The Caribbean pirates, who flourished in the 1660s, and again in the seventeen-teens, made the new liquor a part of their freebooting identity. Sir Henry Morgan (d. 1688) was the best known and most successful example of the first period. Strictly speaking he was not a pirate but a privateer, licensed by King Charles II to fight Spaniards on his behalf and to pay himself from their treasure. Morgan established a base at Port Royal in Jamaica and launched a series of lucrative raids, notable for their brutality, against Spanish possessions in Cuba and Colombia. In 1670 he outdid himself by sacking Panama and burning it to the ground, just after peace had been declared between Spain and England. He was arrested and sent back to England on the frigate *Welcome,* where he was acquitted of piracy, knighted, and returned to Jamaica as its deputy governor. He drank himself to death and was buried in Port Royal, which was wiped off the map by an earthquake four years later. His name and likeness still grace a popular brand of West Indian rum.

The second wave of Caribbean pirates appeared in 1713 as a result of a cessation of hostilities between the various European nations that held islands in the West Indies. Peace created a pool of unemployed seamen, ex–prisoners of war, impressed convicts, and adventurers of every nationality, who took to pillaging minor settlements and merchant shipping. They operated in loose confederations and regulated affairs between themselves according to written *articles,* which were, for the age, models of democracy. They wrote the right to rum into such agreements, as the following extract from the Articles of Captain Roberts illustrates:

I

Every Man has a Vote in Affairs of Moment; has equal Title to the fresh Provisions, or strong Liquors, at any Time seiz'd, and may use them at Pleasure.

Perhaps the most iconic pirate from this second period was Edward Teach, known as Blackbeard, and notorious for his cruelty, concupiscence, and drunkenness. This fiend cut an impressive figure. He was the "embodiment of impregnable wickedness, of reckless daring, a nightmarish villain so lacking in any human kindness that no crime was above him." His eponymous facial hair was luxuriant, and he dressed it for battle with scarlet ribbons and illuminated it with burning matches behind his ears, "which appearing on each Side of his Face, his Eyes naturally looking fierce and wild, made him altogether such a Figure, that Imagination cannot form an Idea of a Fury, from Hell, to look more frightful." Blackbeard lived up to his looks, as the following entry from his journal illustrates:

> Such a Day, Rum all out–Our Company somewhat sober:–A damn'd Confusion amongst us!–Rogues a plotting:–great Talk of Separation. So I look'd sharp for a Prize:–such a day took one, with a great deal of Liquor on board, so kept the Company hot, damn'd hot, then all Things went well again.

For a while, Blackbeard operated out of the Carolinas with the complicity of the colonial authorities, until a warrant for his capture, together with a handsome reward, was issued in Virginia by its governor, Alexander Spotswood. He and his crew were cornered in Okercok Inlet by a superior force, and the pirate died defiant: "*Black-beard* took a Glass of Liquor, and drank . . . with these words: *Damnation seize my Soul if I give you Quarters, or take any from you.*" He then stood his ground and fought "with great Fury, till he received five and twenty Wounds, and five of them by Shot." He was beheaded after death, and his skull continued in service as a receptacle for alcohol. It was converted into a very large punch bowl, called The Infant, "which was used until 1903 as a drinking vessel at the Raleigh Tavern in Williamsburg." According to one account it bore a silver rim on which was engraved "Deth to Spotswoode."

The Carolinas, where Blackbeard drank his last glass of liquor, were emblematic of the progress England's colonies had made in the second half of the sixteenth century. Though none was a match for Barbados in terms of financial clout, they were all flourishing, and expanding in both population and number. The Virginia and the Massachusetts settlements had been joined by Maryland and Pennsylvania, the Dutch had been pushed out of New Amsterdam, which had been renamed New York, New Hampshire had been claimed and settled, and a "great port town" had been founded in Charleston in the

Carolinas. Its first church, St. Philip Episcopal, was financed by a tax of two pence per gallon on rum and other imported spirits.

Rum had a considerable impact on the drinking habits and trading patterns of the American colonies. Its influence was greatest in New England, which became a mercantile nation in its own right as a consequence of the rum trade. One of the first New Englanders to sail down to Barbados had noted that its inhabitants were "so intent upon producing sugar that they had rather buy foods at very deare rates than produce it by labor." The phrase *deare rates* was music to the New England soul. In return for rum, molasses, and sugar, the Massachusetts settlements sent fish, flour, and timber in their own boats. A shipbuilding industry evolved to service this trade, and its captains ranged far and wide in pursuit of profits. As African slaving grew in importance, they entered into the business—indeed they had been involved right from the start. In 1644, John Winthrop of Boston had shipped a cargo of wooden staves to the Cabo Verde Islands, where they were exchanged for slaves, who in turn were traded for sugar in Barbados.

New Englanders started slaving in earnest after it had been discovered that Caribbean rum commanded a premium in Africa. Their presence in the trade was made legitimate in 1689, when the monopoly that the Royal Africa Company held on English slave trading was terminated. Over the next quarter century "about one in seven English slave voyages began in the Americas rather than in England." They loaded up with spirits for the outward journey—according to a current estimate, they carried 1.3 million gallons of them to Africa between 1680 and 1713, which they exchanged for approximately sixty thousand humans.

Africa was a seller's market. Its countries dictated the terms of business on their coasts. With the exception of the Portuguese settlement in Angola, no European nation established more than a toehold on the west coast of the continent before the nineteenth century. Their few forts and trading posts were stationed on islands, such as the English depot at Cape Coast Castle in Ghana, or on narrow, easily defensible peninsulas. Even these were insecure. Ships were regularly cut out, and Europeans were starved or massacred in their fortified settlements. Things had to be done the African way, or not at all. Africans were discriminating in their tastes in trade goods, and these changed from year to year. Their principal demand was for cloth, in very specific colors. The next most important item on their shopping list, more so than guns and gunpowder combined, was rum. It was no use turning up with the wrong goods and expecting to buy slaves. When, for instance, Captain George Scott of Newport arrived with a cargo of bonnets and ribbons, he found few takers, and confided to his diary: "I have repented a hundred times buying... dry goods. Had we laid out two thousand pound in rum, bread, and flour, it would have purchased more in value."

Rum was in demand because, as had been observed by the Portuguese two centuries before, sub-Saharan Africa was populated by drinkers. These consumed alcohol for cultural as well as hedonistic purposes. Most religions in the region postulated life as a voyage undertaken by a soul from and back to the spirit world, and alcohol was thought to ease each soul through the difficult parts of its journey, especially conception, birth, puberty, and death. It was offered to spirits via libations—sprinkled over the foreheads of newborn infants, or on the earth covering a fresh grave. Among the Akan tribe of the Gold Coast, for instance, when a woman gave birth, "all the people—men, women, boys, and girls—come to her.... They give the child a name upon which they have agreed, and swear upon it with the Fetishes and other sorcery... on which occasion they make a big feast, with merry-making, food, and drink, which they love." A similar tradition prevailed at burials: "As soon as the corpse is let down into the grave, the persons who attended the funeral drink palm wine, or rum plentifully out of oxes horns; and what they cannot drink off at a draught, they spill on the grave of their deceased friend, that he may have his share of the liquor." The dead were provided with further drinks at annual ceremonies in their honor. The Akans, who venerated their ancestral stools as being sacred representations of the individuals who once had occupied them, exhibited these heirlooms on specific days every year and splashed them with alcohol. Drink was offered to deities as well as the departed. The serpent gods of Whydah were appeased with gifts of rum, by both native devotees and latterly by visiting slavers, in deference to custom.

Not only was alcohol a trade good in its own right, but it was also an essential *lubricant* of slave trafficking. Time and time again, European merchants found they could not do business without first making presents of rum or similar to local rulers or their representatives. According to a participant in the trade, the African slave seller "never cares to treat with dry Lips." Once lips had been wetted and negotiations concluded, the newly bought slaves were led off to dungeons or holding pens, and thence to the waiting ships. One of them has left us an account of his feelings as he stepped on board in his shackles:

> When I looked round the ship and saw a large furnace or copper-boiling, and a multitude of black people of every description chained together, every one of their countenances expressing dejection and sorrow, I no longer doubted of my fate; and, quite overpowered with horror and anguish, I fell motionless on the deck and fainted. When I recovered a little I found some black people about me. . . . They talked to me in order to cheer me, but all in vain. I asked them if we were not to be eaten by those white men with horrible looks, red faces, and loose hair. They told me I was not: and one of the crew brought me a small portion of spirituous liquor in a wine glass; but, being afraid of him, I would not take it out of his hand. One of the blacks therefore took it from him and gave it to me, and I took a little down my palate, which, instead of reviving me, as they thought it would, threw me into the greatest consternation at the strange feeling it produced, having never tasted any such liquor before.

Some African customs relating to alcohol survived the journey over the Atlantic and took root in the Americas. Slaves on the Caribbean islands were given rum rations by their owners, and although these were meager by the standards of free people—only a gallon or two per head per annum—they managed to hoard some for traditional uses. They were also permitted patches of land on which to grow provisions, and could trade what they grew for drink if they so desired. It seems that when they bought alcohol, they did so to keep their native culture and sense of hospitality alive. Their dedication to these causes was commented on by J. B. du Tertre, a French missionary in the sugar island of Martinique: "I have seen one of our negroes slaughter five or six chickens in order to accommodate his friends, and spend extravagantly on three pints of rum in order to entertain five or six slaves of his country." Du Tertre also noted that slaves celebrated the birth of their children with drinks and would sell "everything they own" to purchase rum for the occasion. They likewise hoarded alcohol to give the soul a proper sendoff on its journey back to the spirit world at death. In Jamaica, slaves buried their own kin with "a pot of soup at the head, and a bottle of rum at the feet." An account of one such funeral shows the persistence of African perceptions of the worth of drink: "Taking a little of the rum or other liquors, they sprinkle it [on the grave], crying out in the same manner, 'Here is a little rum to comfort your heart, good-bye to you, God bless you.'" The toast was returned, on the other side of the Atlantic Ocean, by the Dahomey nation of the slave coast, who chanted:

"The English must bring guns. The Portuguese must bring powder. The Spaniards must bring the small stones, which give fire to our fire-sticks. The Americans must bring cloth and the rum made by our kinsmen who are there, for these will permit us to smell their presence."

It was as well that slaves preserved their own ideologies, for they were debarred from participating in the free drinking culture of the English colonies in continental America, where they were prohibited from entering taverns and ordinaries, lest their presence contradict the spirit of equality that was supposed to rule such places. In order to ensure their absence, tavern owners who served them were fined. While slaves were kept more or less dry, free colonists became increasingly bibulous during the late seventeenth and early eighteenth centuries. Their drinking habits were not homogeneous—a north/south divide was apparent in the kind of alcohol people consumed and in their respective tolerance of drunkenness.

In Virginia, the huge volume of shipping involved in the tobacco trade carried on its outward voyage a variety of British and continental beers, wines, and spirits to tempt the palates of the planters. The colony also imported Caribbean rum. A certain amount of brewing was carried out locally, but Virginian-made beer was reckoned by its inhabitants to be inferior. In 1666 its price was fixed at four shillings or forty pounds of tobacco per gallon, whereas the imported variety cost three times as much. Poor white Virginians made home brews from molasses, corn, potatoes, pumpkins, and Jerusalem artichokes, but otherwise the Virginians produced little alcohol of their own. They were nonetheless creative drinkers, famed for their penchant for combining different liquors to make a variety of flips, punches, and coolers, each of which was credited with special medicinal or stimulatory powers.

Virginia's little sister, Maryland, had similar drinking habits. The emphasis, once again, was on imports. In 1663, it was reported that the Marylanders did not brew at all. As in Virginia, foreign brews were purchased with tobacco. Because of the scarcity of locally brewed beer, both Virginians and Marylanders drank proportionally more spirits than the colonies to the north, and this bias was also evident in the Carolinas. In all three places, there was little or no stigma attached to hard drinking. Each was characterized by small settlements, widely dispersed along rivers rather than roads, so that people gathered together less frequently, and when they visited each other, they vied in demonstration of *Southern* hospitality.

In New England, in contrast, American-made alcoholic drinks were commonplace. Attitudes toward drunkenness were also different: The population was more densely concentrated in villages, towns, and their surrounding farms, and hence opportunities for convivial intoxication were far more numerous, and drunkards were much more visible. Moreover, the reigning Puritan caste had become increasingly antagonistic toward drinking. Instead of perceiving it as a sign of success, indicative of agricultural surpluses and leisure time, they considered it un-American. The pilgrim fathers had got by with cold water and hard work, what now the need for boozing?

An attack was launched on some of the traditional English drinking practices that had been imported to New England, beginning with the custom of paying workers part of their wages in alcohol. In 1645, the "allowance of liquors or wine every day, over and above their wages," was forbidden by the general court of the colony.[20] The Puritans' next target was the excessive drinking that accompanied such communal exercises as raising a barn or meetinghouse, and quasi-public ceremonies, especially weddings and funerals. A supply of alcohol was considered obligatory on all such occasions—witness the funeral bill for David Porter of Hartford, who drowned in 1678:

> By a pint of liquor for those who dived for him—1s
> By a quart of liquor for those who bro't him home—2s
> By two quarts of wine and 1 gallon of cyder to jury of inquest—5s
> By 8 gallons & 3 qts. wine for funeral £1 15s

---

[20] The same prohibition was reenacted in 1672—presumably to remind New Englanders of its existence.

By Barrel cyder for funeral–12s
1 coffin–12s
Winding Sheet–18s

The charge against English-style inebriation while working, marrying, and burying was led from the pulpit. In 1673, Increase Mather (later to preach against another sort of spirits in the Salem witch trials) published his electrifying sermon "Wo to Drunkards," which warned colonial inebriates, in medieval imagery, that while they might succeed in drinking their consciences into comas, when their souls awoke "in the midst of eternal Flames, all the wounds received by this sin will be felt with a witness." His words of wisdom seem to have fallen on deaf ears, for in 1708 his son, Cotton Mather, felt compelled to publish a similar tract against alcohol entitled "Sober Considerations on a Growing Flood of Iniquity."

At the same time as they fulminated against old-fashioned English drunkenness, the Puritans directed their ire against the ordinaries that were popping up like mushrooms all over the country around Massachusetts Bay. While these were impossible to eradicate, since every settlement needed somewhere where visitors might stay, it was possible to limit what people drank in them. In 1645, the Massachusetts General Court forbade ordinary keepers "to suffer anyone to be drunk or drink excessively, or continue tippling above the space of half an hour in any of their said houses." To "drink excessively" was defined as more than half a pint of wine in any one sitting. Transgressors, whether excessive or leisurely drinkers, and the tavern owners who served them, were to be punished with fines.

The enforcement of such remarkable laws was entrusted to a special class of colonial officials, known latterly as *tithingmen,* who were zealous in their duties. Amazed foreign visitors commented on how they had been told to stop drinking, and advised their home audiences to expect unnatural and ill-mannered restraints on their consumption when visiting New England. John Josselyn, writing of Boston in 1663, expressed his disgust at being hounded by one such monitor, who would "thrust himself into the company uninvited, and if [anyone] called for more drink than the officer thought in his judgment he could soberly bear away, he would presently countermand it, and appoint the proportion beyond which he could not get one drop."

Moreover, the licensing procedure for ordinaries was tightened up in 1681. In Boston, the principal town of the region, whose population doubled between 1700 and 1718, the number of taverns grew at a far slower rate—from sixty-three to seventy-four. Thereafter, however, official pressure on the chapels of Satan in New England eased. They were found to be useful venues for discussing British imperial incompetence, and as the merchant element of Boston grew in importance, they were used, like coffee shops in London, as trading centers where bargains could be struck and confidences exchanged.

A measure of the change in priorities, and the balance of power, is apparent in the failure of the "Act Against Intemperance Immorality, and Prophaneness, and for Reformation of Manners," which was approved by the Boston Assembly in 1712, and which included a ban on the sale of distilled liquors in taverns. A glance at the excise levies of subsequent years reveals that taverns continued to sell spirits by the bucket load and that they had enough in their cellars to withstand a siege. In 1715, for example, Thomas Gilbert had 218 gallons of rum, 319 of wine, and 982 of cider in his Boston tavern; and in 1725, Thomas Selby of the Crown Coffee House had nearly 700 gallons of rum and more than 6,000 gallons of wine to hand, which equated to almost a half gallon of wine for every inhabitant of Boston—in one pub. By the time that Selby was storing such prodigious quantities of booze, the number of taverns in Boston had leapt to 134, or one per hundred head of population, i.e., a higher density than that which had prevailed in Elizabethan England.

The excise lists of tavern stocks show, by the relative quantities of various kinds of alcoholic beverage, the prevailing tastes in drink in early eighteenth-century New England. The most popular tipple, in terms of volume, was locally produced cider. Even little settlements produced huge quantities of cider. In 1721 a Massachusetts village of forty families made three thousand barrels—enough for a hundred pints for each family every week throughout the year. In the event, cider became too common and overproduction forced prices down from six shillings per barrel around 1700 to three shillings in 1730. Throughout much of this period, cider served as a currency, like tobacco in Virginia. It was used to pay salaries and levies, and the prices of goods and services were often quoted in barrels of cider.

The cider itself was sometimes transformed into *applejack* by freeze distillation—i.e., by leaving barrels of it outdoors in the winter. This elixir, perhaps the same fluid as Anglo-Saxon *beor*, was easily made by accident in icy New England. It was a farmer's drink, strong, rough, and toxic—applejack hangovers could kill—and was seldom found in taverns, where the most popular liquor was rum. According to *A Trip to New England* (1699) by the English hack journalist Edward Ward, "Rum, alias Kill Devil, is as much ador'd by the American English as a dram of brandy is by an old Billingsgate. 'Tis held as the comforter of their souls, the Preserver of their bodys, the Remover of their Cares and Promoter of their Mirth; and is a Soveraign Remedy against the Grumbling of the Guts, a Kibe-heel or a Wounded Conscience, which are three Epidemical Distempers that afflict the Country." By the time that Ward was writing, New Englanders were making their own rum in Boston. Slave traders found it was less expensive to buy molasses and distil it themselves than to purchase the finished Caribbean spirit. Boston rum had a very poor reputation—a visitor summed up its qualities as "cheap." In 1738 it cost less than two shillings a gallon or about half the price of a similar quantity of beer in Virginia.

Distillation on a commercial scale was also being carried out in New York, which had experienced rapid growth since it passed into English hands in 1664. Manhattan Island had several breweries and produced raw materials for them—hops and barley—in its numerous farms and market gardens. In contrast it imported its wines, for while many had experimented, none had succeeded in making good wine out of native grapes or in keeping foreign vines alive for long enough to produce a vintage. Its inhabitants nonetheless distilled a "brandy" made from grain spirit from 1640 onward, and by the time they had become English subjects "three out of the five breweries in New York also made whisky." However, demand for grain for the stills raised prices to such an extent that there was scarcely enough left for baking into bread, and in 1676 Governor Edmund Andros[21] banned distillation, except with damaged grain. Thereafter, New Yorkers relied on molasses for their stills, whose output was slight in comparison to the volume of rum imported from the West Indies. Like Boston, New York developed large taverns that served as meeting places for its

---

[21] Andros was later satirized as a megalomaniac lunatic in *Androboros* ("Man-eater"), the first play written on American soil. The play also targeted his predecessor, Anthony Colve, who was characterized as Oinoboros ("Wine-eater").

merchants and politicians as well as watering holes for the community at large. In the 1730s, for instance, New York Assembly committees did their business at D'Honneur's Tavern. The size and general layout of such institutions may be gauged from Manhattan's oldest surviving building, Fraunces Tavern, which was built as a house in 1719 and converted to a drinking place in 1762.

The drinking culture of eighteenth-century New York was similar to that which prevailed in the fast-expanding town of Philadelphia, which had been founded in 1682 by William Penn to be the capital of his proprietary colony of Pennsylvania. Its Quaker owner and his coreligionists were peaceful, serious people, who believed in personal communication with, and occasional possession by, the divinity. While they were conscientious investors who would not trade in weapons or participate in war, they accounted wealth no sin and had become a significant force in the English brewing industry.

Penn included a brewery in his own mansion at Pennsbury and recorded, with evident pleasure, that in 1685 an "able man" (William Frampton) had "set up a large *Brew House*," in Philadelphia, "in order to furnish the People with good Drink." Ten years later there were four or five large brewing operations in the town. The beer they produced was reckoned to be "equal in strength to that of London" and was being exported to Barbados, where it fetched a higher price than the English equivalent. While Pennsylvania quickly achieved self-sufficiency in beer, its wine was imported. Like many other European colonists before them, the Quakers had tried and failed to make wine from the native grapes. William Penn planted two hundred acres of his estate with imported vines, but they died, from causes unknown, and the experiment was abandoned. The failure was blamed on the climate, and Philadelphia bought its wines from Europe, the Canary Islands, and Madeira.

The drinking habits of the town were observed, and quite probably shaped, by Benjamin Franklin. Journalism was the first outlet for his energetic genius, and drinking was one of the first topics he addressed. While still a teenager in New England, and writing in the guise of Mrs. Silence Dogood, Franklin contributed a letter to *The New-England Courant*, run by his elder brother, which shows a natural wit, an effective style, and a tolerant approach to alcohol that was to characterize his later work. Its conclusion is typical of Franklin's early style and ordered mind:

It argues some Shame in the Drunkards themselves, in that they have invented numberless Words and Phrases to cover their Folly, whose proper Significations are harmless, or have no Signification at all. They are seldom known to be *drunk,* tho they are very often *boozey, cogey, tipsey, fox'd, merry, mellow, fuddl'd, groatable, Confoundedly cut, See two Moons,* are *Among the Philistines, In a very good Humour, See the Sun,* or, *The Sun has shone upon them*; they *Clip the King's English,* are *Almost froze, Feavourish, In their Altitudes, Pretty well enter'd,* &c. In short, every Day produces some new Word or Phrase which might be added to the Vocabulary of the *Tiplers.*

Franklin moved to Pennsylvania and, after a short spell in London, took over and edited *The Pennsylvania Gazette,* to which he also contributed under aliases. His best-loved alter ego was *Poor Richard,* in whose name an almanac was published every year between 1732 and 1767. The almanac was immensely popular—Poor Richard was the voice of America of his age. In addition to providing weather forecasts and horoscopes for the coming year, the almanac was noted for its aphorisms, which set out in plain English useful behavioral guidelines for the farmers and other colonists who bought it in their thousands. These included maxims about drinking, such as "Take counsel in wine, but resolve afterwards in water"; and "He that drinks his Cyder alone, let him catch his Horse alone."

Franklin also continued to demonstrate an interest in drinking slang. In January 1736 he published the *Drinkers Dictionary,* the most comprehensive collection ever attempted of words and phrases used by drinkers to "cover their Folly." This work, and the aphorisms of Poor Richard, may be taken as being representative of eighteenth-century colonial attitudes to alcohol. Notwithstanding the opposition of a few New England Puritans, occasional drunkenness was viewed with humor and even affection. It was a happy state of relaxation, which might cause people to make temporary fools of themselves, but which did not interfere with their general ability to act as responsible members of the community.

There was, however, one category of drinker whom Franklin felt should be kept away from alcohol at all costs. The Native Americans continued to show an inability to get *groatable* without losing all self-control. This was perceived as a problem throughout the colonies, and Indians, like slaves, were barred from taverns in most places. Numerous laws prohibiting the sale of alcohol to Indians were enacted in various colonies over time: in New Amsterdam in 1643, in Rhode Island in 1654, in Massachusetts in 1657, in Connecticut in 1669, in Pennsylvania in 1701, in New York in 1709.

The problem of Indian drinking worsened as spirits became ubiquitous in colonial America. Since the native tribes had no place for alcoholic drinks in their cultures or diets, they still conceived of them as stimulants and so had a preference for the hard stuff. In 1670 it was reported "that they wonder much of the English for purchasing wine at so dear a rate when Rum is much cheaper & will make them sooner drunk." The same correspondent noted that because they felt the only point in drinking was to become utterly fuddled, if a group of warriors did not have enough to all get drunk, they would choose one person and give their entire stock to him and, if he passed out before finishing it, would hold open his throat and pour in the remainder.

This all-or-nothing attitude was also recorded by French missionaries in Canada. To the Indians, there was "only one sort of drunkenness worthwhile, the sort which they call 'Gannontiouaratonseri,' complete insobriety. And when they begin to feel the effects of the brandy they rejoice, shouting, 'Good, good, my head is reeling.'" The tribespeople themselves acknowledged that alcohol was ruining them. A Delaware Valley Indian, speaking in 1685, lamented that "when we drink it, it makes us mad. . . . We do not know what we do, we abuse one another; we throw each other into the fire, Seven Score of our People have been killed, by reason of the drinking of it, since the time it was first sold [to] us."

The problem was exacerbated by cultural factors. The Native Americans considered drunkenness to be an excuse for any crime—even murder: "A drunken man is a sacred person. According to them it is a state so delicious that it is permitted, even desirable, to arrive at; it is their paradise. Then one is not responsible for his acts." Some observers accused Indians of taking advantage of this exemption, claiming that they got drunk "very often on purpose to have the privilege of satisfying old grudges."

Despite the evident damage that alcohol, especially spirits, was causing to Native Americans, and despite colonial laws against selling it to them, they continued to receive it by the keg. Booze was as essential to the fur trade as to slaving, and the fur trade was likewise a seller's market. The English colonies and the French in Canada competed to buy pelts and found they had to offer rum or brandy in order to secure business. The issue was the subject of an exchange of letters in 1668 between a French official and Governor Dongan of New York. The Frenchman appealed to his rival, on the grounds of piety, to rein in the fur traders who sold liquor to Indians: "Think you, Sir, that Religion will progress whilst your merchants supply, as they do, Eau de Vie in abundance which converts the savages, as you ought to know, into Demons and their cabins into counterparts and theaters of Hell?" Governor Dongan's parry-riposte made the issue one of liberty: "Certainly our Rum does as little hurt as your Brandy and in the opinion of Christians is much more wholesome: However, to keep the Indians temperate and sober is a very good and Christian thing, but to prohibit them all strong liquors seems a little hard."

Commerce was more important than sobriety. When François de Montigny, bishop of Quebec, intervened on the Indians' behalf in 1660 and excommunicated a pair of traders who sold spirits to them, he set off a power struggle with the civil authorities, who insisted that if traders could not offer brandy to Indians there would be no trade at all. The bishop responded with further excommunications in 1662, and in 1668 went one step further by declaring that all brandy sellers were mortal sinners. In the event, pragmatism triumphed over dogma and sales continued.

As the eighteenth century progressed and the Europeans entered into more or less continuous treaty negotiations with various tribes, it became a tradition to offer alcohol as a gift or sweetener, so that in many cases the officials of colonies that prohibited the sale of drinks to Indians broke their own laws when attempting to enlarge their territories. Benjamin Franklin has left a picture of one such encounter—the negotiations held with the Delaware tribe at Carlisle in 1753—which illustrates, with a certain black humor, the double standards of the age. The Indians were told "if they would continue sober during the Treaty, we would give them Plenty of Rum when Business was over." The colonials kept their word, and once negotiations had ended, the Indians set to painting the town red: "They had all made a great Bonfire in the Middle of the Square. They were all drunk Men and Women, quarrelling and fighting. Their dark colour'd Bodies, half naked, seen only by the gloomy Light of the Bonfire, running after and beating one another with Firebrands, accompanied by their horrid Yellings, form'd a scene the most resembling our Ideas of Hell that could well be imagined." The Indians sent a delegation of elders to apologize the next day, who also offered an explanation for their behavior, as follows: "The Great spirit who made all things made every thing for some Use, and whatever Use he design'd any thing for, that Use it should always be put to; Now, when he made Rum, he said, LET THIS BE FOR INDIANS TO GET DRUNK WITH. And it must be so."

13 GIN FEVER

A new Kind of Drunkenness, unknown to our Ancestors, is lately sprung up amongst us, which, if not put a stop to, will infallibly destroy a great Part . . . of our People.

—Henry Fielding

The Native American obsession with self-destructive drinking was considered by Europeans to be a significant point of difference between their respective cultures. It was unthinkable that white Christians could surrender en masse to the same style of inebriation. However, the unthinkable happened in London in the first half of the eighteenth century, when a significant percentage of its population took to drunkenness with an abandon that would have made the most fanatical Native American inebriate wince in shame.

In 1700, with 575,000 inhabitants, London was the largest metropolis in Europe. It was an amalgamation of two cities: London itself, the commercial capital comprising the square mile within the Roman walls, and Westminster, where the court and Parliament were based. The space in between was built over gradually, creating both slums and elegant squares. Affluence and poverty existed side by side in London, especially in its West End, where real estate was booming and mansions and tenements were being thrown up in the few remaining fields. The wealthy found themselves neighbors to laborers: "A Tallow Chandler shall front my Lord's nice *Venetian Window;* and two or three naked Curriers [leather dressers] in their pits shall face a fine lady in her back closet, and disturb her spiritual thoughts."

London was not just the largest, but probably also the most exciting city in the West. It sent ships to India, Finland, Zanzibar, Canada, New England, and the Caribbean, some for commodities, others for luxury goods. It was packed with places to drink, including pleasure gardens, theaters, and its traditional inns, alehouses, and taverns. The Tabard, from which Chaucer had launched his pilgrims, still brewed ale and rented rooms; the Boar's Head, the favorite of Falstaff, still sold sack in Eastcheap. Such now-venerable institutions were augmented by a host of new hostelries, for the collective thirsts of Londoners seemed unquenchable. Beer had overtaken ale as the people's choice, and the average English man, woman, and child got through seventy-five gallons of it each year.

The British prided themselves on their drinking. John Bull was born in 1712 from the pen of John Arbuthnot, and a penchant for inebriation was a part of his and the national character. Foreigners marveled at their consumption. A Swiss traveler wrote home: "Would you believe it, though water is to be had in abundance in London, and of fairly good quality, absolutely none is drunk? The lower classes, even the paupers, do not know what it is to quench their thirst with water. In this country nothing but beer is drunk. . . . It is said that more grain is consumed in England for making beer than for making bread." The same correspondent also listed the kinds of brew that Londoners drank, which ranged from small beer at a penny a pot, to a new brew named porter, which was a "thick and strong beverage" as potent as wine, and cost threepence the pot.

This passion for alcohol was lampooned in *The Spectator,* a daily newspaper founded in 1711 and dedicated to "merriment with decency," which chronicled contemporary manners and foibles in its pages. It documented the drinking preferences of various social classes in a series of articles on English clubs. Londoners rich and lowly were forming convivial associations—aristocrats and intellectuals patronized the Beefsteak and the Kit Cat; the Freemasons were a growing force among tradesmen. The *Spectator* added a few of its own invention, including the *Everlasting Club,* whose hundred members organized a duty rota so that the club was open for drinking 24/7, 365 days per annum. "By this means a Member of the Everlasting Club never wants Company; for tho' he is not upon Duty himself, he is sure to find some who are; so that if he be disposed to take a Whet, a Nooning, an Evening's Draught, or a Bottle after Midnight, he goes to the

Club and finds a Knot of Friends to his Mind." Over the century that the Everlasting was supposed to have been in existence, its members had "smoked fifty Tun of Tobacco; drank thirty thousand Butts of Ale, One thousand Hogsheads of Red Port, Two hundred Barrels of Brandy, and a Kilderkin of small Beer."

Both British and foreign perceptions of their drinking habits were that they drank hard but could hold their liquor, and that drunkenness, though common, was a benign or comical condition. However, this bibulous idyll of clubs and alehouses, of red noses and good cheer, was wrecked in the 1720s by the appearance of a new kind of reckless and nihilistic drinking, centered on the consumption of *gin*. Gin was the English name for Dutch *Genever,* a distilled spirit flavored with juniper, which had been perfected in Holland around 1650 and introduced to England after the Glorious Revolution (1688), when William of Orange was placed on the throne and the Catholic James II ousted.

England had a glut of grain at the time—prices had collapsed after a series of plentiful harvests, to the detriment of England's landowners. Since these comprised the voting class, and new King William owed his throne to them, measures were necessary to prop up their incomes. William had witnessed the phenomenal demand Genever could create for grain in his native Holland and hoped the same might occur in his new kingdom. An "Act for the Encouraging of the Distillation of Brandy and Spirits from Corn"[22] was passed, which allowed anyone in England to distil alcohol using English cereals, upon ten day's notice to HM Excise and payment of a small fee.

The act was a great success, and stills sprang up all over the country. In 1710, the London Company of Distillers issued a celebratory pamphlet, which declared that "the Making of [spirits] from Malted Corn and other Materials, hath greatly increased, and been of service to the Publick, in regard to her Majesty's Revenue, and the Landed Interest of Great Britain." Not only did the new appetite for gin support the general price of corn, it also utilized the damaged grain that bakers and brewers would not buy, thus increasing farmers' and landowners' returns. This useful function encouraged Parliament in 1713 to make explicit the freedom of absolutely anyone to produce spirits: "Any person may distil ... spirits from British Malt." All sorts of people tried their

---

[22] A generic term for wheat, barley, rye, and oats.

hands, using facilities ranging from purpose-built copper stills to con-verted washtubs. Among them they produced a torrent of gin, which was sold from shops, houses, the crypts of churches and inside prisons, from kiosks, boats, wheelbarrows, baskets and bottles, and from stalls at public executions. In the London parish of St. Giles-in-the-Fields, whose fields were now slums, one house in every five retailed gin. Most of it was offered by the *dram,* or quarter pint. It was generally drunk neat and often downed in one. Gin was a cheap, and above all a quick, way of getting drunk. Why work your way through porter at three pence a pot when the same money would buy a pint of gin?

In 1700, the average English adult drank a third of a gallon of gin per annum. By 1723, statistics suggested that every man, woman, and child in London knocked back more than a pint of gin per head per week. This alarmingly high level of consumption generated shocking levels of drunkenness in the capital. Liquor shops were all over town:

> swarming with scandalous wretches ... drinking as if they had no
> notion of a future state. There they get drunk by daylight, and after
> that run up and down the streets swearing, cursing, and talking
> beastliness like so many devils; setting ill examples and debauching
> our youth in general. Nay, to such a height are they arrived in their
> wickedness, that in a manner, they commit lewdness in the open
> streets. Young creatures, girls of twelve and thirteen years of age,
> drink Geneva like fishes, and make themselves unfit to live in sober
> families; this damn'd bewitching liquor makes them shameless.

The problem was aggravated by the squalid living conditions in the slums. Tenement houses were packed from their cellars to their rafters. People dossed down ten to a room, and the only recreation or relief they could afford was drinking gin. A rare account from 1725 of why working women drank is a poignant reminder of how raw Lon-don was: "We market women are up early and late, and work hard for what we have," and "if it were not for something to clear the spirits between whiles, and keep out the wet and cold; alackaday! It would never do! We should never be able to ... keep body and soul to-gether."

The first critics of the *gin craze,* as it came to be known, were the brewers. Despite their new wonder product–porter–they were losing business to gin vendors. In 1726 they sponsored the publication of a satirical pamphlet—*The Tavern Scuffle.* The scuffle of the title was between *Swell-Gut,* a brewer, and *Scorch-Gut,* a gin distiller, who, according to his opponent, was "Scorch Gut by nature; for that his damn'd devil's piss burnt out the entrails of three-fourth's of the King's subjects." Such low blows on gin were countered with reminders from distillers that "the Landed Gentleman must be sensible the distillers work for him, since the distilling trade in and about London only, consumes about 200,000 quarters of corn, and that corn necessarily employs 100,000 acres of land."

Notwithstanding the good news for landowners, all the gin sloshing around London was being linked to a rising crime rate. Britain was an unstable place during the decades when gin drinking was on the rise. There were pretenders to the throne; politics were fiercely bipartisan: The Whigs and the Tories were equally corrupt when in power and equally virulent when in opposition. Religious dissent was on the rise; there had been civil war in the north in 1715 when James Stuart, son of the ousted Catholic king, tried to regain his father's kingdom; and England was at war on the continent between 1702 and 1713. The country was thronged with displaced and discontented people who gravitated toward London.

The town became plagued by thieves, and the roads leading into it were overrun with highwaymen. Members of this latter class of bandit were treated as folk heroes by the poor. In the popular fancy they were all capes and coal-black steeds and "Damn your handsome eyes" spoken through the window of a stagecoach with a pistol pointed at the pounding heart of a beautiful debutante. They were also expected to die well if caught and would dress up for their own executions in white satin. The journey from prison to the scaffold was turned into a procession, during which the condemned man would pause for a few drams of *kill-me-quick*[23] at various gin shops en route. Some even managed a swift one on the gallows itself, where the hangman, quite possibly, also would be drunk. On one notorious occasion a drunken executioner tried to hang the priest who was present on the scaffold to give the condemned the last rites.

Highwaymen were famous both high and low and were the inspiration behind the musical *The Beggar's Opera* (1728) by John Gay,

---

[23] Gin had acquired a variety of nicknames and brands—Old Tom, Strip-Me-Naked, et cetera—most of which alluded to its potency.

which used a cast of robbers, harlots, and fences as mouthpieces to satirize high society, including the country's first prime minister, Robert Walpole. The play oozes gin, whose use is characterized as a feminine trait. Some women drink it on the sly as a pretended cure for turbulent digestion, others are open in their affection for the fluid and do not use their bowels to justify their drams. The following exchange of greetings, between Peachum, a fence and police informer, and Mrs. Trapes, a middle-aged receiver of stolen goods, illustrates the attitude of the shameless kind:

PEACHUM: One may know by your Kiss, that your Ginn is excellent.
MRS. TRAPES: I was always very curious in my Liquors.
PEACHUM: There is no perfum'd Breath like it—I have been long acquainted with the Flavor of those Lips....
MRS. TRAPES: (*holding out cup*) Fill it up—I take as large Draughts of Liquor, as I did of Love.—I hate a Flincher in either.

As the gin craze gathered momentum, the drink itself acquired a feminine identity and became known as *Madame Geneva,* or *Mother Gin.* The sexing can be accounted for by the fact that gin shops were far more unisexual than taverns, alehouses, and other traditional drinking places, and hence people associated gin drinking with the presence of women. However, the true explanation for the feminization of the spirit is more likely to be sardonic. The gin craze coincided with the golden age of English satire. Addison and Steele at *The Spectator,* Arbuthnot, Gay, Dr. Swift, Alexander Pope, Henry Fielding, and many others heaped their abuse on religion, politics, and the human condition. Mother Gin was mother in the sense of a Mama San—the madam of a brothel, a procuress, a deceiver, a female Mephistopheles—but no Gaia.

A year after the first performance of *The Beggar's Opera,* Parliament decided to take action against gin. While the poor were not expected to be perfect, just submissive, their declining standards of behavior had finally caught the attention of their rulers. Madame Geneva was held to blame. It was she who rendered the inferior sorts unfit for useful labor and service and who drove them "into all manner of vices and wickedness." She was attacked with the 1729 Gin Act, which restricted retail sales of gin to licensed premises and set a high price on licenses. These measures were by and large ignored. People still distilled and sold at home, and on street corners, and from under their skirts in the markets. They continued to rob, to prostitute themselves, and to get drunk instead of work. The failure of the '29 Act was recognized in 1733 when Parliament revisited gin. This time, it took a decidedly liberal attitude toward the problem. There was a grain surplus once again. Taxes on distillation were reduced, and provisions were made for export subsidies. As a sop to those in the grip of a gin panic, various petty restrictions on unlicensed gin sellers were introduced.

The '33 Act stimulated supply, and Londoners debased themselves with fresh abandon. The press took up the story. Daily and weekly newspapers were proliferating in London–new titles appeared every few weeks. In the main they were slight compositions–two or four pages interspersed with advertisements–which relied upon scandal or sensation to win readers. Gin horror stories were a favorite stock-in-trade. In 1734, for example, the reading public were gripped by the case of Judith Defour, accused of murdering her own child, with the assistance of a gypsy women named Sukey, then pawning its clothes to buy more gin. Her testimony was printed verbatim: "On Sunday night we took the child into the fields and stripp'd it, and ty'd a linen handkerchief hard about its neck to keep it from crying, and then laid it in a ditch. And after that, we went together, and sold the coat and stay for a shilling, and the petticoat and stockings for a groat. We parted the money, and join'd for a quartern of Gin." Moreover, gin drinkers, like 2-Rabbits, were notoriously accident prone, and their misadventures always made good copy. Tales such as that of a housewife who "came home so much intoxicated with Geneva that she fell on the fire, and was burned in so miserable a Manner, that she immediately died and her bowels came out" captivated an increasingly literate London.

The gin dramas in the press generated sympathy as well as thrills. In 1734, Dr. Stephen Hales published a pamphlet entitled *A Friendly admonition to the Drinkers of Brandy, and other distilled spiritous Liquors.* Hales warned his readers that spirits "coagulate and thicken the Blood, [and] also contract and narrow the Blood Vessels," causing "Obstructions and stoppages in the Liver; whence the Jaundice, Dropsy, and many other fatal Diseases." His Friendly Admonition was based on observation: Hospitals and graveyards were filling up with gin drinkers.

Worse still, teenaged gin moms were breeding sickly infants, who looked "shrivel'd and old as though they had numbered many years." Not only did the wretched creatures look old, they died young. In 1736 the gutter press found a new infanticide with which to stimulate its readers in the form of Mary Estwick, who came home "quite intoxicated with Gin, sate down before the fire, and it is supposed, had [her] child in her lap. Which fell out of it on the hearth, and the fire catched hold of the child's clothes and burnt it to death." Mary, meanwhile slept on without noticing anything was amiss.

In addition to provoking people into fatal errors, gin was discovered to be lethal in its own right. Novices who tried to knock it back like porter sometimes died in their cups. In March 1736, for example, *The London Daily Post* reported the case of Joss the Glazier, who set to drinking half-pints of gin with a bricklayer and a carman "to so great an excess, that Joss the Glazier fell backwards with the eleventh half pint in his hand and died on the spot." Death by sudden drinking was back in the news. Not since it had perplexed the Greeks and led them to conclude it was caused by Bacchic possession had Europeans been so puzzled by an alcohol-related phenomenon. Even doctors were reluctant to admit that drinking alone could cause death instantaneously. Hitherto, it had been thought to need years to work any harm. However, the evidence of their eyes led people to conclude that alcohol could be deadly in what seemed to them to be small quantities—less than a quart of gin could be enough to kill someone. This realization led to a new way of thinking about alcohol. Strong waters, once believed to be composed of the quintessence, the stuff of heaven itself, were clearly nothing of the sort.

Gin was attacked from a new angle in 1736 when Thomas Wilson, an Anglican clergyman, published *Distilled Spirituous Liquors the Bane of the Nation*. This made the novel accusation that gin drinkers were bad consumers—they ate less, and they pawned their clothes instead of buying new ones. Indeed, their failure to purchase the produce of landowners and merchants put the rest of society at risk. The bad consumer argument was further advanced by the parliamentarian Sir Joseph Jeckyll, who noted in his pamphlet *The Trial of the Spirits* that gin was causing the English to neglect their beef: "Why, the miserable creatures, in such a situation, rather than purchase the coarser Joynts of Meat, which the Butchers used to sell at a very easy rate . . . repair to the Gin-Shops, upon whose destructive commodities they will freely lay out all they can rap or rend, till the Parish Work-Houses are filled with their poor, starv'd families, Trade and Country depriv'd of their Manufactures and Labors, while the butchers cannot so much as give these Joynts to the common People . . . but are forc'd, either to bury 'em, or to give 'em to the dogs."

It was evident that a new Gin Act was needed, and in 1736 Parliament voted to clamp down on "strip-me-naked" and its ilk. The act of '36 introduced new and onerous fines for home distilling and raised the license fee for retailing spirits to the huge sum of fifty pounds. It relied on informers for enforcement. These were to be paid a reward of five pounds—as much as a maid might earn in a year—to reveal the identity of miscreants. It was heralded as the end of mother gin—mock funerals for the wicked old lady were staged in London and various other towns, and obituaries were published, including an "Elegy on the Much Lamented Death of the most Excellent, the most Truly-Beloved, and Universally admired Lady, Madam Gineva." A similar pamphlet published the same year painted a desolate picture of the once-thriving gin shops, now "hush'd as death" while the "shrieks of desponding matrons" deprived of their morning tipple rent the air in the streets outside.

In the event, the new act had as little effect as its predecessors. Street traders resumed their business and took the alternative penalty of a few months in the workhouse, rather than paying a fine, if caught. Moreover, a certain rebelliousness had crept into gin drinking. The king, George II, was unpopular, ditto the government, which was perceived as being intent on suppressing the poor. Gin drinking became not only a pleasure but also a political act. Crowds in London chanted, "No gin, no king"—in reference to the fact that the king had gone to visit his relatives in Germany when the act became law, and implying that in the absence of gin, they would not welcome him back.

A struggle between rulers and ruled ensued. There was fresh legislation in 1737 (under the cover of an amendment to the Sweets Act), which tightened the penalties for street sellers—if they could not pay their fines they would not only be sent to the workhouse but whipped until bloody before they were discharged. The '37 Act also made it easier for informers to get their rewards. Informers were a hated species, but the money was good, so many were prepared to risk opprobrium and sell their fellows to the law. For this they were beaten and sometimes killed by gin-drinking mobs. In

1738 another Gin Act appeared, which made it a felony to assault informers, punishable by transportation to the American colonies. The attacks, however, continued, as did the damage attributed to gin. Between 1730 and 1749, 75 percent of all children christened in London died before they reached the age of five, and London parish records from the same period "show twice as many burials as baptisms."

There followed seven years of mayhem, characterized by the familiar levels of excess, before another Gin Act was contemplated. By 1743, the problem was so acute that pamphleteers were predicting an apocalypse for London if gin drinking wasn't reined in: An underground army of zombies with the cadaverous flesh thought typical of gin addicts might "pour forth unexpectedly from their gloomy cells, as from the body of the Trojan Horse, with design to lay the city in flames, that they might share in the plunder."

This time, Parliament was committed to enacting a law that would be obeyed. Lord Lonsdale pointed out during a debate on the matter that the discriminatory nature of prior legislation had made the people "more fond of dram drinking than ever; because they then began to look upon it as an insult upon the rich." Throughout the course of the gin craze, no restrictions had been imposed or even contemplated on the wines and brandy that the upper classes drank in phenomenal quantities. Why should the common people be victimized for their boozing, when their leaders were heroic drinkers, and not merely of spirits? Sir Robert Walpole, for instance, in one year, "paid over £1,000 to one of his five wine merchants for his vintage clarets and Burgundies, and after some months of entertaining at his country estate, returned to the same wine merchant 540 dozen empty wine bottles"—and this was only a fraction of his household consumption, as most of his wine came in barrels, and much of his time was spent in London. The problem was compounded by an urgent need to raise revenues to pay for a new war in Europe. Some voices in Parliament called for a light, patriotic excise on gin. By all means let the poor drink all they desired, so long as they contributed to the support of the nation's armies. Both those in favor of a permissive attitude and their opponents who wanted gin banned accused each other of double standards. It would be hypocrisy to let the rich drink without interference, while the poor were denied their kill-me-quick; and equally, encouraging them to drink for Britain was morally inadmissible.

The case against the tax-and-drink approach was summed up by Lord Hervey:

> We have mortgaged almost every fund that can decently be thought of; and now, in order to raise a new fund, we are to establish the worst sort of drunkenness by a law, and to mortgage it for defraying an expense which, in my opinion, is both unnecessary and ridiculous. This is really like a tradesman's mortgaging the prostitution of his wife or daughter, for the sake of raising money to supply his luxury or extravagance.... The Bill, my lords, is ... an experiment ... of a very daring kind, which none would hazard but empirical politicians. It is an experiment to discover how far the vices of the population may be made useful to the government, what taxes may be raised upon a poison, and how much the court may be enriched by the destruction of the subjects.

Parliament settled on a compromise—a strict licensing system, with affordable licenses and an excise paid at the still-head. Its aims were to restrict demand with high prices, yet not so high as to encourage black market distillation. It also set a precedent by introducing the concept that the taxation of alcoholic beverages should be on a sliding scale and rise in direct proportion to their strength. The 1743 Gin Act was a qualified success. Taverns and other traditional drinking places could afford the new twenty-shilling licenses, and by 1744, one thousand had been taken out in London and twenty thousand nationwide.

This hopeful start was accompanied by encouraging signs that other forces were making headway against the sort of self-destructive spirit drinking that characterized British slums. From 1743 onward, John Wesley and a number of fellow-minded preachers who assumed the name of *Methodists* set out on a mission to convert and reform the urban poor. They found a sizable audience amid the disenfranchised. Wesley attracted crowds of thirty thousand people, which he addressed with no louder instrument than his voice. The crowds were silent and attentive. One of his early sermons, *The Use of Money* (1743), singled out gin selling as a cause of sin: "We may not sell any thing which tends to impair health. Such is eminently all that liquid fire, commonly called drams, or spirituous liquors. It is true these may have a place in medicine.... Therefore such as prepare and sell them only for this end, may keep their conscience clear.... But all who sell them in the common way, to any that will buy, are *poisoners-general*. They murder His Majesty's subjects by wholesale, neither does their eye pity or spare. *They drive them to hell like sheep.*"

Converts to Methodism were expected to steer clear of drinking spirits, unless for medical reasons, as well as from making and selling them. They subscribed to rules that were similar in principle to the articles of the pirates, insofar as they were voluntary restrictions on conduct, and their rules said no to gin:

> You are supposed to have the faith that "overcometh the world." To you therefore it is not grievous:
> 1   To taste no spirituous liquor, nor dram of any kind, unless prescribed by a physician.

It is interesting that spirits were still permitted on doctor's orders, and evidence that even disciplined evangelicals did not envisage banning them completely, despite the horrors of the gin craze. The distinction between acceptable forms of alcohol and liquid hellfire rested on the intention with which they were drunk.

However, the influences of the 1743 Gin Act and the Methodists were diluted by turmoil at home and abroad. A second Jacobite rebellion materialized in 1745 when the Young Pretender, Bonnie Prince Charlie, appeared in Scotland to claim his grandfather's crown. He failed and fled, disguised as a "lady's maid," having got as close to London as Derby. Shortly after the rebellion had ended in Great Britain, and reprisals were over, peace arrived on the continent of Europe. Seventy thousand demobilized soldiers returned to Britain with no jobs to look forward to nor any arrangement for their support, beyond official permission to beg. Disorder returned, which once again was blamed on gin.

By 1750 London had been in the thrall of Madame Geneva for a quarter of a century. She had been legislated against five times, declared the enemy of religion and health, yet persisted nonetheless. Gin had been a constant in an age of change. However, London in 1750 was no longer the rowdy place it had been at the turn of the century. The threat of rebellion had been countered and suppressed, wars had been won in Europe and elsewhere. The best and cruelest work of the golden age of English satire had been written. The epic drinkers who had electrified Parliament with their drunken rhetoric had retired or died. The first half of the eighteenth century had been one of crazes—the South Sea Bubble, lotteries, mad and extravagant fashions, music, the revived theater, and latterly, preaching. By 1750 London had settled down a little. A full third of its population were described as being of the *middling sort,* i.e., middle class. These people had begun to develop an identity and, with it, an ideology. Their priorities may be gauged by the topics of conversation at their dinner parties, which, according to a contemporary observer, were "the fineness or dullness of the weather, beauty of their children, goodness of their husbands, and badness of their several trades and callings."

The emergence of the middling sort, and their humbler relations the respectable poor, as distinct classes from the mass of common people, hitherto perceived of by their rulers as an amorphous mob, was accompanied by a sea change in public opinion toward gin. Gin drinking was no longer conceived of as a way of showing displeasure with government, and the social forces ranged against it combined together for one last push. They found eloquent and popular champions to represent their case in picture and print. Their advocate in prose was Henry Fielding, playwright, novelist, and onetime rake, who had reformed himself and become a magistrate and a fervent opponent of gin. In 1751 he published a pamphlet, an *Enquiry into the Causes of the Late Increase of Robbers,* which was targeted at the pernicious liquid. It portrayed intoxication with that specific drink as a special kind of drunkenness that robbed people of their memories and their ability to distinguish between right and wrong. Gin fanatics seemed to get drunker than other drunks and to do worse things when under the influence. Fielding made a direct link between soaring crime rates in London and gin drinking. His position as magistrate gave his words authority, so that action against gin was also perceived of as action against crime in general.

Public opinion was also influenced by William Hogarth, who produced a pair of satirical etchings—*Gin Lane* and *Beer Street*—which depicted the misery gin drinkers suffered and contrasted them with the good health enjoyed by people who stuck to beer. Hogarth provided Jekyll and Hyde images of drinkers—fat and prosperous, in the case of beer tipplers, but skeletal and damned if they boozed on gin. It's a sunny day in his Gin Lane, with plenty of exposed flesh on view—most of it belonging to the dead or dying. At the center of the panorama is Mother Gin herself, represented as a seminaked woman with syphilitic sores on her legs. She has just dropped her infant son, who hangs in midair, falling headfirst toward a gin shop in a cellar. The scene around her is raging and chaotic—bricks tumble from the buildings as if shaken loose by an earthquake, a child fights a dog for a bone, two little girls in the costume of the foundlings' hospital toast each other with a dram, and a skipping lunatic with a pair of bellows in one hand and a baby on a skewer in the other dances past an open coffin in which an emaciated body is being placed.

In Beer Street, in contrast, even the men look pregnant, and happy to be so. The foaming pots of porter in their hands and by their sides are to scale. There is food all over the picture, and houses are being improved, rather than falling into ruin. The streets are clean, and flags fly from the buildings. These opposing visions of drinking, one of which depicts alcohol as poison, the other as the key to prosperity and good health, sum up the convictions of the age. Gin and beer were utterly different fluids, one malign, the other beneficial, and the evil type needed to be controlled.

The art of Fielding and Hogarth was supported by science. The medical arguments in favor of restraints on distilling and selling gin were compelling. Doctors queued up to give evidence. The physician of St. George's Hospital confirmed that between 1734 and 1749 hospital admission had risen from 12,710 a year to 38,147 "from the melancholy consequences of gin drinking, principally." The economic burden created by sick and dying gin addicts was calculated by Dean Josiah Tucker, who prepared the first estimates of the social costs of drinking and came up with an annual expense of £3,997,619, against a revenue for all forms of taxation on the production and sale of spirits of £676,125. The income was cash, the cost, conjecture, but the figures brought the notion that drinking entailed expenses as well as revenues, and that these might be quantified in monetary terms, to the attention of the public. Finally, a new spirit of humanity was abroad. People could be victims of circumstance and pitied as such, rather than simply being condemned as vicious by nature. Prostitutes, for example, began to attract sympathy for their plight instead of being characterized as impudent hussies. It was the environment that turned people into whores and listless drunks, rather than innate evil.

GIN LANE.

BEER STREET.

In 1751 a new and final Gin Act was introduced, which was both pragmatic and successful. It pushed up duty, controlled licensing, and banned the sale of spirits on credit. In 1751, approximately 7 million gallons of gin were taxed, the following year less than 4.5 million. The fall reflected declining demand, rather a shift from the official to the black market. Best of all, the common people responded positively to the new legislation, indeed, seemed to have lost the desire to debase themselves. Their improvement was commented on by foreign writers, including Giuseppe Baretti, who noted in *A Journey from London to Genoa* (1770) that "in the space of ten years, I have observed that the English populace have considerably mended their manners and am persuaded that in about twenty years more they will become quite as civil . . . as the French and Italians."

14 PROGRESS

Drink success to philosophy and Trade!
—Erasmus Darwin, *1763*

ritish travelers to the continent of Europe, in particular to France, confirmed that the manners of its common sort were indeed far better than those of their native land. Their praise, however, was heavily qualified. France, in the latter half of the eighteenth century, to British eyes, was an impoverished and antiquated place, swarming with well-mannered beggars and surly priests. A trip to the country was a voyage backward in time. Its roads were bad, much of French agricultural practice was medieval, the administration was corrupt, and the calendar was choked with papist feasts, processions, pilgrimages, and spectacles, all of which had vanished in England with the Reformation, but which provided, to the cynical British traveler, "a perpetual comedy."

Perhaps the only feature of France that was more modern than Britain was its police force, founded in 1699 and endowed with intrusive powers of search and arrest. Police spies frequented drinking places, and their presence, which made people guard their tongues when in their cups, together with a thirteenth-century system of guilds and licensing, which gave a monopoly on the retail of spirits to the master lemonade-makers of Paris, thus restricting supply, explains why the French poor did not succumb to a brandy craze. Indeed, the freedom their British counterparts enjoyed to drink themselves to death was indicative of their comparative liberty.

Travelers through this police state were astonished at the wretched quality of the food and drink available en route. As an exception to the general politesse of the people, the manners of innkeepers were execrable, and the fare they offered of a matching standard. According to the Scottish writer Tobias Smollett, en route to Nice in 1763, the food made him ill, and "the wine commonly used in Burgundy is so weak and thin, that you would not drink it in England. The very best which they sell at Dijon, the capital of the province, for three livres a bottle, is in strength, and even in flavor, greatly inferior to what I have drank in London. I believe all the first growth is either consumed in the houses of the noblesse, or sent abroad to foreign markets."

Even in Paris, a foreigner without connections found it hard to eat or drink well. While the French aristocracy were taking the art of dining to new heights in their palaces, the *traiteurs,* or cook shops, of the city sold plain fare, and the wine served in its traditional cabarets and taverns was "very thin." Cheap weak wine was likewise the standard fare at a new class of watering holes–*guinguettes*–that had been established on the outskirts of the town to avoid the heavy Parisian sales taxes. These were large utilitarian places, which offered dancing as well as drinking, and which were patronized by the working poor. Perhaps the only places in Paris where a stranger might get a decent glass of wine were its cafés, whose numbers had multiplied considerably since the now-venerable Procope had introduced coffee to the French capital. These had since assumed a role akin to the coffee shops in London, and served as forums where intellectuals gathered to discuss the news and matters that the royal censors prevented from appearing in print. They offered tea, coffee, chocolate, cordials, wine, and various eaux-de-vie to their clientele and competed with each other for customers with increasingly elaborate interiors. By the date of Smollett's visit some were positively palatial and sported floor-to-ceiling mirrors, gilded cornices, marble counters, and chandeliers. Such splendor, however, was often to no avail, for the Parisians chose where they drank not merely on the grounds of decor but also, and more importantly, on whether or not a café was à la mode.

Parisians were obsessed with novelty. The obsession was a side effect of living under an absolute monarch whose whims counted for more in the formation of public policy than the laws by which he was, by definition, above. Moreover, the medieval notions of showing rank through magnificence in dress persisted, and the French aristocracy distinguished themselves with theatrical and constantly changing costumes and hairstyles. Smollett found such modishness repellent and compared the Parisian ladies of quality, with their painted faces and hair stiffened by "an abominable paste of hog's grease, tallow, and white powder," unfavorably with the Indian chiefs of America, whose makeup he justified on the basis that it was worn to make them look frightening, instead of beautiful. The royal court was the fountainhead of every new trend, including fashions in drinking. Giacomo Casanova, the Venetian man of letters now best remembered for his philandering, provided an example of one such fad in his memoirs:

> The king was hunting, and found himself at the Neuilly Bridge; being thirsty, he wanted a glass of ratafia. He stopped at the door of a drinking-booth, and by the most lucky chance the poor keeper of the place happened to have a bottle of that liquor. The king, after he had drunk a small glass, fancied a second one, and said that he had never tasted such delicious ratafia in his life. That was enough to give the ratafia of the good man of Neuilly the reputation of being the best in Europe: the king had said so. The consequence was that the most brilliant society frequented the tavern of the delighted publican, who is now a very wealthy man.

While Parisians might choose, depending on what was in fashion, between ratafia, a toxic spirit flavored with the kernels of cherries, other species of eau-de-vie, "very good small beer," and brandy, wine was the mainstay of French drinking culture. Notwithstanding the handicaps of being weak and bad, it was plentiful and cheap. In the first quarter of the eighteenth century, a "fury of planting" had taken place all over France, with more and more land being laid out to vines. The consequent surge in production had alarmed the court, which feared there would be a corresponding shortage in grain, and in 1731 the king decreed that no one could plant new vines in France without his express permission. His motive was not merely to prevent famine but also to protect the value of his own and his courtiers' vineyards. The decree was unevenly enforced. In some regions new vines were uprooted; in others, where they had been set in the soil under the protection of the aristocracy, they were allowed to flourish, as was the case in Bordeaux.

In Bordeaux, the fury of planting was concentrated in the Médoc, whose *terroir* had a similar composition to that of established vineyards in Graves. The similarity, it was hoped, would enable the production of wines of comparable quality, which might command equal prices overseas. In the event, the hope was borne out, as is apparent in the comments of Nicolas Bidet (later cellarer to Marie Antionette), writing in 1759: "The Médoc is a canton in favor: The wine which is gathered there is very much in fashion and to the English taste. The proprietors in our Graves have looked with jealousy at the favor the Médoc wines have enjoyed during the last thirty or forty years." The opinion of the English was all-important to the quality producers in Bordeaux. While the bulk of the region's wines still went to Holland, the prestige vintages were aimed at the British market, whose significance was acknowledged by the French commercial council, as was its insistence on excellence and its indifference to price: "It is a generally recognized truth that in all places where the British land they make a great many purchases, raising the price of goods and merchandise and seeking out those which are the most expensive and most perfect. This method is in contrast to that of the Dutch, who spend frugally . . . and are less attentive to the quality of what they buy than to its low price." The vintners of Bordeaux continued to shape their product to British tastes even during the numerous eighteenth-century wars with Britain, and the British continued to buy despite often punitive import duties.

The demand for Bordeaux wine in Britain derived not just from the cellars of its aristocracy and politicians, and the taverns of London, but also from Scotland, where claret was considered *the* patriotic drink, more so than whisky. When Jacobite rebels, in the first half of the eighteenth century, toasted "The king o'er the water,"[24] their cups were usually filled with claret. This preference was celebrated in verse. Whereas, according to William Hamilton of Gilbertfield, whisky was a "duff-draff drink" that made him liable to "bark and yowff," claret gave wings to his muse. The elevating qualities of claret were likewise applauded by the poet Allan Ramsay:

> Gude claret best keeps out the cold,
> And drives away the winter soon;

---

[24] It was treasonous to drink the health of either the old or young pretender, and so Jacobites would toast each other holding their cups above a pitcher of water.

It makes a man baith gash and bold
And heaves his soul beyond the moon.

A love of Bordeaux wines and a penchant for fighting Englishmen were not the only links between Scotland and France in the eighteenth century. Both made substantial contributions to the *Enlightenment*, a coherent cultural movement, whose aim was to provide secular explanations, and scientific solutions, to issues ranging from the place of man in creation to the efficient manufacture of needles. It had been born in England in the second half of the seventeenth century. In the space of forty years the English had killed one king, dethroned another, and experimented with republicanism, before settling on a constitutional monarchy with an impartial legal system and a free press. The various forms of government, and interim anarchy, had resulted in a secular reformation. British thinkers examined the nature of the pact between rulers and their subjects and, while they were at it, the relationship between humanity and God. They concluded that the universe was governed by mechanical principles, and that society should be run on rational ones.

The practical influence of the Enlightenment movement was evident in science, health, education, and agriculture. In all four areas there were consequences for the production of alcoholic drinks and for the culture of drinking. Science was of obvious benefit to the art of brewing, caveat that brewers were a superstitious lot and slow to take advantage of innovations that might assist them in their trade. Although control of temperature is vital to the brewing process, few manufacturers used the newly invented thermometer to help them to improve the consistency of their product. When, for example, an enlightened Hampshire brewer advised Samuel Whitbread, the largest brewer in London, that thermometers were useful, and Whitbread suggested to his directors that they invest in one, he was told to "go home and not engage in such visionary pursuits." However, and despite their disdain for science, the brewers were natural aficionados of Adam Smith and his new discipline of *oeconomics,* and when their technical competitors gained market share with better and more reliable brews, they reconfigured their breweries and their methods.

Breweries also served as laboratories for those in love with progress. In 1771, the philosopher, chemist, and dissenting clergyman Joseph Priestley conducted experiments in a brewhouse in Leeds, whose aim was to isolate the gas given off in fermentation. He succeeded and called it *fixed air*.[25] Further research revealed that the gas was soluble in water, to which it imparted fizz and a faintly acidic taste. After testing the resulting beverage on his friends, who declared themselves enchanted, he wrote a paper, *Impregnating Water with Fixed Air* (1772), which set out a process for making soda water, and suggested that it might be used onboard ships to fight scurvy. Priestley also noted that other liquors might likewise be improved by impregnation with fixed air, thus establishing the basis for artificially carbonated drinks.

Advances in medicine during the Enlightenment era resulted in a diminished role for alcohol in the field of health. The four great London teaching hospitals were established during the latter years of the gin craze, and much of their work involved curing people from booze rather than with it. The folk remedies that had relied on alcohol as a vehicle to distribute various herbal and animal essences through the bodies of patients were consigned to the dustbin of history. The hospitals, however, still considered both beer and wine to have useful therapeutic properties, and provided them to their patients in order to help them to rebuild their strength. Similarly, doctors still prescribed drink to patients for a variety of ailments. When, for instance, the Scottish philosopher David Hume had a nervous breakdown, the prognosis of his doctor was that he had "fairly got the Disease of the Learned," and he was put on a diet of claret and told to take some exercise in order to cure himself.

Medicine also peered into the state of drunkenness. Surely this condition was as susceptible to a scientific explanation as had been blindness or the circulation of the blood? A number of confident theses were advanced. The definition in Ephraim Chambers's *Cyclopaedia* (1728), which aimed to sum up all ancient and modern learning in two volumes, may be taken as typical of the efforts of the time: "DRUNKENNESS, physically consider'd, consists in a praeternatural Compression of the Brain, and a Discomposure of its Fibres, occasioned by the fumes, or spirituous Parts of Liquors." The definition was followed by a description of the mechanics of intoxication: As soon as it had slid down the drinker's throat, liquor underwent "a Kind of Effervescence" in the stomach, whereupon its "finer parts" shot "through the Veins to the Brain," or were "convey'd through the

---

[25] It was carbon dioxide.

Veins to the Heart," and thereafter to the brain via the arteries. More-over, not every kind of liquor was capable of making people drunk. Only those beverages with an excess of sulphur might discompose the drinker. Clearly, there was still progress to be made in unlocking the secrets of Bacchus.

The issue of education attracted the attention of some of the finest minds of the Enlightenment. If children were not to be indoctrinated via catechism and similar forms of superstition and prejudice, then what should they learn and how should they be taught? Should they be allowed to drink? The last question was answered in the affirmative by John Locke's *Some Thoughts Concerning Education* (1693), perhaps the most influential work on the subject for much of the eighteenth century. According to Locke, there was to be no platonic minimum drinking age. Children should be given small beer, but not between meals, indeed only with food, as soon as they could walk. Parents were, however, warned that their offspring should "seldom, if ever, taste any wine or strong drink...but when they need it as a cordial, and the doctor prescribes it." They were also advised to watch their servants, for "those mean sort of people, placing a great part of their happiness in strong drink, are always forward to make court to my young master by offering him that which they love best themselves: and finding themselves made merry by it, they foolishly think 'twill do the child no harm. This you are carefully to have your eye upon, and restrain with all the skill and industry you can, there being nothing that lays a surer foundation of mischief, both to body and mind, than children's being us'd to strong drink."

Whereas enlightened educational methods preserved the ancient British habit of giving alcohol to children, when the same spirit of im-provement was applied to agriculture, it had a negative impact on traditional drinking practices. Nature was perceived of as a resource "for the being and service and contemplation of man," and the En-lightened farmer was "like a god on earth" who "commands this spe-cies of animal to live and that to die." Numerous technical manuals, such as *The Gentleman Farmer; Being an Attempt to Improve Agriculture by Subjecting It to the Test of Rational Principles,* by the Scottish Lord Kames (1776), were published, and with the assistance of the Enclo-sure Acts, vast quantities of common lands were rationalized and im-proved, displacing large numbers of common people. Many rural settlements were turned into pasture or sown with grain. Crofts and houses were abandoned, gardens and village greens were plowed under. With them went numerous rustic alehouses, some of which had existed since the days of *Piers Plowman,* and each of which had been the secular heart of its community. A variety of pastoral drinking practices perished with the alehouses, and the demise of both was lamented by Oliver Goldsmith in his poem "The Deserted Village" (1770). The village of the title had an alehouse, whose ruin Goldsmith brings back to life, in order to show what had been lost:

> Near yonder thorn, that lifts its head on high,
> Where once the sign-post caught the passing eye,
> Low lies that house where nut-brown draughts inspir'd,
> Where grey-beard mirth and smiling toil retir'd,
> Where village statesmen talk'd with looks profound,
> And news much older than their ale went round.

Subsequent stanzas highlighted the social cost to the little community, and the local traditions that had perished with the building itself:

> Thither no more the peasant shall repair
> To sweet oblivion of his daily care;
> No more the farmer's news, the barber's tale,
> No more the wood-man's ballad shall prevail;
> No more the smith his dusky brow shall clear,
> Relax his pond'rous strength, and lean to hear;
> The host himself no longer shall be found
> Careful to see the mantling bliss go round;
> Nor the coy maid, half willing to be press'd,
> Shall kiss the cup to pass it to the rest.

Perhaps the most important influence on British drinking habits during the rush to modernize, secularize, and improve in general was the rise of a beverage that had been associated for millennia past with enlightenment, albeit in Asia. The drink in question was tea, which seemed to possess all the qualities European philosophers most admired: It was both refreshing and stimulating, yet too much of it did not render its drinker tongue-tied and insensible. Tea had been introduced to Europe by the Dutch, who had started drinking it in the 1660s, shortly after they had displaced the Portuguese from their Asian possessions. At first it was an expensive and exotic beverage, which only the very rich could drink. However, increasing trade with the Far East soon brought down the price sufficiently for its use to spread. Those who could afford tea drank it in prodigious quantities. They were urged on by their doctors, who blessed the infusion with medicinal properties. Dr. Cornelis Bontekoe of Amsterdam prescribed a minimum of eight to ten cups each day to his patients and advised them that if they wished to go further, "fifty to two hundred cups" were "perfectly reasonable." Unsurprisingly, it earned the reputation of being a diuretic:

> Tea that helps our head and heart
> Tea medicates most every part
> Tea rejuvenates the very old
> Tea warms the piss of those who're cold.

The next European country to take to tea was France, where it was drunk by the aristocracy, and where Marie de Rabutin-Chantal is credited as being the first to take it mixed with milk. From France it came to England with the Restoration. Initially, it was ridiculously costly. In 1687 the cheapest sort was twenty-five shillings per pound— rather more than a barrel of beer. However, in that age, a high price was an incentive to the upper classes, and in the same decades that England's poor were debasing themselves with drams of gin, a daily dish of tea became a ritual for its wealthy inhabitants. They devised ceremonies around its consumption, which were presided over by women, for tea drinking usually took place in private houses in mixed company, and just as women had acted as cupbearers and peace weavers in mead halls, so they played the same role with tea-pots and dishes of fragrant *bohea*. The rituals invented for tea were satirized by Alexander Pope in his mock-heroic poem the *Rape of the Lock* (1716):

> On shining Altars of Japan they raise
> The silver lamp; the fiery spirits blaze:
> From silver spouts the grateful liquors glide,
> While China's earth receives the smoking tide:

> At once they gratify their scent and taste,
> And frequent cups prolong the rich repast.

After a fashion, tea provided a gateway for female entry into the British Enlightenment. In 1742, Eliza Haywood, best-selling novelist and social commentator, launched a periodical named *The Tea-Table*, which she followed up with *The Female Spectator* (1744–46). Both titles were intended for the expanding circle of educated women in London. Tea featured frequently in their pages, often ironically. According to the *Female Spectator* it was "the utter Destruction of all Oeconomy, the Bane of good Housewifry, and the Source of Idleness, by engrossing those Hours which ought to be employed in an honest and prudent Endeavour."

Tea drinking took some time to spread from the houses of the wealthy to the country at large. The official price of tea was kept at an artificial height by the East India Company, which held a monopoly on its importation, and by heavy duties. However, smugglers took up the slack, and most British tea lovers obtained their supplies on the black market. In contrast to the civilized image the leaf enjoyed among its aficionados, the men who smuggled it were notoriously brutal. In 1747, for instance, a group of Dorset tea contrabandistas known as the Hawkhurst Gang carried out an armed raid on the Poole customs house to reclaim sixty tons of confiscated tea, tortured to death two customs officials who had been sent to investigate them, and killed a poor laborer they suspected of stealing two small bags of tea from one of their caches. The high price of bohea created a market for fakes. Smuggled tea was often cut with leaves from other plants before being offered to the consumer. This problem was common enough to lead to legislation prohibiting the practice, and in 1777, concerned that England was losing its hedgerows, Parliament outlawed so-called *British tea,* the pseudonym for an amalgam of ash, hawthorne and elder leaves, and sheep dung that was sold throughout the nation as a patriotic alternative to the Chinese variety.

Tea did not become acceptable without a struggle. Its detractors attacked both the infusion itself and the people who consumed it. "Were they the sons of tea-sippers who won the fields of Crécy and Agincourt, or dyed the Danube's streams with Gallic blood?" asked Joseph Hanway, a contemporary skeptic, in a 1756 pamphlet aimed at bringing Britons to their senses. Hanway, who pioneered the use of umbrellas in London, was of the opinion that tea would be the ruin of Great Britain. It had already destroyed people's looks: "Men seem to have lost their stature and comeliness, and women their beauty. I am not young, but, methinks, there is not quite so much beauty in this land as there was. Your very chambermaids have lost their bloom, I suppose, by sipping tea." It was also a leading cause of infant mortality: "The careless spending of time among servants, who are charged with the care of infants, is often fatal: The nurse frequently destroys the child! the poor infant, being left neglected, expires whilst she is sipping her tea!"

Hanway's views were challenged in print by Dr. Samuel Johnson, representing the Enlightenment, who confessed to being a "hardened and shameless tea-drinker, who has, for twenty years, diluted his meals only with the infusion of this fascinating plant." Johnson confined himself to tea drinking, as he felt he could not regulate his intake of anything stronger: "I can't drink a little . . . therefore I never touch it." He did, however, live in the Anchor Brewery in Southwark for a number of years and reckoned alcohol to be life's "second greatest pleasure," an opinion shared by James Boswell, his Scottish biographer. Boswell's drinking habits were perhaps more typical of the age and are illustrated by the bottle count in his diary for an evening's drinking with a handful of compatriots in Edinburgh, "the Athens of the North." Together they managed thirty-three pints of Scotch claret, two bottles of old hock and two of port, with a few shots each of brandy and gin on the side. So much alcohol in one sitting had inevitable consequences for the Scotch philosophers, who, had they consulted Dr. Johnson's *Dictionary* (1755), could have chosen between *Fuddled, Fuzzled, Inebriated, Muddled, Tipsy,* or plain *Drunk* to describe their condition.

Although tea affected the daily drinking habits of Britons far more than coffee had—indeed, it came to replace beer for breakfast—its similar failure to inspire, in the sense of intoxicate, meant that the poetick juice of former ages remained the stimulant of choice for enlightened minds. This preference was not limited to the literati who shaped the movement but was also apparent in the middle classes. London was graced with a number of tea gardens, where its population repaired on evenings and weekends to listen to music, enjoy the walks, and to eat and drink. According to an early practitioner of the science of statistics, these entertainment complexes sold more alcohol than infusions. He calculated that on an average Sunday, nearly 200,000

Londoners visited its tea gardens, and "the returning situation of those persons [was] as follows: sober, 50,000; in high glee, 90,000; drunkish, 30,000; staggering tipsy 10,000, muzzy, 15,000, dead drunk, 5,000."

The national penchant for at least mild inebriation during their leisure hours was, after all, consistent with the core philosophy of the British Enlightenment–the pursuit of happiness. As Locke had phrased it in 1717: "The business of men is to be happy in this world by the enjoyment of the things of nature subservient to life, health, ease, and pleasure, and by the comfortable hopes of another life when this is ended."

15 REVOLUTION

IV. However peaceably your Colonies have submitted to your Government, shewn their Affection to your Interest, and patiently borne their Grievances, you are to suppose them always inclined to revolt, and treat them accordingly. Quarter Troops among them, who by their Insolence may provoke the rising of Mobs, and by their Bullets and Bayonets suppress them. By this Means, like the Husband who uses his Wife ill from Suspicion, you may in Time convert your Suspicions into Realities.

—Benjamin Franklin, "Rules by Which a Great Empire May Be Reduced to a Small One," *London Public Advertiser*, September 11, 1773

In 1762, Benjamin Franklin returned to Pennsylvania after a five-year stay in London. In contrast to his first visit, when he had worked as a jobbing printer and had been teased for being a water-drinking American, this time he had traveled as the official representative of the Pennsylvania Assembly to petition the king on its behalf. He was, moreover, a celebrated Enlightenment figure, an Honorary Fellow of the Royal Society, whose experiments with electricity had won him fame throughout Europe. The petition he had been appointed to present related to taxes imposed on Pennsylvania to support the cost of the Seven Years' War, which were considered by the Pennsylvania Assembly to be inequitable.

This was not the only point of difference between Britain and its

American settlements to have emerged during the *French and Indian War*, as it was known in the colonies, whose prosecution had also aggravated preexisting disagreements. One of the principal causes of friction arose from the rum and molasses trade between New England and the French sugar islands. In 1731, an import duty had been imposed by the British on both substances. Despite the volume of the trade, very little duty was collected prior to the outbreak of the war, and during the initial years of the conflict, both French and British colonists kept up their mutually profitable, but doubly illegal,[26] commerce. Rather, however, than continuing their business in a clandestine manner, they took advantage of a wartime convention that allowed combatants to communicate with each other via flags of truce. The convention was intended to facilitate, among other matters, the exchange of prisoners of war. Any ship traveling under a flag of truce was deemed inviolable. A single prisoner of war was enough to earn a flag, and some "prisoners" made a good living voyaging to and fro between the French Caribbean and British mainland colonies. Permits to wear flags of truce were granted by colonial governors, who either sold them by auction or at a fixed price. Only Virginia paid any respect to the sanctity of the institution–indeed, caused a scandal among other colonies when its governor refused a bribe of four hundred pounds to grant a questionable permit.

So successful was this trade that basic foodstuffs from New England were cheaper and easier to find in French Haiti than British Jamaica. Faced with a dearth of rations, the Royal Navy elected to enforce the spirit of the law by breaking it. They sailed into Monte Christi, nominally a neutral port in the Spanish part of Hispaniola, and carried away as prizes all the ships that it contained, including a number of colonial vessels. Although the Admiralty court in London later ordered that some owners be compensated, the raid signaled a change in policy: Royal Naval ships took over the flags-of-truce trade, and smugglers had their vessels sunk or confiscated. In Salem alone, in the last three years of the war, over two hundred boats were taken by the British. These measures had the twin consequences of alienating the owners of the ships and the merchants who traded in

---

[26] French planters were allowed to export neither rum nor molasses, lest they compete with the brandy makers of the parent country.

them, and of causing a shortage of rum in the colonies, thus pushing up the price of this popular fluid.

There was worse to come after the war had ended. Global domination, and the defense of America, had been an expensive exercise. The wise heads in Parliament decided that the grateful colonists would leap at the chance to contribute via duty on imported goods. To this end, they introduced a Sugar Act in 1764, which lowered the rate of duty on molasses, but raised the standards of enforcement by entrusting them to the Royal Navy. Any vessel of less than fifty tons "loitering" within six miles of the coast was deemed to be smuggling and therefore fair game for British warships. Moreover, if the charge could be made to stick in a British Admiralty court, shares in the value of the vessel and its contents were awarded to the officers and crew of its captor. This final provision was considered by the colonists as an invitation to Royal Navy captains to arrest any boat they came across, on the off chance that it carried contraband and so constituted a serious threat to their maritime trade.

The Sugar Act contained a further irritation—it imposed a duty on imported wines, including Madeira, the favorite tipple of the wealthier class of planters. Madeira, the Canary Islands, and the Azores had hitherto been important markets for American produce, and the new duty effectively destroyed the trade. Moreover, while the colonists had been promised in compensation that they would be permitted to import direct from Portugal and Spain, the concession had been sabotaged by London wine merchants. In consequence, they were required to pay more for their imported wines, at the same time as being denied direct access to markets for their own goods. By 1764, Franklin was back in London, once again as representative of the Pennsylvania Assembly, with instructions to remedy this injustice. Despite spirited lobbying, and an eloquent series of letters to the press, the British merchants proved to have greater influence in Parliament, and the restrictions remained. Such discrimination rankled the colonists, who were reminded of it every time they raised a glass of Madeira to their lips or stared at the unsold goods in their warehouses.

The importance of the issue is apparent in the 1765 edition of *Poor Richard's Almanac*, in which Franklin's alter ego provided "a few plain Instructions . . . *First,* for making good Wine of our own wild Grapes. *Secondly,* for raising Madeira Wine in [this] Province. *Thirdly,* for the Improvement of our Corn Spirits, so as they may be preferable to

Rum. And this seems very material; for as we raise more Corn than the English West-India Islands can take off, and since we cannot now well sell it to the foreign Islands, what can we do with the Overplus better, than to turn it into Spirit, and thereby lessen the Demand for West-India Rum, which our Grain will not pay for?"

Colonial tempers were further inflamed by passage of the Stamp Act in 1765, which, like the Sugar Act, was intended to defray the expense of the late war by raising revenue in the Americas. According to its provisions, most official and semiofficial documents, including contracts, liquor licenses, newspapers, and calendars were all required to be stamped, at a cost, before issue. Opposition to the act was universal, and sufficient to provoke a demonstration of unity among the colonists. In November 1765, a Stamp Act Congress was convened in New York to protest the legislation. It was attended by the representatives of no fewer than nine colonies, who adopted a *Declaration of Rights and Grievances* against the British crown.

Hell-bent, so it seemed, on alienating its American subjects, the British government followed up the Stamp Act with the Quartering Act of 1765. Under its provisions, British troops stationed in America were to be accommodated in barns, inns, stables, and the houses of dealers in wine and spirits, and provided with rations, including five pints of beer each every day. The cost was to be borne by the colonists. The New York Assembly refused to comply, and its defiance was celebrated with a street party with "a roasted ox, a hogshead of rum, and twenty-five barrels of ale, which were dispensed freely as long as they lasted."

News of disorder in America, and the clear failure of the Sugar and Stamp acts to raise anything like the projected revenues (the Sugar Act cost eight thousand pounds to administer for every two thousand it raised), persuaded the British government to step back from the brink and repeal the latter act in 1766. It was replaced with the Townshend Acts, which imposed duties on a variety of common products imported into America, and which once again left enforcement to the Royal Navy and the Admiralty courts, effectively removing the right to trial by jury for suspected transgressors. The new acts offered little in the way of concessions for the aggrieved colonists. Their author, Charles Townshend, chancellor of the Exchequer in 1767, was "admired for his ability to make a brilliant speech in the Commons when drunk"; and the legislation that carried his name had a certain inebriated optimism, combined with a *muddled* belligerence, which inspired resistance on the far shore of the Atlantic rather than dutiful acquiescence.

Thus far, alcohol had made a significant contribution to the dispute between Britain and its colonies. The destruction of the rum trade, the closure of markets in Madeira, Portugal, and elsewhere to American produce, and the price inflation of alcoholic beverages had affected the lives and incomes of a majority of Americans. However, tame submission to a parliament in which they had no representation, which had no ear for their grievances, and which, whether by design or accident, threatened to ruin their livelihoods held no appeal to them, and they responded by strengthening the ties among themselves via circular letters and by forming associations dedicated to opposing British injustices, such as the *Sons of Liberty*, which had factions in New York, Boston, and, latterly, Georgia.

The Boston chapter of the Sons of Liberty was founded by Samuel Adams, who ran a malting business in Purchase Street. It met either at the Green Dragon Tavern or the Bunch of Grapes in King Street. The Green Dragon, named after a copper dragon over its door that had oxidized in the rain, was a nursery for revolutionaries. The Sons of Liberty who gathered within its rooms refreshed themselves and inspired their defiance with a specially commissioned punch bowl, made by the silversmith and engraver Paul Revere. Known as the Liberty Bowl, it was in itself an act of political subversion. Engraved on one side was the following:

"TO the Memory of the glorious NINETY-TWO: Members of the Hon. House of Representatives of the Massachusetts-Bay, who, undaunted by the insolent Menaces of Villains in Power, from a Strict Regard to Conscience, and the LIBERTIES of their Constituents, on the 30th of June 1768 Voted NOT TO RESCIND."[27] The back of the bowl bore the legend *No. 45 Wilkes & Liberty* and flags displaying the phrases *Magna Charta* and *Bill of Rights*. The bowl had a capacity of forty-five gills of punch and weighed forty-five ounces. The names of various Sons of Liberty were also engraved around its rim.

---

[27] The inscription refers to a circular letter sent by the Massachusetts Council to the other colonies, objecting to the Townshend Acts, which the governor demanded they rescind. "No. 45" refers to the issue number of *The North Briton* in which John Wilkes, the son of a distiller, published an article on abuses of power that led to his trial for treason and made him a hero of sorts in the Americas.

John Hancock was one of the names inscribed on the Liberty Bowl. Born in Braintree, Massachusetts, Hancock was the wealthiest man in New England, and his wealth had come from trade, principally in various alcoholic beverages. In 1768, one of his ships, the aptly named *Liberty,* was impounded in Boston by British officials for smuggling Madeira wines. Under the cover of a riot, her cargo was liberated by thirsty Bostonians, and the officials were forced to flee the town. Such impertinent disregard for His Majesty's laws and representatives provoked the British to send a man-of-war to Boston to ensure that it was not repeated.

News of this exploit and its consequences spread, and in colony after colony associations were formed, protests staged, and direct action was taken, in the form of a boycott on British goods. This was a powerful weapon. There were by now more than two million people in British America, and while they produced a surplus of commodities, they relied on the metropolitan power for their manufactured goods, which likewise relied on their market for its exports. In 1769, the resolve of the colonists to support nonimportation was tested by the arrival in Philadelphia of the *Charming Polly,* a merchant vessel from Yarmouth with a cargo of best British malt. The city's brewers responded with a written pledge, in which they resolved "that as the load of malt just arrived was contrary to the agreement of the merchants and traders they will not purchase any part of it, nor will they brew the same, or any part thereof, for any person whatsoever." At about the same time, in imitation of the Bostonians, the people of the town liberated a cargo of impounded Madeira from its customs.

Virginia likewise resolved to boycott British products—at a considerable cost to its inhabitants. The colony was still a monoculture, and its tobacco planters sold most of their crop to London merchants, to whom many were heavily indebted, and such voluntary restraints on trade only worsened their financial position. However, whereas the British administration at the time was characterized by the incompetence of its leaders, Virginia, in contrast, was graced with a collection of exceptional individuals, including George Washington, the hero of the French and Indian War, Thomas Jefferson, scholar and planter, and Patrick Henry, lawyer and orator. Such able men saw the dispute with Britain as not merely financial but also constitutional, and under their leadership and inspiration, the Virginia House of Burgesses resolved to oppose the metropolitan power. It was dissolved by the royal governor but reconvened (in true colonial style) in Anthony Hay's tavern, to consider what courses future resistance might take. When the House of Burgesses was permitted to assemble again in 1770, one of its first measures was to execute a nonimportation agreement, which was signed by Washington and Henry and which stated "that we will not hereafter, directly or indirectly, import, or cause to be imported, from Great Britain, any of the goods hereafter enumerated . . . beer, ale, porter, malt."

The nonimportation campaign was a success: In April 1770, the Townshend Acts were repealed, and all duties were eliminated except for those on tea. This concession, however, did not diminish the rising tension. In March of the same year, a company of redcoats quartered in Boston opened fire on a crowd who were pelting them with snowballs, killing three. While the soldiers and their commander were tried for murder, all were acquitted of the capital charge, and only two were lightly punished, by the standards of the age, by being branded with a red hot iron. Such lenience rankled and became the subject of numerous pamphlets demonstrating the cruelty and disregard for human rights by the British.

Whereas the rum trade had been one of the principal initial matters of contention between Britain and her colonies, now it was the turn of a nonalcoholic beverage to provoke discord. In May 1773, the Tea Act came into effect, which imposed a duty of three pence per pound on all tea imported into America. This tax was intended to help the British East India Company through a flat patch of low prices, demonstrating once again that a London-based commercial organization carried more political clout than several million subjects on the other side of the Atlantic. Before it was singled out for a special duty, tea had been a popular drink in the colonies. While its arrival earlier in the eighteenth century had been greeted with almost comical ignorance—according to the reminiscences of a Long Island settler, "One family boiled it in a pot and ate it like samp-porridge. Another spread tea-leaves on his bread and butter, and bragged of his having ate half a pound at a meal, to his neighbor, who was informing him how long a pound of tea lasted him"—it had long since become established as a popular beverage.

However, as soon as tea was selected to carry duty, it became a symbol of oppression, and when three East India tea clippers arrived in Boston Harbor, the colonists resolved to take action. Notices were posted through the town:

FRIENDS! BRETHREN! COUNTRYMEN!
That worst of plagues, the detestable tea, shipped for this port by the East India Company, is now arrived in this harbor. The hour of destruction or manly opposition to the machinations of tyranny stares you in the face.

And a new ballad circulated its streets:

> Rally, Mohawks—bring out your axes!
> And tell King George we'll pay no taxes
> On his foreign tea!
> His threats are vain—and vain to think
> To force our girls and wives to drink
> His vile Bohea!
> Then rally, boys, and hasten on
> To meet our Chiefs at the Green Dragon.
> Our Warren's there, and bold Revere,
> With hands to do and words to cheer
> For Liberty and Laws!

On the night of December 16, 1773, the Green Dragon was packed with colonists dressed up as Indians. "Who knows how tea will mingle with salt water?" they asked, as the Liberty Bowl made its rounds. Late that night, in the words of *The Massachusetts Gazette:*

The Indians, as they were then called, repaired to the wharf, where the ships lay that had the tea on board, and were followed by hundreds of people. . . . The Indians immediately repaired on board Capt. Hall's ship, where they hoisted out the chests of tea, and when on deck stove them and emptied the tea overboard. Having cleared this ship, they proceeded to Capt. Bruce's, and then to Capt. Coffin's brig. They applied themselves so dexterously to the destruction of this commodity, that in the space of three hours they broke up three hundred and forty-two chests, which was the whole number in these vessels, and discharged their contents into the dock.

The British countered this outrage with the Coercive Acts of 1774, which closed the port of Boston and filled the town with troops. Various Sons of Liberty, including Paul Revere, were dispatched posthaste to other colonies to inform them of the "rash, impolitic, and vindictive measures of the British Parliament." A congress with representatives from every colony was convened in Philadelphia, where the delegates surprised themselves with a mutual spirit of cooperation. They discovered they were preparing for war and made appropriate resolutions, including one intended to protect the grain supply in the event of fighting and to keep men sober for the same eventuality: *"Resolved, that it be recommended to the several legislatures of the United Colonies immediately to pass laws the more effectually to put a stop to the pernicious practice of distilling, by which the most extensive evils are likely to be derived, if not quickly prevented."* In the event, none of the United Colonies implemented laws to limit distillation. Rum went well with belligerence.

Meanwhile, back in Boston the tension was rising. The British had prohibited the importation of gunpowder and shot into the colonies and were about to send reinforcements to Fort William and Mary in Portsmouth to protect its magazine. Paul Revere made another ride on April 19, 1775, to advise the local Sons of Liberty that the redcoats were on their way. His first stop was with Isaac Hall, captain of the Medford Minute Men, who gave him a quantity of rum that "would have made a rabbit bite a bulldog." Thus inspired, Revere completed his mission. Patriots raided the fort and emptied its powder store before the reinforcements arrived. It was not long before its contents were being used upon the British. In April 1775 the fighting started. The colonial forces were placed by Congress under the command of George Washington. They surrounded the British troops in Boston, where they dug themselves in and impressed their general with their appetite for alcohol. According to an observer at the siege, "Without New England rum, a New England army could not be kept together." The same writer estimated average consumption to be a bottle per head per day.

A supply of alcohol was no less important to the blockaded British, and the news that they were running short on beef and beer, and that their morale was suffering accordingly, was reported to John Adams by his wife, Abigail, who had remained in the town after the siege had commenced. Contracts were drawn up in London for five thousand barrels of strong beer to be shipped to relieve the redcoats, but a number of resupply vessels were taken by American privateers, including one carrying beer from Bristol in November 1775, and, in the same month, a sloop from the West Indies with "Rum, Sugar, and Fruit on board." The capture of the latter was celebrated in a letter from Horatio Gates to Benjamin Franklin; as was the diversion of its cargo to their cause: "So Wine, and Punch will not be wanting to the Sons of Liberty. Let the Sons of Slavery get them how they can."

In March 1776 the British abandoned Boston. In June of the same year, they landed an army in New York, which was to be their base of operations against their rebellious subjects. The subjects, meanwhile, had resolved to end their association with the mother country. Their *Declaration of Independence* was drafted by Thomas Jefferson in a Philadelphia tavern. The first man to sign it, in a large, clear hand, was the merchant and Madeira smuggler John Hancock. Other signatories included a maltster, a cooper, a distiller, several smugglers, and numerous cider makers.

As the war developed, alcohol continued to play its part. Both sides issued drink rations to their troops, and on occasions the overeager consumption of these influenced the outcome of engagements. Washington's first great victory, at Trenton in 1776 over Hessian mercenaries, was assisted by the drunken condition of his adversaries. At the skirmish of Eutaw Springs, in contrast, the Americans drove a British force from its camp, then paused to consume the rum rations they had captured. The redcoats counterattacked when the Americans had "eaten a toad and a half" and carried the field. Despite such evidence that alcohol might impair the efficiency of fighting troops, General Washington was convinced it was essential to them. The "benefits arising from the moderate use of strong Liquor have been experienced in all Armies and are not to be disputed," he counseled Congress in 1777, and recommended that they ignore their prior resolution against distillation and instead erect "Public Distilleries in different States" to ensure security of supply. Four years later he was still of the same opinion: Soldiers needed spirit rations. In 1781, he advised John Hancock, whose business skills had been applied to sourcing provisions and finance for the Continental army, that "wine cannot be distributed [to] the Soldiers instead of Rum, except the quantity is much increased. I very much doubt whether a Gill of rum would not be preferred to a pint of small wine."

Washington's insistence on spirits for soldiers is interesting, for his own tastes in drink were very broad. At home in Virginia he drank rum, punch, Madeira, and other imported wines, which he supplemented with homemade spirits (he had four stills on his estate), cider, and beer. During the conflict he continued to be catholic in his own tastes, while working to ensure that the spirit rations of his men were maintained. A molasses levy was laid on several states; indeed the substance was treated as a strategic raw material. The taste for spirits that Washington imputed to his troops was shared by his subordinate commanders, especially General Israel Putnam, a thickset, lisping illiterate with "a head like a cannonball" and a good candidate for the title of the hardest man in the entire conflict. Wounded several times, yet still contemptuous of bullets, Putnam is recorded as being distressed in battle only once—when "a shot had passed through his canteen and spilt all his rum."

The entry of France into the conflict settled the result in favor of independence. On the principal that my enemy's enemy is my friend, France had been the first country to recognize the new republic and had supplied it with weapons, advisors, and provisions from 1778 onward. In 1781, the intervention of the French fleet compelled the surrender of an encircled British army at Yorktown, Virginia, which proved to be the last major engagement of the War of Independence. The following year the British parliament voted for peace with its former colonies, and the terms were negotiated in Paris with Benjamin Franklin representing America. The contribution of the rum trade to the origin of the conflict, whose resolution was to have momentous consequences for the global balance of power, was later acknowledged by John Adams: "I know not why we should blush to confess that molasses was an essential ingredient in American independence," for "many great events have proceeded from much smaller causes."

The French financial and military aid that had ensured victory in the War of Independence continued after peace was declared, and the management of the relationship between France and America was vital to the survival of the new republic in its early years. Benjamin Franklin performed this delicate task between 1776 and 1785, when he served as America's representative to the royal court. He occupied a villa in Passy and was a favorite of the modish French. An account of the alcohol consumption in his household has survived, which shows an interesting mixture of colonial potations and those of his host nation. The account, in terms of volume, is topped by Madeira, followed by wine, "cherry wine," cider, and pink champagne. English beer also features on it, as do a few token bottles of rum. It shows that Franklin himself continued to prefer the beverages fashionable in his native land to those more readily available among his nation's allies. His tastes may be contrasted with those of Thomas Jefferson, who replaced him.

Jefferson represented America in France between 1785 and 1789. During this stay he showed the keenest interest in French wine, to the exclusion of other kinds of alcoholic beverage. Jefferson had a lifelong interest in establishing viticulture in America, and in 1787 he took a three-month sabbatical that he spent touring the vineyards of France and Italy. Whereas his stated aims for this journey were to heal an injury by taking the waters at the famous spa of Aix-en-Provence, and to spy on Italian rice growing,[28] to judge by his letters, journals, and actions, he also was on a private mission to discover the secrets of French winemaking.

He kept a diary of his travels, which is notable for its fascination with viticulture to the exclusion of most other matters. It contains a few sketches of the local peasantry and their misery, but wine, winemakers, and the vineyards in which they worked their magic are its principal subjects. Jefferson clearly was thinking of where similar vintages to those he tasted on his tour might be produced in his own country, and when a parallel landscape came to mind, he wrote it down. The Champagne district, for example reminded him of "the Elk Hill and Beaver-dam hills of Virginia." Burgundy and Bordeaux received his special attention. He described not just the look but the feel of their soils, the orientation and elevation of their vineyards, recorded how their vines were trained, how much wine they yielded, and what the wine was worth, both in situ and in Paris.

Jefferson demonstrated a keen palate in his journal—he had become a connoisseur of wine, able to detect the potential for greatness in some of the little-known or forgotten vintages he came across on his tour. Near Turin, for example, he tasted a "very singular" "red wine of Nebiule" of which he wrote, "It is about as sweet as the silky Madeira, as astringent on the palate as Bordeaux, and as brisk as Cham-

---

[28] Italy competed with Carolina in the supply of rice to the slave trade.

pagne." He also showed a detailed knowledge of the esoteric system of ranking wines then prevalent in Bordeaux, and his account of its *premier crus* illustrates his methodical approach to his subject:

> Of Red wines, there are four vineyards of the first quality; viz. 1. *Château Margau,* belonging to the Marquis d'Agincourt, who makes about one hundred and fifty tons, of one thousand bottles each.... 2. *La Tour de Segur, en Saint Lambert,* belonging to Monsieur Miresmenil, who makes one hundred and twenty-five tons. 3. *Hautbrion,* belonging two-thirds to M. le Comte de Femelle, ... the other third to the Comte de Toulouse, at Toulouse. The whole is seventy-five tons. 4. *Château de la Fite,* belonging to the President Pichard, at Bordeaux, who makes one hundred and seventy-five tons. The wines of the three first, are not in perfection till four years old.

In Jefferson's absence, the United States had formulated a constitution, a legislature, and an executive, and had selected George Washington as their first president. Jefferson was eager to convert his fellow Americans to his belief that independence in wine production was of strategic importance. To this end, he sent back samples to taste and vine cuttings to plant. His journal records the pleasure he derived from persuading "our President, General Washington, to try a sample of thirty dozen bottles" of sweet white Sauternes, and other American luminaries were likewise consigned large quantities of the best French vintages.

16   WARRA WARRA

Cut yer name across me backbone
Stretch me skin across a drum,
Iron me up to Pinchgut Island
From today to Kingdom Come!
I will eat your Norfolk Dumpling
Like a juicy Spanish plum,
Even dance the Newgate hornpipe,
If you'll only give me rum!

Whereas alcohol had been associated with the struggle for freedom in Britain's former colonies in America, it was to act as an instrument of oppression in the kingdom's newest territories. Defeat in the War of Independence had led to domestic problems in Britain. The country possessed exceptionally severe criminal laws, which mandated capital punishment for such trivial offences as stealing more than ten shillings' worth of goods, kicking London Bridge, and impersonating a Chelsea pensioner. The death sentence might, however, be commuted to one of transportation overseas, and since it could no longer dump its criminals on America, and its jails were overflowing, Britain cast about for a new depository for them abroad. A penal-colony-cum-naval-station was their ideal, and they settled on Das Voltas Bay, on the Skeleton Coast of Southwest Africa, with Australia (which had been explored and claimed for Britain by Captain James Cook in 1770, but which since had been neglected) a very distant second choice. A reconnaissance mission was sent to scout out Das Voltas, which returned with the unwelcome verdict that it was uninhabitable. The only other option to have been considered was Australia, so Australia it was. A fleet of eleven ships was prepared, loaded with officials including Governor Arthur Phillip, a priest, a regiment of marines and their band, livestock, and tools, and 754 convicts; and on May 13, 1787, it was dispatched to the other side of the world.

The fleet stopped three times en route: at the Canary Islands, to stock up on wine, at Rio de Janeiro in Brazil, to take on the local firewater, and at Cape Town, where livestock, seeds, more provisions, more wine, and some vine cuttings were purchased. The vast quantity of alcohol rations carried by the fleet—three years' worth against a two-year supply of food—was an official concession made to the marines, who had insisted that they could not be expected "to survive the hardships" of Australia without a guaranteed supply of booze.

Eight months and one week after leaving England, having completed, in the words of David Collins, a young marine who was to be judge advocate in the new colony, "a voyage which, before it was undertaken, the mind hardly dared venture to contemplate," the fleet dropped anchor in Botany Bay, on the east coast of Australia. This place had been selected on the recommendation of Cook, who had noted its promise as a port in his journal. However, upon inspection, it was found to be unsuitable for settlement. A neighboring location, Port Jackson, a gap in the cliffs Cook had named as he sailed past, was explored and pronounced perfect. Beyond the gap was a deep, protected harbor, with a spring of fresh water, and dry level land for building. On January 26, 1788, the fleet transferred to Port Jackson. The male convicts were disembarked first and set to work clearing bush for a camp. On February 6, the women were allowed ashore. The event was celebrated with the issue of a double ration of rum. An all-night rutting party between the female convicts, the sailors, and the marines ensued—an evil omen for the future influence of alcohol on an innocent continent. As an eyewitness observed of the preliminaries to the birth of a nation: "It is beyond my abilities to give a just description of the scene of debauchery and riot that ensued during the night."

The morning after was equally appalling. The firewater that the fleet had taken on in Rio gave crushing hangovers. According to a marine officer: "That [Brazilians] have not learned the art of making palatable rum ... the English troops in New South Wales can bear testimony." Unpleasant as it was, the daily aguardiente ration—"half a pint of vile Rio spirits, so offensive in both taste & smell that he must be fond of drinking indeed that can use it"–was cherished by the marines as the single difference in rations between themselves and the convicts. Indeed, for the first precarious years of the penal colony's existence, a rum allowance, as much as a uniform, was the sign of a free man.

In time, a second and a third fleet arrived from Britain, which carried free settlers as well as convicts, the New South Wales Corps who were to replace the marines as guardians of the colony, and plentiful quantities of alcohol. Stocks were further increased by supply ships from Bengal and Cape Town. By 1792, sufficient amounts of booze had been landed for the authorities to decide to conduct an experiment. A license to sell porter was issued, the beverage in question to be taken from the cargo of the *Royal Admiral*. Although only free settlers were allowed to buy it, and only porter was allowed to be sold, "under the cover of this, spirits found their way among the[m], and much intoxication was the consequence. Several of the settlers, breaking out from the restraint to which they had been subject, conducted themselves with the greatest impropriety, beating their wives, destroying their stock, trampling on and injuring their crops in the ground, and destroying each other's property."

While the porter experiment was not quickly repeated, alcohol continued to reach both the settlers and convicts. Fresh supplies kept sailing into Sydney Cove, some from the most unlikely sources. On November 1, 1792, an American ship, the *Philadelphia*, dropped her anchor. Her intrepid owner, Captain Patrickson, had heard from a homebound British supply ship he'd met in Cape Town that the colony in New South Wales paid exorbitant prices for everything, and so had sailed five thousand miles from Africa to Australia with his cargo of American trade goods on spec. His wares were perfect for Australia: "American beef, wine, rum, gin, some tobacco, pitch, and tar." Captain Patrickson had made his enterprising voyage with only thirteen hands, one of whom he'd lost overboard en route. As if to prove it had been no miracle, the following month another Yankee trader put in "the *Hope,* commanded by a Mr. Benjamin Page, from Rhode Island, with a small cargo of provisions and spirits for sale."

Both Americans made handsome profits on their stock, which the military and civil officers of the colony were permitted to purchase for their own use. However, from such nominally responsible owners, "the American spirit . . . by some means or other found its way among the convicts; and, a discreet use of it being wholly out of the question with those people, intoxication was become common among them." Moreover, all the drink sloshing round New South Wales had a perceptible effect on the behavior of its free inhabitants. The familiar 2-Rabbit traits appeared among them, and in 1793 the first drink-related deaths were recorded. Eleanor McCave, her infant child, and "a woman of the name of Green" were drowned in the harbor, after spending all day "drinking and reveling" in Sydney. They were followed to the grave by James Hatfield, "a man who had been looked upon as a sober good character," but who had been waylaid by friends en route from his farm to Sydney, and "partaking intemperately of the American rum, he was seized with a dysentery, which carried him off in a few days." Alcohol claimed a third victim the next month, when the body of John Richards, a settler from Parramatta, was discovered, and an autopsy determined that he had killed himself with rum.

This spate of casualties, and other drink-related disorders, were perceived of as unhappy accidents, to which the authorities responded with appropriate rigor. Convicts who tried to trade for alcohol with the soldiers who guarded them were to be flogged. A licensing system was introduced for the free settlers, and any who attempted "to sell liquor without a licence were to have their stock seized, and their houses pulled down." Notwithstanding such strict limitations on who might buy, sell, or consume alcohol, a free market of sorts in it developed, and in December 1793, a selection of drinks appeared on the official record of market prices in Sydney for the first time:

> WINE–SPIRITS–PORTER
> Jamaica rum per gallon from £1 to £1 8s
> Rum (American) from 16s per gall to £1
> Coniac brandy per gallon from £1 to £1 4s
> Cape brandy per gallon from 16s to £1
> Cherry brandy per dozen £3 12s
> Wine (Cape Madeira) per gallon 12s
> Porter per gallon from 4s to 6s

The prices, allowing for the cost and risk of transport to the colony, were expensive but not ruinous. A gallon of American rum every now and then was within the purses of most settlers, and they used it not only to refresh themselves but to purchase the labor of convicts. The convicts were permitted to offer themselves for work under a "free time" system that had been introduced in 1789–91, when a reduced food allowance had been thought inadequate to maintain them through a full day's worth of punishment, and so they had been given part of each afternoon off to grow their own food. When the ration was restored, the free time remained, which the convicts usually spent in working for reward–preferably rum: "The passion for liquor was so predominant among the people, that it operated like a mania, there being nothing which they would not risk to obtain it: And while spirits were to be had, those who did any extra labor refused to be paid in money, or any other article than spirits."

Widespread intoxication persuaded the new governor, John Hunter, to revise the licensing system. If people had access to legal drinking places–somewhere they might go for a pint or two at the end of each day–they might rein in their drunkenness. Ten men were granted licenses, including James Larra, a French convict who had been transported for stealing a tankard from an alehouse while visiting London, and who had been emancipated the prior year. In 1796, Larra opened Australia's first legal pub, the Masons Arms in Parramatta. In addition to a variety of spirits, he sold imported porter, Madeira, and quite possibly Australian brewed beer. This last beverage was being produced not far away by a Mr. Boston. It was made from "Indian corn, properly malted, and bittered with the leaves and stalks of the love-apple." Despite such unusual ingredients, it was reported that "Mr. Boston found this succeeded so well, that he erected at some expense a building proper for the business."

Unfortunately, instead of responding to the introduction of pubs by drinking moderately, the settlers persisted in indulging themselves "in inebriety and idleness, and robberies." These problems were compounded by the rising price of imported drinks, despite a steady and increasing supply; and drunken convicts left, right, and center, despite the official impossibility of them obtaining alcohol. And the government had been frustrated whenever it tried to solve these conundrums. It was as if a vast conspiracy was at work, which indeed there was.

From the instant of their arrival, the New South Wales Corps had been aware of the extraordinary thirst for alcohol in the colony, and the lengths to which its settlers and convicts would go to get hold of it. Little by little, they had exerted control over the importation and distribution of alcohol in Australia, until they had a monopoly. This process had begun in 1792, when the first governor had returned to Britain, and was completed over the next three years while the colony was administered by Major Francis Grose of the New South Wales Corps. During this period, he and his military colleagues purchased all spirits landed in the colony and chartered boats to bring in more. They started by selling cheap, to fuel demand, then raised prices step by step, until drink was the most valuable thing in New South Wales. By 1795, when Governor Hunter had arrived from Britain, alcohol had become the "recognized medium of exchange. So much so, that even labor could only be purchased with spirits."

In addition to monopolizing the supply of alcohol, the NSW Corps also established control over the workforce. The convicts, as part of their punishment, were required to do hard labor, in theory on farmland and public buildings. They might also be assigned to free settlers and emancipated convicts to help them hew homesteads out of the bush. However, during Grose's tenure as acting governor, they were assigned, almost exclusively, to members of his regiment. "Convict servants were lavishly bestowed, not only upon commissioned officers of the Corps, but also upon sergeants, corporals, and drummers, until scarcely a score of unengaged men remained for any public purposes."

The conflict of interest between public duty and private gain, which would not have been possible in most British regiments, did not trouble the New South Wales Corps. It was hardly an elite unit. Its ranks contained "deserters from other regiments brought from the Savoy" and, horror of horrors, a mutineer; its officers were "old tailors and shoe-makers, stay makers, man-milliners, tobacconists, and pedlars" who made their fortunes in the colony by "extortion and oppression." The extortion and oppression was made the subject of a formal agreement in 1797 when "a combination band was entered into" by the New South Wales Corps, under which they were "neither to underbuy nor undersell each other." It was at about this time that the corps acquired the nickname by which it is known to history—the "Rum Regiment"—an ironic tribute to its status as sole supplier to the colony it was intended to protect. Governor Hunter, to his intense annoyance, found that his power was slight compared with that of the Rum Regiment, who had succeeded in turning a penal colony run on martial lines into a drunken and anarchic hellhole—a sort of Gin Lane by Sea.

Hunter had a particular bête noir among the officers of the rum regiment, Captain John Macarthur, who had been given command of the settlement at Parramatta and who had abused his position of trust comprehensively–buying land, assigning himself convicts to clear and farm it, and paying them with spirits at a 500 percent markup. By the turn of the nineteenth century Macarthur was a wealthy man. He was also a brilliant politician, and as his power grew in New South Wales, he set about undermining that of the governor via a stream of letters to his increasing range of commercial contacts in the City of London. His success can be gauged by Hunter's short tenure–he retired in 1800, an embittered man, and was replaced by Philip King, who had no more success bringing the Rum Regiment to heel than his predecessor.

King began determined to assert his authority and sent Macarthur to Britain to be court-martialed. Unfortunately for King, Macarthur turned out to have the greater influence in the metropolis. He was acquitted and returned to Sydney in 1805 in his own ship, the *Argos,* which bore a golden fleece as its figurehead. Not only had Macarthur been exonerated by the court, but he had also received a land grant of five thousand acres on which to graze the prize merino stud rams he had bought while on trial. The potential of Australia for sheep had aroused more interest among the great and the good in London than any other news from New South Wales. The need for wool was dire in Britain, which was locked in war with Napoleonic France and had lost access to its traditional suppliers in continental Europe. The fact that much of the evidence against Macarthur, including Governor King's report, had been stolen en route between Australia and Britain was overlooked, in favor of the possibility that he might be the man to turn the new colony into a giant "sheep walk."

As well as rewarding Macarthur for his faith in sheep, London decided to remove Governor King, who clearly did not have the measure of his colonists, and to replace him with one of its best sea captains. The man they chose had sailed with Captain Cook, had received the personal thanks of Admiral Nelson for his gallantry during the battle of Copenhagen; had performed one of the greatest feats of navigation of the age, in piloting an open boat 3,618 miles across the open Pacific, and had successfully transported breadfruit from Tahiti to the Caribbean, where it now served as a cheap staple for slaves. Captain William Bligh was fifty-two when he landed in Sydney to take control of New South Wales. He was armed with instructions to clean up the colony, for the complaints of two embittered ex-governors had carried some weight in Whitehall, and while the British were happy to encourage sheep walks, they were also genuinely concerned that their penal colony was full of vice. High on the list of vices to be eradicated was drunkenness. Clause eight of his instructions required Bligh to ensure that no spirits were landed in the colony without his consent.

Once he had had time to form an impression of New South Wales, Bligh wrote to London, setting out the situation as he had found it and his policy for improving the place. He felt that drink was the key issue—the mother of all vices. Booze was the unofficial currency, and its use "as an article of barter had added to its pernicious effects ... beyond all conception." Prices and wages in the colony had become hopelessly skewed because of alcohol: "A sawyer will cut one hundred feet of timber for a bottle of spirits, value 2/6d., which he drinks in a few hours; when for the same labor he would charge two bushels of wheat which would furnish bread for him for two months; hence those who have got no liquor[29] to pay their laborers with, are ruined by paying more than they can profitably afford for any kind of labor ... while those who have liquor gain an immense advantage."

In addition to the evidence of his eyes, Bligh had been presented on arrival with a report on the moral welfare of the colony, prepared by its chaplain, the Reverend Samuel Marsden. Marsden had little good to report of his flock, whom he characterized as depraved and libidinous inebriates. He drew particular attention to the plight of the children born in New South Wales. According to his statistics, the population consisted of 7,000 inhabitants, of whom 395 were married women and 1,035 were concubines. Of a total of 1,832 native-born children, 1,025 were illegitimate. Moreover, there was little available in the way of schooling, and the offspring of convicts tended to reveal their bad blood at an early age. Indeed, intoxicated children had become a feature of Sydney's mud streets.

Bligh developed a five-point plan to revive the penal spirit in New South Wales and to rescue its free settlers from themselves. The extermination of all clandestine trade in alcohol was his first priority. He made rapid progress, and by October 1807 he felt able to report to

[29] I.e., everyone except the Rum Regiment.

London that the barter of rum had been abolished and that sterling had been reestablished as the currency of the colony. In a private letter home he confided that "this sink of iniquity Sydney, is improving in its manners and its concerns." However, a blow struck at rum was not one that the regiment that bore its name was ready to take without retaliation. According to Macarthur, the colony had "become a perfect hell" and the Rum Regiment was "galloping into a state of warfare with the governor." He and his associates decided to engage Bligh where they knew him to be most vulnerable—in the law courts. Bligh was nervous of courts. Sixteen years before he had been subjected to a level of official scrutiny, and public fascination, that few men of his time had had to face. The notorious mutiny that had occurred on HMS *Bounty* when she was under his command had been examined by the Admiralty, sensationalized in the press, and commemorated in poetry, and while Bligh had been exonerated, the stigma of having been on trial in the first place remained.

Testing the authority of Bligh in court not only served the useful purpose of awakening bad memories in the man, it also placed him in a forum where he could not win. The new judge advocate, Richard Atkins, had long been corrupted by the Rum Regiment. By all accounts he was a very public drunk, who committed some spectacular injustices while performing his official duties. He is reported to have sentenced people to death while himself so intoxicated that he could not stand up unaided, and was often too drunk to be able to speak. Bligh considered Atkins to be a "disgrace to human jurisprudence" and had written several letters to Britain requesting a replacement.

The challenge was thrown down to Bligh in October 1807, when Macarthur launched a lawsuit against Robert Campbell, an officer appointed by Bligh to control imports. Macarthur claimed Campbell had illegally seized two copper spirits stills that he was trying to ship into New South Wales. Moreover, not only had Campbell the temerity to detain the stills, but when Macarthur had arranged for the extraction of their boilers from government guard, claiming that they had been packed with medicines, for which he had an urgent need, Campbell had insisted that they be returned. On the face of it the case was absurd: Bligh, as governor, had prohibited the importation of stills, period; and his subordinate had been doing no more than his duty.

The court found, by a majority, the casting vote being delivered by Atkins, in favor of Macarthur. In retrospect, the Rum Regiment and its allies were providing a wonderfully clear message to Bligh—that the courts were utterly corrupt. Another legal challenge to his authority, once again an especially flagrant contravention of the law, was mounted in December 1807. A ship owned by Macarthur had been arrested for exporting a runaway convict. This was an offense of the utmost seriousness—the penal colony was intended to be secure, and shipowners were required to post bonds with the government, which were confiscated if it was proven that they had assisted a convict to escape Australia. Macarthur petitioned to have his bond returned and refused to attend court when requested. He was arrested and charged with sedition.

Events thereafter moved quickly. On January 24, 1808, the New South Wales Corps held a regimental dinner. Its purpose was to rally the troops so that "when heated by wine" they would be encouraged to make "a unanimous resolution of possessing themselves of the administration of the country," i.e., to stage a coup. Thirty-six hours later, on the twentieth anniversary of the foundation of the colony, The New South Wales Corps took part in its only military engagement. While success was complete, the action was hardly glorious—it consisted of the arrest of Bligh in Government House at bayonet point, followed by a celebratory debauch lasting throughout the night. Free drink was handed out to the victorious soldiers, effigies of Bligh were burned in the streets, sheep were roasted, "and those scenes of riot, tumult, and insubordination that are ever incident to the subversion of legitimate government and authority ensued. Macarthur, the hero of the day, paraded the streets, in the most publick parts of which he was always conspicuous."

Bold as they were, the members of the Rum Regiment and their associates did not follow the example of the American colonists and declare independence. They were and knew themselves to be a very privileged minority, who had prospered by exploiting the colonial system and their distance from its center. A free land of equal rights was not at all to their tastes. Once they had Bligh under lock and key they set about justifying their rebellion. Major George Johnston of the rum corps, Bligh's designated successor in the event of his death or absence, was installed as governor. A petition was prepared setting out the reasons for deposing Bligh. It claimed he had been a despot to rival Attila and reveled in commanding the infliction of corporal punishment. As soon as the rebels had knocked their apologia into shape,

Macarthur volunteered to take it to Great Britain and to serve there as a delegate of the leading colonists. He was going anyway–the charge of sedition had already been posted, and the best way to demonstrate innocence was to be present to answer it. Meanwhile, all the old abuses were revived. The Rum Regiment resumed its monopoly on imported spirits, to the distress of the free settlers: "They obtain *Spirits* to what Amount they please, which they sell from five Hundred to a Thousand Per cent for Grain to the unthinking Settlers who have been deprived of procuring a single Drop by any other Channel, since the unfortunate day of the unjust Arrest of His Excellency Governor Bligh."

Such was the time taken for news to travel between New South Wales and London that the second reign of the Rum Regiment endured for nearly two years. Aware that they would have to answer for their actions, they took care to maintain protocol and the semblance of order. In the middle of 1808, Johnston gave way as governor to Joseph Foveaux, technically his superior, who had been away establishing a rule of terror in Norfolk Island at the time of the putsch. Foveaux marked his command by distributing cattle from the government herds among his friends and composing slanderous letters about Bligh to send to Britain. In 1809 Foveaux passed on the command of the colony to another rum corps officer, William Paterson, who was inebriated "the greatest part of his time; so that, from imbecility when sober and stupidity when drunk," he was "a very convenient tool in the hands of Macarthur, or of Foveaux." Under the care of this debauched creature, the colony became a parody of the well-disciplined penal settlement that it was supposed to be. A sketch of prevailing conditions and attitudes appears in a letter of Sir Henry Brown Hayes, an Irish baronet transported for abducting an heiress, who led a comfortable exile on the Vaucluse Estate.[30] According to Sir Henry, "forty thousand gallons of spirits ... were given away to the civil and military officers since Bligh had been deposed, and not anything to the peaceable, industrious individual.... Paterson gets drunk at Government

---

[30] Vaucluse was reputed to have been infested with snakes before Sir Henry took possession and drove them away: He imported five hundred barrels of Irish bog, which was dug into trenches around the perimeter of his property, and which kept all serpents, in obedience to St. Patrick's valediction, off the land they enclosed.

House at Parramatta, and Foveaux is left at Sydney to do as he likes, and he gives pardons, grants, and leases to the whores and greatest thieves. . . . Oh, it has been charming times! . . . Hang half this worthy set and it would be justice, for they have been the greatest robbers."

The idyll that the drink monopoly had generated for the monopolists could not persist. News that Bligh had been deposed had reached London, had been pondered over, and action had been taken. To have one mutiny could be construed as an accident, but two was a record. A new governor, Lachlan Macquarie, accompanied by a pair of British warships, was sent to replace Bligh and restore order. He arrived in December 1809, by which time both Bligh and Macarthur, the principal actors in the drama, had left the stage, Bligh on a naval vessel to Tasmania, where he plotted a countercoup, and Macarthur to London, to explain himself in court.

The new governor was quick to make his mark. The liquor trade was brought under his control and a fair market created. Sunday closing was introduced for taverns to ensure settlers gave their livers a rest on the Sabbath. A number of the ringleaders of the rum mutiny were prosecuted. Instead of working the estates of the officers of the Rum Regiment, convicts were assigned to the deserving smaller settlers, and to serve Macquarie's mania for monumental architecture. During his tenure, Sydney received its earliest public buildings, the first of which was the so-called Rum Hospital. Built in the Georgian style, with Indian touches, it was financed by the grant of a temporary spirits monopoly to its contractors, who were given the exclusive right to sell forty-five thousand gallons of liquor and to receive the proceeds tax free as reward for their labor. Once their funds had been raised, the market set the price for alcohol, and the same bottle of spirits that had sold for twenty shillings in 1808 cost two shillings by the end of Macquarie's tenure in 1821. Once the anxiety over supply had been removed, drinking habits changed. Indeed excessive drinking came to be associated with bad times past—a part of their history ex-convicts wanted to forget. The increased size of the colony was a further stimulus to moderation. Settlers had spread more than a hundred miles from Sydney, over the Blue Mountains and into the virgin bush. It was not possible to visit a tavern every morning in such remote places, nor was it practical to carry kegs of porter on horseback to outlying stations. Their residents learned to ration themselves to a glass or so of rum a day.

The rising generation in Sydney and Parramatta drank beer. Australian brewing had progressed from maize and love-apples to barley malt and hops. Hops first had been cultivated in the colony by James Squire, an emancipated convict, in 1805, and he had been rewarded for his efforts with the gift of a cow from Governor King. The following year he opened a brewery and the *Malt Shovel Tavern* at Kissing Point on the Parramatta River. His pioneering efforts with Australian beer were recorded on his tombstone, and its effects on the drinker inscribed on another nearby, in an early testament to the black humor that has since become a characteristic of Australians:

YE WHO WISH TO LIE HERE DRINK SQUIRE'S BEER

By the 1820s New South Wales was also producing wine. The prime mover was no less than the "great perturbator" John Macarthur, who returned to his sixty-thousand-acre estate from his long exile in London in 1816. Prior to leaving Europe, Macarthur made a trip to France, where he inspected vineyards and collected vines; on the journey back to Australia he had also picked up more vines in Madeira and Cape Town. Although no record of the quality of the wines he produced exists, he built a substantial winery whose ruins still grace the grounds of his palatial home. Wine was also produced by Gregory Blaxland, a settler famous for discovering a route through the Blue Mountains, which hitherto had acted as a barrier to expansion inland. His product—a red wine fortified with brandy—was of sufficient merit to be exported to London, where it was awarded silver (1822) and gold (1828) medals by the Royal Society of Art.

The spirit of intoxication, however, had remained in the land. Exorcised by the Christian immigrants, it now possessed the remnants of the aboriginal tribes of New South Wales. Ab initio, contact between the colonists and aboriginals had been characterized by distrust and violence. Unlike natives on other continents, the aboriginals had displayed little curiosity about Europeans. They did not want to sell their possessions or their women for mirrors or beads. Their first words to the first fleet were "Warra, warra"—"go away." When they were offered alcoholic drinks to taste they spat them out. Their indifference to booze was confirmed when the colonists decided to kidnap some aboriginals, in the hope that these might be tamed to their ways and so as act as ambassadors between the settlers and the tribes.

Accordingly, in 1790, Governor Phillip sent a party of marines to capture some natives. A group of aboriginals was ambushed on a beach and the marines managed to secure one of them. Their hostage was taken to Sydney, washed, shaved, shown a print of Her Royal Highness, the Duchess of Cumberland, and named Manly. He attended dinner at government house on New Year's Eve, where he was taught how to use a napkin. His appetite was observed with the keenest attention. He ate "heartily" of fish and pork, tried to throw his plate out the window when he had finished, but steered clear of the wine. This dislike persisted, even when he trusted his captors enough to reveal to them his name—Arabanoo—and to accustom himself to a British diet: "Bread he began to relish; and tea he drank with avidity: [But] strong liquors he would never taste, turning from them with disgust and abhorrence."

But Arabanoo kept trying to run away. He burst into tears when he was allowed to see his friends from a distance and, unless distracted by the settlers' children, whom he loved, usually was melancholy. A year later he died of smallpox. The colonists replaced him shortly afterward with a pair of orphans, whose parents had perished in the same epidemic. However, these infants did not suit their purpose of acting as a bridge between themselves and the aboriginals, and it was resolved to try and catch some more. Lieutenant Bradley was entrusted with this diplomatic mission "and completely succeeded in trepanning and carrying off, without opposition, two fine young men, who were safely landed among us at Sydney." These were Bennelong and Colbee. Colbee ran away within a week, but Bennelong seemed determined to look on the bright side of captivity: "Though haughty, [he] knew how to temporize. He quickly threw off all reserve; and pretended, nay, at particular moments, perhaps felt satisfaction in his new state. Unlike poor Arabanoo, he became at once fond of our viands, and would drink the strongest liquors, not simply without reluctance, but with eager marks of delight and enjoyment. He was the only native we ever knew who immediately shewed a fondness for spirits: Colbee would not at first touch them."

Bennelong was rewarded for his temporizing with a trip to Great Britain. He accompanied Governor Phillip home, spent several years in

London, where he was taken to a proper tailor, then was sent back to New South Wales with a medal as a keepsake. He died at the handsome old age, according to the best estimates at the time, of forty-one, diseased, crippled, and an alcoholic. Upon his return from Britain, despite his new wardrobe, he was seen to have lost prestige among his fellows. His wife had run off, and he was defeated in the fight to get her back. The injuries he sustained during this combat never properly healed, and it was noted as he drank himself to death that he seemed to be stricken by anomie. He set a precedent that was soon followed by other aboriginals. Long disdainful of alcohol, as epidemics and conflict reduced their numbers, they turned to the drug as a last resort—a final degradation. Like the convicts, they drank to forget; unlike the convicts, they had no other place to remember in their cups. The forests where they had hunted had been cut down and plowed over; the shoreline where they gathered oysters had been covered in wharves. The land could not support both sheep and aboriginals, so these latter were killed, or died of hunger, or drifted into towns.

17   WHISKEY WITH AN *E*

How solemn and beautiful is the thought, that the
earliest pioneer of civilization, the van leader of
civilization, is never the steamboat, never the
railway, never the newspaper, never the Sabbath-
school, never the missionary—but always whiskey!

—Mark Twain

During the same years that the Rum Regiment was establishing
control over the British penal colony in Australia by manipulating
the supply of alcohol, the United States of America also experienced a challenge to the rule of law, which likewise derived from
drink. In 1794, settlers in western Pennsylvania formed a rebel band
named the *Whiskey Boys* and commenced an insurrection against the
federal government. Their cause of war was an excise on domestic
spirits, which had been imposed in 1791 and which was considered on
the western edge of the United States to be unequal, immoral, and
"dangerous to liberty." That freedom from British rule, so recently
won, should not be considered liberty enough, was a matter of serious
concern in Philadelphia, then the capital city of the United States. At
stake was the power of the federal government to tax its citizens—even
if the taxes it chose to impose were not so very different from those
that had been the cause for war with Britain. President Washington
responded to news of the revolt by mobilizing a militia army of thirteen thousand.

In order to understand how a constitutional crisis of such magnitude
had arisen in the new country so quickly, it is necessary to examine the

importance of whiskey to its citizens, especially those on the western fringes of the nation. In the decades prior to independence, and ever since, immigrants had been pushing inland, over the Allegheny Mountains, which had formed a notional border between British colonial limits and land reserved for Native Americans. A high percentage of these settlers were Scottish Irish, to whom free land and no taxes seemed a recipe for paradise, and the inconvenient presence of a few murderous indigenous tribes no worse than what they had left behind. Unlike most immigrants, who acclimatized themselves to their new homeland in its towns or in settled parts of the countryside, the Scots-Irish headed west, toward the interior of the continent, beyond government, where they might live as they wished, in as close to a state of independence as was possible. Their formula for this idyll included self-sufficiency in ammunition (the discovery of "an exceedingly valuable lead mine" south of the Green River was much feted in Virginia), and whiskey.

The art of distilling the water of life was a part of the heritage of the Scotch Irish, and this ancestral solace was prepared wherever they settled. In emergencies, a Scotch Irish could make whiskey using only corn, water, fire, a kettle, and a wet towel. The Wilderness Road, the northern route over the Alleghenies from Virginia, had whiskey for sale at strategic points along its length when it was little more than a path through the forests. In 1775, William Calk, a Virginian moving to what was to become Kentucky, noted its ubiquity in his journal: "Wedn. 22nd we Start early and git to foart Chissel whear we git Some good loaf Bread & good Whiskey." There was also good whiskey to be found upon arrival. In the same year that Calk set out, corn was being grown around the fledgling town of Boonesborough and converted into spirits. Whiskey had great practical advantages on the frontier. It was more valuable, easier to carry, and less likely to spoil than the grain from which it had been made. It also was freely convertible—whiskey could be exchanged for other commodities, for land, for weapons, labor, food, and for luxuries. In consequence, much of the farmland hacked out of the wilderness was planted with grain to produce whiskey, rather than bread.

In the early days of settlement, stills were the largest, most complex, and most valuable man-made objects to be carried over the mountains. A still literally made money. People even traded slaves for them. A 1788 advertisement in the *Lexington Gazette* (by then a town of nearly a thousand souls) offered "a likely young Negroe" man, in exchange for "two copper stills one of about eighty gallons the other about forty gallons." When it was discovered that Kentucky was a heaven for horses, stud fees were also priced in "corn juice." For instance, according to the *Lexington Gazette* of March 17, 1792, the covering charge for "the celebrated swift horse, Ferguson's Gray" was nine shillings' worth of whiskey.

Not only was whiskey ubiquitous in the western settlements, it was considered to be a sacred substance that no democratic government should contaminate with taxation. The Scotch Irish had a history of evading excise in their place of origin, and they intended to continue to do so in the Americas. Indeed, it would have been hard to conceive of a more unpopular way to raise money in the West than a tax on whiskey, which served there as cash, savings, refreshment, and heritage. Many Americans in other states, in particular in the South, felt the same way, and when an excise bill, proposing just such a measure, was introduced into Congress in January 1791, it aroused a storm of protest. The only body of people in America to give it full hearted support was the Philadelphia College of Physicians, which petitioned Congress to tax spirits as hard as they could, on the grounds that they were bad for the health. The bill, and the College of Physicians, met with furious opposition in the House. James Jackson of Georgia described the proposed excise as "odious, unequal, unpopular, and oppressive." The physicians, moreover, were paranoid busybodies who next would want a law "interdicting the use of catsup, because some ignorant persons had been poisoned by eating mushrooms."[31] Representative Parker of Virginia assaulted the proposed tax with classical imagery. It would, he predicted, "let loose a swarm of harpies, who, under the denomination of revenue officers, will range through the country, prying into every man's house and affairs, and like a Macedonian phalanx bear down all before them."

Despite such spirited resistance, the bill was passed on January 27, 1791, and sent to the Senate, where its opponents labeled it an outrage. Its declared purpose was to raise funds for a navy to fight Islamic nations in the distant Mediterranean, which Senator William Maclay of Pennsylvania believed to be spurious: "The trifling affair of our having eleven captives at Algiers . . . is made the pretext for going to war . . .

---

[31] Eighteenth-century catsup was made from mushrooms, not tomatoes.

and fitting out a fleet." If the government was allowed to fill its coffers with excise dollars, who knew what it would attempt next, whether abroad or at home? "Farewell freedom in America," he concluded.

In the event the bill was carried by the unanimous support of the northern states (southern senators voted thirteen to five against it), the country was divided into districts along state lines, and excisemen were appointed, who received a salary and a small percentage of the revenue that they were to collect. The excise was set at between nine and twenty-five cents a gallon, depending on the strength of the whiskey produced, for urban distilleries, and nine cents a gallon for rural stills. When news of this despotic piece of legislation reached the western fringes of American settlement, the people, as their representatives had predicted, were incandescent. A measure of their rage is provided by a contemporary observation that "a breath in favor of the law, was sufficient to ruin any man.... A clergyman was not thought orthodox in the pulpit, unless against the law: A physician was not capable of administering medicine, unless his principles were right in this respect."

When the excisemen appointed in accordance with the new law attempted to exercise their powers in the fall of 1791, they met with a hostile reception. On September 1, Robert Johnson, collector for Washington and Allegheny counties in Pennsylvania, was attacked by sixteen men dressed as women who gave him a symbolic scalping and a layer of tar and feathers. Other collectors received similar welcomes, and very little excise gathering was done over the next two years, during which anger grew against a government that had presumed to tax "We, the People." Discontent was encouraged by the appearance, in January 1793, of Edmond-Charles Genêt, an emissary from revolutionary France. A "dwarfish, dumpy man with dark red hair, coarse features, and a huge mouth from which issued forth a constant stream of passionate oratory in seven languages," Genêt challenged Americans to overthrow their king, guillotine their aristocracy, and murder their tax gatherers. The irrelevant parts of his message were overlooked, his enthusiasm was admired, and the South and western portions of the United States were seized with a bout of Francophilia. Whole towns, stirred by the *partisan* spirit, staged lengthy binges, with bonfires, and whiskey-fueled speeches in favor of liberty from the despots in Philadelphia. President Washington was furious with Genêt: "Is the minister of the French republic to set the

Acts of this Government at defiance, with impunity, and threaten the executive with an appeal to the people?" In the event, he might have spared his anger. Revolutionary France kept on revolting in Genêt's absence, and he was forced to beg asylum in America after his own faction at home was displaced and guillotined.

Genêt married an American heiress and spent the rest of his life as a model citizen. However, the spirit of contention he had encouraged kept on growing. "Democratic clubs" flourished in the backcountry, whose purpose was to oppose anything beyond the bare minimum of government, and any form of taxes at all. The petitions they sent to Congress caused dismay. The United States would fall apart if people rejected a federal power of raising money. Republican newspapers set about vilifying democratic clubs. According, for example, to *The Virginia Chronicle* of July 17, 1794, the local democratic club was a "horrible sink of treason," a "hateful synagogue of anarchy," an "odious conclave of tumult," a "frightful cathedral of discord," a "poisonous garden of conspiracy," and a "hellish school of rebellion and opposition to all regular and well balanced authority." Fearing, perhaps, that hyperbolic abuse might not be enough to convince its readers that democratic clubs were evil, the *Chronicle* appealed to their reason: "Here then is the source from whence all your sedition flows, and until those crotalophorus and ostentiferous institutions are disconcantinated—and the individuals who compose them experience a decollation, their querulous bombilations and debulitions will never cease to obnubilate the prospects of their superiors."

Despite such rebukes, crotalophorus democratic societies increased in number, and the predicted obnubilation over taxes on distillation continued apace. The Excise Act, meanwhile, had begun to divide communities. Some of the larger distillers, especially those with contracts to supply the army, had started to pay their taxes, which inspired opponents of the excise to extend their direct action beyond the people who enforced the act to those traitors who complied with it. Distillers who paid up were tarred and feathered or had their stills shot full of holes. This latter exercise was referred to as "mending" a still, and the marksmen who effected this style of repair adopted a nom de guerre—*Tom the Tinker*. When not occupied in fixing copper vessels, Tom wrote letters to the press in favor of a continuing revolution in the French style.

The volatile mood that prevailed in western Pennsylvania exploded into violence in July 1794, when federal officials were told to collect the excise tax and to serve writs on those distillers who had refused to pay. It was harvest time, and most of the countrymen were engaged in reaping, so that some writs were served in the fields to men surrounded by their families, neighbors, and friends. Such high-handed treatment, reminiscent of feudal Europe, was intolerable to the harvesters, who composed themselves into armed bands and marched on the home of General Neville, the exciseman for Allegheny, Washington, Fayette, Westmoreland, and Bedford counties. They attacked, he killed a pair of them and drove them off, and thus began the *Whiskey Rebellion.*

Instead of returning in peace to their fields, the harvesters sent out riders to gather support, and by the following day they numbered over five hundred. From this point onward, they are known to history as the *Whiskey Boys,* and their first collective act was to renew their attack on Neville. They burned his house and its barns and slave quarters to the ground and, true to their new name, emptied the general's cellar and drank its contents prior to putting the house to the torch. News of this outrage, or brave democratic act, spread through the countryside. Opponents of the excise hastened to join the Whiskey Boys at an assembly in Braddock's Field, close to Pittsburgh, and debated what course of action to pursue. They robbed the mail to find out what news of their disobedience was being spread and decided to march on Pittsburgh, which was the principal metropolis in the region. The rebels formed a line two and a half miles long, for by now there were at least five thousand of them. Once they had reached their objective, which capitulated without a shot being fired, they stood down and set to drinking. The residents of Pittsburgh supplied them with whiskey, gratis. Hugh Brackenridge, editor of *The Pittsburgh Gazette,* explained the reasoning behind such largesse: "I thought it better to be employed in extinguishing the fire of their thirst, than of my house."

So far so good seems to have been the conclusion of the Whiskey Boys, who elected a council and debated their next steps. They considered forming an independent republic and seeking alliances with France, Spain, and/or Britain, but settled for holding another meeting on August 14, at Whiskey Point, close to Pittsburgh, and inviting Virginia to send delegates. The mood at this gathering was bellicose. Brackenridge, after viewing the assembled riflemen, despaired of a peaceful solution. He noted that his fellow westerners were "warlike, accustomed to the use of arms; capable of hunger and fatigue; and can lie in the water like badgers." Moreover, they were "enthusiastic to madness; and the effect of this is beyond all calculation."

Meanwhile, news of the insurgency had reached Philadelphia. President Washington decided that the firmest measures were necessary to enforce the powers of the United States. He issued a proclamation that labeled the Whiskey Boys traitors and sent orders to the governors of Pennsylvania, New Jersey, Maryland, and Virginia to call out their militias. While these forces were being assembled, commissioners were sent to the fractious counties with the offer of amnesty to every insurgent who swore on oath the validity, and his acceptance, of the whiskey excise. The commissioners arrived while the Whiskey Boys were holding yet another meeting and delivered their ultimatum to the assembled masses: obedience or the noose.

Back East, recruitment of the militia was interrupted by protests. Americans resented being called up to fight against each other in favor of taxes. The eastern newspapers thrilled their readers by magnifying the scale of the insurrection. The *Boston Mercury*, for example, credited the rebels with possessing a formal army and a potent navy. Moreover, rumors were printed that the militia were being recruited because further oppressive taxes were on their way, including a one-shilling duty on men's jackets and a fifteen-shilling charge for giving birth to a son.

Despite such negative press, an army of 12,950 had been mustered by October, and Washington traveled to Pennsylvania and to Maryland to inspect its component parts. The Pennsylvanian section was in action almost straightaway, when Governor Mifflin sent some Philadelphia light-horsemen to attack a party of New Jersey troops. Fortunately, there were no casualties and Mifflin issued a formal apology the next day, explaining he had been drunk. In the event, this was the only occasion in the entire campaign that shots were fired and sabers drawn in anger. At the same time as the federal army was being assembled, the Whiskey Boys had put the amnesty that they had been offered to the vote and had decided to capitulate.

This volte-face did not stem from cowardice—the rebels were happy to fight—but rather from the huge changes that had occurred in the short space of time between the excise bill becoming law and the fall of 1794. Settlement had proceeded at an astonishing pace around and beyond the Whiskey Boys. Moreover, they were isolated in their resistance: The Kentuckians, who might have been their allies, were focused on getting free navigation on the Mississippi, which was a federal matter, and potential friends in other states that did not suffer from the handicap of being landlocked simply avoided the excise by smuggling their spirits overseas.

Despite the resolution in favor of submission, there were still many democratic hotheads who opposed amnesty and advocated total war. Tom the Tinker shot up a few more stills and posted notices in which he warned, "My hammer is up and my ladle is hot." As a consequence, when delegates of the Whiskey Boys met with Washington to hand in their resolution to submit, it was decided that their submission was incomplete and unconvincing, and the two wings of the army that had been gathered to enforce the law were dispatched to the backcountry. Along the march the soldiers refreshed themselves morning and night with the substance whose taxation they were there to support. According to the evidence of one of the militiamen, printed in the *American Daily Advertiser,* the campaign held more pleasures than hardships: "No sooner does the drum beat in the morning, than up I start, and away to my canteen, where a precious draft of new distilled whiskey animates and revives me. This being done, away to fire, where in ten minutes you will hear more genuine wit than Philadelphia will afford in a month. When we halt at night, our tents being pitched, we sit down on the straw, cover ourselves with blankets, and push about the [whiskey] canteen so briskly that at length we are obliged to lie down: A sound sleep then enables us to endure a repetition of fatigue–and so on."

When the troops reached the heartland of the revolt they met no opposition. Any who harbored Tinkerish leanings had fled into the woods or down the Mississippi to Spanish New Orleans. The army occupied itself with a show of force and in ensuring that people swore they would pay the whiskey excise. Its officers were impressed with the civilized state of Pittsburgh, where they had a pleasant time, spent, according to one account "in Company with a great number of Gentlemen of and belonging to different Volunteer Corps, in singing and Drinking of Brandy, & C." Less than three weeks later the army marched home. Thirty-three prisoners, some of whom were merely witnesses, were hauled off to Philadelphia and paraded through its streets in triumph. Church bells rang, cannons were fired, and the ships in port dressed themselves in flags. As a coda to the campaign, President Washington set aside February 19, 1795, as a day of national thanksgiving. According to later conspiracy theorists, the Whiskey Rebellion could not have been a more perfect excuse for the federalists to increase their power.

The peaceful conclusion to the Whiskey Revolt coincided with a treaty with Spain that gave America the right to trade on the Mississippi River, and which opened a vast potential market to its western settlements. The Mississippi was the notional limit of America territory. It was a boundary, an inland coastline, which led to the Gulf of Mexico and thence, via international maritime trade, to the rest of the world. Its potential, however, hitherto had been unrealizable. Unlike similar giants such as the Amazon or the Nile, which broaden into deltas as they approach the sea, the Mississippi narrows toward its mouth, and this was guarded by the French/Spanish town of New Orleans. This redoubt of Mediterranean culture had developed in a kind of splendid isolation, and its inhabitants had evolved a unique society, whose mores, dress codes, and drinking habits were utterly different from those of their neighbors upriver.

Founded in 1718 by Jean-Baptiste Le Moyne, Sieur de Bienville, New Orleans was intended to be the principal port and first city of the French province of Louisiana. Some forty-odd years after this territory had been explored and claimed for France, it was decided to establish a colony there to exploit the gold mines and pearl fisheries it certainly must possess. A joint stock company was formed, colonists were collected from the houses of correction in Paris, and a small fleet was sent to settle an area several times larger than France itself. While Parisian financiers sat back and waited for their investments to bear fruit, their colonists ran into trouble. There was no gold, the pearls were bad, and the local Indians were belligerent, had acquired immunity to many European diseases, and had learned to use guns. Moreover, the site chosen for New Orleans was infested with venomous snakes, mosquitoes, and alligators. It flooded nearly every year, at unpredictable times, sometimes making it impossible to plant and at others drowning crops just before they were ripe. To these natural difficulties were added imported problems. The caliber of recruits for the new colony was considered low even by the standards of the age.

The soldiers were weak, badly armed, and short: Only two of them out of a total of three hundred were more than five feet tall. The few women who had been forced to accompany them to America had been obtained from prisons or hospitals and were either immoral, unhealthy, or both. When Lamothe Cadillac, the first governor of the new province, was petitioned by one of his clergy to return any female Louisianan who behaved in an depraved manner to France, he refused. In his opinion, if he sent away "all the loose females, there will be no women left here at all, and this would not suit the views of the king or the inclinations of the people."

Despite such unpromising material, New Orleans, in the style of Jamestown a century before, hung on. By 1743 it had a population of nearly two thousand, including several hundred African slaves. In the same year it received a glamorous new governor, the Marquis de Vaudreuil, who introduced, through personal example, the manners, dress sense, love of pageant, and public corruption that have characterized the city ever since. Among other abuses of power, he allowed the military to corner the alcohol market, so that, for a few years, it resembled a *petit* Rum Regiment. Its officers wandered the streets in dressing gowns and nightcaps, sometimes still drunk from the night before. By 1751, the town had become so decadent that even its money was counterfeit and the languid governor was prompted into action. He instituted a strict criminal code and gave New Orleans its first licensing laws. There were to be six legal taverns, which were not permitted to trade on Sundays, holy days, or after nine in the evenings, and which were prohibited from serving soldiers, Indians, or slaves. In addition, two *cantines*, or liquor shops, were created for the benefit of the soldiers, from which they might purchase wine, brandy, and rum, at the discretion of their commanding officer. These laws were rather honored in the breach than the observance. Unlicensed cabarets (informal drinking houses) proliferated, and did a brisk trade in the sultry summer nights.

In 1763, as part of a post–Seven Years' War global reshuffle of European possessions, New Orleans became Spanish. Its first governor was Don Alexander O'Reilly, an Irishman who had distinguished himself in the military service of the king of Spain. O'Reilly arrived accompanied by a fleet of twenty-four warships and imposed stringent new laws and taxes: It was death to insult the Virgin Mary in New Orleans, and all taverns, cabarets, billiards halls, ballrooms, and cafés had to buy licenses. The variety and number of drinking establishments the city possessed is indicative of the negligible influence that de Vaudreuil's laws had had. The Spanish rebuilt what is now the French Quarter, in their usual colonial style, and added a monumental church to the town. Scarcely had they beautified the place than France took it back, as part of the spoils of the Napoleonic wars. Three years later, in 1803, Napoleon sold it and Louisiana to America for fifteen million dollars, or roughly three cents per acre.

At last, the Mississippi was open, without limitations, to American trade. The pent-up demand was immense. Even without the Louisiana purchase, which doubled the official size of the United States, the country had been expanding at a breakneck rate. Not only did its territory grow but also its population: Whereas in 1800 there had been 5,308,843 Americans, by 1810 there were 7,239,881, and in 1820, 9,638,453. In the same period of time, Ohio, Louisiana, Indiana, Mississippi, Illinois, Alabama, and Missouri (1821) had been added to the union. American territory had been extended further through the occupation of Spanish owned Florida by General Andrew Jackson, and the acquisition via battle and treaty of substantial Indian lands. These new holdings were sold or given to anyone white who wanted them. By the standards of any historical civilization before, or since, the ease of acquiring ownership of land was extraordinary. To Europeans of the time, it was an opportunity that nothing in their history had prepared them for. They took it in their hundreds of thousands and fed the western flow into new states.

The drive west was a matter of amazement to dispassionate observers, who found it strange that immigrants would bypass land that was cheap and scantily settled, by European standards, in favor of a wilderness. A French professor advanced the theory that this was because "man, like the squirrel in a cage, is irresistibly impelled to step westward by reason of the earth's rotation eastward." By 1825 three million Americans had migrated west of the Alleghenies. Together they generated a considerable surplus—of whiskey, tobacco, flour, hogs, and beef; and the forests that they cleared to grow these things produced vast quantities of lumber. The principal outlet for these commodities was New Orleans.

An extraordinary variety of craft took to the Mississippi, carrying the products of the western states to their market. Since this was downstream, no motive power was required for the outward journey.

The river did the work–in theory–for its currents were treacherous and dragged boats onto sandbanks or over snags that tore them open. People built rafts, flatboats, keelboats, longhorns, pirogues, and floated themselves and their goods down the Mississippi. Some settled en route, but most did their business in New Orleans, sold their boats for firewood, then traveled home by land. Prior to steam power, taking a boat back upriver was slow work. Craft had to be punted, towed, or winched, five hundred feet at a time, by their crews. The return journey could take five months.

As traffic on the river increased, the men who steered the boats downstream and dragged them back against the current evolved into a distinct class, renowned for their physical strength and their hard drinking and brawling both ashore and afloat. The largest river craft carried a hundred crew, who received free access to whiskey as part of their wages. Their favorite was Monongahela rye, aka Nongela, and every boat kept a keg of this ambrosia on its deck, with a tin cup attached by a chain, so that crew members might refresh themselves as they felt the need. After boozing, their principal recreation was fighting, which they developed into a highly ritual pursuit, at least in the preliminaries to combat. Challengers took it in turns to dance and boast of their prowess, prior to exchanging blows, kicks, bites, head butts, and knife wounds. Many of them were missing ears, eyes, or noses from prior fights. The champion of each boat wore a red turkey feather in his cap, which entitled him to fight similar paragons. They also fought anyone ashore who would take them on, but these were few.

When the boatmen terminated their downstream trip in *Dixie* (their nickname for New Orleans, after the Creole slang for a ten-dollar note), their wants were simple–drink, sex, and fighting, in no particular order. These were catered for in an area known as the *Swamp,* after the terrain in which it was situated. The Swamp was good value: "For a picayune (six cents) a man could get a drink, a whore, and a bed for the night." It was also, literally, lawless. For the first few decades of its existence, convention, or common sense, dictated that no policeman would enter the area. It averaged half a dozen murders per week. The bodies were thrown into ditches, or left where they fell in bars, for the amusement of customers. The most infamous establishment in the Swamp was the *House of Rest for Weary Boatmen,* a gambling joint where anyone who won too much was killed and left to rot in situ as a reminder of the fickle nature of fortune.

On occasions, the boatmen practiced their Nongela-fueled mayhem beyond the Swamp and terrorized the saner parts of New Orleans. In 1818, for example, several crews banded together and destroyed Gaetano's Circus, which had been a popular family attraction and a fixture of the town since 1804. The attack commenced midperformance. The boatmen were armed with weapons they had captured from the town's constables en route; gentlemen in the crowd fought back with the sword sticks they carried from habit. The rivermen won the day, destroyed the circus ring and its tiers of seats, and as the pièce de résistance, Bill Sedley, a champion fighter with several red feathers in his cap, clubbed its tame tiger and pet bison to death.

The drinking habits of the permanent residents of New Orleans were strikingly different from those of the boatmen. The example set by the elegant Marquis de Vaudreuil was still followed, and while both France and Spain had failed to turn the city into an economic powerhouse, they had introduced a class system, ballroom dancing, opera, theater, and similar trappings of European civilization. Moreover, the city possessed a substantial population of free colored people, who made a significant and vibrant contribution to its culture. The diversity of New Orleans was further increased by the arrival in 1810 of ten thousand Santo Domingans, refugees from slave revolts at home, and latterly Cuba, who were fanatics for etiquette and ostentation.

This splendid mixture of citizens, who looked to France or Spain rather than New England for their fashions, and who thought dressing up and going out to be preferable to hacking themselves farms out of the wilderness, did their drinking in cafés, ballrooms, and other such civilized meeting places, some of which are still extant. The *Absinthe House,* in operation from 1826 onward, as its name suggests specialized in the new French spirit and long, cooling drinks. The *Café des Émigrés* was the haunt of the Santo Domingans and other glamorous exiles. It was famous for a cordial called *le petit gouave.* In addition to such legendary watering holes, New Orleans possessed a series of exchanges—giant bars-cum-auction-houses, where the businessmen of the town, and its politicians and newspaper editors, assembled every day. The most venerable of these institutions was *Malpero's Exchange,* renamed Hewlett's Exchange in 1838. Its principal competitor as a place to do business was the City Exchange, which opened not long after. This was a giant double-storied building with a central rotunda and ballrooms on the second floor. Gumbo, the traditional dish of New Orleans, is said to have been invented in its kitchens; numerous cocktails, including the *Crusta* and *Santini's Pousse-Café*, were created behind its bar. It was also responsible for the institution of the free lunch—whereby food was given for nothing to anyone who bought a drink.

By the 1820s, New Orleans was exporting its elegant style of consumption upriver—a counterculture advancing against the current of whiskey and fighting. This was achieved via steamboats, which commenced operation in 1811. The first example was built from the keel up in Pittsburgh and was named the *New Orleans* after her intended destination. She was an experiment, albeit on a grand scale—148 feet long, capable of carrying seventy-five passengers and twice as many tons of freight. Her maiden voyage commenced on October 20, 1811. The very same week a massive earthquake hit Louisiana, reversing the flow of the Mississippi. This event was interpreted as an act of revulsion by the Father of All Waters, as the river was known to the Indian tribes who had lived along its banks, against the appearance of a mechanical vessel upon its surface.

The *New Orleans* completed her maiden voyage to her namesake on January 12, 1812. She sank on her fourth trip, to the satisfaction of her critics, but her limited success had set an example others rushed to follow. By 1820, 60 steamers were in service on the Mississippi; by 1834, 230. While their design and journey times improved greatly over the period, their safety record remained woeful. In consequence, the superstructures of the boats were as flimsy as stage props, and equally gaudy. They were expected to have short lifespans—on average only three years—and they were built to be pretty rather than sturdy. They did not have to face the ocean and no hull of the time could withstand the force of an exploding boiler, so instead of investing in seaworthiness, competing builders focused on creature comforts. The results were floating versions of the palatial exchanges in New Orleans. They were the most complicated and aesthetic structures that Americans born along the riverbank had ever seen.

Their interiors were as fanciful as their exteriors. Their principal feature was a long slim saloon, elliptical in shape, with cabins around its perimeter. Here, from a man intimately familiar with Mississippi steamboats, is a description of the interior of a typical example: "She was as clean and dainty as a drawing room; when I looked down her long gilded saloon, it was like gazing through a splendid tunnel; she had an oil painting, by some gifted sign-painter, on every stateroom door; she glittered with no end of prism fringed chandeliers; the clerk's office was elegant, the bar was marvelous, and the barkeeper had been barbered and upholstered at incredible cost." The barkeepers on steamboats were usually freelance. They rented their position and made themselves rich by joining forces with professional gamblers, who, alongside exploding boilers and collisions with sandbanks, were the principal source of entertainment onboard. Indeed, the reputation of a boat was determined in part by the length of its drinks list, which could extend to a dozen or more types of cocktail, domestic and imported spirits, and vintage wines. These potions served to while away the monotony of a long river journey and to tempt passengers into gambling.

Conditions on the main deck of these boats below their salons, where most immigrants traveled together with their luggage and livestock, were primitive in contrast, and the only beverages were whiskey and river water. The latter, despite being laden with sediment, had its fans, as the following conversation from a traveler's journal illustrates. The writer, an easterner, has just been offered a glassful of the Mississippi:

> As thirsty as I was, I hesitated to drink the thick muddy water, for while standing in our tumblers, a sediment is precipitated of half an inch. Oh, how I longed for a draft of cool spring water, or a lump of Rockland lake ice! While drinking, one of the ladies advanced for the same purpose.
>
> "Dear me! What insipid water!" she said. "It has been standing too long. I like it right thick."
>
> I looked at her in surprise. "Do you prefer it muddy to clear?" I asked.
>
> "Certainly I do," she replied. "I like the sweet clayey taste, and when it settles it is insipid. Here, Juno!" calling to the black chambermaid who was busy ironing, "Get me some water fresh out of the river, with the true Mississippi relish."

Water drinking was on the rise throughout the United States in the first quarter of the nineteenth century. Piped water had appeared in some cities, following the example of Philadelphia, which had introduced the resource in 1799. Such municipal munificence was rewarded with suspicion: The Philadelphians retained a colonial-era prejudice against water and cautioned newcomers that it was a killer, especially if the drinker gulped it down. According to a French visitor to the city, handbills were distributed each summer to alert people to its dangers: "Strangers especially are warned either to drink grog or to add a little wine or some other spirituous liquor to their water. People are urged to throw cold water on the faces of those suffering from water drinking, and bleeding is also suggested. Sometimes notices are placed on the pumps with the words: 'Death to him who drinks quickly.'"

The lethal reputation of water stands in contrast to the blessings alcohol was believed to bestow upon the human frame throughout America. From Rhode Island to New Orleans, Americans doctored themselves with alcohol, and were prescribed it by their physicians, to treat ailments ranging from bad breath to weak hearts. The new flood of immigrants from Europe, many of whom were unused to the dramatic swings in temperature between American summers and winters, considered alcohol to be absolutely necessary to the process of acclimatization and drank as a defense against the weather, whether it was too hot or too cold. Sufferers of sunstroke and hypothermia alike were treated with a good stiff drink. Moreover, alcohol was often the principal ingredient of American folk remedies. This new species of cure, concocted to replace the British patent medicines that had been popular before independence, kept many invalids drunk. Those who got the eyaws from gulping their medication could avail themselves of further folk remedies intended to cure the condition. The following example, from Kentucky, intended to be consumed in a single draft, probably worked its magic by fright alone:

Recipte for the Eyaws:
take 1 pint of hogs Lard
1 handfull of earth worms
1 handfull of Tobacco
4 pods of Red pepper
1 spunfull of Black pepper
1 Race of Ginger
Stew them well together, & when Applied mix Sum Sperits . . . with it

"Sperits" dominated early nineteenth-century American drinking. As the country grew, and new states meshed with old, they were still the best way of carrying wealth from place to place, or of concentrating the grain harvest on an isolated homestead in a form that would improve in value with age. The volume of production was stupendous. In 1810 federal statistics show that the six main whiskey-producing states together distilled twice as many gallons of whiskey per annum as there were people in America. Ten years later, the notional per capita consumption had risen to more than five gallons per head per annum. According to a later analysis of who was doing the tippling, "Nine million women and children drank twelve million gallons" and three million men accounted for the other sixty million—i.e., by 1829 the average American metropolitan male was drinking as much hard liquor as the average Londoner at the height of the gin craze. If statistics could predict the effect of drink on a population, by rights Americans should have been languishing en masse in emaciated heaps, their birthrate and life expectancy should have collapsed, and crime should have exploded.

That they continued to breed and to enjoy long, healthy, and prosperous lives is explained in part by the fact that they were substituting spirits for other types of alcoholic beverage. Beer, wine, and cider all lost ground to whiskey. The numbers for beer are instructive: In 1810, the same year that the average American man, woman, and child downed sixteen pints of whiskey, they drank only eight pints of beer. According to Treasury figures, America contained a mere 132 breweries, concentrated in Pennsylvania, New York, and Ohio, which together produced the modest total of 185,000 barrels, which was less than any single one of the five largest breweries in London.

The American focus on spirits led to an explosion of creativity in the manner in which they were drunk. The *cocktail* was invented in the United States. Its appearance in the lexicon may be traced to the May 6, 1806, edition of a New York newspaper, *The Balance and Columbian Repository*, which published the drinks bill of a political candidate. The bill included "25 [glasses] cock-tail." The next week, in response to a letter from a curious reader, the paper's editor printed a clarification: "Cock tail, then, is a stimulating liquor, composed of spirits of any kind, sugar water, and bitters . . . it is supposed to be an excellent electioneering potion inasmuch as it renders the heart stout and bold, at the same time that it fuddles the head." Cocktails were ideal for those who could not stomach whiskey solo in the morning. In 1822, breakfast in Kentucky was said to consist of "three cocktails and a chaw of terbacka."

Kentuckians were not the only Americans to start the day with spirits. Indeed, the entire nation was acquiring a reputation for dawn-till-dusk tippling. This trend toward the hard stuff had been detected in its infancy by President Jefferson, who did not wish to see his country become a nation of sots. His years in France, and his love for its wines (he bought over twenty thousand bottles for the use of himself and future presidents), had convinced him that Americans would be better people if they drank vintages instead of spirits. To this end, he argued for reduced duties on imported wines and set out on a quest for an American substitute. Despite sequential setbacks, he never gave up hope that some vigorous native vine might be capable of producing a palatable drink. His persistence is testament to his strength of character: He had watched as the vines he had selected in France, shipped over the Atlantic, and planted in the most promising soil on his own land had died without any clear cause–yet had remained optimistic. He decided that the solution lay in careful hybridizing of native vines. His first all-American hope was the *scuppernong* of North Carolina. It had the potential, he believed, to be "distinguished on the best tables of Europe, for its fine aroma, and chrystalline transparence." He regretted, however, that the "aroma, in most of the samples I have seen, has been entirely submerged in brandy." Sadly, without added brandy, scuppernong was undrinkable. Its grapes gave a tang to wine that experts describe as "foxy."[32]

Whether fortified or not, the crystalline scuppernong did not succeed in weaning Americans off their cocktails. Nor did Jefferson managed to persuade Congress to lower import duties on wine. A decade after first advocating the latter cause, he was still pleading the case. However, in 1818, the legislature appeared to be ready to resolve the matter in his favor. In order to force judgment Jefferson set out his moral and fiscal arguments side by side: Heavy duties on wine were "a prohibition of its use to the middling class of our citizens, and a condemnation of them to the poison of whiskey, which is desolating their houses. No nation is drunken where wine is cheap; and none sober, where the dearness of wine substitutes ardent spirits as the common beverage. Wine is, in truth, the only antidote to the bane of whiskey."

---

[32] "Rank taste when ripe, resembling the smell of a fox"–Robert Beverly, 1795, *History and Present State of Virginia*.

Jefferson was not alone in calling attention to the dangers posed by the rise in whiskey drinking. The Philadelphia College of Physicians, under Dr. Benjamin Rush, a signatory to the Declaration of Independence, had advocated punitive duties on whiskey during the taxation debates in Congress in 1791. Rush considered spirits to be qualitatively different from other kinds of alcoholic beverage and, like Jefferson, was alarmed that Americans were drinking them in preference to beer and wine. When his attempts to win Congress over to his point of view failed, he decided that the only way to battle spirits was by enlisting religion in the fight and addressing "the heads and governing bodies of all the churches in America upon the subject."

To this end, he gathered together a series of articles he had written on the matter into a tract entitled an *Essay on the Effects of Ardent Spirits upon the Human Constitution,* which was published in 1794 and reissued continuously till 1804, by which time its message had begun to take root. The tract was graced with a pictorial representation of the benefits and dangers of alcohol, captioned "A Moral and Physical Thermometer," which divided the world of drinking into two categories–Temperance and Intemperance. Daringly for the time, it suggested that water drinking was conducive to "Health and Wealth." The thermometer evoked Dante in its numerology, setting out, in the temperance section, seven ranks of virtue and, on the intemperance scale, seven descending levels of hell. True to its title, the physical as well as moral consequences of consuming anything more potent than strong beer or wine were provided and, if they were accurate observations of drinkers at that time, suggested that most Americans suffered from "tremors of the hands in the morning, puking, bloatedness, red noses, jaundice, dropsy, and epilepsy."

The accompanying essay, despite being styled as a calm appeal to the reason of its readers, was alarmist in its tone and hyperbolic in its phrasing: "Were it possible for me to speak with a voice so loud as to be heard from the river St. Croix to the remotest shores of the Mississippi...I would say, 'Friends and fellow citizens! avoid the habitual use of those seducing liquors!'" Rush proposed that "to avert this evil," Americans should "unite and besiege the general and state governments with petitions to limit the number of taverns–to impose heavy duties upon ardent spirits–to inflict a mark of disgrace or temporary abridgement of some civil right upon every man convicted of drunkenness; and finally to secure the property of habitual drunkards, for

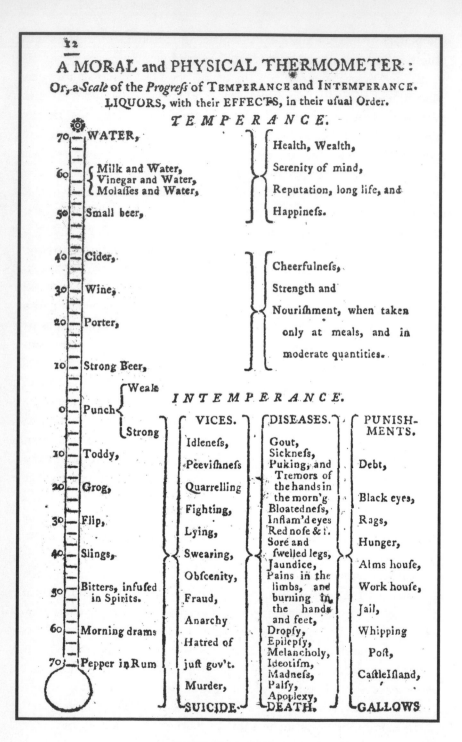

Rush's thermometer

the benefit of their families, by placing it in the hands of trustees appointed for that purpose by a court of justice."

In the western states, where the excise was considered an abridgement too far of civil rights, and ardent spirits were the staple drink, his message fell on deaf ears. In the East, however, where the old Puritan disapproval of drunkenness was alive and well, he found listeners and even disciples. In 1805, America received its first temperance sermon from the lips of Reverend Ebenezer Porter in Washington, Connecticut. His text was Isaiah 5:11: "Woe unto them that rise up early in the morning, that they may follow strong drink; that continue until night, till wine inflame them." According to the Reverend Porter, the prophet Isaiah had had America in mind when he issued his warning to the Israelites. Moreover, "this infant country has reached a maturity in this shameful vice which is without parallel in the history of the world. Probably no nation, ancient or modern, in proportion to its whole population, ever had so many male and female drunkards as this. Certainly in no other have the means of intoxication been procured with so much faculty and used with so little restraint by all sorts of people." It is important to note that, notwithstanding the hyperbole, Porter was advocating temperance with a small *t*–he did not expect his congregation to give up drink entirely, merely to refrain from spirits and inebriation.

Words were followed by deeds: In 1808, the first American temperance society "with a Constitution and by-laws organized for the specific purpose of promoting temperance" appeared. The little town of Moreau, in Saratoga County, New York, had the honor of its birth; Dr. Billy J. Clark, the distinction of paternity. Clark had read Rush, had witnessed the deleterious effects of whiskey drinking on his fellow Moreauvians, and, after wrestling with his conscience in front of a fellow divine one stormy night, felt called to act. He drew up a set of articles and persuaded a number of his flock to subscribe to them. Article IV set out the ground rules of the new society:

> No member shall drink rum, gin, whiskey, wine, or any distilled
> spirits, or compositions of the same, or any of them, except by
> advice of a physician, or in case of actual disease; also, excepting
> wine at public dinners, under a penalty of 25 cents; provided that
> this article shall not infringe any religious ordinance.

The society anticipated disobedience in its members. A second section of its articles imposed a penalty of fifty cents on any member found intoxicated, and Article XI created an obligation to inform on miscreants. The society held its inaugural meeting on August 25, 1808, and elected Dr. Rush as an honorary member.

18 ROMANTIC DRINKING

Gie him strong drink until he wink,
That's sinking in despair;
An' liquor guid to fire his bluid,
That's pressed wi' grief an' care:
There let him booze an' deep carouse,
Wi' bumpers flowing o'er,
Till he forgets his loves or debts,
An minds his briefs no more
   —Robert Burns "Solomon's Proverbs," xxxi, 6,7

The steamboats that plied their way up and down the Father of Waters might have served as a metaphor for the United States in the first part of the nineteenth century–progress and optimism rushing headlong through the wilderness, bearing an ark's worth of livestock and provisions, and a complete spectrum of humanity–planters, preachers, slaves, gamblers, land speculators, merchants, each on a personal mission to occupy and tame the new land. The steamboats were, moreover, representative of progress, in the sense of the advance of technology, and part and parcel of the *Industrial Revolution,* which had been gathering momentum as the century unrolled.

Industry had begun its forward march in England in the 1780s, bringing significant changes to not only naval architecture but also to the production of alcoholic beverages, beer in particular. Breweries were among the earliest modern industrial enterprises. As had been evident since medieval times, there were economies of scale to brewing: The bigger the brew kettle, the more could be made in one go without having to increase the workforce. Moreover, machinery might replace the workhorses which, harnessed to turn-mills, provided most of the mechanical power of the average British brewery. As a consequence, the industry was quick to embrace the age of steam. In 1784, the Red Lion Brewhouse in Wapping installed the first steam engine to be used in brewing, coincidentally the first such device in London. This four-horsepower model, built by Boulton & Watt, was used to grind malt and to pump beer between vats. Within five years every other major London brewer had followed suit.

Improved efficiency, and larger brew kettles, resulted in the production of heroic quantities of beer. This was fermented and matured in immense vats, some of which had a capacity of a million or more pints. They were built from plate iron, encircled with cast iron hoops, and resembled giant metal firkins. Engravings from the period, usually with a diminutive man at their base standing atop a ladder, convey a sense of industry triumphant. One such behemoth, at the Meaux Brewery near Tottenham Court Road in London, was the cause of an early and sensational industrial accident. On October 17, 1814, the twenty-two-foot-tall vessel began to shed its hoops. Shortly afterward, it burst, releasing a tsunami of porter, which flooded the cellars of the surrounding slums, killing eight women and children and demolishing several houses.

In time, however, the Meaux Brewery disaster, when set against the growing casualty register of industrial accidents, appeared unremarkable. Moreover, the loss of a few slum dwellings was soon eclipsed by the wholesale destruction of areas of great natural beauty in the name of progress. People were horrified as much as thrilled by the deforestation and pollution that accompanied the Industrial Revolution, and by the sound of machinery turning, stamping, grinding, day and night. In consequence, a counterculture arose—the *Romantic Movement*—which lamented progress rather than celebrated it. The poets, philosophers, and painters who marched under its banner elevated the environment over engineering, inspiration above patient endeavor, and valued the impulsive behavior of children more than the pedantic logic of adults. Romantic thinking had an important influence on people's perception of alcohol, why they drank it, and what they drank. Certain beverages became popular for their associations as much as for their strength, taste, or effects, and advances made in manufacture, packaging, and distribution by evil industrialization enabled drinkers to indulge their fancies. Thus a Parisian might sip on Scottish whisky and imagine himself to be roaming heather-covered moors, or an English poet drown himself in French wine in order to inspire dreams of the "warm, blushing south." Moreover, there were clear parallels between Romantic values and Bacchic values. Untamed landscapes, the wild-child god, ecstatic self-expression, and other elements of the legend of Dionysus were also part of the Romantic canon.

The roots of Romanticism can be traced to France and Germany. In France, the Swiss émigré Jean-Jacques Rousseau championed the natural goodness of humanity. His two popular romantic novels, *Julie, or the New Heloise* (1761) and *Emile, or on Education* (1762), advocated rustic simplicity, the celebration of mountain scenery, and the superiority of intuition to discipline, especially in the fields of religion and learning. In Germany, the early work of the polymath Johann Wolfgang Goethe, in particular *The Sorrows of Young Werther* (1774), likewise praised nature and elevated emotion above reason. Its sensitive, passionate hero compares his excitability to inebriation and upbraids his contemporaries for being boring and staid: "I have been drunk more than once, and my passion often borders on madness, and I regret neither. Because, in my own way, I have learned to understand that all exceptional people who have created something great, something that seemed impossible, have to be decried as drunkards or madmen. And I find it intolerable, even in our daily life, to hear it said of almost everyone who manages to do something that is free, noble, and unexpected: He is a drunkard, he is a fool. They should be ashamed of themselves, all these sober people!"

Werther's favorite reading was *Fragments of Ancient Poetry* or *The Poems of Ossian* (1760) by James Macpherson. The verses it contained, which sang of mythical Scottish heroes tearing up and down mountains with their deerhounds, falling in love with blondes, and shedding each other's blood in abandon, struck a chord throughout northern Europe. They took the reader away from the artificial manners and obsession with reason that prevailed around them to a landscape where vigor and passion ruled. The Scottish Highlands, in which these fantasies were set, became fixed in minds all over Europe as the ideal romantic landscape. The worship of things Scottish extended to its drinks, which were presumed to be the *uisge-beatha* of the Highland clans, rather than the claret that had been the favorite of the heroes of the Scottish enlightenment. *Uisge-beatha* ("whisky" in Gaelic) was thought to contribute to the poetic physiques typical of the people who inhabited the Highlands, an illusion corroborated by an exciseman in the region, writing before Ossian was published: "The ruddy complexion, nimbleness, and strength of these people is not owing to water drinking but to the aqua vitae, a malt spirit which serves both for victual and drink."

Although the *Poems of Ossian,* which had been presented as genuine translations of ancient Gaelic lays, were discovered to be fraudulent, the sentiments they contained, and the free form of verse that they employed, inspired contemporary poets to seek their inspiration in nature and the common people. In Britain, the fountainhead of Romantic writing was Robert Burns, whose work celebrated the peasants, superstitions, and scenery of his native Scotland in uncomplicated ballad forms. His poetry is deliberately vernacular, nationalistic, and romantic. Unlike Allan Ramsay, whose influence he acknowledged, Burns did not laud claret but rather eulogized whisky and ale, which he believed to be the traditional drinks of his native land. He set out his stall in "Scotch Drink," which commemorates the inspirational powers of fermented grain, while denigrating the fruit of the vine:

> Let other poets raise a fracas
> 'Bout vines, and wines, an' drunken Bacchus,
> An crabbed names an' stories wrack us,
> An' grate our lug
> I sing the juice Scotch bear[33] can mak us
> In glass or jug

Burns was a significant influence over young poets in England, especially William Wordsworth, who acknowledged that the Scotsman had taught him "How Verse may build a princely throne/On humble truth" and, in 1803, made a pilgrimage to the tomb of his hero. He did not include the other Burns shrine in the area, the poet's seat at the bar of the Globe Inn in Dumfries, in his visit, for unlike his mentor, Wordsworth was no fan of drink. He claimed to have been turned against it by an unfortunate experience in his youth. While a student at Cambridge, he was invited to visit John Milton's old rooms, where

---

[33] Barley.

he was tempted to commit what he considered to be sacrilege against the memory of the sober master of English poetry:

> O temperate bard!
> One afternoon, the first time I set foot
> In this thy innocent nest and oratory,
> Seated with others in a festive ring
> Of commonplace convention, I to thee
> Poured out libations, to thy memory drank
> Within my private thoughts, till my brain reeled

The shame of desecrating the "innocent nest" of Milton haunted Wordsworth for the rest of his life. According to his own testimony, and the evidence of his contemporaries, he never was drunk again. He made a virtue of his temperance in his poetry, justifying it on the grounds that since the worship of nature was paramount to poetry, the poet should be in a state of nature when attempting to worship. He postulated a natural kind of intoxication, reached without the aid of "gross and violent stimulants." This drunkenness of the spirit was, according to Wordsworth, the only sort worth enjoying. Not content with trumpeting the virtues of a natural high, he wrote a cautionary poem–"Benjamin the Waggoner" (1819)–against the artificial type, which took its inspiration from Burns's marvelous "Tam O'Shanter," albeit with a very different slant on alcohol. In Burns's poem the eponymous hero is a hearty drinker who declares "Wi' *usquabae* we'll face the deevil," and when confronted by Satan himself, a comely witch in a cutty-sark,[34] and a whole pack of ghouls on his way home from the pub, outruns them all with the aid of his trusty mare Meg. Benjamin the waggoner, in contrast, is a reluctant inebriate, who is forced by a storm to take refuge in a pub, where he is lured into drinking too much by a sailor. His surrender to temptation is inspired by his love for his country–the seaman proposes a patriotic toast, whereupon Benjamin forgets himself:

> "A bowl, a bowl of double measure,"
> Cries Benjamin, "A draught of length
> To Nelson, England's pride and treasure,
> Her bulwark and her tower of strength!"

---

[34] A nightshirt cut very short that scarcely covered the buttocks.

Other bowls follow. The waggoner makes a beast of himself and loses his job as a consequence, to the ruin of his family. Wordsworth's antipathy to drink was noted and criticized by his contemporaries. According to William Hazlitt, a former disciple, "It is because so few things give him pleasure, that he gives pleasure to so few people."

Samuel Taylor Coleridge, a onetime friend of and collaborator with Wordsworth, and fellow Romantic, took a very different position on the importance of alcohol to poetry and poets. Like Wordsworth, he celebrated the common folk, but unlike Wordsworth, his common folk drank for pleasure and did so without coming to grief. Coleridge composed a number of lyrics for drinking songs, which show his love of alcohol and the nostalgia for the preindustrial age so typical of Romantics, as the following duet, a "Song to be Sung by the Lovers of All the Noble Liquors Comprised under the Name of Ale," demonstrates:

> A
>
> Ye drinkers of Stingo and Nappy so free
> Are the gods on Olympus so happy as we?
>
> B.
>
> They cannot be so happy!
> For why? they drink no Nappy.
>
> A.
>
> But what if Nectar, in their lingo,
> Is but another name for Stingo?
>
> B.
>
> Why, then we and the Gods are equally blest,
> And Olympus an Ale-house as good as the best!

Like Burns, Coleridge celebrated native beverages—*Nappy* and *Stingo* were types of strong English ale. However, he differed from the Scot over the value of both wine and the classical heritage. He was happy to employ the Greek pantheon in his poetry and praised wine in verse and in his journals. He mused over its power to inspire: "Wine—some men = musical Glasses—to produce their finest music you must keep them wet." Coleridge felt he was a musical glass and kept himself wet to the extent that Wordsworth ended their friendship, calling him a "rotten drunkard . . . rotting out his entrails with intemperance." He found sanctuary with Charles Lamb in London. Lamb, a noted essayist and drinker, took pleasure writing to Wordsworth to say how happy his guest was: "Coleridge has powdered his head, and looks like Bacchus, Bacchus ever sleek and young. He is going to turn sober, but his Clock has not struck yet, meantime he pours down goblet after goblet, the 2nd to see where the 1st is gone, the 3rd to see no harm happens to the second, a fourth to say there's another coming, and a 5th to say he's not sure he's the last."

Lamb, as his letters reveal, kept an ample cellar, which he used to tempt friends and fellow Romantics into visiting him. Here, for example, he is trying to lure Thomas Manning to London: "You shall drink Rum, Brandy, Gin, aquavitae, Usquebagh, or Whiskey a nights–& for the after-dinner-Trick I have 8 Bottles of genuine Port which mathematically divided gives 1 1/7 for every day you stay, provided you stay a *week*." Manning accepted and afterward invited Lamb to visit *him,* likewise emphasizing the liquid abundance of his home: "The very thoughts of your coming makes my keg of Rum *wobble* about like a porpoise & the liquor (how fine it smells!) goes *Gultch squlluck* against the sides for joy."

The narrow views on drinking displayed by Burns and Wordsworth, the former preaching against wine and the latter against drunkenness, and the inclusive approach adopted by Coleridge and Lamb to any form of alcoholic beverage, may be contrasted with the opinions of John Keats on the value of alcohol to the poet. Like Wordsworth, Keats made a pilgrimage to the tomb of Burns, where he tasted whisky for the first time, "and pretty smart stuff it is." He also included Burns's lodgings and barstool at the Globe Inn in his tour, where he got drunk on beer in honor of his idol–"my pulse is warm with thine old barley-bree."

Notwithstanding the pleasure he gained from evoking the memory of the Scottish master with appropriate beverages, Keats drank wine from preference, specifically claret. A letter to his brother George in America illustrates both his beautiful natural rhythm and his fascination with the red wines of Bordeaux: "Now I like Claret whenever I can have Claret I must drink it.–'tis the only palate affair that I am at all sensual in. . . . For really 'tis so fine–it fills one's mouth with a gushing freshness–then goes down cool and feverless–then you do not feel it quarrelling with your liver—no it is rather a Peace maker and lies as quiet as it did in the grape—then it is as fragrant as the Queen Bee; and the more ethereal Part of it mounts into the brain, not assaulting the cerebral apartments like a bully in a bad-house looking for his trul and hurrying from door to door bouncing against the wainscot: but rather walks like Aladin about his own enchanted palace so gently that you do not feel his step." According to other letters, the poet's favorite Bordeaux was Margaux, and he was sent bottles by well-wishers. His fondness for claret seems to have bordered on the obsessive—a friend related of him that he once "covered his tongue & throat as far as he could reach with Cayenne pepper, in order as he said to have the 'delicious coolness of claret in all its glory!'" However, while Keats acknowledged the contribution of wine to his poetry, he was also careful to distinguish the inebriation it produced from the poetic rapture generated without artificial stimulation in the poet's own mind. In his "Ode to a Nightingale," he contrasts the two forms of intoxication and concludes that the mystic variety is more powerful.

The debate over whether or not to drink, and if so what, among Romantic poets was settled in favor of yes and everything by Lord George Byron, who praised alcohol in his work and lived as he wrote:

> Man, being reasonable, must get drunk;
> The best of Life is but intoxication:
> Glory, the Grape, Love, Gold, in these are sunk
> The hopes of all men, and of every nation;
> Without their sap, how branchless were the trunk
> Of Life's strange tree, so fruitful on occasion!
> But to return,—get very drunk, and when
> You wake with headache—you shall see what then!

Byron's letters reflect his love of the grape, and his disdain for sober romantics, especially Wordsworth and Southey,[35] of whom he commented (1814): "I doubt if either of them ever got drunk, and I am of the old creed of Homer the wine-bibber." His accounts of his drinking exploits with other bibulous writers portray drunkenness as a happy, excited state—a sort of second childhood. After a fashion, Byron brought creative thinking on the benefits of drinking full circle, so that alcohol

[35] Then poet laureate.

was once again the poetick juice that had inspired Restoration-era poets such as Rochester. In the course of this journey, the Romantic poets
had added new reasons for celebrating drinking in their work: It was a
traditional pastime of the rustic laborers many of them chose for subjects, and the regional beverages these drank added color to their
verse. In addition, the power of drink to drown out hated reason and to
stimulate the passions was considered praiseworthy; and finally, intoxication was a useful metaphor for the poetic raptures enjoyed by the
nineteenth-century bard when engaged in the act of composition.

Romantic attitudes to alcohol were also influenced by the appearance
in British society of other kinds of intoxicating substances. These
caused people to reexamine the condition of drunkenness, by comparing it with the altered mental and physical states produced by rival
drugs. Opium was the first competitor to enter common use. It had
long been employed as a medicine before romantic writers began to
take it for recreation. Thomas De Quincey, who had commenced using opium as a painkiller and continued the habit for its pleasurable
side effects, was the first to champion its virtues in print. His *Confessions of an English Opium-Eater* set out the pleasures and the pains he
had experienced with the drug and was a runaway success with the
reading public.

The *Confessions* made comparisons between the effects of opium
and wine, which in themselves represented a landmark in English literature: At last there was a yardstick against which drunkenness
might be measured. De Quincey defined a new kind of intoxication,
which was carefully differentiated from that brought on by drinking:
"Wine robs a man of his self-possession: opium greatly invigorates it.
Wine unsettles and clouds the judgment, and gives a preternatural
brightness, and a vivid exaltation to the contempts and the admirations, the loves and the hatreds, of the drinker: Opium, on the contrary, communicates serenity and equipoise to all the faculties, active
or passive." According to De Quincey, even their similarities emphasized their differences: "Opium, like wine, gives an expansion to the
heart, and the benevolent affections: but then, with this remarkable
difference, that in the sudden development of kindheartedness which
accompanies inebriation, there is always more or less of a maudlin
character, which exposes it to the contempt of the bystander. Men

shake hands, swear eternal friendship, and shed tears—no mortal knows why." The opium eater, in contrast, did not lapse into sentimentality but rather enjoyed clarity of thought and a sensation of transcendental bliss.

In addition to exploring the metaphysics of opium intoxication, De Quincey noted in passing that the recreational use of his favorite narcotic was spreading. Increased supplies from British India had driven down its price, so that even factory workers had access to it and found the "equipoise and serenity" that opium generated to be a cheap alternative to drowning their sorrows. The habit of taking opium after a hard week of work in a factory was, however, seen as a minor problem at the time in comparison to drunkenness. The prices of gin and beer had not kept up with inflation since the gin craze, with the result that they were relatively cheap. In London, in the first quarter of the nineteenth century, a quart of beer cost four and a half pence and a quartern of gin three and a half pence. In consequence, drinking among the working classes was on the rise again. This time it was the manufacturing towns of the north that seemed to be at risk of succumbing to a wave of self-destructive drinking. In contrast, however, to the eighteenth century, those in authority were inclined to look beyond the mere fact of inebriation to its causes, and to look with sympathetic eyes.

This new approach had been stimulated by the advances in medicine that had occurred during the same years that the Romantics were eulogizing nappy ale and "the true, the blushful Hippocrene." In 1804, Dr. Thomas Trotter had published *An Essay, Medical, Philosophical, and Chemical, on Drunkenness, and Its Effect on the Human Body,* in which he asserted that drunkenness was a mental affliction as well as a physical condition: *"The habit of drunkenness is a disease of the mind."* He also noted that drunkards, unlike other people suffering from some debilitating illness, received neither sympathy nor attention from their fellows. If anyone other than a drunk collapsed on the streets, people would rush to his aid; if, however, the individual was intoxicated, he would be "allowed to perish, without pity and without assistance; as if his crime were inexpiable, and his body infectious to the touch."

The concept that drunks deserved assistance and compassion was developed further by Francis Place in his 1829 essay *On Drunkenness.* Place argued that the working-class drunk (whom many commentators still condemned as a worthless brute) merited especial pity, as he was "excluded from all rational enjoyment, shut out from reasonable conversation, doing the same thing, generally in the same place, always against his will ... without hope of bettering his condition and with a conviction that it will become worse and worse as he grows older and his family increases." As a consequence, "no one then need be surprised that they should occasionally get drink, the only matter for surprise is that it should be only occasional. Drinking is the sole means such men have of getting away from themselves, the only resource against the most depressing thoughts."

Further nineteenth-century studies of drinking focused on its economic impact, in particular its ability to cause so-called secondary poverty. Notwithstanding the unpleasant working and living conditions that had accompanied the Industrial Revolution–the sweatshop and the slum–wages were good. The poor had a disposable income that, if spent wisely, would enable them to participate in the consumer revolution–to buy some of the goods they manufactured, and to feed themselves and their families a healthy diet. If, however, in working class parlance, they pissed away their wages against a wall, they were condemned to lifelong poverty and malnourishment. Moreover, they would miss out on the opportunities for self-improvement that were appearing: A diligent, thrifty, and sober worker might rise to the position of overseer–and might even aspire to owning a home.

The subjects of such studies, the workingmen themselves, agreed with the conclusions of their observers, and in 1831 a "self-made cheesemonger" named Joseph Livesey launched a campaign against drinking that attacked the habit from a new and radical angle. Livesey hailed from Preston in northeast England–the heartland of the textiles industry. It was an environment where the benefits of sobriety were immediately evident to both employers and employees: Factory work required precision, concentration, and punctuality, and these qualities were absent in habitual drunks, who were forever holding up production or injuring themselves by sticking their fingers in machines. However, a significant cultural obstacle lay in the way of guarding both productivity and limbs: Drink was still perceived as an absolutely necessary part of the workingman's diet. No one would think of attempting hard labor without fortifying himself in advance with porter, stout, harvest ale, or the local equivalent.

Taking his inspiration from Benjamin Franklin, who had noted in his memoirs that on his first visit to London he had been able to perform the arduous physical tasks required by the printing trade with greater ease than his English colleagues who drank eight pints of beer each working day, Livesey decided to prove that the nutritious qualities attributed to alcoholic drinks were fallacious. The result was the *Malt Lecture,* which he delivered to a mixed audience of workers and philanthropists in his hometown in 1831. He told them that the belief that alcoholic drinks were nourishing was a "great delusion." Using questionable arithmetic, he showed that a gallon of strong ale costing nearly two shillings was less wholesome than a pennyworth of bread. This was revolutionary stuff–in effect, Livesey was advocating a radical dietary change. His numbers were wrong, but the principle was right: A laborer did not need to drink in order to be able to have the strength to work.

There was more: Livesey also demonstrated that the intoxicating element of ale was spirits, by heating up a quart of ale in an alembic and setting fire to the resultant distillate, "to the surprise and conviction of many who saw it." This, too, was a revelation. Hitherto, it had not been generally understood that the intoxicating agent in beer and spirits was one and the same thing. Most people thought they were as different as cats and dogs, and while reformers had been crusading against gin and its ilk for nearly a century, few had dared suggest that good old ale could damage the drinker in exactly the same way. Livesey, by turning beer into spirits before his audience, had made the point that if people should not drink the hard stuff, they should also renounce liquid bread: "Whisky is the soul of beer, and no one can drink beer without drinking whisky." This last point was a "doctrinal innovation" that established a case for total abstinence.

The concept that humanity might live without any kind of alcoholic drink was revolutionary in Western thought. Although self-denial had been argued by early Christian hermits, who subsisted on a diet of bread and water supplemented by the odd handful of berries, mainstream opinion then and ever since had placed booze among the necessities of life. The age of steam, however, seemed receptive to abstinence, and the act of renouncing alcohol absolutely and forever acquired a name–*teetotalism.* The neologism was coined by Richard Turner, a man with a stutter, at a meeting of the Preston Temperance Society in 1833. Converts to abstinence at such events were in the habit of making a public pledge, and Turner stood up before the audience and declared "that he would 'Be reet down out-and-out t-t-total for ever and ever.'"

The Preston teetotalers also innovated by organizing counterattractions to keep the dry out of the way of temptation, including tea parties, meetings, and marches. They refreshed themselves with moral lectures and revived their weary spirits after a long day's work with hymn singing, rather than a gallon of stingo at the local boozer. Their efforts and achievements were observed with the keenest interest by reform-minded men and women in the middle classes. The success of the campaign to end the slave trade in British dominions had been the inspiration for similar crusades in favor of ethical legislation that would impose Christian standards of behavior on the general populace. Societies had been founded to promote church attendance and prohibit commercial activities on Sundays, to prevent cruelty to animals, and to outlaw the barbaric forms of traditional entertainment such as cockfighting, bearbaiting, badger drawing, and chicken stoning that distracted the masses on holidays. Temperance was seized on as the next good cause, and the middle classes formed their own temperance societies, presided over by members of the clergy and wealthy philanthropists. These differed from the working-class organizations in that they promoted the *short pledge*–i.e., abstinence from spirits–rather than the *long pledge*–total abstinence–and some even numbered brewers among their patrons. They employed the techniques of agitation developed by the antislaving campaign, organizing meetings, marches, manifestos, committees, and petitions. The first such, the British and Foreign Temperance Society (BFTS), printed and distributed over two million temperance tracts in the early 1830s and by 1834 had nearly eighty thousand members.

The differences between middle- and working-class temperance societies were not limited to whether their members should give up all drinks or spirits only, but also encompassed how they should promote their messages. Working-class organizations favored dramatic meetings, at which individuals about to renounce the demon drink would stand up and confess their failings before making a tearful promise never to touch liquor again. Such performances had parallels with evangelical Christianity: The drinker played the lost soul, who had seen the light and found the path to redemption, in the manner of the apostle Paul en route for Tarsus. This secular impersonation of religious enlightenment alarmed the clergy, who tended to belong to middle-class temperance societies, and they reacted by preaching against mistaking sobriety for Grace.

The theatrical aspects of working-class meetings, some of which featured singing, dancing, and comic interludes, were also considered distasteful. Moral issues were to be taken seriously, and the music hall atmosphere that prevailed at the workers' gatherings was deemed inappropriate to the seriousness of the subject. Moreover, in an age where it was considered ill-bred to speak of money or its absence, the tendency of teetotalers to emphasize the material gains they had enjoyed since turning abstinent revolted their social superiors. An example of this last sort of behavior was recorded by an appalled member of the professional classes, who attended a midcentury teetotal meeting, which featured a reformed drunk who, "after observing that for many years he had scarcely ever had a decent rag on his back, and was often without food, 'all through drink,' proceeded to dilate upon the fruits of teetotalism: the fruits in his case being … 'this slap-up suit of black and this watch,' pulling the latter article out of his pocket." The reformed drinker then modeled his suit for the audience, told them how much it and the watch had cost, and exclaimed, "There's the fruits of teetotalism for you." As a finale, he waved the watch above his head and shouted, "Who wouldn't be a teetotaler?"

In the event, it required considerable personal bravery to renounce drinking. In addition to being branded as vulgar, working-class teetotalers had to face the opprobrium of their peers. Giving up had social repercussions—teetotalers were often shunned by their fellow workers, who considered their refusal to participate in the traditional drinking rituals (which persisted in almost every trade) offensive. They also took genuine risks with their health, as most urban water supplies were contaminated, and cholera, in some areas, was endemic. They were forced to pay higher premiums for life insurance and, finally, suffered emotional pressure from friends who were genuinely concerned for their safety. At a Preston meeting, for example, as one man was about to take the long pledge, an acquaintance in the audience cried out, "Don't do it, Richard! If tha gives up drinking tha shalt die!"

The evident courage of teetotalers, and their success in persuading their fellow workers to cleanse themselves of their thirsts, inspired contemporary writers to support their cause in print. The horror of drunkenness was the perfect theme for a show of fashionable compassion, for as the nineteenth century progressed, the Romantic Movement turned sentimental. Wild emotions were replaced in works of fact and fiction with proper feelings. This shift is apparent in the work of Charles Dickens, who started out as a court reporter and journalist before progressing to the panoramic novels of metropolitan life for which he is famous. Dickens was first and foremost an urban writer. Instead of focusing on rosy-cheeked peasants living in harmony with nature, he concentrated on the teeming masses in British cities. He aimed for a more accurate picture of the people of his age, especially its working classes, than the Romantics had attempted. He believed in giving detailed and faithful portraits of all his characters and used their drinking habits to assist him. He tells us what was drunk at every level of society and when. We see the survival of old customs and the emergence of new. Alcohol still formed a part of most people's diets— beer was still served to minors. An eight-year-old David Copperfield, for instance, was provided with a half-pint to go with his dinner of mutton chops, and people of all stations punctuated their day with a glass of something here and there.

Dickens is also a mine of information on the places in which people drank. He recorded both traditional watering holes, such as alehouses and coaching inns, and new establishments—*restaurants* and *gin palaces*. The gin palaces, as their name suggests, were ostentatious in their decoration, and since they were usually located in the filthiest slums, their appearance was all the more striking. Dickens pictured one such as a brightly lit and gilded version of hell, where the poor destroyed themselves like moths in a gas lamp. The "Gin Shop" in *Sketches by Boz* (1836) aimed to shock. While it begins with an affectionate scene of Londoners at ease, discussing the pleasures and hardships of life over a dram, it ends with a drunken brawl at closing time: "The potboy is knocked among the tubs ... the landlord hits everybody, and everybody hits the landlord; the barmaids scream; the police come in; the rest is a confused mixture of arms, legs, staves, torn coats, shouting, and struggling. Some of the party are borne off to the station-house, *and the remainder slink home to beat their wives for complaining, and kick the children for daring to be hungry.*"

Dickens drew the curtain over the action after his italics, implying, in true Romantic tradition, that the horrible life of the poor was a "sight to dream of, not to tell." A moral followed: "We have sketched this subject very slightly, not only because our limits compel us to do so, but because, if it were pursued farther, it would be painful and repulsive. Well-disposed gentlemen, and charitable ladies, would alike turn with coldness and disgust from a description of the drunken besotted men, and wretched broken-down miserable women, who form no inconsiderable portion of the frequenters of these haunts; forgetting, in the pleasant consciousness of their own rectitude, the poverty of the one, and the temptation of the other."

Dickens covered similar ground in the same collection of sketches with the fictional "The Drunkard's Death," a masterpiece of sentiment, in which a surprisingly hardy inebriate ruins himself and his family over twenty or so years before fulfilling the promise of the title. The tale inspired a new literary genre—*temperance noir*—adult fairy tales with sots as ogres. Dickens's pioneering work kicks off with a description of the agent of its hero's ruin. Drunkenness was a "fierce rage for the slow, sure poison, that oversteps every other consideration; that casts aside wife, children, friends, happiness, and station; and hurries its victims madly on to degradation and death." Despite such a breathless opening, there was little subsequent hurrying on the part of the doomed drunkard. The action commences at the deathbed of his wife, who is being comforted in extremis by her mother, and four children, all of whom fix accusatory stares at their inebriated father. The instant she expires he returns to his local watering hole; twenty years pass, during which his sons run away, and he beggars his sickly daughter, who works herself to the bone to support him through a misguided sense of duty. One son returns, seeking refuge from the police (a lack of parental guidance has turned him into a murderer), and informs his father that one of his brothers is dead, while the other has emigrated. The father betrays his son to thief takers, the son is tried and executed, the daughter runs away, a few more years pass, during which the drunkard becomes homeless and suicidal and finally, by luck as much as by intent, drowns himself in the river Thames. "A week afterwards the body was washed ashore, some miles down the river, a swollen and disfigured mass. Unrecognized and unpitied, it was borne to the grave; and there it has long since moldered away!"

19 APOSTLES OF COLD WATER

Why are the classical models of the last century
delivered to the moles and the bats, while the
ravings of insanity are admired? Why has the inspiration of the poet degenerated into the vagaries of
derangement? Lord Byron will answer. He confessed
that he wrote under the influence of distilled spirits.
Here the disgusting secret is developed. Authors
drink and write: Readers drink and admire.
—William Goodall, *Reasons Why Distilled Spirits Should
Be Banished*, New York (1830)

On January 22, 1842, Charles Dickens arrived in Boston for a tour of
the United States. He began his visit full of optimism—certain he
would fall in love with the republic and its people. The confidence
was reciprocated—Americans revered his work and gathered in their
thousands for a chance to see the creator of their favorite fictional
characters. On February 14, when he reached New York, Washington
Irving organized the *Boz* ball in his honor at the Park Royal Theater.
Its decoration was themed after Dickens's first transatlantic best-
seller,[36] and in between dances, sketches were acted of popular scenes
from his other works. Despite similarly ecstatic receptions in other cities, and the initial goodwill on both sides, the visit was accounted a
failure. Dickens was accused of disrespect to his hosts for daring to

---

[36] Albeit an image of the hero of "The Drunkard's Death" did not number among
the decorations.

raise the issue of copyright (most U.S. editions of his work were pirated); the author was offended by slavery, by American eating habits, and the twin practices of tobacco chewing and spitting.

The year after his return to Britain, Dickens published *American Notes*—a journal of his experiences that was poorly received on both sides of the Atlantic. In Britain it was labeled "frivolous and dull," in America it was considered to be a shameful abuse of hospitality. Despite such partial criticism, the book provides an instructive picture of American society at the time, including its drinking habits. Like those of many foreign visitors to the United States, Dickens's initial impressions were of wonder at the variety of booze on offer in the republic. Shortly after his arrival in Boston, he noted with pleasure his initiation into "the mysteries of Gin-sling,…Sangaree, Mint Julep, Sherry-cobbler, Timber Doodle," and various other cocktails. He was likewise fascinated by the addition of ice to drinks, which was almost unknown at the time in Great Britain. In New York, in contrast, every bar had a supply of it, a fact Dickens evidently expected would surprise and delight his British readers: "Hark! to the clinking sound of hammers breaking lumps of ice, and to the cool gurgling of the pounded bits, as, in the process of mixing, they are poured from glass to glass!" Ice was commonplace in America as a result of advances in storage technology. A new style of icehouse had been developed that preserved it through the long hot summers, so that every major city had a cheap supply all year round. Yankees were proud of their ice and compared its abundance at home, where "the use of ice … is an American institution," to its rarity in Europe where "the poorer, and even middle classes, know nothing of ice. It is confined to the wine cellars of the rich."

Another peculiarity in American drinking habits to strike Dickens on his tour, especially when traveling between places, was the tendency to serve only water—usually iced—with meals. Moreover, food was consumed in silence, and with what seemed to him to be indecent haste. He found the quiet, barring the sound of mastication, disturbing: "Sitting down with so many fellow-animals to ward off thirst and hunger as a business; to empty, each creature, his Yahoo's trough as quickly as he can, and then slink sullenly away; to have these social sacraments stripped of everything but the mere greedy satisfaction of the natural cravings; goes so against the grain with me, that I seriously believe the recollection of these funeral feasts will be a waking nightmare to me all my life." The contrast to Britain, where meals were convivial affairs, washed down with large quantities of alcohol, and where people lingered at the table over bottles of port after eating, could not have been greater. In America, with the exception of formal dinners, drinking and eating were separated. Whereas a man might spend only quarter of an hour over his food, he would follow up his meal with two hours at the bar, smoking, drinking, and indulging in what Dickens perceived to be the national pastime—talking politics.

In addition to drinking iced cocktails after dinner, Dickens also refreshed himself with imported wines throughout his sojourn, especially champagne. Champagne was very popular in America at the time. According to another British author to have toured the country, "The quantity of champagne drunk is enormous, and would absorb all the vintage of France." That it did not is tribute to the counterfeiting skills of local manufacturers, who produced most of the fizz sold in the United States within its borders: "The small state of New Jersey has the credit of supplying the American champagne, which is said to be concocted out of turnip juice, mixed with brandy and honey. It is a pleasant and harmless drink, a very good imitation."

The domestic wine industry did more than create faux champagne. In the same year that Dickens visited Cincinnati, Nicholas Longworth, its richest resident,[37] had made a breakthrough in the quest to produce an all-American wine, whose taste was not so vile that it needed to be masked with brandy. Longworth had similar hopes to Thomas Jefferson's as to the place that American wine might occupy in American society—both as a healthy alternative to whiskey and as an emblem of civilization. He had begun experimenting with various native and imported vines in 1813 and had had his first qualified success in the 1820s when he planted the *Catawba* grape along the banks of the Ohio. The Catawba had been discovered growing outside a North Carolina tavern by Major Adlum, the same man who had brought the soon-forgotten and unlamented scuppernong grape to the attention of North America. Adlum had experimented with his new contender in Maryland and had sent some of the wine it produced to Thomas Jefferson just before his death, who had pronounced his blessing over it.

Longworth's first few seasons with the Catawba in Cincinnati were disappointing. Its wine proved to be as foxy as the scuppernong.

---

[37] And according to his tax returns, briefly the wealthiest man in the United States.

In the 1830s, suspecting the nasty aftertaste came from the skins of its grapes, Longworth removed them from the must prior to fermentation, with encouraging results: He created a pale, still wine that tasted like artificial strawberries, which found favor with the German immigrants who were settling in the environs of Cincinnati—and no one else. Before, however, Longworth's grand experiment to make a wine his fellow citizens would drink in preference to imports and whiskey failed, fate intervened—a neglected batch of the "strange strawberryish liquor" underwent secondary fermentation, resulting in a clear, effervescent wine, reminiscent of foxy champagne. Longworth sent for winemakers from the Champagne district of France to improve his product and, despite high wastage in the form of exploding bottles (the Catawba sparkled with a true Yankee vigor), succeeded in creating a wine that won not just domestic but international acclaim. By 1850 it was a commercial success and, shortly afterward, an aesthetic triumph. Henry Longfellow, the first great American poet, composed an ode in its favor:

> Very good in its way
> Is the Verzenay
> Or the Sillery soft and creamy;
> But Catawba wine,
> Has a taste more divine,
> More dulcet, delicious, and dreamy.

While Dickens passed through Cincinnati, which he loved (and where he probably met Longworth among its "intelligent, courteous, and agreeable" society), rather than praising its wine in his *American Notes,* he remembered the city with a description of a temperance rally. Although associated through his writing with the same cause in Britain, Dickens chose to emphasize the comical aspects of the marchers and their "banners out of number." His favorite was one portraying "a temperate man with 'considerable of a hatchet' (as the standard-bearer would probably have said), aiming a deadly blow at a serpent which was apparently about to spring upon him from the top of a barrel of spirits." He was also captivated by the appearance of "a huge allegorical device, borne among the ship-carpenters, on one side whereof the steamboat *Alcohol* was represented bursting her boiler and exploding with a great crash, while upon the other, the good ship *Temperance* sailed away with a fair wind, to the heart's content of the captain, crew, and passengers."

Dickens had little time for the American antialcohol movement. Although he spent much of his tour visiting orphanages, lunatic asylums, and other benevolent institutions, he did not honor any of the thriving temperance societies with his company. In retrospect, this neglect was surprising, for temperance was fast becoming the most popular issue in the United States. Its principal activist organization, the American Temperance Society (ATS), claimed one and a half million members by the time of Dickens's visit. The ATS promoted temperance in the sense of abstinence. In 1836 it had published research conducted by the chemist William Brande that proved, as Livesey had demonstrated with his *Malt Lecture,* that weak drinks, in this case wine, contained the same intoxicating substance as whiskey: "The man who drinks wine, drinks alcohol, as really as the man who drinks distilled liquor; and if he drinks his wine clear, and his distilled liquor mixed with water, he may drink quite as much alcohol in one case as in the other."

The news that wine was an ardent spirit in disguise caused consternation in the ranks of temperate Americans, most of whom had been recruited to the cause through their churches. Surely Jesus had not intended his disciples to celebrate his divinity with hard liquor? Many answered this question in the negative and supported their decision by questioning traditional interpretations of the use, and abuse, of wine in the Scriptures. They found themselves on shaky ground. From the days of Noah, the place of wine in Judeo-Christian societies had been a magnificent one, buttressed by divine associations. To rid Christianity of alcohol was a daunting challenge in revisionism. What, for example, about the Eucharist? While most of the sects in America had Protestant roots, and did not believe in the actual transubstantiation of communion wine, it was still served in numerous chapels throughout the country, mocking, as it were, the supposed compatibility of teetotalism and Christianity. Moreover, the Good Book was full of positive thoughts about wine. Of 212 mentions in the Old Testament, the vast majority speak well of "the gift of God." The fact, however, that wine occasionally received a prophet's curse gave hope to the temperance lobby. The Bible was reexamined by Moses Stuart in 1840, and he discovered that *wine* always meant the "liquid fruit of the vine," i.e., unfermented grape juice, on the occasions when it was referred to as a blessing from heaven; whereas when it appeared as Satan's potion and rendered kings or patriarchs unconscious, it meant alcoholic wine.

These imaginative glosses on the Word of the Lord provoked a bitter debate. Dr. John Maclean, professor of ancient languages at the College of New Jersey, took up his pen against revisionism in an 1841 essay, "Bacchus and Anti-Bacchus." It was not merely bad scholarship, he argued, to pretend that the Jesus had not meant alcoholic wine when he made it "the symbol of his shed blood, in the most sacred rite of his holy religion" and commanded "all his disciples to drink of it in remembrance of him" but also bad theology. Despite such principled and erudite opposition, some of the so-called New School Presbyterians switched to nonalcoholic juice of the fruit of the vine for divine service. Together, they created sufficient demand to constitute a target market for entrepreneurs, who invented and promoted tailor-made products with which they might perform their rites. In 1840, for example, *The Charleston Observer* ran an advertisement from Daniel Pomeroy of New York, who offered unfermented grape syrup, guaranteed to remain free of alcohol, for sale to any New School temperates who wished to stay dry in the house of God.

Interestingly, the debate was most intense in Pennsylvania and Kentucky, where temperance flourished at a rate that would have had the Whiskey Boys of 1794 spinning in their graves. In these former frontier states, in whose creation booze had played so central a role, not only was sacramental wine a controversial issue, but so was whether people who sold or manufactured any sort of alcoholic drink could be acknowledged as Christians at all. *No,* said the synod of Pittsburgh in 1841, and anyone who traded in intoxicating beverages should be excommunicated from its congregation. This scorched-earth approach was opposed by William L. Breckinridge, pastor of the First Presbyterian Church in Louisville, who pointed out that biblical lands in recorded history had never produced alcohol-free wine. After adding that Jesus Christ had never forbidden or even criticized drinking per se in any version of the Bible yet published, he concluded "either that we live in a *very* enlightened age, or that all this is profane and blasphemous irreverence toward the Son of God."

While American divines grappled with the theological challenges of abstinence, the nation's drinkers took up the cudgel against alcohol and beat themselves vigorously. They were inspired by the example of half a dozen Baltimore barflies, who had attended a local temperance meeting to laugh but had left as converts. These proceeded to found the *Washington Temperance Society,* named in honor of America's first president, who had led the country to independence from a monarch, and whose spirit they wished to imitate by freeing the United States from the rule of *King Alcohol.* The *Washingtonians,* as they styled themselves, carried the parallel further in a manifesto published in 1841, which parodied the Declaration of Independence: "We hold these truths to be self-evident;–that all men are created temperate; that they are endowed by their Creator with certain natural and innocent desires; that among these are appetites for COLD WATER and the pursuit of happiness!"

Alongside issuing revolutionary propaganda, the Washingtonians staged confessional meetings like those of the northern British teetotalers, at which reformed drinkers would trumpet their prior degradation and present salvation, and which were a novelty in America. While some commentators found their antics disgusting and labeled them as a "scurrilous army of ditch-delivered reformed drunkards (whose glory was in their shame)," their melodramatic assemblies were immensely popular. Within a year, their membership numbered one hundred thousand, and by 1843 there were half a million Washingtonians,* whose leaders were pan-American celebrities. Principal among these was John Bartholomew Gough, a former actor and drunkard, who was renowned for delivering gruesome speeches about inebriates ruining themselves and hurting others. One of his favorite topics was the withdrawal symptoms suffered by alcoholics, which he would demonstrate as he described them: "Did you ever see a man in delirium tremens, biting his tongue until his mouth was filled with blood, the foam on his lips, the big drops on his brow? Did you ever hear him burst out in blasphemy which curdled your blood, and see him beat his face in wild fury?"

Despite its immense popularity, the Washingtonian movement proved short-lived. Away from the excitement and fervor of its meetings, many converts to abstinence relapsed, including Gough, who was discovered dead drunk in a brothel in New York after a weeklong binge. Although Gough tried to paint himself as a victim, claiming

---

* About one in ten of all adult males.

that his cherry soda had been spiked with drugs, his authority was diminished and the torch of abstinence passed back to the ATS. The latter was joined in its fight against alcohol by a number of new organizations, including the American Temperance Union (ATU) and the Sons of Temperance.[38] While these eschewed theatrical or confessional meetings, they nonetheless encouraged melodrama in temperance writing. The ATU resolved to use works of fiction in the battle against alcohol in 1836, and within a decade temperance had become a stand-alone literary genre. The works published in the field fell into two categories: propaganda, such as the *Good Boys' and Girls' Alphabet* (Philadelphia, 1841), whose readers were taught to hate inebriates via "*D* is for Drunkard"; and books with genuine commercial appeal. It was the age of penny dreadful newspapers, which focused on true stories of violent crime, and accounts of the sordid activities of drunkards could tap into the same market, provided that they were sufficiently gruesome in their details. *The Glass; or The Trials of Helen More. A Thrilling Temperance Tale,* by Maria Lamas (1849), is an exemplar of the commercial variety of temperance writing. It features (a rarity) a female alcoholic who shuts her son in a closet while she goes out on a spree and returns to find that he has eaten himself alive: "I unlocked the clothes room door, and there–oh! there bathed in his blood, lay the mangled corpse of my child–murdered by his mother. There he lay, poor slaughtered innocent! starved! starved! starved! His left arm gnawed to the bone–gnawed till the artery had been severed, and he had bled to death."

When temperance societies found they could promote their version of moral ascendancy and make money at the same time, they commissioned both established and up-and-coming authors to create for them. The Washingtonians, for example, in their glory years, paid Walt Whitman to write *Franklin Evans or, the Inebriate*–whose motto was: "Within that cup there lurks a curse." The result was a convoluted tale of drunkenness, Indian wars, and miscegenation, whose orphan hero was redeemed by its sponsors. It had, however, hints of De Quincey, including incitements to voyeurism and flaunting of wounds, in its confessional style of narrative, perhaps because (so Whitman claimed) it had been completed "in three days for money under the influence of alcohol."

---

[38] Who did not abbreviate their name to its initials–SOT.

The flood of temperance writing resulted in a trickle of new ideas in literature. The psychopathic inebriate became a stock-in-trade character, especially for writers in the gothic style. This creature was an altogether more complex type than the bumbling and parasitical individual depicted by Dickens in his groundbreaking "The Drunkard's Death." Active rather than passive, prone to spectacular hallucinations when not drinking, the improved stereotype had wonderful potential. He could kill, go mad, rape his infant daughter(s), repent, suffer the anguish of guilt, digress and forget himself, relapse, and die, shaking, in a maelstrom of nightmares, all in the same book. The promise of such a fictional individual was realized by Edgar Allan Poe in "The Black Cat," whose narrator, addressing the reader from the shade of the gallows, describes the sequence of events that will terminate with his imminent execution. While the plot is ridiculous, the characterization is spectacular: The narrator is a psychopath as well as a drunkard, who murders his pets and feeds his rage with liquor.

Poe knew his business when writing about inebriates. He was as famous, in his lifetime, for his drinking as his composition. Not even his opium addiction could save him from a drunkard's death, around which there remains a mystery similar to those in his best stories. Like the Washingtonian Gough, he vanished for five days, at the end of which period he was found drunk, disheveled, and sick. He died before he sobered up. A theoretical solution to the mystery has Poe captured by the agents of a political party, forced to drink whiskey, then compelled to make multiple votes for their candidate, day after day, until he collapsed, but this was only the most probable of many conjectures.

During the forty years that Poe had lived, American temperance had evolved from a marginal activity practiced by a handful of eccentrics to a mainstream political cause. In addition to indulging in biblical revisionism, and introducing monstrous dipsomaniacs[39] to American fiction, the country's temperance organizations had taken advantage of the federal nature of the United States to propose legislation against drink at the state level. Early victories made them bold. In 1838 they pressured Maine into passing a *Fifteen-Gallon Law*, so-called because it prohibited the sale of ardent spirits in any lesser quantity. This tactic–which aimed

---

[39] A neologism coined in 1843.

to squeeze out small retailers and casual tipplers by putting strong drink beyond the reach of their purses–had been tried before in England at the height of the gin craze and had failed. In the event, the Fifteen-Gallon Law also failed and was repealed within two years as being antidemocratic. The rich drank wine, which was unaffected by the law, and could, if they so desired, scrape together the four dollars or so required to buy fifteen gallons of whiskey. The poor, in contrast, were denied access to their favorite solace.

This setback did not deter the abolitionists nor harm their cause. New temperance societies sprang up like weeds. The Sons of Temperance were joined by the Independent Order of Rechabites, the Sons of Jonadab,[40] the Daughters of Temperance, the Templars of Honor and Temperance, the Colored Temperance Society, and a host of other local, regional, and national organizations dedicated to ridding the United States of alcohol. The ubiquity of the movement was a matter for satirical comment among the majority of Americans who still drank, to whom it seemed that the country was being overrun by the T-word. According to one observer, a typical small town in the East had "temperance negro operas, temperance theaters; temperance eating houses, and temperance everything, and our whole population, in places, is soused head-over-heels in temperance."

The issue even found its way onboard Yankee ships and penetrated American nautical fiction. In *Moby Dick* (1851) Herman Melville made space for arguments pro and contra temperance, albeit largely contra. The subject was raised under the pretext of a discussion as to what was the correct refreshment for a harpooner, while he was guarding the carcass of a whale against sharks. When Dough-Boy, the cabin steward in the book, produces ginger tea for just such an occasion, he is assaulted by the ship's mate:

> "We'll teach you to drug a harpooneer; none of your apothecary's medicine here; you want to poison us, do ye? You have got out insurances on our lives and want to murder us all and pocket the proceeds, do ye?"
>
> "It was not me," cried Dough-Boy, "it was Aunt Charity that

---

[40] The last two named after a band of brothers in the Bible who were the only people in its pages to take a vow of abstinence.

brought the ginger on board; and bade me never give the har-
pooneers any spirits, but only this ginger-jub—so she called it."

"Ginger-jub! you gingerly rascal! take that! and run along with
ye to the lockers, and get something better . . . it is the captain's
orders—grog for the harpooneer on a whale."

While Americans were being depicted in fiction squabbling over
temperance in the distant whaling grounds, at home its proponents
continued to press for legislation at the state level. In 1855 they succeeded in persuading the voters of Maine to ban the manufacture or
sale of alcohol for public consumption. This partial prohibition, which
had little effect on the drinking of its inhabitants, may be seen as both a
public demonstration of virtue and a concession to a fad. Thirteen
other states in the Northeast and Midwest followed suit, as did counties
in various others. The impact of such laws was varied, as were their
provisions. Maine voters were free to import as much liquor as they
wished and might also take advantage of exemptions for cider, and alcohol for medicinal use. Pennsylvania limited its prohibition to sales of
less than a quart of any alcoholic beverage at a time; Michigan, in order
to placate its German immigrants, exempted "beer and wine of domestic manufacture." Its legislators were pilloried for preferring votes to
morality by the Reverend J. S. Smart in his *Funeral Sermon of the Maine
Law and Its Offspring in Michigan* (1858): "It is a pity that a few drunken
Germans should be allowed thus to rule the thousands of American
born citizens in our state. Here, to secure the votes of a few foreigners . . . we have imposed upon us the legal reopening of thousands of
dens of drunkenness in the form of 'Dutch wine halls' and 'lager beer
saloons.'"

The intransigence of immigrant voters was not the only obstacle temperance reformers faced at the polls. American elections were notoriously wet events. Just as Athenian citizens in the days of Plato had
received free wine on important civic occasions, so American voters
were rewarded by candidates to office for participating in the ballot
with as much whiskey as they could hold. The association of alcohol
with elections stretched back to colonial days. It derived from Britain,
where it had long been customary to treat voters with food and drink.
The custom was continued in America, notably in Virginia, where

failure to intoxicate potential voters was regarded as mean-spirited in a candidate and therefore a sign that they were unsuitable for public office. An indication of the importance of alcohol to colonial elections is provided by the entertainments bill run up by George Washington in 1758 when he stood for office for the first time in the Virginia House of Burgesses:

Dinner for your Friends   £3 0s 0d

13 gallons of Wine at 10/   £6 15s 0d

3 pts of brandy at 1/3   £4s 4d

13 gallons of Beer at 1/3   16s 3d

8 qts Cyder Royal at 1/6   12s 0d

30 gallons of strong beer at 8d   £1 0s 0d

1 hhd and 1 barrel of Punch, consisting of 26 gals.

     Best Barbados rum at 5/   £6 10s 0d

12 lbs S. Refd. sugar at 1/6   18s 9d

10 Bowls of Punch at 2/6 each   £1 5s 0d

9 half pints of rum at 7d each   £0 5s 7d

1 pint of wine   30 1s 6d

In return for such extravagance, Washington was elected with 307 votes. His supporters received, on average, a pint of rum, a pint of beer, and a glass of wine each.[41] This method of encouraging voters continued postindependence, indeed, gained fresh momentum, for the American states had larger franchises, and more frequent elections, than anywhere else in the world at the time. And far from casting their vote in accordance with their convictions or consciences, citizens tended to give them away to inappropriate candidates on the spur of the moment for a few drinks.

As the republic aged, the tie between free drinks and the ballot box grew stronger. Voters expected to be treated, and candidates budgeted accordingly. The tie was introduced to new states as they joined the union, as a kind of patriotic institution. In Kentucky, for example, where temperance, in theory, was rampant, King Alcohol still ruled at

---

[41] An expenditure of around $50 per head at current bar prices. For the sake of comparison, the Republican Party spent an average of $12.65 per vote for its victory in 2004.

election time, as the following account of the 1830 polls, from the *New England Weekly Review,* illustrates:

> An election in Kentucky lasts three days, and during that period whiskey and apple toddy flow through our cities and villages like the Euphrates through ancient Babylon.... In Frankfort, a place which I had the curiosity to visit on the last day of the election, Jacksonianism and drunkenness stalked triumphant—"an unclean pair of lubberly giants." A number of runners, each with a whiskey bottle poking its long neck from his pocket, were busily employed bribing voters, and each party kept a dozen bullies under pay, genuine specimens of Kentucky alligatorism.... I barely escaped myself. One of the runners came up to me, and slapping me on the shoulder with his right hand, and a whiskey bottle in his left, asked me if I was a voter. "No," I said. "Ah, never mind," quoth the fellow, pulling a corncob out of the neck of the bottle, and shaking it up to the best advantage. "Jest take a swig at the cretur and toss in a vote for Old Hickory's boys."

George Caleb Bingham's County Election

"Old Hickory" was President Andrew Jackson, whose election campaign had taken alligatorism to new heights. Its manager, Martin Van Buren, a New York politician and power broker, was a master of promotion. Posters of his candidate were distributed across the country and reproduced in local newspapers. Speechwriters and speech makers were hired to refine their message and preach it through the states. The nickname "Old Hickory" was invented, and thousands of miniature hickory sticks were given away at rallies, in addition to sashes, badges, and the customary drinks. When Jackson won, his supporters descended on Washington in their hordes to attend his inauguration. Thirty thousand accompanied him to the Capitol and did their best to follow him into the White House. Those who had succeeded were lured back outside onto the lawn with barrels of whiskey and bowls of orange punch. For months after, Washington was crowded with a host of men from the backwoods, who very quickly drank it dry of booze, while they waited to be given government appointments as rewards for their votes. Most were disappointed—there were not enough minor posts to go around. However, in the higher echelons of the administration, there were sufficient sinecures to satisfy Van Buren and his coterie, who removed sitting officials and took their places for themselves, justifying their venality with the motto, coined by one of their number, "To the victors belong the spoils of the enemy."

The affair between drink and American politics peaked in the election campaign of 1840, when General William Henry Harrison, victor of a frontier skirmish, took on the Democratic Party, which had selected Van Buren as its candidate, at its own game. Armed with the slogan "Tippecanoe and Tyler Too," which referred to the place of his victory, and the name of his running mate, Harrison's campaigners set out to sing the praises of their candidate to the nation. Scarcely had they commenced when their opponents, intending to denigrate, provided them with a more compelling theme. Van Buren labeled Harrison the "Log Cabin and Hard Cider" candidate, expecting that the electorate would associate these things with squalor and inebriation. He was wrong. Americans held both cabins and cider in high regard and responded enthusiastically when the Harrison campaign gave out models of one, and gallons of the other, at its rallies. Voters liked the themes of self-sufficiency and the simple life apparent in these symbols of frontier life and deemed anyone who criticized them effete:

> Let Van from his coolers of silver drink wine,
> And lounge on his cushioned settee;
> Our man on his buckeye bench can recline.
> Content with hard cider is he.

Harrison won by a slender margin of the popular vote. He celebrated his arrival at the White House with some cider, and many other drinks, and died of pneumonia after a month in office.

20 WEST

Notwithstanding the lusty drinking that went on during American elections, they were models of restraint and probity in comparison to the democratic process in Mexico. In 1821, America's southern neighbor had followed it in throwing off the colonial yoke but, rather than organizing itself as a republic, had chosen to be headed by an emperor. Constitutional imperial rule was rejected in favor of a dictatorship two years later, the first of many changes in government that were to enliven Mexican politics for the rest of the century. Twenty-five years after its declaration of independence, a traveling English mercenary estimated that the country had had 237 revolutions over the same period of time.

Excitement in the political sphere was counterbalanced by stability in drinking habits. In order to protect its exports, Spain had maintained severe restrictions on the production of wine and spirits in Mexico almost to the end of its rule, with the consequences that most wine was imported, and most spirits were moonshine. The principal legal drink in Mexico, in terms of volume consumed, was pulque, the favorite moon juice of 2-Rabbits. It was still prepared in a more or less Aztec manner, still spoiled quickly, and its consumption was concentrated in towns. It had come to be perceived of as a type of food, in particular for pregnant women, who were exhorted always to drink at least two cups—one for themselves and one for the child inside them. Pulque was also provided to nursing infants, in the belief that it nourished and strengthened them. This new role had diminished its reputation as an intoxicant and it had become a beverage that anyone, of every age, might enjoy at any time.

Those Mexicans wishing to become their rabbits now drank mescal, i.e., distilled pulque. This was the most common alcoholic beverage in mining communities, and also on the country's vast ranches and in the little villages that grew up to serve them. The rancheros produced mescal for much the same reasons as Kentucky settlers made whiskey: Distillation concentrated their harvest, extended its life, and rendered it transportable. They took pride in their stills and competed in the quality of their product, to which they attributed medicinal as well as organoleptic properties. Mescal was considered good "for everything bad, and for everything good as well." The production of this panacea was concentrated in Jalisco, which had become an official part of independent Mexico in 1821. Jalisco was home to the first licensed mescal distillery in the Americas, founded by José Antonio Cuervo, who had received permission from the Spanish crown to distil "mescal wine" in 1795. Its products, and those of the multitude of other stills that sprang up postindependence, were drunk principally by men, who were expected to comport themselves with courtesy and dignity when under the influence. Mescal was used for ceremonial as well as recreational purposes. The Mexicans had kept many of their pre-Columbian festivals alive in the guise of Christian fiestas, the most important of which were Los Días de Muertos (the days of the dead), staged under the cover of the Catholic festivals of All Souls and All Saints. The dead were assumed to return to the world of the living for the duration of Los Días de Muertos and were supplied with offerings of food and drink. Spirits were the most popular libations, and their tendency to evaporate when left out in a glass was interpreted as proof that the departed had taken a sip.

Notwithstanding the general limitations Spain had imposed on the production of wine in its colonies, the religious institutions it founded in Mexico had been permitted to plant vineyards so as to ensure a supply of wine for the altar. These introduced the grape to the country's largest and emptiest province–California. Spanish California was a sleepy kind of place. While it had been explored in the sixteenth century and named after an imaginary island in a romantic tale, the Spanish had only begun to colonize it in the eighteenth century, and then in a dilatory manner. Settlement had proceeded via a string of military strongholds, or *presidios,* usually coupled with a Franciscan mission. The first of the latter was founded in 1769 at San

Diego, followed by (traveling northward) San Juan Capistrano, Santa Barbara, San Luis Obispo, Monterey, and, in 1776, San Francisco.

San Juan Capistrano, in what is now Orange County, was the first Californian mission to make wine. The man responsible for tending its vines was a young friar named Pablo de Mugártegui. The vines under his care had been delivered by sea in 1779, aboard the *San Antonio,* under Don José Camacho. The first vintage produced at the mission was probably the 1782, for in December 1781, Fra Junipero Serra, the supervisor of the Californian mission chain, had written to it expressing the pious hope that "your vines will survive and bear fruit" as "the lack of wine for the mass is becoming unbearable," thus implying no grapes had been harvested that fall. By 1783, however, Fra Serra's prayers had been answered. Writing from the mission at San Gabriel, once again to regret a dearth of communion wine, he revealed that the shortage had resulted from an accident. When a barrel "was being brought here from San Juan Capistrano it fell off the mule, broke into pieces, and all the wine was lost." There was, however, sufficient wine from the same source at neighboring missions to avert a crisis.

Enthused by the success of San Juan Capistrano, the Franciscans planted vines at every step as the mission chain was extended northward. They were also cultivated by the laity: Don Pedro Fages, *commandante* of Alta California, was growing them in his garden at Monterey by 1783. The vines in question were all the same variety—the *black País*, which became known as the *Mission,* in recognition of the pioneering work of the friars. The principal appeal of its grapes was their fecundity. According to a modern expert, the average example is "an early maturing dark-skinned bag of sweet juice: no more." Few tasting notes on primitive Californian wine exist, and none of them are positive. According to an Englishman who traded for furs on the coast, "with the exception of what we got at the Mission of Santa Barbara, the native wine that we tasted was such trash as nothing but politeness could have induced us to swallow." The shock to the palate may have resulted from the production processes. The wine was trodden by foot and fermented in cowhides slung from poles. It was stored in barrels acquired from the coastal trade, whose prior contents ranged from salted penguins to pickled sardines. Often it was stabilized with the addition of brandy—the friars ran stills at some missions for the production of medicinal *aguadiente,* which also was employed to improve the flavor of the contents of their daily chalice.

However, by 1835, when a Harvard student named Richard Henry Dana visited California, even such unappetizing fluids were in short supply. Postindependence, the Mexican government had expropriated the assets of the Franciscans, and since the missions were the economic as well as spiritual center of each settlement, entropy followed. Dana's account of his visit depicts a vast, almost empty coastline, washed by the long Pacific swells and dotted with occasional settlements, which were falling into ruin. Weeds grew up through the courtyards of their missions, and they were peopled with a few aging friars and their native slaves, and poverty-stricken hidalgos. The only really vibrant places ashore were the bars and grog tents set up by Yankees to cater to the coastal trade.

The principal article of commerce in California was cattle hides, which were taken from the immense herds that roamed free across the unfenced land. Despite the distances (California was as far by sea from the United States as India) and the dangers of doubling Cape Horn, the trade was lucrative, as Dana explained: "The Californians are an idle, thriftless people, and can make nothing for themselves. The country abounds in grapes, yet they buy bad wine made in Boston and brought round by us, at an immense price, and retail it among themselves at a *real* (12½ cents) by the small wine-glass. Their hides, too, which they value at two dollars in money, they give for something which costs seventy-five cents in Boston; and buy shoes (as like as not, made of their own hides, which have been carried twice around Cape Horn) at three or four dollars."

Dana had, however, prophetic words for one place in this dilapidated and sparsely populated part of Mexico. San Francisco, which in his day consisted of a ruined fort, a tumbledown mission, and a grog tent on the beach at Yerba Buena, was blessed with a first-rate natural harbor, and in his opinion, "if California ever becomes a prosperous country, this bay will be the center of its prosperity. The abundance of wood and water, the extreme fertility of its shores, the excellence of its climate, which is as near as to being perfect as any in the world, and its facilities for navigation, affording the best anchoring grounds in the whole western coast of America, all fit it for a place of great importance."

❖ ❖ ❖

While Mexican California slumbered, another of the country's provinces, Texas, attracted hordes of Yankee settlers. They were drawn by the size of the land grants offered by the Mexican government, which came in 4,428-acre blocks. By 1830, three-quarters of the population of Texas was American-born. This influx alarmed the Mexicans, who closed its borders to newcomers and tightened up their political control over the province. Moreover, existing immigrants were required to convert to Roman Catholicism. Texan Americans resented both the autocratic style of government and absence of religious freedom and in 1835, led by Sam Houston, a former governor of Tennessee, they declared independence and the foundation of their own republic.

Mexico responded by sending an army over the Rio Grande that surrounded and massacred a band of settlers who had taken refuge in a fortified mission at the Alamo. Its victims included such luminaries of frontier life as James Bowie and Davy Crockett, who sank his last "horn" of spirits during the siege. They were revenged by Houston, who captured Mexico's dictator, General Santa Anna, and forced him to recognize the new republic. Houston, true to his place of origin, was a renowned drinker, reckoned to consume, in the hyperbolic language of the age, "a barrel of whiskey a day." The American Texans who comprised his forces were as fond of whiskey as their leader. Indeed, the habit of hard drinking was a distinguishing feature of their society and one that bound them together in a new land. As a Texan periodical observed of its readership, "Drinking was reduced to a system, and had its own laws and regulations. Nothing was regarded as a greater violation of established etiquette than for one who was going to drink not to invite all within reasonable distance to partake; so that the Texians, being entirely a military people, not only fought but drank in platoons."

Texas continued as an independent republic until 1845, when it was annexed by the United States to become the twenty-eighth state. The following year, a territorial dispute between Mexico and the United States over their borders led to war. American settlers in California took advantage of the conflict to declare independence in the Bear Flag Revolt of June 1846. The fighting ended quickly with a comprehensive victory for the United States. Peace negotiations and compensation claims took time to reconcile, but in February 1848 Mexico accepted the Rio Grande as its northern frontier and ceded California and New Mexico to the United States.

These territorial gains coincided with the peaceful settlement of the border between British Canada and the United States at the forty-ninth parallel of longitude, effectively extending the existing line between them all the way west across the continent. With the northern and southern limits fixed, and the Pacific fringe in Yankee hands, Americans hurried to occupy the places in between. Their mantra was "Manifest Destiny," for they believed that God had selected them to rule: "This continent was intended by Providence as a vast theater on which to work out the grand experiment of Republican Government, under the auspices of the Anglo-Saxon race." When gold was discovered in California in 1848 it was taken as further proof of divine backing. A stream of Americans and European immigrants flowed west, some of them to settle, others in transit for the gold diggings. They carried copious amounts of alcohol with them, for the spirit of temperance that had possessed people in the eastern states seems to have had little influence west of the Mississippi.

The terrain the migrants crossed was not entirely empty. The United States recognized much of it as belonging to various Indian tribes, seventy thousand of whom it had removed there from their traditional homes. The Indians had been compensated with cash payments and annuities, and assurances that their titles to their new domains would be respected in perpetuity. In the event, few of the transported tribes enjoyed them for more than a generation. The migrants were hot on their heels, and the booze they carried with them contributed to the devastation of Native American culture in the West. Its tribes still exhibited the dipsomaniacal tendencies that had so alarmed white settlers in prior centuries and drank themselves to death with the same abandon. In 1842, for example, David Mitchell, the superintendent of Indian affairs at the St. Louis Agency, advised Washington that over five hundred transported Indian males had been killed by drinking within the past two years and that alcohol was "as destructive and more constant than disease" to the health of his charges.

These casualties had occurred notwithstanding the existence of federal legislation intended to place alcohol beyond the reach of the tribes. In 1802, the government had made it a criminal offence to sell liquor in Indian Country. The laws had been amended, supplemented, and restated in 1822, and again in 1832 and 1834, all to no avail. They were ineffective because liquor was already in Indian country; indeed it had gone west before both the Indian removals and the wagon trains. Lewis and Clark had included whiskey in their rations on their pioneering mission across the continent in 1804. The Yellowstone expedition of 1819–20 found that its taste had not been forgotten. Well west of the Missouri, they had come across a Pawnee warrior who had dropped to his knees in front of them, grabbed his throat with his hands as if dying of thirst, and called out, "Whiskey, whiskey!"

Drink trickled into the Indian lands at the heart of the American continent from all points of the compass. It was introduced from the north via the fur trade, which still considered alcohol to be absolutely necessary to its business. Jacob Astor's American Fur Company, the principal operator in the region, showed a blatant disregard for American law in supplying all its agents with whiskey to exchange for pelts and, when challenged, revived the defense of the seventeenth century— that if it did not offer spirits, the Indians would take their furs to British Canada, which did. Meanwhile, a regular supply of drink arrived from the south, along the Santa Fe Trail, and this trade mushroomed after Texan independence. Distilleries were constructed along the upper Rio Grande and their product soon made a name for itself in the interior. This was the notorious *Aguadiente de Taos*, aka Taos Lightning, renowned for both its potency and its alleged efficacy as an antidote to rattlesnake venom.

However, the principal supply of whiskey to Indian country came from the east, in the wagons of migrants, and courtesy of dedicated merchants. Even after taking into account the dangers and distances involved, ardent spirits were wonderfully profitable trade goods. In the early 1830s, a gallon of whiskey cost twenty-five cents in St. Louis, thirty-four dollars in Fort Leavenworth (thirty miles from Kansas City), and sixty-four dollars by the mouth of the Yellowstone. Anyone willing to risk a few months on the plains could make serious money from selling it. Profit was maximized by dilution. According to one estimate, a barrel of "Pure Cincinnati" could be converted into a hundred barrels of "good Indian liquor." The process was as follows: "A small bucketful is poured into a wash-tub of water; a large quantity of 'dog leg' tobacco and red pepper is then added, next a bitter root common in the country is cut up into it, and finally it is colored with burnt sugar—a nice recipe for a morning's headache!"

At the time of the Indian removals, the American population along the then-frontier had been sparse. However, over the following decades it exploded: The old west in Missouri became a fully developed center for agriculture, with hundreds of thousands of acres under the plow, steam-powered flour mills, and numerous distilleries, which, by 1840, produced over half a million gallons of whiskey per annum among them. Indians living in Indian country close to so much temptation were a natural market, not least of all because they were cash buyers. The federal government paid them their annuities punctually every year, and much of this money was spent on alcohol, resulting in violent, drunken orgies whenever a tribe received its Yankee gold. In consequence, Yankee whiskey traders were blatant in their disregard for the laws. An English traveler was amazed at the flagrant way they went about their business: "The alcohol is put into wagons, at Westport or Independence, in *open daylight* and taken into the territory, *in open daylight.* . . . Two government agents reside at Westport, while six or eight companies of Dragoons are stationed at Fort Leavenworth, ostensibly for the purpose of protecting Indians and suppressing this infamous traffic,–and yet it suffers no diminution from *their vigilance*! What *faithful* public officers! How prompt in the discharge of their *whole* duty!"

In 1847 the laws against selling ardent spirits in Indian country were revised again. For the first time, offenders could be punished with a prison sentence, and as a further innovation, Indians were permitted to appear as witnesses in court. The 1847 legislation also allowed for the payment of annuities direct to Indian families, as opposed to the prior practice of making them to tribal chiefs. Finally, no payments were to be made to drunken Indians, and annuities could be withheld if tribal leaders refused to "pledge themselves to make all proper exertions to prevent the introduction and sale of liquor in their country." The new legislation had as little effect as preceding acts. The sale of liquor in Indian country went on as ever before. The few prosecutions attempted were unsuccessful. The majority of cases were discontinued because the defendant or the witnesses had disappeared into the depths of the Far West. Moreover, juries were biased in favor of liquor sales–they did not see why Indians should not be allowed to drink themselves to death and, given the prevailing level of prejudice against the tribes, considered the facilitation of such an end desirable rather than criminal.

Native Americans were not the only market for whiskey in the West. It had long been penetrated by fur trappers, known to posterity as mountain men. They were followed by fur traders, who set up posts within striking distance of the Missouri River, by boatmen, who plied an intermittent service along the river, by soldiers, and finally by settlers. Each class of migrant had a demand for or brought with them a supply of alcohol, invariably spirits, as the distances were too great to transport any other kind of drink.

As forts and settlements were established along the trails west, so opportunities for drinking increased. The soldiers posted to remote stations killed time with boozing, and the migrants traveling overland to Oregon or California carried a supply of liquor with them intended to last them through the trek. Whenever a group assembled there was usually drinking aplenty—it was a way of forming bonds with strangers, a cultural bridge that united them so far from their places of origin. A picture of such an assembly has been left to us by Francis Parkman, who spent the summer of 1846 on a buffalo hunting trip to the Far West:

> Pushing through a noisy, drunken crowd, I entered an apartment of logs and mud, the largest in the fort; it was full of men of various races and complexions, all more or less drunk. A company of California emigrants, it seemed, had made the discovery at this late day that they had encumbered themselves with too many supplies for their journey. A part, therefore, they had thrown away or sold at great loss to the traders, but had determined to get rid of their copious stock of Missouri whisky, by drinking it on the spot. Here were maudlin squaws stretched on piles of buffalo robes; squalid Mexicans, armed with bows and arrows; Indians sedately drunk; long-haired Canadians and trappers, and American backwoodsmen in brown homespun, the well-beloved pistol and bowie knife displayed openly at their sides. In the middle of the room a tall, lank man, with a dingy broadcloth coat, was haranguing the company in the style of the stump orator. With one hand he sawed the air, and with the other clutched firmly a brown jug of whisky, which he applied every moment to his lips, forgetting that he had drained the contents long ago.

❖ ❖ ❖

Three years after Parkman's excursion, the California gold rush commenced. The prospect of digging a fortune out of the distant hills fired the imagination of all America, and much of Europe. People set off in their thousands, and then their tens of thousands, all animated by the dream of filling their pockets with nuggets that rumor had scattered across the Far West. On one day in August 1850, 39,506 emigrants were counted passing Fort Laramie, and though this flood subsided over the following decade, sufficient numbers of people were crossing the country to change its face forever. The trails west, while arduous, lost some of their notoriety as they were spanned by stage coach services, which ran to fixed timetables and enabled regular communication across the breadth of the continent. The stage routes were supported by long strings of post stations, which, in the case of the central California route, stretched from the Missouri River to San Francisco.

According to the accounts of travelers on the stagecoaches, alcohol was the lifeblood of the service, animating the drivers and tranquilizing the passengers. These two functions were complementary and formed a kind of dynamic equilibrium: The drivers took whiskey for breakfast and drove their teams like furies, the passengers took fright at the pace and calmed themselves with drink. The typical stage driver could "do nothing without whiskey, which he loves to call tarantula juice, strychnine, redeye, corn juice, Jersey lightning, leg stretcher, 'tangle leg' (said to be made of diluted alcohol, nitric acid, pepper, and tobacco), and many other hard and grotesque names." As a consequence, the ordinary passenger suffered a via dolorosa—"twenty-four mortal days and nights . . . through the vilest and most desolate portion of the West"—so that, "becoming crazy by whiskey; mixed with want of sleep," many were "obliged to be strapped to their seats."

While heavy drinking was the norm along the stagecoach routes, it was eschewed in the largest single community in the Far West—Salt Lake City. Founded on July 24, 1847, on what was then Mexican soil, Salt Lake City was intended to be the sacred capital of a new sect of Christians, the Latter-day Saints, known colloquially as *Mormons*. The sect had originated in New York State under the leadership of Joseph Smith, who claimed that Jesus Christ and various angels had directed him to a set of buried golden plates, on which were inscribed a series of revelatory texts. The texts identified the Native Americans with a wandering tribe of Jews and provided a history of their settlement in the New World. They also offered a revised version of Christianity, which permitted polygamy, among other unorthodox practices. After attempting to settle in Missouri, Ohio, and Illinois, and suffering persecution in each place, the Mormons removed to Salt Lake, where they established a community that was distinguished by its order and unity from every other settlement in the West.

The desire of the Mormons to found an independent nation and to insulate themselves from other Christians, whom they termed gentiles, resulted in a brief and nasty conflict with American settlers and soldiers in 1857, at the conclusion of which the United States confirmed its sovereignty over Utah. While nominally under the jurisdiction of an American governor, Salt Lake City was controlled by Brigham Young, the Mormon leader, in accordance with Mormon principles. Since these differed from standard Christianity, the settlement acquired a notoriety, not only in America, but throughout the world. Lurid stories circulated of aging and lecherous Mormon men marrying several generations of related women. They were also rumored to abstain from drinking in their holy city of the West.

Come the hour, come the man. Sir Richard Burton, one of the greatest explorers of the nineteenth century and world authority on sacred places, decided to investigate the sect for himself. Burton had visited Benares in India in his youth, had infiltrated Mecca disguised as an Arab, had "discovered" Lake Victoria in Africa on the expedition that established the true source of the river Nile, and had traveled to and written about a host of other spots noted for their difficulty of access and hostility to unbelievers. Soldier, scholar, linguist par excellence, a man of tested stamina and courage, Burton was the perfect individual to examine the goings-on at Salt Lake City. He even had form, loosely speaking, on polygamy. While only married to one woman, he was a noted philanderer, and his second field of expertise after comparative theology was pornography.

Burton arrived in America in May 1860. It seems that the idea of visiting Utah came to him some time after landing, for according to his diaries, his original reasons for crossing the Atlantic were to escape the controversies surrounding his recent African expedition, to recover his health, and to drown his sorrows: "I'll drink mint-juleps, brandy-smashes, whiskey-skies, gin-sling, cocktail, sherry cobblers, rum-salads, streaks of lightning, morning-glory... it'll be the most interesting experiment. I want to see whether after a life of 3 or 4 months, I can drink and eat myself to the level of the aborigines." Experiment over, Burton set off for Utah via the stagecoach.

Inspired, perhaps, by the cocktails he had tested in the East, Burton paid the keenest attention to the alcoholic and other stimulants he came across while en route. He tasted whatever the staging posts had to offer and also gathered data on native intoxicants. He was fascinated, for instance, by the potential of a "kind of cactus called by the whites 'whiskey-root' and by the Indian 'peioke,'" which was said to act on the system just like whiskey, "only its effects are what I might term a little k-a-v-o-r-t-i-n-g, giving rather a wilder scope to the imagination and actions."

Burton enjoyed his first taste of Mormon liquor while still some distance from Salt Lake City. The beverage in question was Valley Tan whiskey, which Burton, in his mania for comparative analysis, equated to "the korn-schnapps of the trans-Rhenine region." He proceeded to pass three weeks in the City of the Saints, where alcohol, contrary to gentile rumor, was easy to obtain. There were, however, unlike most other American settlements of a similar size, no public bars and no drunks. The principal drink produced and consumed in Salt Lake was lager: "There are two large and eight small breweries in which a palatable Lager-bier is made. The hop grows wild and luxuriant in every kanyon; and there is no reason why in time the John Barleycorn of the Saints should not rival that of the sinners." There seems to have been no stigma attached to the consumption of beer—even Brigham Young took a glass from time to time.

The Mormons were also fond of wine. They had planted Mission, Catawba, and other varieties of grape with the aim of ensuring a supply of communion wine, and imported vintages while they waited for their own vines to bear fruit. Spirits, however, were a different matter, and although the city had a single distillery, the source of Valley Tan whiskey, there was a heavy tax on imported hooch, which when coupled with pressure from the pulpit, meant that few Mormons touched "essence of corn."

In consequence the population of Salt Lake City was, as far as Burton could judge, in a constant state of sobriety and health. Indeed, he was impressed by the general level of well-being, in particular among the British saints who formed a majority of immigrants at the time: "Children and adults have come from England apparently in a dying state, and have lived to be strong and robust men." He attributed their vitality to both the altitude and temperance: "The atmosphere is too fine and dry to require or even to permit the free use of spirituous liquors."

That a colony founded by a religious sect, and intended to be independent from the United States, should be the only place in the West where temperance reigned was a source of irritation to the dry bodies back East and, indeed, in the old West. Why was it that the newest parts of their country were reviving colonial-era attitudes to drinking, instead of choosing contemporary American abstinence? The matter was addressed by the *St. Louis Reporter* in 1858, which concluded that "this state of things is brought about by a variety of causes, not the least of which is the fact that a young man . . . feels that in order to be a true Westerner, he must adopt the free and easy way, and drink whenever asked, throw off all restraint, and 'go it blind,' for the sake of being a 'clever fellow' which means, in these times, a natural fool."

21 THE KING OF
      SAN FRANCISCO

fter refreshing himself in the pure mountain air of Salt Lake City
and taking a last "liquor up" with his traveling companions, Sir
Richard Burton exited the United States via San Francisco. He
paused on his voyage home in Mexico, where, even after eight months
on the road through a nation in the making, he was shocked by the
chaos and took "philosophical consolation in various experiments
touching the influence of Mezcal brandy, the Mexican National drink,
upon the human mind and body." The tumult of Mexico, exaggerated
by mescal, sweetened Burton's perception of America, and in particular the last portion of its soil that he had touched. San Francisco, true
to Richard Henry Dana's prophecy, had become a considerable place,
thanks to the gold rush.

It is hard to overstate the impact of the California gold rush on the
American and global economies. America had always been short of
specie; and now its citizens were digging it by the sackful out of the
California and Nevada mountains—$550 million worth, in 1850s prices,
in the first decade alone. The rumor that America had not just free
land but free gold, too, spread around the world, and people from Pacific and Atlantic nations set out for the new Eldorado. Hundreds of
ships of all descriptions piled into San Francisco Bay, where they were
abandoned by their passengers and crews, who set off for the mines.
Some boats were converted into bars and bunkhouses for the next
wave of arrivals, others were stripped of their timbers, which were
used to construct shanties in the sand dunes ashore. By 1850, a city of
twenty-five thousand people had arisen, which had already won itself

an international reputation as being the most expensive and lawless place on earth. Prices for accommodation, food, and clothing were between ten and a hundred times the prevailing rates in New York. A boiled egg cost a dollar, a quart of whiskey thirty dollars, "the rent of a tiny cigar store barely large enough for one man to stand in was $4,000 a month," and it was cheaper to ship laundry to Honolulu or Canton than to have it done in situ.

The inflated prices were paid without a murmur by miners returning from the Sierras with their pockets full of nuggets and gold dust. Many were rich for the first time in their lives and wished to celebrate by spending their new wealth. Facilities were constructed in San Francisco to accommodate this desire—principally bars. Like the sailors of Dana's generation, who, after months afloat, passed their hours ashore in drunkenness, the miners recovered from a stint in the mountains with a spree in San Francisco. Indeed, the city could be said to have arisen solely for the purpose of encouraging binge drinking, and as it grew it remained faithful to its original spirit.

The population of San Francisco was overwhelmingly male. In late 1849, its female residents were reckoned to number fewer than three hundred, the majority of whom were Hispanic prostitutes. This imbalance could not persist, and from 1851 onward single women arrived in droves:

> The miners came in forty-nine,
> The whores in fifty-one;
> And when they got together
> They produced the native son.

The presence of women did not distract the miners from their drinks: Most of the former were employed gold-digging in bars and brothels, where they were expected to encourage drunkenness in order to facilitate the process of extraction. If their prey showed signs of reluctance, their glasses were spiked with pure alcohol, opium, tobacco juice, or Spanish fly.[42]

As San Francisco sprawled inland from the waterfront, its places of entertainment became concentrated in an area around the base of Telegraph Hill known as Sydney Town, in tribute to the Australian im-

---

[42] Cantharides vesicatoria.

migrants who had settled there, and who came to dominate the San Francisco underworld. Many of these were ex-convicts, or men with experience of exploiting miners that had been gained in the Australian gold rush of 1851. They set up grogeries with colonial names–the Noggin of Ale, the Tam O'Shanter, the Goat and Compass–where they led by example in the art of binge drinking. Their champion was Dirty Tom McAlear, "who for a few cents would eat or drink any sort of refuse offered to him." When arrested in 1852 for "making a beast of himself," Dirty Tom confessed to have been continuously drunk for seven years and not to have washed for at least fifteen. The *San Francisco Herald* has left us a contemporary portrait of Sydney Town in its prime: "crowded by thieves, gamblers, low women, drunken sailors, and similar characters, who resort to the grogeries that line the street, and there spend the night in the most hideous orgies. . . . These ruffian resorts are the hot-beds of drunkenness, and the scenes of unnumbered crimes. Unsuspecting sailors and miners are entrapped by the dexterous thieves and swindlers that are always on the look-out, into these dens, where they are filled with liquor–drugged, if necessary, until insensibility coming upon them, they fall an easy victim to their tempters." In addition to doping, robbing, and murdering their clientele, the *Sydney Ducks,* as the expatriate Australians were known, regularly set fire to other parts of the city, so that they might loot with impunity after the blaze. Their lawlessness resulted in the formation of a Vigilance Committee, which lynched several of the most flagrant offenders and succeeded in imposing order of a sort on San Francisco.

The city expanded at an undiminished rate throughout the 1850s and meanwhile oscillated between calm and chaos. During this period alternative entertainments to drinking appeared, including a circus and a theater, and some of the watering holes upgraded their facilities to cater to a clientele that wished to indulge its vices in respectable surroundings. Foremost among such institutions was the *Eldorado,* which had begun life in 1849 as a grog tent but by the mid-1850s had metamorphosed into an elegant casino, with a resident orchestra and nightly shows featuring well-known entertainers. The Eldorado was further distinguished by the skills of its head bartender, Professor Jerry Thomas, the inventor of numerous cocktails, including the *Blue Blazer.*

The miners who retreated to San Francisco for some R & R, or to dispose of a portion of their newfound wealth prior to shipping for home, also drank at their places of work. Despite the isolation of most of the gold mines, and the high cost of transportation to them, alcohol formed a major component of the loads of the mule trains that picked their way through the forests and over the mountains to the camps inland. Here it served principally as a sedative after heavy labor. Most of the early California mining was carried out on placer deposits—sedimentary pockets of gold that had collected on riverbeds and water courses. The miners either spent their days knee-deep in frigid mountain torrents, washing pan after pan of sediment, or feeding tons of dirt into a sluice box, one shovel-load at a time. The changeable mountain weather made their work all the more arduous. In spring and autumn, they might face blizzards and blazing heat in the same week, in winter they were snowed in for extended periods, and in summer, when the rivers ran low and the miners labored fourteen-hour days to install flumes and dams, flash floods arrived without warning and washed away their handiwork.

The drinking habits prevalent in the California Sierra are depicted in *The Shirley Letters* (1855) by Louise A. K. S. Clappe, who spent 1851 and 1852 at two mining camps in the headwaters of the Feather River. *The Shirley Letters* provide a rare perspective on that isolated and masculine environment, for their author was a respectable woman in a region where such persons were almost unknown. Her appearance at the Indian Bar camp, where her husband worked as a doctor, caused consternation. On the day she arrived she was introduced to one of its founders, who "had not spoken to a woman for two years, and, in the elation of his heart at the joyful event, he rushed out and invested capital in some excellent champagne, which I . . . assisted the company in drinking, to the honor of my own arrival. I mention this, as an instance, that nothing can be done in California without the sanctifying influence of the *spirit;* and it generally appears in a much more 'questionable shape' than that of sparkling wine."

The pervasive influence of alcohol over camp life was reflected in its material culture. The packaging used to carry alcohol to the miners was converted into furniture and decorations. Claret cases were transformed into tables and linen chests, and empty bottles served as window panes, or lamps. On occasions, the ubiquity of used drinking receptacles and associated paraphernalia had a poignant side: Clappe recorded that when she tried to comfort a six-year-old girl whose mother had died, by giving her some little glass scent bottles to play with, the child called them "baby decanters."

On festive occasions, the intensity of the drinking in the mining camps matched or exceeded that which prevailed in San Francisco. Clappe spent Christmas 1851 at Rich Bar, which was cut off by snowdrifts from the world beyond, during which period she was privileged to witness intoxication on a classical scale:

> The saturnalia commenced on Christmas evening, at the Humboldt [saloon]. . . . All day long, patient mules could be seen descending the hill, bending beneath casks of brandy and baskets of champagne. . . . At nine o'clock in the evening they had an oyster-and-champagne supper . . . which was very gay with toasts, songs, speeches, etc. I believe that the company danced all night. At any rate, they were dancing when I went to sleep, and they were dancing when I woke the next morning. The revel was kept up in this mad way for three days, growing wilder every hour. Some never slept at all during that time. On the fourth day they got past dancing, and, lying in drunken heaps about the barroom, commenced a most unearthly howling. Some barked like dogs, some roared like bulls, and others hissed like serpents and geese. Many were too far gone to imitate anything but their own animalized selves.

Clappe further noted that this culture of excess did not admit bystanders. Anyone trying to remain sober during the holiday season was hauled up before a mock vigilance committee, which sentenced them to "treat the crowd." The drunken antics of the miners en masse were sometimes repellent rather than entertaining. Clappe witnessed racially motivated violence against the Chilenos—the South American miners, who were among the first to the gold fields, and who were forced off their claims on the grounds of patriotism by "American," i.e., Anglo-Saxon, newcomers. She was also sickened by examples of frontier justice. At the first trial she attended, the magistrate halted the hearing several times to "treat" the jury to a glass of spirits. At a hanging, the condemned was already nearly lifeless through drink, and the crowd of spectators very close to the same condition, so that their behavior degraded the solemnity of the occasion: "Many of the drunkards . . . laughed and shouted as if it were a spectacle got up for their particular amusement. A disgusting specimen of intoxicated humanity, struck with one of those luminous ideas peculiar to his class, staggered up to the victim, who was praying at the moment, and, crowding a dirty rag into his almost unconscious hand, in a voice broken by a drunken hiccough, tearfully implored him to take his 'hankercher,' and if he were *innocent*... to drop it as soon as he was drawn up into the air, but if *guilty*, not to let it fall on any account."

Clappe left the Sierras in the fall of 1852. The miners at Rich Bar had spent all summer constructing dams and flumes to divert the river from its bed, only to find it held no gold. The camp broke up, and she returned to San Francisco on the last mule train out of the mountains before snowfall closed their passes until spring. As she had observed upon her arrival in the hills, "Gold-mining is nature's great lottery scheme," and the members of the community to which her husband had served as doctor were among its many losers.

In both metropolitan and rural California, heavy drinking was central to the nascent culture. The eastern temperance movement had some western prophets, but their impact on the habits of Californians was minimal. They were received as curiosities rather than crusaders, and their message that drinking was unnecessary and ungodly was a matter of amusement, as opposed to one that inspired sober reflection. Their number included Henry D. Cogswell, the first dentist to set up a practice in San Francisco, who retired a millionaire after decorating gold miners' molars with a portion of their finds. Revolted by the general state of his clients' teeth and their whiskey breath, Cogswell paid for the erection of seven drinking water fountains in the city, each topped with a statue of himself, all of which, in the absence of demand, were destroyed within a decade of his death. In the 1860s fresh attempts were made to limit public drunkenness by "Prayer Bands"– groups of respectable women who infiltrated Sydney Town[43] in the hope of redeeming drunkards with evangelical Christianity. Their favorite tactic upon entering a grogery was to encircle an inebriate and demand in unison, "Have you seen Jesus?" They were not without success. San Francisco was home to many victims of delirium tremens, who suffered vivid hallucinations when deprived of alcohol for more than a few hours, and one Prayer Band even managed to convert Happy Jack Harrington, the manager of a notorious dive, "as he re-

---

[43] By then known as the Barbary Coast.

bounded from the fearsome realms of the pink elephant and the purple crocodile." Sadly for the temperance movement, Happy Jack soon relapsed, and to mark his return to sanity as he knew it, he held a press conference at his bar to alert the world to the evils of sobriety.

"Oh, King Alcohol!" he commenced. "Great is thy sway! Thou makest meaner creatures kings, and the unfortunate fellow of the gutter forget his miseries for a while! ... I was proprietor of one of those popular places of amusement known as dives, and all was serene and calm and I was happy, but they came down and took from me during the night my beautiful place. ... My beautiful soubrettes and Spanish dancers have gone, and when I look back on the scenic effects of these beautiful melodramas,[44] it is no wonder that I stand before you as a rightful example of the destructive effects of temperance. But though crushed to earth, I will rise again!"

The temperance cause in California was further impeded by the buoyant state of Californian viticulture. Within twenty-five years of the gold rush, the undrinkable trash of the Franciscan missions had been superseded by an eminently palatable fluid, and instead of importing wine from Boston, California had become an exporter. The first area of the state to produce pleasant wine in any quantity was the countryside around Los Angeles. The man responsible for the advance in quality was Jean-Louis Vignes, a native of Bordeaux, who fulfilled the promise of his surname when, in 1833, he planted a hundred-acre vineyard to the east of the town. Vignes introduced systematic production methods and experimented with imported varieties of grape. By 1851, his Rancho el Aliso[45] had forty thousand vines and was producing a hundred thousand gallons of wine a year, some of which was noted as being not merely palatable but exceptional.

Inspired by the example of Vignes, other immigrants established vineyards in the vicinity of Los Angeles during the 1840s. Their number included a Swiss, an Irishman, an Englishman, a Scotsman, several Mexicans, and a Kentucky mountain man who reveled in the surname of Wolfskill. Prior to the gold rush, their customers were passing ships and locals, for a majority of the residents of Los Angeles were Hispanic and drank wine as their daily tipple. Post-1849, the flood of immigrants into the north of the state created a huge potential market

---

[44] Sex shows.
[45] Now buried under Union Station in central L.A.

for Southern California wines. The challenge of exploiting it was taken up by two German musicians—Charles Kohler (flute) and John Frohling (violin), neither of whom had any prior connections to the wine trade, but whose profession had given them plenty of opportunity to observe the spectacular thirst for booze in the bars of San Francisco. In 1854 they bought a small vineyard near Los Angeles. Frohling stayed south to supervise production while Kohler returned to the Bay Area to drum up sales. Demand for their wines very quickly outstripped supply, and in order to meet it, the duo purchased a block of land on the Santa Ana River, which they christened Anaheim and subdivided into twenty-acre parcels for sale to German immigrants. The parcels were offered complete with irrigation systems and vines. The venture was a success—by 1862 it was producing three hundred thousand gallons of wine annually and was sending it not only to San Francisco but also to New York.

Production in the rest of California, while widespread, was on a much smaller scale. Some of the mission vineyards continued in operation, and separate centers of cultivation grew up around them, notably in Santa Clara. Immigrants also made independent starts in the mother lode country itself. John Sutter, on whose ranch the gold rush had commenced after the metal was found in his mill race, retired from the ensuing pandemonium to a new holding on the Feather River to grow vines. Adam Uhlinger, a Swiss who had emigrated to California with the express purpose of making wine, established the D'Agostini Winery in Amador County in 1856. By 1860, the gold-producing region had 192,000 vines, or about three percent of the total for the state.

The future of California wine lay in the north, at the limits of Spanish settlement. Sonoma, the last in the chain of missions to be founded, had been equipped with the customary vineyard, and in 1833, together with a further forty-four thousand acres of land, this had passed into the hands of General Mariano Guadeloupe Vallejo, the civil and military governor of Mexican California. Born in Monterrey on July 4, 1807, Vallejo was a pivotal figure in the period of transition between Mexican and American rule, serving Spain, Mexico, and the United States as soldier, administrator, and peacemaker. In 1851, he retired to his estate in Sonoma and dedicated his energies to making wine. While his production methods were primitive, his wine was good—outstanding, perhaps—and its potential was recognized by a Hungarian cavalry officer who had come to pay his respects to the general, and who subsequently was responsible for establishing the reputation of the region in the estimation of wine lovers everywhere.

Agoston Haraszthy (1812–69), the father of modern Californian viticulture, had had enough adventures to fill several normal lives by the time he tasted Vallejo's wine. Unlike so many Europeans who invented a noble background for themselves upon migration to the New World, Haraszthy was a genuine aristocrat, an officer and a gentleman who had served in the imperial bodyguard of the Austro-Hungarian court. Caught up in a political intrigue, Haraszthy had been forced to flee his native country for the United States. He commenced his American odyssey in Wisconsin, where he founded a town named after himself and established several businesses, including a sawmill and a steamboat line. In 1849, he led a wagon train west and settled with his family in San Diego where he ran a butchery, a bus company, and a livery stable, and served as the first sheriff of San Diego County. In 1852, he moved to San Francisco, where he again held various official positions, including the supervision of the San Francisco mint. Five years later, after being tried for and acquitted of embezzling from the mint (his smelters had run too hot and vaporized $151,000 worth of gold, which was distributed by the winds over the streets of San Francisco), he paid his fateful visit to General Vallejo and, after sipping his wine, bought 560 acres adjacent to the general's estate. The land came complete with a small vineyard and a derelict winery.

Haraszthy threw his customary energy into developing and expanding his new property. Within a decade he owned six thousand acres around Sonoma, of which four hundred were planted with vines, and had built himself an Italianate villa and an elaborate system of underground tunnels in which to store his vintages. He cemented his friendship with Vallejo by marrying two of his sons, Arpad and Attila, to a pair of the general's daughters at a joint wedding ceremony on Vallejo's estate. He also introduced important technical improvements in viticulture to the region. His vines were planted on dry slopes and were not irrigated, they were fermented in redwood vats instead of raw hides, and he had experimented with a wide range of imported grapes.

News of his experiments, and the excellence of his wine, prompted the California legislature, in 1857, to employ him to examine how the quality of its viticulture might be improved. The following year,

Haraszthy delivered a "Report on Grapes and Wines of California," which provided practical advice on vines and soil types and was distributed to prospective planters. These latter were further encouraged with fiscal incentives: In 1859 the state legislature decreed that the first four years of production at new vineyards were to be tax free. Haraszthy, meanwhile, believed that there was still much more to be learned and in 1861 persuaded the governor of California to send him on a tour of the European wine-growing regions. He accomplished his assignment with typical vigor, gathering information and over a hundred thousand vine cuttings of some three hundred varieties, which were delivered via the Wells Fargo Company the following year. Haraszthy's personal charm and perhaps some samples he brought with him to Europe made an impression on the French, for in 1862 the *Revue Viticol* was kind enough to suggest that California wines might be "capable of entering into competition with the wines of Europe," albeit "in the distant future." Upon his return to Sonoma, Haraszthy produced a second comprehensive report for the state agricultural board–*Grape Culture, Wines, and Winemaking* (1862)–which laid the foundations for the scientific production of wine in America.

Sadly, 1862 proved to be the zenith of Haraszthy's career. The state of California refused to pay him for the vines he had collected in Europe; two years later, a collaborative venture with silent financial partners, intended to fund an ambitious program of expansion at his Buena Vista Winery, failed, and Haraszthy was squeezed out by his investors. In 1866 he left California for Nicaragua, where he established a distillery and a sawmill, and where he met his end in 1869 when he fell into a river infested with alligators.

In the same decades that Vallejo and Haraszthy were developing viticulture in Sonoma, other entrepreneurs were planting vines in the adjacent Napa Valley, led by George Yount, an ex–trapping partner of the same William Wolfskill who had settled down to make wine in Los Angeles. Yount had arrived in Napa in 1838 armed with a land grant of twelve thousand acres from General Vallejo and a new Christian name–Jorge de Concepción–after having been baptized a Catholic and confirmed as a Mexican citizen. The region was untamed country at the time, with more grizzly bears than settlers. Yount is reputed to have killed several of the former while engaged in the process of clearing his land. He founded a town named after himself, as was the custom, and established a small vineyard on his acres. In 1849, an apostate Mormon named Samuel Brannan set up at the north end of the Napa where he, too, founded a town—Calistoga.

Brannan had ambitious plans for his new settlement, which he intended to develop as a West Coast Saratoga for the wealthy inhabitants of San Francisco. At the ground-breaking ceremony, Brannan is claimed to have been overcome with drunken exuberance and to have sworn he would create "the Calistoga of Sarafornia." The name stuck, and when Calistoga opened for business in 1862 it featured a sizable hotel, landscaped grounds, a racetrack, a swimming pool, a skating rink, and a goldfish pond. Over the following decade the Napa Valley filled up with settlers and was divided into a patchwork of small farms and ranches. A large proportion of the immigrants were Germans, a number of whom established little vineyards in which they attempted to replicate the delicate white wines of their native land, thus introducing another style to the region.

The net effect of the émigrés, visionaries, financiers, and mountain men on the production of Californian wine was enormous. By 1862, the state was home to 10.5 million vines—a 40 percent increase in just two years. This created problems of success—first in the matter of labor. Few emigrants would deign to sully their hands tending vines or grape picking for the low wages offered by winery owners. Moreover, many of the people who had arrived in California were professionals—doctors or lawyers who followed the sensible philosophy that it was easier to obtain gold from miners than from the ground. Haraszthy solved the problem on his estate by recruiting Chinese labor, at eight dollars a month with board, via a contractor in San Francisco named Ho Po, who sourced agricultural workers from Guangdong Province in China. Initially, such guest workers were welcomed in the Golden State, as unobtrusive, law-abiding "coolies," who were usually kept secluded from "proper," i.e., white, immigrants. Their anticipated role in the future was set out in the pages of the *California Farmer,* which hoped that they should be to the state "what the African has been to the South," but with the advantage that they went back to China at the conclusion of their contracts.

However, a number of Chinese came to California to settle as well as to perform labor for a fixed term, and they introduced their own drinking customs to the state, and indeed to America. These were more or less unchanged from those that had been observed by European visitors to China in the sixteenth century. Much of their drinking was therapeutic, and when they wished to become intoxicated they smoked opium in preference to getting drunk. Their favorite drinks were rice or plum wine, imported from their homeland, which were consumed in small measures, and with a degree of ceremony. They also imported medicinal beverages, including snake wine, which they believed to be a cure for rheumatism. Its reputation as such spread beyond the Chinese community, and other Americans began to manufacture imitations, which they sold under the generic name of *snake oil*.

While Chinese labor enabled the California wine industry to keep growing, Chinese Americans were of little assistance in solving the second problem generated by the success of the industry as a whole, which was how to dispose of its increased production. The eastern states of America, which might have been expected to be buyers on patriotic grounds alone, were perceived of in California as being obsessed with whiskey, if they drank at all. In the opinion of Arpad (son of Agoston) Haraszthy: "The great obstacle to our success, is that the average American is a whiskey drinking, water drinking, coffee drinking, tea drinking, and consequently a dyspepsia-inviting subject, who does not know the use or value of pure light wine taken at the proper time and in moderate quantities. The task before us lies in teaching our people how to drink wine, when to drink it, and how much of it to drink."

In the event, California demand accounted for much of its new production. By 1861, the state had over 380,000 inhabitants, compared with a little less than fourteen thousand immediately prior to the gold rush. Many of the newcomers were from wine-drinking cultures in Europe who considered the fluid to be a necessity of life. Furthermore, the surprising number of professionals who'd trekked across the prairies or shipped around Cape Horn also had at least a familiarity with wine, and once in California they drank the local vintages. The prestige attached to wine drinking also made it attractive to miners. Those wishing to distribute some of their newfound wealth felt they made a better show if they bought claret or champagne with their gold dust. That much of what they drank was made in California mattered less than labels declaring it to be French. Finally, any surplus in production was taken up by distillation. For those die-hard Yankee immigrants who considered spirits to be the only drink worthy of the name, overproof brandy was as good as a similar beverage distilled from corn, and if the vintners occasionally labeled their product whiskey, few of its end consumers noticed the deception.

22 GOOD TASTE

The discovery of a new dish confers more happiness
on humanity than the discovery of a new star.
                        —Anthelme Brillat-Savarin

Man's frenzied love of all substances which exalt his
personality, whether healthy or dangerous, bears
witness to his greatness.
                        —Charles Baudelaire

In the same decades that Americans were forging trails over and building towns in wildernesses, the French were aspiring to civilize their already-settled nation and to perfect every detail of sedentary life. Even such biological imperatives as eating and drinking were scrutinized and transformed, so that a meal or a bottle of wine no longer served merely to fill the belly or to quench a thirst, but was also expected to provide an aesthetic experience. There was artistry in cooking and winemaking, and nineteenth-century French connoisseurs trained their senses to identify, to appreciate, and to applaud it. His or her training ground was comprised of the restaurants of Paris, which were appearing in their dozens all over the City of Light. They were the creatures of the French Revolution. Some were started by the cooks of the nobility who had lost their places when aristocratic households were broken up, many more were opened to satisfy a growing desire for equality of access to luxury: Citizens with the money and inclination to indulge their taste buds should have the opportunity to do so in the ideal republic.

The new restaurants were theaters of gastronomy. The machinery and the raw materials with which their chefs worked their magic were banished from the stage—the kitchen itself was hidden behind closed doors, through which wondrous culinary creations would emerge, perfect and complete, paired with wines absolutely suited to their complex flavors. As the nineteenth century progressed, they became social and cultural institutions, with their own vocabulary and, indeed, ideology. To the connoisseurs, or *gourmands,* who patronized them, an exquisite dinner at a legendary restaurant was a quasi-religious experience.

The discipline of the gourmand was pioneered by Alexandre Balthasar Grimnod de la Reynière, who published his gustatory adventures in his *Almanach des gourmands* (1803). The *Almanach* purported to be a guide to the best food in Paris and to have invented the literary genre of the restaurant review. Unlike prior commentaries on eating, which sought to combine consumption with moral, economic, or medical observations—the wastefulness of the rich, the brutishness of the poor, the dangers posed by red wine and radishes to people of a phlegmatic disposition—the *Almanach* portrayed a good meal as an end in itself. The book was both successful and controversial. Its opponents claimed it encouraged the sin of gluttony by promoting an unhealthy obsession with delicacies. Gourmands who "build the weaknesses of their private lives into doctrines and propound them in a public forum" were fetishists of the worst order. Controversy stoked sales, and the *Almanach* ran through eight editions by 1808, by which time it was established as a reference work and was taken perhaps more seriously than its author had intended. It possessed more than a streak of gothic fiction in its style. The judgments contained in the *Almanach* were claimed to have been pronounced by an anonymous jury of taste, a gastronomic grand inquisition, whose seventeen members met every Wednesday at an undisclosed location to consider, in conditions of strictest secrecy, the offerings of the best chefs, confectioners, pastry cooks, and wine merchants in Paris. Moreover, there is a love of the macabre, and the revolting, in the text. Readers of the *Almanach* were advised, for instance, that the best way to tell if a turkey carcass was fresh or not was to insert a finger into its anal cavity and then lick the finger.

The cult of restaurant-going that Grimnod had encouraged gave rise to a new occupation—that of the *sommelier.* The word derives from Old French, where it served as the title of the individual in a noble household responsible for the management of pack animals and provisions. Over time, in the same manner as the English *butler* came to denote a domestic servant entrusted with the provision of drinks to the dinner table, the sommelier became charged with the care and presentation of wine. After the Revolution, many attached themselves to the restaurants opened by the chefs they used to work alongside, and with the appearance of *gourmandisme,* their role was elevated to a level of similar consequence. The sommelier's tasks included the purchase of appropriate wines, their storage under suitable conditions, and the provision of advice to customers as to which wines matched which foods. Their prophet was André Jullien, author of the *Sommelier's Manual* and the *Topography of All the Known Vineyards.*

Once it was established that there was a genuine public interest in the critical appraisal of good food and drink, fresh publications on the subject expanded its scope, from the what, where, and when of gourmandizing to the why. The *Physiology of Taste* (1825), subtitled *Transcendental Gastronomy,* by Anthelme Brillat-Savarin, was the first to attempt to codify its ethos. Brillat-Savarin believed that prejudice had grown against the art of discrimination, to the detriment of civilization: "I have looked through various dictionaries for the word *gourmandise* and have found no translation that suited me. It is described as a sort of confusion of gluttony and voracity. Whence I have concluded that lexicographers, though very pleasant people in other respects, are not the sort of men to eat a partridge wing gracefully from one hand, with a glass of Lafitte or Clos de Vougeot in the other."

In order to remedy this sorry state of affairs, Brillat-Savarin, via a series of anecdotes (including one concerning a wild turkey hunt in Connecticut, where he spent several years in exile), and meditations on such ancillary aspects of gourmandise as dreams and obesity, aimed to create a philosophy that justified the pleasures of discrimination. When it came to drinking, the watchword was to do so slowly: "True [gourmands] sip their wine. Every mouthful thus gives them the sum total of pleasure which they would not have enjoyed had they swallowed it at once." Furthermore, the aspiring sensualist should never tipple to the point of intoxication, and those who did so were "utterly ignorant of the true principles of eating and drinking." While he ruled out drunkenness, Brillat-Savarin expected his disciples to have strong heads—any man in good health should be capable of drinking two bottles of wine every day, and those of exceptional constitutions considerably more. An example of this latter class was provided in the person of General Bisson, a French hero of the Napoleonic wars, "who drank eight bottles of wine at dinner every day, and who never appeared the worse for it. He had a glass larger than usual and emptied it oftener" but nonetheless "he could jest and give his orders as if he had only swallowed a thimbleful." The concept of *savoir boir*—to know how to drink—was further illustrated by an anecdote from Brillat-Savarin's years in the United States, where he and a pair of fellow French exiles had drunk a collection of American planters under the table, by controlling the speed at which they consumed and by lining their stomachs with appropriate foods prior to the contest.

The devotees of gourmandise, if they paid close attention to the philosophical and practical advice in the pages of the *Physiology of Taste,* might aspire one day to possessing the powers of the elect of the discipline, who could "tell the latitude in which any wine ripened as surely as one of Biot's or Arago's disciples can foretell an eclipse." They were also taught how to steer clear of bad wines, such as the infamous *vin blanc* of Surenne. According to Brillat-Savarin, three things were needed to get rid of a single glass of this fluid: "A drinker, and two men to hold him down in case his courage fails."

Both gourmands and the restaurants that nourished them continued to thrive as the nineteenth century progressed, whatever the political climate. They multiplied under the Bourbon and Orléans monarchies and survived the revolution of 1848, so that by the advent of the Second Republic Paris was recognized as the culinary capital of the world. This eminence was a matter of national pride, which itself was a sentiment that Napoléon III, who ruled France between 1852 and 1870, did his best to encourage in his subject-citizens. Louis Napoléon was a modernizer. Under his guidance, France was to have factories, steam trains, and businessmen. Gourmands were natural supporters of his program. The spreading railway network whisked delicacies from the provinces to the capital in so short a time that they could be served in its restaurants while still fresh. A gourmand need no longer take to the countryside in pursuit of exquisite, if highly perishable, game such as ortolans when they could be had without effort in Paris with their blood still warm.

In order to fix an affection for progress in those French who were not enthusiasts for it, Napoléon III decided to arrange a Universal Exposition in Paris in 1855, which would serve as a showcase for industrial might and human ingenuity. It was to be modeled on "the Great Exhibition of the Works of Industry of All Nations" that had been staged in London in 1851. The British example, while bristling with machinery, had had very little on show for the gourmand. There were no fine wines, for the temperance brigade had sought a bar on alcohol beverages. Their general absence from the exhibits was lamented in the press as being wrong in principle: "Regardless of their value in the arts, or as an article of food or medicine, they were not allowed to be exhibited, because they are sometimes turned to a bad purpose. For similar reasons, types might have been prevented, because bad books were sometimes printed." The few examples of alcoholic drinks that managed to slip through the temperance net and into the Crystal Palace would have made a gourmand blanch: "Six bottles of champagne wine manufactured in England from rhubarb stalk."

In Paris matters were to be different. The "Preparation and Conservation of Alimentary Substances" category of exhibits had "Fermented Drinks" as a subcategory. When invitations were sent out to every area of France, asking that regional officials consider what items of manufacture they could submit to the exhibition, both Burgundy and Champagne replied that they would send their wines. Bordeaux, in contrast, rummaged around for something suitably industrial and considered sending samples from its rope factories. However, when representatives from Burgundy got in touch with the idea of a joint display of fine wines, a notice was published in the local papers inviting Bordeaux's vintners to a meeting to discuss the matter. These latter were enthusiastic about showing their products at the Exposition, and it was decided that a display dedicated to the wines of the region, of all qualities, should be prepared.

Once the decision had been taken to send wine instead of ropes to the Universal Exposition, a problem emerged that threatened to scupper the plan. For nearly a century the wines of Bordeaux had been subject to an informal classification based on the concept of *cru,* or growth. Wines belonging to the *premier cru* commanded higher prices than those of the second or third class; indeed the pricing for each year's vintage was made with reference to the amount paid for the first growths. Winemakers were exceedingly jealous of their rankings, and it was feared that some might try to take advantage of the exposure they would receive in Paris to manipulate their position. The dilemma was summed up by the Bordeaux Chamber of Commerce. While it believed that "this solemn occasion should not be missed to remind our compatriots, and especially foreigners, that in the production of wine, France, and the Gironde in particular, is one of the most favored regions in the world," if "the proprietors of a particular region seek to profit from the Exposition to mount a fight among themselves with the aim of destroying a classification based on the experience of long years, we would not hesitate to declare that it would be better, in our view, that none of our wines appear at the Exposition."

This informal "classification," which was deemed more important than a Universal Exposition, was the result of the careful compilation of prices paid for the various wines of the region over the years by its wine merchants and brokers. Thomas Jefferson's notes from his visit to Bordeaux in 1787 had reproduced it in part, and versions had been set down in the wine guidebooks that had become popular in the first half of the nineteenth century. The most complete of these was contained in the *Treatise on the Wines of the Médoc and the Other Red Wines from the Gironde Department* by William Franck, a wine merchant of Bordeaux, which, by its third edition in 1853, listed sixty-two *crus* divided into five classes. A number of variants on it appeared in other guidebooks, but all reflected a near consensus in the proper ranking, at least at the top of the *cru* pyramid. They were all agreed that there were only four first growths—Château Lafitte, Château Margaux, Latour, and Haut-Brion, and more or less ten second *crus*. Below the third tier, however, they often differed.

This, then, was the position of the classification of Bordeaux wines at the time of the Universal Exposition. It was a controversial matter: A superior ranking, even among its lowest echelons, meant belonging to a higher price bracket. Hence the trepidation of the Chamber of Commerce in Bordeaux about allowing any of its wines to be exhibited. The solution it settled upon was a single large display containing all the wines of the region, which were to be labeled with their place of origin and rank, but not the name of the producer. A giant map—a *Carte Vinicole*—was also to be prepared, whose key linked the bottles on show to the communes in which they had been produced. Thus, visitors would receive a striking visual impression of the variety and excellence of Bordeaux wines, and gourmands would be able to point out the plots of land where their favorites were produced and plan tours of the vineyards.

Producers were invited to submit their wines, and the Carte Vinicole was commissioned. Whereas the response to the request for samples was disappointing, the great map promised to be sensational. It showed road and rail links to Bordeaux and was decorated with engravings of three famous châteaux, surrounded by their vines. In order to furnish a key to the Carte Vinicole, the Chamber of Commerce wrote to its union of wine brokers, asking it to provide a "list of all the red classed growths in the department, as exact and complete as possible, specifying to which of the five classes each of them belongs and in which commune they are located." A fortnight later the brokers responded with a six-page document listing fifty-seven red wines divided into five *crus,* and twenty-one whites separated into three classes. This was the now-legendary *classement.* At the time, it was considered a temporary expedient, which no doubt would be altered in the near future. The 1868 edition of *Cocks & Féret,* the most influential guidebook of the age, commented that "like all human institutions" it was "subject to the laws of time, and every so often it must certainly be revised, [and] brought up to the level of progress." The same phrase appeared in subsequent editions of the guide for the following century, during which the classification remained intact. Indeed, it has only been altered once since it was written down by Georges Merman on April 18, 1855.[46]

The Universal Exposition was a runaway success. Five million visitors queued up to admire its working steam engines, take balloon flights, and buy machine-made souvenirs. The newly classified wines of Bordeaux won several prizes for excellence and the table wine of the region, exhibited in the Gallery of Domestic Economy, received a special award on account of its medicinal qualities. In the opinion of the prize jury, it was impossible not to place so excellent a fluid "among the most useful of nutrients for people in good health, and, more often, for invalids and convalescents."

The scientific display of wine at the great exposition and the gourmand fashion for depicting it as an affair of the senses alone infuriated many educated French people. It was an insult to classical civilization, and to France, to suggest that the appreciation of wine was the province of nutritionists, fanatics, and invalids and that no one should ever drink for the

---

[46] By the elevation of Mouton Rothschild to the category of first growths in 1973.

sole and express purpose of becoming intoxicated. Wines might possess a universe of flavors, but that was not what they were for, and it was intellectual suicide to pretend that vintages were uncorked simply to reveal their bouquets. What was wrong with drinking in the style of Socrates, or Alexander, or General Bisson? Whoever heard of a sober poet?

Charles Baudelaire, decadent and immortal bard, led the charge against progress, *gourmandisme,* and sober drinking. He deployed his spleen in an essay, *On Wine and Hashish,* initially against Brillat-Savarin, who had presumed to define wine as "a liquor made from the fruit of the vine," invented by Noah. What, inquired Baudelaire, would a visitor to planet Earth from the moon, or a more distant place, "who has vaguely heard of the delicious liquors with which the citizens of this globe procured for themselves as much courage and as much gaiety as they wanted" learn about wine from the author of *Transcendental Gastronomy*? Might they mistake it for a type of food?

To Baudelaire, the principal purpose of drinking was intoxication, or as he termed it, "sailing in the gutter." He felt that the relationship between humanity and wine was an affair of the heart, not the head, and, through his writing, gave wine a voice to express its affection for its creator: "My beloved, I want to sing out to you, despite my prison of glass and my bolts of cork, a song of fraternity, a song full of joy, light and hope.... You gave me life and I will reward you. I will pay off my debt to the full." Wine sang not only of its pleasure in refreshing humanity in general and the "sublime dance" it performed inside each drinker, but also drew attention to its powers of consolation. Through intoxication, it gave solace even to those employed in the meanest occupations. Baudelaire depicted this last power with the figure of a ragpicker, wandering through the Parisian night, sorting over refuse in the hope of finding something of modest value to sell, sustained in his wretchedness by wine. Under its benign influence, the ragpicker's stick becomes an emperor's scepter, and he imagines that he is riding through the city at the head of an army: "His heart swells with happiness. He listens with delight to the acclamations of an enthusiastic public. Any moment now he will be dictating a law code superior to all codes known hitherto. He swears solemnly that he will make his peoples happy."

❖ ❖ ❖

While the debate raged between gourmands and decadents as to the true purpose of wine, the single most important breakthrough in human understanding of alcoholic drinks—a complete and accurate scientific explanation of why they are alcoholic—was achieved in France. The genius responsible for the advance was Louis Pasteur. Prior to his definitive studies, no one in history had been able to describe precisely how grape juice turned into wine. For all they knew, it might have been the invisible hand of Bacchus or some other form of divine intervention. Pasteur made his breakthrough by building on the work of Antoine-Laurent Lavoisier, the father of modern chemistry, who had discovered that the process of fermentation consisted of the conversion of carbohydrates to carbon dioxide and ethanol, which he named alcohol, thereby introducing the Arabic name for the substance to the West. Unfortunately, his research was carried out at the height of the French Revolution, and as Lavoisier was a tax collector as well as a scientist, his career was cut short by the guillotine in 1794. An appeal for clemency on the grounds of his exceptional discoveries was fruitless. "The Republic has no need of geniuses," observed the court, and beheaded him the same day.[47]

The next step toward understanding fermentation was taken in 1836 by a German physiologist, Theodor Schwann. Schwann determined that yeast was a microorganism, named it *Saccharomyces*—Latin for sugar fungus, after its eating habits—and noted that it excreted alcohol after consuming its favorite food. The final breakthrough came in 1862, when Pasteur combined his predecessors' discoveries and demonstrated that it was yeast that converted the sugars in wine and beer to alcohol. For the first time in history, vintners and brewers understood the magic behind their products. Pasteur conducted further, specific research for each trade, published as *Études sur le vin* (1866) and *Études sur la bier* (1871). Each of these studies addressed the issue of quality control—why certain batches of wine or beer went bad, and how this might be foreseen and prevented. The answer in most cases was bad yeast, or bacterial contamination. To combat the latter, Pasteur invented the process that bears his name—pasteurization. Simply stated, pasteurization involves heating a liquid to sixty-four degrees Celsius for thirty-two minutes,

---

[47] Lavoisier is rumored to have carried out his last experiment at his own execution. Its purpose was to determine how long a severed head remains conscious. An assistant stood by the basket at the foot of the guillotine and counted how many times Lavoisier's head blinked its eyes before they closed forever. Apparently he managed fifteen.

which kills any bacteria it may contain, and if the liquid is subsequently sealed hermetically no microbial activity will reoccur.

In 1867, shortly after Pasteur had revealed the secret processes that gave wine its voice, Paris staged another Universal Exhibition. The city had been extensively remodeled since 1855, under the guidance of Baron Haussmann, prefect of the Seine Department. Haussmann had envisaged Paris "as a perfectly regulated instrument ... free of traffic jams or slums." His grand motif was the boulevard, and under his direction Paris received two hundred kilometers of new streets, many of them broad avenues, "lined by 34,000 new buildings containing 215,000 new apartments." There were changes below as well as above boulevard level. Paris was equipped with piped water delivered via a chain of aqueducts from sources up to 235 kilometers away. Its sewerage system was revamped, and the fetid smells that had characterized the city since medieval days were banished into history.

While some visitors to the exhibition of 1867 enjoyed guided tours of the new waterworks, more put time aside for a trip to one of the capital's famous restaurants. The temples of *gourmandisme* had become celebrated in foreign guidebooks as cultural landmarks, on a par with Notre Dame and the Louvre, with the advantage over such venerable rivals that they required no more than a good appetite to appreciate. For many American visitors, they also possessed a novelty value. While the first French-style restaurant (Delmonico's, run by two Swiss Italians) had opened in New York in the 1820s, there were as yet few imitators, and the concepts of choosing one's meal and eating it at a leisurely pace, with wine, were alien to most Americans. When they crossed this cultural divide in Paris, they wrote agitated letters home. The presence of women, and even children, in restaurants was a common topic in such correspondence. Could this be proper? The American institution that most resembled a French restaurant was a gambling-house-cum-bordello in the West, and it was hard to imagine respectable women, or children of any condition, in such establishments. Such qualms were not entirely unjustified. Savoir faire dictated that one passion leads to another, and Parisian restaurants usually offered *cabinets*–private dining rooms, which ranged in size from cubicles to spaces capable of seating several dozen people–where customers might indulge what Brillat-Savarin termed the sixth sense–the urge to procreate–over lunch, or dinner. Cabinets also served as chapels of drunkenness for the students of the city, whose

How young people study law in Paris

dedication to wine, whether as apostles of science or Baudelaire, was caricatured in satirical magazines of the age.

While the French carried off prizes for wine and luxury goods at the Universal Exhibition of 1867, they lagged in other categories, notably industrial machinery and weapons. The steel artillery pieces exhibited by Krupp, a Prussian firm, were emblematic of the difference in focus between pleasure-loving France and military-minded Prussia. Three years after the exhibition, the same brand of howitzers that had been displayed in Paris were employed against the French capital at the conclusion of a brief but decisive Franco-Prussian War, which established the Prussians as the major land power in Europe, at the head of a unified Germany.[48] The *Second German Empire,* which was constituted in Versailles shortly before France surrendered, was a novelty.

---

[48] The great restaurants of Paris kept serving throughout the German siege, albeit with improvised menus. Voisin offered roast cat garlanded with rats, accompanied by Bollinger Champagne.

From the Dark Ages to the Napoleonic Wars, Germany per se had been a patchwork of independent kingdoms. In order to inspire a sense of nationalism in the citizens of the new entity, it was necessary to invent them a common identity. Prussian concepts of what it meant to be German were used to shape the new ideal.

Beer drinking was high on their list. It had been confirmed as a Teutonic trait by the hero of Prussian militarism, King Frederick the Great (d. 1786), who had set out his views on the matter in his *"Coffee and Beer" Manifesto* of 1777, which was intended to dissuade Prussians from drinking infusions instead of brews: "His Majesty was brought up on beer and so were his ancestors and his officers. Many battles have been fought and won by soldiers nourished on beer, and the king does not believe that coffee-drinking soldiers can be depended on to endure hardship or to beat his enemies." Moreover, beer drinking was a pan-Germanic pastime. Bavaria, once Prussia's greatest rival for Teutonic hegemony, had spent much of the nineteenth century developing a regional identity centered on beer. Its principal festival, the Oktoberfest, while established to honor the nuptials of King Ludwig I in 1810, had since evolved to become a beer-soaked celebration of Bavarianness. A similar passion for suds was evident in the myriad of smaller states incorporated into the new German Empire. Their collective beer love had been nourished during the Napoleonic Wars, when the French had occupied some of them, forced others into alliances, and set about rearranging their frontiers, laws, roads, and social institutions. The hated new rulers were wine drinkers and this preference had been seized on as a cultural point of difference. In consequence the new model German, *Deutsche Michel,* as he was styled at the time, was defined in part by what he opposed. He was simple, well-natured, and strong, in contrast to the effete and arrogant French. Similarly his diet was plain and nourishing—the antithesis of gastronomy. Michel enjoyed his rude good health from eating sausages and drinking beer, rather than picking at partridge wings and sipping Lafitte.

The Napoleonic rearrangement of Germany had influenced not just the prejudices of its inhabitants but also its brewing industry. Local feudal and ecclesiastic privileges were abolished, petty rulers were stripped of their wheat-beer monopolies in addition to their titles and kingdoms, and the monasteries were disbanded and their breweries sold to merchants. Market liberalization continued after the defeat of

Napoléon, and in 1834 Prussia had formed a *Zollverein,* or customs union, with Bavaria and Württemberg, which reduced or removed tariffs on trade between its parties, and constituted the first step toward political union. The Zollverein was expanded in 1836 and again in 1838, and beer flowed across the old borders between German states. In the absence of medieval restrictions and import duties, small and inefficient breweries could not compete with larger better-capitalized operations, and their number declined. Munich, for example, which had had sixty breweries in 1790, had only thirty-five in 1819 and fifteen in 1865. The fewer survivors serviced larger markets. For the first time in centuries they could export to neighboring states and beyond. Concurrent advances in distribution—better roads with fewer tolls, and railways, encouraged the trend. The first freight to be carried by rail in Germany consisted of two casks of beer, which were transported from Nuremberg to Fürth on July 11, 1836.

In order to win and keep customers in a free market, German brewers needed to produce a consistent, stable product. To this end they embraced advances in science and technology. The malting process was improved by the introduction of indirect hot-air kilns that dried the grain with warm dry air instead of smoke, which tainted it with combustion residues. They bought thermometers and hydrometers and kept a close eye on innovations overseas. When an Australian named James Harrison constructed a refrigeration device for a brewery in Sydney in 1851, the Spaten Brewery in Munich followed suit a few years later with a "cold machine," the forerunner of the modern refrigerator. Temperature control enabled German brewers to focus on lager beer, whose bottom-fermenting yeasts work best close to the freezing point and which, hitherto, they had only been able to brew with confidence in the winter months.

German lager was improved by the use of recipes from Czechoslovakia and Austria. Principal among these was *pilsner,* which had been created in the Czech city of Plzen by a Bavarian brewmaster named Josef Groll in 1842. Pilsner[49] was brewed with Saaz hops, soft water, and German bottom-fermenting yeast and was a pale, dry beer with a delicate flavor. The town of České was thought to produce the best Pilsner beer, known as *Budvar* in Czech and *Budweiser* in German.

---

[49] Urquell, the original Pilsner brewery, is still in production and is still celebrated for the excellence of its beer.

This ambrosia seems to have had a particular appeal to aristocratic households and acquired the nickname "the beer of kings" in recognition of its hold on stately palates. Its name was Germanicized to pilsener, or pils, after its adoption by the Prussians and its quality enhanced yet further with the invention, in 1878, of the beer filter. The end result was a dry, clear golden brew, served chilled, and manufactured in accordance with a centuries-old purity law[50] and new Prussian-inspired legislation imposing national quality standards.

While beer took precedence over wine in the German psyche, German winemaking also flourished throughout the nineteenth century. The Prussian-inspired Zollverein stimulated the art of viticulture as well as that of brewing. Free trade encouraged growers to focus on quality, and German wines began to impress visiting gourmands, who had hitherto believed them (with a few glorious exceptions) to be weak, thin, and acidic. By the time that André Jullien, the pioneer sommelier, toured Germany in the 1840s, he was able to advise his fellow countrymen that change was afoot. Some of its vintages possessed a remarkable bouquet, "equaling, if not surpassing, that of our best wines," and good or bad, all had the virtue of being weak so that they did not "attack the nerves or trouble the reason when one has drunk too much."

The improvements Julien had noted were most in evidence in the Rheingau region, whose vintners had discovered the beneficial powers of the noble rot *(Botrytis cinerea)*—a fungus that shrivels grapes and ferments their juices while they are still on the stalk, and which imparts sweet flavors to their wines. Some Rheingau wines were made with hand-selected bunches of such grapes, and the best were pressed from berries chosen individually. These delicacies sent those lucky enough to drink them into raptures. Agoston Haraszthy sampled some on his fact-finding visit to Europe in 1861 and confessed that "to describe [them] would be a work for Byron, Shakespeare, or Schiller, and even those geniuses would not do full justice until they had imbibed a couple of glasses. . . . As you take a mouthful and let it run drop by drop down your throat, it leaves in your mouth the same aroma as a bouquet of the choicest flowers will offer to your olfactories."

The general trend toward the production of superior wines in Germany was further encouraged through the foundation of a wine school

---

[50] The Bavarian Reinheitsgebot of 1516.

at Geisenheim and the creation of model German wineries near Trier. These latter concentrated on producing a dry Riesling, whose flavors became more subtle and delicate as it aged. By the time that the Second German Empire celebrated its tenth birthday, its inhabitants could celebrate their patriotism with perhaps the best beer in the world, and wine manufactured to the most fastidious of standards.

23 EMANCIPATION

The same spirits which make a white man drunk
make a black man drunk too. Indeed, in this I can
find proof of my identity with the family of man.
—Frederick Douglass

When there shall be neither a slave nor a drunkard
on the earth—how proud the title of that Land,
which may truly claim to be the birthplace and the
cradle of both those revolutions, that shall have
ended in that victory. How nobly distinguished that
People, who shall have planted, and nurtured to
maturity, both the political and moral freedom of
their species.

—Abraham Lincoln

Many American visitors to the Universal Exhibition in Paris in 1855 were likely to have carried one or both of two recent publishing sensations as reading material for the transatlantic voyage. While one of these books, *Uncle Tom's Cabin* (1852), by Harriet Beecher Stowe, was also a best-seller in Europe, the other, *Ten Nights in a Bar-Room* (1854), by T. S. Arthur, was famous only in America, where four hundred thousand copies were in circulation. A strangely compelling and stridently Prohibitionist novel, *Ten Nights in a Bar-Room* was indicative of the differences in attitudes toward alcohol that had developed between the United States and France. Its readers were concentrated in the eastern and old western states, where the myriad temperance organizations founded in the first half of the nineteenth century had succeeded in turning their cause from a moral into a political issue. The debate had moved on from Communion wine to coercion. Drink was bad, and since people were too weak to resist it, it must be denied to them. Wherever there was alcohol on sale there would be drunkards and wherever there were drunkards there was poverty, squalor, and violence. The only way, therefore, to forestall impending chaos was to outlaw drinking places. Temperance candidates stood at every election, great or small, with the aim, if successful, of prohibiting the retailing of alcohol.

The temperance platform was dramatized in *Ten Nights in a Bar-Room,* most of whose action takes place in the Sickle and Sheaf Tavern in a small town named Cedarville, which the narrator visits over a period of ten years, during which time the inhabitants of the once-pretty settlement are gradually ruined by the malevolent influence of the drinking house in their midst. The book features all the established emblems of temperance noir writing—the corruption of youth, several murders, a drunk redeemed at his daughter's deathbed, d.t.'s-inspired hallucinations (including a giant toad under the bedclothes), and so on; it also rehearses protemperance arguments by placing them in the mouths of casual drinkers, as the following example, masquerading as a conversation about politics between strangers, illustrates:

"Did not you vote the anti-temperance ticket at the last election?"

"I did," was the answer; "and from principle."

"On what were your principles based?" was inquired.

"On the broad foundations of civil liberty."

"The liberty to do good or evil, just as the individual may choose?"

"I would not like to say that. There are certain evils against which there can be no legislation that would not do harm. No civil power in this country has the right to say what a citizen shall eat or drink."

"But may not the people, in any community, pass laws, through their delegated law-makers, restraining evil-minded persons from injuring the common good?"

"Oh, certainly—certainly."

"And are you prepared to affirm, that a drinking-shop, where young men are corrupted, aye, destroyed, body and soul—does not work an injury to the common good?"

"Ah! but there must be houses of public entertainment."

"No one denies this. But can that be a really Christian community which provides for the moral debasement of strangers, at the same time that it entertains them? Is it necessary that, in giving rest and entertainment to the traveler, we also lead him into temptation?"

The discussion ends with the temperance advocate predicting an apocalypse for the United States unless action is taken against taverns:

Of little value, my friend, will be, in far too many cases, your precepts, if temptation invites our sons at almost every step of their way through life. Thousands have fallen, and thousands are now tottering, soon to fall. Your sons are not safe; nor are mine. We cannot tell the day nor the hour when they may weakly yield to the solicitation of some companion, and enter the wide open door of ruin. And are we wise and good citizens to . . . hesitate over some vague ideal of human liberty when the sword is among us, slaying our best and dearest? Sir! while you hold back from the work of staying the flood that is desolating our fairest homes, the black waters are approaching your own doors.

The other great political issue of the day was slavery, the principal theme of *Uncle Tom's Cabin*. Superficially, the prohibition and abolition movements had much in common. Each perceived their cause as being a moral crusade, and a number of individuals served both. The Reverend Henry Ward Beecher, for example, brother of the author of *Uncle Tom's Cabin*, preached temperance and raised funds to arm abolitionists in Kansas. However, many temperance agitators thought it more important to free the southern states from the curse of drinking than to encourage them to free their slaves, and they indulged in shameful equivocations in order to keep abolition and abstinence apart. According, for example, to John Gough, the Washington celebrity, alcoholism was by far the worst kind of servitude: "Ah, yes, physical slavery is an awful thing," he noted in *Platform Echoes,* a volume of memoirs, but a "man may be bought or sold in the market and yet be a freer man than he who sells him."

Not only did the temperance movement place politics before humanity, it also rejected an entire community of potential supporters.

IN THE MONSTER'S CLUTCHES.
Body and Brain on Fire.

African Americans, free or in bondage, were staunch opponents of alcohol. Drink had grim historic links with their presence in the United States—many had ancestors who had been traded for a keg of rum. Furthermore, slaves with drunken owners often suffered arbitrary acts of brutality, which contributed to their loathing of alcohol. Finally, drink was used as an instrument of oppression on the plantations. At Christmas, slaves were given "holidays," supplied with spirits, and encouraged to get drunk, in the belief that if allowed to indulge themselves every now and then, they would see their enslavement as less cruel. According to Frederick Douglass, the aim of this practice was to "disgust the slave with freedom, by allowing him to see only the abuse of it."

Sobriety, alongside education and domestic economy, had been recognized at the 1831 First Annual Convention of the People of Color, held in Philadelphia, as a key attribute most likely to raise African Americans to "a proper rank and standing amongst men." They were, however, forced to form their own temperance organizations, and these were sometimes the objects of racist violence, as for example in 1841, when a white mob attacked the members of the Moyamensing Temperance Society who were celebrating the final manumission of slaves in British dominions. Despite such harassment, free blacks kept faith with abstinence, hoping by their sobriety to prove they were worthy of equality.

The pursuit of temperance in the United States was sidelined by its Civil War, during which a laissez-faire approach to drinking prevailed. Convictions pro and contra alcohol were held with equal force and were equally tolerated by each side. Lincoln was a teetotaler, as was Confederate general Thomas J. "Stonewall" Jackson, who explained his abstinence thus: "I like strong drink–so I never touch it." General Ulysses S. Grant, in contrast, was very nearly an alcoholic. Whether or not a man took liquor was up to him, and if it helped him to function better, it was accepted as a harmless idiosyncrasy. The spirit of the times is reflected by the response of Abraham Lincoln to a complaint that General Grant drank too much. Rather than promising to make him abstain, Lincoln vowed that he would ask "the quartermaster of the army to lay in a large stock of the same kind of liquor, and would direct him to furnish a supply to some of my other generals who have never yet won a victory."

Both sides supplied their troops with alcohol. An unofficial whiskey ration was issued to the Union army,[51] and the Confederates supplied their men with spirits from time to time. In terms of supply, the Union armies were ahead. Despite the Maine law and its cohorts, there were still more distilleries north of the Mason-Dixon Line than in the Rebel states. Moreover, after it had assumed command of the ocean and the Mississippi River, the Union could import at will and deny the South the same resource. This blockade, in combination

---

[51] And refused by the soldiers of the Temperance Regiment raised by the governor of Maine, who had pledged to serve dry.

with the deliberate despoliation of agriculture in Confederate territory, dried up the Rebel supply of alcohol, so that by the time of the war's conclusion many Confederate soldiers had become temperate through force of circumstance. Indeed, fluctuations in the supply of alcohol in the South closely reflected its fortunes in the war.

At the beginning of the conflict, the mood of the Confederate volunteers who had flocked to its banner had been buoyant. Sixty percent of them were farmers or their sons, in the majority from small communities, who had seldom, if ever, seen a city or a crowd. A holiday atmosphere prevailed as they assembled and traveled to the front. The excitement of events led many who had been temperate at home to experiment on the way to war and to fall "into the delusion that drinking was excusable, if not necessary, in the army." The initial elation, and a ready supply of alcohol with which to sustain it, alarmed the Confederate command. In 1861 General Braxton Bragg prohibited the sale of alcohol within five miles of Pensacola, where his troops were stationed. Drunkenness, in his opinion, was causing "demoralization, disease, and death" among them: "We have lost more valuable lives at the hands of the whiskey sellers than by the balls of our enemies." His example was recommended to his fellow officers, and similar prohibitions were installed in other Rebel camps. They do not seem to have been enforced with any great severity. Alcohol was smuggled into camp, at times blatantly, at others discreetly–injected into a watermelon (a large one could absorb a half gallon of whiskey) or tipped down the barrel of a musket that was held at present arms until its bearer reached his tent. Punishments for carrying liquor into camp were not, by military standards of discipline, severe. No one was flogged or shot for drinking. Private Henry Jones, for instance, found guilty of drunkenness at his post in Tullahoma, Tennessee, was made to spend two hours a day, every day for a month, standing on the head of a barrel with an empty whiskey bottle hanging from his neck.

The first Christmas of the war was celebrated in the South with spirits and song. Whiskey acquired the nickname among some Rebels as "Oh-be-joyful," under which guise it pops up in their letters home. Quality, however, was on the wane: "The general Davis sent up a barrel of whiskey to the camp," reported one trooper, "but it was such villainous stuff that only the old soakers could stomach it." The following year whiskey could still be found to celebrate the Nativity, but shortages of other supplies rendered its enjoyment imperfect. One

Texan rebel's diary entry for December 25, 1862, lamented the absence of eggs to make eggnog and observed, "If it was in my power I would condemn every old hen on the Rio Grande to six months confinement in close-coop for the non conformance of a most sacred duty." By 1863, however, not only the mixers but also oh-be-joyful was in short supply. Post-Vicksburg, the Mississippi was controlled by the Union, thus cutting off Taos Lightning and other such delicacies, and within the Confederate heartland stills were being broken up for their copper, which was used to forge bronze cannon.

At the same time that supplies of liquor were diminishing, the temperance movement began to appear in force in Southern camps. While Bibles had been issued to every soldier by various benevolent societies at the start of the conflict, these were neglected in initial years, when it seemed that the next Rebel victory would force the Union to sue for peace. However, as reverses on the battlefield increased, a religious revival took place among the Confederate ranks, which was supported by a plethora of religious tracts, whose publishers maintained a more efficient distribution network than the suppliers of such secular comforts as clothing and rations. These tracts provided moral as well as spiritual guidance to the Rebel troops and sought to arm them against the evils of swearing, gambling, and drinking. One such, *Lincoln and Liquor,* put a new spin on the slave-to-alcohol argument—why fight for freedom from Washington, only to surrender to the whiskey bottle? The pamphlet also predicted crop failures if they continued to be wasted in the manufacture of "distilled damnation." The revival and the pamphleteering seem to have diminished demand for now-scarce alcohol. One rebel soldier wrote to his mother and sister from the front thanking them for various gifts, including some whiskey, but warning them, "The Whiskey you may depend will be used moderately as I belong to the Temperance society of whom Gen Braxton Bragg is president."

Throughout the conflict Southern officers had better access to alcohol than their men and did not experience the same vicissitudes in supply. Not all of them followed the example of Bragg; indeed, some abused the privilege. This was resented in the ranks, whose scorn for inebriated superiors is apparent in the diary entry of an anonymous Louisiana soldier for October 25, 1863, apropos of his new brigadier: "From what I can tell [he] is better able to command a bottle of whiskey than anything else." Confederate physicians also had privileged access to alcohol. It was employed as a panacea against ailments ranging from camp itch to malaria, and when supplies of anesthetics dried up, it served as an analgesic during surgery. The Civil War created nearly half a million cripples. Fear of wounds turning gangrenous made amputation the operation of choice, and accounts from both sides describe the horror of seeing cartloads of freshly severed human limbs stacked up outside operating tents. More often than not the only sedative a wounded Confederate received before his arm or leg was sawn off was a mouthful of spirits. Like the officers, the physicians were suspected of exploiting their advantages. Indeed, some confessed to drinking a fair proportion of their own medicine under the strain of work.

While the South burned, the cocktails still flowed in Washington. Nathaniel Hawthorne advised visitors to Willard's Hotel, which served as an informal center of operations in the capital, to "adopt the universal habit of the place, and call for a mint julep, a whiskey skin, a gin cock-tail, a brandy smash, or a glass of pure Old Rye, for the conviviality of Washington sets in at an early hour, and, so far as I had an opportunity of observing, never terminates at any hour." Moreover, as victory for the North became inevitable, there was no equivalent religious revival in the Federal camps and no attendant blip in temperance. Indeed, the movement received a serious setback when a tax was imposed on beer and distilled spirits in the Union states, thereby conniving at their manufacture and sale.

American drinking habits shifted in the aftermath of the Civil War. Lager beer replaced whiskey as the national beverage of the workingman. The change was caused by a number of factors. The excise tax introduced by the Union to help pay for its armies had pushed up the price of spirits, so that they were no longer much cheaper than sodas. The price of beer, meanwhile, was traveling in the opposite direction. Although it had likewise been subjected to a tax (of one dollar per barrel) the net effect of the imposition over the following decade was to focus brewers on making the production, distribution, and sale of their merchandise vastly more efficient. Attendant benefits in both quality and availability resulted in a surge in consumption. Whereas in 1860 there had been 1,269 breweries in the United States, with a total output of one million barrels, by 1867 output had risen to six million barrels, and by 1873, 4,131 brewers produced nine million barrels of beer among them. Most of this growth was accounted for by lager beer, in the pilsner style, and much of it came from towns in the old West such as Pittsburgh, Cincinnati, Milwaukee, and Chicago.

The switch to lager from colonial favorites such as ale, porter, and stout resulted partly from demographics, and partly from changing tastes among consumers. The flood of German immigrants in the mid-nineteenth century had created a naturalized American market for lager. Over the next two decades Teutonic entrepreneurs established large breweries dedicated to their native brews in towns where fellow Germans had settled in numbers. Some of their enterprises remain household names: In 1855 Frederick Miller took over the Menomonee Valley Brewery in Milwaukee, and lent the enterprise his name, the following year Joseph Schlitz started brewing in the same town, and in 1857 Eberhard Anheuser acquired a small brewery in St. Louis, which, with the assistance of his son-in-law Adolphus Busch, he converted to the production of Anheuser-Busch pilsner. In addition to introducing German beer to America, immigrants also established Bavarian-style beer gardens where they might gather in their leisure hours. The Bowery district of New York was graced with a number of these institutions, which won the approval of the press of the city for the orderly conduct of their patrons. They were "immense buildings, fitted up in imitation of a garden," which could accommodate "from four hundred to twelve hundred guests. Germans carry their families there to spend a day or an evening." These drinking places usually provided music to entertain their clients, which was judged to be "exquisite in some places, especially in the Atlantic Garden." However, they also attracted criticism for being foreign to the American way. They were child-friendly, did their best business on Sundays, and were notoriously peaceful places where, despite the quantity of alcohol consumed, good humor and decency prevailed. Such qualities provoked both the ire of the temperance movement, who reviled the clientele of beer gardens for Sabbath breaking and for drinking in front of their wives and children, and the prejudice of non-German Americans, who held up the different customs of the minority for ridicule.

After lager and beer gardens, German immigrants introduced a third innovation to American drinking: organization. When the Civil War tax on beer was introduced in 1862, thirty-seven New York lager brewers had arranged a national convention to consider the matter, which was attended by brewers from other Union states. The convention was repeated the following year, and the next, by which time it

had acquired a title–the United States Brewers Association (USBA)–
and a mission, which was to influence America's elected politicians in
favor of beer. From the start, the members of the USBA had been diligent in paying their taxes and asking that they might be reduced.
They were also conscientious in documenting their financial contribution to the war, and to postwar reconciliation, and this record formed
the bedrock on which the beer lobby was raised. In addition to singing
the praises of liquid bread, the USBA launched a preemptive strike on
temperance, whose resurgence it feared. According to its secretary,
speaking at the 1866 convention, "Just now a note of war is heard
coming against us by fanatics who, in pretending to support Sunday
and temperance laws, are in fact trying to annihilate the self-respect
and independence of mankind, and liberty of conscious, and of trade."
Its response, made formal in Chicago in 1867, was the resolution:
"That we will use all means to stay the progress of this fanatical party,
and to secure our individual rights as citizens, and that we will sustain
no candidate, of whatever party, in any election, who is any way disposed towards the total abstinence cause."

At the same time as declaring war on temperance, America's
brewers industrialized their businesses. European innovations such as
steam engines and microscopes were introduced, and the ever-growing
railway network was used to extend distribution. Contemporary advances in cooling technology and ice storage enabled them to produce
lager all year round, and their consistent, refreshing product made
many converts to the German way of brewing. Once they had stimulated demand, the brewers sought to control it. They became apostles
of vertical integration, buying saloons in imitation of the tied pub system of their British counterparts. These profited at the expense of independent competitors by a combination of lower prices and clever
marketing strategies, which latter included washing the sidewalk in
front of the saloon with beer so that its compelling aroma, mingled
with the scent of alcohol evaporating in the sunlight, would lure
drinkers in through the doors.

Saloons superseded the colonial tavern as the archetypal American
drinking place. Unlike taverns, the average saloon was not expected to
serve as a multipurpose institution–a place in which to lodge strangers,
judge witches, plot independence, and serve travelers the odd pint of
strong waters or cider. The ideal shifted from Elizabethan inn to gin
palace. Instead of a warren of rooms, the action was concentrated in a

single large space serviced by a long bar. The counter itself was often decorated in an ornate style, with carved facings, a brass footrail, and spittoons of the same material tastefully disposed about its base. An alluring display of bottles and, from 1879 onward, a cash register, backed by a wall of mirrors, drew the eye of the drinker toward the obliging bar-staff.

In metropolitan saloons, the free lunch pioneered by the City Exchange in New Orleans became an institution. Working hours were changing. Gone were the fourteen-hour days of the first flush of the Industrial Revolution, when there had seemed to be no limit to the capacity of the laborer for labor. Employers let their workers rest at noon and set them free in the evenings, thus creating two fixed periods when they might relax and refresh themselves. The opportunity to eat for free for the price of a few beers drew hungry men to drink at lunchtime for the sake of food, and they rewarded such largesse with their loyalty in the evenings.

Saloons, more so than taverns, relied on men for their clientele. Throughout the nineteenth century, American women had been drifting away from public drinking places, and the new model was developed with their absence in mind. It transpired, however, that America's brewers had neglected its women at their peril. In 1873 they rose en masse and attacked the manufacturers and retailers of alcohol with an unprecedented fury. As the Brewers Association had prophesized, the dormant heresy of temperance was revived, and its flame of intolerance rekindled, albeit by unexpected hands. The Woman's Temperance Crusade of 1873–74, during which "hundreds of thousands of women, in a paroxysm of activity and prayer, closed thirty thousand saloons and initiated a generation of female leadership in the temperance movement" was as unwelcome a development as it had been unforeseen.

The crusade was the brainchild of Dr. Dioclesian Lewis, a Boston minister who had learned his temperance at the hands of a drunken father. Lewis made a living as a traveling lecturer, and his favorite themes were the education of women and the social evils caused by alcohol. His eloquence persuaded a band of women in Hillsboro, Ohio, to march into a saloon to reclaim their menfolk, and once the crusade had been set in motion, it snowballed into a national campaign. Across the United States, groups of women invaded saloons. Once inside, their preferred tactics were to sing hymns or fall on their knees in prayer. If prevented from entering, they would occupy the sidewalk outside and raise the doxology. On the occasions that their piety persuaded the saloon keeper that he was an inadvertent ally of Satan, redeemers and redeemed would roll out the barrels and bottles of liquid perdition and empty their contents on the road.

The women of America had taken to the front line of the war on alcohol because they considered themselves to be its voiceless victims. They were beaten and impoverished by drunken husbands, with little opportunity for legal protection or redress. Divorce was rare, and alcoholism did not yet constitute proper grounds for separation. Women could not vote, and hence they were as helpless to prevent the supply of drink as they were to escape its consequences. And so they seized on temperance as a cause to rally around. With temperance they could test their collective power to influence the behavior of American men, by persuading them to deny themselves their saloons. If we could vote, they declared, we would vote for temperance. Indeed, the female quest for an alcohol-free America was seen by many of its participants as the first step in the quest for female suffrage.

In retrospect, the brewers should have anticipated the danger. A fair number of women's temperance societies had flourished prior to the Civil War. While organizations such as the Daughters of Temperance acted as dutiful sisters to their fraternal orders, others were protest groups, established by women who had been excluded from making a common cause with teetotal men, such as the Woman's New York State Temperance Society. The WNYSTS was the creation of Susan B. Anthony and Mary C. Vaughn, both former Daughters of Temperance, who had been banned "from speaking at a Sons of Temperance convention in Albany (in 1852) because of their sex." The new society had progressive views on divorce, which it advocated should be permitted to a woman married to an alcoholic. It also passed opinions on matters other than temperance, including slavery and, by extension, universal suffrage. It was, however, ahead of its time, and its members were not consistent in their opinions. Susan B. Anthony, for instance, limited the intended beneficiaries of her demand for votes to black men and white women.

Despite their noble aims and impressive membership rolls, women's temperance societies had been passive creatures prior to the Civil War. The Woman's Temperance Crusade of 1873–74 taught them the use of their teeth, and the newly established Women's Christian Temperance Union (WCTU) gave them a tongue. The WCTU quickly established supremacy among women's temperance bodies and within a decade was a power in national politics. Its rise to influence and fame was managed by Frances E. Willard, who acted as its national president between 1879 and 1898, and whose motto was "Do Everything!" No measure was spared in the effort to drive out alcohol. Towns were encouraged to build drinking-water fountains; *temperance restaurants,* a combination of words that would have been oxymoronic to a gourmand, were established; and the free lunch offered by saloons was attacked as a wicked ruse whose hidden costs included the risks of drunkenness and damnation. Moreover, abstinence was idolized and drinking demonized in the promotional material that the WCTU prepared for and taught in American schools. Young girls were trained to withhold their kisses from any with alcohol on their breath via the slogan "Lips that touch liquor shall never touch mine!" Finally the WCTU borrowed some of its opponents' tactics—like the brewers, it scrutinized the stance on abstinence of every candidate for election and stigmatized any whom it judged to be insufficiently dry.

Temperance was once again a hot topic in national as well as local politics. A Prohibition Party was established in 1869 as a breakaway from the Republicans, who were not prepared to adopt state-enforced abstinence as official policy. Many within its ranks, however, practiced temperance, and in 1876 Americans elected their second dry Republican president, Rutherford B. Hayes, who, unlike Lincoln, enforced his own self-denial on the White House and entertained domestic luminaries and visiting dignitaries alike with alcohol-free fruit punches and sodas. His wife, Lucy, also teetotal, passed around the jugs. In recognition of her unbending commitment to abstinence, she was given the nickname of *Lemonade Lucy* by a grateful WCTU.

However, while the temperance movement was advancing on several fronts, it was forced to give ground to the beer lobby in other places. It had been the fervent hope of the drys that the American Centennial Exhibition, staged in Philadelphia in 1876, would be an alcohol-free event, and they lobbied to have brewers excluded from its agricultural displays. However, they were outflanked by their opponents, who petitioned for, and were awarded, a separate edifice of their own—the Brewers Hall, a magnificent structure of wrought iron and glass. It was graced with a monumental portico, reminiscent of Napoléon's Arc de Triomphe, which sheltered an immense statue of

Gambrinus, the medieval king and legendary beer drinker of Bohemia, represented in a posture of victory. The Brewers Hall was one of the most popular attractions of the Centennial Exhibition, in particular its icehouse, which featured chilled beers from around the world. In addition to refreshing their visitors, the brewers supplied them with propaganda, which explained that the duties they paid were by far the largest source of internal revenue in the United States: That "a brewer is just as necessary to the commonweal as a butcher, a baker, a tailor, a builder, or any other economic industry, is proven by the present position of the trade in the United States."

24 IMPERIAL PREFERENCE

Here with a loaf of bread beneath the Bough,
A Flask of Wine, a Book of Verse, and Thou
Beside me singing in the Wilderness
And Wilderness is Paradise enow.
                              —Edward FitzGerald

Whereas the British and American temperance movements had marched hand in hand during the first half of the nineteenth century, exchanging ideas, sharing tracts, and lending each other their orators, by the 1870s, when American women were invading saloons and American men were electing a dry president, their paths had diverged and the British temperance movement was in retreat. Although on paper its armies were intact, it had lost the fight for the hearts and minds of Britons to the nation's brewers. Its defeat may be attributed in part to its reliance upon child soldiers, whom it had deployed in so-called *Bands of Hope*. The first Band of Hope, a temperance society dedicated to recruiting minors to the cause, was founded in Leeds in 1847 and within two years had "pledged 4,000 children between the ages of 6 & 16." It was imitated the length and breadth of the land, and by 1860 there were 120 Bands of Hope in London alone, and several hundred thousand British children had committed themselves, or had been pledged by their parents, to a lifetime of total abstinence. Their faith in temperance was sustained throughout infancy and adolescence with propaganda and group outings. They were taught temperance songs and read temperate fairy tales, which had been revised to admit a bestiary of drunks and inebriated ogres. George Cruikshank, who illustrated many of the works of his friend Charles Dickens, was among the revisionists.[52] He had taken to abstinence with the fanaticism of a convert and expressed his new convictions through his art. Cruikshank dedicated two years of his life to a single giant allegorical painting, the *Triumph of Bacchus*. This shocking canvas, containing several hundred figures, has a monumental statue of the Greek deity of the title as its focus, raising a goblet of liquid perdition atop a pyramid of wine casks, from which issue fountains of the same fluid, which are distributed to the crowds at its base and thence throughout the rest of the canvas, to the general ruin of society. Fearful, perhaps, that he had not made the message clear, Cruikshank followed up with a series of engravings entitled *The Bottle*, which depicted the step-by-step ruin of a respectable family through the drunkenness of its breadwinner.

Despite mobilizing the children of the nation and issuing lurid propaganda, the British temperance movement failed to convert its aspirations into laws. Its lack of success was not for want of trying. Enthused by the triumph of their American cousins in Maine, the plethora of British temperance and abstinence societies had paused in their turf wars to throw their support behind the United Kingdom Alliance (UKA), which was founded in 1853 "to outlaw all trading in intoxicating drinks" and to create thereby "a progressive civilization" in Britain. The UKA spent the first four years of its life perfecting its publicity; then, in 1857, it turned to action. A bill was presented by a tame MP to the House of Commons that sought to limit the sale of alcohol via a so-called *Permissive Act*. Despite the promise of its name, the proposed act was anything but liberal. Its aim was creeping Prohibition—if enacted, a two-thirds majority of voters in an area would be empowered to ban drink shops within their locality. Critics

---

[52] His monomania alarmed Dickens, who thought Cruikshank had gone too far in the name of a good cause. In 1853 he issued a gentle rebuke, which accused him of introducing "a Whole Hog of unwieldy dimensions into the fairy flower garden." Dickens accompanied his rebuke with a mock-temperance version of *Cinderella*, whose politically correct heroine was as dull as she was dry.

Cruikshank's The Bottle

outside the temperance movement pointed out that since the franchise was limited to adult males who owned property, a Permissive Act would enable 2/15ths of the population to "dictate to the remaining 13/15ths." It also received fire from its own side. Teetotalers thought it did not go nearly far enough and resented the fact that it had been drafted by a brewer. In the event it got nowhere, and no farther when it was reintroduced in 1858, and every subsequent year until 1872, by which time its presentation had become a curious annual exercise in futility.

While the UKA was engrossed with its Permissive Act, and its constituents were busy recruiting hordes of children, British wine merchants were prospering with the encouragement of queen and country. In 1860, after fortifying himself with "a great stock of egg and wine," Prime Minister William Ewart Gladstone delivered his budget speech, in which he announced a cut in duty on French wines. Britons responded favorably to this largesse and, by 1866, had doubled their consumption and revived the economy of Bordeaux, which was going through a rough patch, at the same time. The 1860s and

'70s were also a golden age for brewing. British beer had never been better or more popular. Production raced to keep pace with demand. Between 1859 and 1876 annual per capita consumption rose from 23.9 to 34.4 gallons—about three times as much as was drunk by the average American. The statistics for spirit drinking were similarly encouraging. While they lagged their eighteenth-century ancestors and contemporary Americans by some distance, by 1875 the average Briton had rebuilt his or her average intake to 1.3 gallons of liquor per annum.

In retrospect, data showing that consumption of alcohol and membership in temperance societies were both trending in the same direction should have awakened the suspicions of each side, for they either implied that fewer people were drinking more or that many people who had pledged themselves to abstinence still drank. The truth was put to the test in 1872, when, in addition to the ritual submission of a Permissive Bill to Parliament, a Licensing Act intended to reform both the drinking laws and drinking habits of Great Britain was also introduced.

It was an emotive area of legislation, which demanded the modification of some of the oldest statutes in English law still in use, which, since their earliest forms, had protected the rights of access of the common man to good ale at a reasonable price and his freedom to consume it at his leisure. The nonvoting majority of the British public were notoriously sensitive to political tinkering with the licensing laws, and rioted if they thought that their rights to drink were likely to be abridged. Their point of view was shared even by temperance advocates such as Bishop Magee, who expressed his unease with the concept that Queen Victoria's government should dictate the drinking habits of her subjects: "If I must take my choice . . . whether England should be free or sober, I declare—strange as such a declaration may sound, coming from one of my profession—that I should say it would be better that England should be free rather than that England should be compulsorily sober. I would distinctly prefer freedom to sobriety, because with freedom we might in the end attain sobriety; but in the other alternative we should eventually lose both freedom and sobriety."

The debate over the merits of the 1872 Licensing Bill was extended by the beer, wine, and spirits interests, who accused its sponsors of being inspired by French radicalism. Liberal commentators further muddied the waters by suggesting that the bill was a Tory Trojan horse with capitalism hidden in its belly. Seduced by the alleged social benefits of temperance, Parliament might overlook the social problems caused by long hours, poor working conditions, wretched accommodation, and the absence of any fulfilling leisure activities other than drinking, and so mistake a symptom for the disease. Abstinent capitalists were the real enemies of British society, not the alcohol that the oppressed multitudes drank for solace.

Finally, nonconformists became entangled in the debate. Joseph Livesey, the original malt lecturer, accused evangelicals of hijacking his movement, claiming that teetotalism had become "a useful expedient only, for the furtherance of denominational religion." Radical Protestant theologians, meanwhile, locked horns in a side quarrel as to the literal truth of the Bible, and indeed its relevance to the age of steam. Instead of trying to prove that the Old and New Testaments meant grape juice when they said wine, some extremists acknowledged their potency and held it out as evidence that the Good Book was nonsense on stilts and that its failure "to censure Noah for his drunkenness" was "only one of the numerous instances" of its "imperfect and perverted morality."

The net result of so many conflicting interests was paralysis. The difficulty of trying to accommodate them all was summed up later by Lord George Cavendish: "If an angel from heaven were to come down and bring in a Licensing Bill, he would find it too much for him." A Licensing Act of sorts was passed in 1872, which took, among others, the important steps of prohibiting the sale of ardent spirits to children under the age of sixteen[53] and clarifying statutory opening times for public houses. The act was roundly criticized by all parties and anathematized by temperance organizations. Keeping fifteen-year-olds away from gin was no great legislative leap forward toward a dry Britain. A single statistic explains best why their hopes were doomed to slaughter, with or without angelic assistance: In 1870, exactly a third of all British national tax revenues derived from the manufacture and sale of alcoholic drinks. Abstinence would bankrupt the nation. British brewers, distillers, and wine merchants made this important fact very clear to voters when they treated them in pubs during the 1874 election season. Gladstone, who lost,

---

[53] They could still buy beer at any age.

attributed his defeat to the power of the British drink industry and complained, "We have been borne down on a torrent of gin and beer."

The death of temperance as a political cause in Great Britain was accompanied by an intellectual backlash against institutionalized sobriety. This process had commenced in 1859, when Edward FitzGerald's *Rubaiyat of Omar Khayyam* introduced the Arab *khamriyya* form of poetry to English literature. The *Rubaiyat* was as much invention as translation–FitzGerald intended to produce a single coherent piece rather than to revive the ad hoc structure of Omar Khayyam's work. He was, however, careful to preserve the defiant tone of the original, with its emphasis on enlightenment through drinking rather than via philosophy or religion. The Christian audience whom FitzGerald addressed were challenged to consider the poem in the light of their own beliefs, rather than to dismiss it as Muslim fulminations against the limitations of Islam. As such, it was strong stuff–a frontal attack on the Christian doctrine of the resurrection of the body, which was then enjoying a surprising vogue, and indeed, on belief in an afterlife at all, whether corporeal, spiritual, or a combination of the two:

> Ah, fill the Cup:–what boots it to repeat
> How Time is slipping underneath our Feet:
> Unborn TOMORROW, and dead YESTERDAY,
> Why fret about them if TODAY be sweet!
> One moment in Annihilation's Waste,
> One Moment, of the Well of Life to taste–
> The Stars are setting and the Caravan
> Starts for the Dawn of Nothing–Oh, make haste!

The *Rubaiyat* was a commercial triumph and ran through five editions in FitzGerald's lifetime. He altered the poem in successive texts, and some of the changes were made to emphasize that the wine it referred to was real wine, not a metaphor for divine inspiration, as had been suggested by hopeful temperates, and as such was proof that God connived at drinking:

> Why, be this Juice the growth of God, who dare
> Blaspheme the twisted tendrils as a snare?

A Blessing, we should use it, should we not?
And if a Curse—why, then, who set it there?

However, while British politics, philosophy, and literature were turning against temperance, medicine gave it some welcome support. In 1860, French scientists had proved that the perceived warming qualities of alcohol were illusory, and thus killed off the so-called "heroic cures" that prescribed heroic amounts of alcohol to victims of "cooling" diseases like dysentery.[54] The mechanics of cirrhosis of the liver were explored and documented, experiments were carried out on animals, with sobering results: Alcohol, in the right doses, was a killer. No wonder the faces of gin drinkers, who still were common in mid-Victorian Britain, were "apoplectic and swollen, the scarlet color so dense that it is almost black; eyes dead, bloodshot, like those of a raw lobster."

The field of nutrition also provided backing to opponents of alcohol. For much of its existence, the British temperance movement had been handicapped by the prejudice of the average Briton in favor of corpulence. Stout equaled healthy, and abstainers found it hard to match the obese, ruddy John Bulls paraded by the brewers with champions from their own ranks. However, as competitive sports, whose contestants were leaner than the medieval ideal, became popular spectacles, public perception changed and figures such as W. G. Grace, the first cricketing superstar, six-two and a mere 250 pounds, came to represent the trim new model of physical excellence. Athletes slaked their thirsts with tea instead of ale, and the rapid growth in popularity of the infusion gave hope to the temperance movement. British per capita consumption of tea more than doubled between 1850 and 1875. The leap in demand, however, was rather the consequence of economic factors than closet abstinence. Duty on tea had been reduced over the same period, and plantations of it had been established in India. Cheap, plentiful Indian tea flooded the home market. Not only was it of excellent quality, it also had the benefit of being produced within the bounds of the jewel in the crown of the British Empire, so that to drink a British Indian cuppa was an act of imperial patriotism.

---

[54] Prince Albert, spouse of Queen Victoria, was one of the last to be treated with this therapy, and was prescribed six pints of brandy per day in the hope of defeating the waterborne ailment that ultimately killed him.

The merchant ships that carried tea from India to Great Britain were loaded with beer for the voyage out. Expatriate Britons in the subcontinent had prodigious thirsts for their native brews and paid the highest prices for any that reached them without spoiling. The passage to India crossed the equator twice, via some of the calmest and roughest parts of the Atlantic and Indian oceans, and exposed the outbound cargo of beer to extreme variations in temperature and motion. In order to survive, it had to be brewed in a particular style, which came to be known as India Pale Ale, or *IPA*. The recipe for IPA was based on the traditional English October ale, a strong (OG 1140 or more), heavily hopped brew, matured in the barrel for a year, then aged in bottles for up to ten more, which had been the favorite style of the eighteenth-century country squire. When a freshly made batch of this nectar was first shipped to India, it was discovered that, unlike most beers, which deteriorated on the journey, October ale improved. It underwent an accelerated process of maturation so that it was ready to drink upon arrival and was the equal of brews that had spent years in English cellars.

Hodgson's Brewery in London was the beneficiary of this discovery and, for the first two decades of the nineteenth century, had a near monopoly on the India market. The arrival of a fresh shipment of its ale was trumpeted in the expatriate press. *The Calcutta Gazette* of January 20, 1822, for example, carried a notice advising its readers that a cargo of "Hodgson's warranted prime picked pale ale of the genuine October brewing ... fully equal, if not superior, to any ever before received in the settlement" had appeared in port. However, such preeminence was resented by rival brewers in Britain, and when Hodgson's decided to charter ships and do its own exporting to India, it also made enemies in the Honorable East India Company, whose employees hitherto had made substantial profits from the carriage of beer. In 1822, Campbell Majoribanks, a director of the East India Company, invited Samuel Allsopp, a brewer from the town of Burton-on-Trent, to attempt the manufacture of a competitor. By coincidence, the hard water of the Burton wells was perfectly suited to the IPA style, and when Allsopp's new pale ale was shipped to India, it generated fan mail in return. It was, according to one grateful empire builder, "almost universally preferred by all old Indians[55]

---

[55] In the sense of British expatriates.

to Hodgson's." It also found favor at home in Burton-on-Trent, and a pair of local brewers, Bass & Ratcliff and Salt, produced imitations of Allsopp's brews. By the 1830s exports to India were dominated by Burton breweries. IPA was also the rising star of the British beer market. Strong in alcohol, dry in flavor, and pleasantly effervescent, it established itself as a refreshing alternative to sweet, glutinous stouts. Production in Burton-on-Trent rose from 300,000 barrels in 1849 to 1.75 million in 1869, by which time Bass & Co., which ran three breweries in the town, had become the largest brewer in the world.

In addition to changing British tastes in beer, the Indian market also influenced the way in which Britons consumed their spirits. India was administered from Calcutta, where malaria, typhoid, hepatitis, and various other killers were endemic. The local water had a reputation for unwholesomeness worse than that of raw sewage. It was a time-honored maxim of the expatriate community that alcoholic beverages were the only safe drinks, and they were consumed with vigor. Indeed, Anglo-Indians ate and drank as if the key to health on the subcontinent was to consume heavy meals, rich in meat, thrice a day, to wash these down with plenty of fortified wines and spirit-based punches, and to supplement them with more alcohol at other fixed hours. Every evening, they would participate in the ritual of the *chotapeg*, during which they protected themselves against malaria with a dose of quinine, whose bitter, astringent flavors were made more palatable by mixing it with gin. The therapeutic part of the combination was improved by Jacob Schweppe, a manufacturer of aerated waters, which launched an *INDIAN quinine TONIC* in 1870 and exported it to its place of inspiration. It was immediately popular as the perfect partner for gin, and a taste for this medicinal mixture was carried back to the United Kingdom by retiring empire builders, where the *gin and tonic* was added to the list of "traditional" British drinks.

The expanding empire did more than supply Britons with cheap tea and new recipes for long drinks. In Australia, a long-held imperial ambition was finally realized when its inhabitants started to produce marketable volumes of decent wine. The dream of securing an independent supply of wine had been one of the first motors of British imperialism, a driving force behind the movement to acquire territory and establish settlements in distant lands. The Virginia Company had been instructed to plant vines, in the hope that its vintages would one day reduce England's reliance on its enemies in Catholic Europe; and subsequent settlements were likewise encouraged to cultivate the grape. The dream came true, at last, in Australia.

Vines had been carried to the New South Wales colony by the first convict fleet. There were some early successes in the manufacture of wine, but it was not until the settlement of the Hunter Valley in the 1830s that terrain suited to making good wine was planted with quality grapes. The following decade, aiming to wean its population off a lingering taste for rum, the government of New South Wales encouraged the plantation of more vines by enabling vintners to sell wine without requiring a publican's license. Production boomed, reaching a hundred thousand gallons by 1850.

The vine was introduced to other areas of Australia as they were settled. Adelaide, founded in 1836, was ringed with vineyards within a few years. By 1844, one of its growers (Walter Duffield) had sufficient confidence in his product to send a case of it to Queen Victoria as evidence of the fertility of her latest colony. He was rewarded with a gold medal from Prince Albert and a prosecution in South Australia for making wine without a license. In the 1840s a number of Silesians settled in the Barossa Valley and introduced the Riesling grape and Rhine styles of wine to Jacob's Creek. At about the same time, Dr. Christopher Rawson Penfold laid out a vineyard in Magill, aiming to produce fortified wines for his patients. By the middle of the century South Australia had several thousand acres of vines and was producing a wide variety of styles, including Australian sherry, Málaga, Burgundy, port, and brandy.

The grape was introduced to the neighboring state of Victoria following its gold rush in 1851. As had been the case in California, the immigrants who came in search of nuggets also planted vines. Although the earliest Victorian vineyards were small, and intended to supply their growers rather than function as commercial operations, the first governor of the state was a wealthy Swiss, who saw its promise for wine and encouraged planting on a larger scale. He persuaded several compatriots to emigrate to join him; they also formed equally high opinions of its potential, and one of their number, Paul de Castella, imported twenty thousand vines from the venerable Château Lafitte to his station at Yering. Planting in Victoria took off following the Duffy Land Act of 1862, which provided incentives to cultivate hitherto wild land, and two thousand acres were laid to vines within four years.

Eager to let the world know of their success with the grape, Australians sent their wines to the international exhibitions that were so popular in the late nineteenth century. They were shown in Paris, in a display shaped like a giant bottle, at the Exposition Universelle of 1855. The tasting notes of its judges on the offerings from the Hunter Valley illustrate the diversity and quality of a single region: They included "white wines akin to those of the Rhine; red light wines like those of Burgundy; Mousseux varieties with a bouquet, body, and flavor equal to the first Champagnes; Muscats, and other sweet wines." They also featured at exhibitions in London in 1862, Vienna in 1873 (where a Victorian red won a prize), and the Centennial Exhibition in Philadelphia in 1876.

By 1885, Australia had twenty-two thousand acres planted to vines and was exporting nearly fifty thousand gallons of wine per annum to London. Some of its output, moreover, was gaining an international reputation for quality, especially the reds produced in the state of Victoria. In 1889, one of these, named St. Huberts, won a gold medal in Paris, and seemed to be the first New World wine ready to challenge the dominance of Europe in the production of superior vintages. However, this proved to be its swan song: A deadly parasite appeared amid the Victorian vineyards and, by 1900, had destroyed most of their rootstock.

25   LA FÉE VERTE

The parasite responsible for murdering the hopes of Australian vintners in the state of Victoria had already been at work elsewhere; indeed, by the time it was killing vines in the Southern Hemisphere it had brought French wine production to its knees. *Phylloxera vastatrix,* the *devastator,* a diminutive if ravenous species of vine louse, had been restricted to the eastern portion of the United States until 1862, where it had been the mysterious cause of the death of imported vines, including those of William Penn and Thomas Jefferson. It was introduced to Europe by a vintner of Roquemaure in the Rhône Valley, within a shipment of American vine cuttings. The result was an ecological disaster. The *phylloxera* louse is not only voracious but also wonderfully prolific. A single female, breeding without the help of a mate, can, with the aid of successive generations, produce 25.6 billion descendants within eight months. Part of its life cycle is spent on wings, and it spread itself with ease through France's vineyards. By 1869 it had reached Bordeaux, by 1874 it had created such a panic at the French Ministry of Agriculture that a reward of three hundred thousand francs had been offered to anyone who could halt its progress, and by 1884 it had destroyed 2.5 million acres of French vines and was eating its way through a further 1.5 million.

The French sought to combat this scourge with both science and folklore. Chemists discovered that a sulphur compound, injected into the soil around the roots of each vine, kept the devastator at bay, but the process was expensive, harmful to the environment, and had to be repeated every year. Folklorists had no such success. Holy water was found to be entirely ineffective, as were whale oil, cow urine, and even human urine. Schoolboys in Beaujolais were led out to treat the vines after classes, to no avail. In desperation the French were forced to accept that their only defense against an American pest was to graft onto American vines, whose roots were immune to *phylloxera* attacks. While this option had been open from the 1870s, it had required the decimation of French vineyards, and the sacrifice of French pride, to make it acceptable.

The diminished supply of good French wine forced the country's citizens onto other beverages, one of which, *absinthe,* caused a spirits craze in France. The event had a very Gallic flavor to it that distinguished it from past Anglo-Saxon adventures with liquor drinking en masse. Absinthe, a distilled, flavored liquor, takes its name from the French word for the *wormwood* plant, which was considered to be its principal active ingredient, and which derives ultimately from the Greek *apsinthion,* meaning "undrinkable," in reference to its ultrabitter flavor. Notwithstanding the taste, wormwood had been reputed to possess therapeutic properties since pharaonic times and had been employed against afflictions as diverse as indigestion, scabs on virgins, intestinal worms, and rheumatism. It was associated not only with herbalists but also witches, who were reckoned to use it to help them to fly, and this risqué connection gave it an exciting potential as an ingredient of a drink. The potential was realized in 1792, when Dr. Pierre Ordinaire, a French royalist refugee in Switzerland, combined wormwood with other herbs and 120° proof alcohol and started to sell his creation by the bottle. The people loved it, so that soon there were rivals and, by 1800, industrial-scale absinthe distilleries, including that of Pernod in France, which exported their products to places as far away as New Orleans.

Absinthe first made an impression in Paris in the 1840s. It had been issued as a water purifier to French troops in North Africa, who had developed a taste for it and demanded it when they returned to their capital in triumph. The presence of these uniformed heroes in cafés, calling for their favorite refreshment, gave absinthe a new appeal—a glass might evoke the romance and excitement of fighting Arabs among the sand dunes of the Sahara. It received a further boost when it was adopted as their favorite drink by both Parisian poets and painters, who represented it in their art as liquid inspiration. It will come as no surprise to learn that Charles Baudelaire was an *absintheur*[56]—indeed the rise of absinthe could be said to mark the triumph of his vision of the proper purpose of alcohol in civilization. An anecdote of the period describes Baudelaire rushing into his favorite café, apparently dehydrated, but insisting that the water jug be removed from his table because "the sight of water upsets me." The jug gone, the poet quenched his thirst by downing several absinthes "with a detached and insouciant air."

Baudelaire's fellow *absintheurs* were quick to blame their fascination for the fluid on its entrancing color. It was a pale green, like liquid emeralds, and when it was mixed with a little sugar and water, it became opalescent. It acquired nicknames—la Fée Verte, the Sorceress, the White Witch, and the Charenton Omnibus. With the exception of the last, which refers to the lunatic asylum at Charenton, where many of its fans spent their final days, its monikers show that absinthe was conceived of as a woman, a younger and sexier Mother Gin, with bright green eyes and spellbinding powers. These last were no mere enchantment: While spirits were made strong at the time, absinthe could be anything from 120° to 180° proof: The Green Fairy punched above her weight. The poet Paul Verlaine was among the first to acknowledge the power of her blows. Afflicted by a number of personal sorrows in the late 1860s, he sought to drown them in absinthe: "It was on absinthe that I threw myself . . . absinthe day and night." Already violent, he became more so when struggling with the green deceiver—he would stab his friends with his sword stick, for instance, if they attempted to get between him and his bottle.

After spending two years recovering from this first bout with absinthe, Verlaine came across an ideal sparring partner in Arthur Rimbaud and prepared for another contest. Rimbaud was significantly less stable than his new friend and lover. In addition to attacking people with sword sticks, he cut at them with knives or put sulphuric acid in their beer. He was a vigorous proponent of intoxication. In his own words, "The poet must make himself a seer by a long, immense, and reasoned derangement of all the senses . . . they must be roused! Drugs, perfumes! The poisons taken by the Sybil!" Verlaine and Rimbaud enjoyed a tempestuous

---

[56] As was his American hero—Edgar Allan Poe.

affair that took them to a surprisingly ordinary series of places, including Tottenham Court Road in London and Belgium, where Verlaine shot Rimbaud in the wrist. The state of mind of Rimbaud during the liaison, during which he, too, took sanctuary in absinthe, can be gauged by the following letter, written to a friend, at its height:

PARISHIT, JUNISH 72

My friend,

. . .

There's one watering hole here I prefer. Long live the Academy of Absomphe, despite the malevolence of the waiters! It is the most delicate and most tremulous of garments, drunkenness thanks to that sage of the glaciers, absomphe! Only, afterward, to go to bed in shit!

Rimbaud was burned-out by the age of twenty. He gave up poetry and started a new life as an adventurer and arms trader in Africa. Verlaine became a schoolteacher, although his absinthe habit, which rendered him incapable every afternoon, and his affair with one of

The master at work with his muse

the boys entrusted to his care, soon lost him his job. Thereafter he dedicated his hours to the cafés of the Latin Quarter, where he became part of the literary tourist trail. Visitors recorded sightings in their diaries; journalists went in search of him. He was a fixture well into the 1890s and might be spotted scribbling away with a glass of the good fairy on the table beside him.

French painters were likewise entranced by absinthe and paid homage to their muse with portraits of absintheurs. Edouard Manet led the field with *The Absinthe Drinker* (1859), a Goyaesque canvas of a Baudelarian ragpicker, with a glass of the sorceress by his side. This vessel emits a pale green light, and like a candle, it casts no shadow of itself. The subject's arms are wrapped inside his cape, and his shadow on the wall behind him resembles the silhouette of a woman, sitting back to back against him, as if she were a spirit that had arisen from his drink. There is yet more allegory. The drinker's left leg sticks out toward the viewer with its foot at an odd angle, as though it had been paralyzed by a stroke. A splash of green, between trouser and shoe in the same place, echoes the color of his pick-me-up. It is possible to read the painting as a temperance tract. The venom in the glass beside the ragpicker has crippled him and filled his head with delusions, the demons once imprisoned in the empty bottle at his feet have escaped and done their work. In its time, *The Absinthe Drinker* received more criticism than praise. It was considered to be coarse and drab, and very different from the prevailing views in France as to what constituted a great painting.[57]

Manet and his fellow Impressionists assembled in the Café Guerbois in the evenings, which, like other Parisian cafés of the period, served as a nursery to the arts. Each one attracted distinct cliques of painters, poets, critics, and grisettes.[58] Absinthe was a fixture on all their drinks lists. It was pictured in its element by Edgar Degas in *Dans un café* (1876), which shows a couple sitting together, but apart, at a marble table in a café, each privately meditating on some mutual disappointment. The girl has a full glass of absinthe in front of her, but even this happy

---

[57] The taste then was for ultrarealist pictures of romantic or historical subjects—Salomé in Spanish costume, Napoléon on a stallion. Few bourgeois could imagine hanging the portrait of a common and elderly drunkard in their drawing rooms.

[58] Nineteenth-century French slang for a flirtatious and attractive woman.

prospect is not enough to make her smile. Despite its innovative use of perspective, the painting drew critical fire, principally because it showed miserable people in a humdrum setting. That it portrayed a sickly-looking grisette doing the drinking attracted little comment, for women had been acknowledged as patrons of Parisian cafés and participants in the absinthe craze ever since their respective inceptions.

Frenchwomen were considered to have an irresistible weakness for absinthe—more so than for any other drink. Although the wormwood that gave it its identity had long been associated with the feminine—the Greeks, for instance, prescribed *apsinthion* to relieve the pains of periods and childbirth—the fondness of Parisiennes for the emerald goddess was attributed to modern causes: It would be more comfortable, in the imagination of male commentators, to get tipsy inside a corset on absinthe than on wine or beer. Alongside convenience, women were believed to prefer absinthe for its influence over the emotions, because, according to a later writer, it "accentuated certain traits of the capricious temperament."

While the unisexual appeal of absinthe was an echo of the gin craze, the enthusiasm of the French public for the Charenton Omnibus was very different from the affection that British drinkers had bestowed on their Old Tom and Strip-Me-Naked. Absinthe was considered to provide an aesthetic, rather than brutish, kind of intoxication. This difference was made plain in the last part of the nineteenth century, when absinthe drinkers let go their inhibitions, with the aim of fusing their lives with their art. From the 1880s onward a fresh generation of absintheurs, including Alfred Jarry and Villiers de L'Isle-Adam in writing, and Henri Toulouse-Lautrec, Vincent van Gogh, and Paul Gauguin in painting, gave both creativity and absinthe drinking a bad name.

Alfred Jarry set the benchmark for both disciplines. He hated water, "that terrible poison, so solvent and corrosive that out of all substances it has been chosen for washings and scourings" and which, perhaps the worst of its many sins, when "added to a clear liquid like absinthe, makes it muddy," and did his best to live without it. His consumption of alcohol, in contrast, was prodigious. A contemporary recorded that on an average day he drank two liters of white wine first thing, followed by a swift three large absinthes. At lunch he took wine and absinthe with his food and rounded off the meal with a few café-Cognacs. Dinner was accompanied by "at least two bottles of any vintage, whether good or bad." Thus fortified, Jarry was ready for a proper night's drinking. The same writer also noted that she "never saw him really drunk, except on one occasion when I took aim at him with his own revolver, which sobered him up instantly."

It is interesting to imagine what an American temperance writer of the same period would have made of Jarry. Prima facie, he was a fine example of the dangers of alcohol—a talented young man who frightened others and destroyed himself before he had realized his potential. Unfortunately, his appearance (a dwarf, he usually exaggerated his diminished stature by dressing in a cape and a top hat), his obsession with bicycle racing and physical fitness, his deliberately robotic speech and penchant for firearms, all militated against a place for him in a temperance novel—he was far too exciting to be a credible fictional character.

Jarry's masterpiece, the play *Ubu Roi,* premiered in 1896 with a set decorated by Henri Toulouse-Lautrec, his closest equivalent among painters as an excessive absinthe drinker. Toulouse-Lautrec, also stunted, took Impressionism back indoors, to Parisian dance halls such as the Moulin Rouge. "Nature has betrayed me," he claimed, alluding to his deformity, and he ignored it in return. His work, which focuses on artificial paradises of the night filled with spectral hedonists, as they might appear to someone on the spot and equally drunk, has been described as having been "entirely painted in absinthe." When he felt the need for a glass of his muse, Toulouse-Lautrec would declare an urge to *"étouffer un perroquet"* (strangle a parakeet)—a slang term for the liquor then in use around Montmartre. Syphilis and parrot-wrestling soon ruined his health, and his behavior under their influences embarrassed his aristocratic family. His father, who was fond of dressing up in chain mail and carrying around a sword an ancestor had employed in the conquest of Jerusalem in the First Crusade of 1096, complained, "Why doesn't he go to England? They scarcely notice the drunks over there." An attempt was made to dry him out, which Toulouse-Lautrec frustrated with his absinthe cane, which had been hollowed out to conceal a flask containing nearly a pint of the fluid. He died in 1901, convinced he was being hunted by dogs and the elephant from the Moulin Rouge.

By the time that Toulouse-Lautrec and Jarry had been laid to rest, absinthe had acquired an evil reputation among the medical profession in France. Parisian physicians, alarmed that an Anglo-Saxon-style spirits craze was in progress, published warnings as to the damage that too much of the green stuff could cause. Their prophet was Dr. Auguste Motet, who contended that absinthe, more so than any other alcoholic drink, caused rage and decay in the drinker. His disciples followed up his work by killing animals with extract of absinthe. Its effect on guinea pigs in particular proved to be startling, and cautionary cartoons were drawn up for distribution to French soldiers, which showed the little creatures dancing with their paws held high, before keeling over dead after being injected with too stiff a measure. The change in perception toward absinthe in the closing decades of the nineteenth century was summed up by a Dr. Ledoux. Whereas "our fathers still knew the time when absinthe was an elegant drink—on the cafe terraces, old Algerian warriors and bourgeois idlers consumed that louche beverage with the aroma of mouthwash"—it had since become a favorite of degenerates and the proletariat, whom it hastened to their ruin.

Opposition to absinthe was not limited to the medical profession. As the casualty register of famous or notorious people who were reckoned to have succumbed to this most virulent of drinks lengthened, politicians and journalists also raised their voices against the sorceress. Their hysterical tone was caricatured by Gustave Flaubert in his *Dictionary of Received Ideas:* "ABSINTHE: Exceedingly violent poison. One glass and you're dead. Journalists drink it while writing their articles. Has killed more soldiers than the Bedouins. Will be the destruction of the French army."

Although absinthe was considered to be uniquely dangerous on account of the wormwood it contained, other kinds of alcoholic drink also started to receive a negative press in France. Intoxication was portrayed not merely as a state of aesthetic rapture, or a necessary preliminary to artistic composition, but also as a curse, albeit principally of the laboring class of citizen. The coal miners of Émile Zola's novel *Germinal,* for instance, drink themselves into beer-bloated stupors on their rare holidays: Like the slaves on an American plantation they gain a temporary illusion of freedom via intoxication. In Zola's other works, alcoholics destroy themselves, their families, and their descendants. Moreover, their drunkenness is of the degrading sort that characterized the villains of Anglo-Saxon temperance noire. Hitherto, the disgusting, obsessive alcoholic had been rare in French literature, just as the miser, a stock-in-trade character of French novels, was similarly rare in English books.

However, negative sentiments about alcohol in some quarters were outnumbered by positive and even rapturous feelings toward it in others. Absinthe continued to receive the homage of poets, and, a result of the phylloxera-induced shortage of wine, beer began to acquire a reputation as a civilized drink in France. Its progress is apparent in the paintings of the Impressionists. *The Luncheon of the Boating Party* (1881) by Auguste Renoir shows a group of young people drinking under the striped awning of a riverside inn on a sunny summer afternoon. The men are in singlets and straw boaters, the women wear elaborate dresses hemmed with frills and sport bouquets and ribbons in their hats. Their faces are flushed, their expressions convivial. A certain relaxation in their features confirms that they are tipsy—that happy state in between sobriety and intoxication—and at the focus of the work a pretty girl is draining a glass of beer.

Manet also celebrated beer in his canvases. His late masterpiece, *Bar at the Folies-Bergère* (1882), shows a tired and pensive young waitress with her hands on the marble bartop of the celebrated nightclub. Neatly arranged on its surface are bottles of champagne, rose wine, absinthe, and Bass IPA, brewed in Burton-on-Trent, with its venerable red triangle trademark. This detail is emblematic of the great changes that had occurred in French art and society, post-phylloxera and -absinthe. It is hard to imagine David, the champion of vast and epic canvases, depicting French heroes at crucial moments, including anything but French wine in his paintings, let alone a Swiss cordial or an English brand of beer.

The market for Bass IPA in Montmartre was not entirely French, for the district had become a tourist attraction in its own right. It was home to nightclubs, the cancan, absintheurs, poets, and impressionists galore. Visitors from Europe, Africa, and the Americas poured into Montmartre and Paris during the 1870s and came in torrents for the Centennial Exhibition of 1889, which celebrated the temporary end of the French monarchy a hundred years before. The exhibition was crowned with a newly built monument—the Eiffel Tower. This enchanting folly, a celebration of iron in the same material, evoked mixed reactions among Parisians. The Church and traditionalists hated it. According to the men of God it was "a hideous, horrible phallic skeleton," which left, in the opinion of establishment writers such as Alexandre Dumas and Guy de Maupassant, "a stain on the honor of Paris." The common people, in contrast, were delighted with the erection, and their hearts beat with pride when the French tricolor was hoisted at its pinnacle, and its engineer boasted to the world, "This is the only flag to fly on a staff three hundred meters long." The general enthusiasm for the Eiffel Tower was reflected in material culture: Its silhouette was adopted as a motif for absinthe spoons; indeed, it soon became a quintessential symbol of the city itself.

After the exposition of 1889, Paris waited until the next century to play host again to the exhibition-goers of the world. These returned in 1900 to find that its artistic center of gravity had shifted to Montparnasse; that Impressionism had drifted into Postimpressionism en route to somewhere entirely new; that modern had replaced decadent in poetry; but that absinthe was still drunk with the same abandon, indeed, if anything, had become more popular. This last perception was supported by statistics: In 1874, at about the time that Degas was painting his uncomfortable couple, France drank roughly seven hundred thousand liters of absinthe per annum; by the end of the first decade of the new century it was consuming nearly thirty-six million liters in every year.

The export market for absinthe, in contrast to its domestic counterpart, matured at a sickly pace. Overseas demand was greatest in French imperial possessions, including Vietnam and Tahiti, where the Postimpressionist painter Paul Gauguin kept his habit alive, and in expossessions, like New Orleans. However, it made slow progress outside of Francophone places. The British, as a rule, with the exception of a few poets and their single Impressionist of merit, Walter Sickert, did not take to it. Perhaps its reputation for filling the drinker with thrilling gothic visions was the problem. Why flirt with the occult when one already lived in Stygian gloom? Most British cities, including the capital, were choked with smog for weeks on end. The streetlamps in London were still on at noon, but even so, visibility was measured in yards, and after dark Jack the Ripper butchered women on the sidewalks. Conditions were too ugly to risk seeing on absinthe.

To each culture, a counterculture. The Aesthetic Movement, with figures such as Oscar Wilde and Aubrey Beardsley in its prows, sailed into the gloom of late Victorian London, bearing the important news of the discovery that the point of life was to admire, and to enjoy, everything beautiful in it. The concept of beautiful extended to stimulants such as cocaine, cigarettes, ether, and absinthe. Aesthetes were enchanted by the daring reputation the green-eyed temptress had acquired in France, and felt they should drink her in preference to the Highland whisky of neoromantics or the bottled ale of retrospective country squires. This sense of duty was articulated by Oscar Wilde: "I could never quite accustom myself to absinthe, but it suits my style very well." He slipped it neatly into his philosophy via an anecdote, which dressed absinthism in Aesthetic costume: "Three nights I sat up all night drinking absinthe, and thinking that I was singularly clearheaded and sane. The waiter came in and began watering the sawdust. The most wonderful flowers, tulips, lilies, and roses sprang up and made a garden of the café. 'Don't you see them?' I said to him. *'Mais non, monsieur, il n'y a rien.'*" ("No sir, there's nothing there.")

26 HATCHETATION

I can resist everything but temptation.
—Oscar Wilde

In 1882, Oscar Wilde took his message of flower power on a coast-to-coast tour of the United States. He found decadence alive and kicking at the sunset end of the Anglo-Saxon diaspora. The people of California and its neighboring states maintained a gold rush mentality toward drinking–more was their eternal ideal and more there was. Whiskey aplenty arrived by rail, and the West itself produced ever-increasing quantities of wine, brandy, and beer. Wilde got his first taste of western hospitality during a visit to the Matchless silver mine in Leadville, Colorado. "At the bottom of the mine," he recorded, "we sat down to a banquet, the first course being whiskey, the second whiskey, and the third whiskey."

Other British writers followed Wilde west, and all were equally enamored with the liquid hospitality they received in Pacific America. Rudyard Kipling, who found San Francisco a "mad city–inhabited for the most part by perfectly insane people whose women are of remarkable beauty," was much taken by the *Pisco punch,* a drink then in vogue, whose principal ingredient was a clear Peruvian brandy. Sweet to the taste, yet highly potent, this ambrosia inspired Kipling to speculate on its composition: "I have a theory it is compounded of cherubs' wings, the glory of a tropical dawn, the red clouds of sunset, and fragments of lost epics by dead masters."

The idyllic countryside outside San Francisco, and the wines produced there, also attracted the praise of visitors. In 1880, Robert Louis

Stevenson spent several months in the upper Napa Valley with his new American spouse. He dedicated part of *The Silverado Squatters,* his account of his stay, to the winemakers around him, whom he conceived of as prospectors searching the valley and its surrounding slopes for the ideal *terroir,* which might impart unique flavors to their vintages: "Bit by bit, they grope about for their Clos de Vougeot and Lafitte, those lodes and pockets of earth, more precious than the precious ores, that yield inimitable fragrance and soft fire; those virtuous Bonanzas, where the soil has sublimated under sun and stars to something finer, and the wine is bottled poetry." Stevenson was certain of their eventual success: "The smack of Californian earth shall linger on the palate of your grandson." This was a prayer as much as a prophecy. He hoped Napa wines might one day replace the great French clarets and burgundies whose vineyards were then being wiped out, forever as it seemed at the time, by phylloxera. The vineyards of California did not escape the dreaded pest, but it arrived in the state after the discovery that foreign vines grafted onto native American rootstock were immune, and the devastation France had suffered was avoided.

The science of winemaking in California had come a long way since the days of Agoston Haraszthy. A research facility dedicated to oenology had been established at the state university, whose studies made an immediate contribution to the fecundity of local vineyards and the quality of their wine. By 1887, California production was fifteen million gallons per annum, four years later it had risen to twenty million, and in 1897–a freak year–it touched thirty-four million gallons, which resulted in a price crash. Between 1858 and 1890, some of the state's most famous producers commenced operation, including Charles Krug, Karl Wente, and Jacob Beringer.

California brewing grew at similar pace to Californian winemaking. Its specialty was *steam beer,* so named because of its ultrahigh level of carbonation: When a barrel of the stuff was tapped there was an explosion of foam, like steam from a ruptured boiler. The carbonation was natural and resulted from the addition of a quantity of green wort to each barrel (a German technique, known as *krausening*), which caused a second bout of fermentation. Steam beer was a relic from the gold rush era. The first brewers in San Francisco, faced with a burgeoning thirst and a shortage of both raw materials and of ice for cooling, had been forced to adopt the practice of krausening, which enabled them to manufacture a lager style of beer at high speed, in hot conditions, that was ready for drinking within twelve days, i.e., less than half the time of traditional lagers. Its distinctive properties and low price won it a place in the hearts of Californians, so that by the time that ice was plentiful, and California was bulging with capital for new breweries, steam beer, an invention born of necessity, continued to be manufactured in preference to alternatives of better quality.

The new states to the east of California also experienced a brewing boom. The mining towns that sprang up around productive veins were invariably adorned with saloons and breweries. Perfect brewing conditions in and around Denver encouraged German immigrants to put aside their picks and washboards and turn their hands to making lager. One such, Adolph Coors, who set up in Golden, Colorado, in partnership with another German, turned out a brew of such exceptional quality that within a year, according to the *Colorado Transcript,* "Messrs. Schuler and Coors have leaped to the front rank of brewers ... and their beer is regularly sold in Denver and the mountain and valley towns." Arizona and Washington enjoyed similar surges in production. In Phoenix, the Arcade Brewery, once again run by Germans, was considered one of the wonders of the territory and a tribute to the thirst of its few citizens. So great was their love of beer that they paved the sidewalk of First Street with empty bottles, packed neck down into the dirt. According to eyewitness accounts, this produced a durable, if irregular, surface: "The walk was so uneven a person felt as if afflicted with the blind staggers when walking over it."

The output of local breweries in former wildernesses was supplemented by imports delivered by the spreading railroads. From the 1880s onward national brewers emerged in America, whose brands of beer were available from coast to coast. While there was a degree of consolidation within the industry, most brewers expanded their production and reach through organic growth. The nation seemed to be possessed with an insatiable thirst for beer. Between 1880 and 1910, U.S. official production increased at more than twice the rate of the country's population: from 13 million barrels per annum to 59.5 million. The numbers were enough to attract syndicates of investors from the London Stock Exchange, who among them spent a fortune in the early 1890s acquiring American brewers. The foreign interlopers did not, however, succeed in capturing any of the national champions, who responded to the new competition by streamlining their distribution and perfecting their brands. Pabst of Milwaukee, distinguished by the blue ribbon on its label, was the first brewer to manufacture a million barrels of beer in one year (1893), followed by Anheuser-Busch, with its signature "A and Eagle" and the trademark *Budweiser,* and by Schlitz, the beer with the globe on its bottles, emblematic of the confidence and ambitions of the American brewing industry.

While such confidence was scarcely misplaced in the West, whose population drank with a rare vigor, in the midwestern and eastern states opposition to King Alcohol was rising. The temperance movement had grown into a serious political force. It had focused its efforts on the so-called local option, i.e., the prohibition of the retail of alcohol at the state, city, and county level. Following up on their initial success in Maine, temperance organizations had succeeded in persuading voters and state assemblies in Kansas, Iowa, Maine, New Hampshire, and Massachusetts to incorporate prohibition within their constitutions. Although such bans were often no better than legal fictions—it was easy to find public drinking places open in territories that, officially, were alcohol free—they were important precedents: If Americans could vote to live in a nominally dry state, then they might, one day, vote to live in a dry country.

In addition to plugging away at the local option, the temperance movement stepped up its efforts in the field of indoctrination. The women of the WCTU had decided that education was the key to victory in the fight for an alcohol-free America. To this end, they established a *Department of Scientific Temperance Instruction in Schools and Colleges* within their organization, under the command of Mrs. Mary Hannah Hunt. Her mission was to instill a prejudice against alcohol into American children through compulsory propaganda. Mrs. Hunt envisaged a future when "from the schoolhouses all over the land will come trained haters of alcohol to pour a whole Niagara of ballots upon the saloon." She succeeded in embedding temperance in the school curriculum in every state except Arizona. It was taught to children disguised as personal hygiene or physiology. If they started drinking, they were told, they would grow up stunted, foul-breathed, and mad; they would beat their spouses, if they were lucky enough to marry; and would harm themselves and those around them until claimed prematurely by the grave. Such fictions were presented as scientific facts, which were proven with theatrical demonstrations of the deadly powers of alcohol. Many young Americans were treated to a show in which a slice of raw calf brain was immersed in a jar of spirits. It turned gray and blotchy at once, and the students were advised that the same would happen to their brains the instant they took a sip of liquor. Alcohol, they were taught, scorched the skin of the drinker's throat, hence the burning sensation. It also turned the blood into water, and the heart into fat: "Such a heart cannot be so strong as if it were all muscle. It is sometimes so soft that a finger could easily be pushed through its walls." Scientific temperance was augmented by mathematical temperance, of a similarly wretched standard of probity, as the following example, from the "Think a Minute" series for first-grade students, illustrates:

> Daddy was disgusted with neighbor Jones. "Swigs beer like a sponge! Drank ten glasses, one after another—made a fool of himself—and had to be carried home dead drunk!"
>
> Billy asked, "Daddy, how much did you drink?"
>
> "Only one glass," said Daddy virtuously.
>
> Billy has been studying fractions. "One glass is ten percent of ten glasses," he calculated. "Mr. Jones was a fool to drink ten glasses. Were you ten percent of a fool, Daddy?"

The good work of the Department of Scientific Temperance Instruction was supplemented by informal material, similar to that prepared for the British Bands of Hope. There were temperance nursery rhymes, temperance camp songs, temperance wall charts, temperance spelling books, and temperance medals. Newly born infants had the white ribbon of the WCTU tied to their swaddling clothes, a prayer read over them, and their name entered on the Cradle Roll. As soon as they could walk and sing they were deployed against drinkers, especially during elections. They were assembled around polling booths, dressed in their Sunday school best, issued with little American flags, and, when a known sot arrived to vote, would surround him and break into song. The effect could be sinister, as is apparent in Tobias Wolff's depiction of the junior wing of the WCTU at work: "Swirling round the marked man in a wild elves' dance, they sang with piping empty violence:

> We are some fond mother's treasure
> Men and Women of tomorrow,

> For a moment's empty pleasure
> Would you give us lifelong sorrow?
> Think of sisters, wives, and mothers,
> Of helpless babes in some low slum,
> Think not of yourself, but of others,
> Vote against the Demon Rum.

An entire generation of American children was conditioned to fear alcohol and to feel guilty when they drank it. Many, however, of the *Men and Women of Tomorrow* got over their indoctrination. According to federal statistics, per capita consumption of alcohol was creeping back up in the 1880s and '90s to pre–Civil War levels, notwithstanding the fact that several states were officially dry. This worrying trend was blamed by temperance advocates on the pernicious influence of saloons and their illegal counterparts in those places where they were banned. The saloon became, to the abstinent-minded, a symbol for all that was evil about booze.

The case against these establishments was not without foundation. The American saloon of the 1890s was an equivocal place. While some served similar community roles to colonial-era taverns, functioning as social centers, labor exchanges, and offering a space where people could gather to celebrate christenings and weddings, they were outnumbered by squalid corner bars that dealt plainly and simply in intoxication. Although the principal clientele of this latter category was male, they also sold beer to local women and children, who bought it by the bucketful out the back door. *Rushing the growler,* as the practice was known, was particularly common in New York. While their counterparts in Ohio were wearing white ribbons and watching their teachers pickle calves' brains in grain spirit, children in the tenements of the Bronx were drinking deep. Even the poorest families could afford a daily binge: A saloon keeper of the time observed that rushing the growler was "an inexpensive mode of becoming intoxicated. On thirty cents a whole family of topers can become drunk."

Many of the less-salubrious kind of saloon harbored brothels and, if they could not accommodate prostitutes in-house, operated sister businesses where they might send their drunks. They also served as recruiting grounds on polling days, for the practice of buying votes with drinks was still common in urban America. Finally, they were often stinking eyesores surrounded by crawling drunks. A really nasty saloon was a tableau vivant of temperance noir. Their existence anywhere in America, and persistence in states where they had been outlawed, pricked the consciences of many drys, especially those of a religious bent, who perceived them to be the terrestrial colonies of hell. From the insulted ranks of temperate Americans, a heroine emerged to take the fight to the saloons, who gave their movement the excitement that hitherto it had lacked.

Sensation, in the imposing shape of Mrs. Carry A. Nation, helped drinking to become the first American political issue of the twentieth century. Born Carrie Amelia Moore to a Kentucky slave owner, this future scourge of saloons had good reason to hate alcohol. After a peripatetic childhood, during which she suffered from a mysterious and debilitating bowel ailment, and an unhappy adolescence, which she spent caring for her insane mother who suffered from the delusion that she was Queen Victoria of England, Carry made an unhappy marriage to an alcoholic doctor, who died of the delirium tremens shortly after the birth of their first and only child. The child, a daughter, suffered from a disfiguring abscess, which caused her right cheek to fall off, and which prevented her from opening her jaws for eight years. Carry attributed the affliction to the drunkenness of her husband: "The curse of heredity is one of the most heartbreaking results of the saloon. Poor little children are brought into the world with the curse of drink and disease entailed upon them."

Carry remarried to a preacher and attorney named David Nation and moved to Kansas, where she absorbed the propaganda of the WCTU. This she combined with her individual version of radical Christianity to create a personal doctrine of direct action against alcohol. She was physically well-equipped to put it into effect—six feet tall, approximately 180 pounds, strong of arm, with a piercing voice, false teeth, and a face whose jowls resembled those of a bulldog. Moreover, Medicine Lodge, the nominally dry town where she lived, was full of provocation—its prison, which she visited in an evangelical role, was packed with drunkards; and its flamboyant, if illegal, saloons did a roaring trade, even on the Sabbath day.

Carry flowered into violence in late 1899, when she attacked Mart Strong's saloon in her hometown one Sunday afternoon. Accompanied by fellow female advocates of temperance, who supplied background music on a melodeon, and singing what was to become her

battle song,[59] she advanced into the bar and chased out all its customers. Encouraged by her success, she marched on all the remaining
saloons in Medicine Lodge in subsequent weeks, and on the local
drugstore, where she smashed a keg of medicinal whiskey with a
sledgehammer and set its contents on fire. Once she had cleared
Medicine Lodge of alcohol, Carry meditated on action against other
hotbeds of sin nearby.

The next place to feel the strength of her arm was Kiowa, a neighboring hamlet in Barber County. She set off in a buggy loaded with
stones and other missiles and, in the course of a single morning,
smashed up the fixtures, fittings, and windows of no fewer than three
saloons. After Kiowa, she moved on Wichita, the state capital, whose
illegal drinking joints operated within walking distance of the legislature that had outlawed them, and which were renowned for their ostentatious architecture and interiors. First stop was the Carey Hotel,
which featured a magnificent oil painting by John Noble, entitled
Cleopatra at the Bath or *The Temptress of the Nile,* behind its bar. Such
prurient canvases were common in the saloons of the period and drew
Mrs. Nation's particular ire. "It is very significant," she wrote, "that
pictures of naked women are in saloons.... The motive for doing this
is to suggest vice, animating the animal in man and degrading the respect he should have for the sex to which he owes his being; yes, his
Savior also!" She treated Cleopatra to a volley of stones, then raged
through the saloon with an iron bar, shattering bottles, decanters, and
tumblers, while shrieking, "Glory to God! Peace on earth, goodwill to
all men!" at the top of her voice. She was arrested while in the process
of battering the cherrywood bar counter with a brass spittoon.

Once they had her in custody, Wichita officials were confronted
by a legal conundrum: Strictly speaking, joints were banned in Kansas, and to prosecute someone for damaging one would be to admit to
their not-so-clandestine existence. The police chief offered to pay her
fare home, but she refused to go, and so she was sent to Sedgwick
County Jail while they worked out what to do with her. She caused
similar headaches among policemen, sheriffs, and county attorneys
throughout and beyond the state after she was bailed, not least of all
because the press detected greatness in Carry Nation and encouraged

---

[59] Who hath sorrow? Who hath woe?/ They who dare not answer no;/ They
whose feet to sin incline,/ While they tarry at the wine.

her into newsworthy behavior. The exciting reports they published of her exploits caused mobs to form wherever she appeared. She adopted the hatchet as her signature weapon and sold little replicas made of pewter to help finance the battle against jointists and "hellions." Moreover, she was fearless: In the course of her crusade she was arrested twenty-five times, had her nose broken by the wife of a saloon keeper, her head cracked open by the wife of a cigar-store owner,[60] her wrist shattered by a bartender in Ohio, had been horsewhipped in Kansas, pistol-whipped in Texas, had a chair broken over her head in Kentucky and her false teeth knocked down her throat in Trinidad, Colorado.

Had she been a man, it is probable that Mrs. Nation's career would have been ended with a bullet or two in the first saloon that she attacked. However, protected by her sex, she spent several years assaulting bars, drinkers, smokers, and tobacconists in the United States and abroad, during which time she became an international celebrity, albeit a figure of ridicule as much as praise. The WCTU and other temperance organizations, while acknowledging the publicity she generated for their cause, distanced themselves from its source: Carry Nation did not personify the dry ideal.

Indeed, the liquor barons were more effusive in their praise of the woman who described herself as "a bulldog running along at the feet of Jesus, barking at what He doesn't like." She was offered considerable sums to represent various brands of beer, and several whiskey manufacturers sent her kegs of their product in the hope that she would destroy them in front of the drinking public. Whenever she smashed a bar the debris was collected and sold as relics; many saloons were named after her, and the Big 803 in Topeka, Kansas, displayed a hatchet, captured from her in 1901, in pride of place behind its counter.

Despite the indifference of the WCTU, and the unwanted admiration of the liquor interests, Carry had a real impact on the illegal saloon trade, in particular during the first year of her crusade, when she and imitators wrecked nearly fifty bars, causing hundreds of thousands of dollars in damage, and cleared over thirty counties of drinking places. She was a champion to many dry eyes, and her admirers

---

[60] She also crusaded against smoking.

broadcast her virtues in print. The *Topeka State Journal,* for example, lavished hyperbole on her efforts:

> Carry A. Nation, prophetess of God and prohibition, came suddenly like the furious driving Jehu. Her cyclonic joint smashing shook the rum power of the United States from apex to foundation stone. The great American god Bacchus turned pale on his throne. Gambrinus and his thirty thousand white-aproned priests of debauchery and licentiousness trembled in every saloon and bagnio throughout the Union.

However, in states where saloons were legal, Carry was treated as a figure of fun. When she found her preferred style of direct action barred, she took to the stage and became a popular vaudeville attraction. She justified her cooperation with the forces of darkness on the grounds that that the American theater-going public constituted "the largest missionary field in the world. No one ever got a call or was allowed to go there with a Bible but Carry Nation. The door was never opened to anyone but me. The hatchet opened it." Her most popular role was as Mrs. Hammond in the stage version of *Ten Nights in a Bar-Room,* whose plot had been altered to include a saloon-smashing scene, which Carry performed with practiced grace. Offstage, she continued to preach wherever anyone would listen. She was the victim of numerous hoaxes, in particular at the hands of students. She was invited to Yale, for instance, by a letter that complained that the students were being forced to consume alcohol in their food. Menus featuring dishes such as roast ham with champagne sauce were included in the letter. She duly traveled to New Haven and was chaperoned around campus by the members of the Jolly Eight drinking club. When she tried to give a speech she was drowned out by drinking songs. She posed for a formal photograph, and just before the shutter clicked, the students assembled behind her pulled out concealed mugs and bottles. She left convinced that Yale was "a school of vice to a great extent."

Carry even took her message to Great Britain in 1908. She set out full of hope and got off to a good start by smashing the bar mirror in the steamship *Columbia,* which carried her over the Atlantic. She was arrested several times during the course of her visit, and while she received a positive welcome from British temperance organizations, she was treated to a barrage of eggs and vegetables by London theater-goers when she appeared onstage at various music halls. When asked her opinion of the British upon her return to the United States, she characterized them as tea fiends and claimed that their addiction made them nervous and affected.

Carry died the following year of a stroke, possibly complicated by congenital syphilis. Her final written assessment of the temperance issue was prophetic: "I now feel that this great wave of prohibition which is sweeping over the whole land, propelled by a mighty power of public sentiment, will go on and on until national prohibition will be the ultimate outcome."

❖   ❖   ❖

Although the art of hatchetation perished with its founder, the temperance movement kept her spirit alive by concentrating its forces on saloons. These open sores on America's fair face were visible proof of the damage wreaked by alcohol. The Anti-Saloon League (ASL), a relatively young association of drys, was in the van of the attack. The ASL had been founded in Oberlin, Ohio, a hotbed of sobriety, in 1893. It was conceived of as a political weapon, forged for a single purpose— to end drinking in the United States. It perceived, correctly, that temperance had become a pivotal issue in federal politics. The short-lived National Prohibition Party, while it had attracted few votes, was believed to have influenced the outcome of the presidential elections of 1884 and 1888, in the first case giving a narrow victory to the Democrat Grover Cleveland, and, in the second, to the Republican Benjamin Harrison. The Prohibition Party itself was supplanted as a third force in American politics by the rise of the Progressives, but both Democrats and Republicans had learned to pay at least lip service to Prohibition.

The ASL set out to exploit each party's anxieties over the temperance vote, and by the end of the nineteenth century it had become a power broker at both state and federal levels. It owed its eminence to two men: Wayne Wheeler and Richmond Pearson Hobson. Wheeler could make or break candidates for office, Hobson could swing thousands of voters with a single speech. Wheeler had achieved his leverage by creating a network of ASL supporters among Protestant churches in rural areas, whose collective congregations were sufficiently numerous to influence both local and national elections. The same churches provided meeting places where the ASL might tell its followers how to vote and were also a source of the donations with which the ASL underwrote its activities. By 1912 the ASL was supported by nearly sixty thousand congregations, who among them gave two million dollars per annum to its coffers and as many votes when it came to polling time.

This was power that the liquor lobby might only dream of, and it was exploited with Machiavellian skill by Wayne Wheeler. According to his biographer, over a twenty-year career spent in the persecution of alcohol he "controlled six Congresses, dictated to two Presidents of the United States, directed legislation for the most important elective state and federal offices, held the balance of power in both Republican and Democratic parties, distributed more patronage than any other dozen men, supervised a federal bureau from the outside without official authority, and was recognized by friend and foe alike as the most masterful and powerful single individual in the United States."

Not only was the ASL powerful, it was also wealthy by the standards of a political organization of the age. The donations it gathered from its supporters were spent on propaganda, and its publishing arm spewed out over 250 million pages of temperance writing each month. This blizzard of print was directed at white Protestant men and women in the old western and northeastern states. These people were believed to resent the changes that were occurring in America and to be ready to accept that drunkenness might be behind such phenomena as industrialization, the rise of megacities, and their population with hordes of Roman Catholic immigrants. In consequence, ASL periodicals, pamphlets, and its touring speakers made eugenics a central theme in their case against drink. The speakers peppered their discourses with racism and images of the decline of the breed. According, for example, to Richmond Pearson Hobson, the ASL's star orator, "In America we are making the last stand of the great white race, and substantially of the human race. If [alcohol] cannot be conquered in Young America, it cannot in any of the old and more degenerate nations. If America fails, the world will be undone and the human race will be doomed to go down from degeneracy to degeneracy till the Almighty in wrath wipes the accursed thing out."

In addition to providing an apocalyptic vision of the threat posed by alcohol to future generations, Hobson stimulated his audiences by linking drinking with the great taboo topic of the age—venereal disease. Both syphilis and gonorrhea were rampant in the United States, with infection rates ten times those of the present day, and both, then, were almost incurable. According to Hobson, "Probably, certainly, more than fifty percent of adult males are tainted with some form of terrible vice disease, the whelp of liquor." The baneful influence of alcohol over sexual behavior was likewise highlighted in ASL publicity. Posters were distributed warning that it could override the will, with potentially dreadful consequences:

> I   ALCOHOL INFLAMES THE PASSIONS, thus making the temptation to sex-sin unusually strong.
> II   ALCOHOL DECREASES THE POWER OF CONTROL, thus making the resisting of temptation especially difficult....
> AVOID ALL ALCOHOLIC DRINK ABSOLUTELY.
> The control of sex impulses will then be easy and disease, dishonor, disgrace, and degradation will be avoided.

By 1913, the ASL felt the time was ripe to disclose its true objective. At its twentieth annual conference in Columbus, Ohio, delegates made the unanimous resolution to seek the prohibition of the sale of alcohol throughout the United States by constitutional amendment. An appropriate amendment was drafted and delivered to the steps of the Capitol in December of the same year, accompanied by a troop of schoolgirls dressed in white and a regiment each of ASL and WCTU supporters. It was received by Senator Morris Sheppard, of Texas, and Richmond Pearson Hobson, in his capacity as congressman for Alabama.

Once the draft was in safe hands, the ASL mobilized its supporters, who were instructed to bombard the government with letters, telegrams, and petitions in its favor. In the words of Wayne Wheeler, "From that December day in 1913, when we wired back to our people in every State in the Union, 'Open fire on the enemy'... the country kept up a drumfire upon Washington." This furious assault caught the liquor lobby off guard. They were so confident of the significance of the contribution made by taxes on beer and spirits to the federal budget, which, between 1870 and 1915 provided more than half of the internal revenue of the United States, that they dismissed the proposed amendment as a publicity stunt. They politely drew the attention of legislators to their contributions and launched a counterattack against the ASL. Instead, however, of copying the modern campaigning methods of their opponents, they resorted to the old-fashioned techniques of bribing journalists and poll rigging, which backfired.

There was a growing desire for probity in American politics at the time, and the ASL took pleasure in disclosing the clumsy attempts of brewers and distillers to influence editors and buy voters with money and free booze. Whether they drank or not, Americans were tired of corruption and suspicious of big business. In various industries ranging from oil to tobacco, monopolies, in the form of trusts, had been established that set prices, forced down wages, and created a dependent underclass of worker/consumers who were slaves in all but name. Moreover, there was a certain fin de siècle weariness in America after all the excitement of the nineteenth century. The western quest had ended, the Indians had been confined to reservations, and the continent been tamed. Drunkenness seemed to belong to the pioneers and frontiersmen of the past, not to the present ordered nation with its network of great cities and small towns.

The mood of the age is apparent in *John Barleycorn, or Alcoholic Memoirs* (1913), by Jack London, the best-selling literary author of the day. The book reviews all the contemporary arguments against alcohol and illustrates them with anecdotes from the author's life, beginning with the first time that he got drunk, at the age of five. Although, by his own confession, London did not start drinking heavily until he was fifteen, he quickly made up for lost time. Thereafter he enjoyed a love/hate relationship with alcohol, alternating between long wet and dry stretches. He felt his drinking habits were typical of his age and that they were the result of the ubiquity of booze, and the central role of saloons in male society. He had little time for the predestination theories of the temperance movement, which considered everyone to be a drunk in waiting: In London's view "comparatively few alcoholics are born in a generation. And by alcoholic I mean a man whose chemistry craves alcohol and drives him recklessly to it. The great majority of habitual drinkers are born not only without desire for alcohol but with actual repugnance toward it." This innate repugnance was overcome by repeated exposure to drink and to drinkers, commencing in childhood. London's father used to take him into saloons, and he found them magical places—beacons of hospitality, quite unlike other public institutions such as shops or libraries, which never "let me warm by their fires or permitted me to eat the food of the gods from narrow shelves against the wall." The special status of saloons was reinforced as London progressed into his teens, when he perceived them as symbolic of the adult world to which he wanted to belong. He yearned to be among the men he saw in bars who "talked with great voices, laughed great laughs." Indeed, even "the sots, stupefied, sprawling across the tables or in the sawdust, were objects of mystery and wonder."

The fascination that saloons held for young men, and their ubiquity, were, in London's opinion, the prime cause of the sort of destructive drunkenness that he hoped to see eradicated in America. Moreover, he believed that only Prohibition would achieve this aim: "All the no-saying and no-preaching in the world will fail to keep men, and youths growing into manhood, away from John Barleycorn when John Barleycorn is everywhere accessible, and where John Barleycorn is everywhere the connotation of manliness, and daring, and great spiritedness."

When he wrote *John Barleycorn,* Jack London had less than four years to live. He managed to fit in a stint as a war correspondent in Mexico, to write six further books, to sail around Cape Horn, and to spend a year cruising the Pacific in his own yacht, before his kidneys packed up–possibly from too much alcohol,[61] possibly from one or a combination of the tropical diseases he'd caught when traveling, and the arsenic- and mercury-based medicines he had taken to cure them. *John Barleycorn* was intended not for his generation but for people of the future, for whom it had a plain message: "The only rational thing for the twentieth century folk to do is to cover up the well; to make the twentieth century in truth the twentieth century, and to relegate to the nineteenth century and all the preceding centuries the things of those centuries, the witch-burnings, the intolerances, the fetiches, and, not least among such barbarisms, John Barleycorn."

---

[61] When he was in drinking mode, London expected his liquor to kick. By his own high standards, absinthe was for lightweights: "The trouble I had with the stuff was that I had to take such inordinate quantities in order to feel the slightest effect."

27   IN THE CHALK TRENCHES OF CHAMPAGNE

The twentieth century was quick to differentiate itself from those that had preceded it, albeit not in the manner in which Jack London had hoped. The year after *John Barleycorn* was published, he was approached by *Collier's* magazine to act as their war correspondent in Europe, where a conflict of unprecedented magnitude had erupted. His ill health prevented his acceptance and spared him the horror of bearing witness to slaughter on an industrial scale. The First World War claimed thirteen million victims in the four years between 1914 and 1918, a quarter of them in a small patch of France and Belgium, where the British and French and their German opponents settled into a static war of attrition.

In order to maintain this standoff, and to supply their millions of troops with weapons, sustenance, and replacements, the resources of the combatant nations were organized for battle. Among the consequences of putting entire economies on a war footing were restrictions on the use of alcohol for recreational purposes. The production of food was accorded a greater priority than brewing, and distilled alcohol was diverted to be used for making fuel and explosives. The little left for drinking was rationed, and directed toward where it was needed most. Interestingly, there was a near unanimity among the parties to the conflict that the best place for whatever alcohol could be spared for booze was the front line. At the point of impact between armies, where soldiers died in their hundreds of thousands–gassed, bombed, bayoneted, machine-gunned–and where many millions more were mutilated, blinded, or condemned to spend the remainder of their lives in wheelchairs, drink was distributed alongside such other necessaries as food and ammunition.

In Britain, the Royal Navy continued its centuries-old tradition of a daily rum ration. The nation's soldiers also received a regular supply of rum. The army quota consisted of one gallon per day for each company of sixty-four men—the equivalent of two ounces per head. It was delivered in stoneware jugs marked with the initials S.R.D., which stood for Services Rum (Diluted), or, according to the soldiers for whom it was intended, Seldom Reaches Destination. The rum was West Indian, although whisky and cognac were sometimes provided as substitutes. Teetotalers were under no obligation to drink their daily allowances—according to an official memorandum, "the individual man is in all cases free to refuse the issue of rum if he so desires"—but most of them gave in: "This option is only exercised in a few instances."

Extra shots of spirits were issued prior to and directly after combat. Liquor was considered to be good for modern soldiers: "The comfort, efficiency, and fighting value of the troops are greatly increased by the issue of fortified alcohol." The troops themselves seconded the opinion of their officers. Even those who had been temperate drinkers before the war, whatever their rank, confessed to the worth of the water of life in the front line. The British poet Siegfried Sassoon, for example, writing of one of his first combat experiences—a night raid on the German trenches—reflected on the respect he had developed since for spirits: "It surprises me when I remember that I set off without having had a drink, but . . . in those days the helpfulness of alcohol in human affairs was a fact which had not yet been brought home to me. The raiders had been given only a small quantity, but it was enough to hearten them as they sploshed up the communication trench." The value of strong drink to the men in the trenches was reiterated in numerous testimonials. According, for example, to a Canadian fighting at Passchendaele: "Under the spell of this all-powerful stuff . . . one almost felt that he could eat a German, dead or alive, steel helmet and all."

Spirits, in addition to serving as stimulants, were also used to bring comfort to the wounded and the dying and to proof the senses of the burying details who covered over the mutilated and rotting remains of their comrades. Even after they had become hardened to the task, these working parties were given rum afterward, in order, as one of them expressed it, "to take the taste of dead men out of my mouth." Rum was also issued as an emetic to some of the victims of gas attacks. While chemical weapons killed relatively few combatants, they maimed in the most horrible and painful manner and created terror in the ranks whenever they were deployed. The following account, by the victim of a gas attack, highlights the use of rum as a remedy: "The gas was phosgene, and we were all sick, choking, when the QM arrived with rum. We swallowed some and the fumes of the rum and gas made us horribly sick and we vomited most of the gas out. After a couple of hours we only had a bad headache and didn't go out of action."

On the rare occasions that alcohol was forbidden to fighting troops, they resented its absence. Sassoon, returning to action after being wounded, and forced to serve in a different battalion, noted that its commander "had made himself obnoxiously conspicuous by forbidding the Rum Ration" and that "the 'No Rum Division' failed to appreciate their uniqueness in the expeditionary force."[62] Official rations were supplemented with private stocks: Cherry brandy in silver hip flasks, a bottle of whisky hidden under a trench coat, a tin cup of bartered wine. Moreover, a market economy of sorts was in action behind the lines, and resting troops might spend their wages as they pleased. Most of those stationed in France gravitated toward the *estaminets*– cafés set up by enterprising civilians in the villages and towns close to the fighting that sold simple foods such as eggs and fries, and beer and wine. The latter was usually sweetened with sugar, as the British Tommies found the thin *vin du pays* too sour for their taste. Unable to pronounce *vin blanc,* they called it *plonk,* a name still in service for cheap wine of indifferent quality.

Plonk, and whatever else was available, was consumed principally for its intoxicating effects. However, British soldiers did not drink to forget, or for temporary oblivion. They drank to bond–to confirm the friendships they had formed in the trenches. Their accounts praise and elevate this camaraderie as the only redeeming feature of the conflict. Their attitude was shared by their French allies. The *poilus,* or French common soldiers, also received an alcohol ration, consisting of a quarter liter of *pinard* wine per man per day. They were further

---

[62] Sassoon records that the same commander tried to ban smoking among his men and prevent the issue of steel helmets lest these would "make them soft."

entitled to brandy, though this was issued irregularly–witness the complaint of a poilu in Henri Barbusse's *Under Fire*, the first novel to be written during the war to picture the savagery of the western front: "We have the right to get [Cognac] in the trenches–seeing how it was voted somewhere, I don't know when or where, but I know it was–and in the three days we've been here they've been dishing out our brandy ration on the end of a fork." Like their British counterparts, the French soldiers supplemented their alcohol rations with purchases whenever they had the opportunity to buy. Since they were fighting on native soil they acquired their wine from householders as well as cafés, estaminets, and itinerant vendors. Wine held a special value to the French soldiers–as part of their heritage, it was one of the things they were fighting for. This sentimental aspect is apparent in *Under Fire*, in which the poilus reminisce about the local wine of their various parts of France–its relative strength, and flavors, and the memories associated with it: "To drink some wine from the South–and even from his own special South–and drink a lot of it . . . How great it would be to see life in the best of colors again, if only for a day! Ah, yes! He needs wine! He dreams of getting drunk!–when the war is over. . . ."

On the other side of no-man's-land, German front-line troops were also issued alcohol. In the first year of fighting, according to one combatant, "there were liberal helpings of a pale red brandy, which had a strong taste of methylated spirits, but wasn't to be sneezed at in the cold wet weather. We drank it out of our mess-tin lids." While the regularity of supply suffered as the war wore on, the Germans did their best to ensure that hard liquor reached the trenches, in the belief that it was of benefit to the morale of the fighting soldier. However, as such issues became rare, the troops took the appearance of spirits as a signal that they were soon to be sent over the top, and considered them to be a benediction for the damned.

The Germans also provided alcoholic drinks to soldiers resting behind the lines. Indeed, the ancient association of drinking and fighting in German warrior culture seems to have been encouraged. According to the writer Ernst Jünger, when he was sent to an officer training school after distinguishing himself in action: "By day, the young people were honed into soldiers by all the rules of the art, while in the evenings, they and their teachers assembled around vast barrels brought over from the stores . . . to display much the same degree of discipline and commitment—to drinking." Jünger also noted that some units possessed their own Beer King, who was responsible for punishing breaches of drinking etiquette among his subjects. The Beer Kings were modeled on their counterparts at German universities, and the respective monarchs of different units would challenge one another to duels, which were settled with snowballs or similarly inoffensive weapons. The persistence of such peacetime traditions in a war zone had no parallel among the officers of French or British troops, who practiced less formal styles of collective intoxication. The habit, however, of meeting to drink to their fallen acquaintances was common to all, and Jünger speaks for both sides when he declares that "such libations after a successfully endured engagement are among the fondest memories an old warrior may have. Even if ten out of twelve men had fallen, the two survivors would surely meet over a glass on their first evening off and drink a silent toast to their comrades."

The situation on the home fronts of the combatant nations was very different. In many of them World War I represented a turning point in governmental attitudes toward drinking. "Whole industrial societies were engaged against one another, their lives organized for war virtually from top to bottom," and in order to control these machines, state intervention escalated. Limitations were imposed on freedom of movement, of association, and of expression; rationing and other austerity measures were introduced. In some countries public drunkenness was made a criminal offense for the first time, and everywhere resources were diverted from the manufacture of alcoholic beverages to the production of explosives, food, and fuel.

In Great Britain, taxes on beer were raised, drinking hours were curtailed, and output was restricted. Curbs on civilian drinking commenced in 1914 with the Defense of the Realm Act, which in combination with the Intoxicating Liquor (Temporary Restrictions) Act of the same year, cut the opening hours of British pubs from seventeen and a half hours per day to five and a half hours on weekdays and five hours on Sundays. Even tighter restrictions were imposed around munitions factories, whose workers were rumored to prefer the charms of Bacchus to those of Mars and to be turning out dud shells after their liquid lunches. In some areas where munitions were produced, such as Gretna Green in Scotland, the government nationalized the pubs and breweries so as to ensure it had direct control over local drinking habits. The British temperance movement enjoyed a brief wartime revival. Enthused by the comments of David Lloyd George, the munitions minister, who declared that "we are fighting Germans, Austrians, and Drink; and, so far as I can see, the greatest of these three deadly foes is Drink," two million people signed a petition calling for total Prohibition, which was delivered to Parliament in 1916.

Although the temperance petition was ignored, steps were taken to reduce the volume of brewing. By 1917, brewers were allowed to produce only one-third of the quantity of "standard" beer, which was deemed to have an OG of 1055, that had been brewed prewar. Since the restriction was based on strength, the brewers tried to keep volume up by making weaker beer, which used less grain. Production nonetheless fell from thirty million barrels in 1914 to nineteen million in 1917, and the resulting "Government ale," or "Lloyd George's beer," which was only three-quarters of the strength of prewar brews, was mocked in the press and the music halls. Despite its feeble kick, demand outstripped supply, and the Ministry of Food was reduced to issuing notices to hoteliers requesting them to ask their presumably middle-class guests to "refrain from drinking beer, in order that there may be more beer for the working classes." To add insult to injury, the duty on beer was increased from seven shillings nine pence per barrel in 1914 to two pounds ten shillings in 1918, which more than doubled the price of a pint. Many of the wartime austerity measures survived the conflict—duty was ramped up again in 1919 and again the following year, the "Temporary Restrictions" on pub opening times remained in place until 2005, and Britons were condemned to drinking weak, expensive beer for generations to come.

The production and sale of beverage alcohol was also curbed in Commonwealth countries, notably in Canada. Distilled alcohol was an important raw material, after conversion to acetone, in the manufacture of the smokeless explosive cordite. Competition between drinkers and munitions for the same fluid was resolved in favor of the war effort and Alberta and Ontario introduced Prohibition in 1916, followed by Quebec in 1918. Canada had flirted with Prohibition before the war—a referendum had been held on the matter in 1898 that had revealed a majority in favor of a ban in all provinces bar Quebec, but no action had been taken at the federal level, and only Prince Edward Island had proscribed drinking. Prohibition was repealed postwar in all provinces, although it was retained in Prince Edward Island until 1948.

The advent of mechanized warfare likewise led to limitations on recreational drinking in France. Absinthe was banned in 1915: The nation could not afford to lose potential soldiers to the debilitating influence of la Fée Verte. The licensing system of cafés was revised in the same year, with the aim of reducing their numbers, and public intoxication was deemed a crime for the first time. Moreover, prostitutes were banned from cafés, as well as barmaids under eighteen years of age, unless they belonged to the family of the owner. While such legislative measures were debated with a great deal of passion and enacted with some fanfare, they had less effect on the number of drinking places than the conflict itself. Entire villages and towns were obliterated in the Somme and the Marne regions of France, and the country lost perhaps an eighth of its watering holes to enemy action. Its vineyards also suffered: Those in the Champagne district, in particular, were the scenes of intense combat. In September 1914, the Germans occupied Reims, the principal city of the region. When they were forced back out by a counterattack, many were found to be so drunk on looted champagne that they could not use their weapons and, according to a French officer, were "harvested like grapes." Fighting raged around the town for a further three and a half years, during which 40 percent of the surrounding vineyards were destroyed and the city itself flattened by artillery bombardments. The extensive network of chalk cellars under Reims was converted into a subterranean fortress, with field hospitals and barracks situated among the champagne bins. The winegrowers, however, still tended their surviving vines, and the vintages of 1914, 1915, and 1917 turned out to be some of the best of the twentieth century.

Vineyards in other parts of France suffered from a shortage of labor, and the war years saw an overall decline in wine production. Consumption, however, remained fairly constant, thanks to the estaminets, the pinard ration of the poilus, and government support: In 1917 the French National Assembly voted to give a bottle of champagne to every one of its seven million servicemen. French consumption of alcoholic beverages other than wine, in contrast, fell precipitously—the quantity of beer drunk dropped by a third and that of spirits by nearly two-thirds.

In Germany, the civilian supply of alcoholic drinks collapsed during

World War I. By 1918 beer production was only 25 percent of prewar levels, and the output of wine was substantially reduced when Germany was forced to cede Alsace and Lorraine back to France at the end of the conflict. The deprivation suffered by German drinkers was, however, light in comparison to that of their Russian counterparts. Following the Bolshevik Revolution of 1917, "the first workers' and peasant's government" outlawed vodka and other forms of alcoholic drinks, and the ban remained in place until 1924. Draconian as such measures seemed, they, too, paled in comparison to the restrictions suffered by both the soldiers and civilians of the last Allied power to join the fighting.

In April 1917, following German submarine attacks on American shipping, the United States entered World War I against the aggressor and prepared to send an American expeditionary force to fight in France. It was an immense challenge: The American prewar army had a total strength, including national guardsmen, of just over two hundred thousand—a tiny force in comparison to the millions of men fielded by the European powers. Moreover, its weapons and tactics had become superseded by new developments since 1914. The American army had no tanks, only a handful of machine guns, ancient artillery, and was organized according to drills perfected in the Civil War. Despite the logistical difficulties of recruiting, training, equipping, and transporting a viable fighting force to Europe, five regiments under General Pershing were shipped to France in June 1917, and by October the first units of the AEF were in action on the western front.

Unlike their British and French allies, the *doughboys,* as American soldiers were known, were expected to serve dry. They did not receive alcohol as part of their rations, nor could they obtain it in camp. This deprivation resulted from the Canteen Act of 1901, a piece of ASL-inspired legislation, which prohibited "the sale of, or dealing in, beer, wine, or any intoxicating liquors by any person in any post exchange or canteen or army transport or upon any premises used for military purposes by the United States." The Canteen Act was strengthened in 1917 on the eve of battle by Section 12 of the Selective Service Act, which established a total prohibition zone within a five-mile radius of American camps. The same law also made it illegal for anyone anywhere to sell intoxicating beverages to a member of the armed forces in uniform. The aim was to give America "the soberest, cleanest, and healthiest fighting men the world has ever known."

Not only was Prohibition decreed by law, but the benefits of total abstinence were also lauded in army manuals. Chapter II–"Personal Hygiene"–of the *U.S. Army Manual of Military Training* gave the following directions regarding booze to its readers: "Do not drink whiskey or beer, especially in the field. It will weaken you and favor heat exhaustion, sunstroke, frostbite, and other serious troubles. Alcohol muddles the mind and clouds thoughts, and so causes a feeling of carelessness and silliness that may ruin some military plan, or give the whole thing away to the enemy and with it the lives of yourself and your comrades. The soldier who drinks alcohol will be among the first to fall out exhausted."

Notwithstanding official sanctions, the doughboys, as their journals and letters reveal, did have access to alcohol in France. Bottles of wine were pressed on them by grateful French civilians, they were toasted by their allies, and they came across caches of temptation in the ruins of villages and farms. The Ninth Infantry, for example, en route to the front line, paused in the abandoned town of Montreuil, where they discovered substantial stocks of wine, cider, and brandy. When they resumed their march, "inebriated comics in some squads [were] now caparisoned in corsets, lace-trimmed drawers, and large organdy hats."

In recognition of the ubiquity of alcohol on the western front, and of the near impossibility of keeping his men abstinent, General Pershing ordered that troops on active service in France might have access to light wines and beer. This practical measure attracted the ire of Prohibitionist congressmen, who demanded that the president censure Pershing. However, while politicians squabbled over the hygiene and morals of America's fighting men, the troops themselves took solace from a bottle when the going was tough. The following extract from the diary of First Lieutenant Elmer Hess, Fifth Field Artillery, for May 31, 1918, illustrates the boost that they gained from a drink in the combat zone:

> I went over to Major Bailey's headquarters and was there when he was visited by a French Colonel and his Adjutant. Through the interpreter, Major Bailey was begged to remove his battalion across the River Marne to the hills overlooking the river on the south bank. This Major Bailey refused to do, stating that his orders were to take these positions, and until his Colonel countermanded his orders, he would stay here. The French Colonel then informed us

that outside of the detachments of French cavalry, there was no infantry in front of the 1st Battalion; the Germans at any moment might sweep through this sector. He begged us to cross the river immediately as he expected to blow up the bridge which, he said was our only avenue of escape. Again Major Bailey refused to withdraw. An hour later we heard a terrific detonation which we knew meant the destruction of the bridge over the Marne and our supposed last avenue of escape. Lieutenant Peabody, who was in the kitchen of the farmhouse, raised a bottle of wine and drank a health to the bridge in which we all joined before the reverberations of the explosion had passed away. At three o'clock in the morning we were up again. We assembled in the yard of a farmhouse, lined up, and roll call was taken. Our rolls were dropped and piled up. Later we would come back and get them if we lived that long.

28 AMPHIBIANS

the season 'tis, my lovely lambs
of Summer Volstead Christ and Co.
the epoch of Mann's righteousness
the age of dollars and no sense.

—e. e. cummings

First Lieutenant Elmer Hess lived long enough to collect his bedroll, finish the campaign, and return to a hero's welcome in the United States, his chest decorated with the Silver Star and the French Croix de Guerre. However, by the time demobilization was complete, returning veterans were unable to toast their achievements on home soil with anything stronger than *Bevo,* a nonalcoholic malt liquor brewed by Anheuser-Busch. While the doughboys had been away fighting, America's drys had achieved a victory as complete as that of the Allied powers in Europe. According to the Eighteenth Amendment to the Constitution, "the manufacture, sale, or transportation of intoxicating liquors within, the importation thereof into, or the exportation thereof from the United States and all territory subject to the jurisdiction thereof for beverage purposes is hereby prohibited." The demobilized veterans reacted to the introduction of Prohibition with amazement and disbelief. Could it be true that a majority of their fellow citizens hated alcohol so much that they did not want a drop of it in their country? Had there been a vote? In retrospect, their suspicions were justified and their surprise was foolish. There had been no vote, but the country had been creeping toward Prohibition throughout the war years. State after state was turning dry: In 1912 there had been twelve dry states, by 1914 there were fourteen, and by 1916 twenty-three had amended their constitutions or introduced legislation to outlaw alcoholic drinks.

Moreover, Prohibition had been a key issue in the 1916 presidential elections. The ASL had become the best-organized lobbying machine in the United States. Its influence was such that at the eve of the elections it was indifferent as to which party won: Whatever the color of the next administration, Congress would be packed with ASL supporters. Before the results were announced, in the words of Wayne Wheeler, the svengali of the ASL, "the dry workers throughout the country were celebrating our victory. We knew that the Constitutional Amendment would be submitted to the states by the Congress just elected."

When, in 1917, the issue of Prohibition had been threatened to be overshadowed by the entry of the United States into World War I, the ASL had turned the conflict to its advantage. The drain on resources created by alcoholic beverages was exaggerated in the most lurid language by ASL propagandists: "Brewery products fill refrigerator cars, while potatoes rot for lack of transportation, bankrupting families and starving cities. The coal that they consume would keep the railways open and the factories running." Abstinence, meanwhile, was promoted as the key to victory over the beer-swilling Germans: "Prohibition is the infallible submarine chaser we must launch by thousands. The water-wagon is the tank that can level every Prussian trench. . . . Sobriety is the bomb that will blow kaiserism to kingdom come."

The first wartime legislation to be used as a Trojan horse for Prohibition was the 1917 Food Control Act, whose aim was to husband the country's resources for the war effort. Despite the fact that America was in no danger of famine, the drys ensured that the conversion of food into distilled liquors was forbidden by the act—a de facto prohibition on spirits. The Food Control Act further allowed the president, at his discretion, "to limit or prohibit the manufacture of beer or wine as he saw fit." In the event, President Wilson decided to introduce a British-style restriction on American brewers in December 1917. The quantity of grain they were allowed for brewing was cut by 30 percent, and a legal maximum strength for beer was fixed at 2.75 ABV. In 1918, further austerity measures and restrictions were introduced via the Food Stimulation Act, which proscribed the use of grain for brewing until the war had ended and demobilization had been completed.

Although the brewers tried to fight back, they were tainted by their German heritage, which they had done so much to promote before the war. After 1917 they were forced to keep their heads below the parapet, as the American wartime press demonized Germany and its culture. Things Teutonic were boycotted or renamed–sauerkraut, for instance, became "liberty cabbage." The drys were quick to identify this weakness and exploit it. In addition to linking beer drinking and kaiser culture in ASL propaganda, Wheeler wrote to the federal custodian of alien property to alert him to the menace posed to America by traitors in its midst.

> Dear Mr. Palmer:
> I am informed that there are a number of breweries in this country which are owned in part by alien enemies. It is reported to me that the Anheuser Busch Company and some of the Milwaukee Companies are largely controlled by alien Germans.... Have you made any investigation?

Palmer duly investigated and concluded that the brewing companies, while American owned, had done their best to encourage kaiserism: It was "around the sangerfests and sangerbunds and organizations of that kind, generally financed by the rich brewers, that the young Germans who come to America are taught to remember, first, the fatherland, and second, America."

At the same time as they were denying Americans access to spirits via food control legislation, and attacking brewers in the name of patriotism, the drys kept working on their principal objective–Prohibition via constitutional amendment. In August 1917 a bill was introduced to the Senate, where the prevailing mood was favorable. No one knew how long the war might last, and a measure that could only increase the fighting efficiency of the nation merited careful attention. Moreover, many senators felt the bill would "not really enact prohibition, but merely [submit] it to the states," and that the states would never all go dry. Sensing that they were in a minority, and that the bill would be passed, wet politicians tabled an amendment that set a time limit of seven years for individual states to ratify the bill, which they believed would be insufficient for the required three-quarters majority to do so, and which therefore would prevent it from becoming law. The vote was taken, and the amendment adopted. The following December the bill was put to Congress, where it was approved by 282 votes to 128. *The Washington Times* insinuated that this apparently healthy majority reflected fear rather than a genuine interest in Prohibition: "Every Congressman knows that if the ballot on the constitutional amendment were a secret ballot, making it impossible for the Anti-Saloon League bosses to punish disobedience, the amendment would not pass." To the consternation of the wets, the amendment was ratified by thirty-six states within fourteen months, followed quickly by nine more,[63] and on January 16, 1919, the Eighteenth Amendment of the Constitution of the United States became law–America was officially dry.

Like medieval sumptuary laws, and unlike prior amendments to the Constitution, the Eighteenth was a proscriptive piece of legislation, which took away rights rather than guaranteed them. The restrictions it introduced had to be implemented, and the Volstead Bill, named after its sponsor, Andrew Joseph Volstead of Minnesota, and drafted by Wayne Wheeler, set out the mechanics of enforcement. Its sponsor, although partial to an occasional drink, was a disciplinarian at heart who believed "law regulates morality, law has regulated humanity since the Ten Commandments," and hence had no qualms in attaching his name to what he considered to be a useful exercise in social engineering. The bill was debated at length in Congress and subjected to a string of amendments. President Wilson vetoed it in its final form for technical reasons, but the House and the Senate overrode him and the Volstead Act was adopted in October 1919.

It was prima facie a Draconian piece of legislation: Violators of its provisions might be punished with substantial fines, prison terms, and confiscation of their property; and infringements were to be investigated by a force of fifteen hundred agents, who were endowed with intrusive powers of search and seizure. It was also horribly flawed: Two classes of Americans–medical patients and religious communicants–were still allowed to purchase alcohol for pleasure. The distillation of alcohol for industrial purposes was also exempted, as was home brewing and cider making, for the Volstead Act envisaged a damp, not dry, America. It was no crime under its provisions to drink alcohol–people

---

[63] The amendment was eventually ratified by every state except Rhode Island and Connecticut.

were permitted to consume their pre-Prohibition stocks and any other booze they might come across. Its potential for confusion was immense and its oppressive nature was bound to be resented. Congressman Crago of Pennsylvania predicted, while the act was being debated, that it would result in "a discontent and disregard for law in this country beyond anything we have ever witnessed before." He was right.

The start of Prohibition, in January 1920, was marked by Americans in a variety of ways, some auspicious, others less so. The drys were jubilant. Church bells rang out to commemorate victory; Billy Sunday, the celebrity dry evangelist, staged a mock funeral for John Barleycorn in Norfolk, Virginia. "The reign of tears is over," he claimed. "The slums will soon be only a memory. We will turn our prisons into factories and our jails into storehouses and corncribs." Some communities really believed that all crime was alcohol-inspired and sold off their jails. The wets, in contrast, were pragmatic, or opportunistic. The Yale Club laid down a sufficient stock of wine to last for fourteen years; and within a minute of the Volstead Act coming into effect six armed bandits robbed two railroad cars in Chicago of a hundred thousand dollars' worth of whiskey intended for medical use. Before the law was twenty-four hours old, two similar robberies had occurred in the same city—a foretaste of the crime wave to come.

Since it was not an offense to drink per se, and the act had not—as if by magic—dried up the thirst of the country's wets, anyone willing to take the risk of supplying them with hooch could be certain of handsome rewards. Demand was vibrant: After all, once Americans had liquor in their clutches they could drink it with impunity at home. The Volstead Act created its own species of criminal—the bootlegger—a smuggler ready to disobey the Constitution in order to sell alcohol to his or her countrymen. The subcategory who specialized in international trade, known as rum-runners, were the most glamorous class of bootleggers, especially those who ran in their goods by water—over the warm blue Caribbean, the steel-gray St. Lawrence, across the Gulf of Mexico, and through Pacific swells. America's neighbors took advantage of their activity. The Bermudas, and various small Caribbean islands, developed statistically prodigious thirsts; Canadian provinces quickly repealed their own Prohibition laws in order to profit from tax revenues on liquor sales south.

The prince of the rum runners, whose surname has entered the language as a byword for quality, was William S. McCoy. An ex-merchant seaman, McCoy was working as a yacht builder in Florida at the outbreak of Prohibition. Sensing the opportunities for gain, he purchased an old fishing schooner, the *Henry L. Marshall*, registered her in the Bahamas under the British flag, loaded her holds with scotch, and set sail for the Georgia coast. He dropped anchor in St. Catherine's Sound and disposed of his cargo to a prearranged buyer for a price that covered the cost of his boat. Over the next three years, McCoy expanded his fleet, acquiring the *J. B. Young*, *The M. M. Gardener*, and his favorite, the schooner *Arethusa*. After the loss of his original boat, which was taken by the U.S. Coast Guard while under the command of a subordinate, he did all his business from international waters, i.e., more than three miles offshore. His customers would motor, row, or sail out to him to make their purchases: "They would come wobbling and bouncing out in their little open craft, one man steering, the other pumping for dear life, and swing in under my schooner's lee. Usually it was too rough to tie up. Four of us would hold the skiff away from our side with oars and boat hooks, and we would throw the . . . liquor out to the crew. The buyer would toss a roll of bills to me. 'Twelve thousand dollars for two hundred cases, Bill,' he would shout. . . . My reputation and the white form of the *Arethusa* riding on the Row was all the advertisement I needed." McCoy never watered his liquor and never dealt with gangsters, hence his reputation for probity and the birth of the term *the real McCoy* for an article of genuine quality. In 1924 he was captured aboard the *Arethusa* by the Coast Guard, tried for violations of the Volstead Act, and spent eight months in jail. Upon release he retired from rum-running and passed the remainder of his life as a real estate investor in Miami. The adventures of McCoy and his fellow rumrunners captured the imagination of the public to the extent that *Outlook* magazine commented in 1924 that prohibition was satisfying "three tremendous popular passions . . . the passion of the prohibitionists for law, the passion of the drinking classes for drink, and the passion of the largest and best organized smuggling trade that has ever existed for money."

While the smuggling trade was significant, for the first few years of Prohibition the largest source of bootlegged hooch was industrial alcohol. Production of this useful chemical increased several fold, despite the reduced need for cordite in peacetime. Indeed, by 1926, American industry was consuming 150 million proof gallons of it annually, of which perhaps a third was diverted to the beverage market. As a precaution against such an eventuality, the Volstead Act had required that industrial alcohol be *denatured,* i.e., adulterated with chemicals that made it unpleasant or impossible to drink. However, the bootleggers soon learned how to remove, neutralize, or dilute denaturants, and their customers were prepared to put up with any traces that remained. Each gallon of industrial alcohol produced three gallons of mock whiskey, gin, or brandy, so that the overall volume of the illicit market equaled that of legal production prior to Prohibition.

The second largest domestic source of bootlegged booze was moonshine, i.e., spirits from clandestine stills. Moonshine had a long and honorable connection with the Appalachian Mountain region, where it had been made in significant quantities since the nineteenth century, and where craft distilleries rose to the occasion when demand leapt in 1920. The scale of the expansion of the moonshine industry can be gauged from the statistics of the Prohibition Bureau: In 1921 a total of 95,933 illicit stills were seized; in 1925 the figure was 172,537, and by 1930 it was 282,122. Moonshine could be rough stuff. Quality was sacrificed to quantity once the Volstead Act came into force. Distillers could not take the risk of aging their product to improve its flavor, so they added dead rats and rotten meat to it to achieve the same effect. The average glass of moonshine was on a par with gin-craze gin, and its pet names—Panther and Goat whiskey, Jackass brandy, Yack Yack bourbon—all suggesting a coarse strength, were similar in spirit to those that had emerged in eighteenth-century England. Moonshine and imperfectly renatured industrial alcohol poisoned thousands of Americans. Their deaths were given lurid coverage by the press, but instead, as the drys had hoped, of evoking disgust among readers, they attracted sympathy: It was wrong that people should have to risk their lives for a drink. Fortunately, the quality of moonshine improved with the increased availability of corn sugar, the production of which (a rare example of Prohibition benefiting the white economy) expanded sixfold between 1921 and 1929.

Both moonshine and industrial alcohol were often repackaged prior to sale. Since the real McCoy commanded higher prices than a quart of Jackass brandy, Appalachian hooch was often labeled as imported whiskey, rum, brandy, or gin. It was, after all, a sellers' market, and powers of discrimination were on the wane. The process of making such delights was described by a Prohibition administrator in

Pittsburgh to a Senate subcommittee in 1926: "You sent in an order for gin, and they would open a spigot on this big tank, run out so much alcohol, and so much water, and so much flavoring extract and coloring fluid, and throw that into the gin. If you wanted a case of scotch, open the same spigot, run the recovered denatured alcohol into a container in whatever quantity they wanted, the addition of water, a few drops of creosote or essence of Scotch, and a little caramel, and it would come to the bench for scotch."

The wholesale trade in beverage alcohol catered not only to the home consumer but also to a thriving retail trade. The saloon was dead, long live the speakeasy! Americans did not wish to bid farewell to sociable drinking, and as saloons across the country closed, or struggled on as soda fountains, a multitude of illegal drinking places sprang up as substitutes. Speakeasies ranged from single rooms in tenement dwellings to palatial institutions equipped with restaurants, dance floors, and jazz bands. In New York, for example, illegal drinking establishments such as the Cotton Club, the Stork Club, El Morocco, and 21 were the first true nightclubs the city had seen, offering food, drink, dancing, and entertainment to their clientele. They were patronized not only by the wealthy and dissipated but also by Broadway stars and by New York's intelligentsia, who were dubbed "gintellectuals" by the pioneer of American celebrity journalism, Walter Winchell. Speakeasies were staple fodder for the New York press, which reported who had been spotted where in its gossip columns, and noted the police raids on various joints in its crime pages. Collectively, they formed a never-ending carnival, which people might either join in or look on as observers through the eyes of their favorite columnists. Upton Sinclair, novelist, dry, and activist, suggested that they had dragged Bacchanalia into the twentieth century and that "Wine, Women, and Song" had been "modernized" into "gin, janes, and jazz."

Unlike the saloons they replaced, speakeasies were patronized by both sexes. American women had expanded their domain beyond the home during the war. They had become wage earners in their own right and, courtesy of the Nineteenth Amendment to the Constitution, had gained the right to vote. They began drinking in public in numbers during the Prohibition years; indeed, the removal of the prior taboo on women in saloons can be counted as one of the triumphs of Prohibition. Not only did women begin to tipple away from home during the Volstead era, they also started drinking ardent spirits. It made little sense to bootleg beer or other weak drinks, and the standard fare at respectable speakeasies was cocktails. The fruit juices, bitters, and sugar they contained masked the dubious pedigree of the alcohol that gave them their kick.

Cocktails spread from the public to the private sphere during Prohibition. Far fewer American households had servants in the 1920s and the formal dinner parties that had characterized the Victorian Age were impossible to stage without them. Instead, people entertained each other with cocktail parties, which required, in comparison, minimal preparation. By 1923 a journalist was able to comment, "There are not many ladies in well-to-do houses now—certainly in the Eastern States—who are not experts at mixing cocktails." The trend did not pass unnoticed by federal authorities. In 1924, the Prohibition commissioner, Roy Haynes, appealed to the patriotism of women tempted to serve "pre-Prohibition" (i.e., alcoholic) cocktails because of the demands of fashion: "It is outrageous that in any American home the household should feel more ashamed of not having liquor to serve their guests than ashamed to violate and trample under their feet the Constitution of the United States." Such views, however, were contrary to the spirit of the age. A retrospective article published in *Vogue* in 1930 identified cocktail drinking as a key attribute of the "secure leaders of fashion" who were idolized by young American women: "They are athletic. They were the first to smoke because they liked it, and probably the first to drink cocktails."

The demand for cocktails stimulated invention. New recipes were created, and old ones improved, including the dry martini. This faultless elixir was developed in New York in the 1920s and celebrated by its gintellectuals. According to H. L. Mencken, the dry martini was "the only American invention as perfect as a sonnet"; and Ogden Nash lauded the mixture in "A Drink with Something in It":

> There is something about a Martini,
> A tingle remarkably pleasant;
> A yellow, a mellow Martini;
> I wish I had one at present.
> There is something about a Martini,
> Ere the dining and dancing begin,
> And to tell you the truth,

It is not the vermouth—
I think that perhaps it's the gin.

Dorothy Parker, epitome of the modern girl, immortalized its effects in a ditty:

I like to have a Martini
Two at the very most.
After three I'm under the table.
After four I'm under the host.

America's women were imitated by its students. Drinking flourished on hitherto dry campuses, and students paid their way through college by bootlegging or bartending in speakeasies. During their vacations they flocked to fashionable watering holes in the great cities, adding their thirsts to those of the resident multitudes. So great was the demand in New York that in 1929 its police commissioner estimated it was home to thirty-two thousand drinking places—double the number of saloons and illegal joints it had contained in the pre-Prohibition era.

Americans who lacked the time to visit speakeasies could buy their liquor at other retail outlets. These were numerous, if not ubiquitous: At the height of Prohibition *The New York Telegram* sent a team of reporters to investigate where alcohol was for sale in the city. They found it on offer in "dancing academies, drugstores, delicatessens, cigar stores, confectionaries, soda fountains, behind partitions of shoeshine parlors, back rooms of barbershops, from hotel bellhops, from hotel headwaiters, from hotel day clerks, night clerks, in express offices, in motorcycle delivery agencies, paint stores, malt shops, . . . fruit stands, vegetable markets, groceries, smoke shops, athletic clubs, grillrooms, . . . chophouses, importing firms, tea-rooms, moving van companies, spaghetti houses, boarding houses, Republican clubs, Democratic clubs, laundries, social clubs," and last, but not least, "newspapermen's associations."

By 1923, America was considered by one observer to be neither wet nor dry, but rather "amphibious." Perhaps the archetype of its amphibians was President Harding, who set a bad example to the nation by drinking in the White House while vowing to enforce the Volstead Act in the role of chief executive. Whiskey was his favorite poison, which he knocked back in his "study" with his gang of Ohio cronies. An account of this place shows that saloon style had not perished with the saloon: "Trays with bottles containing every imaginable brand of whiskey stood about, cards and poker chips ready at hand," and there was "a general atmosphere of waistcoat unbuttoned, feet on the desk, and the spittoon alongside." When Harding died midterm, his successor, Vice President Calvin Coolidge, who was reelected as president in 1924, pursued a policy of benign neglect toward Prohibition. With such mixed messages from the top, even the Prohibition bureau developed amphibian traits. For instance, the director of Prohibition enforcement in northern California confessed in public "that he did drink occasionally because San Francisco is a wet community, and that he also served liquor to his guests because he was a gentleman and 'not a prude.'"

Widespread and flagrant disobedience to the Volstead Act was made easier by the incompetence of the federal body that had been created to enforce it. Ever since its inception the Prohibition Bureau had made a reputation for itself as being violent, inefficient, and corrupt. Its organization was flawed, and its agents were second-rate. Their average wages—between twelve hundred and two thousand dollars a year in 1920—"compared unfavorably with those of garbage collectors." Not only were the rewards poor, the work was also dangerous. By 1923, thirty Prohibition agents had been killed in action. They had taken quite a few civilians with them, indeed had committed some spectacular murders that had turned public opinion against them. In consequence, a career in Prohibition enforcement offered little to an honest man. Turnover was rapid, and one in twelve agents was dismissed for cause. Recorded grounds for dismissal included "bribery, extortion, theft, violation of the National Prohibition Act, falsification of records, conspiracy, forgery, [and] perjury."

There were honorable exceptions, such as Izzy Einstein and Moe Smith, who between them arrested nearly five thousand violators and confiscated five million bottles of illicit booze. They worked as a team, often in disguise, and their disparate physical appearances gave them the appeal of a double comedy act. The newspapers followed their raids, noting new disguises or ruses that had enabled them to deceive bootleggers and speakeasy proprietors. Izzy, labeled "the master mind of the Federal rum-ferrets," often tipped off reporters before a bust, and this hunger for publicity led to his downfall. In 1925 both he and Moe were dismissed "for the good of the service"—their stellar performances had set their colleagues in too unfavorable a light.

The disappointing form of Prohibition agents was outstanding in comparison to the other groups of people whom the Volstead Act had envisaged would assist in its enforcement. State legislatures were dilatory in introducing the necessary supplementary legislation, even those that had been dry pre-Prohibition. Some, like New York, legislated for state Prohibition only to withdraw it. The Mullan-Gage Law it passed in 1921 was repealed in 1923 after it had paralyzed the courts with liquor offenses. Private citizens were disinclined to inform on or to testify against bootleggers, and juries were loath to give guilty verdicts. Dry sentiment, when put to the test, had evaporated.

The organizations and individuals who had campaigned for Prohibition found themselves on the defensive in the 1920s. They were held accountable for the failings of an unenforceable law as well as the culture of violence it had spawned. They responded by going into denial: In 1925, for instance, faced with evidence that that the nation's youth were turning to the bottle, Wayne Wheeler claimed that things had never been so good. Prohibition-era drinks were so bad and so expensive that no one could fall in love with them: "The cost and quality of post-Volsteadian drinks does not create a habit as did the licensed intoxicants," ergo: "The American youth problem is less serious than that in other countries."

Moreover, America underwent profound changes in the Prohibition years, but these were not the changes for which the drys had hoped. Instead of becoming pious models of self-restraint, Americans had launched themselves into a frenzy of crime and consumerism. Although the drys held their noses and tried to reconcile such behavior with temperance, they misinterpreted the spirit of the age, and their post-Volsteadian publicity only succeeded in demonstrating the extent of their anachronism. A 1924 *Atlantic Monthly* article on the impact of *consumptionism*, for example, predicted that this new phenomenon would lead to voluntary abstinence. At its dry author saw it, consumptionism, defined as "the science of compelling men to use more and more things," was "bringing it about that the American citizen's first importance to his country is no longer that of citizen but that of consumer." And "consumptionism cannot suffer drink because in drink men find a substitute for that satisfaction which is in the acquiring of luxuries." In other words, the opportunity to go shopping would extinguish the desire to binge. After all, "The purpose of Prohibition was not to make more valuable citizens. The purpose was to make for valuable consumers."

The item most American consumers aspired to purchase was an automobile. In 1921 the nation had nine million cars; by 1929 over twenty-six million of them were on its roads. Prior to this expansion, it had been hoped that driving would discourage drinking. Temperance was "the friend of machinery," and no sane person would wish to compromise the pleasures of driving by getting *stewed to the gills*[64] before taking to the road. However, the reverse proved to be the case. Automobiles facilitated bootlegging. If Prohibition had been introduced in the age of the horse and cart it might have stood a chance of success, but cars enabled bootleggers to cover vast distances quickly. They often worked in armed convoys and held regular firefights with Prohibition agents, whose trigger-happy ways led to a fashion in Michigan for windshield stickers reading, DON'T SHOOT, I'M NOT A BOOTLEGGER.

The rapid increase in the number of automobiles extended the reach of bootleggers into small rural communities, whose residents hitherto had had to rely on the exemptions to the Volstead Act in favor of sacramental wine and medicinal hooch when they wanted a drink. The exemption in favor of religious drinking was exploited with considerable zeal: In 1925 the Federal Council of Churches reported to its members that "nearly three million gallons of sacramental wine were taken out of government warehouses in 1924," only a quarter of which had ended up on the altar. A similar proportion of medicinal alcohol went astray. Together the markets for communicants, Jews, and invalids, whether genuine or bogus, enabled a number of California winemakers to hang on through Prohibition. While their overall number declined by 80 percent post-Volstead, the quantity of wine they made under bond did not decrease proportionally. Indeed, the average annual output of bonded wineries during Prohibition was eight million gallons, much of which was consumed by healthy atheists.

Those California vineyards that did not supply the bonded market prospered by going into the juice grape business. Whereas many had anticipated ruin in the Volstead era, instead they enjoyed a boom. The

---

[64] Prohibition had created a host of new synonyms for intoxication.

total area of vineyards in the state increased from 300,000 acres in 1919 to 400,000 in 1923, to 650,000 acres in 1928. Not only were more grapes planted under Prohibition, but the prices they commanded soared. In the best pre-Prohibition years prices had been twenty-five dollars a ton. The first Prohibition era harvest averaged fifty dollars a ton; in 1921 it hit a Prohibition high of eighty-two dollars a ton. It fell back from this spike, but for most of Prohibition prices exceeded those commanded when America had been wet.

Demand for grapes was driven by the "nonintoxicating cider and fruit juices" exemption to the Volstead Act, which allowed the manufacture of such drinks for use in the home. The principal out-of-state destination for California "juice" grapes was New York, followed by Chicago. These places were supplied via a market at the Pennsylvania Railroad yard, to which growers shipped their products in refrigerated cars. The scale of business was titanic: "In 1928 one buyer bought 225 carloads (3,100 tons) of grapes in a single purchase." As *Business Week* observed, "The only inference is that these grapes went to someone who is manufacturing wine in vast quantities." The periodical labeled the Penn yard "the Wall Street of the grape auction business" and described the procedure by which grapes were sold on to the public: "The ordinary speculator buys two or three cars and has them shipped to a siding in his own neighborhood. Then he sends word around and families gather for the year's supply of wine. To cart away their purchases they come with toy wagons, wheelbarrows, and even baby buggies." The Manhattan Produce Yard became so clogged up with prams when a grape delivery arrived that its administration banned them altogether from its grounds.

In order to exploit the juice grape market systematically, and to utilize winemaking equipment lying dormant, the Californian Vineyardists Association (CVA) was organized in 1926, with the intention of producing and selling concentrated juice. Despite the probability that such concentrate would be used to make wine, the legality of manufacturing it was cleared with Washington. The CVA established a commercial subsidiary, Fruit Industries, Inc., to sell its new product, which it branded Vine Glo. Advertisements were placed in local and national media that hinted at its potential:

> Now is the time to order your supply of VINE-GLO. It can be made in your home in sixty days—a fine, true-to-type guaranteed beverage

ready for the Holiday Season. VINE-GLO . . . comes to you in nine
varieties, Port, Virginia Dare, Muscatel, Angelica, Tokay, Sauterne,
Riesling, Claret, and Burgundy. It is entirely legal in your home–but
it must not be transported.

Americans wishing to enjoy some "true-to-type" port or claret
could purchase by mail order or through pharmacies. They were delivered a five- or ten-gallon keg by Fruit Industries personnel, who would
add water to the concentrate, start fermentation and return in sixty
days to bottle the product and retrieve the keg. Vine-Glo was a commercial success and inspired copycat products, including Bacchus wine
bricks, which were marketed as "solidified merriment." Such was the
impact of juice grape and concentrate sales that American per capita
consumption of wine grew while the Volstead Act was in force.

Nineteen twenty-eight, the year that wine bricks hit the market, was a
watershed year for Prohibition. The drys, on the defensive, succeeded
in strengthening the mechanics of enforcement; the wets, bolstered by
explicit backing from labor organizations and prominent capitalists,
began to build up momentum toward repeal. Moreover, Prohibition was a pivotal issue in the 1928 presidential election. For the first
time since its introduction, voters could chose a self-confessed wet
candidate–the Democrat, Alfred E. Smith. His Republican opponent,
Herbert Clark Hoover, was, in contrast, in favor of continuing Prohibition, which he described as "a great social and economic experiment,
noble in motive and far reaching in purpose," and vowed to improve
the enforcement of the law as it stood. The election was notable for
the malicious personal attacks on Smith, a Catholic, who was vilified
as a papist drunk intent on turning America into a Vatican fiefdom.
The popular historian H. L. Mencken summed up the state of the nation on the eve of the polls: "If Al [Smith] wins tomorrow, it will be
because American people have decided at last to vote as they drink. . . .
If he loses, it will be because those who fear the pope outnumber
those who are tired of the Anti-Saloon League." Smith lost by a convincing margin.

True to his word, Hoover reformed Prohibition enforcement. Attempts were made to raise the abysmal standards of Prohibition Bureau agents. The entire service was made to sit the civil service exam.

Only 41 percent passed after two attempts. Most of those who failed were dismissed and replaced. In 1929 the Jones Act was introduced, which stiffened penalties against violators of the Volstead Act. An amendment to it raising the appropriations of the Prohibition Bureau to the stupendous sum of $256 million (from around $12.5 million) was approved, then dropped—the drys were leery of making an unpopular law an expensive one. They had claimed that Prohibition would be cheap and virtually self-enforcing, which clearly had not been the case. Most important, in May 1929, Hoover appointed a commission under George W. Wickersham to perform the first federal review of law enforcement in the United States. Violent crime, much of it related to bootlegging, had become the principal domestic political issue since his election. On February 14 of the same year, members of the gang of Alphonse Gabriel "Scarface" Capone had lined seven members of a rival organization against a warehouse wall and gunned them down. The circumstances of the murders caught the imagination of the public—the St. Valentine's Day Massacre was symptomatic of everything that had gone wrong in America since Prohibition had been introduced. The man behind the massacre likewise typified the kind of citizen who was profiting from the blunder. Al Capone was a second-generation Italian American who had left school at fourteen after beating up a teacher, and who seemed destined for a career in petty crime until the Volstead Act appeared. Thereafter, his star ascended, until he was accounted Public Enemy Number One. Capone, never shy of publicity, put his philosophy on record: "I make my money by supplying a public demand. If I break the law, my customers, who number hundreds of the best people in Chicago, are as guilty as I am. The only difference between us is that I sell and they buy. Everybody calls me a racketeer. I call myself a businessman. When I sell liquor, it's bootlegging. When my patrons serve it on a silver tray on Lake Shore Drive, it's hospitality."

29 LOST

Wine inspires gaiety, strength, youth, and health. It
is bottled sunshine.

—Professor P. Pierret

"That's what you are. That's what you all are," Miss
Stein said. "All of you young people who served in
the war. You are a lost generation."
"Really?" I said
"You are," she insisted. "You have no respect for
anything. You drink yourselves to death."

—Ernest Hemingway

The "great social and economic experiment, noble in motive and
far-reaching in purpose," which President Hoover had been
elected to defend, was being abandoned as a failure in the few
places where it had been attempted outside of the United States. By
the time Hoover assumed office, Communist Russia had re-legalized
beer and wine and was about to commence the state manufacture of
vodka by the workers for the workers. Iceland and Norway had flirted
with and given up on Prohibition, Sweden had decided against it in a
1922 referendum; indeed, only Finland and the Canadian province
of Prince Edward Island soldiered on as dry lands. Although drink
control legislation brought in as austerity measures during World War
I lingered on the statute books in Great Britain, in general the waters
of temperance were receding. They never had been very deep in
France, and while absinthe remained banned, drinking was otherwise

encouraged in the Roaring Twenties. French winemakers, who had lost two of their principal export markets—claret to America and champagne to Russia—sought to compensate through the promotion of their product to their fellow countrymen. Their efforts were supported by a state *Office International du Vin* whose mission was to endorse the benefits of wine drinking. The government also took steps to improve the quality of French wines. The concept of the present-day *appellations controlées* was introduced, which decreed that only wines from carefully defined regions might be labeled as such, and furthermore that the growers in each region were limited to using "grape varieties hallowed by local, loyal, and established custom." The improved product was marketed as quintessentially French, the key to good health, amiable humor, and long life.

Lest any French person doubt the benefits that flowed from drinking French wine, medical, martial, and cultural evidence in its favor was brought to their attention. The medical case for wine was established by the testimonials of doctors. According to one such pundit, "Urban and rural people can and should drink a liter of unfortified wine per day with meals for their own good and the prosperity of the land." French wine drinkers interested in the technical details of how wine improved their well-being were advised by Dr. Jean-François-Napoléon Dougnac that it was a "radioactive foodstuff, for grapes store solar radiation and devour mineral elements from the soil." At the time a mild dose of radioactivity was thought to be good for one—various continental spas boasted of the Geiger count of their mineral water, but in the opinion of Dr. Dougnac this was nothing compared to the potency of wine, whose "radioactive properties" stimulated the organs and glands, augmented the red blood cell count, positively influenced the nutritional process, and regulated "the tone of the vagosympathetic system." As proof of such stimulatory powers, Dr. Dougnac cited the case of an "American teetotaler who was cured of his fatigue and neurasthenia by Saint-Émilion." Moreover, wine was not merely a restorative but also a prophylactic against various waterborne diseases. "If you drink Chablis with your oysters," French seafood lovers were counseled, "you will never get typhoid fever."

Statisticians also chipped in in favor of wine by pointing to its beneficial effects on the human lifespan. From 1928 onward, medical students in Paris were taught that wine drinkers had an average life expectancy four years greater than water drinkers, and that the longest-lived people in France were the inhabitants of Bordeaux. The raw data was supported with anecdotal evidence: The centenarian Dr. Guéniot, author of *Living to Be One Hundred*, recommended the consumption of wine with meals to those who wished to imitate him.

Wine, according to its supporters, not only enabled the French to live longer, it also enhanced their fighting qualities. According to the testimony of a doctor who had served on a recruiting board during World War I, "We were able to note that among the young men called for army duty, those from wine growing regions were the most muscular, alert, and lithe, as well as the strongest, biggest, and leanest." French poilus who had lacked such congenital advantages were nonetheless thought to have benefited from their pinard ration. Indeed, such was the battlefield reputation wine had won in World War I that should there be another war, it would be at the top of any French general's requisition list. According to no less of an authority than Marshal Philippe Pétain, "Of all the supplies sent to the army during [WWI], wine was surely the most highly anticipated and appreciated by the soldier." Finally, arguments were advanced in support of the significance of French wine in Gallic culture. An expert warned that without wine "the French race would lose its true character and become a bland people without any personality." French drinkers responded to the advice of their doctors, politicians, and nationalists by upping their consumption, from about 120 liters per head per annum prior to the war, to 168 liters a decade later, confident that wine was both a healthy and patriotic beverage.

The French postwar drinking culture demonized abstinence. People who chose to live without alcohol were condemned to be fat, ugly, and weak. Water drinkers had the worst of it, for "water tends to thicken the flesh." This, according to Dr. Dougnac, was a defensive mechanism: "Fat is formed and intervenes in water drinkers, to neutralize the poisons derived from food that are not destroyed by internal secretions. These secretions are insufficient due to the lack of a stimulant like wine." To be thin was to be chic in the 1920s, and unfashionably obese water drinkers were ostracized. They were also reckoned to suffer facial disfigurement as punishment for their temperance: "Wine takes its revenge on those who don't drink it by covering their faces with acne, pimples, and red blotches." Last but not least, dry people were believed to be feeble. According to a publication sponsored by a French wine merchant, "Since Prohibition, the Americans have retrogressed in sports. They have lost their superiority in world boxing championships and [can] only maintain their superiority in footraces over short distances."

Wine was perhaps the only constant in French culture during the 1920s and '30s. Whereas its visual art underwent radical transformations—Fauvism and Cubism and other rebellions against Impressionism were succeeded by neoclassicism and Dada—its creators kept on drinking. Pablo Picasso paid homage to Bacchus in his drawings; Henri Matisse took inspiration from the ecstatic bacchantes on Greek friezes to create exquisite representations of dancers; Pierre Bonnard learned to draw as an illustrator of champagne ads. Even the Dadaists found time for wine amid the chaos. French literature underwent similar convulsions to its art over the same period, during which decadence and symbolism gave way to surrealism, whose apostles made a place for wine in their ethos. According to André Breton, author of the *Surrealist Manifesto,* the perfect example of a surreal sentence was "The exquisite corpse will drink new wine."

Paris, the epicenter of all the artistic turmoil, was reckoned by both its inhabitants and a large community of expatriates to be the cultural capital of the Western world. It was cheap and permissive, and these qualities attracted creative sorts from all around the globe. The American presence and influence was notable. Gertrude Stein made the international reputations of Picasso and Matisse as artists, and her own as a writer; Ernest Hemingway, Ezra Pound, and Scott Fitzgerald produced some of their best work in France. In some cases, Prohibition at home was a contributing factor to self-imposed exile among American authors. Although it was easy enough to get a drink almost anywhere in the United States, the laws against doing so were perceived as both oppressive and offensive. According to Malcolm Cowley, "Our own nation . . . passed the Prohibition Amendment as if to publish a bill of separation between itself and ourselves; it wasn't our country any longer." In Europe, by contrast, drinking was out in the open, and all the more pleasant for it, especially to those who drank hard. The difference in attitudes toward alcohol on opposite sides of the Atlantic was spelled out by Ernest Hemingway: "In Europe . . . we thought of wine as something as healthy and normal as food and also as a great giver of happiness and well-being and delight. Drinking wine was not a snobbism nor a sign of sophistication nor a cult; it was as natural as eating and to me as necessary, and I would not have thought of eating a meal without drinking."

Hemingway presented the value of wine in the diet and elsewhere to an American audience in his first successful novel, *The Sun Also Rises* (1926). It is a Bacchic tale, whose centerpiece is the fiesta in honor of San Fermín at Pamplona. It has scarcely a page without a drink on it, and every character of importance is paralytic at least once in the story. American readers were reminded, via sideswipes at Prohibition and Wayne Wheeler, that the events recorded in *The Sun Also Rises* would not have been legal in the United States. Moreover, the demented, wine-soaked festival at its heart had no real counterpart in America's heritage. Its depiction caused many of Hemingway's countrymen to reexamine their culture, and those who found it desiccated followed the author to Spain in search of something more authentic.

As well as using intoxication as an aid to characterization, and as a cultural marker, Hemingway discriminated between the types of drunkenness caused by specific drinks, as if each different potion had its own special magic. Absinthe, for example (then still legal in Spain) knocks out every character in *The Sun Also Rises*, including its narrator, whereas even a skinful of wine causes no such trauma. Fastidious descriptions of drink and drinkers were common to Hemingway's subsequent work; indeed it is hard to imagine a Hemingway novel without alcohol. This focus on booze, and its ability to alter the character of the drinker, was also apparent in the work of many of Hemingway's contemporaries; indeed was typical of the so-called Lost Generation of writers who rose to prominence after the First World War. Their number included Scott Fitzgerald, who joined Hemingway in Paris in 1926, shortly after finishing his third novel, *The Great Gatsby*.

A masterpiece of the Jazz Age, written in the south of France and Italy about Prohibition America, *The Great Gatsby* is awash with drinking scenes and drunks. It features all the emblems of the Roaring Twenties—extravagant automobiles, the cult of celebrity, conspicuous consumption, and fortunes won by dubious means. Jay Gatsby, the central character, has elements of Trimalchio, the slave made good in the *Satyricon* of Petronius; indeed, the original title of the novel was *Trimalchio in West Egg*. Gatsby, like his Roman equivalent, serves only the best, in oversized cups. His champagne glasses are the size of finger-bowls and are endlessly replenished.[65] The intoxication it engenders in his guests is of the amiable, albeit vacuous kind. They are mindless hedonists, typical of their venal era.

The depiction of the influence of alcohol in Fitzgerald's next novel, *Tender Is the Night,* was far more critical. Drinking humiliates and ruins the hero of the book and kills a minor character outright. Set on the French Riviera, which Fitzgerald and his wife, Zelda, helped establish as a popular summer resort, the novel commences in splendor and ends in sorrow. It took Fitzgerald nine years to write, during which period his own equilibrium vanished and he fell victim to his bottled muse. According to Hemingway, Fitzgerald never had been able to take his drink. Without warning, he sometimes underwent a dramatic and sinister transformation after only one or two measures. His wife was also a problem drinker, and in the opinion of Hemingway, her habit aggravated that of Fitzgerald, to the detriment of his writing: "At this time Zelda could drink more than Scott could, and Scott was afraid for her to pass out in the company they kept that spring and the places they went to. Scott did not like the places or the people and he had to drink more than he could drink and be in control of himself, to stand the people and the places, and then he began to drink to keep awake after he would usually have passed out. Finally he had few intervals of work at all." Zelda, like the heroine of *Tender Is the Night,* required medical treatment for her mental health. Scott, like Dick Diver, his fictional hero, went into physical decline. The book itself is a tour de force, although Fitzgerald himself felt its last section had been compromised by his drinking habits: "I would give anything if I hadn't had to write Part III of *Tender Is the Night* entirely on stimulant. If I had one more crack at it cold sober I believe it might have made a great difference."

By the time of its publication, Fitzgerald had returned to the United States for good. His creative powers were fading, largely as a result of his drinking. He made a living by selling short stories, including one entitled "An Alcoholic Case," which, in contrast to the cheerful roles allotted to drink in his first three novels, portrays the fluid as addictive and destructive, in the style of temperance noir. He also supported himself by going to work as a scriptwriter in Hollywood, like

---

[65] Champagne had a good Prohibition. It is estimated that dry-era America got through seventy-one million bottles—equivalent to a 300 percent increase in annual consumption when compared to pre-Volstead years.

his fellow dipsomaniac, William ("Civilization begins with distillation") Faulkner.

Faulkner kept the whiskey flag flying throughout Prohibition. While alcohol plays a far less important role in his work than that of Hemingway and Fitzgerald, he exceeded them both in personal consumption. He drank steadily while composing and binged furiously when not. A friend from his New Orleans days described how they prepared booze in bulk at the height of Prohibition: "The favorite drink at that time was Pernod, made right there in New Orleans, and it cost six dollars a bottle. We made it up in great pitchers for all our parties. We also made gin in the bathtub using five gallon cans of Cuban alcohol and adding the proper little bottle of juniper essence, which you could buy at the corner store." In addition to making a portion of his liquid inspiration, Faulkner also ensured a steady supply through bootleggers, buying whiskey by the gallon so as to be sure he could get suitably "corned up" before putting pen to paper.

Hollywood, where not only Fitzgerald and Faulkner but a host of other established authors were lured to write scripts, had emerged as the dominant cultural power in America during the 1920s and '30s. As such, its influence over people's perception of alcohol was all-important. Since the movies had come of age during Prohibition, they might have been expected either to damn liquor or be altogether dry of it. Celluloid had been considered the ally of temperance in its infancy. No fewer than three film versions of *Ten Nights in a Bar-Room* had been made by the time the saloons closed their doors forever, and other box office hits such as *The Saloon Keeper's Nightmare* and *Distilled Spirits* helped create a subgenre of temperance movies. Such high-minded entertainments portrayed alcohol as a menace that wrecked lives. Films were also considered protemperance because they offered Americans a counter-attraction to the saloon. The country had twenty-one thousand picture houses by 1916, and these were family places, whose sober audiences sat still in silence for the show. However, moviemakers quickly found that cinemagoers responded positively to comic, and even sympathetic, images of drunkards. Charlie Chaplin broke into movies on the strength of his stage portrayal of an inebriate, which he repeated for the cameras in *His Favorite Pastime* (1914), *A Night Out* (1915), and *One A.M. (1916)*. The circus clown was reborn as a drunkard on the screen.

As the twenties progressed, filmmakers pandered to their audiences with movies showing the excitement, glamour, immoral behavior, and heavy drinking at the pinnacle of American society. *Alimony* (1925), for example, offered moviegoers "brilliant men, beautiful jazz babies, champagne baths, midnight revels, petting parties in the purple dawn, all ending in one terrific smashing climax that makes you gasp." The drys complained and threatened legislation to curtail the representation of drinking in a positive light; in response Hollywood adopted self-censorship (in 1926) in the form of the Hays restrictions, which forbade the depiction of "drinking scenes, manufacture or sale of liquor, or undue effects of liquor which are not a necessary part of the story or an essential element in the building up of the plot." Some studios held the line—drinkers turned their backs on the camera before taking a cocktail—but others decided drink was a necessary part of most stories, whether it was shown as the devil in a keg of bootleg whiskey, or heaven in a cocktail glass. It appeared in the former role in the first all-talking movie, *Lights of New York* (1928), which depicted Gotham as a blot on American values, overrun with speakeasies and murderous gangsters. Its two provincial heroes who get sucked into this black hole of vice are advised by a streetwise cop at the end to "get on the first train to the mountains an' the flowers an' the trees, an' leave the roarin' parties of the city to roar on without ye."

However, the burden of relevance was reinterpreted in subsequent flicks, which did not center their plots on drinking per se. Hollywood decided it simply was not possible to make contemporary dramas featuring men and women who didn't booze. "Lunch is poured," announces a title card in the opening scenes of *Our Modern Maidens* (1929), whose titular virgins proceed to drink, dance, and seduce their way through the film with deranged abandon. The movie was well-received by the critics, one of whom described it as "this vivid picture of ultramodern youth." Thereafter, realism triumphed over self-censorship. Actors and actresses were shown drinking and enjoying doing so, especially if they were heroes or heroines. Villains, in contrast, drank water or nothing. By 1930, when the fifth celluloid version of *Ten Nights in a Bar-Room* hit the screens in New York, its dry sentiments were dismissed by critics as archaic and ridiculous, although "those who come to laugh will probably stay to laugh."

The movies had a huge influence over America. According to a 1932 report commissioned by President Hoover, "for the vast audience the pictures and 'filmland' have tremendous vitality. Pictures and actors are regarded with a seriousness that is likely to escape the casual observer who employs formal criteria of judgment. Editors of popular motion picture magazines are deluged with letters from motion picture patrons, unburdening themselves of an infinite variety of feelings and attitudes, deeply personal, which focus around the lives and activities of those inhabiting the screen world. . . . These [letters] are filled with self-revelations which indicate, sometimes deliberately, more often unconsciously, the influence of the screen upon manners, dress, codes, and matters of romance." Filmland was also an influence over people's attitudes to alcohol. Indeed, shortly after the repeal of constitutional Prohibition via the Twentieth Amendment, a director of MGM stated his belief that "it was the motion picture, showing that in spite of prohibition liquor was an immense factor in American life, that had a great deal to do with changing sentiment on the question."

While drinking on the silver screen helped sway public opinion in favor of the repeal of Prohibition, the actual termination of the noble experiment was the work of former groups of drys who turned against the monster they had created. Business was the first to rebel against the Eighteenth Amendment, followed by American women, and, finally, organized labor. The defection of industry to the wet cause came as a shock to the drys: Industrialists had been among their most ardent supporters, and the concept that drinking and operating machines did not mix had been vital to their case: In the words of Henry Ford, "We must give up drink or industrialism." However, in 1928 the Du Ponts, hitherto staunch Prohibitionists, assumed leadership of the Association Against the Prohibition Amendment (AAPA). Their stated reason for this volte-face was to preserve the freedoms guaranteed by the Constitution; their tacit motivation was a desire to reduce their tax bills by restoring liquor revenues. They were joined by senior management from other large businesses, including Western Union and Standard Oil. By the end of the year the AAPA had among its members 103 directors serving "on the boards of businesses with two million employees and assets of forty billion dollars." This development occurred at a time of weakness for the drys. Wayne Wheeler had died of a heart attack in the same year, and his replacement, Bishop Cannon, lacked the political clout of the pioneer of pressure politics.

However, when American women turned against Prohibition,

through the formation (in 1929) of the Women's Organization for National Prohibition Reform (WONPR), which was headed by a cast of New York socialites, the drys rallied on the moral high ground and attacked the traitors to their cause. The *American Independent,* a dry rag, was of the opinion that "these wet women, though rich most of them are, are no more than the scum of the earth, parading around in skirts, and possibly late at night flirting with other women's husbands at drunken and fashionable resorts." However, by 1932 the WONPR had over a million members, and the drys had lost their moral authority: Bishop Cannon had been uncovered as a stock market speculator, a black market profiteer during World War I, a gambler, and an adulterer who had kept his mistress on diocesan funds.

Unlike its women and its industrialists, America's workers had never been part of the Prohibition camp. In 1922, the American Federation of Labor passed a resolution supporting modification of the Volstead Act to permit beer and light wines; the same resolution was passed every subsequent year. Prohibition was perceived as discriminatory against urban and factory workers, who had drunk beer in saloons rather than cocktails and so had suffered more than the rich, whose tastes in drinks were better catered to by bootleggers. The workers not only had to endure thirst but also violence as a result of Prohibition. Organized crime, flush with money from selling alcohol, moved into the strikebreaking business. Union leaders were murdered and workforces cowed by gangsters hired by unscrupulous industrialists. This unintended consequence of the great moral experiment sickened many Americans, as did the never-ending casualty register caused by toxic bootleg.

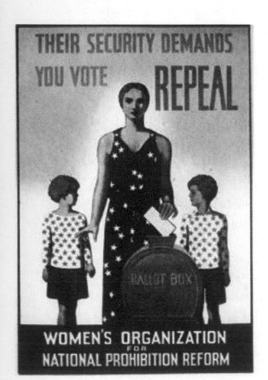

In 1930, America suffered the worst outbreak of mass poisoning it had yet experienced, which crippled perhaps fifty thousand people for life. The culprit was a patent medicine, Jamaican ginger extract, known colloquially as *jake,* which was available without prescription from pharmacists as a remedy for coughs. Jake was up to eighty-five percent alcohol. It was legal under the medicinal alcohol exemption of the Volstead Act, although federal law required that such "tonics" contain at least five percent solids after an evaporation test, that they be unpalatable, and that they be packaged in small containers to dissuade people from buying them by the pint. However, the criminals who moved into the market for tonics found such limitations irksome. They added plasticizer chemicals from the photographic industry to their product, which enabled them to cheat federal tests and to sell what were in essence bottled shots at drugstores up and down the country. The chemicals, however, were highly toxic: Contaminated Jake permanently damaged its victims' central nervous systems. Its usual symptoms were a loss of control of the muscles in the feet, forcing those afflicted by it to walk on their ankles until the ligaments had been ripped to shreds, and thereafter to crawl. This condition was known as jake leg, or jake foot. Jake also made men blind and impotent. As the outbreak occurred in the days before class action suits, there are no precise figures for how many people were poisoned. The greatest number of victims were in the southern and southwestern states, and many of them were African Americans. The progress of jake leg was recorded in blues songs such as "Jake Leg Blues" by Willie Loften & the Mississippi Sheiks. Although the source of the contamination was traced, and one of the bootleggers responsible for such misery sentenced to two years in prison, the outbreak helped to turn small-town America against Prohibition.

The failings of the Volstead Act were brought to the attention of the federal government by the Wickersham Commission, which concluded its two-year scrutiny of Prohibition and reported its findings on January 7, 1931. Although it recommended that America continue to be dry, albeit with more diligent enforcement, the body of evidence in its report showed that Prohibition was a failure. In the opinion of the Wickersham Commission, "The Eighteenth Amendment and the National Prohibition Act" had come into existence "at the time best suited for their adoption and at the worst time for their enforcement." It was, in essence, oppressive wartime legislation introduced after peace had been declared, and as such had been resented from the start.

Thereafter, matters went from bad to worse. The United States had changed so much since 1920. Automobiles, airplanes, cinema, and radio had connected rural and urban America, and metropolitan values had spread at the expense of rustic fanaticism. The commission noted the appearance of "new standards of independence and individual self-assertion, changed ideas as to conduct generally, and [a] greater emphasis on freedom and the quest for excitement since the war." Such new standards had influenced people's perception of alcohol: "It is safe to say that a significant change has taken place in the social attitude toward drinking. This may be seen in the views and conduct of social leaders, business and professional men in the average community. It may be seen in the tolerance of conduct at social gatherings which would not have been possible a generation ago. It is reflected in a different way of regarding drunken youth, in a change in the class of excessive drinkers, and in the increased use of distilled liquor in places and connections where formerly it was banned." As a result of all these changes, it was evident to the commission that, "taking the country as a whole, people . . . are drinking in large numbers in quite frank disregard of the declared policy of the National Prohibition Act."

After picturing Prohibition as a hated anachronism, which was held in contempt by Americans of either sex and every age, the Wickersham report drew attention to its discriminatory nature, so alien to the principles of America. It noted that it had been "easier to shut up the open drinking places and stop the sale of beer, which was drunk chiefly by working men, than to prevent the wealthy from having and using liquor in their homes and in their clubs. . . . Thus the law may be made to appear as aimed at and enforced against the insignificant while the wealthy enjoy immunity. This feeling is reinforced when it is seen that the wealthy are generally able to procure pure liquors, where those with less means may run the risk of poisoning through the working over of denatured alcohol or, at best, must put up with cheap, crude, and even deleterious products."

Moreover, popular hatred of Prohibition had been inflamed by the oppressive manner in which it had been enforced: Homes had been searched, telephones tapped, innocents murdered by Prohibition agents.

Americans were disgusted with the "informers, snoopers, and under-cover men unavoidably made use of if a universal total abstinence is to be brought about by law," and were furious at the "inequalities of pen-alties, even in adjoining districts in the same locality." There was also the little matter of corruption, evidence of which was hard to ignore: "It is sufficient to refer to the reported decisions of the courts during the past decade in all parts of the country, which reveal a succession of prosecutions for conspiracies, sometimes involving the police, pros-ecuting, and administrative organizations of whole communities . . . to the revelations as to police corruption in every type of municipality, large and small, throughout the decade . . . to the evidence of connec-tion between corrupt local politics and gangs and the organized un-lawful liquor traffic, and of systematic collection of tribute from that traffic for corrupt political purposes." Such ubiquitous graft had clogged up the courts at the state and federal level, resulting in real damage to the efficiency and integrity of the administration of justice in the United States.

The Wickersham report made sobering reading for the shrink-ing number of dry Americans. It concluded that Prohibition would only succeed if it was enforced by an expensive army of trained agents, assisted by the cooperation and blessings of the general pub-lic. And as the report had pointed out, the likelihood of the latter helping the cause in either deed or thought was slim. However, sin-cere efforts were made to carry out the commission's recommenda-tions. The federal courts went into overdrive to prosecute bootleggers and owners of speakeasies. The number of convictions for liquor of-fences, which had averaged about 35,000 per annum during the Roar-ing Twenties soared to 61,383 in 1932. Jail sentences rocketed from around 12,000 to 44,668. This last flurry of prosecutions proved to be the dying convulsions of Prohibition. By the end of 1932, America had sunk into the Great Depression. A quarter of the workforce was unemployed, industrial production had fallen by more than half, and two million people were homeless. In this changed climate, it was useless to persist in enforcing an expensive and unpopular law, when the country might plug the gaping hole in its revenues with taxes on drinking.

President Hoover himself acknowledged "the futility of the whole business," and repeal was a central issue in the election of 1932. The

Democratic Party adopted it as a plank of its platform, and when its candidate, Franklin Delano Roosevelt, declared, "I pledge you, I pledge myself, to a new deal for the American people," the new deal included the termination of Prohibition. Hoover, in contrast, wobbled on the issue. New Yorkers joked that the new bridge from Fort Tryon to the Palisades should be named after him, "since it was wet below and dry on top and straddled the river with a foot on either side." The Republicans eventually settled for a moist compromise—resubmission of the Eighteenth Amendment to the states, with the caveat that whatever the states decided, the saloon would remain banned. Roosevelt won by a landslide.

On December 6, 1932, Senator John J. Blaine of Wisconsin drafted a Twenty-first Amendment, to be submitted to the states, which would nullify the Eighteenth. It was quickly adopted by both houses and sent to state governors in February 1933. Each state was to hold a referendum on the matter and a three-quarters majority of states was required for ratification. The process was expected to be slow, and as an interim measure, Congress sought to modify the Volstead Act, via the Cullen Bill, to permit the sale of beer with an ABV of 3.2 percent. Its aims were made clear by Congressman La Guardia: It was before the House "first, by reason of the great need of additional revenue; second, owing to the complete failure of prohibition enforcement; third, by reason of the changed attitude of the American public." The bill provided for a federal tax of five dollars per barrel of beer and became law on April 7, 1933. The surviving breweries turned off their de-alcoholizing units in preparation, Anheuser-Busch arranged a floodlit ceremony, attended by thirty thousand people, for 12:00 P.M. on the sixth of April, and *The New York Times* carried the headline BEER FLOWS IN NINETEEN STATES AT MIDNIGHT.

Drinkers wanting something stronger did not have long to wait: The Twenty-first Amendment to the Constitution of the United States was ratified with the same alacrity as had been the Eighteenth. By December 1933, thirty-five states had consented, with Utah standing in the wings, determined to be remembered as the thirty-sixth to do so: "No other state shall take away this glory from Utah." At 5:32 P.M. on December 5, Utah cast its ballot. At 7:00 P.M. President Roosevelt signed the proclamation that banged a stake through the heart of Prohibition. The death of the monster was generally quietly received. Although New Orleans greeted it with a twenty-minute cannonade, most places and people kept their heads. H. L. Mencken, the Sage of Baltimore, celebrated with a glass of water and the comment that it was "my first in thirteen years." Prohibition had lasted thirteen years, ten months, and eighteen days, fifty-odd days less than the fourteen years' supply of wine laid down by the Yale Club back in 1920.

30 CRIME AND PUNISHMENT

In the same year that America cut back on state intervention in the personal habits of its citizens, Germany opted to travel in the opposite direction. Its new chancellor, Adolf Hitler, had a vision of greatness for his country, based on the sacrifice of individual rights to what he perceived to be the common good. Hitler had spent most of his adult life dry. He had sworn to live sober after getting drunk for the first time in 1905, to celebrate passing an exam, and waking up the next morning in a ditch with a hole in his memory. He did not, however, attempt to enforce his preferences in the matter of drinking upon Germany, for it would have been impossible to remove beer from the Teutonic ideal, based on racial purity and total devotion to his wishes, which he aimed to create. Indeed, he exploited the historic importance of beer to the national psyche by staging his first attempt at power in the Bürgerbräukeller—a Munich brew cellar. The location was chosen not only on account of its size—it accommodated several thousand drinkers—but also for its patriotic decor, which Hitler believed would make his audience receptive to his strident brand of nationalism. The putsch failed, and Hitler spent some months in prison, where he resolved to achieve power through legal means. His philosophy began to find favor with Germans in the late 1920s, principally for economic reasons. The country had yet to recover from the onerous restitution provisions of the Treaty of Versailles that had ended World War I, and when the Great Depression struck, Hitler's *Nazi* Party, with its declared aim to restore Germany to its former eminence, attracted increasing support. By 1932 the Nazis were the largest party in the Reichstag.

A propaganda picture-book, intended to endear Hitler to his countrymen, was published in the same year and made a virtue of his abstemious habits: "It is almost unknown that Hitler does not drink alcohol or smoke, or that he is a vegetarian. Without insisting that anyone follow his example, even in his closest circle, he holds like iron to his self-established principles." There were pragmatic reasons, other than cultural, for not insisting that the rest of the nation also renounce alcohol, for the manufacture of beer, schnapps, and wine made an important contribution to the German economy. In 1933, the drinks industry employed over a hundred thousand workers, representing 2.2 percent of the entire German workforce, and spending on alcohol accounted for 9 percent of the country's national income in the same year. Interestingly, Hitler's holier-than-thou approach had enormous appeal. It was as if his self-denial was a sacrifice made on behalf of all Germans—while they did their best to drown their sorrows, the little Austrian was dedicating every waking hour to the welfare of the nation.

In 1933, Hitler assumed totalitarian powers and set to fashioning his new Reich in accordance with his ideals. His chosen tools were *gleichschaltung* ("synchronizing"), eugenics, and militarism. The *gleichschaltung* policy involved the elimination of non-Nazi organizations, including trade unions and other political parties, and the institution of various Nazi youth and cultural programs in their stead. The eugenics program focused on sterilization. Hitler had declared in his autobiography, *Mein Kampf,* that "whoever is not bodily and spiritually healthy and worthy, shall not have the right to pass on the suffering in the body of his children." Alcoholics were considered to belong to this caste of undesirables and were included as a category within the Law for the Prevention of Hereditarily Diseased Offspring, which decreed "whoever suffers from severe alcoholism can be sterilized." An initial quota of 10,000 alcoholics, out of a estimated total of 410,000 "defectives," was set. The sterilization program did not achieve its targets—it was supplanted by genocide—but several thousand irredeemable drunks were nonetheless neutered. Hamburg was the most dangerous place for hard drinkers to live: "By 1935, 561 (or 41 percent) out of the 1,364 biologically defective persons who had been sterilized were severe alcoholics."

Undesirable citizens who did not quite merit sterilization were sent to concentration camps. These were managed by Heinrich Himmler, dry Obergruppenführer of the SS, and commenced operations in March 1933. Here Jews, gypsies, Mormons, homosexuals, trade unionists, and avid drinkers could be detained indefinitely, for no cause. Each group of deviants was labeled with a colored triangle. Alcoholics wore a black one. They formed a small minority of inmates, for as Hitler consolidated his power over Germany his propagandists succeeded in attaching a mild stigma to drinking. Booze was painted as a threat to education—a poison that might impede the training of young Germans. "The Educational Principles of the New Germany," published in a Nazi women's glossy (1937), advocated abstinence for the warriors in waiting: "The idea of the healthy and strong German should not be mere empty talk. Parents can help here. They will train our youth in simplicity and cleanliness. They will train them, even when they are older, not to waste their spare time by dubious or even harmful activities such as card playing, drinking alcohol, and bad music, but rather to prepare their bodies for their future tasks."

The future tasks the article had in mind were martial. In 1938 Hitler forced Austria into unification with Germany and annexed parts of Czechoslovakia. *Time* magazine made him man of the year. In 1939 he followed up by occupying Prague and invading Poland, an ally of both Britain and France, thus precipitating World War II. As France prepared for war, considerable attention was paid to ensuring that its soldiers would receive the all-important wine or *pinard* ration. By 1939 its reputation as a military beverage had been inflated to heroic proportions. Pinard, it was believed, had saved France in the last war, and a regular supply of wine would be vital to national survival in the forthcoming conflict. A lobbying organization was established to promote this notion, and it staged a gala in November 1939, attended by Parisian high society and various government ministers, at which soldiers were served warm and aromatic pinard from vats by models dressed in French blue. In 1940, only weeks before the fighting commenced, the French Chamber of Deputies was advised that "wine, the pride of France, is a symbol of strength; it is associated with warlike virtues," and it was predicted that the beer-drinking Germans would have no chance against the poilus. The deputies took heed and earmarked transport to ensure enough wine got to where it was needed. Over a third of all railroad cars designed to carry liquid in bulk were requisitioned for the carriage of pinard, much of which, in the event, was abandoned to the Germans shortly after its arrival at the front.

France folded against the Nazi blitzkrieg within two months. In the scramble for excuses, the wine ration was singled out for special abuse. France had failed because its soldiers had been drunk at critical moments. Under the terms of its armistice, the country was divided into occupied and unoccupied zones. The Germans took back the provinces of Alsace and Lorraine outright and occupied north and northwestern France and its entire Atlantic coast. The remaining 40 percent of the country was left under the *Vichy* regime of Marshal Philippe Pétain. Vichy France moved quickly against drinking. Pétain, who had written eulogies to pinard prior to the war, now blamed alcoholism for "undermining the will of the army." In August 1940 the sale of booze was prohibited "in cafés and restaurants on Tuesdays, Thursdays, and Saturdays." The same laws also introduced, for the first time in French history, a minimum drinking age: No one under fourteen was permitted to consume alcohol.

More repressive legislation followed. In September 1941 drinking places were divided into five categories, ranging from those that sold no alcohol, through cafés offering beer and wine, to full-service bars. No new examples of this last category could be opened at all, and severe quotas were placed on all establishments serving drinks. In 1943 more legislation was introduced to aid enforcement: Prefects could close a café for up to three months and the secretary of the interior for up to a year "to preserve order and health." In consequence of these measures, the number of drinking places in Vichy France fell by a third between 1940 and the end of the war.

While the Vichy regime was denying wine to its own countrymen, the Germans who occupied France were helping themselves to it. They associated drinking with victory, rather than defeat, and shortly after the armistice Nazi agents were appointed for the Burgundy, Bordeaux, and Champagne regions. Their duties were to source fine wines for the German administration and its armed forces. Between them they managed to extract an average of nearly nine hundred thousand bottles a day for the duration of the occupation. Producers in each of the regions were obliged to sell their vintages to them at debased rates of exchange. Demand was vast, especially for champagne. More than two million bottles of it had been looted in the first fortnight of the occupation alone–a notable exception to the German policy of behaving well in occupied France. The agent selected for the Champagne region, Otto Klaebisch, was expected to source a further half-million bottles per week.

Resistance, overt and covert, was immediate. Faced with the choice of selling their stocks of vintage champagne to the Germans, or relabeling the 1939, which was almost undrinkable, as "Special Cuvée for the Wehrmacht" they chose the latter course. François Taittinger, of the eponymous producer, was imprisoned for selling champagne so bad it tasted like "fizzy ditch water" to the Reich. He did not help his case by riposting, "Who cares? It's not as if it's going to be drunk by people who know anything about champagne!" when accused of the crime. His spirit was typical of the district. Since champagne was used to celebrate fresh Nazi victories, the destination to which it was shipped served as a clue as to where they would strike next. The French resistance passed this information on to British intelligence, who were warned of the impending North African campaign when they received the news in late 1941 that thousands of cases of fizz had been requisitioned for "a very hot country."

A similar spirit of defiance prevailed in Bordeaux and Burgundy. Whenever possible, trash wine was substituted for good, or barrels were drained of their vintages and filled with water before they were sent to Germany. Producers hid their best wine—in caves, under woodpiles, in walled-up cellars. They also sheltered Jews, a number of whom had owned vineyards in Bordeaux. Nazi policies toward Jews were applied in France: Their property was confiscated, or *Aryanized,* and they themselves were deported to concentration camps. The Vichy regime itself "Aryanized" several important Jewish-owned estates, notably those of Baron Philippe de Rothschild, proprietor of Château Lafitte and Château Mouton Rothschild, although this step was taken to keep them under nominally French control.

The years 1939–41 were bad vintages in most French regions on account of the weather. Moreover, yields were low, so that in order to maintain their quotas producers were forced to sell their reserves. Delicacies such as Pol Roger '28 were shipped to Germany, from whence they were dispersed to combat zones and private cellars. The redistribution of French wine was managed by Herman Goering, who was all for wringing France dry of its last drop of "bottled sunshine": "In the old days, the rule was plunder. Now, outward forms have become more humane. Nevertheless, I intend to plunder, and plunder copiously." He accumulated more than ten thousand bottles of prime French vintages (some of which was "ditchwater" relabeled) for his own cellar. The rest was directed to fellow officers in the Luftwaffe, the Werhmacht, and the *Shutzstaffel,* or SS.

The SS were the executors of the Holocaust. In late 1941, the Nazis adopted a program of genocide against Jews and other *untermenschen* ("subhumans"): "The Führer has ordered that the Jewish question be solved once and for all and that we, the SS, are to implement that order." Initially, massacres were carried out with firearms. Women, children, and those too old to be used for slave labor were machine-gunned in batches and buried in communal graves. The work, however, sickened even the Aryan volunteers detailed to carry out the task. According to a Nazi report, "Many members of the Einsatzkommandos [SS death squads], unable to endure wading through blood any longer, had committed suicide. Some had even gone mad. Most of the members of these kommandos had to rely on alcohol when carrying out their horrible work."

The death squads were not the only wing of the SS to try to drown their humanity with drink. A portion of the vintages commandeered from France was supplied to the officials of concentration camps, where the process of exterminating *untermenschen* was expedited by the use of gas chambers. The selection of victims for the chambers was carried out by qualified doctors, who also supervised their operation and in some cases provided death certificates. The inconsistency of such activities with the Hippocratic oath need not be elaborated. According to their own accounts, doctors had to drink heavily in order to dull their feelings: "The selections [of people to be gassed] were mostly an ordeal. Namely to stand all night. And it wasn't just standing all night–but the next day was completely ruined because one got drunk every time.... A certain number of bottles were provided for each section and everybody drank and toasted the others.... One could not stay out of it." Auschwitz doctors also drank deep when off duty. The officers' club was stocked with champagne and cognac, and they used these to acclimatize newcomers to the total absence of ethics. One old hand recalled the process: After a few glasses, an Auschwitz debutante would ask, "How can these things be done here?" Then there was something like a general answer ... which clarified everything. "What is better for him [the prisoner]–whether he croaks in shit or goes to heaven in [a cloud of] gas?"

❖ ❖ ❖

Great Britain was the last European bastion against the Nazis. Throughout 1940 and 1941 it was attacked by waves of German bombers whose aim was to kill and cow as many civilians as possible, as much as to destroy military targets or attain the air superiority deemed necessary for an invasion. Shipping convoys carrying essential supplies to Britain were likewise bombed from the air, and torpedoed by German submarines, resulting in the imposition of rationing for the entire nation. As had been the case in World War I, austerity measures were introduced to preserve grain for food instead of brewing. This time, however, such measures recognized that alcohol could help morale on the home front. This more relaxed attitude toward drink was embodied in the figure of Sir Winston Churchill, who explained his philosophy thus: "My rule of life prescribe[s] as an absolutely sacred rite smoking cigars and also the drinking of alcohol before, after, and if need be during all meals and in the intervals between them." Churchill usually began each day with a glass of champagne,[66] or a weak whisky and water. He drank wine with his lunch and dinner, and more whisky and water in between times. Despite the steady intake, he was seldom intoxicated, indeed, expressed his abhorrence for the state: "My father taught me to have the utmost contempt for people who get drunk."

Churchillian attitudes to alcohol permeated government. Booze was considered a necessity rather than a luxury. In May 1940, the minister for food set out the official position on wartime drinking, with regard to the nation's favorite beverage: "It is the business of the government not only to maintain the life but the morale of the country. If we are to keep up anything like approaching normal life, beer should continue to be in supply even though it may be beer of a rather weaker variety than the connoisseurs would like." The resulting brews were indeed feeble–Victorians would have hesitated to offer them to their children. They were, on average, a full 30 percent weaker than the typical nineteenth-century pint and, in the last year of the war, had an average OG of only 1034.5. They were also expensive. Beer duty more than doubled, raising the price of a pint from five pence prewar to a

---

[66] His favorite, which he drank by the pint, was Pol Roger '28.

shilling at its conclusion. Supplies of this weak and costly substance were reduced by enemy action: In London alone, breweries receiving direct hits from German airplanes included Barclay Perkins, Taylor Walker, Whitbread, Watneys, Youngs, Fullers, Charringtons, Guinness, and Ind Coope. Pubs also suffered: By 1943 thirteen hundred throughout the country had been obliterated by enemy action.

Austerity measures were also imposed on whisky makers in Scotland, restricting the amount of beverage alcohol they could produce. The larger distilleries kept going by producing industrial alcohol for propellants and explosives. Many of the small malt stills, however, were forced to close their doors. Although much of Scotland was spared the blitz, on September 29, 1940, one of the few Nazi bombs to fall on Edinburgh hit the warehouse of the Caledonian Distillery, destroying 1.2 million gallons of whisky. The following year distilleries were bombed in Glasgow and Greenock, and during the course of the war a further 4.5 million gallons of scotch in government storage were lost to Nazi air raids. Taxes were hiked on the little whisky available for sale: At the outbreak of war, the duty per gallon had been £3 12s 6d, or £4.12 in modern sterling. By 1943 it had nearly doubled to £7.87.

While the high price of scotch was beyond the pockets of most Britons, it did not deter American servicemen, who had begun to arrive in the United Kingdom from 1942 onward, following Germany's declaration of war against their country. In contrast to the position in the First World War, when Americans in uniform overseas had been expected to stay dry at all times, it was now anticipated that they would tipple when off duty, and to this end they were issued with a brief guide to British etiquette, which included advice on where and what to drink with their hosts. The where was in pubs: "A pub, or public house, is what we call a bar or tavern." The what was whisky, which was admitted to be rare, or beer. The guide elaborated on the latter fluid, probably to forestall the inevitable disappointment that its readers would experience after their first sip of "bitter," and also cautioned them not to drink too much, for although it was "now below peacetime strength, [it] can still make a man's tongue wag at both ends."

The new relaxed attitude toward alcohol among the American high command was nowhere better demonstrated than in the material broadcast on official radio for the entertainment of the troops. The centerpiece of one wartime Christmas transmission was a "Temperance Lecture" delivered by W. C. Fields. Fields had made his reputation playing drunks in the movies and was famed for his bon mots on the subject of intoxication. His lecture, which would have been blasphemy to the ears of an ASL supporter, sketched a few comic incidents of his failure to stay dry and concluded, "Now, don't say you can't swear off drinking; it's easy. I've done it a thousand times." Clearly, it was now considered safe to represent tippling in a positive light to the troops.

The entry of America into the war in Europe changed the course of the conflict. Superiority was attained in the air and at sea. Weapons and other materiel were shipped in huge quantities to Russia, which had joined the Allies against the Nazis in 1942, and whose troops were pressing in on Germany from the east. In 1944, American, Canadian, New Zealand, and British troops were gathered on the south coast of England to invade France. The British were prepped for their encounter with Gallic culture through the issue of a guidebook, *Instructions to British Servicemen in France,* which warned its readers not to expect to be drowned in celebratory drinks once they had crossed the Channel: "The Germans have ... drunk the wine or distilled it into engine fuel. So there are only empty barrels to roll." Moreover, "the idea of the French living in a glorious orgy of 'wine, women, and song' never was true, even before the war. The French drink wine as we drink beer. It is the national drink and a very good drink, but there was far less drunkenness in peacetime France than in peacetime England." After explaining that wine would be rare and was different, the instructions, at the top of its list of don'ts, warned the 1944 generation of Tommies against knocking back too much of it: "Don't drink yourself silly. If you get the chance to drink wine, learn to 'take it.'"

As the Allies liberated France during the course of 1944, they received a truly Gallic welcome. Bottles and barrels of alcohol hidden from the Germans were unearthed and offered around. Bars closed by the Nazis or the quisling Vichy regime served drinks once again, often after a symbolic liberation. Ernest Hemingway, over as a war correspondent, performed the ceremony at Jimmy's American Bar in Paris. The Allies also captured German stockpiles of looted drink, some of which was carried back to Britain, to the chagrin of its customs officials. Duties on wines, beers, and spirits made an important contribution to the war effort. The Americans were perceived to be the worst offenders, not least of all because their camps were beyond the jurisdiction of British bureaucracy. After a thousand bottles of champagne were discovered in a U.S. airfield in Essex, the British Secret Service was detailed to investigate. Colonel J. H. Adam reported that "American officers are bringing wines and perfumes into this country without any Customs formality" and warned, "It will clearly not be long before British officers, realizing the position, will hand such articles to an American officer on the 'plane' and ask him to take them to London." How could Britain expect to repay its lend-lease debts if its officers started to behave like American airmen?

As the Allies approached the borders of the Third Reich, riding high on a wave of liberated alcohol, Germany's civilians were plunged into drought. The output of domestic breweries had dried up under the pressure of Allied carpet bombing, and for lack of raw ingredients. The strength of beer had dropped precipitously, from a prewar average OG of 1048 for strong beer, to 1030 in 1942, to 1012 in 1943, or below the strength where its alcoholic content can generate intoxication. Brewing ceased altogether in 1944. German wine production was similarly affected. In 1942 the Hitler Youth had dug out all the hybrid vines in Alsace, to be replaced with Aryan strains. The luxury of time they had anticipated—a thousand-year Reich—was over three years afterward—too soon for the replacements to come into service. Domestic supplies of drink were further reduced to feed the Nazi war machine. Distilled alcohol was needed for munitions and as fuel, notably for the V2-rocket bombs. The small quantity of looted or stockpiled booze remaining was diverted to the armed forces and the Nazi elite.

Indeed, the only parts of Germany where alcohol was freely available were those under Russian control. After their victory at Stalingrad in 1942, the Soviet armies had pushed the Nazis out of Russia and forced them back into their own territory. The dry policies of the Bolsheviks were a thing of the past: From 1942 onward, Russian soldiers were provided with a vodka ration of a hundred grams per man per day. It was issued in bottles and shared out among sections. The ration was intended to improve morale and to be a source of food: Prewar Soviet research into the nutritional benefits of alcohol had concluded that a small quantity gave the drinker a shot of energy and might therefore boost the performance of the fighting soldier. In the event, however, an allowance of vodka resulted in a culture of drunkenness among Red Army troops, who supplemented their rations with whatever came to hand, including industrial solvents and antifreeze. Large numbers were killed or incapacitated by such poisons, and intoxication was also responsible for numerous accidental shootings. By the time the Soviet armies entered Germany in 1945, their discipline had been visibly compromised by drinking. According to an allied observer attached to the Soviets, "Russians are absolutely crazy about vodka and all alcoholic drinks. They rape women, drink themselves into unconsciousness, and set houses on fire."

This culture was prevalent among officers as well as common soldiers. Intelligence reports on the performance of officers in the field employed the euphemism "went off to have a rest" to signify that their subjects had been blind drunk. There was plenty of temptation lying around, for the retreating Germans had left alcohol stocks intact, in the belief that a drunken army could not fight. This was a grave error: The Russians had so great an advantage in men, tanks, artillery, and aircraft that they could tolerate a degree of intoxication in the ranks, and the German civilian population, especially its women, suffered at the hands of drunken and vengeful Russians. Over two million were raped during the Soviet advance through Germany to Berlin.

The scene in the capital of the Reich, in the last weeks before its fall, as the Russians fought from street to street toward its center, blasting buildings into rubble with their tanks and heavy artillery, was apocalyptic. In the Nazi bunkers, a kind of *danse macabre* occurred. The champagne flowed, and Nazi girls, determined to lose their virginity before a Russian stole it, engaged in drunken fornication with state officials and strangers. Hitler married his mistress, Eva Braun, celebrated the event with a champagne breakfast, then the couple shot themselves. Their bodies were laid in a shell crater and incinerated. Outside the bunkers, among the rubble and ruined houses, whose atmosphere was thick with dust and suffused with the stench of dead bodies, the Russian soldiers drank captured alcohol as if the world were about to end and hunted through the ruins for German soldiers and women. A snapshot of the chaos is provided by a letter written by Vladimir Borisovich Pereverzev, a Soviet front-line soldier, or *frontski*, in Berlin:

> Hello my nearest and dearest ones. So far I am alive and healthy, only I am slightly drunk the whole time. But this is necessary to keep up your courage. A reasonable ration of three star cognac will

do no harm.... You write that part of the kitchen ceiling collapsed, but that's nothing! A six-story building collapsed on us and we had to dig our boys out. This is how we beat the Germans.

Pereverzev was dead before his letter reached his nearest and dearest.

The war in Europe ended on May 8, 1945. The Russians had discovered Hitler's remains and certified them through his dental records a few days previously. His jaws were stored in a little red satin-lined box, "the sort used for cheap jewelry," and attended, in their container, Russian vodka-fests celebrating the overthrow of fascism. On such occasions a culture of drunkenness united generals and the *frontskis* who served under them, and was condoned at the highest level. When the British foreign minister, Anthony Eden, raised his eyebrows at the spectacle of Field Marshal Voroshilov "being carried out feet first from an inter-Allied banquet," Stalin explained that in his opinion, his generals "fought better when they were drunk." The end of the war in the west was commemorated throughout Europe. In Great Britain, it was honored with a public holiday, which was distinguished by its euphoric crowds and mass inebriation. However, after the celebrations were over, and people had turned their thoughts to reconstruction, the prospects appeared bleak.

31   THE BOTTLE

W hile Europeans contemplated their ruined cities, whose breweries, wine cellars, and drinking places had been bombed into
dust, their allies in America enjoyed an increased, rather than a
diminished supply of alcohol. American per capita consumption rose
by nearly 50 percent during World War II, and this rise had the tacit
blessing of the federal government. Unlike 1917, there were no austerity measures to limit brewing, distilling, or the constitutional right to
alcoholic beverages, and the expectation that American troops would
drink off duty while serving overseas reflected this sea change in attitude. Prohibition was remembered as an unpleasant anomaly, and
the sooner that it could be forgotten the better.

The official revival of the love affair between Americans and alcohol was documented in the movies, the plays, and the books of the
1930s and '40s. The initial response to repeal in Hollywood had been
to resurrect the comic drunk of the early years of the silent era. W. C.
Fields, whose Christmas temperance lecture had so amused the
troops, was the king of the genre. A heavy drinker offscreen, Fields
perfected a celluloid alter ego with the same habit, to which were
added misanthropy, misogyny, and a hatred of children and dogs.
The comic aspects of drunkenness were also explored in cartoons,
notably in Walt Disney's *Dumbo* (1941), whose infant elephant hero
drinks, by accident, a bucketful of water laced with moonshine.
Spectacular hallucinations follow. Dumbo starts blowing bubbles,
one of which mutates into a pink elephant, which clones itself via its
trunk, as does its clone, and the trio launch into a jazz arrangement,

perform mitosis, melt and blend, then explode into a golden flower, and so on. There could be no better advertisement for the beneficial effects of alcohol upon the imagination. Booze, literally, teaches Dumbo how to fly.

However, by the middle of the 1940s, celluloid topers were being presented in a tragic as well as a Falstaffian light. Repeal had placed not just drinking but drunkenness out in the open, and the latter could no longer be explained away in the language of temperance as the aberrant behavior of a handful of criminals, sinners, and perverts. It was a phenomenon that America had to face, examine, and, if possible, understand. Hollywood rose to the challenge with *The Lost Weekend*, directed and cowritten by Billy Wilder, which won four Oscars, including best picture and best script, in 1946. *The Lost Weekend* dramatizes the psyche and the motives of a compulsive drinker. Its central character is Don Birnam, a handsome, charming alcoholic with ambitions to become a writer, who claims to have been driven to the bottle by lack of confidence—or the realization that he is bereft of talent. While Don is the ghost of temperance noir, equipped with the usual catalog of clichés—vivid d.t.'s, drastic lapses in coordination, cold sweats, blackouts, and a tendency to petty theft—he is nonetheless a sympathetic character, whose insecurity is a matter for pity.

Changes in the treatment of drinking also occurred in playwriting. The transformation is apparent in the work of Eugene O'Neill, himself a recovered alcoholic, whose late, great dramas—*The Iceman Cometh* (1939), *Long Day's Journey into Night* (1940), and *A Moon for the Misbegotten* (1943)—focus on the horrors rather than the wonders of intoxication. *The Iceman Cometh* mocks the repetitive speech and mental vacuity of habitual drunks; *Long Day's Journey* highlights their sense of guilt and state of denial; and *A Moon for the Misbegotten* argues that they are already as good as dead. Jim Tyrone, hero of this last play, is abandoned by its heroine at the conclusion: Despite his wit, despite his wealth, despite her love, he is lost. "May you have your wish and die in your sleep soon, Jim, darling. May you rest forever in forgiveness and peace," she reflects, as the curtain falls.

O'Neill's representation of alcoholics as soulless shells, automatons who had lost their ability to love, was strong stuff, even by the standards of ASL propaganda. A similar trend was apparent in fiction. The comic or macho drunks who had graced the pages of Ernest Hemingway were replaced by an altogether darker style of inebriate. Instead, however, of showing the collateral damage drinkers could cause, à la *Ten Nights in a Bar-Room,* and using this to imply their black hearts, novelists went inside their characters' heads, sometimes sympathetically, and portrayed the personal suffering that alcoholics endured. *Under the Volcano* (1947) by Malcolm Lowry typifies the change in treatment.

Set in Mexico in 1938, *Under the Volcano* follows the last day in the life of an alcoholic British consul who has been posted to a provincial town, in order to keep him from embarrassing his country. According to Lowry, "The idea I cherished in my heart was to create a pioneer work in its own class and to write at last an authentic drunkard's story." Much of the action is presented through the eyes of the consul, who drinks steadily, if not to say spectacularly, from page to page. Guilt and hopelessness are his principal emotions; like Faust, he feels he has made a pact with the devil and placed himself beyond redemption. In his creator's opinion, "the agonies of the drunkard find a very close parallel in the agonies of the mystic who has abused his powers"; and while the consul puts on a brave face, he is certain he is damned:

> Closing his eyes again, standing there, glass in hand, he thought for
> a minute with a freezing detached almost amused calm of the
> dreadful night inevitably awaiting him whether he drank much
> more or not, his room shaking with daemonic orchestras, the
> snatches of fearful tumultuous sleep, interrupted by voices which
> were really dogs barking, or by his own name being continually
> repeated by imaginary parties arriving, the vicious shouting, the
> strumming, the slamming, the pounding, the battling with insolent
> archfiends, the avalanche breaking down the door, the proddings
> from under the bed, and always, outside, the cries, the wailing, the
> terrible music, the dark's spinets: he returned to the bar.

Lowry himself was an alcoholic who completed his novel in a driftwood shack on the coast of British Columbia, as far away from daily temptation as he could place himself. His addiction to the bottle was typical of the rising generation of authors, who seem to have received Hemingway's advice to Fitzgerald, that "all good writers are drunks," as a mantra. Some took it to extremes, such as Dylan Thomas, Welsh lyrical poet, who killed himself with alcohol in 1953, aged thirty-nine. Just days before he slipped into a fatal coma after a drinking session in the White Horse Tavern in Greenwich Village, he proclaimed, as a matter

of pride, "I've had eighteen straight whiskies. I think this is a record"—
sad words from the man who advocated fighting time until the end.

In the same years that writers were exploring the psychology of heavy
drinking in their lives and in their work, a growing number of Americans were joining a new resistance movement against it: Alcoholics
Anonymous, a voluntary, altruistic organization that traced its origin
to June 10, 1935, the day on which one of its founders took his last
drink. The AA was the brain child of two ex-alcoholics, Bill Wilson, a
Wall Street speculator, and Dr. Bob Smith, a medic from Ohio. It
aimed to help people cure themselves of their longing for drink
through a program of mutual aid. In 1939 it published a manifesto,
Alcoholics Anonymous, known by its devotees as the *Big Book,* which set
out a "spiritual toolkit" with which dipsomaniacs might reform themselves via a twelve-step program. The toolkit, which laid a fundamental emphasis on belief in God, was derived from the teachings of the
Oxford Group, a Christian cult that had flourished in the mid-1930s.

The AA targeted hopeless alcoholics. Unlike the temperance
movement, it made no attempt to brand anyone who drank as a fool
committing a potentially fatal error. Instead, it divided drinkers into
three classes: those who could take it or leave it; those who couldn't
leave it but could take it, albeit at the risk of some damage; and those
who could not take it at all and therefore must leave it. A snapshot of
the third category of individual was provided in the Big Book:

> He is a real Dr. Jekyll and Mr. Hyde. He is seldom mildly intoxi-
> cated. He is always more or less insanely drunk. His disposition
> while drinking resembles his normal nature but little. He may be
> one of the finest fellows in the world. Yet let him drink for a day, and
> he frequently becomes disgustingly, and even dangerously, antiso-
> cial.... He uses his gifts to build up a bright outlook for his family
> and himself and then pulls the structure down on his head by a
> senseless series of sprees.

In the opinion of the AA, such all-or-nothing drinkers were actually
victims, cursed with flawed personalities, which rendered them incapable of resisting alcohol. *"The fact is that most alcoholics, for reasons yet ob-
scure, have lost the power of choice in drink. Our so-called willpower becomes*

practically nonexistent. . . . We are without defense against the first drink." This
no-fault diagnosis, in contrast to the stigma nineteenth-century drys
had attached to drunkards, won the AA many converts; as did the tactic of sending reformed drunks to assist those who still suffered. Whereas
in 1941, the AA had a mere two thousand members, by 1950 it had
nearly ninety thousand, in three thousand separate groups across the
United States. Moreover, chapters had been started in twenty-six foreign countries, and in 1950 the AA held a First International Convention.
Attendance was strongest from the Anglo-Saxon diaspora and Scandi-
navian countries, and almost negligible from the wine-drinking regions
of old Europe.

The progress of Alcoholics Anonymous in America was recognized
in print by *The Saturday Evening Post:* "To anyone who has ever been a
drunk or who has had to endure the alcoholic cruelties of a drunk–and
that would embrace a large portion of the human family–90,000 alcoholics reconverted into working citizens represent a massive dose of pure
gain. In human terms, the achievements of Alcoholics Anonymous stand
out as one of the few encouraging developments of a rather grim and
destructive half century." The magazine also noted that the membership
of the association had become, since its inception, progressively younger
and increasingly feminine. Average age had dropped from forty-seven to
thirty-five, and women comprised 15 percent of total membership, although in New York City a full 30 percent were female. Other such regional variations were apparent across America. While, in accordance
with its name, the AA shielded the identity of its members, groups in
Los Angeles were happy to flaunt their status as recovered drunkards.
They staged mass meetings of up to a thousand ex-inebriates, and wore
gold rings with an AA monogram, and stickpins in their ties, set with
various precious stones whose color announced how long they had been
dry. In New England, in contrast, AA goers treasured their anonymity.

However, certain aspects of the modus operandi of the AA attracted criticism, in particular its insistence on the acknowledgment
of the existence of God as a prelude to sobriety. In the words of the *Big
Book:* "We believe there is no 'middle-of-the-road solution' and that
salvation is not possible without spiritual help. Morals and philosophy
on their own are not enough." The organization itself recognized that
such insistence acted as a deterrent to agnostic and atheist drinkers,
who might otherwise benefit from its aid. It advised members, when
proselytizing, to "stress the spiritual feature freely" and to emphasize

to a potential convert "that *he does not have to agree with your conception of God*. He can choose any conception he likes, provided it makes sense to him. *The main thing is that he be willing to believe in a Power greater than himself and that he live by spiritual principles*." For those unwilling to believe, the AA recommended tough love: Leave them in their misery until they're ready.

The AA's perceived support of the alcoholism-as-disease theory was also controversial. Medical science had made considerable advances since the days of Benjamin Rush, pioneer of the idea, and Mary Hannah Hunt, the WCTU firebrand who had got it onto the school curriculum. Drinking did not fit easily with modern concepts of disease. It made no sense to equate a dry martini to the cholera bacteria either in its nature or effects. Moreover, if alcoholism really was a disease, why didn't every drinker catch it? However, the belief that the AA endorsed the concept, combined with its evident success in curing drunks, led to a vogue for the theory in the press and attracted criticism from more sober observers. While Bill Wilson later clarified the official position of the AA, his clarification was ambiguous enough to please each side in the controversy: "We AAs have never called alcoholism a disease because, technically speaking, it is not a disease entity. For example, there is no such thing as heart disease. Instead there are many separate heart ailments or combinations of them. It is something like that with alcoholism. Therefore, we did not wish to get in wrong with the medical profession by pronouncing alcoholism a disease entity. Hence, we have always called it an illness or a malady—a far safer term for us to use."

Despite such equivocation, the disease theory of alcoholism gained increasing credence in the 1950s. In 1951, the World Health Organization acknowledged alcoholism to be a serious medical problem, and in 1956 the American Medical Association classified it as a treatable sickness. Moreover, the disease theory was accepted as true by a new federal organization, the National Council for Education on Alcohol (NCEA), and adopted as the flagship policy of the Center of Alcohol Studies at Yale University, led by E. M. Jellinek. In 1960, Jellinek published *The Disease Concept of Alcoholism*, which defined the affliction by its symptoms, which included an insatiable thirst and erratic behavior.

A number of treatments were developed to combat the new illness. The first was a pharmacological version of electrotherapy, which hitherto had been a common remedy for drunkenness. A high-voltage charge across the frontal lobes sometimes converted inebriates to abstinence at the flick of a switch. Sadly, such conversions were rare, and hence the appearance of a drug promising the same transformations in behavior was greeted with excitement in the medical profession. The drug was disulfiram, a patented version of which, called Antabuse, was offered to American alcoholics in 1951. Antabuse plus even small amounts of booze generated an instantaneous and violent hangover in the drinker, who could expect to enjoy hot flushes, a throbbing head, copious vomiting, hyperventilation, tachycardia, hypotension, syncope, vertigo, and confusion, all within a few minutes of sneaking a drink. Not only did Antabuse make drinking painful, but it was also on occasions fatal—negative reactions to it included "acute congestive heart failure, unconsciousness, convulsions, and death." Such strong medicine clearly was not suited to every alcoholic, and experiments were made with other drugs, notably LSD.

The treatment of drunks with LSD was pioneered by Dr. Humphry Osmond in Saskatchewan, Canada, in the early 1950s. Osmond, who coined the term *psychedelic* and defined it in a ditty ("To fathom hell or soar angelic, just take a pinch of psychedelic"), tested LSD on schizophrenics before moving on to alcoholics. His patients included Bill Wilson, one of the founders of AA, who was still lapsing fifteen years on, and he claimed a 50 percent success rate overall. Osmond, together with Abram Hoffer, also investigated the potential of nicotinic acid and its amide, aka niacin, as a cure for the disease of alcoholism. Wilson once again volunteered as guinea pig and reported favorably. He reintroduced the name Vitamin B_3 for niacin and recommended it to fellow alcoholics as an antidote to the anxiety, tension, and depression to which they were prone. However, the AA did not endorse his views on either LSD or Vitamin B. If effective pharmacological therapies existed for alcoholism, then what need for a belief in God and the twelve steps? LSD fell further out of favor when nonalcoholics started taking it for fun.

Disease or not, drinking was infecting an increasing number of Americans at the midpoint of the twentieth century. According to federal figures, annual per capita consumption had doubled from a post-Prohibition low of roughly a gallon of pure alcohol in 1934 to 2 gallons in 1950—about the same level as it had been in 1916, when teetotalers were predicting an imminent collapse in the morals and economy of the country.

Beer was America's favorite beverage—in 1950 the average drinker got through 23 gallons each year, supplemented with 1.73 gallons of liquor and 1.27 of wine. The demand for beer was supplied by national brewing companies, who sold uniform products coast to coast. Advances in the chemical processing of water had made it possible to produce homogeneous beer wherever—California Budweiser could be identical to Virginian. Once they had established complete control over their product, the brewers sought to gain market share through national advertising campaigns—in periodicals, on the radio, at the movies, and via the newfangled television. Whereas in 1938 the industry spent six million dollars per annum on advertising, by 1950 it was spending over fifty million. It also became involved in the sponsorship of sporting events. The link between beer drinking and athleticism had been established by Colonel Jacob Ruppert, beer baron and owner of the New York Yankees. Ball games were perfect events at which to promote and to sell beer, and other brewers followed suit.

The trend toward homogeneous national brands was assisted by advances in packaging. The beer can, invented in 1935, took off in the 1950s. It was the ultimate portable and disposable beer delivery system, and perfectly suited to the growing home-consumption market. The trend toward drinking at home was driven by changing leisure patterns: The neighborhood saloons that had dominated recreation pre-Prohibition did not return in similar numbers post-repeal, and instead of rushing the growler, beer lovers bought cans by the case in drive-through liquor stores, which they consumed in front of the television. Home drinking was also boosted by the persistence of local prohibition—in 1959 nearly 14.5 million Americans still lived in areas that were still officially dry. They could, however, import with impunity, and liquor stores thrived on the wet borders of such regions.

The ownership of TV sets spread at a lightning pace in the 1950s: In 1952, 15.3 million Americans owned TVs; by 1955, 32 million had been sold; and by 1960, 90 percent of households had them. Television offered wonderful opportunities to drink manufacturers to place an image of their products in the front rooms of American households. This alarming prospect stirred what was left of the temperance movement into action. Between 1947 and 1958 they forced nine congressional committee hearings on their legislative proposals to ban alcohol advertising. However, their influence had so waned that no action resulted. No legislator wished to revive Prohibition. Besides, beverage producers had forestalled the drys with self-regulation. The Distilled Spirits Institute (DSI), the main trade association of American distillers, imposed an advertising code on its members that prohibited radio and television advertising, the depiction of women in print advertising, and the placement of hard-liquor ads in religious publications. Their decision not to advertise on TV was subsequently confirmed by a ban from the National Association of Broadcasters. The brewers, in contrast, allowed themselves to advertise on broadcast mediums and to show women in beer ads. Budweiser was the first U.S. brewer to sponsor a network TV show (the Ken Murray show on CBS in 1951), and others followed suit. They were, however, cautious in the way they presented their product and, in 1954, complied with a House Commerce Committee suggestion by agreeing not to feature anyone actually drinking beer in their ads. This restriction was intended to prevent the brewers from seducing juveniles and natural-born drys with images of actors expressing joy after a mouthful of suds. Temperance may have faded but the paranoia that had given birth to it remained: Humanity, born in sin, needed protecting from its evil nature.

Early TV programs did not feature much drinking and, when they did, tended to represent it in a humorous light. The vaudeville inebriate, rather than the red-eyed home breaker, was the face of alcohol on the small screen. *I Love Lucy,* the most popular program in America, which ran from 1951 to 1957, used intoxication to garner laughs, most memorably so in the "Lucy Does a TV Commercial" episode of May 5, 1952, in which Lucy gets the part of the "Vitameatavegamin girl" to promote an eponymous tonic. As Lucy rehearses the tongue-twisting script and drinks the beverage—which, in the style of traditional American tonic drinks, is highly alcoholic—she gets progressively drunker, until she mangles her lines into comic innuendo:

Well, I'm your vitavitevegivac girl, are you tired run-down listless?
Do you pop out at parties? Are you unpoopular . . . well are you? . . .
the answer to all your problems is in this little ol' bottle. Vitameatavegamin (LOOKS AT BOTTLE) . . . that's it. Vitameatavegamin
contains vitamins, meat, megitables, and vinerals . . . hmm
(HICCUP).

The trend toward tippling outside of bars, saloons, and taverns was also fueled by a rise in underage drinking. After repeal, the age of consent for alcohol had been set at the federal level as twenty-one. Americans could have sex and marry at fourteen, drive a car at sixteen, be called up for military service at eighteen, but could not drink until they were old enough to vote. Not all of them waited. They had unprecedented freedom of movement and spending power. Manufacturers of automobiles and other consumer goods identified and targeted the new teenage market. Its constituents were fond of dressing up and dancing; they also believed learning to smoke and drink to be rites of passage into the adult world they rebelled against yet imitated. The teen world was explored by Hollywood in *Rebel Without a Cause* (1955). Its opening scenes feature a drunken teenager, Jim Stark, played by James Dean. While Jim is arrested and taken to the police station, he is treated sympathetically, and when his family arrive to claim him, they try and pass off his inebriation as no more than youthful high spirits. There is not an ounce of temperance sentiment in the scene—the fact that Jim is drunk is presented as unremarkable. His reasons for getting drunk receive greater attention. They are depicted as a mixture of nihilism and escapism, and established teenage angst as a proper motivation for drinking.

Teenagers also worked up a thirst by dancing. A new strain of music—rock 'n' roll—was emerging, whose practitioners were deified or demonized, depending on the age of the listener. Rock 'n' roll had alcohol in its blood. The forms of music it was created from, especially blues and country, acknowledged booze as an inspiration, and a number of early rock 'n' roll stars continued the tradition. Jerry Lee Lewis personified the new breed of hard-drinking rocker. In contrast to Elvis Presley, who drank more Pepsi than anything else in his initial years of fame, Jerry Lee seldom let such childish refreshments pass his lips. By the time he achieved national recognition in 1957 with the hits "Great Balls of Fire" and "Whole Lotta Shakin' Goin' On," the twenty-two-year-old Lewis was on his third marriage, to his thirteen-year-old second cousin. Although he had been drinking legally for only fourteen months, he had developed a whiskey habit, which he supplemented with pharmaceuticals, as did Gene Vincent, a contemporary star in the teenage firmament. The author of "Be-Bop-A-Lula" (1956) acquired his taste for alcohol, tranquilizers, and amphetamines after breaking his leg in a motorcycle accident. The tranquilizers were prescribed, the amphetamines were taken to counter the lethargy they engendered, and the whiskey served to take the edge off the speed.

As rock 'n' roll and its mixture of black and white performers and influences became a fact of life in America, attempts were made to sanitize its performers in order to maximize sales. If they could be represented as clean-living young men and women, and their music as an encouragement to rhythmic exercise, then parents would approve and let their children buy and play rock 'n' roll records. This proved to be uphill work. While performers such as Elvis Presley toed the line and might, in their early years, be characterized as the soda fountain faces for the new genre, others were less malleable. Gene Vincent "turned out to be willful, difficult, often drunk, and possibly a little insane. Where Elvis attempted to be all things to all people, Gene embraced the evil heart of rock 'n' roll."

The lyrics of most fifties rock songs were dry. Dating, automobiles, music, and dancing were their principal themes. Sex and teenage ine-briation had to be expressed in innuendo. But little by little, the bottle crept in—the spirit of Cecil Grant's "Nashville Jumps" (1949)—

> Seen ya goin' up Cedar Street hill,
> I know you've got your whiskey from Jack Daniel's still!
> Nashville really jumps, really jumps all night long

and was revived by Chuck Berry in "Rock and Roll Music" (1957), and thereafter drink was celebrated in rock with increasing frequency. It was the ideal balm for teenage angst, for the lovesick, for the would-be rebel. It was an antidote to milk bars and soda fountains and prom queens.

32   RECONSTRUCTION

Europe lagged behind America in the introduction of new consumer goods such as television sets and record players. Its inhabitants had far less disposable income during the 1950s than their transatlantic counterparts. The continent had to rebuild itself before it could advance into a brave new world of rock 'n' roll and beer commercials. The task of reconstruction post–World War II had been vast: Cities and infrastructure had to be rebuilt from the ground up, factories retooled to make civilian goods, fields and waterways cleared of mines and munitions, and in order to achieve such renewal, near-dead economies had to be jolted back to life.

In the event, the economic revival was completed with remarkable speed. Boosted by American aid, by 1951 the output of many European nations exceeded prewar levels, though on a per capita basis they were still a long way behind the United States. The process of renewal, however, was uneven. The continent had been divided into a capitalist West and a Communist East under the de facto control of Soviet Russia. Those countries on the Communist side of the Iron Curtain did not enjoy the same dynamic growth as their Western counterparts, and any surpluses they generated were siphoned off by the USSR as war reparations. Moreover, in the booming West, certain industries, notably that for beverage alcohol, lagged behind the general trend.

One of the priorities of European reconstruction had been fixing and improving the water supply. Prior to World War II, a majority of European households did not have a piped source of potable water. During the war, a significant number of the casualties had been caused by malaria, or waterborne diseases. On some fronts, such as the Italian, these had killed more soldiers than had died in action. The provision of safe water took precedence over the redevelopment of breweries and distilleries. In 1951, German beer production was half of what it had been when Hitler had invaded Poland. However, it recovered quickly thereafter and, in the western portion of the divided nation, had reached 150 percent of prewar levels for the entire country by 1960. Thirty-two hundred breweries had risen from the rubble to supply demand. The picture in East Germany, under Soviet control, was very different. Weak beer dribbled out of a mere 212 breweries, which together generated only two-thirds of the volume that the region had produced in 1939.

In France, the restrictions imposed by the hated Vichy regime on cafés and other watering holes were continued for a decade after the war. Winemaking, however, was encouraged, and the state took steps to ensure that its vineyards focused on quality as much as quantity. A new interim grade of French-made wine—Vins Délimités de Qualité Supérieure (VDQS)—was introduced to work alongside the AOC system of 1935. The VDQS stamp enabled producers in areas not yet designated as *Appéllation Controlée*—90 percent of France in 1950—to achieve higher prices than mere *vin du table,* and assured patriotic Frenchmen that the juice in the bottle was French-bred. This and other policies were so successful that by 1953 France was drowning in wine, and supply management measures were instituted. Growers were set targets, and if they exceeded these, they had to deposit any surplus production with the government, which used it as buffer stock or distilled it for industrial use.

No sooner had the state intervened to manage the fertility of French vines than nature struck back with harsh winters and late frosts, causing a general shortage, forcing prices through the roof, and incidentally creating one of the greatest vintages of the twentieth century (that of 1955) in Bordeaux. The government responded to the crisis with more legislation, which it alternately repealed or enforced in subsequent years, until 1964, when it decided to focus on regulation instead of market manipulation. The decision was taken as a consequence of France's membership in the European Economic Community (EEC), an entity established by the Treaty of Rome in 1957, to encourage free trade between a number of European countries. Italy, also a member, produced cheaper wine than France, which, according to free market principles, would force French growers out of business. This menace was held off with import quotas for a few years and killed, finally, with French-inspired, pan-European quality control legislation, which required Italy, and other EEC members, to register their vineyards, grade their wine, and perform other costly, time-consuming measures, in the name of harmonization.

In the same years that French legislators were equivocating on whether to control prices or output, French scientists continued to investigate the salutary properties of the national beverage. In 1951, Jean Lancepleine proved that the bactericidal properties of French white wine were not simply the result of its being alcoholic. His work was followed up by Hélène Jensen, who demonstrated that the antibacterial properties of red Bordeaux were even better, and better still if the wine was between seven and ten years old. Scientific proof that the addition of wine to contaminated water might make it drinkable confirmed one of the oldest human prejudices over the fluid—that the mixture was safer than untreated water. The French, as in the past, responded favorably to the good news by drinking more wine. Per capita consumption rose steadily until 1962, when it peaked at just over twenty liters of pure alcohol equivalent—or nearly 170 bottles each for every French person over the age of fifteen.

Despite such high levels of consumption, the French did not experience an epidemic of alcoholism, nor did they rush in their thousands to join the French arm of Alcoholics Anonymous. The idea that drinking might be a kind of disease did not occur to them. On the contrary, in the opinion of Roland Barthes, writing in 1955, "to believe in wine [was] a coercive collective act" in French society, and unbelievers were described as "sick, disabled, or depraved." Conversely "an award of good integration is given to whoever is a practicing drinker: Knowing *how* to drink is a national technique which serves to qualify the Frenchman, to demonstrate at once his performance, his control, and his sociability." Barthes thought that French attitudes derived in part from their belief that intoxication, far from being the primary aim of the drinker, was a side effect of no more than incidental importance: "What is characteristic of France is that the converting power of wine is never openly presented as an end. Other countries drink to get drunk, and this is accepted by everyone; in France, drunkenness is a consequence, never an intention. A drink is felt as the spinning out of a pleasure, not as the necessary cause of an effect which is sought: wine is not only a philter, it is also a leisurely act of drinking."

Similar views toward wine and intoxication prevailed in Italy, where levels of consumption likewise rose in the 1950s and continued to do so for the following decade. However, the demographics of the country changed markedly over the same period as Italians emigrated from rural areas into cities, resulting in changes in drinking habits. Whereas in rural Italy wine had been a type of food, a part of every meal, and served as such, albeit in diluted form, to children as well as adults, in the fast-growing cities eating and drinking came to be perceived of as separate acts. Moreover, the new metropolitans were nakedly materialist and took their cultural inspiration from the United States, which further weakened the customary link between the bottle and the dining table.

An unflattering picture of the changing values of the period is provided in the film *La Dolce Vita* (1960), which represents the Romans of its age as obsessed with celebrity, cars, and sensation. The film also reflects unfavorably on shifting attitudes toward alcohol. Whereas, traditionally, Italians had frowned on public displays of drunkenness, this ugly phenomenon is shown to be gaining acceptance in contemporary society, principally as a result of American influences. The film chronicles the exploits of Marcello, a journalist, as he chases scoops and celebrities through the streets of Rome and the neighboring countryside. In early scenes, the only overt drunks are American visitors who show no shame in their condition, indeed advocate it as an acceptable state. Toward the end of the film Marcello has acquired the same habit, and becomes aggressive and irrational when under the influence.

La Dolce Vita also illustrates the penetration of foreign drinks in Roman society. Its fashionable characters drink vodka, gin fizzes, and named brands of scotch whisky. In contrast, the unfashionable, such as Marcello's father, a traveling salesman, stick to traditional stimulants such as champagne when they want to celebrate. There are, finally, hints of the revival in Italian wines that occurred in the decade following the release of the film. In response to EEC legislation, a quality regime was introduced—the *Denominazione d'Origine Controllata* (Denomination of Controlled Origin or DOC), loosely based on the French AOC model, which defined regions, grapes, and production methods for wines such as Barolo and Barbaresco from Piedmont, and

Brunello di Montalcino from Tuscany. Although the DOC regime was slow to be implemented—indeed, has yet to be applied to the entire country—Italian production increased, quality improved, and Italians were prepared to pay more for good wines from their own soil.

The French-inspired concept that only wine from a specific geographical area made in accordance with local practice might be allowed to call itself, say, champagne, while a matter of law in France and the EEC, was something of a novelty beyond the country itself and its new European partners. It was tested in the British courts in 1958, when the French government brought a criminal suit against a British importer of fizzy wine from Spain which he sold under the label of "Spanish Champagne." The suit failed, but the following year a civil action against the same wine merchant succeeded, which established an important precedent; namely that a foreign country might recognize and protect, as if it were a commercial brand, the intellectual property created by the AOC system or one similar. Only champagne made in Champagne in accordance with French regulation might be sold as such. The decision caused heated debate in the British press. Some foresaw a world where protectionism reigned and even basic foodstuffs such as walnuts might be patented, while others considered the ruling an affront to the poor.

Great Britain took a long time to recover from World War II. Food rationing persisted until 1952, and beer output fell steadily between 1945 and 1951. Although its potency rose, so did its price, and the availability of potable water at home was no consolation. In addition to constraints upon supply, which meant that that pubs frequently ran dry of beer, restrictive opening times remained in force so that even if a pub had suds, its customers were forced to squeeze their drinking into narrow slots. The writer George Orwell considered the British drinking experience to be unpleasant enough to dissuade tourists, whose presence, it had been hoped, would speed up reconstruction, from visiting the country: "Apart from the many other difficulties, our licensing laws and the artificial price of drink are quite enough to keep foreigners away. Why should people who are used to paying sixpence for a bottle of wine visit a country where a pint of beer costs a shilling? But even these prices are less dismaying to foreigners than the lunatic laws which permit you to buy a glass of beer at half past ten while forbidding you to buy it at twenty-five past." As an incentive to fight this evil, Orwell offered a literary picture of his ideal pub, the Moon

Under Water, a sort of drinker's Eden, where English beer lovers of every caste might relax in unison with their spouses and offspring.

The miseries endured by postwar English beer drinkers were slight in comparison to the torments suffered by Scottish whisky lovers. Most production was diverted to the export market to earn foreign currency for reconstruction, and whisky for home consumption was rationed until 1960. The anguish that afflicted scotch aficionados deprived of their daily drams was caricatured in the movie *Whisky Galore!* (1949). Set on a small island in the Hebrides during the Second World War, and based on a true incident, *Whisky Galore!* depicts the attempts of whisky-starved islanders to salvage the cargo of a ship that has run aground with fifty thousand cases of the water of life on board and which is protected by the British home guard. The movie provides an affectionate view of drinking, indeed proposes that life without whisky is not worth living. "Some men are born a couple of drams short of par," opines the local doctor of the tight little island, as he makes up the natural shortfall with a glass of scotch.

As the economic climate improved in the late 1950s, British drinking underwent a revival. Beer consumption returned to prewar levels in the middle of the decade, and home consumption of whisky did the same in 1961. The fifties also witnessed the appearance of a novelty in the British beer market—lager. This cold, fizzy substance, the antithesis of bitter, had first been brewed in Britain on a commercial scale in 1949. The market leader, Skol, was targeted at younger drinkers who were thought to find the powerful taste of bitter off-putting. Despite having a market share of only 1 percent in 1960, lager was heavily promoted, attracting 19 percent of all the advertising spent on beer in the same year. Since lager had no traditional associations in the mind of the British drinker, these had to be invented. Its comparative lack of flavor was turned to its advantage. Ads focused on its refreshing qualities rather than its taste and depicted it as perfectly suited to the exciting new era of television and rock 'n' roll that Britain, belatedly, had joined.

Notwithstanding the recovery in consumption, the British were still drinking less than a third of the amount of booze on a per capita basis as their counterparts in France—the equivalent of a mere seven and a half liters of pure alcohol per annum against twenty-five. Despite such comparative abstinence, they nonetheless perceived of themselves as being heavy drinkers, a perception that was reflected in the plays, fiction, and films of the period. The movie *Saturday Night and Sunday Morning* (1960), for instance, which chronicles the life of a young factory worker in Britain in the fifties, presents alcohol as an anesthetic against the pain and boredom of a futile existence. Drunkenness allows its hero a temporary refuge in oblivion, and the condition is his principal aim when drinking. Such a mentality was the polar opposite of that which prevailed in France, where people drank for taste first and stimulation second.

A kinder picture of British tippling was presented in *Coronation Street,* the longest-running soap opera on British television, first broadcast in December 1960. The show is set in a terrace of houses in a northern town and features a neighborhood pub, the Rover's Return, where its characters socialize en masse. In addition to drinking and gossiping they play darts and other traditional pub games. The Rover's Return serves them as a home away from home—a kind of community center very much in the style of the village alehouse. On the rare occasions when one of its clientele has one too many, a motive, other than the mere desire to see double, is provided. People drink to compensate for disappointment, or to celebrate success, and alcohol, by offering consolation, or enhancing merriment, is presented as serving a useful role in society.

While overall consumption patterns in Great Britain in the 1950s were closer to those portrayed in *Coronation Street* than *Saturday Night and Sunday Morning,* there were exceptions, notably in Soho, London, where the rising stars of literature and painting met to drink deep. The epicenter of their boozing was the Colony Room, run by the formidable Muriel Belcher, who encouraged her customers to be as rude to each other as possible when in their cups, and who led by example. The Colony's clientele included the painter Francis Bacon, who was provided with free drinks in return for introducing new customers. Among the other heavy-drinking artists he brought to the club were Frank Auerbach, Lucien Freud, and Patrick Caulfield. Indeed, painters, whether figurative or abstract, seem to have taken to the bottle with the same abandon as writers during the middle decades of the twentieth century: The consumption of the principal British artists of the period was matched and perhaps exceeded by America's Abstract Impressionists—Rothko, Pollock, and De Kooning were all alcoholics.

The binge drinking practiced in Soho was also a feature of Britain's institutions of higher learning, where the competitive forms of consumption that had been typical of the eighteenth century were revived and improved. Although the average Briton may have been sober compared to his or her continental counterpart, British students drank in defiance of the trend. Their teachers, too, were fond of their sauce, as is illustrated in the first British campus novel—*Lucky Jim*, by Kingsley Amis. Set in a red brick university at the turn of the 1950s, the novel follows the fortunes of Jim Dixon, a young lecturer who, in contrast to the older members of his faculty, prefers pop songs to English classical music and who would rather spend time drinking pints in a pub than sipping sherry in a drawing room. The novel employs inebriation both as a deus ex machina to manage the plot and as a device to permit Jim to speak his mind. It also features one of the most memorable descriptions of a hangover in literature, as Jim awakes to find he has set his bed on fire: "Not for him the slow, gracious wandering from the halls of sleep, but a summary, forcible ejection. He lay sprawled, too wicked to move, spewed up like a broken spider crab on the tarry shingle of the morning. The light did him harm, but not as much as looking at things did; he resolved, having done it once, never to move his eyeballs again. A dusty thudding in his head made the scene before him beat like a pulse. His mouth had been used as a latrine by some small creature of the night, and then as its mausoleum."

Campus drinking rituals, especially at Oxford and Cambridge, were matters of fascination to foreign visitors. An Australian studying at University College, Oxford, for instance, recorded his bemusement when ordered to drink a "sconce" of two and a half pints of beer as a penalty for appearing at dinner without a gown. He did so, in the then–world record time of eleven seconds. Bob Hawke, the drinker in question, prime minister of Australia between 1983 and 1992, later acknowledged that "this feat was to endear me to some of my fellow Australians more than anything else I ever achieved."

Hawke had honed his speed-drinking skills as an undergraduate in his native Australia, which, at the close of World War II, had one of the most restrictive liquor licensing regimes in the world. Public houses throughout the nation closed their doors at 6:00 P.M. Rather, however, than persuading Australians to drink less, it caused them to drink faster, resulting in the notorious "six o'clock swill," when workers would try to fit a full evening's drinking into the hour between finishing work and closing time. The public bars of Australian hotels were designed to accommodate rapid, perpendicular drinking. Few had any furniture or interior fixtures at all, beyond a shelf around the wall where customers might rest their glasses in between drafts. Beer was dispensed from a device resembling a gasoline pump. The floors and the walls were tiled so that they might be hosed down after each session. Perpendicular speed drinking led to horizontal drinkers: "When the pubs closed, the streets filled with wild cries and the gutters ran with chunder."[67] This "unedifying spectacle" and an epidemic of automobile accidents involving drunks, led to the appointment of a royal commission, which reported in 1954 that "there are evils associated with six o'clock closing which ought not to be tolerated in a civilized community." New South Wales civilized its licensing laws in 1956, but Victoria and South Australia did not follow suit until 1966 and 1967 respectively.

Despite the persistence of restrictive laws in much of the country, Australian per capita beer consumption rose steadily, if not spectacularly, throughout the 1950s and '60s. Whereas it had been a mere twelve gallons per person per annum immediately prior to World War II, by 1953 it had risen to more than twenty and, by the mid '60s, was nudging thirty gallons. While beer was considered the national beverage, wine consumption was also on the up over the same period. This increase resulted in part from changing demographics: In the decade following the war more than a million continental European immigrants arrived in Australia, many of whom came from wine-drinking cultures. Their presence revitalized Australian wine production. Prior to 1957, Australia produced more fortified wine than table wine. The switch from empire standards such as Australian port and sherry to lighter styles was driven by demand from non–Anglo-Saxon Australians, and by an increase in the number of Australian women who drank. The latter had been notable by their absence in the ritual of the six o'clock swill, except behind the bar; indeed, midcentury Australian drinking was by and large an all-male ritual, in which mates took turns to "shout" each other rounds of beer before crawling home. However, a fashion for *pearl* or *perle* wines in the 1950 converted many Australian women to the pleasures of the grape. These were produced using temperature- and pressure-controlled fermentation, resulting in a light, naturally effervescent drink reminiscent of weak champagne.

---

[67] Vomit.

The brand leader was Barossa Pearl, introduced by Gramps in 1957. Barossa Pearl was drinkable rather than beautiful—"a sort of feminine substitute for beer," according to an observer of the period.

Although Pearl wines were representative of the general standard of Australian winemaking at the time, some producers were setting their sights far higher. Foremost among these was Max Schubert of Penfolds in Southern Australia. Schubert believed that Australia was capable of producing a truly great wine that might rival the *premier crus* of Bordeaux. The idea had taken seed in 1950, when Schubert had visited the major growing regions of Europe and had tasted some forty- and fifty-year-old Bordeaux wines that still retained "magnificent bouquet and flavor." On his return to South Australia, Schubert decided to use Shiraz grapes and fermentation techniques he had learned in France to produce a "big, full-bodied wine, containing maximum extraction of all the components in the grape material used." Nineteen fifty-one was the year of his first vintage, which was matured in untreated oak hogsheads for eighteen months, then bottled and stored. The process was repeated each year until 1956 when the directors of Penfold, curious to know what kind of wine was filling up its cellars, called for a tasting. Various Australian wine luminaries were invited to Adelaide and all the vintages produced to date were sampled. No one liked any of them. One taster described Grange Hermitage, as the new wine had been named, as *"A concoction of wild fruits and sundry berries with crushed ants predominating"*; while another remarked to its creator, *"Schubert, I congratulate you. A very good, dry port, which no one in their right mind will buy—let alone drink."*

Schubert was instructed to cease production. He disobeyed orders and continued to make smaller quantities clandestinely between 1957 and 1959. Happily, by 1960, the first vintages were beginning to settle down, becoming "less aggressive and more refined," and official production resumed again in 1960. In 1962 the '55 vintage won its first gold medal. It collected another fifty-four gold medals in various contests over the next fifteen years, indeed, was only withdrawn from contests so that other vintages of Grange Hermitage could win gold instead. A single bottle of the '51 now sells for forty-five thousand Australian dollars, and the wine has realized its creator's dream of making an Australian wine to rival the best of Bordeaux.

33 FLASHBACKS

> I hate to advocate drugs, alcohol, violence, or
> insanity to anyone, but they've always worked
> for me.
>
> —Hunter S. Thompson

In the same year that Grange Hermitage won its first gold medal, America elected a glamorous young president, put the first man in space, and its population and economy were booming. The highway construction program instituted by the Federal Aid Highway Act of 1956, which had pledged twenty-five billion dollars to construct forty-one thousand miles of interstate roads over ten years, was close to completion, enabling Americans to explore their country with unprecedented ease. In this heady domestic atmosphere, where the watchword was optimism, the consumption of alcohol, which had paused for breath at the end of the 1950s, recommenced its upward trend. However, the debate on the pleasures and hazards of drinking was sidelined for much of the 1960s as the national passions for novelty and stimulation spilled over into the field of intoxicants. New rivals to drunkenness emerged as matters for celebration or demonization, besides which getting corned up seemed reassuringly quaint.

The quest for novelty had a prophet, Jack Kerouac, whose groundbreaking novel *On the Road* (1957) unrolls like an excited conversation in a bar. It is a poem to the continent—to freedom of movement—to turn the ignition key and go! It is also gloriously wet, a booze-soaked odyssey back and forth across the republic, a *Sun Also Rises*, grounded on American soil, that acknowledged the debt to Hemingway in the conversational exchanges of its characters. The book represents alcohol as the solvent of melting-pot America. All over the nation, rednecks, intellectuals, black bluesmen, and Mexicans swallow it together in the cauldron of integration. And not only is it the misfits who hum a different tune to mainstream America, but also the ordinary Joes who join in the bacchanalia: "Americans are always drinking in crossroads saloons on Sunday afternoon: They bring their kids; they gabble, and brawl over brews; everything's fine. Come nightfall the kids start crying and their parents are drunk. They go weaving back to the house. Everywhere in America I've been in crossroads saloons drinking with whole families."

In addition to spontaneity, Kerouac and his fellow Beat writers valued honesty. *On the Road* includes scenes which show that alcohol can debase as well as elevate: "I drank sixty glasses of beer and retired to the toilet, where I wrapped myself around the toilet bowl and went to sleep. During the night at least a hundred seamen and civilians came in and cast their sentient debouchments on me until I was unrecognizably caked. What difference does it make after all? anonymity in the world of men is better than fame in heaven."

Not only did *On the Road* salute old-fashioned inebriation via alcohol, it also made a bow in the direction of a fast-growing rival—*tea,* i.e., marijuana. While smoking tea had long been a pastime of black urban American communities and had appeared sporadically on the drug lists of socialites, in the late 1950s and early '60s the habit spread rapidly. Getting high became the new drunk. The experience, however, was qualitatively different. It was quicker: A single marijuana cigarette made its smoker stoned before they'd finished it, whereas a practiced drinker needed half an hour, an empty stomach, and several drinks to achieve the same sense of dislocation. It also had a lighter touch, making people happy, passive, and mildly neurotic. Marijuana lovers were more prone to fits of the giggles than to brawling, and Kerouac noted the differences in effect in his prose.

On the Road was a bridge over change. Hitherto, pace De Quincey, writers had relied primarily on drunkenness as a device to alter the mental states of their characters. However, from the sixties onward, other drugs were substituted for good old-fashioned John Barleycorn. Marijuana, in particular, received widespread coverage and its style of intoxication was presented as being more cerebral than the howling and primitive state brought on by a bottle of rye. The difference between the two conditions, high or flayed, was emphasized in the movie *Easy Rider* (1969), which chronicles the adventures of two hippies, Billie and Captain America, as they travel to New Orleans on their customized Harley-Davidsons. Arrested in a small town on the specious charge of "parading without a permit," they meet George, a local attorney, in the cells, who is sleeping off a whiskey binge. While George's drinking is acceptable in his community, the hippies, despite their peaceful demeanor, are personae non grata on account of their long hair. George befriends them, gets them out of jail, and agrees to accompany them to New Orleans. He tries some weed on the first night on the road and launches into a charming monologue of how he and his cousin saw forty-one UFOs flying in formation over Mexico, and how their alien occupants will bring peace and discipline to the world. Marijuana, it is implied, stimulates the brain in places that alcohol seldom reaches.[68]

Easy Rider also features an acid trip. LSD was no longer just a drug for schizophrenics and chronic alcoholics—it had been adopted by hippies as the key to the doors of perception. The headquarters of recreational tripping was San Francisco, the western capital of the Beat empire. Its epicenter, where the hippies gathered, was Haight-Ashbury. Their curious dress and strange behavior drew a host of journalists, including Hunter S. Thompson, who noted their indifference to alcohol: "There are no hippy bars, for instance, and only one restaurant above the level of a diner or lunch counter. This is a reflection of the drug culture, which has no use for booze and regards food as a necessity to be acquired at the least possible expense." Bemoaning their sobriety, Thompson observed that "prior to the hippy era there were three good Negro-run jazz bars on Haight Street, but they soon went out of style. Who needs jazz, or even beer, when you can sit down on a public curbstone, drop a pill in your mouth, and hear fantastic music for hours at a time in your own head? A cap of good acid costs $5, and for that you can hear the universal symphony, with God singing solo and the Holy Ghost on drums."

The behavior of the hippies seemed evidence for Dr. Humphry

---

[68] Interestingly, much of the vocabulary of drug use was borrowed from the language of drinking. *High* appears in the 1927 *Lexicon of Prohibition*, as does *splifficated; buzzing* features in Benjamin Franklin's *Drinker's Dictionary*, and *stoned* dates back to Jacobean England as a term for lustful drunkenness.

Osmond's theory that LSD and alcohol did not mix. However, and despite its potential to control alcoholism, acid was outlawed in 1966. Its prohibition was accomplished almost without resistance. The general public perceived it to be a dangerous drug, on a par with other proscribed substances such as heroin and cocaine. While the ban was not an immediate success–by the time Hunter S. Thompson was writing of its ubiquity in the Hashbury, it had been illegal for a year–its use declined, probably from natural causes as much as federal prohibition. Its tendency to make its devotees imitate schizophrenics, especially after repeated use, caused demand to tail away–it was scarcely worth bootlegging. According to Thompson, writing in 1971, the decline was due to a different Zeitgeist in America: "The big market, these days, is in Downers. . . . What sells, today, is whatever Fucks You Up– whatever short circuits your brain and grounds it out for the longest possible time. . . . Uppers are no longer stylish. Methedrine is almost as rare on the 1971 market as pure acid. . . .'Consciousness Expansion' went out with LBJ . . . and it is worth noting, historically, that downers came in with Nixon."

In the event, the dip in the popularity of alcohol among the young, and a general fashion for alternative intoxicants, proved to be temporary. Some had never abandoned booze: Thompson displayed a steadfast devotion to the bottle and, in his novel *Fear and Loathing in Las Vegas,* argued its utility in mitigating the effects of psychedelic drugs. He also advised new readers that if they wanted to appreciate his style, which he christened *gonzo* journalism, they should inject a halfpint of rum, tequila, or bourbon "straight into the stomach" in order to approach the material in the proper frame of mind. The dominant sentiment in *Fear and Loathing* is pessimism. In contrast to the optimism of *On the Road,* and even *Easy Rider,* both of which hoped to inject new vigor into the American Dream, *Fear and Loathing* was written as its requiem. The psychedelics' visions for their country had been impractical and unpopular. Many of their icons turned to drink. Jim Morrison, aka the Lizard King, lead singer of the Doors, who once sang about getting high on *The Ed Sullivan Show,* was getting drunk in front of seven thousand fans at the Dinner Key Auditorium in Miami by 1969. Janis Joplin, whose soulful voice had tantalized hippies at the Monterey Festival in 1968 and at Woodstock in '69, was a diehard fan of Southern Comfort; the same nectar was also the favorite of Ronald C. "Pigpen" McKernan, who augmented it with Thunderbird tonic wine, and who died of his drinking habit in 1973. His tomb was inscribed:

RONALD C. MCKERNAN

1945–1973

PIGPEN WAS

AND IS NOW FOREVER

ONE OF THE

GRATEFUL DEAD

While the hippies were growing their hair, espousing Eastern mysticism and peace, and tripping out on contraband acid, a far larger number of their peer group were having their heads cropped and their bodies disciplined and dressed in uniforms in preparation for a tour with the U.S. armed forces in Vietnam. Between 1964, when America first started sending significant numbers of troops to the country, and 1973, when the last of its forces were withdrawn, over two million Americans served in the Vietnam War. The majority of the combatants were conscripts; their average age was nineteen. Despite their youth, they were provided with a beer ration; indeed, beer was considered to be sufficiently important to their well-being to be helicoptered into battle zones alongside food. The standard issue was two cans per man per day. If possible, a hundred-pound block of ice per platoon was also provided so that the brews could be enjoyed at the right temperature.

Those serving in Vietnam could augment their fighting rations at the post exchanges, or PXs. Lest they overindulge, their purchases of beer were restricted to three cases per month. They were also provided with drinking places. Private soldiers could buy beer, by the can or case, at the EM (enlisted man) clubs, aka malt shops. Two grades of brew were available, regular (costing $2.40/case) and premium ($3.00). Quality was an important issue in Vietnam. The local beer, Ba Mu'o'i Ba, or "33" lager, was nicknamed "tiger's piss" and considered to be about as drinkable. Some American brands, according to correspondents of the age, were treated with the preservative formaldehyde, to proof them against the agitation and high temperatures they would encounter on military bases. This additive was reputed to make drinkers lightheaded and served as a scapegoat for drunkenness.

The presence of so much alcohol in a war zone, especially on the big firebases, sometimes led to confusion. The journalist Michael Herr recorded visiting one such camp where booze had got the upper hand: "The colonel in command was so drunk that day that he could hardly get his words out, and when he did, it was to say things like, 'We aim to make good and goddammit sure that if *those guys* try *anything cute* they won't catch us with our pants down.' The main mission there was to fire H & I, but one man told us that their record was the worst in the whole Corps, probably the whole country, they'd harassed and interdicted a lot of sleeping civilians... even a couple of American patrols, but hardly any Viet Cong."

Vietnam was a relatively wet war. The tropical climate encouraged the consumption of cold drinks, and intoxication relieved the stress of combat among troops when they were off duty. While some resorted to marijuana, more chose alcohol as their transport to amnesia. Their preference had the tacit support of high command. It was better that fighting men bonded over a few cans or a bottle than that they smoked themselves into introspection and started to question why they were there. Indeed, mass sessions of drunken bonding seem to have been permitted, on appropriate occasions, as being useful to morale. The writer Tim O'Brien pictured one such event–the Christmas festivities at LZ Gator–in *If I Should Die in a Combat Zone:*

> Now and then, to help slice the monotony into endurable segments, floor shows came to LZ Gator. Korean girls, Australian girls, Japanese girls, Philippine girls, all doing the songs and routines and teases that must be taught to them in some giant convention hall in Las Vegas.... Each show started with one of those unrecognizable acid-rock songs, faded off into "I Want to Go Home–Oh, How I Want to GO Home," then a medley of oldies-and-still-goodies, none of them very good. Then some humor, then–thank God, at last–the stripper.... Everyone drank. Most of us drank in excess, but the colonel would kill one beer and stop there. Then the climax came. The men, roaring drunk, with tears in their eyes, would plead with the stripper–beg her, bribe her–to finish the job. But nothing ever came of it. We went away exhausted.

In addition to providing such home comforts as were feasible to combat troops, the authorities gave them local leave–in Vietnam, in other Asian countries, in Australia–and in every place, whether feted as heroes, fleeced as tourists, or hated as invaders, they won a reputation as hard drinkers with their thirsts. Asian children lined up to sell them liquor in the streets, Australians welcomed them into their veterans' halls and plied them with beer. However, when many of the same men got back to the United States, they were denied entry to bars on account of their youth. The minimum drinking age in America remained at its post-Prohibition high of twenty-one, as, indeed, did the age at which its citizens could vote.

These discrepancies became important political issues in the United States. It was wrong to require people to fight, without giving them a say in whether their country went to war. In 1971 the franchise was extended to eighteen-year-olds by the Twenty-sixth Amendment to the Constitution. A similar line of reasoning was applied to drinking. If you could trust a nineteen-year-old with an M16 or a fighter jet, then why not with a can of beer when he got home? Moreover, some of the men then in power could remember coming back from World War I to Prohibition. Why inflict the same letdown on your own grandchildren? If they were old enough to fight, they were old enough to drink. In the early 1970s, thirty states decided to correct the anomaly and lowered their minimum drinking ages to eighteen.

In the same decade that grunts in Vietnam were sipping on their beer rations and the hippies of the Hashbury were eschewing alcohol for acid, a quiet revolution took place in the vineyards around the San Francisco Bay. California wine production had been growing steadily since repeal. In 1946, it had passed a hundred million gallons for the first time and in 1971 broke the two-hundred-million-gallon barrier. Most of this growth had come from fewer, larger wineries–America's vintners, like its brewers, had consolidated. However, a counterculture emerged in the late sixties in the form of small boutique wineries, dedicated to excellence rather than volume. The prophet of quality was Andre Tchelistcheff, who came from France to the Beaulieu Winery, one of the few class vineyards to survive Prohibition, in 1937. He was horrified at the crude production methods then current–people grew port grapes next to Riesling vines, they flung sackloads of sulphur and chunks of ice into the must as it fermented, and pumped the resulting mess into concrete tanks to mature. Little by little over the following decades, Tchelistcheff succeeded in sorting out his vineyards, brought the concept of temperature control into the process of fermentation, and introduced oak barrels in which the improved juice might settle and become an attractive wine.

His apostles were assisted in their quest for excellence by the research of Dr. Albert Winkler at UC Davis, who invented a *heat summation* system to determine what type of grape would be best suited to a particular area of California. Heat summation quantified the number of "degree days" of sunshine the area received, matched these against European equivalents, and recommended appropriate grapes and methods of cultivation. Bordeaux, for instance, had two thousand five hundred degree days per annum, the same as Napa, suggesting that the valley and nearby Sonoma could be perfect for Cabernet Sauvignon vines and claret-style reds, while the flanks of their enclosing hills had a similar profile to those in Burgundy, where Chardonnay was planted to make white wines.

A few veterans of Prohibition, including Inglenook, Krug, and Mondavi, were quick to follow the trail blazed by Tchelistcheff and Winkler. They were joined in the 1960s by a fresh generation of American winemakers who were intent on creating spectacular vintages. The newcomers extended the hippy mantra then current across San Francisco Bay into something positive–tune in, turn on, drop out, make wine. There was also something of the frontier spirit at work among them. Hugh Johnston, writing of a visit made to the vineyards of northern California in 1963, declared himself to be "enthralled . . . with what I had tasted" but "appalled at the lack of interest and recognition by the public, or facilities for them to visit the Napa Valley with the slightest degree of comfort."

The facilities may have been primitive, but the New Age winemakers were not. Following Winkler's data, they ranged up and down the Pacific Coast. In the late 1950s, a UC Davis graduate, Richard Sommer, scouted north, making wine in Oregon and Washington, before setting up the Hillcrest Vineyard in the Umpqua Valley. In 1965, David Lett planted Pinot Noir at his Eyrie Vineyard in Oregon. Meanwhile, in Sunnyside, Washington, a group of wine-loving professors at the state university planted a handful of acres with vines with the aim of producing what they termed *varietals*, i.e., wines made from a single type of grape and intended to exhibit its ideal characteristics. The Sunnysiders crafted their first vintages in a garage in Seattle and soon had enough fans to turn their hobby into a business–the Columbia Winery.

By the early 1970s the fruits of the American quality revolution were apparent. Boutique wineries were making spectacular varietals, some of which reflected the best properties of the European wines on which they had been modeled. Cabernet Sauvignons and Chardonnays showed especial promise. Hugh Johnston was followed by other foreign oenophiles to Napa, and California wines acquired a cult status overseas. Some were so good, it was rumored, that they eclipsed their French prototypes. The issue was put to the test in 1976 when Steven Spurrier, an English wine merchant based in Paris, organized a blind tasting of California's best, pitting them against some of France's grandest *crus*. He lined up six American Cabernets against such elixirs as Mouton Rothschild '70, and a Haut-Brion of the same year, and six Chardonnays against four white Burgundies. He assembled a jury of nine French men and women, the crème de la crème of French wine tasting, including growers from Bordeaux and Burgundy and the sommelier of the Tour d'Argent Restaurant in Paris. While a number of journalists were invited, only one, George M. Taber of *Time* magazine, attended. Although his two-thousand-word report on the tasting was slimmed down to a four-paragraph article in the June 7 edition of *Time*, the event turned out to be the biggest story of the twentieth century in the world of wine. In Taber's words, "The unthinkable happened: California defeated all Gaul."

Taber's account of the contest suggests that the most respected connoisseurs of wine in France were unprepared, both in mind and in palate, for the possibility that French wine could be made better somewhere else: "As they swirled, sniffed, sipped, and spat, some judges were instantly able to separate an imported upstart from an aristocrat. More often, the panel was confused. 'Ah, back to France!' exclaimed [a French judge] after sipping a 1972 Chardonnay from the Napa Valley. 'That is definitely California. It has no nose,' said another judge— after downing a Bâtard-Montrachet '73. Other comments included such Gallic gems as 'This is nervous and agreeable,' and 'This soars out of the ordinary.'" When the scores of the judges were compiled, the "top-soaring" red was a 1972 Cabernet Sauvignon from Stag's Leap Wine Cellars. American Chardonnays, meanwhile, took four out of the first five places among the whites. Robert Louis Stevenson's prophecy that "the smack of California earth will linger on the palate of your grandson" had been fulfilled.

The results of the Judgment of Paris were played down in France.

They received little immediate coverage, and subsequently were explained away as having been rigged by pitting California's best years against unusually weak French vintages. French producers, however, took notice, and some invested in Californian soil, following a lead established by the champagne producer Moët Hennessy, which had bought land in Napa in 1973. In the same year that the global arbitrators of taste in wine had chosen California as the best source of Bordeaux-style reds, and Burgundy-style whites, Moët released a Napa Valley Brut, which hinted at the potential of the Golden State for making outstanding fizz. It was good enough to induce Piper-Heidsieck, another French champagne house, to invest in neighboring Sonoma, and to provoke the curiosity of the Coca-Cola Company, which bought two California wineries in 1977.

International fame and an increasing domestic appetite for American wine led to rapid growth in production. In 1979 California created 314 million gallons of poetic juice—half as much again as the year in which Stag's Leap '72 had been born. Most of this went down American throats: Between 1969 and 1979 per capita consumption close to doubled. While Thomas Jefferson's dream that the United States might one day become a nation of vintners and wine drinkers had yet to be fulfilled, progress toward its realization was, at last, apparent.

34 WESTERNIZATION

The spirit of curiosity that had led Americans to experiment with alternative intoxicants and to perfect their winemaking skills was also at work in Asia over the third quarter of the twentieth century. It was strongest in Japan, where it took the guise of an ardent desire to embrace all things Western. This longing extended to Western drinks, which were perceived of as being essential to the culture of the Occident—as important as wearing an English suit or adopting American business practices. Western temperance, in contrast, was not considered to be a vital part of the dynamic culture the Japanese wished to imitate. In consequence, they started drinking beer and whisky in preference to sake and their other traditional beverages.

Their motivations for switching to beer were reflected in the ways in which it was promoted in Japan. Beer was portrayed as cool, modern, and American—as the lifeblood of that go-getting nation, whose industrial prowess the Japanese were keen to rival. The Asahi Brewing Company introduced canned suds to Japan in 1958, and the product was a runaway success: What better symbol could there be of economic vigor than the convenient, hygienic, transportable, and disposable beer can? The importance of an American connection was apparent in Sapporo beer's advertising campaign of the same year, built upon the slogan "Munich, Sapporo, Milwaukee." This was a clever bridge between the pre–World War II perception of beer in Japan as a traditional Teutonic brew and the new and desirable Yankee dynamism. The urge to imitate was apparent among corporations as well as consumers. Following the introduction of a minimum-level-of-production law in 1959–no brewery could make less than two million liters (528,000 gallons)–the Japanese brewing industry underwent an American-style consolidation, and the country's brewers contracted into five: Asahi, Kirin, Sapporo, Suntory, and Orion.

Whisky was also adopted as a symbol of the West, where whisky drinking, like playing golf, was believed to be the hallmark of every successful businessman. Whisky became the darling of Japanese white-collar workers, to whom it was an aspirational drink that conferred an aura of power upon its consumer. The market, thanks to tariff barriers, was dominated by domestic brands. Suntory led the field. In 1950 it released what was to become its flagship marque, Suntory OLD. This proved so popular that by 1961 it was being exported to the United States.[69] While OLD and its ilk were packaged to resemble scotch, their flavor profiles were different from the fluids they had been created to emulate. The Japanese drank not just for show, but also for pleasure, and their tastes were dissimilar to those of the average Pittsburgh steel magnate. The difference, according to Hideaki Kito, a master blender for Kirin whisky, was dictated by the Japanese diet. In his opinion, the taste of authentic Japanese whisky had to be based on "Japanese culture, Japanese food. We eat a lot of fish, for example, therefore we have to create a match for this with the whisky. Our research showed that clean and estery whiskies are much better suited to the Japanese palate."

While the Japanese were happy to switch to Western beverages, their traditions as to who might drink alcohol remained unchanged. Boozing was regarded as a male prerogative. Women were permitted, indeed were expected, to serve alcohol to men but to avoid it themselves, unless they were old or sick. They were also expected to tolerate drunkenness among their husbands, fathers, brothers, and sons, in particular if these were white-collar workers or *salarymen*. The salaryman, like his drinking habits, was a hybrid of East and West–modern in appearance, yet traditional in action. His employers had adopted American corporate structures with neat hierarchies, in which, according to Japanese custom, employees ascended according to age and years of service, unless they were women–in which case they did not rise beyond the typing pool. Superficially, such a chimera seemed

---

[69] It is currently the largest-selling brand of whisky in the world.

doomed to sterility. Old men do not think outside the box. However, during the 1970s and early 1980s, the rate of Japan's industrial growth surpassed that of any other industrialized country, and alcohol was the lubricant that enabled the Japanese business machine to run smoothly. While the gerontocracy demanded and received respect for their years when behind their desks, after work, off premises, and over a drink, they let their young Turks speak.

The Japanese divided business into two parts: "dry" relations, i.e., meetings during office hours; and *mizu shobai,* or the "water trade," which took place at night in bars. For the dry portion of each working day, salarymen maintained the ancient ethos of seniority through age, and juniors were expected to refrain from passing an opinion. However, at postwork drinking sessions, after a single drink, the same subordinates were deemed to be "drunk" and given license to speak their minds. This convention allowed ideas to flow between different levels of staff that might otherwise have been stifled by tradition. Therefore, in order to make an impression, an aspiring salaryman was required to drink and to be theoretically, if not actually, drunk most evenings. Indeed, the wives of young executives who came home sober would worry that their spouses' careers were faltering.

The obligation to drink with colleagues or clients after work was reflected in Japanese consumption statistics by age, which resembled, for men, a bell curve. Their boozing was limited in their teens[70]–a 1980 survey into the drinking habits of fifteen- to eighteen-year-olds in Japan found only 0.8 percent of the boys and none of the girls were daily drinkers–began to rise as they commenced their careers as salarymen, got heavy as they entered their forties, peaked between ages of fifty and fifty-nine, remained heavy for another decade, then tailed away upon retirement. The profile of Japan's few female drinkers, in contrast, was a gently rising curve, with women more likely to drink between the ages of seventy and seventy-nine than in their twenties and thirties.

The importance of alcohol to Japanese business culture resulted in a public tolerance of drunkenness far in excess of that which prevailed in America. It was no crime to be intoxicated and no shame to vomit or urinate in the streets. Alcohol was readily available for those of an

---

[70] The legal drinking age in Japan has been twenty since 1922.

age to drink it—no license was required to sell it, and in addition to countless bars, restaurants, and grocery stores, beer was sold from vending machines for those wishing to refresh themselves while on the move.

In addition to drinking for the good of their careers, urban salarymen did so for hedonistic reasons, often at one of the growing number of karaoke bars. These venues, which commenced life in the mid-1970s, supplied taped background music over which drinkers took turns singing lyrics. Their delivery was often compromised by the bottle, in accordance with the Japanese concept of *jogo,* i.e., "the tendency to change character when drunk." Jogo recognizes three subcategories: the *warai-jogo* (happy drunk), the *naki-jogo* (lachrymose drunk), and the *neji-jogo,* or nasty drunk. Depending upon his jogo, the salaryman might be expected to giggle, frown, or rage when he crooned. A small percentage of Japanese drinkers suffered a supplementary transformation to that occasioned by mal *jogo* when in their cups. Their faces would *makkaka naru,* i.e., turn red. This condition results from the genetic disability of some Japanese to digest alcohol. Those possessed of this hereditary trait do not produce acetaldehyde dehydrogenase and so cannot properly metabolize acetaldehyde, and hence suffer some of the same problems as alcoholics on Antabuse when they take a drink, including an instantaneous *futsukayoi* or hangover.

While the metropolitan salarymen tippled on Western booze in drinking places that fused domestic and imported rituals, their compatriots in rural areas favored traditional beverages, which they employed to guard the integrity of native styles of drunkenness. *Sake* was the staple drink outside of cities. Brewed from rice, to an ABV ranging from 18 to 25 percent, and with a flavor profile radically different from Western beverages, which sought to balance "sweetness, sourness, pungency, bitterness, and stringency," sake was Japanese to the bottom of the flask. In contrast to the limited selection of beers produced by the brewers' cabal, it was available from thousands of manufacturers, in a wide range of styles, some of which were intended for consumption on highly specific occasions. For instance, *iwai-sake* (celebration sake) was brewed for use in Shinto festivals and purification rituals; other kinds were fermented for the sole purpose of being offered to Akiyasama, the fire goddess, or to Ebisusama, the god of trade.

Sake was a secular as well as sacred fluid in rural parts of Japan. Its consumption was obligatory to commemorate rites of passage—births, marriages, deaths; and to seal business transactions. It was the correct present to give on certain calendar holidays, and, finally, it was the cause of endemic drunkenness. According to a study of an agricultural community in the Ono Valley in Kyushu, the use of sake was ubiquitous both in space and time. Like Holland in its golden age, men drank at the slightest provocation. Moreover, they used alcohol to regulate formal matters among themselves and, like their salarymen kin, set aside time for feigned or real intoxication, which they used to express the feelings that they were otherwise expected to conceal.

The form for such official binges in Kyushu was as follows: All the men in the village would convene at the house of one of its principal landowners, where they were seated, according to precedence, at low tables laid out in a horseshoe shape. The eldest man sat at the top of the curve, the next eldest to his right, the third to his left, and so on. They were followed down the arms of the horseshoe by the women, who also sat according to age. The host would open proceedings with a brief speech of welcome, which was answered by his oldest guest. Sake was poured for the men by the women, and once everyone had a full cup the host would issue the command *"Kanpai!"* ("Glasses dry!") and his guests would drain them in unison.

Once the preliminaries were out of the way, the rituals changed. The men did the pouring, and toasting became one-on-one instead of universal. An older man might invite a junior several stations below him at the table to take a cup of sake, and since this involved the presentation of said cup from hand to hand, which the recipient downed in one and then reciprocated, the established order of the community that the seating plan had represented was broken as the old circulated among the young. Moreover, freedom of speech was deemed to be in operation, and discussions between participants became heated and even violent, with fights breaking out across the tables.

These formal parties served the same purpose as the Tokyo bar sessions that businessmen staged in order to learn the opinions of their juniors. An egalitarian spirit prevailed, and men without status in the village might say what they thought without undermining the traditional hierarchy, because the sessions themselves were an integral part of custom and began with a display of precedence. Moreover, they served to reinforce the conviction among their participants that they were "part of a (threatened) underclass rural population, which continue[d] to practice a traditional and 'truly Japanese' way of life . . . distinct from both urban lifestyles and Western customs and practices."

◈　◈　◈

The hybrid drinking culture that developed in Japan during the second half of the twentieth century had parallels elsewhere in Asia. In Hong Kong, a curious example of fusion drinking emerged in the 1970s, centered on the consumption of luxury French Cognac. By 1981, 5 million Hong Kong Chinese were drinking more of the distilled grape spirit than 120 million Japanese, and by the mid–1980s they were the heaviest per capita consumers of Cognac in the world. This obsession with Cognac, and not just any Cognac, but luxury brands, stood in marked contrast to their limited interest in other Western drinks. Beer aside, which was consumed as if it were a type of soda, none of the empire standards such as scotch, gin, and port had ever garnered much of a following among the Chinese residents of the British colony.

Prior to the adoption of Cognac, prevailing drinking practices in Hong Kong were based on traditional Chinese custom, which was best characterized, in terms of wet or dry, as constantly damp. While total consumption was low, imbibing was frequent and usually undertaken for ritual or health rather than for the express purpose of becoming drunk. Alcohol, or *jiu,* was an integral part of Chinese medicine and religion, a necessary ingredient of Chinese hospitality, and a vital ingredient in the celebration of rites of passage. When and how to drink was first formalized in the *Book of Rites,* a pre-Christian Confucian work, whose precepts set down, for instance, what an old man should drink in winter, who should prepare it for him, who serve it to him, and so on. Confucianism also regarded heavy drinking as one of the Four Vices or Disasters, and Confucius himself counseled dutiful sons against the bottle. Public drunkenness, moreover, was perceived of as disgraceful: To be drunk alone out of doors was to lose face. *Jiu,* therefore, was a necessary, if equivocal, fluid to the Chinese: Ritual and medicine demanded that they drink, without appearing to be drunk. Historically, jiu was divided into three classes: fermented grain drinks–*huang jiu,* usually brewed from rice, sorghum, or millet; distilled drinks–*bai jiu;* and *yao jiu*–medicinal alcohols, which were distilled spirits infused with herbs or animal parts. These last were highly specific beverages, formulated to take account of the intended drinker's age, sex, and well-being.

Perhaps the most common form of *yao jiu* in use in Hong Kong was snake wine. This salutary beverage could be served aged or fresh, depending upon the ailment it was expected to treat. The aged variety was prepared by seeping the gutted bodies of dead snakes in grain alcohol for several years. Different species of snakes imparted distinct therapeutic qualities to the liquor. Fresh snake wine was made by cutting the gall bladder out of a living snake, squeezing its bile into a shot glass, and adding alcohol to taste. Hostelries dedicated to these beverages could be found in the center of high-rise Hong Kong. They usually consisted of a long wooden counter with a row of large glass jars, each stewing some variety of snake, or other kind of creature, including ravens, scorpions, and rat fetuses. Behind the bar would be floor-to-ceiling wooden drawers, with brass ventilation grilles on their faces, and various kinds of live snakes inside. An invalid in need of fresh snake wine could select a cobra, a python, a krait, or a pit viper, have it vivisected before his eyes, and finish his drink before the animal was dead.

In addition to taking a large proportion of their medicine with jiu, the Hong Kong Chinese employed alcohol in their relations with the supernatural world. It was necessary to present some to the ancestors at the annual festival of Ching Ming, when participants would disinter their forebears after they had been in the ground for seven years, polish their bones, and offer them libations. Similarly, on the night of the Hungry Ghosts, when the spirits of those neglected by their descendants roamed the streets, little offerings of food and alcohol would be left out to placate the unhappy phantoms. Drinks were also served to the dead at the Dragon Boat Festival; and to the spiritual guardians of the community, and of the households it contained, at Chinese New Year. Alcohol was ubiquitous in Hong Kong Chinese culture and available 24/7 everywhere, to more or less anyone of any age with the money to pay for it. There was little overt drunkenness, however, because of the potential loss of face. Even when occasion demanded more than a ritual drink, it was anathema to behave in a boorish manner as a consequence.

Until the 1970s, there had seemed little place for Western booze in such a tightly regulated drinking culture. However, by the end of the decade, Cognac had been adopted by the Hong Kong Chinese as part of their identity, and their penchant for the stuff was acknowledged by other Chinese communities as being unusual. Why was Cognac so special? The answer was its price. The Hong Kong Chinese considered it a social duty to show their wealth. Ostentation was achieved through consumption, and Cognac was the most expensive form of Western alcohol. Moreover, thanks to rigorous French classification, it was graded by quality, thus enabling it to express distinctions in wealth. Those on middle incomes could serve VS, those with more money VSOP, the truly wealthy XO, and the super rich could offer crystal decanters of Cognac distilled in the reign of the last French king. Brands of Cognac became as well known as Coca-Cola and acquired specific identities among the Chinese. Rémy Martin, for instance, was *Yan Tau Ma* ("Human-Head Horse"), after the centaur on the label. The drink itself was attributed with medicinal qualities, to assist its absorption into Chinese society. According to a local expert, "The Chinese associate the grape with hot foods, which are essentially fiery, masculine, potent." Cognac was thought to work directly on the male sex drive and to be a defense against impotence. The very rich would add a rare and costly piece of ginseng to a similarly expensive bottle of Cognac in order to create a deluxe aphrodisiac. Whisky, in contrast, was reckoned to have the opposite effect. The Hong Kong Chinese associated it "with cool elements, feminine elements, so it has never been seen as a man's drink here."

The integration of Cognac was also assisted by its amber color. To the Chinese eye it looked expensive, unlike, say, the empire-standard gin. According to an agent for Hennessey Cognac, "No businessman here would think of opening a good bottle of vodka or gin at an important dinner.... It's colorless and looks like a cheap Chinese liquor, so nobody would be impressed." With white spirits condemned on account of their transparency, and whisky because it was effeminate, Cognac had the field to itself. Its properties and virtues had been established in traditional terms and differentiated from other Western spirits. It could be drunk—it should be drunk—but when? Banquets were the answer, especially wedding banquets, which were the prime opportunities for showing wealth. Traditionally, families had prepared a special rice wine upon the birth of a daughter, called *Nuerhong* (Red Daughter) or *Nujiu* (Daughter's Wine), to serve at her wedding. As Hong Kong became increasingly crowded, so that it was more or less impossible to brew and store large quantities of Red Daughter, commercial varieties appeared. But these were no match for Cognac, which became de rigueur at wedding banquets and spread to other types of feast where communal drinking took place.

At banquets to mark the Chinese lunar new year, the French spirit was also consumed with especial fervor. Bottles were placed on each table of guests, for use in toasts. Toasts were frequent: to the host, to the other tables one at a time, to circulating dignitaries, and to each of the twelve courses upon arrival. Toasts were bumpers—participants were required to charge their glasses together, say, "Yum sing," i.e., drink up, then empty them in one. Even careful drinkers could get through a quarter bottle of Human-Head Horse over dinner. So much liquor, in a relatively short space of time, inevitably led to intoxication and the consequent need for strategies for appearing sober after the banquet had finished. In order to avoid the loss of face from being drunk in public, many guests would jettison their cargo of alcohol in the toilets as soon as they left the banquet.

By 1980, Cognac had become part of the identity of the Hong Kong Chinese. It was something to aspire to, and if a street sweeper dreamed of winning the Lucky Six lottery, there would be a place in his dreams for a specific brand of Cognac. The position for his fellow Chinese in the People's Republic of China, however, was very different. China's economy had flatlined between 1952 and 1978, and few of its inhabitants could dither over whether to buy XO or something more expensive for their second daughter's wedding. In the sixties and seventies, when Hong Kong's economy took off, at least thirty million Chinese died from starvation due to the failure of the so-called Cultural Revolution. This *folie de grandeur* featured the 1968 Down to the Countryside Movement, which was neither a hippy nor an Arcadian idyll but the forced reeducation of the country's intellectuals in the ways of its peasants. While Chairman Mao declared the revolution over in 1969, its philosophy persisted until his death in 1976.

Over these years, alcohol production was something of a star performer in an economy crippled by dogma, and output doubled between the start of the Cultural Revolution and its conclusion. Chinese per capita consumption also rose and, by 1976, had reached 1.34 liters per annum, against 10.18 for the average American, 5.23 for a Japanese, 4.7 for a Hong Kong Chinese, and 21.1 for the inventors of Cognac. Over 90 percent of this small total was derived from traditional beverages, with beer making up the remainder. Western-style beer had been produced in China since 1903, when the Germans had taken control of Shandong Province and installed breweries. Interestingly, beer was not condemned alongside other imperialist fluids as a capitalist poison during the Cultural Revolution, and new breweries were built in all China's provinces except Tibet. The star brew of Communist China was *Tsing Tao,* made with Lau Shan mineral water to a German recipe. Its quality was sufficient to attract attention outside China, and in 1972 it was exported to the United States to help reduce the Chinese trade deficit.

Tsing Tao was not the only Red Chinese beverage to make a name for itself overseas. *Mao-tai,* the prestige liquor of the glorious revolution, was also in demand. Distilled from brewed sorghum, mao-tai is a clear, sour-smelling spirit, as strong as nineteenth-century absinthe and notoriously inflammable. It was served to President Nixon and his entourage on his 1972 visit to China and made a lasting impression on every American who drank it. Dirck Halstead, a reporter covering the event, described mao-tai as "a highly combustible rice wine that was essentially sake–times ten." Henry Kissinger, Nixon's national security advisor, was equally impressed by mao-tai, as the following transcription from dinner in April 1974 at the Waldorf Astoria with Chinese Vice Premier Deng Xiaoping illustrates:

KISSINGER: I think if we drink enough mao-tai we can solve anything.

DENG: Then when I go back to China, I must increase production of it.

KISSINGER: You know, when the president came back from China, he wanted to show his daughter how potent mao-tai was. So he took out a bottle and poured it into a saucer and lit it, but the glass bowl broke and the mao-tai ran over the table and the table began to burn! So you nearly burned down the White House!

35   MESSAGES

While Asian nations were incorporating Western beverages within their own drinking cultures, research in America was uncovering some disagreeable information about the same drinks. In 1973, Kenneth Lyons Jones and David W. Smith, two dysmorphologists at the University of Washington, identified a pattern of deformation common to eight children born to alcoholic mothers that they named *fetal alcohol syndrome* (FAS). Their findings corroborated similar work carried out in France in 1968 and were confirmed by a Swedish study in 1979. These investigations, together with further research on primates, established an unpleasant truth about alcohol—that it was a *teratogen*. The word derives from Greek and its literal meaning is "monster maker." It is used to describe substances or processes that cause congenital malformations. Other teratogens include the antiacne drug Accutane, the rubella virus, and atomic weapons. The existence of FAS gradually crept to the attention of the public. In 1975, *Time* magazine ran an article entitled "Liquor and Babies," which explained that alcohol "easily crosses the placenta from mother to child," gave an example of a drunkard's child born with the smell of liquor on its breath, and claimed, on medical advice, that prospective mothers should "consider having abortions if they become pregnant while addicted to alcohol." Similar articles in other publications followed, and by 1977 FAS had grown into a sufficiently important public health issue to appear on television. In May of that year *NBC Evening News* included pictures of Melissa, a baby girl afflicted with the syndrome. Her features were described to the television audience as follows: "She's very, very small . . . she has microcephaly, which means that her head is very small. She also has short palpebral fissures or small eye slits, and she is mentally deficient." The broadcast was followed by a Pabst beer commercial.

The news that alcohol could damage unborn children was received with alarm. It was infinitely more sinister than the temperance movement's creed that drunkards fathered drinkers. Could martini moms beget monsters? The night after Melissa was presented to the American public, Barbara Walters on ABC and Walter Cronkite on CBS reported that, according to the National Institute on Alcohol Abuse and Alcoholism (NIAAA), any pregnant woman who had more than two drinks a day risked giving birth to a handicapped child. Walters added that "the dangers of drinking during pregnancy are so serious, therapeutic abortion for alcoholic women may be advised." Abortion had not been legal for long in the United States and the issue remained highly contentious. How likely was it that drinking damaged fetuses so badly that they should be exterminated in the womb? It was an era of health scares. A number of commonplace things, notably tobacco, had been found to be cumulative and deadly poisons. Was drinking as bad for you as smoking, if you were pregnant? According to the surgeon general it was. In 1981 he issued the warning that mothers who drank gave birth to undersized children, echoing a similar warning he had issued to cigarette smokers in 1964.

While some of the earliest research into FAS had been carried out in Europe, doctors and news anchors there did not rush to tell pregnant drinkers to seek therapeutic abortions, nor did their equivalents of the surgeon general advise abstinence in expectant mothers. The evidence in the case was different from that against smoking. While FAS was real, and caused terrible handicaps, it appeared to afflict only very heavy drinkers who took "eight to ten drinks or more per day." In consequence, European health professionals felt the risk was slight when compared to the beneficial properties of alcohol, specifically beer and wine, for expectant and nursing mothers. A glass or two a day might help ease their stress, and in Germany beer was recommended in modest portions to breast-feeding mothers. In America, in contrast, concern over FAS continued to mount. In 1982, the commissioner of the FDA suggested alcoholic beverages should carry warning labels, a theme taken up by Senator Strom Thurmond, the controversial

Republican from South Carolina who had proposed just such a measure every year since 1967.

The image of alcohol in America received a further dent at about the same time from a new group: Mothers Against Drunk Driving (MADD). MADD was formed by a Californian named Candy Lightner, whose thirteen-year-old daughter had been run down and killed by a drunken driver in 1980. Lightner resolved that she "would fight to make this needless homicide count for something positive in the years ahead," and through grassroots activism and media exposure, MADD quickly became a political force. It was a popular cause—in 1982, a total of 26,173 Americans were killed in alcohol-related road accidents. The bloodbath was worst among young Americans and was concentrated along state lines. Some of the states that had lowered their Minimum Drinking Age (MDA) during the Vietnam war had since raised it again, but others had not, so that an eighteen-year-old in a state with an MDA of twenty-one could get a drink at a bar in a neighboring state, then drive home. Such anomalies led to the emergence of so-called *blood borders*. One such border ran between Wisconsin and Illinois. In January 1980, the Prairie State had raised its MDA to twenty-one, while that of Wisconsin remained at eighteen. Within a year, alcohol-related crashes in Badger State border communities involving nineteen-year-olds from Illinois rose from just under a third to nearly one half.

Young American drinkers were also killing themselves and others in the centers of states, which led to the perception that boozing was on the rise among eighteen- to twenty-four-year-olds wherever they lived,[71] a perception assisted by changes in the portrayal of drinking by Hollywood, whose drunken teenagers were at last beginning to look their age. The exemplar of the genre, the comedy *Animal House* (1978), glorified frat house drinking, featured a drunken road trip, and inspired a generation of male students to try to crush newfangled aluminum beer cans against their foreheads, in imitation of the actor John Belushi. *Animal House* also made a bow in the direction of the Western cultural roots of drinking in its toga party scenes, in which Belushi appeared as Bacchus, with a wreath of ivy round his temples. Literature also continued to set a bad example. By the 1980s the reading lists for

---

[71] The actual drinking habits of American college students changed very little between 1973 and 1983.

high school curricula were dominated by drinkers, including Poe, London, Hemingway, Fitzgerald, Faulkner, Steinbeck, O'Neill, Kerouac, Capote, Gregory Corso, Tennessee Williams, Norman Mailer, and Edward Albee.[72]

In 1982, President Reagan appointed a commission to investigate drunk driving. The following year he broadcast its findings to the nation in a holiday season radio address. The statistics were horrifying: "We've lost more than a quarter of a million of our countrymen to drunk drivers in the last ten years. That's five hundred every week, seventy every day, one every twenty minutes." The casualty register for nonfatal injuries was even more appalling: "Every year, nearly seven hundred thousand people are injured in alcohol-related crashes. Every one of these casualties is someone's son or daughter, husband or wife, mother, father, or friend. The personal tragedies behind the statistics are enough to break your heart." Reagan concluded his broadcast with an indication that he intended to take action: "Some of our citizens have been acting irresponsibly. Drinking and driving has caused the death of many innocent people. It is up to us to put a stop to it, not in a spirit of vengeance but in the spirit of love."

The love was already being manifested in a 1983 U.S. Department of Transportation ad campaign, which—under the tagline DRINKING & DRIVING CAN KILL A FRIENDSHIP—targeted the country's sixteen- to twenty-four-year-olds, who now accounted for 42 percent of all fatal alcohol-related car crashes. After love came coercion. Reagan perceived the problem stemmed in part from the "crazy-quilt of different state driving laws," and although twenty-six of the twenty-nine states who'd lowered their minimum drinking age had reraised them by 1984, he decided a uniform federal MDA of twenty-one would be the first step toward its resolution. Reagan took pains to explain why this decision was not inconsistent with his policies in general:

> Now, some feel that my decision is at odds with my philosophical
> viewpoint that state problems should involve state solutions and it
> isn't up to a big and overwhelming government in Washington to

---

[72] "By nature, I am a gentle, responsible, useful person, with a few special insights and gifts. With liquor, I am insane."

tell the states what to do. And you're partly right. But the thing is, this problem is much more than a state problem. It's a national tragedy involving transit across state borders. Beyond that, there are some special cases in which overwhelming need can be dealt with by prudent and limited federal action. And in a case like this, where the problem is so clear-cut and the benefits are so clear-cut, then I have no misgivings about a judicious use of federal inducements to encourage the states to get moving, raise the drinking age, and save precious lives.

Prudent and limited federal action consisted of the National Minimum Drinking Age Act of 1984, which required all states to raise the minimum age for the purchase and "public possession" of alcohol to twenty-one. In order to avoid a constitutional minefield, the act refrained from labeling any states that did not comply as rebels, nor did it seek to punish them with coercion or fines. Instead, it specified a 5 percent reduction in federal highway funding to any recalcitrant states, and this incentive persuaded them all to raise their MDA to twenty-one by 1988. The new act did not envisage total prohibition for any American under the age of twenty-one. Volstead-style exemptions were made in favor of religious communicants, and the medicinal use of alcohol, and drinking in private clubs was also exempted. Moreover, people under the MDA might still drink at home. Lest young Americans be tempted to explore such loopholes, the publicity campaign against drunk driving continued with redoubled force. Celebrities joined its vanguard, contributing their talents to the cause for free. In 1985, the singer Michael Jackson received the personal thanks of President Reagan at the White House, for donating his Grammy Award–winning single "Beat It" for use in public service announcements on television and radio aimed at dissuading young people from touching alcohol.

The forces of temperance were on the rise in the 1980s, and better provided than ever before with medical and statistical ammunition to take on the demon drink. Moreover, a dry spirit permeated the age. American consumption was in decline. From a post-Prohibition peak of 2.75 gallons of alcohol per head per annum (10.45 liters) in 1981, it fell to 2.3 gallons (8.74 liters) in 1991. Hard liquor suffered the most, dropping 30 percent over the same period. Consumer tastes were changing. It was chic to look tanned, trim, and toned. People went to aerobics classes after work and drank mineral water, instead of heading to a bar for a few happy-hour martinis. The interest in bottled water was something new in the United States. While its citizens had long been devoted to their sodas, the notion of paying a premium price for a drink that fell out of the sky for free was alien to them. Their minds were changed by fashion—it became all the rage to drink European spa and mineral waters, from "sources" such as Perrier, which were promoted and sold as a kind of cleansing elixir. Bottled water was perfectly suited to the spirit of the eighties. The nourishing, and therefore fattening, qualities of alcoholic drinks worked against them, and designer water had a freshness, an implied vitality to it that was better suited to consumers' aspirations than the deadening consequences of drunkenness. In a decade dedicated to appearances, drunks were considered unhealthy. Swollen, pitted noses laced with exploding veins, slurred speech, trembling hands, tendencies toward violent rage or clumsy overaffection, sewer breath, and liquid bowels were all at odds with the new ideal. Health consciousness also affected the tastes of those who still drank. Instead of choosing dark, strong, traditional pick-me-ups like whiskey, they called for light rum and white wine coolers. Even the beer market was affected. Brewers were forced to introduce "lite" brands, which featured less color and flavor, and (critically) fewer calories.

The beverage alcohol industry found itself under siege in the 1980s. Its products deformed unborn children, turned drivers into killers, and ruined peoples' looks and waistlines. A change of image was in order. Booze needed a new appearance to tempt back deserters and make its steady friends consume more. Its manufacturers placed their hopes in lifestyle advertising. If drinking could be associated with activity and adventure, with skydiving, car racing, and rodeos, then people might love it once again. The new approach was commented on by *Advertising Age* magazine in 1984: "More and more it seems that the liquor industry has awakened to the truth. It isn't selling the bottle or the glass or even liquor. It's selling fantasies. Life-style approaches have come into favor as the most effective way for the liquor industry to promote its wares. Psychologically, for consumers to be attracted to these ads, they need to be attracted to the people in them, to identify with the fantasies they create."

Perhaps the most effective lifestyle advertising campaign of the period was the *Spuds MacKenzie* series for Bud Lite, featuring an English bull terrier with a black patch of fur around one eye. Billed as the ultimate party animal, Spuds was introduced to America during a commercial break in Super Bowl XXI of 1987. Spuds (in real life a bitch named Honey Tree Evil Eye) had an entourage of three beautiful and scantily clad young women–the Spudettes–who accompanied him on various adventures. The idea of representing the ideal drinker as an animal in broadcast media ads had been pioneered in Great Britain, where Hoffmeister beer had chosen a bear called George as its archetypal customer. George (an actor in a bear costume) was represented as a natural leader among a gang of young men, the best at darts and hoops and finding excitement and girls. The campaign's tagline was *Follow the bear.* Spuds resembled George in many aspects– he was leader of his peer hierarchy, irresistible to women, and his life was spent in having fun. The ads appealed to Americans of all ages. A later survey showed that 88 percent of fifth- and sixth-grade schoolchildren could match the slogan "Spuds McKenzie, the original party animal" with Budweiser the brewer.

Neo-Prohibitionists, concerned that children might be persuaded into drinking beer by a pet dog, revived the alcohol advertising debate of the 1950s. What was to stop infants, inflamed by Spuds, from raiding their parents' fridges for Bud Lite? The matter was raised in Congress. Dr. Jean Kilbourne advised the chamber that drink ads created "a climate in which dangerous attitudes toward alcohol are presented as normal, appropriate, and innocuous. Most important, alcohol advertising spuriously links alcohol with precisely those attributes and qualities [like] happiness, wealth, prestige, sophistication, success, maturity, athletic ability, virility, creativity, sexual satisfaction, that the misuse of alcohol usually diminishes and destroys." Not only was such advertising dangerous, it was ubiquitous. Alcohol was promoted on a scale similar to food and cosmetics. In 1988, over eight hundred million dollars was poured into television promotions for wine and beer. And ads weren't the only problem. It was estimated that America's brewers "paid for about 10 percent of all sponsorships of athletic, music, cultural, and other special events" in the country; and that many of these events attracted "large audiences of underage drinkers."

In response to such alarm calls for action, Congress considered two categories of marketing control measures that might be applied to alcohol: Restrictions on advertising, including mandatory counterpropaganda; and health warning labels, as had been imposed on tobacco packaging. The issue was raised in the Senate by Strom Thurmond, who singled out Spuds MacKenzie for an especial curse and berated a cardboard cutout of the animal during a speech from the floor. By 1989 opinion in both houses had tilted in favor of some form of control. The drinks lobby fought back by pointing out that per capita consumption and advertising spending were contrary trends: They were competing harder for fewer customers. Moreover, in their opinion, "to blame advertising for the tragic effects of alcohol abuse" would be "to controvert the best available social science." Images of bull terriers in midget submarines did not turn people into alcoholics. However, sentiment in Washington was against them. The dangerous consequences of drinking, whether provoked by advertising or not, were highlighted by the Carrolton bus disaster of 1988, when a drunk traveling the wrong way down a highway collided head-on with a school bus on hire to a church youth club, causing twenty-seven fatalities and fifty-four other injuries. It was the worst such accident in the country's history, horrible in excess of the neo-Prohibitionists' predictions.

Action against alcohol became inevitable. In 1988, Strom Thurmond introduced a bill to the Senate, supported by Orrin Hatch, Ted Kennedy, and Al Gore, that aimed to place a two-part warning on all drink packaging, which, in its final form, was as follows: "(1) According to the Surgeon General, women should not drink alcoholic beverages during pregnancy because of the risk of birth defects. (2) Consumption of alcoholic beverages impairs your ability to drive a car or operate machinery, and may cause health problems." The bill was signed into federal law in 1989. In retrospect it was a victory for the alcohol lobby. Pregnant women had never been a major market, and the warning against drunk driving absolved brewers, distillers, and winemakers of any potential liability to the relatives of the victims of drunk drivers. Moreover, the debate about booze advertising had revealed weaknesses in the arguments of their opponents, many of which were founded on the disease theory of alcoholism that had risen to prominence in the 1950s. If alcoholism was a disease, then how did someone catch it from a TV commercial? The idea that Spuds, or his successors, the Singing Frogs, might trigger an innate and insatiable lust for drink, as strobes set off epileptics, was the best explanation neoprohibitionists could offer, but it was not enough to convince the legislature to act against drink advertising.

The appearance of warnings had no evident effect on the nation's drinking. The gently declining trend in consumption did not suddenly plunge, and its continuance downward was best explained by changes in corporate attitudes toward drinking. Alcohol, and alcoholism, were considered backward in the brave new world of globalization and information technology. Drinking was regarded as a juvenile activity—something to be experienced at college but abandoned once upon the corporate ladder. Multinational companies evolved antialcohol policies that their employees were expected to follow for the good of their careers. The three-martini business lunch was consigned to history, as were many corporate cocktail cabinets. The new ethos was apparent in the 1985 movie *Wall Street,* a Faustian tale about Bud, a young stockbroker eager to share in the immense fortunes being made in the markets at that time. Bud solicits the attention of Gordon Gekko, a corporate raider, who epitomizes the new model capitalist. "Lunch is for wimps," he declares at their first encounter, and Bud pointedly calls for Evian when he meets Gekko in a restaurant at night. The old order is represented by Bud's father, a union leader at Bluestar Airlines, who does his business with the men he represents over a few beers in the local bar. Gekko aims to take over Bluestar in order to break it into pieces and rob its pension fund, and Bud is forced to choose between old-fashioned beer-drinking, metal-bashing America and the greed-is-good philosophy of Gordon Gekko. After a bottle of whiskey he decides to do the right thing—intoxication leads to an epiphany that restores his moral perspective.

There were genuine monetary benefits to be gained from alcohol-free workplaces. Companies that introduced such policies found their workers had fewer accidents, thus reducing insurance premiums and compensation payments, and that they had to sack fewer workers for drunkenness, enabling savings in termination costs and the expenses of recruiting replacements. IBM, then the most profitable industrial company in America, was a shining example of an efficient alcohol-free corporation. It had long frowned on drinking among its employees, to whom it issued etiquette manuals that set out appropriate hairstyles, advised them not to wear a blue suit with brown shoes, and pointed out that being "under the influence of or affected by alcohol" constituted "inappropriate conduct" and was grounds for dismissal.

The private-sector move toward alcohol-free workplaces was followed by federal regulation. The Omnibus Transportation Employee Testing Act of 1991 required alcohol testing of safety-sensitive transportation employees in aviation, trucking, railroads, mass transit, pipelines, and other transportation industries. The act affected several million workers, any of whom, subject to appropriate procedure, could be tested for drink at any time while on duty. Despite the eminently sensible nature of the legislation, it was controversial. How far should the government, or an employer, be permitted to pry into the personal habits of a worker? The contract between employer and employee was a commercial arrangement and should not dictate the latter's conduct outside of working hours. Vows of sobriety—or chastity for that matter, for the country was in the middle of the AIDS panic and compulsory testing was being considered for that too—were more appropriate to monasteries than to capitalist nations.

The Omnibus Transportation Employee Testing Act rounded off ten bad years for alcohol in America. There had been, however, a few bright spots in the gloom. The television series *Cheers,* which, after a poor first season in 1982, had shot up the ratings and spent eight years as one of the ten most-watched programs in America, was one such glimmer of hope. Almost all of its action took place in a barroom, which was modeled on the Bull & Finch Pub in Boston. Despite the promise this location offered for bottle fights between aging rummies, or as a hangout for the unemployed, *Cheers* focused on social drinking. The bar's clientele were rarely shown under the influence, and when they were they were credited with motives, like promotion at work. *Cheers* appealed to the 66 percent of the American population aged fourteen years and over who admitted to drinking. The program was rewarded for its realism with twenty-six Emmy Awards over its eleven-season lifespan.

The final episode of *Cheers,* broadcast on May 23, 1993, was the most-watched TV show of that year. For most of its run the habit it portrayed had been demonized and regulated against. Just as in the glory days of the WCTU, children were being taught, as fact, that alcohol led to mental and physical ruin. If they started drinking they would move on to crack and quite possibly catch AIDS en route. The bias against alcohol was apparent at the highest level. The federal government's *Dietary Guidelines for Americans,* issued in 1991, advised adults as well as children not to drink at all. Alcoholic beverages had "no net health benefit"; they were "linked with many health problems," were "the cause of many accidents," and could "lead to addiction." "Their consumption is not recommended," the guidelines concluded. However, and in the same year in which they were published, evidence to the contrary was broadcast on prime-time television, which was so persuasive that the minority of Americans who did not drink might have been expected to buy a bottle or two and toast farewell forever to abstinence.

The revelations were contained in the November 17, 1991, edition of *60 Minutes,* hosted by Morley Safer. Its subject was a health conundrum, known as the *French Paradox,* which Safer phrased as follows: "So why is it that the French, who eat 30 percent more fat than we do, suffer fewer heart attacks, even though they smoke more and exercise less? All you have to do is look at the numbers: If you're a middle-aged American man, your chances of dying of a heart attack are three times greater than a Frenchman of the same age. Obviously, they're doing something right—something Americans are not doing." Safer examined several possible theories as to what that something could be. Was it because the French ate more fruit and vegetables, or that they lingered over their meals instead of bolting them down standing up, or could it be because they drank ten times as much red wine? In the opinion of *60 Minutes,* the solution to the French Paradox was hidden in a bottle: "There has been for years the belief by doctors in many countries that alcohol, in particular red wine, reduces the risk of heart disease. . . . Now it's been all but confirmed."

The program featured two medical experts, Dr. Curtis Ellison of Boston, who confirmed the potential of wine to protect against heart disease, but also drew attention to "the tremendous problem of alcohol abuse"; and Dr. Serge Renaud of the French health service, who was more bullish on the issue, and who was happy to state, "It's well-documented that a moderate intake of alcohol prevents coronary heart disease by as much as fifty percent." At the show's conclusion, Safer raised a glass of red wine to the camera and commented, "So the answer to the riddle, the explanation of the paradox, may lie in this inviting glass." The program was watched by an estimated 33.7 million Americans, who responded positively to the good news. Within a month of the broadcast, sales of red wine increased by 44 percent.

Morley Safer was honored with a special prize from LVMH Moët Hennessy Louis Vuitton, the French champagne and luxury goods producer.

While the idea that drinking might be good for you came as a surprise to most Americans in 1991, the evidence had been around for a while; indeed, ever since the depths of Prohibition. In 1926, Raymond S. Pearl, biologist, pioneer researcher into aging, wine lover, and *bon viveur,* had published *Alcohol and Longevity,* in which he demonstrated that moderate drinkers outlived both alcoholics and abstainers. The book had been inspired by research Pearl had carried out into chicken breeding. He had decided to test the hypothesis that alcohol affected the birds' fertility, and noted that those chickens that had been made to drink "far outlived their untreated brothers and sisters." Moving on to humans, he examined the data from a survey made in Baltimore on tuberculosis, involving 3,084 men and 2,164 women, and found that, after disregarding other factors, those of his subjects who treated themselves with bootleg hooch also outlived the dry members of their peer group.

Pearl's findings—that moderate drinkers lived longer—were confirmed again and again over the next seven decades. However, and unlike his discovery that smokers died younger, they had little impact in the sphere of public health during the same period. No matter how much evidence was heaped up in favor of booze, the federal government refused to recommend it to the people. Sadly, those most in need of learning about the life-sustaining properties of drink were the least likely to have come across the issue before it appeared on TV. Abstinence was most common among Americans "with less than a high school degree," 51 percent of whom were dry, compared to only 20 percent of college graduates. The category who'd spent fewer years in education already had a shorter life expectancy than their better-educated peers—why hold back from helping them toward equality?

Once the health benefits of alcohol were well and truly in the public domain, California's winemakers explored ways of keeping them there by reminding drinkers of the salutary properties of their product. Since they were compelled to warn drinkers about the dangers of DUI and FAS, might they not also warn them wine was good for their hearts? Despite the evidence in favor, they were not hopeful. The federal regulator, the Bureau of Alcohol, Tobacco, and Firearms (BATF), did not allow alcohol manufacturers to make "therapeutic or curative claims" about their products. Past attempts by people in the wine trade to add positive statements to their labels had been rejected, notably in the case of Kermit Lynch, an importer, who had sought and been refused permission to quote Thomas Jefferson ("Wine from long habit has become an indispensable for my health"), Louis Pasteur ("Wine is the healthiest, most hygienic beverage known to man"), and 1 Timothy ("Drink no longer water, but use a little wine for thy stomach's sake") on his merchandise.[73]

Initial attempts to incorporate quotations from or references to *60 Minutes* into publicity material were rebuffed by the BATF. The Leeward Winery of Ventura, California, which summarized the program and the benefits of drinking in its March 1992 newsletter, was told to stop distributing it. Mondavi, which had added neck hangers to its bottles referring to *60 Minutes*, was also ordered to desist. However, in October of the same year, Beringer Estates of St. Helena succeeded in getting approval for a neck hanger with quotes from the program, one of which was Dr. Ellison's reference to the "tremendous problem of alcohol abuse." Despite being given the go-ahead, Beringer decided not to proceed, fearful of inflaming the ire of federal agencies other than BATF, among whom antipathy toward alcohol was universal, no matter how much evidence had piled up in favor of moderate drinking. By 1993, studies involving a total of more than half a million subjects of "varying ages, both genders, and different economic and racial backgrounds," adjusted "for concurrent risk factors—including diet, smoking, age, high blood pressure, and other medical conditions—and to allow for separate analyses of lifetime abstainers and ex-drinkers, drinkers who reduced their consumption for health reasons, all nondrinkers, and coronary-artery-disease-risk candidates" had "consistently found coronary artery disease risk is reduced by drinking." Indeed, when taken together, the studies made "the risk-reduction link between alcohol and coronary artery disease close to irrefutable."

Notwithstanding such persuasive numbers, numerous official and independent bodies in the health care industry continued to attack alcohol and lobbied for a "sin tax" on the fluid to pay for the Medicaid reforms proposed by the new Democrat administration under Presi-

---

[73] Lynch later pointed out to BATF that "your office should proceed with caution when deciding whether Thomas Jefferson's writing is too dangerous to be read by the American public."

dent William Jefferson Clinton. The liquor industry lobbied back, and both sides watched anxiously to see which one of them he would believe. Their mutual curiosity was satisfied in February 1993, when a delegation from the Wine Institute met with the president at the White House. According to a reporter at the scene: "With flash bulbs popping, Wine Institute President John A. De Luca told the forty-six-year-old Clinton about recent medical research revealing potential health benefits from moderate alcohol consumption. Clinton interrupted, noting appreciatively that he had reached the age that when all this health data comes out, I want to take another glass of wine.... Before Clinton could even finish his sentence, the group erupted in applause. The president grinned, beating his chest, thump, thump, thump, like a healthy heart."

36 SINGLETONS, WINE LAKES, AND THE MOSCOW EXPRESS

The American samples that I have defined as "problem drinkers" in my treatment studies have reported . . . an average consumption of approximately fifty drinks per week. In Norway and Sweden, the audiences tended to be shocked by this amount of drinking and argued that my samples must consist of chronic addicted alcoholics. In Scotland and Germany, on the other hand, the skepticism tended to be aimed at whether these individuals had a real problem at all because this level was regarded as quite ordinary drinking.

—American clinician on tour in Europe in 1983

The numerous studies which had concluded that alcohol could enhance longevity all noted that its benefits were greatest for moderate drinkers. But what constituted moderate drinking? Not finishing the bottle every night? A sip of champagne on New Year's Eve? Raymond Pearl had chosen vernacular definitions in his pioneering study: "Surely it is in accord with common usage to call a person who gets drunk a heavy drinker. Also it is common usage to call a person who drinks a little but never gets drunk a moderate drinker." While perfectly intelligible to the average drinker, such definitions were too imprecise to issue to individuals wishing to take up alcohol or cut down their consumption. Numerical guidelines were required, so that people might count their drinks as they did their calories. Moreover, such guidelines needed to provide for the different strengths of spirits, wine, and beer. The solution to the latter problem was the *standard drink,* a hypothetical measure of alcohol that could be equated to a glass of wine, a beer, or a shot of spirits. The issue was addressed by governments worldwide, resulting in a variety of standards. The most generous definition was made in Japan, where a splendid twenty-eight grams of pure alcohol was chosen as being a representative drink. The meanest was poured in Austria, where a mere 5 grams counted as a measure. America came to rest in the middle: standard serving sizes of beer (12 ounces), wine (5 ounces), and spirits (1.5 ounces) were all officially defined as containing the equivalent of 14 grams of ethanol.

But how many of these standard drinks could people consume and protect their hearts without compromising their livers? In Great Britain, which had settled on an austere measure called the *unit—*containing only 0.8 grams of pure alcohol, equivalent to a little glass of 11 percent wine, a small measure of spirits, or a half pint of weak beer—the Royal College of Physicians (RCP) had a stab at the task of quantifying safe limits. In 1982 it settled on fifty-six units per week, or roughly nine bottles of wine, for an adult male. This wonderfully liberal allowance, construed by some as an invitation to drunkenness, was reviewed in 1987 when the RCP published *A Great and Growing Evil: The Medical Consequences of Alcohol Abuse,* which cut it by more than half. The new report set the maximum recommended weekly intake at twenty-one units for men, and fourteen for women.[74] A member of the working party responsible for the cuts later described how they had been calculated: "Those limits were really plucked out of the air. They were not based on any firm evidence at all. It was a sort of intelligent guess by a Committee." Better that people were made to veer in favor of caution on the basis of false figures than be allowed to make up their own minds on the best available evidence. Although statistics suggested, and

---

[74] Lower limits were prescribed for women because they tend to weigh less and to have a greater percentage of body fat than men, leading to higher concentrations of alcohol in the blood and tissues after the same number of drinks.

some doctors protested, that up to forty-two weekly units of alcohol were better than none at all in terms of protecting against heart attacks, the invented limits were nonetheless confirmed as government gospel.

Twenty-one units a week, although a mere three and a half bottles of wine, or only half a bottle a day, could, however, still cause problems if a drinker decided to knock it all back at once. Many tried: Britons did not consume alcohol at a uniform rate–they tended to drink most at the end of a working week, and (unlike their ancestors) very little on Monday mornings. On their weekend sprees they clogged up the country's emergency wards to have their stomachs pumped, their bones set, their burns treated, and their cuts stitched. This style of drinking was particularly common in northeast England, where the principal function of alcohol was considered to be to produce drunkenness. The culture of the age and the place was reflected in the pages of *Viz*, a Newcastle-based adult comic, whose readers competed in its letters columns as to which of them had wasted most of their pay on booze.

Curious to relate, the episodic style of drinking that was commonplace in Newcastle had not been considered as a factor in determining safe limits until the 1990s, when health care professionals and statisticians decided to look at drinking occasions, and at people's reasons for drinking, as opposed to weekly or annual averages. They found that in the real world, a third of the people might drink two-thirds of the alcohol in one country, whereas in another, two-thirds drank seven-tenths–on Friday and Saturday nights. In extreme cases, such as the Feria de San Fermín in Pamplona, the scene for Hemingway's *Sun Also Rises*, almost the whole town, and people from miles around, got drunk for an entire week every July. Such sporadic excess was labeled *binge* drinking, and the concept of safe limits was modified to take account of the phenomenon.

In 1995, the British government refined its guidelines in accordance with the new thinking. Instead of suggesting no more than twenty-one units per week, it advised that men should drink no more than three to four units each day, and women only one or two. It emphasized that a man downing more than ten units in one sitting, and a woman more than seven, were, technically, on a binge with a capital *B*. Bingers were advised to detoxify themselves at once by abstaining from alcohol for at least the next forty-eight hours. However, while the ten-unit definition of bingeing for men

A strip from Viz magazine

had seemed plausible when it represented ten separate drinks, the average strength of these had been rising, especially in the case of beer.

British brewing underwent radical changes in the last quarter of the twentieth century. In the 1970s, the market had been dominated by large brewers and their tied pubs. In order to maximize profits, the brewers had attempted to replace traditional "live" beers, so-called because they continued to ferment in their casks after delivery to pub cellars, with "nitrokeg." This latter style, of which Watney's infamous *Red Barrel* was the exemplar, was pasteurized, filtered, then packaged in steel or aluminum kegs and delivered to the tap by forcing compressed nitrogen into the beer. Nitrokeg was a modern, stable beverage, less wasteful than real ale, and easier to transport and store. It lacked, however, the delicate and changing flavor of traditional living beers. Its introduction prompted howls of outrage from purists, who formed the *Campaign for Real Ale* (CAMRA), whose mission was to protect the quality and diversity of British beer. CAMRA became the most successful single issue consumer group in the country, and through its efforts real ale was rescued from the edge of extinction. Diversity was also protected by the Thatcher administration, which issued legislation known as the *Beer Orders* in 1989, whose purpose was to end the cartel in tied houses run by a handful of large brewers. The orders forced any brewer owning more than a thousand pubs to sell down to that limit. It also required tied houses to offer guest beers. It inspired a renaissance in craft brewing and also, as Britons revived the beer recipes of their ancestors, a return of the alcoholic strength of the average brew to pre–World War II levels.

The increase in potency was also prompted by the growth in lager sales. This once-alien beverage had gained market share from both real ale and nitrokeg at an explosive rate. Whereas in 1970 only 7 percent of pints drunk in English pubs were lager, by 1996 it accounted for more than half of all beer sold. Although early British lagers were weak, rising demand inspired foreign brewers to enter the market, and their products were, to a nation used to 3.2 percent beer, very strong. *Holsten Pils,* the pioneer in this new sector, weighed in at 5.5 percent ABV. While Germans drank it for breakfast by the liter, in Britain Holsten Pils was sold in 275-milliliter bottles in deference to its relative kick. Incidentally, it was also marketed as a lite drink, in the sense of being low in calories: "Holsten Pils, the beer where more of the sugar turns to alcohol." Bottled lagers, which eventually settled around 5 percent ABV for taxation reasons, pushed up the strength of draft lager, which pulled up the strength of bitter.

In consequence, the average pint was no longer two units but three and a bit, which meant that any man who drank more than two and half pints of beer was, officially, bingeing. Hitherto, to binge, in English, had implied great, glorious, or self-destructive excess, and bingeing had been the province of Vikings, Reformation poets, and sybarites, of Eric Bloodaxe, the Earl of Rochester, and Lord Byron. The suggestion that someone who had a pint at lunch, a second after work, and then opened a can of beer in front of the television at home with his dinner was embarking on a binge was open to criticism. The body digests about a unit an hour, so that by the time the two-and-a-half-pint binge drinker[75] had finished his spree he would be sober enough to pass a drunk-driving test; indeed, if he stretched out the latter part of his binge over three hours, he would never be drunk enough to fail one.

Some, however, still flew the flag for the old-fashioned meaning of *binge,* notably Jeffrey Bernard, "Low Life" columnist for the *Spectator* magazine, who chronicled his daily dissipation at the Coach and Horses pub in Soho between 1975 and his death from alcohol-related illnesses in 1997. Described as "a suicide note in weekly installments," Bernard's column set out the pains as well as pleasures of drinking. As his medical problems worsened (he had one leg amputated in 1994) he became something of a sainted figure—a man whose eyes were fixed on imminent death and so able to provide an unbiased view on life. Interviewed by the *Idler* magazine in 1995, when diabetes and a recurrent kidney problem had forced him to be dry, the dying sage set out what to him were the powers of alcohol to improve or diminish the quality of existence:

IDLER: What's it like not drinking?
BERNARD: Awful. Boring. Miserable. Lonely. It's like being half dead.
IDLER: What does drinking give people?
BERNARD: A cerebral kick, a lift. Confidence. The ability to chat up
    crumpet. Oh, to me not drinking is like being dead, almost. I sit
    here taking endless journeys down memory lane.

---

[75] A female *binger* needed less than two pints of beer, or three small glasses of wine, in an evening to qualify for the soubriquet.

Bernard, however, was perceived as something of an anachronism— a relic of the old school that held it morally permissible to drink oneself into the grave. Most Britons, like Americans, were drinking in different ways than preceding generations. They, too, had fallen in love with bottled mineral water, and spritzers, and light spirits instead of dark; their preference for pale lager over amber bitter has been documented above. In contrast to Americans, however, they were consuming more alcohol, not less, and slowly reascending the league table of drinking nations. Despite all the good advice on safe limits, British per capita consumption of alcohol climbed in the 1980s and 1990s.[76] The nation's schoolchildren led the trend. According to the RCP, the number of twelve- to thirteen-year-old boys and girls who admitted to drinking in the preceding week rose from 29 percent of boys and 26 percent of girls in 1996, to 38 percent and 30 percent respectively three years later. In 1998, the equivalent figures for fourteen- to fifteen-year-olds were 55 percent and 53 percent. They were encouraged in their habits by the appearance of a new style of beverage—*alcopops*—or alcoholic sodas. The first in the class was *Two Dogs* alcoholic lemonade, 4.8 percent ABV, which adults drank au naturel, or mixed with their white rum or vodka. Two Dogs soon had a pack of imitators. Engineered to appeal to the sweeter tooth, alcopops, unlike beer, did not taste very different from sodas; indeed a child might guzzle one without realizing his or her mistake. Alcopops also helped grown-ups who could not stomach real ale to graduate from soft drinks to wet ones.

The rate of growth in alcopop sales was matched by that in wine consumption. The nation's adults, once they had outgrown bingeing, drifted into lifestyle drinking. The British were told on television and in books that French, Italian, and Spanish peasants lived happier and longer lives than white-collar workers in London because of their diet, part of which was wine. Annual per capita consumption rose to more than twenty-five bottles. Much of the new demand was accounted for by British women, who, as the statistics for teen tippling revealed, were starting younger and drinking more. Sixty-nine percent of them drank wine, against 62 percent of men, and they were responsible for over 70 percent of wine purchases in supermarkets.

---

[76] And continues to do so in the present decade.

Their fictional role model was Bridget Jones, a thirtysomething working girl whose adventures in love, and attempts to control her intake of calories, cigarettes, and units of alcohol, were chronicled by Helen Fielding in *Bridget Jones's Diary* (1996). Despite her resolution to stay within the government's "sensible drinking" guidelines of no more than 14 units per week, Bridget often exceeded her quota in a single night, and managed 3,836 of them in less than one year, or just under 74 a week, enough for two "Heavy" drinkers as defined by the RCP. She also underestimated her unit count. A Bridget unit was a bottle of strong beer, a big swig out of a vodka bottle, or a large glass of Chardonnay, each one of which was more than an official measure. In this respect, she was representative of her fellow Britons, who confessed to drinking far less than they actually did. Indeed, if UK General Household Survey reports could be believed, then, in the words of the RCP, "surprisingly, it appears that nearly half the alcohol on which duty is paid is not consumed."[77]

Drinking with her urban family was Bridget's principal leisure activity. She and her fellow singletons viewed it as an essential rite of friendship, a preliminary to sex, and a passport to amnesia when they were disappointed in love. Although they had harsh words for its effects on their heads the next morning and on their behavior the night before, they criticized alcohol far less than they praised it or consumed it. Indeed, their compulsive drinking set them apart from their parents' generation.

Bridget Jones's Diary, its sequel, *Bridget Jones: the Edge of Reason*, and the movies of each struck a chord among young, single postfeminist metropolitan women throughout the Anglo-Saxon diaspora. They had not lost their mothers' aspirations to be mothers, but they had gained a male confidence in their pursuit of their careers, their partners, and their drinking habits. Their behavior resembled that of the angry young men of their fathers' generation—they swore, smoked, had extramarital sex, they suffered hangovers, and they owned their own houses. They were conscious of being different. Bridget Jones, though happy to admit to frequent bingeing in her diary, did not ex-

---

[77] The problem of underreporting was not confined to Britain. A 1986 survey of drinking habits in Tucson, Arizona, revealed that while 85 percent of respondents said they did not drink beer, 75 percent of the city's trash cans had empty beer containers in them.

pect it from her mother: "My mum has drunk nothing but a single cream sherry on a Sunday night since 1952, when she got slightly tipsy on a pint of cider at Mavis Enderby's twenty-first, and has never let herself or anyone else forget it. 'There's nothing worse than a woman drunk, darling.'"

The favorite tipple of Bridget and real-life female singletons was white wine. Their enthusiasm for New World Chardonnays altered British tastes so much that in 2004, Australia displaced France as the principal supplier of wine to the UK. The shift was dramatic–whereas in 1997, 35 percent of the wine drunk in Britain was French, by 2004 this figure had declined to 20 percent, against a 21 percent share for Australia. Falling demand abroad for French wine was exceeded by falling demand at home. Once the champions of the league table of drinking nations, the French had tumbled to eighth place by 2003, just below Great Britain. The fall was occasioned by a collapse in wine consumption, which dropped by more than a third in the last two decades of the twentieth century. The quintessentially French beverage, celebrated by the country's poets, statesmen, and medics as liquid inspiration, no longer commanded the affection of the masses. Their novel indifference was accounted for in part by *gastro-anomie*:[78] Instead of sitting down to a three-course lunch with wine each day, the French grabbed a burger and fries at McDonald's and lubricated their throats with water or sodas. Another factor in declining wine consumption was the introduction of strict legislation against drunk driving.

France had famously grim drunk-driving statistics. The annual holiday migrations to and from its coasts, which migrants punctuated with long and liquid lunches, were spattered with the blood of fatal accidents. In 1995, the government acted to reduce the carnage by redefining what constituted drunk driving. The permissible blood alcohol content (BAC) was lowered to 0.05 grams per liter–half the level in the United States at the time. The new lower limits were enforced with roadside checks and stiffer penalties for infringements, and resulted in an immediate 5 percent reduction in fatalities. The decline thereafter, however, was slow. The one-or-more-for-the-road mentality died hard and took with it some celebrated victims, notably Diana, Princess of Wales.

---

[78] A fatal weariness with *gourmandisme*.

Although French traffic fatalities declined by a fifth between 1993 and 2003, the country still had one of the worst road safety records in Europe. Twice as many French people were killed in automobile accidents than in Britain, and they were twice as likely to be drunk at the time. However, a fresh propaganda campaign from the government, which caused an immediate drop in restaurant wine sales, drew protests from the country's vintners. It was wrong, in their opinion, to tell French people to drink no alcohol before they got behind the wheel. They issued counterpropaganda, reminding drivers that although the legal BAC was low, it was better than nothing at all, and recommended they should consider two or three glasses of wine, with food, whenever they broke their journeys.

The French wine industry was in a desperate state. Supply had not slumped in sympathy with demand. In the same years that the French and foreigners drank less French wine, their country was producing more and more of it. The problem, moreover, was trans-European: Italians and Spaniards were also making more, and drinking less, and wanted to sell their surplus in France. Further complications arose from the appearance of New World wines in French supermarkets. The very existence of such fluids, let alone the notion that patriots might prefer them to the offerings of their native land, was an insult to French winemakers and a threat to the Gallic way. In the words of a Languedoc vintner, "Each bottle of American and Australian wine that lands in Europe is a bomb targeted at the heart of our rich European culture."

Fortunately for the producers, *rich European culture*, as interpreted by the European Union, meant providing subsidies to agriculture. In the case of wine, the EU operated an intervention mechanism to buy up surplus production. This was *crisis distillation*, introduced in 1982 as a measure for use only in emergencies, but operated in twenty-two of the twenty-six years since, and which made the supranational entity the biggest buyer of French, Italian, and Spanish wines in the world. Presently, one in every six bottles of European wines is bought by the program for conversion into ethanol for use in fuel additives, industrial disinfectant, and vinegar. Alcohol fuels not just the driver but also the automobile in France. One percent of all French gasoline comes from crisis-distilled wine—each bottle being good for a few kilometers' travel down the autoroute.

Crisis distillation was not popular in the sunny vineyards of

Languedoc-Roussillon, whose proud vintners did not welcome the forced conversion of their liquid artistry into petrol, aftershave, and antiseptic. Their government had betrayed them by permitting competition. If foreigners were barred from the market, then all would be well once more. A resistance was formed, which attacked the bastions of free trade and of government authority. It called itself the *Comité Régional d'Action Viticoles* (CRAV). CRAV's clandestine operatives, some of whom had learned their trade against the Germans in World War II, hijacked bulk transporters of foreign wines, and French wines from different regions, and emptied their contents into the drains. They dynamited government offices and set fire to police cars; they organized riots and sent death threats. This display of brute force by militant vintners focused the French government on their woes. Studies were made and it was concluded that image was the problem in Languedoc-Roussillon. Few foreigners knew where it was in France, its wines were too heterodox, and their labels were confusing. They lacked the clarity of New World wines, most of which were marketed as varietals—Chardonnay or Pinot Noir, for example. French state funds were dispensed to reform the image, and in 2006 the pending introduction of a new generic appellation, *South of France*, was announced. According to Jacques Gravegeal, the man behind the uberbrand, these three words would turn consumers on the proper way: "Languedoc-Roussillon is still the biggest wine-producing region in the world, but it is a hidden region of France. No one knows where it is. When you talk about the South of France it is different, it creates an image in peoples' minds."

The problems of the south were also present in the west. Even Bordeaux was suffering. While its best wines fetched record prices,[79] its table wines were being crisis-distilled. The strict rules of the various AOCs limiting how wines could be made meant that many areas could not produce the single-grape varietals that were most in demand. The sheer number of producers (Bordeaux had over seventeen thousand) also worked against the region. New World vintners were winning market share by offering a few clearly branded products—Paul Masson Chardonnay, for example, was the best-selling wine in Bordeaux's oldest overseas market. Such problems were compounded by

---

[79] Château Pétrus 2005 (rated 96–100 by Robert Parker) costs $4,000 per bottle.

complacency among the region's vintners. "We thought we were the king of carrots," one confessed. "We just didn't see the others coming.... We never bothered about consumers. Now we're beginning to wake up. We understand that the consumer is what really matters. We can make the best wine in the world, but if nobody buys it, it's useless."

Other regions were suffering alongside Bordeaux and Languedoc-Rousillon. In 2006, France was subsidized by the EU to crisis-distill 150 million liters of quality wine, and an equal amount of table wine. Italy, also in a glut, was paid to refine 250 million liters of table wine and a further 10 million of quality vintages. The exceptional cost to the EU, mostly borne by countries making little or no wine of their own, was 131 million euros. The community also spent 220 million on maintaining its so-called *wine lake,* a network of warehouses that contained 1.5 billion liters of unwanted wine, i.e., more than four bottles a head for every living European. Such wastage was prodigal even by its own standards. According to Mrs. Fischer Boel, the official charged with formulating a new policy on wine for the EU, it was "a ridiculous way to use taxpayers' money.... We are producing too much wine for which there is no market." She proposed the destruction of up to four hundred thousand hectares of vines within the EU. Their crop was worthless and it would be cheaper to pay their owners to grow nothing.

While the EU struggled with overproduction, in the USSR the reverse was the case. In consequence, its leaders started to lurch toward capitalism, intending to embrace it. The process commenced under President Gorbachev in 1986, after the failure of a last-ditch effort to save the Soviet Union for Communism by making its comrade citizens sober. The Kremlin had decided that the West was winning the cold war because its workers did not mix vodka drinking with making computers. Taxes were raised on alcohol, new criminal offenses for drunkenness were introduced, and drunks were censored out of movies. Male life expectancy leapt by three years, from sixty-two to sixty-five. However, the antialcohol campaign had little impact on Russian productivity and provoked a public backlash against the system that had initiated it. Popular discontent, in combination with economic stagnation, forced Gorbachov to introduce *Perestroika* (economic restructuring) to Soviet territories.

Perestroika was painful. The temporary restrictions on the manufacture and supply of alcohol had driven its production under-ground. *Samogon* (moonshine) poured out of illicit stills, whose operators did not care if their raw materials were toxic so long as they were cheap. Together with crisis sources (there was no such thing as a Communist wine lake) of alcohol such as aftershave and brake fluid, samogon killed tens of thousands of Russians every year. Moreover, temperance reforms attached to perestroika, including the prohibition of alcohol at state functions and the promotion of tea-houses and ice-cream parlors, drove drunks into each other's homes, or onto the streets, where they drank openly, for oblivion, and per-sonified the atomization of Soviet society. Their poet was Venedict Erofeev, whose *Moscow Stations* depicts the failed rail journey of a Moscow drinker to meet his sweetheart in Petushki. The book is distinguished for its black humor and alarming cocktail recipes. Its narrator considers himself a scientific alcoholic who is inspired to drink deep by a chorus of loving angels in his head. Whether taking his morning pick-me-up in the corridor of the train or sneaking in a swift one in the lavatory, he celebrates their guidance in a dramatic fashion: "I drank straight from the bottle, tossing my head back like a concert pianist, aware of great things just beginning, and those still to come. . . ." The narrator is catholic in his tastes and will "drink anything that burns." He believes most Russians share the same compulsion to get drunk and reflects on the effect that this has had on their culture: "It's weird, nobody in Russia knows how Pushkin died, but everybody knows how to distil varnish." The fruits of such knowledge were genuinely frightening potations, including the nar-rator's favorite:

Dog's giblets, the drink that puts all others in the shade! It's not just a drink, it's the music of the spheres! What's the most beautiful thing in life? the struggle to free all mankind. But here's something even more beautiful—write it down:

     Zhiguli beer   100 g
     Sadko the Wealthy Guest shampoo   30 g
     antidandruff solution   70 g
     superglue   12 g
     brake fluid   35 g
     insecticide   20 g

Let it marinade for a week with some cigar tobacco, then serve.

The process of dismantling the Soviet behemoth begun by Gorbachev was finished by his successor, Boris Yeltsin, in 1991. In addition to terminating the USSR, he also abolished the state monopoly on the manufacture of vodka. The result was a collapse in tax revenues and a new flood of samogon. Yeltsin followed up in 1993 with a privatization program intended to distribute state property among the people, most of whom received a voucher representing their share in the nation's industry and infrastructure. These were bought up by entrepreneurs—the street price for each was a bottle of vodka—with the result that a few became fabulously wealthy, the owners of oil fields and gold mines, while the government went bankrupt. Its president, already known to be fond of a drink, pursued his hobby with increased vigor and a disdain for public sobriety. He raised eyebrows on state visits abroad when he stumbled and slurred his way through official appointments, or missed them altogether because he was drunk. His penchant for intoxication was tolerated by other heads of state: "At least Yeltsin's not a mean drunk," observed President Clinton, after being advised of his guest's antics while on an official visit to the United States in 1994.

Yeltsin staggered on with his reforms until 1999, when power passed to Vladimir Putin. Within a year of his taking office, a state holding company for alcohol had been established—*RosSpirtProm,* which presently accounts for close to 50 percent of Russian alcohol production. This measure induced tax revenues to flow once more—in 2003, 2.2 billion liters of taxed vodka were sold in Russia, or about fifteen liters per *head* of population, including babies. However, and notwithstanding the ready availability of white-market vodka, tax-free samogon continued to flood the market. Gin-craze conditions appeared—the birthrate plummeted, and male life expectancy dropped back to sixty-one years. In the first four months of 2005 more than thirteen thousand people died of drinking poison hooch. In response President Putin, notably more sober than Yeltsin, proposed a new state vodka monopoly. Rigorous central quality controls, plus affordable pricing, would put an end to the use of perfume and varnish as beverages.

Private enterprise also came to the aid of Russians struggling with their drinking. A hangover cure developed in KGB laboratories, which had enabled its agents to outdrink their capitalist adversaries, was patented and marketed to bear-headed Russians and, after 2003, to people overseas under the brand name *RU 21*. RU 21 was said to work by neutralizing the body's ability to metabolize alcohol. Its principal active ingredient, succinic acid, hindered the production of alcohol dehydrogenase, the enzyme responsible for converting alcohol into acetaldehyde, the compound that turns drinkers into quivering catatonics the morning after.

37 FIAT LUX

For is not the life of man simply the soul's sidelong glance? the soul's eclipse? We're all of us drunk, each in his own way, only some have imbibed more than others. And that's how it affects people: Some laugh right in the world's face, others cry on its shoulder.

— **Venedict Erofeev**

The principal export market for RU-21 was America, where the declining trend in alcohol consumption that had commenced in 1980 bottomed out in 1997. Thereafter, it rose slowly, reaching the equivalent of 2.22 gallons of pure ethanol per head per annum in 2003. There appears to have been a 9/11 effect—the incidence of heavy drinking increased by nearly 10 percent in 2002 over the preceding year. The recovery of American drinking, and consequent need for hangover cures, was achieved in the face of spirited resistance from opponents of alcohol. Indeed, the controversy over whether it is a friend or foe of mankind has been debated with especial vigor over the last decade. Enemies of the demon drink have sought to limit its availability and promotion and have emphasized its negative impact on health, while its manufacturers and advocates have fought to maintain their markets, and to spread the news of certain positive discoveries as to the worth of alcohol to society in general.

The increase in consumption was broad-based, and led by demand for hard liquor and wine. The spirit revival was largely the work of

African Americans, a demographic class hitherto indifferent, statistically, to alcohol, but who tuned into lifestyle drinking in the last decade of the twentieth century. By 1995, black males aged eighteen to twenty-nine had overtaken their white counterparts in "Frequent heavy drinking." The shift was inspired by popular music. Rap and hip-hop dominated the charts, and their artists were advocates of alcoholic beverages, the more expensive the better. Such talents as Snoop Dogg, P. Diddy, and Biggie Smalls were dandy disciples of premium Cognacs. They trumpeted their good taste in song. An analysis of a thousand of the most popular tunes from 1996 and 1997 revealed that 47 percent of rap songs (against 13 percent for country & western and only 4 percent for heavy metal) referred to alcohol, most to a specific brand such as Rémy Martin.

By happy coincidence, rappers and their disciples were the saviors of the French Cognac industry. In the late 1990s, Asian economies nosedived and, with them, demand for VSOP. Weddings were postponed to a more auspicious date, Chinese New Year celebrations were muted. Without the Hong Kong market, grape growers in the Cognac region of France were facing ruin. After rioting in the best of French traditions, they demanded compensation and subsidies from the EU. In the event, crisis redistillation of brandy to make it suitable for automobile fuel proved unneeded. Tunes such as "Pass the Courvoisier" (2001), a duet featuring Busta Rhymes and P. Diddy, sang them out of trouble.

Rap put a flame under the tail of American demand, which rose nearly threefold between 1993 and 2003 to account for 36 percent of global Cognac consumption. African Americans were responsible for roughly three-quarters of the sales of the market leader Hennessy. When growers in the Cognac region were asked what they thought about their new customers, they replied that they viewed them with "equipoise and serenity." Theirs was a quality product, which did not require a specific setting or a time of day for its perfect enjoyment. It was appropriate to the bucolic, urban, and even ghetto environments.

African American patronage was also an influence in the champagne market. The rappers' favorite brand was Cristal by Louis Roederer, which had been invented for Czar Alexander II of Russia in 1876 and made exclusively for the czars until the revolution in 1917, whereupon production ceased. The brand was reintroduced and offered for sale to the public for the first time in 1945. It remained a rare, expensive, and relatively unknown tipple until the later 1990s, when rap artists adopted it as a token of success. It appeared as *Cris* or *Crissy* in their lyrics, notably in Jay-Z's number-one hit "Hard Knock Life (Ghetto Anthem)" (1998): "Let's sip on the Cris and get pissy-pissy." By 2003, Cristal had become the seventh most-mentioned brand in Billboard's Top 20 chart, one place behind Prada but ahead of Hennessy, Lamborghini, and Chevrolet. Unfortunately for Cristal, when the French managing director of Louis Roederer was asked what he thought of its new clientele, he implied he would rather not have their business and regretted that "we can't forbid people from buying it." The racist insult incensed his best customers: Jay-Z called for a boycott, and both he and P. Diddy included the phrase "Fuck Cris" in the lyrics of subsequent songs.

While the decision to boycott Cristal was one that only a few Americans were rich enough to make, most were in a position to afford beer, and the brewers solicited their custom with considerably more energy and tact than French champagne producers. In contrast to rising demand for spirits, the beer market was flat. Competition for drinkers was intense, and advertising expenditure reached new highs. In 2004, the top ten brewers spent $1.14 billion in reaching out to beer lovers across the nation. Anheuser-Busch, which occupied the number-one slot, got through $412 million on its own. Such colossal sums, and the apparent ubiquity of beer advertising, provoked the ire of opponents of drinking. It was impossible, they argued, to protect the nation's youth, i.e., those under the minimum drinking age of twenty-one, against such a barrage. They pointed to statistics showing that 76 percent of American children had had their first drink, usually beer, before they left high school, and they demanded an increase in regulation.

The style and content of brewers' promotional material were largely determined by self-regulation, in accordance with the Beer Institute Advertising and Marketing Code of 1997. This voluntary code, whose preamble noted the "ancient origins" of beer, and that it had "held a respected position in nearly every culture and society since the dawn of recorded history," was a reasonably stringent document, whose overriding aim was to "portray beer in a responsible manner." It forbade the depiction of underage drinking, drunk driving, or intoxication in any form, and provided a myriad of other limitations on what ads might show, and when they could be shown. There were to be no kisses, no cartoon characters, no Santa Claus, and no promises of success in business or in love. Last but not least, "Beer advertising and marketing materials should not depict the act of drinking."

Most of the code was dedicated to ensuring that beer ads were kept out of sight of underage drinkers. This was to be achieved by limiting their appearance to shows, events, and publications where the brewers could be certain that at least 50 percent of the audience was over twenty-one. The compliance of the industry with this so-called *placement standard* was questioned by the Center for Alcohol Marketing and Youth, which published a series of studies with alarming titles suggesting that the brewers, and indeed the liquor industry in general, were in breach of their own codes. Papers such as "Television: Alcohol's Vast Adland" (2002) and "Radio Daze: Alcohol Ads Tune in Underage Youth" (2003) sought to demonstrate that self-regulation was at best ineffective and, at worst, a license to corrupt.

The matter was considered by the Federal Trade Commission in 1999 and again in 2003. Its conclusions made disappointing reading to the opponents of alcohol advertising. It found that, on the evidence, the brewers had achieved 99 percent compliance with their own codes and that such codes made them models of corporate responsibility. Moreover, in response to the investigation, they had voluntarily raised the placement standard from a 50 percent adult audience to 70 percent, beyond which, in the opinion of the commission, it would be hard to venture without impeding their lawful ability to promote a legal product.

Although this round went to the brewers, the victory was technical rather than moral. By coincidence, perhaps, many of their ads appealed strongly to juvenile minds. While they did not feature adults kissing or making money, they abounded in animals. Budweiser, for instance, had expanded its menagerie. Spuds MacKenzie and the singing frogs had been succeeded by twin Dalmatians, a trained mouse, a ferret, and a pair of lizards. A 2005 study into how children responded to beer ads found that they had an overwhelming preference for those that featured their four-legged friends. The ads that interested juniors least, in contrast, were those that focused on the brewing process and the quality of the resulting product.

They did not have to sit through many of them. Quality, in the sense of a superior pint, and variety, too, had by and large been filtered out of American brewing in the fifty years following repeal. By 1984, the four largest brewers controlled 94 percent of the market. Over the following decade, when the fashion for lite beers emerged, their products, while consistent, carefully engineered fluids, had little appeal to a connoisseur. In consequence, discriminating adult beer drinkers took matters into their own hands and set up their own breweries—in their backyards, in bars, and in commercial lots. These craft brewers were inspired by the example of Fritz Maytag, a Stanford graduate who had bought 51 percent of the Anchor Brewing Company in San Francisco for a few thousand dollars in 1965. Anchor had been brewing continuously since 1896 but had hit rock bottom just before Maytag invested. He became its sole proprietor in 1969 and thereafter flourished. His flagship product was bottled Anchor Steam Beer, modeled on the staple brew of the gold rush era, which won itself space in California restaurants and bars both on account of its quality and its difference from the lite brews promoted with animals on television.

After quality came diversity. Anchor introduced new styles of brews, including *Liberty Ale,* which was released on April 18, 1975, to commemorate the bicentennial of Paul Revere's rum-stoked gallop, and *Ninkasi,* made to the recipe implicit in the hymn to the ancient Sumerian goddess of brewing. Such superior products, and commercial success, prompted a host of other Americans to try their hand at making beer. Craft brewers sprung up all over the land in the early 1990s. Anchor Steam was joined by Chelsea Sunset Red, Sierra Nevada Pale, Pete's Wicked Blonde, BridgePort India Pale Ale, Brooklyn Black Chocolate Stout, and dozens of other novel labels.

The craft beer movement, however, ran low on steam toward the turn of the millennium. Its growth decelerated from a 50 percent year-on-year rate to only 5 percent in 1997. Several factors contributed to the loss of momentum. Ironically, quality was one of them. Some of the new breweries made bad, strange, or temperamental beer, and whatever its critics said about Bud Lite, it was a wonderfully consistent and stable product. A sour pint of "Alligator's Breath" or suchlike might put a prospective convert off craft beer for life. A second factor was intrasector competition. The new brewers weren't fighting only the majors but also their peers for market share. Competition was encouraged through beer shows and prizes. Beer critics such as Roger Protz and Michael Jackson issued tasting notes and ratings, and brewers with better scores won customers from their lesser-ranked brethren.

The beer *gourmandisme* awakened by the craft sector also turned Americans on to foreign suds. Many of the new styles had been inspired by German lagers and British ales, and converts to quality beers were tempted to taste the original models of their locally made favorites. In consequence, imported brews led the charge against the bland majors in the second half of the 1990s, doubling their market share between 1995–96 and 2001. By 2005, imports accounted for 12 percent of the American market, against a 3.5 percent share for the 1,371 breweries of the craft sector. The remaining 84.5 percent was supplied by a mere thirty-eight major breweries. The market itself was a behemoth. In 2005, just under three hundred million Americans drank 6.35 billion gallons of beer worth $82 billion between them, equating to more than thirty gallons per head for those of either sex of drinking age.

The rebirth of American craft brewing inspired a revival in that most puritan of beverages, hard cider. The staple of colonial farmers had been killed off as a commercial drink by Prohibition. Orchards were felled, and by the 1950s people had forgotten even the taste of President John Adams's breakfast tipple. The hard cider market slept for another forty years until awoken in the early 1990s through the introduction of brands such as *Woodchuck Cider* from Middlebury, Vermont, and *George Hornsby Draft Cider*, made by the Californian vintners E. & J. Gallo. The Boston Beer Company, a small brewer responsible for Samuel Adams Ale, also entered the market with *Hardcore Crisp*, which, as its name suggests, was targeted at a different market than its beer. Neo–cider drinkers were perceived of as being in their early twenties, dynamic in character, futuristic in outlook, and metropolitan in culture. The branding and marketing of new products were therefore aimed at white collar urban males. However, it was women who loved them, and by the law of unintended consequences that seems to apply to alcohol advertising, they became the principal consumers of hard cider. From a very low base of a quarter of a million gallons in 1990, the American market grew to 3.6 million in 1995 and 10.35 million gallons in 2001.

Women were also responsible for growth in wine consumption, which climbed from 464 million gallons in 1995, or 1.77 per head of population, to 703 million gallons (2.37) in 2005. As in Britain, a Bridget Jones factor was at work, which gave America's women the confidence to drink like men as well as work like them. Their self-belief, and thirsts, were reflected in books, movies, and on TV. The soap opera *Sex and the City,* which ran from 1998 to 2004, pictured its four career-women heroines lubricating their discussions of love and life with a profusion of cocktails and wine coolers.

American demand for wine, especially California wine, continued to be stimulated by its craft wineries, whose numbers increased year after year. All over the state, people were prospecting for that perfect *terroir* that might one day produce a vintage to equal or exceed a 1955 Haut-Brion, or a 1972 Stag's Leap Cabernet Sauvignon. A new spirit of wine *gourmandisme* appeared that was caricatured in the movie *Sideways* (2004), which laid bare the passion and antics of twenty-first-century American oenophiles. *Sideways* is the story of two college friends, Miles and Jack, who spend a stag week in wine country before Jack's wedding. Miles is an aspiring novelist, a wine lover, and neurotic; Jack is calm, a working actor, and wants to spend his last days before marriage in promiscuity. Although both boys meet girls and sleep with them, wine love has all the best lines; indeed, the film gives lessons in the art. Maya, Miles's paramour, whose heart melts when she hears him speak with feeling about Pinot Noir, betters him in her response, when she describes what passes through her mind as she takes her first sip of some exceptional vintage: "I like to think about what was going on the year the grapes were growing, how the sun was shining that summer or if it rained.... I think about all those people who tended and picked the grapes and, if it's an old wine, how many of them must be dead by now. I love how wine continues to evolve, how every time I open a bottle it's going to taste different than if I had opened it on any other day. Because a bottle of wine is actually alive—it's constantly evolving and gaining...."

The upward trend in wine consumption was also helped along by more good news on the matter of the French Paradox. Proof of the beneficial powers of wine in particular, and alcohol in general, had continued to mount over the years since Morley Safer and *60 Minutes* had brought it to the attention of the nation. In 1995, the U.S. Dietary Guidelines included for the first time, alongside its usual strident warnings, a cautious endorsement of alcohol, as follows: "Current evidence suggests that moderate drinking is associated with a lower risk for coronary heart disease in some individuals." The guidelines also hinted that the fluid might just possibly have a cultural value: "Alcoholic beverages have been used to enhance the enjoyment of meals by many societies throughout human history." Winemakers in California were delighted. Surely they could direct their customers to the good news, now that it was official, via a few short words on their labels? Laurel Glen Winery applied to the BATF with samples and, in 1998, got clearance for a label encouraging drinkers to "consult your family doctor about the health effects of wine consumption."

This modest concession evoked a tempest of protest from American drys, who could not countenance any praise of alcohol, however fainthearted, in any publication whatsoever. They were led by the evergreen senator Strom Thurmond, who was still utterly opposed to letting adult Americans know that a glass of wine a day might help them live longer. The ninety-six-year-old teetotaler held up treasury appointments and threatened to remove jurisdiction of wine labeling from the BATF to the Department of Health and Human Services unless the approval was rescinded. The BATF backed down and suspended clearance until hearings had been staged in 2000. The key test was whether a message suggesting a wine buyer speak to his or her doctor about the "health effects" of wine contravened the Federal Alcohol Administration Act, which stipulated that the manufacturers of alcoholic beverages should not claim their products had curative properties.

Prima facie, the evidence was on the side of California's vintners. "Health effects" was, after all, a neutral phrase. Following the rules of chance, a prospective drinker might well consult a teetotal doctor, who was only interested in showing them pictures of damaged livers and alcohol-induced automobile crashes. The matter, however, continued to be stalled until Senator Thurmond retired in January 2003, a month after his hundredth birthday. It was settled in favor of wine later that year by the Tax and Trade Bureau (TTB), which decided that scientifically truthful statements in their proper context might appear on labels, so long as they also warned of the risks of drinking and included a disclaimer such as "This statement should not encourage you to drink or to increase your alcohol consumption for health reasons." It was a victory for principle–the TTB had made the formal admission that alcohol could be good for people–but in practical terms it was a defeat. There was scarcely enough room on a magnum-size bottle label for the "health effects" suggestion, the necessary warnings, a disclaimer, and a modicum of information about the type of wine inside. There was, however, space on promotional material such as posters to advise Americans thinking of buying wine, in wording simultaneously prosaic and suggestive, to see a doctor.

Ridiculous as the dispute may seem, it was indicative of the reviving power of the antialcohol lobby. Neotemperance was in tune with neoconservatism. President George W. Bush, who stopped "heavy drinking" in 1986, after a booze-soaked youth, was emblematic of the new dry minds, and federal policies toward alcohol reflected the influence of the health care industry, whose focus was on treating problem drinkers. The hand of neotemperance was apparent in new restrictions on drinking among members of the U.S. armed forces, whose personnel, like the doughboys of 1917, were compelled, by a change in law, to stay dry while on active duty. Those serving in Iraq, where the cult of Ninkasi had originated, and one of the few Muslim countries to have had a tolerant attitude toward alcohol in the present millennium, were restricted to "near beer" on base and, unlike in Vietnam, could not rehydrate themselves with slabs of Bud from the PX. Combat troops were also vetted before deployment. According to official guidelines, a Marine who drank a couple of six-packs in the week before going overseas was "at risk," faced "a potential problem with alcohol," and should be pointed toward a remedial program rather than a war zone.

Similarly Draconian interpretations of problem drinking were applied in Texas, where, in 2006, the Texas Alcoholic Beverage Commission (TABC) launched *Operation Last Call,* whose aim was to root out drunkenness at its source. A team of undercover agents was sent to patrol bars, arrest any people they deemed to be drunk, and haul them in for a breath test. Those with a blood alcohol content too high to drive were liable to fines up to five hundred dollars for public intoxication, even if they didn't possess a car. According to Captain David Alexander of the TABC, "Going to a bar is not an opportunity to get drunk. . . . It's to have a good time, but not get drunk." While many drinkers might disagree with the suggestion that being drunk and having a good time were mutually exclusive, Operation Last Call was pursued with sufficient vehemence as to raise an outcry among liberty-minded Texans. Bar owners, in contrast, were afraid to complain, mindful of the fact that TABC was also responsible for issuing liquor licenses. "Do you think I want a half dozen of these baboons camped on my doorstep?" said one, speaking anonymously. "They can close me down in a New York minute."

The hand of neotemperance was also apparent in the 2005 edition of the U.S. Dietary Guidelines, which declared in the preamble to its section on alcohol that nearly half–"forty-five percent of U.S. adults"– did not drink at all. According to sources as diverse as the World Health Organization, the NIACC, the *Encyclopaedia Britannica,* and U.S. household surveys, perhaps 33 percent of Americans over the age of fourteen are dry–a statistic that would have amazed the Founding Fathers, but which is nonetheless well short of nearly half. Moreover, 83.1 percent of Americans confess to having used alcohol at least once in their lives, as do 90.2 percent of the coming generation.[80] The neotemperance influence over the 2005 guidelines extended beyond the preamble. The cautious cultural blessing of 1995–that people had been recorded as drinking alcoholic beverages with their food throughout history–had been censored, and the proven protection such drinks offered against heart attacks had been watered down. This is the current wording :

> Moderate alcohol consumption may have beneficial health effects in some individuals. In middle-aged and older adults, a daily intake of one to two alcoholic beverages per day is associated with the lowest all-cause mortality. More specifically, compared to nondrinkers, adults who consume one to two alcoholic beverages a day appear to have a lower risk of coronary heart disease. In contrast, among younger adults alcohol consumption appears to provide little, if any, health benefit, and alcohol use among young adults is associated with a higher risk of traumatic injury and death. . . . Furthermore, it is not recommended that anyone begin drinking or drink more frequently on the basis of health considerations.

The last nonrecommendation, advising nondrinkers not to start, may be contrasted with the position in Great Britain, where, despite a government-inspired binge-drinking scare, the Royal College of Physicians nonetheless advised dry British subjects to get wet for the good of their hearts.

The appearance of neotemperance resulted in a revival of the temperance genre in fiction. Once again, Americans were able to titillate themselves with stories of raging drunks harming themselves and terrorizing others. However, twenty-first-century examples of the genre

---

[80] Those between twenty-one and thirty-one in 2002.

tended to give more weight to redemption than Victorian-era tomes, with degradation serving as a prelude to uplifting demonstrations of willpower. *A Million Little Pieces* (2003) by James Frey, initially presented as a true story, was typical of the new wave of temperance fiction. The book chronicled the efforts of its author to overcome alcoholism and addiction at a treatment center modeled on Hazelden in Minnesota. Written in direct and effective prose, *A Million Little Pieces* offered willpower as a way of escaping the treadmill of alcoholism. It was, moreover, critical of the AA twelve-steps program, which formed the core of treatment at Hazelden in real life: "I have been to AA meetings and they have left me cold. I find the philosophy to be one of replacement. Replacement of one addiction with another addiction. Replacement of a chemical with God and a Meeting. The Meetings themselves made me sick. Too much whining, too much complaining, too much blaming. Too much bullshit about Higher Powers. There is no Higher Power or any God who will cure me. There is no meeting where any amount of whining complaining and blaming is going to make me feel any better. I am an Alcoholic and a Drug Addict and a Criminal....I want a drink. I want fifty drinks...."

In addition to stimulating a revival in temperance noir, contemporary attempts to demonize alcohol provoked a counterculture, which glorified booze and drunkenness. Publications such as *The Modern Drunkard* magazine (motto: "Say it loud, say it plowed") celebrated the pleasures of overindulgence and intoxication, highlighted some of the excesses of the neotemperance brigade, and also served the serious purpose of questioning the power and influence of campaigning bodies such as Mothers Against Drunk Driving. MADD had proved to be an extremely effective lobbyist in the decades since its formation. It had fought for and won stricter federal controls over drunk driving. By 2002, all states had lowered the Blood Alcohol Content, above which drunk driving became a per se offence, to 0.08. MADD's present ambition is to prevent any drinker from ever driving at all, through further reduction of the permissible BAC, stricter penalties for drivers who exceed it, and compulsory ignition interlock devices to be fitted to every auto in America. The program is justified by the MADD assumption that even one is too many. According to Penny Wagner, a MADD chapter president, "once you've consumed your first drink, you've lost that ability to make a sound judgment," which is simply untrue. Analyses of accident statistics suggest that impairment commences when the driver's BAC is above 0.1, so that the current limit of 0.08 has a built-in safety margin. Moreover, should MADD's ambitions to lower the BAC to .02 be realized, the result would be a law that declared sober people to be drunkards,[81] denied them their driving privileges, punished them with fines and prison sentences, and robbed them of their civil rights, not least of all the presumption of innocence until proven guilty in criminal trials.

Notwithstanding the efforts of the neotemperance movement to demonize America's favorite recreational drug and to introduce discriminatory legislation against those who used it, the opening years of the new millennium were full of good news for drinkers. The three-quarters-plus of American adults who drank, over 90 percent of whom did so in moderation, were found to be calmer, healthier, longer-lived, richer, and cleverer than their dry compatriots. In the years when Strom had raged against wine labels, further positive "health effects" of alcohol had been uncovered, including evidence that it offered some protection against a malady afflicting millions of Americans—stress. A 1999 paper concluded that "studies of the relationship between alcohol and stress suggest that drinking can reduce stress in certain people and under certain circumstances," particularly "people who have difficulty controlling their behavior, are highly self-conscious, or have difficulty organizing new information when sober." While the stress survey must be characterized as pioneering, rather than definitive, the body of evidence that had continued to accumulate in favor of the ability of all types of alcohol to reduce heart disease was now so substantial as to be irrefutable. Moreover, research into the mechanics of the protection offered by a drink or two every day was uncovering new and exciting potential in alcoholic beverages, especially wine.

Experiments carried out in 2006 on a special breed of mice, genetically hardwired for obesity, revealed that if their diets were supplemented with resveratrol, a compound that occurs naturally in grape skins and red wine, they lived longer and more fulfilling lives than their obese peers, without themselves having to lose weight: "Fat-related deaths dropped 31 percent for obese mice on the supplement,

---

[81] A large cup of mouthwash can generate a BAC reading greater than .02.

compared to untreated obese mice, and the treated mice also lived long after they should have." The overweight overachievers on massive doses of resveratrol were also conspicuous for their activity. According to Dr. David Sinclair of Harvard Medical School, "These fat old mice can perform as well . . . as young lean mice." In his opinion, his program had found "the Holy Grail of aging research."

There was plenty more good news for alcohol fans. The same demographic surveys which showed that college graduates were much more likely to drink than the rest of the population revealed the truth that abstainers risked not only their health, but also their wealth, every time they said no to the bottle. According to a 2006 study of the relationship between alcohol and affluence, "self-reported drinkers earn 10–14 percent more than abstainers" and "males who frequent bars at least once per month earn an additional 7 percent on top of the 10 percent drinkers' premium." The premium mostly applied to moderate drinkers, and since these constituted the majority, "drinking and socializing" was a "potentially productive investment that positively influences future earnings." The report concluded that "anti alcohol campaigns can be considered harmful to individuals and the economy as a whole."

In addition to improving the mental, physical, and financial well-being of drinkers, and contributing to the prosperity of the nation, alcohol also seemed to make its aficionados brighter than their sober peers. In 2004, a decades-long survey of 10,000 British civil servants concluded that even those who drank only one glass of booze a day had "significantly sharper thought processes than teetotalers."

Established drinkers, and abstinent people tempted into joining them, enjoyed access to an unparalleled choice of drinks in the opening years of the present decade. American craft brewers and wineries produced thousands of idiosyncratic brands between them, the major manufacturers created an annual Niagara of beverages that were models of homogeneity and sheer drinkability, and domestic choices were supplemented by a host of beers, wines, and spirits of every grade of quality, from all over the world. Good news, and good booze, led to a sea change in official attitudes toward alcohol around 2005. It was recognized at the federal level that drinking was not just part of people's lives, but also beneficial to the economy, beyond being a simple source of revenue. It was time to start to praise and encourage domestic manufacturers of alcohol, rather than to launch another doomed investigation into their advertising practices. On June 6, 2006, the House of Representatives gave its unanimous consent to *Resolution 753*, which put it on record that "American craft brewers promote the Nation's spirit of independence through a renaissance in hand crafted beers like those...produced here by the Nation's founding fathers, including George Washington and Thomas Jefferson, for the enjoyment of the citizenry." The resolution further observed that the craft brewers' diverse and "flavorful" beers had made the United States "the envy of every beer-drinking nation in the world," and commended them for "providing jobs, improving the balance of trade, supporting American agriculture, and educating Americans about the history and culture of beer while promoting the responsible consumption of beer as a beverage of moderation."

American craft brews, excellent as they were, were nonetheless outshone by California wine. In May 2006, The *Judgment of Paris* contest between the best California Cabernet Sauvignons and Premier Crus of Bordeaux was re-adjudicated using the same ten wines, all now more than thirty years old, and the court found, once again, in favor of California. This time the Californians improved their rankings, winning all the first five slots. Best overall was Ridge Vineyards Monte Bello '71, with Stags Leap '73, the victor of 1976, in second place.

Interestingly, and despite their tested excellence, for most of the life of wines such as Ridge Vineyards Monte Bello '71 it had been impossible for most Americans to obtain them through the mail. The sale of alcohol followed the repeal era three-tier system, composed of producers or importers who sold to wholesalers, who sold to retailers, who sold to individuals. Sending wine through the mail or via a common carrier direct to a drinker was illegal in twenty-three states and a felony in some, including Florida, Kentucky, and Utah. This meant that drink manufacturers were effectively excluded from selling via catalogs or on the Internet, and the issue was tested in the Supreme Court in 2005. Its justices held that states must allow direct shipment by out-of-state wineries if (indicative of a lingering nervousness about alcohol) they allowed them by instate wineries. The new ruling had been recognized by thirty-three states by January 2007, enabling many Americans, at last, to order their own country's wines direct. Small vineyards without national distribution and connoisseurs living far from their favorite wineries may now trade to their mutual satisfaction, unless they live in such recalcitrant states as Kentucky, where anyone caught ordering non-Kentuckian wine more than once still faces a felony charge.

A three-tier retail system was not the only hangover from the Volstead era in Kentucky. As of August 2005, 54 out of its 120 counties prohibited the sale of alcohol, and a further 36 had restrictions of some kind on its retailing, including 19 where residents might only drink on golf courses. Indeed, and unbeknownst to many Americans, Prohibition lingers on in many parts of their native land, principally in the southern states. Most of the northern counties of Alabama are still dry, as are nearly half of all counties in Mississippi, and Tennessee and Texas both still harbor large numbers of alcohol-free jurisdictions. Ironically, Lynchburg, Tennessee, home to Jack Daniel's whiskey, is dry. The grandchildren of the Prohibition era find such dinosaurs amazing, not to say infuriating, when they chance across them. Here, for example, are the reactions of the writer Tucker Max to discovering that a part of the country he loved forbade the sale of booze:

> I had heard about "dry counties" before, but they were still an abstract and foreign concept to me. I thought of them as silly anachronisms from a long distant prohibitionist past, something only found in the pages of *National Geographic*. I was wrong. Evidently, every county along I-75 from Richmond, KY, to the Tennessee border is dry. THIS INFURIATED ME. I almost got into a fight with the redneck checkout woman when she told me I have 40 more miles to go before I could buy liquor.
>
> "HOW AM I SUPPOSED TO ARRIVE DRUNK IF YOU WON'T SELL ME LIQUOR?? WHAT KIND OF BARBARISM IS THIS??"

Fortunately for the rising generation of drinkers, dry areas, gradually, are being submerged. The Pacific Coast has been all wet since 2003 when Monmouth, Oregon, voted to license drinking. Most of the former temperance heartlands in the Midwest and Northeast have also been flooded, including such shining examples of self-denial as Slippery Rock, Pennsylvania, which had been dry since its foundation by Zebulon Cooper in 1789. Slippery Rock went under in 2001, for entirely commercial reasons: It wished to attract business and development but felt these would not come unless there were places to drink after work. Paradoxically, the same logic was used in Bridgewater, the last dry town in Connecticut, as a reason for staying arid. According to an official of the Bridgewater Historical Society, "We're not looking for development. . . . We're not looking for a way to bring bigger, better businesses to this place." Anyone from Bridgewater wanting a drink must travel four miles out of town, despite the fact that it contains a winery within its jurisdiction. There remain other notable strongholds of temperance in the East, whose persistence might have given the pioneers of Prohibition some consolation. Ocean City, New Jersey, founded in 1879 by a quartet of Methodist ministers as a "moral seaside resort," is still dry; a liquor barn sits just outside the city limits on the only causeway in. Consolations aside, a metaphorical stake was driven through Wayne Wheeler's dead heart in January 2006 when Westerville, Ohio, former headquarters of the Anti-Saloon League and once known as the "dry capital of the world," licensed the sale of beer for the first time since 1875. The first legal glass for 130 years fetched $150 at auction. Its buyer toasted his fellow citizens before he drank to the end of more than a century of paranoia over alcohol. "Here's to a new tradition in Westerville," he said.

From a cultural perspective, $150 is a small price to pay for the reintroduction to Westerville of a substantial chunk of heritage. Alcohol has been one of the building blocks of Western civilization and continues to be an important ingredient of both our diet and our culture. While its contribution to nutrition is often overlooked, it is nonetheless significant. In 2004, average American per capita consumption of alcohol was 2.24 gallons, equating to 67,524 calories every year, or about 7.4 percent of each drinker's annualized RDI (recommended intake of calories). In addition to sustenance, alcohol also provides an aesthetic experience—drinking is an affair of the palate, as much as of the stomach or the head: A chilled beer, a glass of fine wine, a shot of bourbon, all stimulate the senses in unique and pleasing ways. Moreover, the power of alcoholic drinks to lessen inhibitions and facilitate self-expression, continues to associate their consumption with friendship, and artists in every medium still pay homage to their liquid muses. Finally, there is yet a place for intoxication in modern society. We resort to the bottle when our passions are high—we drink to celebrate, and to drown our sorrows.

Attempts to ban alcohol in the West have all, like the noble experiment of Prohibition, failed. As the legend of Bacchus illustrates, drink must be accommodated within society, for, like the Greek god, it also has a dark side, and if its production and consumption are forced underground, chaos results: Witness recent conditions in Russia, where excessive drinking has had a substantial negative impact on the well-being of an entire nation. However, in most countries with long-standing drinking traditions, moderate tippling has a positive effect on health. Although the mechanisms by which alcohol increases longevity when taken in small, if regular, doses have yet to be determined, its beneficial side effects are readily apparent: It eases the stresses of coexistence, it helps us to relax when we are tense, it restores life's luster when we feel sad.

There seems to be a universal desire to add ceremony to the consumption of alcohol—to acknowledge that under its influence, drinkers will let down their guard and say what they really think. In consequence, most cultures have specific phrases or words to accompany the raising of a glass, whose usual sentiment is to wish good health to the drinker and his or her companions. Whatever your background, whatever your poison, let me propose a toast for sharing the journey of this inspirational, if equivocal, fluid through history: *Salud, Kan pei, Chin-chin, Prost, Yum sing, Skol, Slainte, À votre santé, Na zdrowie,* The king o'er the water, or just plain Cheers!

NOTES

1 THE GRAIN AND THE GRAPE

1 **Ancient beverages:** *Ancient Wine, The Search for the Origins of Viniculture*, Patrick E. McGovern, Princeton University Press, 2003.

2 **Jiahu, "China":** Fermented beverages of pre- and proto-historic China, Cheng, Zhijun Zhao, Changsui Wang Moreau, Alberto Nuñez, Eric D. Butrym, Michael P. Richards, Chen-shan Wang, Guangsheng Fa, Patrick E. McGovern, Juzhong Zhang, Jigen Tang, Zhiqing Zhang, Gretchen R. Hall, Robert A., published online December, 8, 2004.

5 **"Enkidu knew nothing":** *The Epic of Gilgamesh*, Trans. Maureen Gallery Kovacs, Stanford University Press, 1989.

8 **"vineyard of the red house":** *Gods, Men and Wine*, William Younger, The Wine and Food Society Limited, London, 1966, p. 33.

8 **Egyptian beer:** "Beer from the early dynasties (3500–3400 B.C.) of Upper Egypt, detected by archaeochemical methods," Salwa A. Maksoud, M. Nabil El Hadidi, and Wafaa Mahrous Amer, *Vegetation History and Archaeobotany*, Vol. 3 No. 4, December 1994.

5 **Heirakonpolis interactive dig online at:** www.archaeology.org/interactive/hierakonpolis/.

9 **Skara Brae:** "Barley, Malt, and Ale in the Neolithic," Merryn Dineley, *BAR International Series*, Vol. 1213, 2004.

10 **Mayan drinking:** *The Blood of Kings: Dynasty and Ritual in Mayan Art*, Linda Schele and Mary Ellen Miller, Thames & Hudson, London, 1992.

2 BACCHANAL

11 **"But when Orion and Sirius are come into mid-heaven":** *Works and Days ll, Hesiod, pp. 609–617.*

13 **"Wine is like fire":** II 4 *Deipnosophists Athenaeus*, Trans C. D. Yonge, London, 1854.

13 **"There is a wine which *Saprian*":** 1 Yonge, I 52.

13 **"drive men out of their senses":** 1 Yonge

15   "But even so it was the remark and not its target that became notorious": 1 *Courtesans and fishcakes, the consuming passions of classical Athens*, James Davidson, Fontana Press, London, 1998, p. 151.

16   "If with water you fill up your glasses": Yonge, II 9.

16   "But that water is undeniably nutritious": Yonge, II 26.

16   "Wine lays bare": Yonge, II 6.

16   "so that it may not be discovered what sort of a person you really are, and that you are not what you pretend to be": Yonge, X 31.

17   "This is the monument of that great drinker": Yonge, X 48.

17   "and in every kind of luxury and amusement": Diodorus of Sicily, quoted in *Bacchus, A Biography*, Andrew Dalby, The British Museum Press, London, 2003, p. 51.

19   "ritual dance of the *tragos*": Ibid., p. 81.

20   "When a man has reached the age of forty": Plato Laws, from Yonge.

23   Ithyphalloi: *Wine in the Ancient World*, Charles Seltman, Routledge & Kegan Paul Ltd, London, 1957, p. 150.

24   "a man of violent temper": Yonge, X 46.

24   "If the wine be moderately boiled": Yonge, X 34.

25   "If an important decision is to be made, they discuss the question when they are drunk": *Herodotus, The Histories*, Penguin Classics edition, Trans. Aubrey de Selincourt, London, 2003, p. 62.

25   "wanted the tales of the god's wanderings": quoted in *Alexander the Great*, Robin Lane Fox, Penguin, London, 1994.

26   "Of those who entered for the prize": Yonge, X 48.

Euripides and Dionysus: R. P. Winnington-Ingram, Cambridge University Press, 1948.

3 IN VINO VERITAS

29   "care of armies": *The History of Rome*, Livy, Book 39.13.

29   "at Rome, women": *Natural History*, Pliny, Trans. John F. Healy, Penguin Classics, 1991.

31   "Whither, O Bacchus": Horace, *Odes* III xxv, *Odes and Epistles*, Trans. C. E. Bennett, Loeb Classical Library, 1978.

31   "from the moment Liber": Horace, Epistles XIX.

31   "Let Moderation Reign": Horace, Odes xxvii.

31   "It unlocks secrets": Horace, *Epistles* V.

33   "There's not a man been born": 1 *The Satyricon*, Petronius, Trans. William Arrowsmith, Meridian Classics, New York, 1959, p. 55.

33   "assumed the entire garb of Bacchus": *Athenaeus*, Trans. Charles Burton Gulick, William Heinemann Ltd, London, 1927: IV, 148. *Lucius Junius Moderatus Columella: On Agriculture* (1954), Translated by E. S. Forster and Edward H. Heffner (Loeb Classical Library).

34   "Wines from Pompeii": Pliny, p. 70.

34   "without putting on a stitch of clothing": Ibid.

36   "Whatever Fame sings of": 1 *Epigrams*, Martial Trans. Walter C. A. Ker, Loeb Classical Library, 1979.

36   "Daedalus, now thou art": *Epigrams,* Martial VIII.

37   "They gained so rapidly in corpulence": Dionysius of Halicarnassus, Roman Antiquities.

37   "liquor drunk in the houses of the rich": Gulick IV 151.

38   "savage people of great bravery": XV Book II De Bello Gallico, Julius Caesar, Trans. W. A. MacDevitt, Project Gutenberg etext.

38   "a liquor prepared": Tacitus, *Germania*, The Oxford Translation Revised–Project Gutenberg etext.

39   "Who the first inhabitants": Tacitus, *Agricola* the Oxford Translation Revised–Project Gutenberg etext.

40   Vindolanda: http://vindolanda.csad.ox.ac.uk/.

4 WINE, BLOOD, SALVATION

44   Justin Martyr: *Apologia*, Trans. Rev. S. Thelwall, online at www.earlychristianwritings.com.

45   Clement–pedagogia: Book II Chapter II, online from the Catholic Encycolpedia, www.newadvent.org.

48   Early Christian ritual: *Roots of Christianity*, Michael Walsh, Grafton Books, London, 1986.

5 BARBARIANS

50   "The public halls were bright, with lofty gables,": *Exeter Book*: R. Hamer, London, 1970, a choice of Anglo-Saxon Verse.

51   barbarian invasions: *The Fall of the Roman Empire*, Peter Heather, Macmillan, London, 2005 *Ausonius,* with an English translation, Hugh G. Evelyn–White, W. Heinemann, London, 1919.

53   "Drinc heil": 1 *Beer and Britannia an Inebriated History of Britain*, Peter Haydon, Sutton Publishing Limited, Stroud, 2001, p. 20.

54   beor: "Old Englsh Beor," Christine E. Fell, Leeds Studies in English, New Series Vol. VIII 1975.

56   "So his mind turned": *Beowulf,* a verse translation, Seamus Heaney, W. W. Norton & Company Inc., New York, 2002.

58   *hemina*–Benedictine rule: XL–of the quantity of food and drink for Benedictine Rules see www.osb.org.

58   "Ale is drunk around Loch Cuain": 1 *Beer, the Story of the Pint,* Martyn Cornell, 2003, Headline Book Publishing, London, p. 29.

59   "If anyone because of drunkenness": *Gildas, de excidio,* Trans. J. A. Giles, G. Bell & Sons, London, 1891.

59   "They had placed in their midst": 1 *The Barbarian's Beverage–a History of Beer in Ancient Europe,* Max Nelson, Routledge, Oxford, 2005, p. 95.

61   *Colloquy of Aelfric*: Garmonsway, G. N., ed. *Colloquy. Ælfric.* 2nd ed. 1939, University of Exeter, 1999.

61   "pregnant women should not drink to excess": Fell, p. 86

63   "It was the custom at that time": *Heirnskringla, the Ynglinga Saga,* Snorri Sturlson, Trans, Samuel Laing, London, 1844, 41.

6 ISLAM

65   "How I wish": *Abu Nuwa: A Genius of Poetry,* Philip F. Kennedy, Oneworld Publications, Oxford, 2005 p. 60.

65   "perfect physical specimins": "Ibn Fadlan and the Rusiyyah," James E. Montgomery, online at www.uib.no/jais/v003/montgo.1.pdf.

67–68   Koran references:
         2;219–"They ask concerning wine and gambling
         (5;90) "Strong drink, games of chance, idols and divining arrows
         78;31: "As for the righteous"
         47:15) "rivers of wine, delicious to drinkers"

69   "celebrated for refusing": *The Decline and Fall of the Roman Empire,* Vol. 5, Edward Gibbon, Everyman's Library Edition, J. M. Dent & Sons Ltd. London, p. 334.

69   "Drink the wine, though forbidden": Kennedy, p. 15.

70   "I wish that I were the Eucharist": Ibid, p. 56.

70   "Quick to your morning drink": Ibid., p. 61.

70   "she is so antique that": Ibid., p. 71

71   "A wine both frisky and quiet": Ibid., p. 66.

73   "Tonight I will make a tun of wine": *The Rubaiyat of Omar Khayyam,* Trans. Peter Avery and John Heath-Stubbs, Allen Lane, London, 1979, p. 77.

73   "They say there is Paradise with the houris and the River": Ibid., p. 67.

74   "Vladimir listened to them": *The Story of Wine,* Hugh Johnson, Mandarin, London, 1989, p. 99.

7 BREWS FOR BREAKFAST

77   "as holy writ saith": *The Travels of Sir John Mandeville,* Project Gutenberg etext.

78   "The people of the region": *Alcohol in western society from antiquity to 1800,* Gregory Austin, 1985, Clio Press Ltd, Oxford, p. 94.

79   "the largest vine-growing establishment": Johnson, p. 138.

79   "send ships forthwith": *Alcohol, Sex and Gender in Late Medieval and Early Modern Europe,* A. Lynn Martin, Palgrave, Hampshire, 2001, p. 6.

82   "almost every other household": *Ale, Beer and Brewsters in England: Women's Work in a Changing World,* Judith M. Bennet, Oxford University Press, 1996, p. 19.

84   "in the public house to die": *Wine, Women and Song,* John Adddington Symonds, Chatto & Windus, London, 1925.

86   "When by law or custom of the Church men fast": *Literature and Pulpit in Medieval England,* G. R. Owst, Cambridge University Press, 1933, p. 435.

87   "paler than that of the infirm": Ibid., p. 443.

87   "Thou arte lord of great power": Ibid., p. 310.

88   "By God's blood, this day is unhappy!": Ibid., p. 423.

88   "Hick the horse dealer and Hugh the needle seller": *Piers Plowman* Passus 5, Trans. Donald and Rachel Attwater, Ed. Rachel Attwater, Everyman's Library, J. M. Dent, London, 1957.

General:

Margery Kirkbride James, *Studies in the Medieval Wine Trade,* Ed. Elspeth M. Veale, Clarendon Press, Oxford, 1971.

Christopher Dyer, *Standards of Living in the Later Middle Ages,* CUP, 1989.

8 A NEW WORLD OF DRINKING

91   "it truly is most friendly": Austin p. 97.

91   "There is undoubtedly something to be said for inebriation": Ibid., p. 97.

91   "Marvelous medicament": Ibid., p. 96.

92   "In view of the fact": Ibid., p. 140.

92   "It eases diseases coming of cold.": Ibid., p. 141.

96   "up to now no tribe has been found": *Alcohol in Ancient Mexico,* Henry J. Bruman, University of Utah Press, 2000, p. 48.

96   "every third day, the women": Ibid.

96   "have solemn festivals of drunkenness": Ibid., p. 38.

97   "dance after drinking repeatedly": Ibid., p. 92.

98   "there are no dead dogs, nor a bomb,": Ibid., p. 17.

98   "Once they were all intoxicated they began to sing;": *A History of Ancient Mexico,* Bernardino Sahagun.

99   "would not look for anything else in life": Sahagun, Book IV Ch IV, p. 212.

100   "As soon as the presentation of gifts was over": *The Fables and Rites of the Yncas,* Christoval de Molina, Trans. Clements R. Markham, London, 1873, p. 313.

101   "a liquor which they brew of rice": *The Travels of Marco Polo,* Trans. Henry Yule, Project Gutenberg etext.

102   "that they say that more than one-third of the rice grown": *Joao Rodrigues's Account of Sixteenth Century Japan,* Ed. Michael Cooper, Hakluyt Society, Series III, Vol. 7, p. 252.

102   "first and chief courtesy": Ibid., p. 238.

102   "In Europe it is a great disgrace": Ibid., p. 236.

102 "and so they are obliged to drink": Ibid.
103 "that from the time they returned home": Ibid.
103 "They seem to do this on purpose in order": Ibid., p. 238.
103 "various properties, natural powers, and benefits of Cha": Ibid., pp. 277–78.

General:
Portuguese Voyages, Pero Vaz de Caminha, Ed., Trans. Charles David Ley, Everyman, London, 1947.
"Flopsy, Mopsy and Tipsy (interpretation of the rabbit symbol in Aztec iconography)," Patricia Rieff Anawalt, *Natural History,* April 1997.

9 WATKIN'S ALE

106 "we ought to give thanks to God": Martin Luther, "Sermon on Soberness and Moderation against Gluttony and Drunkenness," May 18, 1539.
110 Church ales: *The Voices of Morebath, Reformation and Rebellion in an English Village,* Eamon Duffy, Yale University Press, New Haven and London, 2001.
107 "heathens and not Christian": "Wine, Beer and the Reformation in Europe," Mack P. Holt, in *Alcohol: A Social and Cultural History,* Ed. Mack P. Holt, Berg, Oxford, 2006, p. 32.
110 "The multiplying of taverns is evident cause": *A History of the English Public House,* H. A. Monckton, Bodley Head, London, 1969, p. 38.
112 "ale for an English-man is a natural drink.": *A Dyetary of Helth,* Andrewe Boorde (1547), Ed. F. J. Furnivall, N. Trubner & Co., London, 1870, Kessinger Publishing reprint, p. 256.
112 "He took this maiden then aside": Ballad with music online: www.biostat.wustl.edu/~erich/music/songs/watkins_ale.abc.
113 "A good sherris-sack hath a twofold operation": *King Henry IV,* Part 2, Act IV, iii, The Yale Shakespeare, ed. Wilbur L. Cross and Tucker Brooke, Barnes & Noble, 1993.
115 "to borrow a rank": *The English: A Social History 1066–1945,* Christopher Hibbert., W. W. Norton & Company, New York, 1987, p. 225.

10 PILGRIMS

117 "so full of grapes": *Arthur Barlowe First Voyage to Virginia,* online at http://etext.lib.virginia.edu/etcbin/jamestown-browse?id=J1014.
118 "He was of so hard a complection": *Big Chief Elizabeth: The Adventures and Fate of the First English Colonists in America,* Giles Milton, Picador, London, 2001, p. 80.
119 "We made of the same in the country some mault": "Thomas Harriot: A Brief and True Report of the New Found Land of Virginia," online at http://digitalcommons.unl.edu/cgi/viewcontent.cgi?article=1020&context=etas.

119   "sugarcandie": Milton, p. 281.

120   "neither taverne, [nor] beere-house": Ibid., p. 268.

120   "To plant a Colony by water drinkers": *Brewed in America: A History of Beer and Ale in the United States,* Stanley Baron, Little Brown and Company, Boston, 1962, p. 6.

120   "There are about three hundred men there more or less": Ibid., p. 4.

121   "been the death of two hundred": Ibid., p. 6.

122   "the change of air, diet": *Of Plymouth Plantation 1620–1647,* William Bradford, The Modern Library, New York, 1981, p. 27.

122   "inns to entertain or refresh their weather-beaten bodies": Ibid.

122   "our victuals was only biscuit": *Mourt's Relation–a relation or journal of the beginning and proceedings of the English plantation settled in plimouth in New England,* online at http://etext.virginia.edu/users/deetz/Plymouth/mourt1 .html.

123   "As this calamity fell": Bradford, p. 86.

123   "gave him strong water": *Mourt's Relation.*

123   "After salutations, our governor kissing his hand": Ibid.

124   "6th Obj.: The water is not wholesome." Bradford, p. 158.

124   "as healthful, fresh, and lusty as they that drink beer.": Baron, p. 8.

124   "If barley be wanting to make into malt,": *Drinking in America: A History,* Mark Edward Lender and James Kirby Martin, Macmillan Inc., New York, 1987, p. 5.

125   "Morton became Lord of Misrule": Bradford, p. 227.

125   "Give to the Nymph that's free from scorn": Ibid.

126   "drank so much strong water": Baron, p. 9.

127   "it is ordered that no person that keeps an ordinarie": Ibid., p. 11.

127   "1. Wm, Renolds is presented for being dru1nck": *The Liquor Problem in All Ages,* Daniel Dorchester, D. D. Phillips & Hunt, New York, 1884, p. 109.

127   "set up a brew house at his great charge,": Baron, p. 11.

128   "the island where we": John Heckewelder, quoted in *Drink: A Social History of America,* Andrew Barr, Carrol & Graf, New York, 1999.

129   "They never make wine or beer": *Description of the New Netherlands,* Adriaen Van der Donck, Trans. The Hon Jeremiah Johnson [c. 1642], p. 69.

129   "covered with their cuirasses": *Deadly Medicine: Indians and Alcohol in Early America,* Peter C. Mancall, Cornell University Press, Ithica, 1995, p. 139.

129   "what he thought the brandy he was so fond of": Ibid., p. 75.

130   "simply to become intoxicated": Ibid., p. 75.

11 RESTORATION

133   "All these gentlemen of the Netherlands": *The Embarrassment ment of Riches,* Simon Schama, Vintage Books, 1997, p. 180.

134   "I do not believe scarce a sober man": Ibid., p. 190.

134   "men drink at the slightest excuse": Ibid., p. 200.

136   "our drunkenness as a national vice takes its epoch": *A Brief Case of the Distillers and the Distilling Trade,* Daniel Defoe, London, 1726, p. 17.

136   "in a course of drunken gaiety": Samuel Johnson, *Lives.*

136   "Cupid and Bacchus my saints are": Upon His Drinking Bowl

137   "frantically fashionable": Johnson, p. 228.

138   "You have made us drunk with *the juice*": "The politics of Drink in Restoration Drama," Susan J. Owen, in *A Babel of Bottles: Drink, Drinkers and Drinking Places in Literature,* Eds. James Nicholls and Susan J. Owen, Sheffield Academic Press, 2000, pp. 45–46.

138   "freedom from the illegal and intolerable": Cornell, p. 82.

139   "a simple innocent thing": *The Social Life of Coffee: The Emergence of the British Coffeehouse,* Brian Cowan, Yale University Press, New Haven, 2005, p. 95.

140   "thick as puddle water": "A Character of Coffee and Coffee Houses" 1661, London, electronic edition prepared and edited by Emily Clark.

140   "First, Gentry, Tradesmen, all are welcome hither": Cowan, p. 102.

12 RUM

142   "The chief fuddling they make": *Rum: A social and Sociable history of the Real Spirit of 1778,* Ian Williams, Nation Books, New York, 2005, p. 28.

143   "For when their spirits are exhausted": Ibid., p. 44.

143   "This drink is of great use to cure": Ibid.

143   "the best way to make ... their strangers welcome": Ibid., p. 53.

143   "lately supplied the Place of Brandy in Punch": Ibid., p. 52.

144   "Every Man has a Vote in Affairs of Moment": *A General History of the Pyrates,* Daniel Defoe (1724), Dover Publications Edition, New York, 1999, p. 211. [Note: Roberts, the most successful pirate of his period, was fond of tea and drank it from a china service, which his crew had voted to his special use from general plunder.]

144   "embodiment of impregnable wickedness": Ibid., p. 85.

145   "Such a Day, Rum all out": Ibid., p. 86.

145   "*Black-beard* took a Glass of Liquor": Ibid., p. 80.

145   "as a drinking vessel at the Raleigh Tavern": "When Blackbeard Scourged the Seas," George Humphrey Yetter, *Colonial Williamsburg Journal,* Vol. 15, No. 1 (Autumn 1992), pp. 22–28.

146   "so intent upon producing sugar": Williams, p. 37.

146   "about one in seven": *The Rise of African Slavery in the Americas,* David Eltis, CUP, 2000, p. 127.

147   "I have repented a hundred times": *Rum, Romance and Rebellion,* Charles William Taussig, Milton Balch & Company, New York, 1928, p. 36.

147   "all the people–men, women, boys": *Spirits and Spirituality: Alcohol in Caribbean Slave Societies,* Frederick H. Smith, essay, www.kislakfoundation. org/prize/200102.html.

147   "As soon as the corpse.": Ibid.

147   "never cares to treat": Ibid.

148   "When I looked round the ship": *The Interesting Narrative of the Life of Olaudah Equiano, or Gustavus Vassa, the African.* Written by himself. New York: Printed by William Durell, 1791, electronic edition from Early Americas Digital Archive.

148   "I have seen one of our negroes slaughter.": Smith.

148–49 "a pot of soup at the head": Ibid.

149   "Taking a little of the rum or other liquors": Ibid.

149   "The English must bring guns": Ibid.

150   "allowance of liquors or wine every day": "Puritans in Taverns: Law and Popular Culture in Colonial Massachusetts, 1630–1720," David W. Conroy, in *Drinking, Behavior and Belief in Modern History,* Eds. Susanna Barrows and Robin Room, University of California Press, 1991, p. 42.

150   "By a pint of liquor for those who dived for him": Taussig, pp. 218–19.

151   "in the midst of eternal Flames": Conroy, p. 44.

151   "to suffer anyone to be drunk": Taussig, p. 210.

151   "thrust himself into the company uninvited,": Ibid., p. 212.

154   "a large *Brew House*": Baron, p. 45.

155   "It argues some Shame in the Drunkards themselves": *New England Courant,* September 10, 1722.

155   "Take counsel in wine": *Poor Richard's Almanac,* 1733.

156   "that they wonder much of the English": Mancall, p. 70.

156   "only one sort of drunkenness": Ibid., p. 69.

156   "when we drink it, it makes us mad": Ibid., p. 96.

156   "A drunken man is a sacred person": Ibid., p. 81.

156   "very often on purpose": Ibid., p. 80.

157   "Think you, Sir, that Religion": Taussig, pp. 24–25.

157   "if they would continue sober during the Treaty": Franklin, autobiography, Project Gutenberg etext.

Colonial Taverns: *Becoming America: The Revolution before 1776,* Jon Butler, Harvard University Press, Cambridge, Massachusetts, 2000.

13 GIN FEVER

159   "A Tallow Chandler shall front my Lord's nice *Venetian Window*": "Beer Street: Gin Lane Some Views of 18th Century Drinking," T. G. Coffey, *Quarterly Journal of Studies on Alcohol* 27 (1966), p. 670.

160   "Would you believe it, though water": Cesar de Saussure, quoted Hibbert, p. 376.

160   "By this means a Member of the Everlasting Club": *The Spectator,* No. 72, May 23, 1711, Project Gutenberg etext.

161   "the Making of [spirits] from Malted Corn": *Craze, Gin and Debauchery in an Age of Reason,* Jessica Warner, Profile Books, London, 2003, p. 33.

162   "swarming with scandalous wretches": *The Much Lamented Death of Madame Geneva*, Patrick Dillon, Review Books, Headline Publishing, London, 2002, p. 22.

162   "We market women are up early": Ibid., p. 20.

163   "Scorch Gut by nature": Ibid., p. 62.

163   "the Landed Gentleman": Coffey, p. 673.

164   "One may know by your Kiss, that your Ginn is excellent": *The Beggars' Opera*, John Gay, Project Gutenberg etext.

164   "into all manner of vices and wickedness": Dillon, p. 90.

165   "On Sunday night we took the child into the fields and stripp'd it": Dillon, p. 96.

165   "came home so much intoxicated": Warner, p. 68.

166   "shrivel'd and old as though": Coffey, p. 671.

166   "quite intoxicated with Gin": Dillon, p. 115.

166   "to so great an excess, that Joss": Ibid.

166   "Why, the miserable creatures": Warner, p. 113.

167   "hush'd as death": Dillon, p. 148.

168   "show twice as many burials": Coffey, p. 672.

168   "pour forth unexpectedly from their gloomy cells": Dillon, p. 229.

168   "more fond of dram-drinking": Ibid., p. 164.

168   "paid over £1,000 to one of his five wine merchants": Coffey, p. 682.

169   "We have mortgaged almost every fund": *Parliamentary History*, 1743.

169   "We may not sell any thing": DD, p. 107.

171   "the fineness or dullness of the weather": Dillon, p. 268.

172   "from the melancholy consequences of gin-drinking": Ibid., p. 254.

174   "in the space of ten years, I have observed": Ibid., p. 273.

Also: Henry Fielding, *An Enquiry into the Causes of the Late Increase of Robbers* (1751), Clarendon Press, Oxford, 1988.

14 PROGRESS:

175   "a perpetual comedy": *Travels through France and Italy*, Tobias Smollet, Project Gutenberg etext.

176   "The wine commonly used in Burgundy": Smollet.

177   "The king was hunting, and found himself": *Memoirs of Jacques Casanova de Seingalt 1725–1798, to Paris and Prison*, Volume 2a–Paris, Trans. Arthur Machen, Project Gutenberg etext.

178   The Médoc is a canton in favor": 1855: *A History of the Bordeaux Classification*, Dewey Markham Jr., John Wiley & Sons, Inc., New York, 1998 p. 46.

178   "It is a generally recognized truth": Ibid., p. 45.

178   "duff-draff drink": *To the King o'er the Water, Scotland and Claret*, c. 1660–1763, Charles C. Liddington, Holt, p. 170.

178   "Gude claret best keeps out the cold": Ibid.

179   "go home and not engage in such visionary pursuits": Cornell, p. 109.
fixed air: http://dbhs.wvusd.k12.ca.us/webdocs/Chem-History/Priestley-1772/Priestley-1772-Start.html.

180   "fairly got the Disease of the Learned": *The Creation of the Modern World,* Roy Porter, W.W. Norton & Company, New York, 2001, p. 89.

180   "DRUNKENNESS, physically consider'd": *Cyclopaedia* (1728) Vol. I, p. 249, online at http://digital.library.wisc.edu/1711.dl/HistSciTech.Cyclo paedia02.

181   "seldom, if ever, taste any wine, John Locke, *Some Thoughts Concerning Education,* Section 19, 1692, etext http://www.fordham.edu/halsall/mod/1692locke-education.html.

181   "for the being and service and contemplation of man": Porter, p. 299.

181   "commands this species of animal to live": Ibid., p. 306.

183   "Tea that helps our head and heart": Schama, p. 172.

184   "Were they the sons of tea-sippers": *A Journal of Eight Days' Journey,* London, Jonas Hanway, 1756.

185   "hardened and shameless tea-drinker": Review of *A Journal of Eight days' Journey, The Literary Magazine* 2, No. 13, Samuel Johnson, 1757.

186   "the returning situation of those persons": DD, p. 97.

186   "the business of men is to be happy": Porter, p. 100.

15 REVOLUTION

187   "IV. However peaceably your Colonies have submitted": "Causes of the American Discontents before 1768," Benjamin Franklin, *The London Chronicle,* Jan. 5–7, 1768.

190   "a roasted ox, a hogshead of rum": Baron, p. 71.

191   "TO the Memory of the glorious NINETY-TWO": John Singleton Copley, *New England Silver & Silversmithing 1620–1815,* Eds. Jeannine Falino and Gerald W. R. Ward, The Colonial Society of Massachusetts, distributed by the University Press of Virginia, 2001, pp. 135–151.

192   "that as the load of malt just arrived": Baron, p. 93.

193   "that we will not hereafter": Ibid., pp. 91–92.

193   "One family boiled it in a pot": Barr, p. 312.

194   "Friends! Brethren! Countrymen!": Ibid., p. 315.

195   "rash, impolitic, and vindictive measures": *Essex Gazette*, May 30, 1774.

195   "*Resolved,* that it be recommended": DD, p. 120.

195   "would have made a rabbit bite a bulldog": Williams, p. 172.

195   "Without New England rum": *1776*, David McCullough, Simon & Schuster, New York, 2005, p. 19.

196   "so Wine, and Punch will not be wanting": Letter, Horatio Gates to Benjamin Franklin, November 7, 1775.

196   "Public Distilleries in different States": Williams, p. 173.
196   "wine cannot be distributed": Ibid., p. 174.
197   "a head like a cannonball": McCullough, p. 35.
197   "a shot had passed through his canteen": Williams, p. 173.
197   "I know not why we should blush to confess": Barr, p. 310.
198   "the Elk Hill and Beaver-dam hills": Thomas Jefferson, *Memoranda Taken on a Journey from Paris into the Southern Parts of France, and Northern of Italy, in the Year 1787*, Vol. II, Memoir, Correspondence and Miscellanies, edited by Thomas Jefferson Randolph, Boston, 1830.

16 WARRA WARRA

200   "Cut yer name across me backbone": *The Fatal Shore*, Robert Hughes, Vintage Books edition, New York, 1988, p. 292.
201   "a voyage which, before it was undertaken": *An Account of the English Colony in New South Wales*, Vol. 1, David Collins, London, 1798, Project Gutenberg etext.
201   "That [Brazilians] have not learned the art": Hughes, p. 80.
201–02   "half a pint of vile Rio spirits": Ibid., p. 97.
202   "under the cover of this": Collins.
202   "American beef, wine, rum, gin": Ibid.
202   "the *Hope*, commanded by a Mr. Benjamin Page": Ibid.
203   "the American spirit ... by some means or other": Ibid.
203   "a woman of the name of Green": Ibid.
204   "Indian corn, properly malted": Ibid.
205   "recognized medium of exchange": *Rum, Rebellion*, H. V. Evatt, Australia's Great Books Edition, Silverwater, NSW, 1984, p. 26.
205   "Convict servants were lavishly bestowed": Ibid.
205   "old tailors and shoe-makers": Ibid., p. 29.
205   "a combination band was entered into": Ibid., p. 30.
207   "as an article of barter": Ibid., p. 109.
208   "this sink of iniquity Sydney": Ibid., p. 113.
208   "become a perfect hell": Ibid., p. 120.
209   "when heated by wine": Ibid., p. 192.
209   "and those scenes of riot, tumult": Ibid., p. 221.
210   "they obtain *Spirits* to what Amount": Ibid., p. 312.
210   "the greatest part of his time": Ibid., p. 342.
210   "forty thousand gallons of spirits ...": Ibid., p. 328.
213   "Bread he began to relish": *A Complete Account of the Settlement at Port Jackson*, Watkin Tench, London, 1793, Project Gutenberg etext.
213   "and completely succeeded in trepanning": Ibid.
213   "Though haughty, [he] knew how to temporize": Ibid.

17 WHISKEY WITH AN *E*

215 "How solemn and beautiful is the thought,": *Life on the Mississippi,* Mark Twain (1883) Penguin Classics edition, New York, 1986, p. 411.

216 "an exceedingly valuable lead mine": *The Discovery, Settlement, and Present State of Kentucky,* John Filson, 1784, p. 290–etext on www.americanjourneys.org.

216 "Wedn. 22nd we Start early": *Kentucky Bourbon: The Early Years of Whiskeymaking,* Henry G. Growgey, University of Kentucky Press, 1971, p. 23.

217 "a likely young Negroe": Ibid., p. 53.

217 "odious, unequal, unpopular, and oppressive": *Whiskey Rebels–The Story of a Frontier Uprising,* Leland D. Baldwin (Revised Edition, 1968), University of Pittsburgh Press, p. 64.

217 "let loose a swarm of harpies": Ibid., p. 65.

217 "the trifling affair": Ibid., p. 67.

218 "a breath in favor of the law": Ibid., p. 80.

218 "dwarfish, dumpy man with dark red hair": *A History of the American People,* Paul Johnson, HarperPerennial edition, New York, 1999, p. 224.

218 "Is the minister of the French republic": Ibid.

219 "horrible sink of treason": et seq, Baldwin, p. 94.

220 "I thought it better to be employed": Ibid., p. 162.

221 "warlike, accustomed to the use of arms": Ibid., p. 178.

222 "my hammer is up": Ibid., p. 204.

222 "No sooner does the drum beat": Ibid., p. 232.

222 "in Company with a great number": Ibid., p. 252.

224 "all the loose females": *The French Quarter: An Informal History of the New Orleans Underworld,* Herbert Asbury, 1936, 2003, Thunder's Mouth Press, New York, p. 4.

225 "man, like the squirrel in a cage": Ibid., p. 72.

226 "For a picayune": Ibid., p. 101.

228 "She was as clean and dainty as a drawing room": Twain, p. 303.

229 "As thirsty as I was": *Come Hell or High Water,* Michael Gillespie, Great River Publishing, Stoddard, Wisconsin, 2001, p. 156.

230 "Strangers especially are warned": Barr, p. 38.

230 "Recipte for the Eyaws": Growgey, p. 73.

231 "Nine million women and children": *The Alcoholic Republic: An American Tradition,* W. J. Rorabaugh, Oxford University Press, New York, 1979, p. 11.

231 "three cocktails and a chaw": Johnson, p. 402.

232 "distinguished on the best tables of Europe": Ibid., p. 383.

233 "Were it possible for me to speak": DD, p. 174.

235 "this infant country has reached a maturity": Ibid., p. 169.

235 "with a Constitution and by-laws": Ibid., p. 181.

235 "No member shall drink rum, gin, whiskey": Ibid., p. 182.

18 ROMANTIC DRINKING

239 "I have been drunk more than once": *The Sorrows of Young Werther,* Johan Wolfgang von Goethe, trans. Catherine Hutter, New American Library Edition, New York, 1962, p. 58.

240 "The ruddy complexion, nimbleness, and strength": *Scotch: The Whisky of Scotland in Fact and Story,* Sir Robert Bruce Lockhart, KCMG, Putnam & Company, London, 4th Edition 1970, p. 8.

240 "Let other poets raise a fracas": *A Choice of Burns's Poems and Songs,* Faber & Faber, London, 1966, p. 103.

241 "O temperate bard!": William Wordsworth, Prelude III 304–07.

241 "gross and violent stimulants": *Bacchus in Romantic England: Writers and Drink, 1780–1830 (Romanticism in Perspective),* Anya Taylor, Palgrave Macmillan, 1998, p. 39.

242 "It is because so few things give him pleasure": Ibid., p. 57.

242 "Ye drinkers of Stingo and Nappy so free": Ibid., p. 95.

242 "Wine – some men=musical Glasses": Ibid., p. 100.

243 "rotten drunkard . . . rotting out his entrails": Ibid., p. 103.

243 "You shall drink Rum, Brandy": Ibid., p. 76.

243 "The very thoughts of your coming": Ibid.

243 "and pretty smart stuff it is": Taylor, p. 58.

243 "now I like Claret whenever I can": Ibid., p. 172.

244 "covered his tongue & throat": Ibid., p. 173.

244 "Man, being reasonable, must get drunk": *Don Juan* CLXXIX.

245 "Wine robs a man of his self-possession": *Confessions of an English Opium Eater,* Thomas De Quincy, Penguin Classics edition, p. 73.

245 "Opium, like wine, gives an expansion": Ibid., p. 84.

247 "excluded from all rational enjoyment": Taylor, p. 24.

247 "self-made cheesemonger": *Drink and the Victorians: The temperance Question in England, 1815–1872,* Brian Harrison, Faber and Faber, London, 1971, p. 117.

248 "to the surprise and conviction": Ibid., p. 122.

248 "Whisky is the soul of beer": Ibid., p. 125.

248 "that he would 'Be reet down out": Ibid., p. 126.

250 "after observing that for many years": Ibid., p. 128.

252 "Drunkards' Death": *Sketches by Boz,* Charles Dickens, Project Gutenberg etext.

19 APOSTLES OF COLD WATER

253 "Why are the classical models of the last century": Rorabaugh, p. 199.

254 "frivolous and dull": *Star Spangled Eden,* James C. Simmons, Carroll & Graf Publishers, Inc., New York, 2000, p. 127.

254 "the mysteries of Gin-sling": *American Notes,* Charles Dickens, Project Gutenberg etext.

254   "the use of ice . . . is an American institution": Barr, p. 54.

255   "The quantity of champagne drunk is enormous": Frederick Marryat, quoted in Barr, p. 101.

255   Nicholas Longworth: "The Late Nicholas Longworth," *Harper's Weekly*, Vol. VII, No. 323, March 7, 1863.

256   "strange strawberryish liquor": Johnson, p. 374.

256   "Very good in its way": "Ode to Catawba," 1854.

257   "The man who drinks wine": Barr, p. 176.

259   "We hold these truths to be self-evident": "Slaves to the Bottle," John W. Crowley, in *The Serpent in the Cup: Temperance in American Literature*, Ed. David S. Reynolds and Debra J. Rosenthal, University of Massachusetts Press, Amherst, 1997, p. 122.

259   "scurrilous army of ditch-delivered": "Black Cats and Delerium Tremens," David S. Reynolds, in *Serpent*, p. 26.

259   "Did you ever see a man in delirium tremens": Ibid., p. 27.

260   "I unlocked the clothes room door": Ibid., p. 28.

260   "in three days for money": Ibid., p. 50.

262   "temperance negro operas": Ibid., p. 22.

262   "we'll teach you to drug a harpooneer": *Moby Dick*, Herman Melville, 1851, Bantam Classic edition, New York, 1981, p. 339.

263   "It is a pity that a few drunken Germans": Barr, p. 244.

264   "Dinner for your Friends £3 0s 0d": Williams, p. 83.

265   "An election in Kentucky lasts three days": Simmons, p. 11.

266   "To the victors belong the spoils of the enemy": Johnson, p. 340.

267   "Let Van from his coolers of silver drink wine": Barr, p. 88.

20 WEST

269   "for everything bad": *Intoxicated Identities: Alcohol's Power in Mexican History and Culture*, Tim Mitchell, Routledge, New York and London, 2004, p. 95.

270   "your vines will survive and bear fruit": "Alta California's First Vintage," Roy Brady, in *The Book of California Wine*, Ed. Doris Muscatine, Maynard A. Amerine, and Bob Thompson, University of California Press, Berkeley, 1984, p. 13.

270   "was being brought here from San Juan Capistrano": Ibid., p. 13.

270   "an early maturing dark-skinned bag": Johnson, p. 386.

270   "with the exception of what we got at the Mission": Ibid., p. 388.

271   "the Californians are an idle, thriftless people": *Two Years before the Mast*, Richard Henry Dana, Jr., Penguin Classics edition, New York, p. 125.

271   "if California ever becomes a prosperous country": Ibid., p. 305.

272   "a barrel of whiskey a day": Johnson, p. 374.

272   "Drinking was reduced to a system": Barr, p. 375.

273   "This continent was intended by Providence": Johnson, p. 371.

273   "as destructive and more constant than disease": *White Man's Wicked Water: The Alcohol Trade and Prohibition in Indian Country, 1802–1892,* William E. Unrau, University Press of Kansas, 1996, p. 52.

274   "Whiskey, whiskey!": Ibid., p. 20.

274   "A small bucketful is poured": *The City of the Saints,* Sir Richard Burton (1862), reprinted University Press of Colorado, Niwot, Colorado, p. 81.

275   "The alcohol is put into wagons,": Unrau, p. 87.

275   "pledge themselves to make all proper exertions": Ibid., p. 58.

276   "Pushing through a noisy, drunken crowd": *The Oregon Trail,* Francis Parkman, Project Gutenberg etext.

277   "do nothing without whiskey": Burton, p. 24.

277   "twenty-four mortal days and nights": Ibid., p. 3.

278   "I'll drink mint-juleps, brandy-smashes": Eden, p. 189.

279   "kind of cactus called by the whites": Burton, p. 64.

279   "the korn-schnapps of the trans-Rhenine": Ibid., p. 320.

279   "There are two large and eight small breweries": Ibid.

279   "Children and adults have come from England": Ibid., p. 277.

280   "this state of things is brought about by a variety of causes": Unrau, p. 84.

21 THE KING OF SAN FRANCISCO

281   "philosophical consolation in various experiments": Burton, p. 501.

282   "the rent of a tiny cigar store": *The Barbary Coast,* Herbert Asbury, 1933, Alfred A Knopf, Inc., Thunder's Mouth Press, New York, p. 16.

282   "The miners came in forty-nine": Ibid., p. 35.

283   "who for a few cents would eat": Ibid., p. 51.

283   "crowded by thieves, gamblers, low women": Ibid.

284   "had not spoken to a woman for two years": *The Shirley Letters* (1854–5), Louise A.K.S. Clappe, Peregrine Smith Books, Salt Lake City, p. 27.

285   "The saturnalia commenced on Christmas evening": Ibid., p. 92.

285   "many of the drunkards": Clappe, p. 87.

286–
87   "as he rebounded from the fearsome realms": Asbury, p. 116.

287   "Oh, King Alcohol!": Ibid., p. 117.

291   "what the African has been to the South": Brady, p. 26.

292   "The great obstacle to our success": Barr, p. 397.

22 GOOD TASTE

294   "build the weaknesses of their private lives": *The Invention of the Restaurant: Paris and Modern Gastronomic Culture,* Rebecca L. Spang, Harvard University Press, Cambridge, Mass., 2001, p. 160.

295 "I have looked through various dictionaries": *The Physiology of Taste,* Anthelme Brillat-Savarin—Project Gutenberg etext.

297 "Regardless of their value in the arts": Markham, p. 8.

297 "this solemn occasion should not be missed": Ibid., p. 32.

299 "list of all the red classed growths": Ibid., p. 98.

299 "like all human institutions": Ibid., p. 183.

299 "among the most useful of nutrients": Ibid., p. 149.

300 "a liquor made from the fruit of the vine": *On Wine and Hashish,* Charles Baudelaire, Trans. Andrew Brown, Hesperus Press, London, 2002, p. 3.

300 "My beloved, I want to sing out to you": Ibid., p. 6.

300 "His heart swells with happiness.": Ibid., p. 8.

302 "as a perfectly regulated instrument": *Paris: Capital of the World,* Patrice Higonnet, Trans. Arthur Goldhammer, The Belknap Press of Harvard University Press, Cambridge, Mass., 2002, p.177.

302 "lined by 34,000 new buildings": Ibid., p. 186.

303 "roast cat garlanded with rats" Johnson, p. 367.

306 "equalling, if not surpassing": Ibid., p. 420.

306 "to describe [them] would be a work for Byron": Ibid., p. 422.
German beer: *Prost! The story of German Beer,* Horst D. Dornbusch, Brewers Publications, Boulder, Colorado, 1997.

23 EMANCIPATION

308 *"When there shall be neither a slave":* Serpent, p. 123.

309 "Did not you vote the anti-temperance ticket": *Ten Nights in a Barroom,* T. S. Arthur, Project Gutenberg etext.

310 "Ah, yes, physical slavery": Serpent, p. 124.

312 "disgust the slave with freedom": *Narrative of the Life of Frederick Douglass, an American Slave,* Project Gutenberg etext.

312 "a proper rank and standing": Serpent, p. 110.

312 "the quartermaster of the army": Wiliams, p. 247.

313 "into the delusion that drinking was excusable": *The Life of Johnny Reb,* Bell Irvin Wiley, Louisiana State University Press, Baton Rouge (1943) 2000, p. 40.

313 "the general Davis sent up a barrel": Ibid., p. 167.

314 "If it was in my power I would condemn": Ibid.

314 "The Whiskey you may depend": Ibid., p. 187.

314 "From what I can tell [he] is better able": Ibid., p. 237.

316 "immense buildings, fitted up in imitation of a garden": Baron, p. 180.

316 "exquisite in some places,": Ibid., p. 181.

317 "Just now a note of war": et seq., Ibid., p. 220.

318 "hundreds of thousands of women": *Domesticating Drink: Women, Men, and Alcohol in America, 1870–1940,* Catherine Gilbert Murdock, John Hopkins University Press, Baltimore and London, 1998, p. 18.

319   "from speaking at a Sons of Temperance": Murdock, p. 26.

321   "a brewer is just as necessary": Baron, p. 226.

24 IMPERIAL PREFERENCE

322   "Here with a loaf of bread": *The Rubaiyat of Omar Khayyam,* 1st (1859) and 5th (1889) editions, Edward Fitzgerald, Dover Publications, Inc. New York.

322   "pledged 4,000 children between": Harrison, p. 192.

323   "a Whole Hog of unwieldy dimensions": "Household Words," Charles Dickens, No. 184, Vol. VIII.

323   "to outlaw all trading": Harrison, p. 197.

324   "dictate to the remaining 13/15ths": Ibid., p. 209.

324   "a great stock of egg and wine": Ibid., p. 248.

325   "If I must take my choice . . .": Ibid., p. 293.

326   "a useful expedient only, for the furtherance": Ibid., p. 190.

326   "to censure Noah for his": Ibid., p. 186.

326   "If an angel from heaven": Ibid., p. 277.

327   "Ah, fill the Cup:- what boots it to repeat": Fitzgerald.

328   "apoplectic and swollen": Younger, p. 436.

329   "Hodgson's warranted prime picked pale ale": Cornell, p. 135.

329   "almost universally preferred by all old Indians": Ibid., p. 137.

330   Australia: *The Wine Industry of Australia 1788–1979,* Gerald Walsh, Wine Talk A.N.U. Canberra, 1979.

332   "white wines akin to those of the Rhine": Johnson, p. 373.

25 LA FEE VERTE

333   *Phylloxera: Phylloxera: How Wine Was Saved for the World,* Christy Campbell, HarperCollins, London, 2004.

335   "the sight of water upsets me": *The Book of Absinthe: A Cultural History,* Phil Baker, Grove Press, New York, 2001, p. 63.

335   "it was on absinthe": Ibid., p. 67.

335   "The poet must make himself a seer": Ibid., p. 75.

336   "Parishit, Junish 72": Rimbaud–to Ernest Delahaye, *Selected Poems and Letters,* Arthur Rimbaud, Trans. Jermey Harding and John Sturrock, Penguin Classics edition, London, 2004, p. 249.

338   "accentuated certain traits": Baker, p. 118.

338   "that terrible poison,": et seq., Ibid., p. 88.

339   "entirely painted in absinthe": Ibid., p. 129.

340   "our fathers still knew the time": Ibid., p. 124.

340   "ABSINTHE: Exceedingly violent poison.": "Green Gold: The Return of Absinthe," Jack Turner, *The New Yorker,* March 13, 2006.

341   Manet *The World of Manet,* Piere Schneider, Time-Life Books, Alexandria, Virginia.

341   "a hideous, horrible phallic skeleton": Higonnet, p. 358.

343   "I could never quite accustom myself to absinthe": Baker, p. 30.
Absinthe–health campaigns and manufacturers' promotional material:
Virtual Absinthe Museum, www.oxygenee.com.

26 HATCHETATION

344   "I have a theory it is compounded": Asbury, p. 227.
345   "Bit by bit, they grope about": *The Silverado Squatters,* Robert Louis
Stevenson (1883), Project Gutenberg etext.
346   "Messrs. Schuler and Coors": Baron, p. 250.
346   "The walk was so uneven": Ibid., p. 255.
347   "from the schoolhouses all over the land": *Prohibition: The Era of Excess,*
Andrew Sinclair, Faber and Faber Ltd., London, 1962, p. 56.
348   "Such a heart cannot be so strong": Sinclair, p. 58.
348   "Daddy was disgusted with neighbor":: *Ardent Spirits: The Rise and Fall of
Prohibition,* John Kobler, Da Capo Press, New York, 1993, p. 139.
348   "Swirling round the marked man": Sinclair, p. 119.
349   "an inexpensive mode": Kobler, p. 180.
350   "The curse of heredity": *Carry Nation: The Woman with the Hatchet,*
Herbert Asbury, Albert A. Knopf, New York, 1929, p. 41.
351   "It is very significant": Ibid., p. 101.
351   "Glory to God! Peace on earth": Ibid., p. 103.
352   "a bulldog running along": Ibid., p. xvii.
353   "Carry A. Nation, prophetess of God": Ibid., p. 211.
353   "the largest missionary field in the world": Ibid., p 256.
353   "a school of vice to a great extent": Ibid., p. 267.
354   "I now feel that this great wave": Ibid., p. 303.
355   "controlled six Congresses": Kobler, p. 182.
355   "In America we are making": Sinclair, p. 62.
356   "Probably, certainly, more than fifty percent": Ibid., p. 64.
356   "I ALCOHOL INFLAMES THE PASSIONS": Ibid., p. 65.
356   "From that December day in 1913": Kobler, p. 201.
357   "comparatively few alcoholics": *John Barleycorn, or Alcoholic Memoirs*
(1913), Jack London, Signet Classics edition, New York, 1990, p. 17.
357   "let me warm by their fires": Ibid., p. 36.
358   "talked with great voices": Ibid., p. 37.
358   "All the no-saying and no-preaching": Ibid., p. 115.
358   "The trouble I had with the stuff": Ibid., p. 202.
358   "The only rational thing": Ibid., p. 115.

27 IN THE CHALK TRENCHES OF CHAMPAGNE

360   "the individual man is in all cases free": "Rum in the Trenches," Tim
Cook, *Legion Magazine,* Defence Today, September/October 2002.
360   "It surprises me when": *Memoirs of an Infantry Officer,* Siegfried Sassoon,
Faber and Faber, London, 1997, p. 18.

360   "Under the spell of": Cook.

361   "to take the taste of dead men": Ibid.

361   "The gas was phosgene": Williams, p. 187.

361   "the 'No Rum Division'": Sassoon, p. 122.

361   "*estaminets*": *Her Privates We,* Frederic Manning (1929), Serpent's Tail edition, London, 1999.

362   "We have the right to get": *Under Fire,* Henri Barbusse (1916), Penguin Classics edition, Trans. Robin Buss, London 2003, p. 21.

362   "To drink some wine from the South": Ibid., p. 128.

362   "there were liberal helpings": *Storm of Steel* (1920), Ernst Junger, Trans. Michael Hofmann, Penguin Books, London 2003, p. 12.

362   "By day, the young people": Ibid. p. 16.

363   "such libations after": Ibid., p. 140.

363   "Whole industrial societies were": *The Penguin History of the Twentieth Century,* J. M. Roberts, Penguin, London, 1999, p. 250.

364   "we are fighting Germans, Austrians": Cornell, p. 184.

364   "refrain from drinking beer": Ibid., p. 187.

365   "harvested like grapes": *Champagne,* Don and Petie Kladstrup, John Wiley & Sons, Chichester, 2006, p. 163.

366   "the soberest, cleanest": Sinclair, p. 128.

367   "inebriated comics": *The Doughboys,* Laurence Stallings, Popular Library edition, New York, 1964, p. 106.

367   "I went over to Major Bailey's": Elmer Hess, May 31, 1918, diary online at www.landscaper.net/ww1memoirs.htm#1st%20Lieut.%20 Elmer %20Hess,%2015th%20Field%20Artillery.

Soviet prohibition: *A History of Vodka,* William Pokhlebkin, Trans. Renfrey Clarke, Verso, London, 1992.

28 AMPHIBIANS

370   "the dry workers throughout the country": Baron, p. 300.

370   "Brewery products fill refrigerator": Sinclair, p. 133.

371   "Dear Mr Palmer": Baron, p. 305.

371   "around the sangerfests": Sinclair, p. 132.

371   "not really enact prohibition": Ibid., p. 171.

372   "Every Congressman knows": Kobler, p. 210.

373   "a discontent and disregard for law": Sinclair, p. 182.

373   "The reign of tears is over": *The Great Illusion,* Herbert Asbury, Doubleday & Co., New York, 1950, p. 144.

374   "They would come wobbling": Kobler, p. 259.

374   "three tremendous popular passions": Sinclair, p. 198.

376   "You sent in an order for gin": Kobler, p. 249.

377   "There are not many ladies": Murdock, p. 110.

377   "It is outrageous": Ibid., p. 99.

377   "They are athletic": Ibid., p. 110.

377 "the only American invention": PJ, p. 707.

378 "dancing academies, drugstores": Kobler, p. 234.

379 "Trays with bottles": Sinclair, p. 271.

379 "that he did drink occasionally": Murdock, p. 99.

379 "compared unfavorably with those of garbage": Sinclair, p. 199.

379 "the master mind of the Federal": Kobler, p. 297.

380 "The cost and quality of post-Volsteadian": Sinclair, p. 251.

380 "science of compelling men to use more": "Things Are in the Saddle," Samuel Strauss, *The Atlantic Monthly,* November 1924, pp. 577–88.

381 *stewed to the gills:* "The Lexicon of Prohibition," Edmund Wilson, March 9, 1927, in *The American Earthquake: A Documentary of the Twenties and Thirties* (1958).

381 "Don't shoot, I'm not a": Sinclair, p. 335.

381 "nearly three million gallons of sacramental wine": Ibid., p. 304.

382 "In 1928 one buyer bought 225 carloads": "The Volstead Act: Rebirth and Boom," Ruth Teiser and Catherine Harroun, in *California Wine.*

383 "a great social and economic experiment": Sinclair, P. 315.

383 "If Al [Smith] wins tomorrow": Ibid., p. 318.

384 "I make my money by supplying a public demand": *The Americans: The Democratic Experience,* Daniel J. Boorstin, Vintage Books, New York, 1974, p. 84.

29 LOST

385 "Wine inspires gaiety, strength, youth": *Mon Docteur le Vin* (1936), Trans. Benjamin Ivry, Distributed by Yale Unversity Press, New Haven, 2003, p. 11.

385 "That's what you are. That's what you all are": *A Moveable Feast,* Ernest Hemmingway (1936) Arrow Books, 2004, p. 18.

386 "grape varieties hallowed by local": PJ, p. 478.

386 "Urban and rural people can": Ivry, p. 1.

386 "radioactive properties": Ibid., p. 2.

386 "American teetotaller": Ibid., p. 6.

386 "If you drink Chablis with your oysters": Ibid., p. 4.

387 "We were able to note that among": Ibid., p. 18.

387 "Of all the supplies": "Wine and Health in France, 1900–1950," Kim Munholland, in *Alcohol: A Social and Cultural History,* Ed. Mack P. Holt, Berg, Oxford, 2006, p. 77.

387 "the French race would lose": Ibid., p. 79.

387 "water tends to thicken": Ivry, p. 13.

387 "Wine takes its revenge on those": Ibid., p. 14.

387–
  88 "Since Prohibition, the Americans": Ibid., p. 17.

388 "The exquisite corpse": *Manifesto of Surrealism,* André Breton, 1924.

388   "Our own nation . . . passed": *Exile's Return,* Malcolm Cowley Penguin edition, New York, 1994, p. 47.

388   "In Europe . . . we thought of wine": Hemingway, p. 97.

390   "At this time Zelda": Ibid., p. 108.

390   "I would give anything if I hadn't": *Tender Is the Night,* Scott Fitzgerald, Scribner Paperback Fiction edition, New York, Introduction, p. xv.

391   "The favorite drink at that time": *The Thirsty Muse: Alcohol and the American Writer,* Tom Dardis, Ticknor & Fields, Boston, 1989, p. 42.

392   "brilliant men, beautiful jazz babies,": Sinclair, p. 336.

392   "drinking scenes, manufacture or sale of liquor": "The Movies and the Wettening of America: The Media as Amplifiers of Cultural Change," Robin Room, *British Journal of Addiction* 83:11–18, 1988.

392   "get on the first train": Sinclair, p. 337.

392   "this vivid picture of ultramodern youth": *Alcohol in the Movies, 1892–1962,* Judy Cornes, McFarland & Company, Inc., Jefferson, North Carolina, 2006, p. 37.

392   "those who come to laugh": Room.

392   "for the vast audience": Ibid.

393   "it was the motion picture": Ibid.

393   "on the boards of businesses": Sinclair, p. 103.

394   "these wet women, though rich most": Ibid., p. 358.

395   jake leg: "Jake Leg: How the Blues Diagnosed a Medical Mystery," Dan Baum, *New Yorker,* September 15, 2003.

395   "at the time best suited for their adoption": Wickersham Report, available online at: www.drugtext.org/library/reports/wick/Default. html.

398   "since it was wet below and dry on top": Sinclair, p. 386.

398   "first, by reason of the great need": Baron, p. 320.

398   "No other state shall take away": Kobler, p. 353.

399   "My first in thirteen years": Ibid., p. 384.

30 CRIME AND PUNISHMENT

401   "It is almost unknown that Hitler": *The Hitler No-one Knows (Hitler wie ihn keiner kennt)* Heinrich Hoffmann, Berlin: "Zeitgeschichte" Verlag, 1932.

401   "whoever is not bodily and spiritually": "A Sober Reich? Alcohol and Tobacco Use in Nazi Germany," Jonathan Lewy, *Substance Use and Misuse,* 41: 1179–95, p. 1186.

401   "whoever suffers from severe alcoholism can be sterilized": Ibid., p. 1185.

402   "wine, the pride of France": "Mon Docteur le vin, Wine and health in France, 1900–1950," Kim Munholland, in Holt, p. 84.

403   "in cafés and restaurants on Tuesdays": Ibid., p. 139.

404   "Special Cuvée for the Wehrmacht": *Wine and War: The French the Na-*

zis, and France's Greatest Treasure, Don and Petie Kladstrup, Hodder and Stoughton, London, 2001, p. 105.

404 **"Who cares? It's not as if"**: Ibid., p. 93.

404 **"a very hot country"**: Ibid., p. 94.

404 **"in the old days, the rule was plunder"**: Ibid., p. 54.

405 **"The Führer has ordered"**: *The Nazi Doctors: Medical Killing and the Psychology of Genocide,* Robert Jay Lifton, Macmillan Books, London, 1986, p. 157.

405 **"Many members of the Einsatzkommandos"**: Ibid., p. 159.

405 **"The selections were mostly"**: Ibid., p. 193.

405 **"would ask, 'How can these thing'"**: Ibid., p. 196.

406 **"It is the business of the government"**: Cornell, p. 197.

407 **"A pub, or public house"**: *Instructions for American Servicemen in Britain 1942,* Bodleian Library, Oxford, 1994.

408 **"The Germans have ... drunk the wine"**: *Instructions for British Servicemen in France 1944,* Bodleian Library, Oxford, 2005.

409 **"American officers are bringing wines"**: "Why War Was Raged over RAF's Brandy Run, Neil Tweedie, *Daily Telegraph,* March 24, 2004.

410 **"Russians are absolutely crazy about vodka"**: *Berlin: The Downfall,* 1945, Anthony Beevor, Penguin Books, London 2003, p. 36.

410 **"Hello my nearest and dearest ones"**: Ibid., p. 349.

411 **"the sort used for cheap jewelry"**: Ibid., p. 400.

411 **"being carried out feet"**: *Whisky,* p. 129.

31 THE BOTTLE

413 **"May you have your wish and die in your sleep soon"**: *A Moon for the Misbegotten,* Eugene O'Neill, Nick Hern Books edition, London, 1992.

414 **"the idea I cherished in my heart"**: Malcolm Lowry, September 1948, preface to the French edition of *Under the Volcano.*

414 **"Closing his eyes again"**: *Under the Volcano,* Malcolm Lowry, Penguin Modern Classics, London, 2000, p. 343.

415 **"He is a real Dr. Jekyll and Mr. Hyde"**: Ch. 2, Alcoholics Anonymous online: http://www.aa.org/bigbookonline/.

415 *"The fact is that most alcoholics"*: Ch. 2, AA.

416 **"To anyone who has ever been"**: Jack Alexander, *The Saturday Evening Post,* April 1, 1950.

416 **"stress the spiritual feature freely"**: Ch. 7, AA.

418 **Vitamin B$_3$**: "Niacin and its Amide," A. Hoffer, MD, Ph.D., text online: http://www.doctoryourself.com/hoffer_niacin.html.

422 **"Turned out to be willful, difficult"**: Gene Vincent, Mick Farren, Sex, Drugs and Rock and Roll, Robinson, London, 2001, p. 46.

422 **The evolution of Rock and Roll**: *Country: The Twisted Roots of Rock and roll,* Nick Tosches, Da Capo Press edition, New York, 1996.

422   **Disease Theory of alcoholism**: "The Cultural Context of Psychological Approaches to Alcoholism," Stanton Peele, *American Psychologist*, 39, 1984, 1337–351.

32 RECONSTRUCTION

425   **"to believe in wine [was] a coercive collective act"**: *Mythologies*, Roland Barthes, Trans., Annette Lavers, Vintage Books edition, London, p. 59.

427   **"Apart from the many other difficulties"**: George Orwell, "As I please," *Tribune*, August 18, 1944.

430   **"Not for him the slow, gracious wandering"**: *Lucky Jim*, Kingsley Amis (1954), Penguin Classics edition, London, 2000, p. 61.

431   **"when the pubs closed, the streets filled"**: "Drinking the Good Life: Australia, 1880–1980," Diane Erica Kirkby, in Holt, p. 210.

431   **"there are evils associated"**: Ibid., p. 216.

432   **"a sort of feminine substitute for beer":** Ibid., p. 217.

432   **"big, full-bodied wine"**: Max Schubert A.M., "The Story of Grange"–paper delivered to the Australian National University Wine Symposium, Canberra, 1979.

432   **Consumption statistics for France, Italy, UK, Germany**: www.eurocare .org/pdf/profiles.

432   **French regulations**: *Oxford Companion to Wine*, Jancis Robinson,. ed, Oxford, 1999.

432   **Medical discoveries re alcohol**: *Bacchic Medicine*, Harry W. Paul, Editions Rodopi, Amsterdam–New York, 2001.

33 FLASHBACKS

433   **"I hate to advocate drugs, alcohol, violence"**: introduction to *Fear and Loathing in Las Vegas*, Hunter S. Thompson, Harper Perennial Modern Classics edition, 2005.

434   **"Americans are always drinking in crossroads saloons"**: *On the Road*, Jack Kerouac (1957) Penguin, London, p. 89.

434   **"I drank sixty glasses of beer"**: Ibid., p. 231.

435   **"There are no hippy bars"**: "The Hashbury is the Capital of the Hippies," Hunter S. Thompson (From the *New York Times Magazine*, May 14, 1967) in *The Great Shark Hunt*, Picador London, 1980, pp. 407–08.

436   **"The big market, these days, is in Downers"**: *Fear and Loathing*, p. 202.

438   **"We aim to make good and goddammit sure"**: *Dispatches*, Michael Herr, Picador, London, 2004, p. 12.

438   **"Now and then, to help slice the monotony"**: *If I Die in a Combat Zone*, Tim O'Brien (1969), Flamingo Modern Classic edition, London, 1995, p. 179.

440   **"enthralled ... with what I had tasted,"**: *California Wine*, p. xxxii.

441   **"As they swirled, sniffed, sipped, and spat"**: *Time* magazine, June 7, 1976.

Californian Wine: "The Volstead Act, Rebirth and Boom, Ruth Teiser and Catherine Harroun, *California Wine*, pp. 50–81.

Consumption statistics: National Institute on Alcohol Abuse and Alcoholism: www.niaaa.nih.gov/Resources/DatabaseResources/QuickFacts/AlcoholConsumption/.

34 WESTERNIZATION

444   "Japanese culture, Japanese food": "In the Shadow of Mount Fuji," David Broom, *Whisky Magazine*, Issue 57.

445   *mizu shobai* "Drinking Country, Flows of Exchange in a Japanese Valley," Brian Moeran, in *Drinking Cultures*, Ed. Thomas M. Wilson, Berg, New York, 2005, p. 26.

446   "sweetness, sourness, pungency": Ibid., p. 37.

447   *"Kanpai!":* Ibid., p. 31.

447   "part of a (threatened) underclass rural population": Ibid., p. 38.

448   *huang jiu*": "Cognac, Beer, Red Wine or Soft Drinks? Hong Kong Identity and Wedding Banquets," Josephine Smart, in Berg, pp. 107–128.

449   Snake wine–Author's observations.

450   "The Chinese associate the grape with hot foods":, "Where the VSOP Goes Down ASAP," Barbara Basler, *New York Times*, October 28, 1992.

450   "No businessman here would": Ibid.

450   "*Nuerhong* (Red Daughter) or *Nujui* (Daughter's Wine)": Berg, p. 115.

452   "highly combustible rice wine": "With Nixon in China: A Memoir," *by* Dirck Halstead *Digital Journalist*; January 2005.

Fusion drinking: *Drinking Occasions, Comparative Perspectives on Alcohol and Culture*, Dwight B. Heath, Brunner-Routledge, New York and London, 2000.

Consumption trends: WHO Global Status Report on Alcohol, 2004, Country Profiles: Japan, China.

Japanese youth drinking: "Young People's Drinking Behavior in Japan," Susumu Higuchi, MD, Ph.D., Kenji Suzuki, MD, Sachio Matsushita, MD, Yoneatsu Osaki, MD, Ph.D., text at: www.icap.org/portals/0/download/Kobe/Higuchi_WASP.pdf.

Hong Kong Drinking: "Alcohol–Is There or Will There Be a Drinking Problem in Hong Kong?," S.P.B. Donnan, *Journal of the Hong Kong Medical Association*, Vol. 11, No. 1, 1989. "Cultural Aspects of Drinking Patterns and Alcohol Controls in China," Ian Newman, *Globe*, 2002 Issue 1, online at www.ias.org.uk/resources/publications/theglobe/globe200201/gl200201_index.html.

35 MESSAGES

453   "easily crosses the placenta": "Liquor and Babies," *Time Magazine*, July 14 1975.

454   "She's very, very small": "An argument That Goes Back to the Womb: The Demedicalisation of Fetal Alcohol Syndrome, 1973–1992," Janet Golden, *Journal of Social History* 33 (1999) 269–98.

454   "the dangers of drinking during pregnancy": Ibid.

454   "eight to ten drinks or more per day": Ibid.

455   The actual drinking habits of American: Ruth C. Engs, and David J. Hanson, "The Drinking Patterns and Problems of College Students: 1983," *Journal of Alcohol and Drug Education*. 31(1):65–84, 1985.

456   "We've lost more than a quarter of a million": Ronald Reagan, Radio Address to the Nation on Drunk Driving, December 17, 1983; www.presidency.ucsb.edu/ws/index.php?pid=40875.

456   "Now, some feel that my decision": Ronald Reagan, speech, June 20, 1984 River Dell High School, Oradell, New Jersey.

458   "More and more it seems": "The Evolution of U.S. Temperance Movements Since Repeal: A Comparison of Two Campaigns to Control Alcohoic Beverage Marketing, 1950s and 1980s," Pamela Pennock, *The Social History of Alcohol and Drugs* 20 (2005) 14–65.

459   "a climate in which dangerous attitudes": "Alcohol Advertising: A Call for Congressional Action." Statement of Jean Kilbourne, Ph.D., to the Committee on Governmental Affairs of the United States Senate, June 29, 1988.

459   "paid for about 10 percent of all": "Are We Addicted to Alcohol Advertising? (1989), Christine Lubinski, www.health20-20.org/are_we_addicted_to_alcohol_advertising.htm.

460   "To blame advertising": Pennock.

465   "your office should proceed with caution": "BAFT out of Hell," Jacob Sullum, *Reason,* May 1994.

465   "varying ages, both genders": "The Conflict Between Public Health Goals and the Temperance Mentality," Stanton Peele, *American Journal of Public Health,* 83:803–10, 1993.

466   "reached the age that": Ben Sherwood, *Washington Monthly,* 1993.

Consumption trends: "A 10-Year National Trend Study of Alcohol Consumption, 1984–1995: Is the Period of Declining Drinking Over?" Thomas K. Greendfield Ph.D, Lorraine T. Midanik, Ph.D., John Rodgers, MA, *American Journal of Public Health,* Vol. 90, No. 1, January 2000.

Consumption statistics: National Institute on Alcohol Abuse and Alcoholism: www.niaaa.nih.gov/Resources/DatabaseResources/QuickFacts/AlcoholConsumption/.

36 SINGLETONS, WINE LAKES, AND THE MOSCOW EXPRESS

Standard drinks for various countries: International Center for Alcohol Policies: www.icap.org.

UK Safe Limits: *Sensible Drinking: The Report of an Inter-Departmental* Working Group, Department of Health, December 1995.

Alcohol absorption rates: "Alcohol in the Body," Alex Paton, *BMJ,* Vol. 330, January 8, 2005.

Safe Limits: "Current Weekly Limits Too Mean," J. C Duffy, *BMJ* 1994; 308:270–271.

468   **"Those limits were really plucked":** Richard Smith, reported on *Sky News,* October 20, 2007.

472   **"Idler: What's it like not drinking?":** "Conversations," Jeffrey Bernard, *The Idler,* February 8, 1995.

474   **"surprisingly, it appears that nearly half":** *Alcohol–Can the NHS Afford It?* A Report of a Working Party of the Royal College of Physicians, February 2001.

475   **"My mum has drunk nothing but a single cream sherry":** *Bridget Jones's Diary,* Helen Fielding, Picador, London, 1996, p. 47.

475   **"gastro-anomie":** "Consuming Wine in France, the 'Wandering' Drinker and the Vin-anomie," Marion Demossier, in Berg, pp. 129–154.

476   **"Each bottle of American and Australian wine":** "Wine War," *Business-Week* September 3, 2001.

477   **"Languedoc-Roussillon is still the biggest wine-producing":** "South of France Wine Brand Gets Green Light," Chris Mercer, www.beveragedaily .com, July 20, 2006.

478   **"We thought we were the king of carrots":** "Too Much of a Good Thing, Peter Gumbel, *Time Europe,* October 30, 2006, Vol. 168, No. 19.

478   **"a ridiculous way to use taxpayers' money":** "Brussels Tells Wincmakers to Face Up to New World Challenge," David Rennie, *Daily Telegraph,* June 23, 2006.

Drunk driving, France: "Alcohol is the Main Factor in Excess Traffic Accident Fatalities in France, Michel Reynaud, Patrick Le Breton, Bertrand Gilot, Françoise Vervialle, and Bruno Falissard, *Alcoholism: Clinical and Experimental Research.* 26(12): 1833–39, December 2002.

"France's Wine Industry Encourages Drinking and Driving," Associated Press, November 17, 2003.

479   **"I drank straight from the bottle":** *Moscow Stations,* Venedict Yerofeev, Trans. Stephen Mulrine, Faber & Faber, London, 1997, p. 27.

479   **"it's weird, nobody in Russia knows":** Ibid., p. 48.

479   **"Dog's giblets, the drink that puts all others in the shade!":** Ibid., p. 50.

000   **Russian drinking crisis:** "Kicking the Vodka Habit," M. Lawrence Schrad, *St. Petersburg Times,* November 7, 2006.

480   **"not a mean drunk":** *The Russia Hand: A Memoir of Presidential Diplomacy,* Strobe Talbot, Random House, 2002.

37 FIAT LUX

482   **"for is not the life of man simply the soul's sidelong glance?":** Yerofeev, p. 123.

482   **9/11 effect:** "Prevalence of binge drinking and heavy drinking among adults in the United States, 1990–2004," Centers for Disease Control and Prevention, online at: www.cdc.gov/alcohol/datatable.htm.

483 **"Frequent heavy drinking"**: "Exposure of African American Youth to Alcohol Advertising, 2003 to 2004," Center on Alcohol Marketing and Youth, Georgetown University, available at http://camy.org/research/afam0606/afam0606.pdf.

483 **"equipoise and serenity"**: "Hip Hop Fridays: How Rap Music Saved Cognac," John Carreyrou and Christopher Lawton, *Wall Street Journal*, July 2003.

484 **"we can't forbid people from buying it"**: "Bubbles and bling," Gideon Rachman, *The Economist*, Summer 2006.

484 **"ancient origins"**: Beer Institute Advertising and Marketing Code, online at: www.beeresponsible.com/advertising/AdAndMarketing Code. html.

485 **Alcohol Advertising and youth**: "Alcohol Advertising: What Makes It Attractive to Youth?" Chen, et al., *Journal of Health Communication*, 10:553–65, 2005. Online at: http://resources.prev.org/documents/AlcoholAdvertising_Youth.pdf.

487 **Craft brewing statistics**: http://www.beertown.org/craftbrewing/statis tics.html.

487 **Senate resolution for craft brewing**: http://www.beertown.org/pdf/ACBW_Resolution_753.pdf.

490 **"a potential problem with alcohol"**: "Substance Abuse in the Deployment Environment," *Iraq War Clinician Guide*, R. Gregory Lande, DO FACN, Barbara A. Marin, Ph.D., and Josef I Ruzek, Ph.D., p. 79, XII.

490 **"Going to a bar is not an opportunity to get drunk"**: "Texas Police Look in Bars for Signs of Drunkenness," Hugh Aynesworth, *Washington Times*, March 29, 2006.

491 **"Moderate alcohol consumption may have beneficial health"**: U.S. dietary guidelines online: http://www.health.gov/dietaryguidelines/dga2005/document/html/chapter9.htm.

492 **"I have been to AA meetings and they have left me cold."**: *A Million Little Pieces*, James Frey, Hodder Headline, London, 2004, p. 90.

493 **"studies of the relationship between alcohol and stress"**: "Does Drinking Reduce Stress?" Michael A. Sayette, Ph.D., Alcohol Research and Health, Vol. 23, No. 4, pp. 250, 255.

494 **"Fat-related deaths dropped 31 percent"**: "Wine Extract Keeps Mice Fat and healthy," Seth Borenstein, Associated Press, 2006.

494 **"self-reported drinkers earn 10–14 percent more than abstainers"**: "No Booze? You May Lose: Why Drinkers Earn More Money Than Nondrinkers," Bethany L. Peters, Edward Stringham, Reason Foundation, Policy Brief 44, September 2006.

495 ***Judgement of Paris***: "Judgement of Paris Revisited: California in Pole Position Yet Again," Jane Anson, *Decanter Magazine*, October 24, 2006.

496 **"I had heard about 'dry counties'"**: *I Hope They Serve Beer in Hell*, Tucker Max, Penguin Books, London, 2006.

497   **"We're not looking for development . . .":** A State's Last Dry Town Asserts a Right to Hold On to Tradition, William Yardley, *New York Times* December 26, 2005.

497   **"Here's to a new tradition in Westerville":** "Dry Capital of the World No More," *Chicago Sun-Times,* January 15, 2006.

Wet and dry Kentucky counties: http://www.abc.ky.gov/NR/rdonlyres/ 88403470-8A7E-410C-9816-8B520F7649C8/0/WetDryList.pdf.

Dry counties: David J. Hanson, Ph.D., at http://www2.potsdam.edu/hansondj/ Controversies/1140551076.html.

INDEX